Pink Floyd

The Press Reports

1966 - 1983

By Vernon Fitch

We acknowledge the financial support of the Government of Canada through
the Book Publishing Industry Development Program for our publishing activities.
Published by Collector's Guide Publishing Inc., Box 62034, Burlington, Ontario,
Canada, L7R 4K2
Printed and bound in Canada
Pink Floyd — The Press Reports (1966-1983)
by Vernon Fitch
ISBN 1-896522-72-6

Pink Floyd

The Press Reports

1966 - 1983

By Vernon Fitch

Table Of Contents

Acknowledgements

Pink Floyd-The Press Reports would not have been possible without the dedication of the numerous music journalists who have written articles about Pink Floyd over the years. Accolades go to the following journalists for their contributions to the written history of Pink Floyd. Sid Adilman, Michka Assayas, Aldo Bagli, Lynden Barber, Ron Base, Alan Betrock, Michael Bloom, Chris Bohn, Derek Boltwood, Bruno Bornino, Caroline Boucher, Bill Boyles, Michael Branton, Christine Brown, Mick Brown, Roy Carr, Chris Charlesworth, Jay Cocks, Ray Connolly, Philippe Constantin, Richard Cook, Sally Cork, Karl Dallas, Dai Davies, Robin Denselow, Dennis Detheridge, Dave DiMartino, Norrie Drummond, Ben Edmonds, Pete Erskine, Jim Farber, Bob Farmer, Mick Farren, Hugh Fielder, Howard Foster, Johnny Fox, Noel Gallagher, Armando Gallo, John Gibson, Mikal Gilmore, Lon Goddard, Peter Goddard, Jim Green, Richard Green, David Griffiths, Loyd Grossman, Martin Hayman, Richard Hogan, Roy Hollingworth, John Hopkins, David Hughes, Martha Hume, Chris Jagger, Derek Jewell, Thomas Johnson, Allan Jones, Nick Jones, Nick Kent, Bruce Kirkland, Stephen Lavers, Kurt Loder, Derek Malcolm, Bill Mann, Robert Martin, Lynn Van Matre, Diana Maychick, Dave McCullough, Ian McDonald, Paul McGrath, Lisa Mehlman, Martin Melhuish, Drew Metcalf, Miles, Richard Milner, Brian Mulligan, Charles Sharr Murray, Michael Oldfield, Peter Overton, Alan Parker, Peter D. Parks, Richard Patterson, Steve Peacock, Wilder Penfield III, Ian Penman, Neil Peters, Steve Pond, Bill Provick, Chuck Pulin, Mike Quigley, Mike Richardson, Giorgio Rivieccio, Ira Robbins, John Rockwell, Juan Rodriguez, Frank Rose, Penelope Ross, Clint Roswell, Cal Rudd, Jane Scott, Stella Shamoon, Roy Shipston, Sylvie Simmons, Debbie Smith, Simon Stable, Don Stanley, Ben Steelman, Tony Stewart, Tom Stock, Greg Stone, Todd Tolces, Tony Tyler, Tommy Vance, Alan Walsh, Jeff Ward, Michael Watts, Chris Welch, Penny Weston, Richard Williams, Tony Wilson, Archer Winsten, Jim Wright, and many others.

The various articles on which this book has been based have been sourced from my personal library, and various other individual collections. Special thanks go to Robert Godwin, Doug Hext, Jon Rosenberg, Richard Mahon, Steve Benson, and Andre Terhorst for their assistance with this project.

Introduction

A study of the numerous press reports written about Pink Floyd throughout the years provides an interesting glimpse into their history. Nowhere else can you find information about their activities as they were taking place, or how music journalists viewed the band in the context of what was occurring at the time. To better understand how the press perceived the band during its many phases, it is best to start at the beginning.

Pink Floyd began as a rhythm and blues based band in Great Britain in the mid 1960s. Their rise to stardom started in 1966 with a shift from rhythm and blues to improvised experimental music. Experiments with light and sound gained them a local following in London and began attracting initial press coverage of the band.

In 1967, the psychedelic music scene in London was expanding rapidly and Pink Floyd appeared at the forefront of the scene. They played regularly in the clubs of the London underground, and gained notoriety with frequent press reports about their activities. Hardly a week went by without some mention of Pink Floyd in the British music papers. This led to a wider following for the band, and their London club shows became events of significant proportions. By the time of the release of their first album, The Piper at the Gates of Dawn, in August 1967, the band were well known in the British press, and European and American papers began to take notice of the group. A ten-day tour of America in November 1967 introduced American audiences to the band, and brought about the first concert reviews of Pink Floyd by the American music press. But on their return to Britain, problems within the band began to damage the perception of the group.

At the beginning of 1968, Syd Barrett, their main songwriter, guitarist, and vocalist was replaced by David Gilmour. The press, which had, up until this time, praised Pink Floyd's and Barrett's innovative musical style, were suddenly confronted with a Pink Floyd line-up that no longer included the musician that they had considered the driving force behind the band's music. Numerous journalists believed that this signaled the demise of the group and press reports about the band diminished. It wasn't until the Pink Floyd free concert in Hyde Park, London, and the release of the second Pink Floyd album, A Saucerful of Secrets, in June 1968, that the press began to, once again, praise the activities of the band. It was also at this time that Pink Floyd did a second tour of the United States, in July and August 1968, which resulted in the second series of published reviews of Pink Floyd concerts by the American music press.

In 1969, the band built on the success of A Saucerful of Secrets, and the press began to eagerly follow their activities. News articles covered their innovations, such as a new sound system called the Azimuth Co-ordinator, the use of pre-recorded tapes and electronic sounds, and the accompaniment of members of the London Philharmonic Orchestra at certain live performances. They also reported that Pink Floyd was participating in two film projects, and that they completed a new album that featured the musical talents of each of the four band members, called Ummagumma. The press praised Ummagumma as a high point of the psychedelic period. In 1970, two new solo albums by former Pink Floyd member, Syd Barrett, were released, causing a renewed interest in Barrett, and various interviews with Barrett were published. The press also reported about work by Pink Floyd on a new cartoon soundtrack project and a ballet project, another Hyde Park free concert, plus the release of the album, Atom Heart Mother, which featured the title song on an entire side of the album, complete with an orchestra and choir. They followed its release with tours of the U.S., Great Britain, and performances at various European festivals. Press reports about the album and concerts proliferated.

1971 brought the release and reviews of the Pink Floyd album Meddle. Meddle is perhaps the definitive release from this period of the band and featured the song Echoes, which captured the band at it's improvisational peak. Reports also surfaced that work had begun on a new project, one that would become Dark Side of the Moon.

In 1972, Pink Floyd began touring their new piece, Dark Side of the Moon, and it was greeted with numerous press reviews. Pink Floyd also released another soundtrack album, Obscured by Clouds, an album that was embraced by the press. But things were about to change drastically for Pink Floyd the following year.

In 1973, the album Dark Side of the Moon was released. Dark Side of the Moon is a concept album about the stresses of life, and today it is regarded as perhaps the defining recorded legacy of the 1970s. This album brought Pink Floyd enormous commercial success, something that they had been striving for, but it also changed the band due to the pressures and problems associated with its success. The press greeted the album with mixed reviews, but the public embraced the album, and Pink Floyd concerts moved into large, ten to fifteen thousand seat arenas that were sold out instantly. No longer was Pink Floyd considered an underground band. From here on, they were squarely in the public eye. This brought turmoil to the band, and the band members began to question their reasons for being in the band. They scaled back on their public appearances at a time when the press and public desired more from them. Reports of their demise once again began to appear in the music papers.

In early 1974, the press lacked relatively any new subject matter to report on, as the band disappeared from public view. Journalists were forced to write recaps of the band's history or occasional reports of session work by band members. All the while, the success of Dark Side of the Moon was generating an increased interest in the band. Then, in November 1974, exactly one year after their last performance in Britain, Pink Floyd returned to the concert stage in Britain for a two month British Winter tour with three new songs. Although the shows sold out immediately and were received well by the public, the press was less than enthusiastic about the performances. Reports were published stating that the new material was tedious and boring, and that the musicians seemed not to care about their performances.

In 1975, Pink Floyd toured the United States and Canada to mixed reviews and sold-out stadium audiences. They also released the follow-up album to Dark Side of the Moon, titled, Wish You Were Here, about absence and the impersonal recording industry machine. The initial reaction to the album in the press was generally good, although not every reporter felt that it was up to what they expected of Pink Floyd.

The band spent 1976 writing music for a new album, while David Gilmour mixed a couple of songs for Hawkwind and produced an album for the band Unicorn. Articles about the band's history were commonplace.

In 1977, Pink Floyd released the album, Animals, a musical statement about a society that is divided into classes of animals. They followed its release with a world tour that included performances in huge stadiums, often breaking attendance records. At this time, the press was also covering the ongoing punk movement, and conflicting reports about the scaled down, no-frills punk bands were mixed with articles about the gigantic spectaculars of Pink Floyd. During this time Pink Floyd virtually denied all requests for press interviews, to the dismay of many music journalists.

1978 brought solo records by David Gilmour and Richard Wright, and with them press reviews and occasional interviews. The press also reported at this time that Roger Waters was working on a new piece, which was to become Pink Floyd's next concept album.

In 1979, the band released The Wall, an album that explored the mind of a rock musician who succumbs to the pressures of life by building a wall around himself. The Wall is considered by many people the zenith of the band. It received generally positive reviews by the music press, although some journalists failed to agree with its message.

In 1980 and 1981, the press reported on live performances of The Wall. They also reviewed the release of Nick Mason's solo album, Fictitious Sports, in 1981. The Wall movie was completed and released in 1982. Press reviews were mixed but often included interesting commentary by the films collaborators. The Final Cut album was released in 1983, and was generally criticized by the press, although one journalist called it a rock and roll masterpiece.

The press coverage of Pink Floyd during the years 1966 through 1983 is entertaining and enlightening. These reports give a unique insight into the band and provide a look at how Pink Floyd was perceived during its formative years. Since interviews with band members are often included in these press reports, many facets of the band can be discovered, as told by the band members themselves. As such, it is an interesting glimpse into the life and times of Syd Barrett, Roger Waters, David Gilmour, Richard Wright, and Nick Mason.

Pink Floyd, 1968. Left to Right: Roger Waters, Nick Mason, Rick Wright, David Gilmour.

Foreword

Pink Floyd – The Press Reports consists of a chronological listing of significant newspaper and magazine articles written about Pink Floyd by the music press during the years 1966 through 1983. Although there have been thousands of articles written about Pink Floyd during this time period, this book focuses mainly on articles from Britain, primarily because they have provided the most complete coverage over the years. Special attention has been given to articles containing band interviews and record reviews. Some concert reviews of major concerts have also been included to provide an additional basis of historical events.

For reasons pertaining to copyright, the information in these articles has been summarized. In the case of interviews, the questions have been paraphrased, although the replies are reprinted word for word. In summarizing these articles, I have made every effort to include all the historical aspects of the stories and to maintain the original intent of the authors. Articles containing both praise and criticism have been included for the sake of historical perspective.

It was my intention in compiling this book that it would serve as an historical reference work on Pink Floyd. Significant events can be traced back to their origins in print, and factual issues can be researched by reading comments by the band members. By reading this book, you will be exploring the history of Pink Floyd from 1966 through 1983, often times as told by the band members themselves.

1966
. . . to the Beginning

October 14, 1966 - International Times (U.K.) published an ad for an all night rave on Saturday, October 15, 1966 at the Chalk Farm Roundhouse to launch the International Times. The rave featured a performance by the Pink Floyd, plus strips, trips, happenings, and movies. You were asked to bring your own poison & flowers & gas-filled balloons & submarine & rocket ship & candy & striped boxes & ladders & paint & flutes & feet & ladders & locomotives & madness & autumn & blowlamps. Pop / Op / Costume / Masque / Fantasy Loon / Blowout / Drag Ball. Surprise for the shortest, barest costumes. Advance tickets are 5/-.

October 21, 1966 - International Times (U.K.) reviewed the Pink Floyd concert at the Roundhouse in London on October 15, 1966. They wrote, "The Pink Floyd, psychedelic pop group, did weird things to the feel of the event with their scary feedback sounds, slide projections playing on their skin (drops of paint run riot on the slides to produce outer space/prehistoric textures on the skin), and spotlights flashing on them in time with a drum beat."

October 30, 1966 – The Sunday Times (U.K.) reported on the Pink Floyd concert at the Roundhouse in London on October 15, 1966 to launch the International Times newspaper. They wrote that Pink Floyd played "throbbing music" while "bizarre colored shapes" were projected on a screen behind the band. People at the show ate a mound of jelly at midnight. As for being psychedelic, manager Andrew King stated, *"We don't call ourselves psychedelic. But we don't deny it. We don't confirm it either. People who want to make up slogans can do it."* Bass player Roger Waters added, *"It's totally anarchistic. But it's co-operative anarchy, if you see what I mean. It's definitely a complete realization of the aims of psychedelia. But if you take LSD, what you experience depends entirely on who you are. Our music may give you the screaming horrors, or throw you into screaming ecstasy. Mostly it's the latter. We find our audiences stop dancing now. We tend to get them standing there, totally grooved with their mouths open."*

November 18, 1966 - The Gazette, Kent (U.K.) reported that the Pink Floyd, from London, will be performing at the Technical College dance tomorrow night, and will be supported by the Koalas.

November 23, 1966 - The Herald, Kent (U.K.) published an article titled, "The psychedelic sound comes to Canterbury" that reviewed the Pink Floyd concert at the Canterbury Technical College on November 19, 1966. The psychedelic music of Pink Floyd is different, but the reviewer liked it and

PSYCHEDELICAMANIA
DOUBLE - GIANT - FREAK - OUT - BALL
AT THE ROUND HOUSE CHALK FARM NW1

FRI. 30TH DEC.
ALL NIGHT RAVE 10 P.M. – ON...

GENO WASHINGTON
& RAM JAM BAND

THE CREAM

ALAN BOWN SET

SAT. 31ST DE
NEW YEARS EVE
ALL NIGHT RAVE 10 P.M. – ON...

THE WHO

THE MOVE

THE PINK FLOYD

LATE BARS CENTRAL HEATING
PSYCHEDELIC LIGHTING
NEW IMPROVED ENTRANCE

TICKETS FROM INDICA BOOKS HOUSEMANS BETTER BOOKS COLLETS BIBAS BOUTIQUE

wanted more. The visual and audio effects coordinated with movement, and weird music together with strange projected slides of coagulating colors, may induce the audience to dance.

After the show, the reviewer spoke to the band about their use of amplifiers and colors. The group consists of five people, with light man, 17-year old Joe Gannon, the fifth member of the band. Without his psychological visual effects, the act would not be the same. The organ is the most powerful instrument in the band, played by Rick Wright. He uses it to build up loud, vibrating sounds and continuous drones. Roger Waters on bass guitar, and Syd Barrett on lead guitar also do vocals, which are strong and produce a somewhat melodic sound that blends perfectly with the presentation. Nick Mason plays drums, spasmodic cymbal swishes, and loud crashes.

Asked about their music, Rick Wright said, "*It does sometimes get to a point where it is a wow. That is when it works, which is not always. Then we really feel the music is coming from us, not the instruments, or rather the instruments become part of us. We look at the lights and the slides behind us, and hope that it all has the same effect on the audience as it does on us.*" Asked how this type of music started, Wright replied, "*It was completely spontaneous. We just turned up the amplifiers and tried it, thought about it, and it developed from there. But we still have a long way to go before we get exactly what we want. It must develop still further. There is probably more coordination between the members of our group than in any pop group. We play far more like a jazz group than anything else. Because we have to be together to produce the right sound, we have come to think, musically, together. Most of our act is spontaneous and unrehearsed. It just comes when we are on stage.*"

Asked about the lighting effects, Joe Gannon explained, "*I design the slides, basing them on my idea of the music. The lights work rhythmically. I just wave my hand over the micro-switches and the different colors flash. We have only been using the lights for one month. But before that, we were concentrating on starting with the right equipment. The lighting is so much a part of the group that it had to be good before it could blend properly*

1967
Arnold, Emily, Piper and Apples

with the music." His ambition is to create a new medium with a direct link between the audio and visual effects. And the band wants to project films on the wall behind them instead of slides. Gannon thinks that this would make more of an impression on the audience. Since the equipment the band uses is so expensive, the band is currently putting any money they make towards better lighting equipment and more powerful amplifiers.

Asked about audience reactions to their performances, Wright said, "As we are a comparatively new group and are projecting a really new sound, most people just stand and listen at first. What we really want is that they should dance to the music and with the music, and so become a part of us. When some people do experience what we want them to, it gets a bit of a jungle, but it is harmless enough because they are wrapped up in the music and themselves. It is a release of emotion, but an inward, not an outward, one, and no one goes into a trance or anything."

December 12, 1966 - International Times (U.K.) reviewed the Pink Floyd concert at the London Free School Sound/Light Workshop. They wrote, "Since I last saw the Pink Floyd they've got hold of bigger amplifiers, new light gear and a rave from Paul McCartney. This time I saw them at Powis Gardens W.11, on Tuesday 29th, the last of their regular shows there. Their work is largely improvisation, and lead guitarist Sid Barrett shoulders most of the burden of providing continuity and attack in the improvised parts. He was providing a huge range of sounds with the new equipment, from throttled shrieks to mellow feedback roars. Visually the show was less adventurous. Three projectors bathed the group, the walls and sometimes the audience in vivid colours. But the colour was fairly static, and there was no searching for the brain alpha rhythms, by chopping the focus of the images. The equipment that the group is using now is infant electronics: lets see what they will do with the grownup electronics that a colour television industry will make available."

January 2, 1967 - The Daily Mail (U.K.) reviewed the Pink Floyd concert at the Roundhouse in London on December 31, 1966. The article stated that the music and lights were set up to create psychedelic sensations, similar to those experienced on an LSD trip. The music was extremely loud, with the decibel level at 90 or more, and the Pink Floyd reached 120 at the Freak-out.

January 7, 1967 - Melody Maker (U.K.) reported on the Psychedelicamania concert at the Roundhouse in London on December 31, 1966. Bands performing at the 'Giant Freak-Out All Night Rave' included Pink Floyd, The Who, and The Move. Nick Jones wrote that Pink Floyd have "a promising sound" and "groovy picture slides that merge, blossom, burst, grow, divide, and die." Proceeds from the show went to Centre 42.

January 1967 - Rave Magazine (U.K.) reported that Pink Floyd are "a name to watch in the new year."

January 14, 1967 - Melody Maker (U.K.) published an article titled, "Who's Psychedelic Now? – Spotlight on The Pink Floyd and The Move" by Chris Welch and Nick Jones. These days, bands have to bombard an audience's senses with flames, light, and fiendish noises. If they do this, they are on the road to success. One such semi-pro band, The Pink Floyd, were unheard of a few weeks ago, but now have a residency at the Marquee Club in London.

Originally an R & B band, Pink Floyd began experimenting with light and sound at the Hornsey College of Art Light-Sound workshop. Nick Mason explained, "We were very disorganized then until our managers materialized and we started looking for a guy to do the lights full-time. The lighting man literally has to be one of the group. When we were in our early stages, we didn't play a lot of our electronic interstellar music, and the

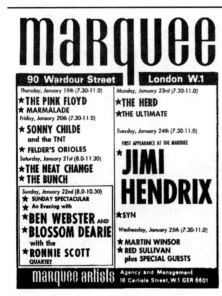

slides were still rather amateurish. However, this has developed now and our 'take-off' into the mainly improvised electronic scenes are much longer, and, of course, in my opinion, the slides have developed to something out of all proportion. They're just fantastic."

As far as being labeled psychedelic, Mason stated, *"You have to be careful when you start on this psychedelic thing. We don't call ourselves a psychedelic group or say that we play psychedelic pop music. It's just that people associate us with this and we get employed all the time at the various freak-outs and happenings in London. Let's face it, there really isn't a definition for the word 'psychedelic.' It's something that has taken place around us, not within us."* Roger Waters added, *"I think the reason is that we've been employed by so many of these freak-out merchants. I sometimes think that it's only because we have lots of equipment and lighting, and it saves the promoters from having to hire lighting for the group. A freak-out, anyway, should be relaxed, informal, and spontaneous. The best freak-out you'll ever get is at a party with about a hundred people. A freak-out shouldn't be savage mobs of geezers throwing bottles."*

January 21, 1967 - Melody Maker (U.K.) published an ad for the Pink Floyd concert at the Marquee Club on 90 Wardour Street on Thursday, January 19, 1967, and at the UFO

Club on Friday, January 20, 1967, admission 10/- for members, and 15/- for guests. Also in this issue is an add stating that the Pink Floyd announce that their sole agents are the Bryan Morrison Agency.

January 28, 1967 - Melody Maker (U.K.) published an ad for "Another Mammoth All-Night Rave" at the Queen's Hall Leeds on Friday, February 3, 1967 to Saturday, February 4, 1967. The rave will feature four stages, dancing for 10,000, 12 groups, and will continue for 10 hours non-stop. Groups performing include The Cream, "Plus! Plus! Plus! It's happening! Schizophrenic, Psychedelic, freak out – schmeak out! A whole show in Lighting, Music, Films, and Colour by Pink Floyd for the first time ever outside London." There will be a fairground, barbeque, and early-morning breakfasts. "We're letting a live Gorilla loose in the crowd at midnight."

February 27, 1967 - International Times (U.K.) published an ad for The UFO Club, with "The Return of the Invisible Pink Floyd" on February 24, 1967.

March 10, 1967 - The Gazette, Kent, England (U.K.) reported that Pink Floyd will be performing at the Canterbury Technical College dance on March 11, 1967. The band use two electricians and artists to get the hall ready for their show. The band is quoted as saying, *"I suppose that if we had to have some kind of definition, you could say the Pink Floyd were lights and sounds. The two mediums compliment each other and we definitely don't use them together as a gimmick. Our aim is simply to make our audiences dig the effect."*

March 11, 1967 - Melody Maker (U.K.) reviewed the Pink Floyd's first single, 'Arnold Layne.' They called the single a very good record with an amusing and weird story.

Also in this issue is an ad for the UFO Club and a Friday allnite concert with Pink Floyd. "See the Pink Floyd go pop." The show will feature a promo film for 'Arnold Layne.' Admission is 10/- for members, and 15/- for guests.

New Musical Express (U.K.) published a half-page ad for the new Pink Floyd single, 'Arnold Layne.'

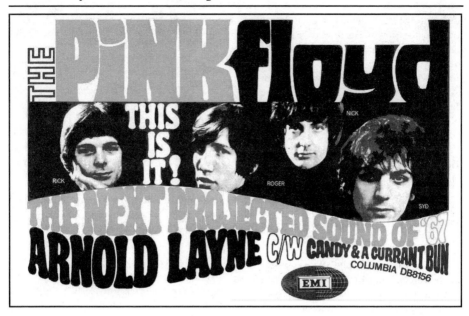

March 13, 1967 - International Times (U.K.) published an article titled, "The Pink Floyd versus Psychedelphia" by John Hopkins.

"The Pink Floyd group specializes in psychedelic music" - News of the World. "The Pink Floyd does not know what people mean by psychedelic pop, and are not trying to create hallucinatory effects on their audience" - EMI handout. Censored, censored, censored, censored, censored – Pink Floyd Candy and a Currant Bun, uncensored version.

Publicists, agents and record executives play out their games attempting to prove that the Pink Floyd haven't really got much connection with anything. A nice, clean, music-for-the-family image, art for arts sake. Oh yes, and "musical spokesman for a new movement which involves experimentation in all the arts, including music," blab, blab, blab. While all this has been going on like a storm in a teacup somewhere in EMI House, the Pink Floyd have done it again. Their first record, a single called 'Arnold Layne,' is about a clothes fetishist. Don't believe it? Read on.

Arnold Layne had a strange hobby, Collecting clothes, Moonshine, Washing Line, Suit him fine. On the wall hung a tall mirror, Distorted view, See through baby blue, He dug it. Now he's caught, A nasty sort of person, They gave him time, Doors bang chain gang, He hate it. Oh Arnold Layne, it's not the same, Takes two to know, two to know, two to know, Why cant you see. Arnold Layne don't do it again."

All of which leads me to believe that EMI will shortly be denying things again (it's already been banned on Radio London for being 'smutty.') Actually I think I prefer it when the Floyd give me hallucinations. Here are a few more hallucinations for the record. The Pink Floyd had been gigging around for a year or two on the London Art College Scene when Steven Stollman got them to play at one of his Marquee Club happenings. That was almost exactly a year ago. Somehow word got around that what they were doing was different. It was. They played mainly instrumentals, and numbers would sometimes last for half-an-hour each. Guitars played with cigarette lighters, etc.

The word was out, but it wasn't till last October that they got a regular job, playing weekly at the London Free School. One evening, Joel and Toni Brown, an American couple, brought their slide projector and gassed everyone by putting on a light show with the music. When the Browns returned to Millbrook, New York, Jack Bracelin took over and began to develop his own light show (which is now one of the attractions of the UFO all-nighter).

On October 27th, 2500 people heard

them at the International Times launching party at the Round House, Chalk Farm. [Ed. note: The International Times launch party actually took place on October 15, 1966.] A few days later they played for Oxfam at the Albert Hall, and then for Psychedelphia versus Ian Smith, at the Round House again. By early November, the Floyd had signed a management contract with Andrew King and Peter Jenner, and had acquired 17-year-old Joe Gannon to work their lights. Gannon quickly caught on and produced what is the basis of their light now. Two projectors from the back of the hall illuminate the stage with multicolored liquid moving slides. Occasionally colored lights flash on stage, or a movie is shown.

Back to the plot. By December the band were getting out-of-town gigs and the Free School had virtually disbanded. Just before Christmas, UFO opened on Friday nights with the Pink Floyd as main attraction. Hundred-watt amplifiers, ear-splitting vibrations, liquid light that takes your breath away. In February they turned professional, got blasted by the gutter-press News of the World for being social deviants. Two weeks later, the newspaper retracted its statement, which nevertheless had delayed their EMI signing. But by this time they had produced their first single, which they sold to EMI. This isn't a record review, but their record is worth hearing, if only to see how a group playing mainly instrumentals and relying on a light show for in-person attraction can make a single with sales potential. Try Radio Luxemburg any day at all, and Caroline when the payola has been fixed.

Record details: Arnold Layne c/w Candy and a Currant Bun, By The Pink Floyd. Composer Syd Barrett. Produced by Joe Boyd for Blackhill Enterprises, released on Columbia DB 8156. The Pink Floyd: Roger Waters, Syd Barrett, Nick Mason, Rick Wright. All except Rick have green eyes.

Footnote: what is psychedelic pop? "Turn off your mind relax and float downstream" – The Beatles, Revolver LP, words taken from The Psychedelic Experience. "The Psychedelic Experience - a sort of textbook for the LSD cult" - News of the World. "I'm very stoned" – The Beatles, Strawberry Fields Forever. The Beatles also record for EMI.

March 15, 1967 - The Herald, Kent (U.K.) published an article titled, "The pagan effect of The Pink Floyd." Pink Floyd's performance in Canterbury on November 19, 1966 was good, but their recent performance on March 11, 1967, was even better. Live, their music consists of high droning sounds with exciting build ups, combined with unusual colors projected onto the stage behind the band. However, the band's records are different from their stage act. Asked about their new single, 'Arnold Layne,' Syd Barrett replied, "*I listened to it a couple of times and discovered that it was good.*"

March 18, 1967 - New Musical Express (U.K.) reviewed the Pink Floyd single, 'Arnold Layne,' writing that 'Arnold Layne' is an unusual song, but not psychedelic. It has off-beat weird lyrics, great organ work, and a spine-tingling build. The flip side, 'Candy and a Currant Bun,' has a jaunty beat, fuzz guitar, with strange oscillating chanting. This song is more like psychedelia.

March 25, 1967 - Disc and Music Echo (U.K.) published an article titled, "Meet the Pinky Kinkies (in Sound and Vision, that is)" by Bob Farmer. Pink Floyd's new record, Arnold Layne, has been banned by Radio London, and Roger Waters commented, "*We can't think what Radio London are so perturbed about. It's a song about a clothes fetishist who's obviously a bit kinked. A very simple, straightforward song about one sort of human predicament.*"

Their stage act is becoming very popular, as Roger Waters explained, "*Ours is a sort of light-sound show. As for our music, it's pop but very free and full of improvisation. Some of our numbers have been known to run for at least half an hour.*" The lighting effects are a main attraction for the group, and light man Pip Carter is considered as the fifth group member. Their light show includes projectors, spot lamps, and liquid slides. Noted Roger Waters, "*We started on this lighting idea a couple of years ago. It seemed that visual images are just as good a thing to give an audience as sounds. Visual images can be really stimulating to you when you're up on stage playing.*"

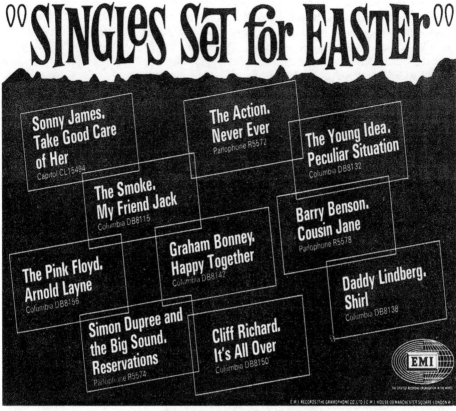

A rare EMI ad for the first Pink Floyd single

Another rare EMI ad for The Piper At The Gates Of Dawn album.

Melody Maker (U.K.) reported that Pink Floyd have completed five songs for their first album. Paul McCartney is reported as having attended several of the recording sessions.

New Musical Express (U.K.) published an ad for the Bryan Morrison Agency Ltd. and listed The Pink Floyd as one of their acts.

Record Mirror (U.K.) reported that the new Pink Floyd single, 'Arnold Layne,' is doing very well. The group is quoted as saying, *"If we have to have some kind of definition, you could say we are lights and sounds. The two mediums compliment each other and we definitely don't use them together as a gimmick. Our aim is simply to make the audience dig the effect."*

April 1, 1967 - Disc and Music Echo (U.K.) published an article titled, "Beatles, Cream lap up Pink!" by Chris Jagger. Jagger wrote that Pink Floyd is becoming popular due to their new single, but their success is due to their stage act, which includes 700 watts of amplification, weird music that is largely improvised, and lighting that includes slide projections and melting oil paints. The sheer volume will blow you out. The band members lose themselves in their music on stage and try to absorb the audience's minds also. Although they mainly play in London, they have also received excellent receptions in Leeds and Southampton. But they do have problems getting all their equipment to their gigs, and have a road manager that can't drive.

The band has a new single out, 'Arnold Layne,' and EMI have put up the money for the production of an independent album by the group, which they have started recording. They also have been involved in a movie about the London scene, starring Michael Caine and Julie Christie. Pink Floyd has an original sound, write all their own songs, and experiment with sound on stage. Other musicians who think that Pink Floyd have a promising future are Paul McCartney, Eric Clapton, and Peter Asher.

Melody Maker (U.K.) published an article titled, "Freaking out with the Pink Floyd" by Nick Jones. Jones interviewed the band at Syd Barrett's house near Cambridge Circus in the middle of London's West End. Barrett's front door was painted purple.

Asked why he wrote such a dirty song as 'Arnold Layne.' Barrett replied, *"Well, I just wrote it. I thought 'Arnold Layne' was a nice name, and it fitted very well into the music I had already composed. I was at Cambridge at the time I started to write the song. I pinched the line about 'moonshine washing line' from Rog, our bass guitarist, because he has an enormous washing line in the back garden of his house. Then I thought, 'Arnold must have a hobby,' and it went on from there. Arnold Layne just happens to dig dressing up in women's clothing. A lot of people do, so let's face up to reality. About the only other lyric anybody could object to is the bit about 'it takes two to know, takes two to know,' and there's nothing smutty about that. But then, if more people like them dislike us, more people like the underground lot are going to dig us, so we hope they'll cancel each other out."* Rick Wright continued, *"I think the record was banned not because of the lyrics, because there's nothing there you can really object to, but because they're against us as a group and against what we stand for."* Barrett added, *"It's only a business-like commercial insult anyway. It doesn't affect us personally."* Roger Waters explained, *"Let's face it, the pirate stations play records that are much more 'smutty' than 'Arnold Layne' will ever be. In fact, it's only Radio London that have banned the record. The BBC and everybody else plays it. I think it's just different politics, not anything against us."*

Syd Barrett then played some tapes of songs from the upcoming Pink Floyd album, including "Interstella" and "Flamin," which the writer thought was interesting pop music. The band then went to a pub for drinks with the writer, and then to EMI Studios for a recording session.

Asked where they fit in musically, Nick Mason replied, *"We would like to think that we're part of the creative half in that we write our own material and don't just record other people's numbers, or copy American demo discs. Our album shows part of the Pink Floyd that haven't been heard yet."* Roger Waters continued, *"There's parts we haven't even heard yet."* Nick Mason added, *"It's bringing into flower many of the fruits that*

Syd Barrett, 1967.

have remained dormant for so long." And Syd Barrett added, "*It all comes straight out of our heads, and it's not too far out to understand. If we play well on stage, I think most people understand that what we play isn't just a noise. Most audiences respond to a good act.*"

New Musical Express (U.K.) published an article titled, "School inspired Pink Floyd." Pink Floyd are four off-beat students who developed a technique described as a "fusion of light, colour, and music." It was developed at Hornsey College when Syd Barrett and Nick Mason saw potential in the light and sound laboratory. It features projected images and weird luminous effects. But it's not psychedelic. This new music form was begun a few months ago, and has gained acceptance among students. Fans include Paul McCartney. The band plays all original material, including their single 'Arnold Layne.'

Also in this issue is the NME Top 30 chart for the week of March 29, 1967, with the Pink Floyd record, 'Arnold Layne,' entering the chart for the first time at No. 26. Also in the chart for the first time is the Jimi Hendrix record, Purple Haze, at No. 25, and the Turtles, Happy Together, at No. 30.

April 8, 1967 - Disc and Music Echo (U.K.) published an article titled, "They're all in the Pink!" The article examined each member of Pink Floyd.

Lead guitarist Syd Barrett was born in Cambridge and is the best looking band member. He began playing music when he was seven and took piano lessons that ended two weeks later. He attended art school in Cambridge and then London, and became involved in Pink Floyd because he lived next to Roger Waters. Barrett said, "*Teenagers in Britain are great. Possibly, they are not buying the bulk of records, but they come to life as audiences. Just because Humperdinck, closely followed by the Ken Dodds, is doing so well is not indicative of apathy on the part of the teenagers.*" Barrett wears black corduroy jackets, wine-red pants, and white shoes. Barrett said, "*Freedom is what I'm after. That's why I like working in this group. There's such freedom artistically.*"

Organist Rick Wright is quiet,

easygoing, and absent minded, having locked the keys in the group's car. He attended Haberdashers. Wright continued, *"Then I went to Regent Street Polytechnic to study architecture and gave up in boredom after a year. So I started going abroad to places like Greece, then came home to earn a bit of money in jobs like interior designing and private decorating. But I was very unhappy and turned to studying music. I gave that up two months ago but only because the Pink Floyd had become a full-time occupation."* Someday he wants to "write a symphony or something." Speaking about Pink Floyd, Wright said, *"We're playing something completely different from what has gone before. Like jazz musicians, we improvise all the time, both vocally and instrumentally."*

Bass player Roger Waters began by stating that, *"I lie and am rather aggressive."* He was born in Great Bookham and moved to Cambridge when he was still very young. He later attended Regent Street Polytechnic. As for Pink Floyd, Waters explained, *"We give the public what they can see for themselves. We don't want to manufacture an image. We don't want to be involved in some publicity build-up."* Asked about their clothes image, Waters replied, *"We dress as we feel at the time."* Asked about the concept of their stage act, Waters added, *"There is no concept about it. Our music just comes from the fingers. There's no preconceived arrangement. Perhaps there was an idea dreamed up in as much as we use images as well as sounds, but otherwise it's all improvisation."* Speaking about whether he had any musical background in his family, Waters replied, *"Well, my mother's stone deaf, my fathers dead, and my grandmother bought her first pop record last week. It was a disc called 'Arnold Layne.'"*

Drummer Nick Mason is from Birmingham and describes himself as a "very mediocre, ordinary youth." His grandfather once wrote a "fine, regal march" called 'Grand State March.' Explained Mason, *"I take life easy, but I am a bit paranoic. I feel everyone has a down on me. I want to be successful and loved in everything I turn my hand to."* Asked about working in Pink Floyd, Mason replied, *"I had studied architecture for three years at the Polytechnic and then spent a year working in an office. It's only just lately, in fact, the*

Pink Floyd have been doing much work. In the past we played about one date a fortnight and spent the rest of the time sitting in pubs and saying how nice it would be to be famous. Only when we got a manager who started organizing us did we get beyond just dreaming."

Melody Maker (U.K.) reported that The Pink Floyd were scheduled to make their TV debut on Top of the Pops on Thursday, April 6, 1967, with 'Arnold Layne.' The article was accompanied by a picture of the band from the Arnold Layne promo film. Tour dates were listed.

The article also reported that sequences for the bands first feature film were scheduled to begin shooting on April 24, 1967. The working title of the film is 'The Life Story of Percy the Ratcatcher.'

Also in this issue is an ad for The Pink Floyd at the Roundhouse on Saturday, April 8th, 10 pm till dawn. Admission is 5/-.

Record Mirror (U.K.) published an article titled, "Ladies clothes, free form music, anarchy and the Pink Floyd." The band is surrounded by controversy, with their new single, 'Arnold Layne,' being banned on certain radio stations. The band maintain that the song, which is about a bloke who nicks ladies clothing off the washing line, is not "smutty," saying, *"It's more because people are against us as a group. Nothing to do with the material we use."*

Talking about experimentation in their music, Roger Waters stated, *"We play what we like and what we play is new. I suppose you could describe us as the house orchestra of this new movement because we're the only people doing what the fans want to hear. We're really part of the whole present pop movement. We're not, repeat not, an anti-group. In fact, we're very much in favor of a lot of things, including freedom and creativity, and doing what you want to do, but, of course, tempered by social conscience. We're not really anarchists."*

Speaking about their live performances, Waters explained, *"We take all the lighting equipment and get it set up before the show starts. Then our lighting manager takes over while we're playing and it's up to him to choose the light sequences which strike him as being harmonious with the sounds being produced by us. Before we start, the whole room is blacked out and then the lights go into operation. We link sounds together which are not usually linked, and link lights which are not usually linked."*

About their music, Nick Mason commented, *"We are relying a lot on our album to show what we're really trying to say. We try to develop. We don't have much time for people who just copy other artists, or get hold of an American record and just put it down, note by note."*

About their goals, the group said, *"Our aim is not to create hallucinatory effects on our audiences. We want only to entertain."* The band members are Roger Waters who is a science fiction reader, Syd Barrett who likes fairy stories, Nick Mason who hates "nasty people," and Rick Wright who hates crowded pubs. Their upcoming album has not been scheduled for release by EMI yet.

April 15, 1967 - Melody Maker (U.K.) reported that Pink Floyd were dropped at the last minute from appearing on Top of the Pops. Stanley Dorfman, the producer of the show, stated "We filmed the Floyd and the Move before last week's show because they were both playing out of town on Thursday night. Naturally we wanted to get the film in the can in case their new records entered the chart. In fact, on our combined chart, the Floyd dropped three places so it ruled them out of the show."

April 22, 1967 - New Musical Express (U.K.) reported that Pink Floyd will be among thirty groups performing at a 14-hour, all night rave at London's Alexander Palace on April 29, 1967. The event is being described as a "Technicolour dream."

Trend (U.K.), a British teen girls magazine, published an article titled, "Toes Blossom and the Floyd is Pink." They wrote, "A group that relies to an enormous degree on the visual aspect to engender excitement is the Pink Floyd. Please don't be too startled when I say that I actually like them. My tastes aren't nearly as negative as I might sometimes indicate. I have seen them work three or four times, and they are always interesting. When I

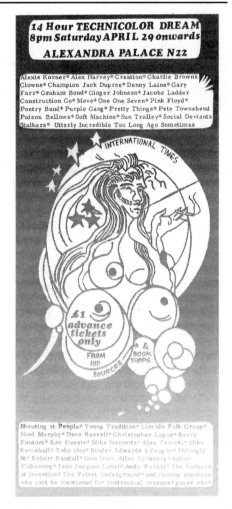

first watched them at the Marquee (still the best club in London), I thought the weird lighting effects would soon pall. They haven't. They remain totally fascinating and engrossing. Anyone who hasn't yet caught the Pink Floyd should do so immediately. Don't be put off by their first record, 'Arnold Layne,' which, though not bad, doesn't really indicate what they are all about. They're a new sensation."

Valentine (U.K.), a British teen girls magazine, published a picture of The Pink Floyd and an article titled, "Colourful!" They wrote, "TV is going into color, though that won't really happen for a year or so, and so is pop. There is this group called The Pink Floyd whose first disc was `Arnold Layne'/`Candy and a Currant Bun.' The Pink Floyd do pop in color. I quote their own words about their stage show: *"We are lights and sounds. The two mediums compliment each other, but we definitely don't use them together just as a gimmick. Our aim is simply to make our audiences dig the effect."* Their stage presentation consists basically of the playing of the usual group instruments, but combining their sounds with various lighting sequences which are projected onto both the group and their audience. Still with me? What I want to know is what happens if your make-up, shades, and dress color don't suit the lighting The Pink Floyd project on you? A lot of girls are going to look awful."

May 6, 1967 - Melody Maker (U.K.) **reported** on the Technicolour Dream concert held at the Alexandra Palace, London, on April 29, 1967. Nick Jones called the concert, at which Pink Floyd performed, "the beginning of a healthy young attitude towards total freedom for the individual."

May 1967 - Beat Instrumental (U.K.) **published** an article titled, "Arnold Layne was just us say The Pink Floyd." *"Psychedelic? We don't know what it means. If it means flashing lights, then we're a psychedelic group. If it doesn't, then we're not."* So say the Pink Floyd, the group hailed as the first big break-through for psychedelic music. But what of their hit record? *"'Arnold Layne' is nothing but a pop record. It wasn't intended to represent anything in particular. It's just us."*

How did 'Arnold Layne' come into existence? Says composer Syd Barrett, *"I wasn't influenced by anything, if that's what you mean. The title came first, and the rest just followed. Yes, we all write songs. In fact, our first album will consist of nothing but originals. About nine by me, and the rest by the others."* The group maintains that much of the disc's success was due to the sound obtained in the Sound Technique recording studio. *"We went in, played the number, and the sound just came. We never go into the studio with any particular aim, except to turn out a good commercial record."* Apart from writing, the boys also act as their own producers and arrangers. *"Whoever writes the song, produces it."*

When did the Pink Floyd realize that some form of stage act was necessary? *"We believe that music works in conjunction with the lights,"* said organist Rick Wright. *"We don't go on stage with anything worked out. The decision to include some form of visual effects was made some time ago. Hence the lights. That is our act really. Just lights."*

Would they have had so much success with this, their first record, without so much advance publicity? *"It's very hard to say,"* said the thoughtful Roger Waters. *"The radio stations won't play your record unless you're known. You're not known until you do something different. You don't get publicity without doing something different. You're not known until you get some publicity. And a record helps you to get publicity. But the record won't be played without people knowing who you are. The whole thing goes round in a circle, and becomes very complicated."*

"Incidentally," continued Roger, *"the next record will probably be completely different. We don't want to get stuck in a rut with just one sound. What sound it will be, we just don't know. All we'll do is go into the studio with an arrangement, and see what sounds appear. If we think it's right for that particular time, we'll use it. If not, we'll try something else."*

May 13, 1967 - The London Financial Times **(U.K.) reported** on the Pink Floyd 'Games for May' concert at the Queen Elizabeth Hall on May 12, 1967. Flowers were thrown at the audience, followed by darkness, hysterical laughter and the music of Pink Floyd. Colors were projected on the backcloth, with amoeba like shapes ebbing and flowing. At times, the band members wandered the stage playing with friction cars and blowing bubbles. The show was billed as a salute to spring.

May 19, 1967 - International Times (U.K.) **published** an article titled, "Floyd Play Games" that reviewed the Pink Floyd 'Games for May' concert at the Queen Elizabeth Hall on May 12, 1967. They wrote, "The choice of the Queen Elizabeth Hall for the Games for May event was really good thinking, for it was a genuine twentieth-century chamber music concert. Acoustically, the hall is probably better for amplified sound than natural sound and the cleanness of presentation of the hall itself was perfect for the very loose mixed media. The performance consisted, basically, of the Pink Floyd, a tape machine, projections, flowers, and the Queen Elizabeth Hall, all combined rather leisurely. The first half was a fairly straight presentation of their sound and light show, but the second half moved right into the hall and into the realm of involvement. Musically, the second half was really bordering on pure electronic music, and very good at that. On the whole, it was good to see the strength of a hip show holding its own in such a museum-like and square environment."

May 20, 1967 - Melody Maker (U.K.) reported that Pink Floyd will finish the recording of their new single and album this week. Peter Jenner stated, *"We will complete about fourteen tracks altogether and then take a new single and the album from that."* The single should be released on May 26, 1967, or June 2, 1967, with the album scheduled for release in mid-June. Also reported in this issue is that the Pink Floyd are planning a 'Games for June' happening at Chiswick House.

New Musical Express (U.K.) published an ad for Barbeque '67, a concert at the Tulip Bulb Auction Hall, Spalding, Lincs., on Spring Bank Holiday, Monday, May 29th, featuring the Jimi Hendrix Experience and The Pink Floyd. Admission was £1.

Trend (U.K.), a British teen girls magazine, published a full-page full color picture of the Pink Floyd and an article titled, "The Pink and Their Purple Door" by Penny Weston. Weston wrote, "Think of the Pink Floyd and your mind boggles and conjures up weird ideas of strange sounds and lighting effects. Then think of Arnold Layne and you become more puzzled. Who is Arnold Layne you ask yourself? Does he really exist?

Determined to find out the true identity of Arnold we asked the Pink Floyd up to our offices. When they trooped in one afternoon, in an orderly crocodile fashion, we were pleasantly surprised. Where were the four eyes and Dracula teeth? Instead we were confronted with four friendly, good-looking boys who didn't quite live up to our image of

terrifying, psychedelic monsters. Syd Barrett, the lead guitarist, plonked himself down into a seat next to me and began to explain. *"We're not really a psychedelic group,"* he said in a calm, matter-of-fact voice. *"People seem to have given us the wrong label. We do use strange lighting techniques on stage, but this is to complement our music and not to create hallucinations."*

Then we talked about their record, 'Arnold Layne,' which, incidentally, is their first release and has been quite a success. I didn't miss my cue. "Who is Arnold?" I asked excitedly. There was a pause and then Roger, the bass guitarist, laughed rather shyly. *"He doesn't exist at all. He's purely fictitious."* There were disappointed mumbles from all the office staff who were secretly hoping that the Floyd would have brought Arnold with them. *"No, you see,"* said Syd, staring at me with his large green eyes, *"I wrote Arnold Layne into the song because the words just fitted with the music."*

As a songwriter, Syd has some strong views on music. *"I think that you need a really good stage act to back up a song,"* he explained. *"When we use odd lighting combinations on stage we're trying to paint a picture in the audience's mind. Our music is like an abstract painting, it should suggest something to each person."* Syd is an ex-art student so he's qualified to speak about abstract paintings. Drummer Nick Mason, and Roger Waters, bass guitarist, were both studying architecture before they met up with Syd and Rick Wright, who plays the organ.

The group live in a flat in London's West End. *"We all get on very well,"* boasted Nick. *"Of course, we have the usual rows that other people in flats have, but apart from that, we get on fine."* Incidentally, their front door is painted purple. Very fitting, we thought.

I asked the Floyd what they thought of their record being banned on Radio London. Rick acted as spokesman, saying, *"I don't think the record was banned because of the lyrics, because you can't really object to them,"* he said. *"I think they must be against us as a group. They don't seem to like what we stand for."* Roger agreed and nodded his dark, shaggy head. Dangling his long legs precariously over the side of a desk, he said, *"I think it's something to do with different policies. Nobody else has banned our record so it's not really affecting us."*

At the moment, the Pink Floyd are recording their first album. Everything is very hush-hush but they assure us it will be quite unique. *"We play what we like, and when we like,"* said Syd. We're sure that the Pink Floyd's album will be a big winner, and it's refreshing to hear of a group who really like the music they play."

Also in this issue is a letters page with two pictures of the Pink Floyd, and readers letters that are answered by Pink Floyd.

A CHANGE FOR THE BETTER. Tastes change as we mature - little girls love dolls, little boys like soldiers. When they grow up the position is reversed, girls prefer the soldiers and boys go for the dolls. - Eda Aslett, Momton Headi, Surrey.

Syd: *"No wonder all the boys are dressing in military style and the girls have wooden legs."*

SQUARE PEG. I was pegging out some of my brother's socks when I ran out of pegs. My nine-year-old brother was outside so I asked him to hold them while I went and found some more pegs. I turned my back on him and went over to the other line to get the pegs. When I looked back there were the socks on the line supported by suspenders. - Ann Wightman, Maidstone, Kent.

Pink Floyd: *"Your brother must be a proper 'Arnold Layne!'"*

STOMACH THIS! When my family and I were out one day we were wondering where we could go for our dinner. A man overheard us talking and he said to us, "I suggest you go into the cafe around the corner, my father has stomach trouble and he always goes there." Not a very good recommendation was it? - Carol Conchie, Wirral, Cheshire.

Rick: *"What was on the menu, 'Alka-Seltzer' and chips?"*

SWITCHED OFF. When our radio went wrong, our next-door neighbor lent us a very old one. The next day mum was listening to it and it was playing a lot of Oldies. She yelled to my aunt, "That radio must be old, hark at the tunes its playing." I always thought that she was mad but now I know it. - Miss P. Davis, Gillingham, Kent.

Pink Floyd: *"Take it from us, your mum must be a bit switched off."*

MISTAKEN. My little brother brought some math homework home. He did it and took it to the teacher the next morning to be marked. In the evening he came running into the kitchen shouting, "My teacher loves me so much, she put a kiss beside every sum I've done." You should have seen my mums face when she opened his book and saw that they were all wrong – Tony, London, N.8.

Pink Floyd: *"I expect your mother was very X?"*

NOTHING'S IMPOSSIBLE. The other day I went to see the film The Ten Commandments. When it came to the dividing of the seas (which in the film is trick photography) a little boy behind me said, "Well, it just shows that it can be done." – R. Little, Windsor, Berks.

Pink Floyd: *"Who said 'The camera doesn't lie?'"*

DOUBLE-DUTCH. How many people, I wonder, have been to as many different schools as my sister? She started at a Dutch Nursery School, from there she moved to a Chinese Nursery School. Every evening she would come home jabbering away in Chinese! When the school closed down, my sister was placed in an Indonesian-speaking school. Then we moved to Europe and my sister went to a German school where, after a few months, she had picked up the language. Now we live in England and my sister will be taking her GCEs. You might think that she was a clever linguist, but the only language she can speak fluently is English. - G. Fjoa, Kenton, Middx.

Pink Floyd: *"We bet she can speak fluent Double-Dutch!"*

WORTH MORE THAN A PENNY. In our town there is a sign, which reads 'CAR PARK multi-storey TOILETS.' Whatever next! - Pauline Drake, Luton, Beds.

Pink Floyd: *"You should see what's written on band room walls!"*

SLIP-UP. For my birthday, recently, I received an orange silk mini-skirt. I thought that it was gorgeous and wore it shopping the next day. Imagine my horror when I walked into a clothes store and saw it displayed in the lingerie department as a mini-slip! - Lyda Boocock, Ontario, Canada.

Roger: *"Sounds to us as if Lyda made a 'mini slip-up!'"*

Romeo (U.K.), a British teen girls magazine, published "The Romeo File on Pink Floyd" on the back cover. It featured a picture of the band, plus biographical information on each band member. Band "likes" are listed. Roger likes sunshine, large cars, Chelsea buns, and science fiction novels. Rick likes sun, freedom, and Beethoven. Nick likes Christmas, and November 5th. Syd likes fairy stories, and painting.

June 1967 - International Times (U.K.) reviewed the happenings at the UFO Club on June 2, 1967. They wrote, "The Pink Floyd played to the largest crowd that UFO has ever held. At times, queues stretched for yards up Tottenham Court Road, and twice the box office had to close because the floor was completely packed. The audience included Jimi Hendrix, Chas Chandler, Eric Burdon, Pete Townshend, and members of the Yardbirds. Appeals by Susy Creamcheese and Joe Boyd were made to the rather emotional crowd to prevent them taking any action against John Hopkins' imprisonment until after his appeal had been heard. It is a pity that with all this happening, the Pink Floyd had to play like bums. The Soft Machine also appeared briefly to perform a poem for John Hopkins, and The Tales of Ollin dance group played for about 40 minutes and completely captured that audience's imagination. Also on the bill was Hydrogen Jukebox."

June 10, 1967 - New Musical Express (U.K.) reported that Pink Floyd have a new single scheduled for release next Friday, June 16, 1967, called 'See Emily Play.'

June 17, 1967 - New Musical Express (U.K.) reviewed the Pink Floyd single, 'See Emily Play,' with an article titled, "Melody Survives Pink Floyd's happening." 'See Emily Play' is full of weird oscillations, reverberations, electronic vibrations, fuzzy rumblings, and appealing harmonies. It should do well. The flip side, 'The Scarecrow,' is interesting, has fascinating harmonies, and a nice acoustic guitar.

Record Mirror (U.K.) reviewed the Pink Floyd single, 'See Emily Play/The Scarecrow.' 'See Emily Play' is Pink Floyd's best so far and should be a substantial hit. 'The Scarecrow' is stronger lyrically than the melody. Tipped for the top 50.

July 1, 1967 - New Musical Express (U.K.) published an article titled, "Nothing nasty behind our light and colour effects" by Norrie Drummond that featured an interview with Roger Waters. Waters explained, "*We are simply a pop group. But because we use light and color in our act, a lot of people seem to imagine that we are trying to put across some message with nasty, evil undertones.*"

The Pink Floyd use equipment that throws liquid abstract shapes on to the stage as they play. This has caused the band members to be seen as mystical, since they can't easily be seen. Waters replied, "*It sometimes makes it very difficult for us to establish any association with the audience. Apart from the few at the front, no one can really identify us.*"

The band, which turned professional less than four months ago, has already had two medium hits. Waters said, "*We're not rushing into anything. At the moment we want to build slowly and I think we're doing not too badly. The important thing is that we're doing what we want to do. We record the numbers we want, and fortunately they seem to be the ones that people want. No one interferes with us when we're in the studio. They just leave us, more or less, alone to get on with what we want.*"

Pink Floyd pay little attention to the record charts. Waters explained, "*We listen to Radio London and the other stations, but we don't really concern ourselves with what other groups are doing. The Chart puzzles me because I just can't imagine the type of person who would buy Engelbert Humperdink's record, and the Cream's. That is, if there is such a type.*"

Asked about the type of audience they attract, Waters replied, "*We recently played a concert at the Queen Elizabeth Hall, and that's usually where string quartets play. The people who came to see us there were a very mixed lot, some really way-out people with bare feet, and a few old women who always go to the Queen Elizabeth Hall no matter what's on. But mostly they were average men and women, between 17 and 25, mixed with a few teeny-boppers.*"

Pink Floyd would like to play more concerts like that in the autumn. Waters revealed, "*We'd like to play the major centers like Manchester, Liverpool, and Glasgow, doing our own two-hour show. You see, contrary to what some people think, it's not just the Southern audiences that we appeal to. In fact, the further North we go, the better the reception. We played in Belfast recently, and the reception there was great. The same thing happened when we played in Abergavenny. We had screamers and everything. It really astonished us."*

Waters then is quoted as saying to manager Andrew King, *"I've just remembered a great idea I had last night. I was driving down the M1, and a wing mirror on a lorry in front was vibrating finely. It was reflecting all the other lights on the road, winking indicators, stop lights, and so on. Now supposing we were to . . . "*

Also in this issue is the NME Top 30 chart for the week of June 28, 1967, with the Pink Floyd record, 'See Emily Play,' entering the chart for the first time at #27.

July 8, 1967 - New Musical Express (U.K.) reported that Pink Floyd are planning a tour of provincial cities in the late summer. The shows will be similar to their 'Games for May' presentation. Pathe Pictorial is currently making a short color film of 'Scarecrow' for the ABC circuit. The bands first LP, tentatively titled, 'Astronomy Domine,' has been completed and is planned for release at the end of the month. The album cover has been designed by lead guitarist, Syd Barrett.

Record Mirror (U.K.) published an article in which writer David Griffiths wrote about his luncheon with Roger Waters, Nick Mason, Peter Jenner, and Andrew King.

Asked about his architecture training, Mason responded, *"Mind you, the best chance for an architect to find clients is in show business. I'm always on the lookout for someone who has half a million pounds to spare and wants me to design him a house. Please tell the readers of the Record Mirror to get in touch with me if they are affluent enough to need my services."*

Asked about their first single, 'Arnold Layne,' and the fact that it was not a hit, manager Andrew King explained that it was destined to have a minority appeal. King added, *"It certainly fulfilled its destiny."*

As for their new single, 'See Emily Play,' Roger Waters stated, *"When you record a single, you are not interested in showing the public how far you've advanced since the last record. You've got to please the recording company apart from any other consideration, otherwise they won't release it."*

Although the writer has never been to a Pink Floyd concert, he has been told that they are extremely exciting. Mason said, *"You should come to one of our concerts. In clubs we play louder, partly to hold attention. In concerts, where everybody is seated and, we hope, seriously listening, we perform with greater range. We use a box, called the Azimuth Co-ordinator, which was designed for us and which enables us to throw stereo effects around a hall."*

Their recent performance at the Queen Elizabeth Hall in London was a sell out, but they are now banned from holding any future shows there because they threw flowers. Waters explained, *"It seems we contravened a regulation. We were told that people might have slipped on the flowers we threw into the audience."* The audience for the concert included both young and old people. Waters said, *"Someone I know was sitting next to two old ladies who sat there, still and silent, until the interval. Then one turned to her friend and said, 'They're very good, aren't they?'"* This type of response is not always automatic. *"Even fans don't always understand what we're trying to do,"* stated Waters. *"We had some photographs done, only in black and white, using a psychedelic slide superimposed on us. Some fans, who'd written asking for pictures, wrote back asking if we'd spilt something on the pictures. They really believed something had gone wrong."*

As for hostility directed towards the band, manager Peter Jenner stated, *"The Pink Floyd are a very good target, though we always get along well with promoters who have a professional approach. But we do run into those who say 'Whatever it is, it isn't music.'"*

July 15, 1967 - Romeo (U.K.), a British teen girls magazine, published a picture of the Pink Floyd with a letter in "Romeo Readers Meet the Pops." The letter read, "One night my friend Janice and I went to see the Pink Floyd at the Floral Hall, Belfast. After their performance, we went backstage to their dressing room. They were very nice to us and gave us their autographs. When they said goodbye in their lovely accents we found ourselves crying and we begged them to stay. But they had to go. Because of this, we missed the transport home, so we began to walk. As we passed a nearby hotel we saw two of the group coming out of the drive! Janice ran for the car, and they opened the door to let us in. She got in first and there was no room for me, so I sat on the singer's knee! As we were getting out of the car he kissed me, and said goodnight. We ran home to my house, and we both couldn't stop crying. *M. Moore, Belfast, 15.*"

July 22, 1967 - Disc and Music Echo (U.K.) published an article titled, "Pink Floyd: Freak out comes to town" by David Hughes. The article focused on the musicians in the band, with comments by Peter Jenner.

Asked about them being an R & B group that likes to improvise, Jenner replied, "*My guess is that this was not even intentional. They are a lazy bunch, and could never be bothered to practice. So they probably had to improvise to get away with it. We knew that this was what interested them and wanted to encourage them to play what they wanted, rather than what their public wanted. The Floyd are one of the few groups who can appreciate that electric instruments are more than just ordinary instruments with amplification.*"

Talking about concert venues, Jenner added, "*Pink Floyd music is an environment. They much prefer playing in a concert hall, where any atmosphere is created solely by them and their music.*"

On touring as a traveling freak show, Jenner explained, "*A freak-out could be as grand an occasion as a fair or a circus, and we'd like to have a large marquee and travel the country. 'The Freak-Out Comes to Town' it could be called.*"

Roger Waters is a blues man, obsessed with cars, and might end up as a business manager. Syd Barrett is a gypsy at heart who loves painting, music, fairy tales, outrageous clothes, and total freedom. Nick Mason wants to be rich and famous, and would like to write film scripts. Rick Wright is very

moody, a musician, wants to buy a Mellotron, and has written hundreds of songs that will never be heard. Peter Wynne Wilson is the light man and wants to design a machine that will turn sound into light.

Also in this issue is an ad for the album, 'Piper at the Gates of Dawn,' coming shortly.

Melody Maker (U.K.) published Blind Date with Syd Barrett in which Barrett was played a number of records, and he gave his opinions on them without knowing who they were.

Art - 'What's That Sound (For What It's Worth)' Barrett said, "*Good. I don't recognize it and I've no idea who it is, but it drives along. Liked the instrumental sound. A medium hit. I suspect it to be American. I dug.*"

Gene Latter - 'A Little Piece Of Leather.' Barrett said, "*It's a great song. That's nice. It's on the soul scene and I think people will go on digging the soul scene. I hope the people who listen to us will listen to this as well. The new wave of music is all-embracing. It gets across and makes everybody feel good. I don't think this will do well in the chart but it'll be okay for the clubs. I nearly guessed who it was - Gene Latter?*"

Jim Reeves - 'Trying To Forget.' Barrett said, "*Very way out record. I think I tapped my foot to that one. I don't know who it was. Let me think. Who's dead? It must be Jim Reeves. I don't think it will be a hit. It doesn't matter if an artist is dead or alive about records being released. But if you're trendy, this doesn't quite fit the bill. It's another that would sound better at 33 1/3.*"

Barry Fantoni – 'Nothing Today.' Barrett said, "*Very negative. The middle jazzy bit was nice. Apart from the saxophone bit, it was morbid. I don't know what it was all about. It seemed to be about somebody kissing somebody's feet. I don't want to hear it again. Maybe it should be played at 78.*"

Alex Harvey - 'The Sunday Song.' Barrett said, "*Nice sounds, yeah. Wow. Lot of drums, but it avoids being cluttered. The people in the background seem to be raving a bit more than the people in front. English? One of those young groups like John's Children? It moved me a little bit, but I don't think it will be a hit. Very snappy.*"

Tom Jones - 'I'll Never Fall In Love

Again.' Barrett said, "*I detect a Welsh influence in the strings. I feel it's one of those numbers you should play at slow speed, or backwards, or upside down. It's Sandy McPherson. Everyone knows who it is. It won't be a hit because it's too emotional. It'll sell a lot, but I wont buy one.*"

Blues Magoos - 'One By One.' Barrett said, "*It's got a message, but it didn't really seem to branch out anywhere. It's nice, and I dug it, but it won't do anything. No idea who it was. You're going to tell me it's the Byrds. I really dig the Byrds, Mothers Of Invention, and Fuggs. We have drawn quite a bit from those groups. I didn't see any reason for this record being a big flop or a big hit. It was a nice record.*"

Oliver Nelson - 'Drowning In My Own Despair' (Polydor). Barrett said, "*Crazy, yeah. If pressed to think about it, I would suggest it was the Four Tops. So, it's not the Four Tops. If you want a hit, it's best to make your own sounds. The label is a pretty color.*"

Vince Hill - 'When The World Is Ready' (Columbia). Barrett said, "*Fade it out. Vince Hill. I didn't understand the lyrics at all. It's very well produced and very well sung. It may be a hit, but I shouldn't think so, because the lyrics are so unconvincing.*"

David Bowie - 'Love You Till Tuesday.' Barrett said, "*Yeah, it's a joke number. Jokes are good. Everybody likes jokes. The Pink Floyd like jokes. It's very casual. If you play it a second time it might be even more of a joke. Jokes are good. The Pink Floyd like jokes. I think that was a funny joke. I think people will like the bit about it being Monday, when in fact it was Tuesday. Very chirpy, but I don't think my toes were tapping at all.*"

New Musical Express (U.K.) published an ad for the 7th National Jazz-Pop-Ballads & Blues Festival to be held at The Royal Windsor Racecourse on August 11-13, 1967. Scheduled for Saturday August 11, 1967, were The Pink Floyd. Tickets for a single day are 20p.

July 24, 1967 - Eastern Evening News (U.K.) reported on the Pink Floyd concert at the Floral Hall, Norfolk on July 19, 1967. The article stated that 800 people attended the concert, and were subjected to mind expanding trans-psychedelic influences before the band

came on. BBC2 had a camera crew at the show to record the freak out for television. A young girl, supervised by the bands art director, was running slide projectors using colored slides with tints and potions. The curtains on the stage parted, and Pink Floyd began their first song, a shuddering number, with flashing green lights from all angles, in time to the music, casting shadows around the hall. The second song used colored slides, projected across the whole stage, like globular brain cells. The vocals were disappointing due to the sound system, but the band was interesting and exciting.

After the show, Roger Waters explained that they were planning to tour the country circus-style, under a large marquee. Waters said, "*Although we have not yet approached them, we have thought of asking the Cream to join us, and we have been in touch with Andy Warhol's group. The snag is on one-nighters. You can't be sure the places where you play will be suitable for our projectors and other gear, to have the full effect.*"

July 28, 1967 - International Times (U.K.) published a full-page ad for the Love in Festival featuring Pink Floyd at the Alexandra Palace on July 29, 1967, and a large ad for the UFO Club with the Pink Floyd on July 28, 1967.

July 29, 1967 - Disc and Music Echo (U.K.) published an article titled, "Och Aye . . . Scotland goes Pink." Pink Floyd played at the Red Shoes Ballroom, in Elgin on July 20, 1967. Band members were quoted as saying, "*We've never played on a smaller stage.*" "*The audience was very cool to us.*" "*Some actually danced while we played.*" "*Hey, what was that guy saying 'do ye ken I could sing better in ma wee bath?'*" They added, "*Terrible stage. We're going to give up ballroom gigs. Conditions are so bad. We'd really like to set up in a big tent, circus style, and take our show around the country.*" "*I suppose it's odd, us being up here when we've got a big hit going. Still, we're staying up here a couple of nights. Be a break, really. No, the hotel people don't mind our clothes and hair. Think they'd be a bit disappointed if we didn't turn up in fancy dress.*"

New Musical Express (U.K.) reported that Pink Floyd will perform at the 1968 Mexico Olympic Games to be held in Mexico City next June. They will be playing at an official "youth culture" festival of music at the games. Also upcoming for the band is a concert tour of major British cities in September, with a new single likely to be released at the same time. The band hope to play additional overseas shows prior to their appearance in Mexico, although they may instead do a second British tour following their September shows. BBC-2 television filmed the Pink Floyd's concert at the Roundhouse in London recently. The footage is to be used in a special show about the Roundhouse, to be shown during the BBC-2's "Man Alive" series sometime during the next month. Pink Floyd's new album, 'Piper at the Gates of Dawn,' is to be released next week.

Also in this issue is an ad for the Bryan Morrison Agency Ltd., with Pink Floyd listed as one of their acts, and an ad for the Love in Festival at the Alexandra Palace on July 29, 1967, that included Pink Floyd. Tickets are £1.

August 4, 1967 - Go Magazine published an article titled, "The Pink Floyd is London's Answer to West Coast Sound" by Debbie Smith. Although Pink Floyd have never been to the United States, they look like they could have just come off the stage at the Fillmore. Included in the article are interviews with band members, done in the studio during the recording of their first album.

Syd Barrett talked about Pink Floyd's stage presentation, saying, *"We use lights to get the audience used to the type of music we play. It's hard to get used to it, actually, because it's a new type of idea, a loose, free-form music. But because it is a new type of music we realize that it takes a lot more time to get used to it. The crazy lights help, I think. Anyway, I like looking at them."*

Rick Wright talked about audiences, saying, *"You just can't come into a place where we're playing and order a drink and have a chat. You have to concentrate on what we're trying to say."*

Syd Barrett on labeling it psychedelic music, said, *"People can call it*

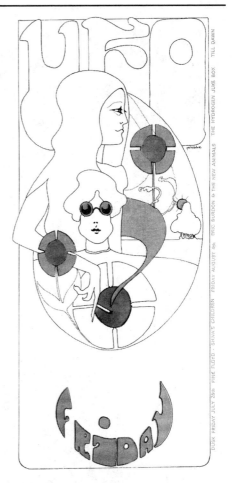

anything they like. We don't like labels to be stuck on things, but as long as they listen, I don't object." Rick Wright on labeling it psychedelic music, said, *"The word, psychedelic, means mind-expanding, or at least it did when they started it out. But in Britain if you say 'psychedelic' you mean 'drug taking', and that's a scene we wouldn't want to be identified with."*

Roger Waters on going to America, said, *"We are working on our manager to get us over to the West Coast. We don't get many records of those groups over here and we do want to see it for ourselves."*

Nick Mason on the future, said, *"I can't imagine myself doing this in 45 years time. But then, I can't generalize, can I?"*

Syd Barrett on goals, said, *"It's better not having a set goal. You'd be very narrow-minded if you did. All I know is that*

I'm beginning to think less now. It's getting better."

Syd Barrett on the suggestion that if he stops thinking completely, he might as well be a vegetable, replied, *"Yeah!"*

August 5, 1967 - Disc and Music Echo (U.K.) reported that Pink Floyd are planning to turn concerts into a circus-style act, to be held under a big tent. They hope to debut it in Paignton at the end of August and, if successful, will tour with it beginning in late September. Said co-manager, Peter Jenner, *"This could be the biggest thing to happen in pop."* Currently Pink Floyd are taking a break with the exception of finishing a new single. Jenner explained, *"We're dropping out for a bit because, lately, the strain has been such that the boys haven't been enjoying their work. We want to enjoy it, so we're stopping until that enthusiasm has returned."*

Melody Maker (U.K.) published an article titled, "The Great Pink Floyd Mystery." Pink Floyd concerts are hideous with "a thunderous, incomprehensible, screaming, sonic torture that five American doctors agree could permanently damage the senses."

Roger Waters stated *"We're being frustrated at the moment by the fact that, to stay alive, we have to play at lots and lots of places and venues that are not really suitable. This can't last, obviously, and we're hoping to create our own venues. We all like our music. That's the only driving force behind us. All the trappings of becoming vaguely successful, like being able to buy bigger amplifiers, none of that stuff is really important. We've got a name of sorts now among the public so everybody comes to have a look at us and we get full houses. But the atmosphere in these places is very stale. There is no feeling of occasion. There is no nastiness about it, but we don't get rebooked on the club or ballroom circuit. What I'm trying to say is that the sort of thing we are trying to do doesn't fit into the sort of environment we are playing in. The supporting bands play 'Midnight Hour,' and the records are all soul, then we come on. I've got nothing against the people who come and I'm not putting down our audiences. But they have to compare everybody. So-and-sos group is better than everybody else. It's like marking exercise*

books. Dave Dee, Dozy, Beaky, Mick, and Tich get a gold star in the margin, or 'Tich – very good.'"

Waters continued, *"On the club scene we rate about two out of ten and 'Must try harder.' We've had problems with our equipment and we can't get the PA to work because we play extremely loud. It's a pity because Syd writes great lyrics and nobody ever hears them. Maybe it's our fault because we are trying too hard. After all, the human voice can't compete with Fender Telecasters and double drum kits. We're a very young group, not in age, but in experience. We're trying to solve problems that haven't existed before. Perhaps we should stop trying to do our singles on stage. Even the Beatles, when they worked live, sounded like their records. But the sort of records we make today are impossible to reproduce on stage, so there is no point in trying."*

Asked if this was being dishonest, Waters replied, *"This is the point. We don't think so. We still do 'Arnold Layne,' and struggle through 'Emily' occasionally. We don't think it's dishonest because we can't play live what we play on records. It's a perfectly okay scene. Can you imaging somebody trying to play 'A Day in the Life?' Yet that's one of the greatest tracks ever made. A lot of stuff on our LP is completely impossible to do live. We've got the recording side together, and not the playing side. So what we've got to do now is get together a stage act that has nothing to do with our records, things like 'Interstellar Overdrive,' which is beautiful, and instrumentals that are much easier to play."*

Asked if it makes them depressed when they don't communicate with an audience, Waters replied, *"It's sometimes depressing and becomes a drag. There are various things you can do. You can close your mind to the fact you're not happening with the audience and play for yourself. When the music clicks, even if it's only with ten or twelve people, it's such a gas. We're trying to play music of which it can be said that it has freedom of feeling. That sounds very corny, but it is very free."*

As to the future, Waters explained, *"We can't go on doing clubs and ballrooms. We want a brand new environment, and we've hit on the idea of using a big top. We'll have a huge tent and go around like a traveling circus. We'll have a huge screen, 120-feet wide and 40-feet high inside, and project films and slides. We'll play the big cities or anywhere and become an occasion, just like a circus. It'll be a beautiful scene. It could even be the salvation of the circus! The thing is, I don't think we can go on doing what we are doing now. If we do, we'll all be on the dole."*

Also in this issue is a review of the Pink Floyd concert at the UFO Club by Roger Simpson. Multi-colored projected lights were a background to a cacophony of sound. The band played two sets, but did not play either of their two hit singles. Songs they performed included 'Pow R Toc H,' and the debut of a new song called 'Reaction in G' that was written in reaction against their Scottish tour when they had to play 'See Emily Play.' They drew every conceivable sound from their instruments and they were an impressive scene.

Also in this issue is an ad for the Pink Floyd album, 'The Piper at the Gates of Dawn.' Available now.

New Musical Express (U.K.) reported that the Pink Floyd had to cancel a promotional visit to Hamburg, Germany, that would have included an appearance on the TV show 'Music for Young People.' They also had to cancel a concert on Monday at the Torquay Town Hall. Rumors that Syd Barrett had quit the group were denied by manager Andrew King, who stated, *"It is not true Syd has left the group. He is tired and exhausted, and has been advised to rest for two weeks. We have decided the whole group will holiday for the next fortnight, and any bookings which have to be cancelled during this period will be rearranged for a later date."*

Also in this issue is an ad for the Pink Floyd album, 'Piper at the Gates of Dawn,' available now.

August 12, 1967 – Record Mirror (U.K.) published a full-color picture of The Pink Floyd on the front cover.

August 19, 1967 - Melody Maker (U.K.) published an article titled, "Pink Floyd Flake Out!" Syd Barrett is reported as suffering from "nervous exhaustion" and, as a result, the Pink Floyd has cancelled all shows for the rest of

August, including the Windsor Jazz Festival. Appearances will resume in September with a concert on September 1, 1967 in a special cinerama tent in Paignton, Devon, England. The cinerama tent will feature special lighting effects and films, and if it works out, will be taken on the road.

The Pink Floyd recorded songs for their next single earlier this week, and it will be a Syd Barrett composition scheduled for release on September 8, 1967. Upcoming tours include five days in Denmark beginning September 8, 1967, and four days in Ireland starting September 15, 1967.

Mirabelle (U.K.), a British teen girls magazine, published a full page picture of The Pink Floyd as part of the Mirabelle Scrapbook, with the warning: "Don't gaze too long, or you'll get hooked too!"

New Musical Express (U.K.) published "Life Lines of Pink Floyd," listing hobbies, ('dreaming' for Richard Wright), favorite colors ('multi' for Roger Waters), personal ambitions ('rule the world' for Nick Mason), and pets ('cat called Rover' for Syd Barrett), of the group members.

Valentine (U.K.), a British teen girls magazine, published a full-page black and white centerfold picture of The Pink Floyd.

August 26, 1967 - New Musical Express (U.K.) reported that the venue for The Pink Floyd's UFO Festival on September 1 & 2, 1967 has been changed to the Chalk Farm Roundhouse in London. It was originally planned to be held under a canvas at Paignton, Devon, but was moved because the owners of the marquee didn't want it to be used for a psychedelic festival. Manager Andrew King stated, *"Presenting a show under canvas would have been a completely new experience. We are now negotiating with other firms to find a suitable marquee for a future festival."*

August 31, 1967 - International Times (U.K.) published an ad for the new Pink Floyd album, 'The Piper at the Gates of Dawn,' and a concert ad for the UFO RAI Festival featuring Pink Floyd on September 1 and 2, 1967.

September 1967 - Beat Instrumental (U.K.) published an interview with Rick Wright done in the Top of The Pops Television Studio. Asked about their single, 'See Emily Play,' Wright said, "*It was recorded in the Sound Technique Studios in Chelsea. Although it sounds a bit gimmicky, hardly any special effects were used. Take that 'Hawaiian' bit at the end of each verse, that was just Syd using a bottleneck through echo. The part that sounds speeded up, John Woods, the engineer, just upped the whole thing about an octave. On stage, we have to cut that particular bit out, but then I don't think the audience minds if our reproduction isn't 100 percent accurate. They realize that many groups use weird effects, and don't expect to hear them all in a ballroom. I don't think the success of 'See Emily Play' has affected us personally. Sure, we get more money for bookings, but the next one could easily be a flop. When I first heard the playback in the studio, I had a feeling it would go higher than it did, but I'm not complaining.*"

Pink Floyd recorded their album, 'The Piper at the Gates of Dawn,' at EMI studios. Wright explained, "*We decided to use both studios. I don't think one is necessarily better than the other, but they've both got different atmospheres, and it makes a change to keep swapping around. Norman Smith, our producer, is very keen on Sound Technique, but he also likes the EMI studios. In the future, we'll be using both. Originally, we were recommended to Sound Technique. Can't remember who by, but they hadn't been open very long. I think we were one of the very first groups to use it, but now a lot go there because of our success.*"

Asked if Pink Floyd played most of their concerts in London, Wright replied, "*We only play in London about once a month. Then it's at the UFO in Tottenham Court Road. The rest of our time is spent doing ballrooms up and down the country. We've also got quite a bit of work lined up abroad, but that doesn't mean we're going to forsake England. It's just a pity that some of the ballrooms are so bad, especially the stages. But we've got an idea which could put an end to all that. There could well be a Pink Floyd circus soon. We've got this massive Big Top capable of holding 6,000*

people, which we intend to take around the country. You know, find a field outside a town, set up, and play. Just like a proper circus. We've got this huge cinemascope screen for all the flashing light bit, and we'll make it into a complete show. There'll be us, of course, plus a few other acts. It's something that's never been done before, but we think it'll work.*"

September 2, 1967 - New Musical Express (U.K.) reviewed the Pink Floyd album, 'Piper at the Gates of Dawn.' They wrote that the music is varied, from outer-space, to Arabic, to jazz. The album features rasping guitar by Syd Barrett, distorted vocals, shouts, laughs, and raving organ from Rick Wright. 'Interstellar Overdrive' takes up most of side two, with weird overtones. The drum effects by Nick Mason on 'Scarecrow' are good. Four stars.

Also in this issue is an ad for the U.F.O. Festival at the Roundhouse on Friday and Saturday. Pink Floyd will be performing on both nights. The concert is a benefit for Release. Tickets are 25p, or 15p for UFO members.

Record Mirror (U.K.) reviewed the new Pink Floyd album, 'Piper at the Gates of Dawn,' writing that their psychedelic image really comes to life on the album, which showcases their talent and recording technique. The record features mind blowing sounds and is performed extremely well. Four stars.

September 1967 - Rave Magazine (U.K.) published an article titled, "The Big Pop Movement" by Jeremy Pascall about the new pop scene. Included is a full-page color picture of The Pink Floyd from the Piper at the Gates of Dawn photo session.

September 9, 1967 - Melody Maker (U.K.) reported that Pink Floyd are flying to Denmark for four days, then on to Sweden for one day, before returning to Britain. And on September 14, 1967, they fly to Ireland for four days, then to Belgium on the 18th for a television show.

New Musical Express (U.K.) published an ad for Bryan Morrison as sole agent for Pink Floyd.

September 11, 1967 - Aarhus Stiftstidende (Denmark) reported on the concert at the Boom Dancing Center in Aarhus, Denmark on September 10, 1967. More than 1,000 people attended the show. The band performed three songs from their record, but they were all treated so you could not tell which. Asked if it was strange that their vocals could not be heard, the band replied "*Not that strange. The microphones did not work. Eventually we shut them off.*" Syd Barrett remarked after the concert, "*How the audience screamed. Don't people ever clap their hands in this country?*"

September 12, 1967 – BT, Copenhagen (Denmark) reported on the concert held at the Star Club in Copenhagen, Denmark on September 11, 1967. Bands want to give the audience a total experience in both visuals and sound effects, and Pink Floyd have come very far in doing this. They played instrumental pieces, and the one recognizable song was 'Set the Controls for the Heart of the Sun.'

September 16, 1967 - New Musical Express (U.K.) reported that the first Radio 1 edition of the Top Gear Show will debut on October 1, 1967, from 2-5 p.m. with host Pete Drummond, and will include a session by Pink Floyd.

Also reported in this issue is that the Pink Floyd will be doing a five-day tour of Ireland, beginning at the Belfast Starlite on Friday, September 15, 1967, followed by the Ballymena Flamingo on the 16th, and the Cork Arcadia on the 17th. A Belgian television promotional appearance is scheduled for Monday the 18th.

September 23, 1967 - Melody Maker (U.K.) reported that Pink Floyd are finishing negations for their first tour of the United States. Beginning in November, they are scheduled for two weeks at the Fillmore in San Francisco, one week in Boston, and a few days in New York. Their album, 'Piper at the Gates of Dawn,' is selling well on the West Coast.

Also in this issue is an ad that reads, "EMI proudly congratulate their top line artistes chosen by you in the pop poll." Pink Floyd is among the artists listed.

September 30, 1967 - Billboard Magazine (U.S.) reported that Pink Floyd have set the dates for their first U.S. tour, which will begin in San Francisco on October 26, 1967, with a week at the Fillmore Auditorium. Other dates on the four-week tour include performances in Boston, Los Angeles, and New York. General Artists Corp. is handling the group's bookings. Pink Floyd's co-manager, Peter Jenner, is in New York meeting with The Richmond Organization, Pink Floyd's publishers. Jenner has also been working on promotion plans with Hugh Dallas of Tower Records for the upcoming U.S. release of the Pink Floyd album, 'The Piper at the Gates of Dawn.'

Melody Maker (U.K.) reported that Pink Floyd are planning a European television tour beginning in early November, that will include dates in Holland, Germany, Denmark, Sweden, Belgium, and France. Agent Bryan Morrison said, "*This tour is an entirely new concept to us. It is planned as a sort of TV blitz intended to get through to as many people as possible in the shortest possible time.*" The band is also working on a new single, with 'Emily' moving up the American charts. Morrison added, "*There has been tremendous demand for their LP on the West Coast.*"

October 7, 1967 - Disc and Music Echo

(U.K.) reported that Pink Floyd have finalized arrangements for four spectacular concerts next March. The shows will feature Pink Floyd, plus a 100-voice choir and a small choral orchestra. Venues and dates for the performances are Manchester Free Trade Hall on March 2, 1968, Liverpool Philharmonic on March 9, 1968, the Royal Albert Hall on March 15, 1968, and Birmingham Town Hall on March 16, 1968.

Also reported in this issue is that Pink Floyd will play at the Fillmore Auditorium in San Francisco during a four-week tour of America starting at the beginning of November. The band have not decided on what song to release as their new single, although several Syd Barrett songs have been recorded.

Melody Maker (U.K.) reported on the Pink Floyd concert at the Saville Theater on October 1, 1967. Pink Floyd began their set with lights "flickering nervously" at their feet, playing an eerie song. The opening impact disappeared for the rest of their performance, with their faces in the dark resulting in an impersonal performance. Their music is "shatteringly original," using unexplored electronic ideas, but their song order lacked direction and didn't seem to go anywhere.

New Musical Express (U.K.) reported that Pink Floyd will put on four concert spectaculars in major concert halls next March, that will feature a small orchestra and a 100-voice choir. The concerts are slated for Manchester Free Trade Hall, Liverpool Philharmonic Hall, London Royal Albert Hall, and Birmingham Town Hall. The band will also do a regular tour in the early part of the year, possibly with the Incredible String Band. Next week the band will be recording a new single, another Syd Barrett song. The latter part of the month will be spent playing for German and Belgian television on the 17-20th, and at concerts in Paris, France on 22-26th. Additional television and concert appearances are scheduled for Holland on November 8-12th, and the group will be leaving for an American promotional tour on November 20th.

Also in this issue is a review of the Pink Floyd concert at the Saville on Sunday, October 1, 1967. Hippies and beautiful people

turned up to see the Pink Floyd and their light show, which they have down to a fine art. Flashing patterns and waving silhouettes accompanied their music, which was very loud and primarily instrumental.

Record Mirror (U.K.) reported that the Pink Floyd will be performing a number of "spectaculars" in March, that may include a 100-piece choir and a small chamber orchestra. The spectaculars will begin on March 2, 1968 at the Manchester Free Trade Hall, followed by the Liverpool Philharmonic Hall on the 9th, the Royal Albert Hall on the 15th, and the Birmingham Town Hall on the 16th. This coming Monday, the band will be trying out the new Unit Delpha four computer at the BBC's Radiophonics Workshop.

October 14, 1967 - Melody Maker (U.K.) reported that Pink Floyd are recording the soundtrack to a new BBC Colour TV series at the BBC Radiophonic Workshop.

New Musical Express (U.K.) reported that the Pink Floyd have been added to the Jimi Hendrix/Move/Amen Corner tour as a replacement for the Turtles who dropped out. The tour will begin on November 14, 1967 at London's Royal Albert Hall.

Valentine (U.K.), a British teen girls magazine, published a picture of The Pink Floyd and reported that, "The music, the sound, and the lights of groups like Zoot Money's Dantalian's Chariot and The Pink Floyd can be said to blow your mind. They are also liable to blow all the electrical fuses in the places they are playing. So a new problem arises to natter at these groups and their faithful road managers. The Pink Floyd experienced it a few weeks ago when they were due to give a big show in a marquee at a summer resort. When the marquee owners realized the nature of the Floyd's performance they called the date off, saying a canvas tent was not the place for it. So, the Floyd went into a mighty circular brick building in London's Camden Town called the Roundhouse, once a railway loco depot. Tough walls and good lighting circuits."

October 1967 - Beat Instrumental (U.K.)

reported that most guitarists start their musical career on a piano. But not Syd Barrett. He launched out on a banjo. *"I'm not quite sure why,"* Barret said. *"It just seemed a good idea at the time. I picked it up in a second hand shop and plunked away quite happily for about six months. Then I decided to get a guitar. The first one was a Hofner acoustic, which I kept for a year. Then I joined a local Cambridge group called Jeff Mott and the Mottos and splashed out on a Futurama 2. At the time I thought it was the end in guitars, fantastic design and all that. Incidentally, Jeff Mott was a great singer. Wonder what happened to him? We did a lot of work at private parties. And some of our material was original, but mostly we stuck to Shadows' instrumentals and a few American songs. Eventually the group dissolved and I moved into the blues field, this time playing bass. It was another Hofner, and I played that for a couple of years. One day I met a guy called Roger Waters who suggested that when I came up to a London Art School, we got together and formed a group. This I did, and became a member of the Abdabs. I had to buy another guitar because Roger played bass, a Rickenbacker, and we didn't want a group with two bass players. So I changed guitars, and we started doing the pub scene. During that period we kept changing the name of the group until we ended up with The Pink Floyd. I'm not quite sure who suggested it or why, but it stuck."*

Barrett continued, *"A couple of months ago, I splashed out a couple of hundred on a new guitar, but I still seem to use that first one. It's been painted several times, and once I even covered it with plastic sheeting and silver discs. Those discs are still on the guitar, but they tend to look a bit worn. I haven't changed anything on it, except that I occasionally adjust the pickups when I need a different sound."*

Barrett continued, *"Who are my idols? Well, Steve Cropper is an obvious choice, and so is Bo Diddley. In the old days, he was a great influence on both me and the group. No, I don't think they influence me now. At least I'm not conscious of it. Apart from being a good guitarist, I don't really have any ambitions, yet! I haven't been in the business that long."*

October 21, 1967 - Melody Maker (U.K.)

reported that Pink Floyd were recording a new single in London the previous week, to be released on November 13, 1967. They will also be doing a U.S. tour, returning to Britain on November 13, 1967.

Record Mirror (U.K.) published an article titled, "'We Feel Good' say the Pink Floyd" by Derek Boltwood. Pink Floyd has combined light and sound in their performances and are now considered one of the best of the new-wave groups.

Talking about their performances, Roger Waters stated, *"We play what we like, and what we play is new. I suppose you could describe us as the movement's house orchestra because we were one of the first people to play what they wanted to hear. We're really part of the whole present pop movement, although we just started out playing something we liked. We're not an anti-group. In fact, we're very pro lots of things, including freedom and creativity, and doing what you want to do, but tempered by social conscience. We're not really anarchists. But we're in a very difficult position, because the sort of thing we do comes over best in concert, rather than in clubs or dance halls. We gave a concert a short while ago at the Royal Festival Hall, and although we learnt a lot from it, we also lost a lot of money on it. We had to give up a week's work in order to arrange everything, and so on. 'Games for May,' as it was called, was on in the evening, and we went onto the stage in the morning to try and work out our act. Up till then we hadn't thought about what we were going to do. Even then we only got as far as rehearsing the individual numbers and working out the lighting. So when it came to the time of the performance in the evening, we had no idea of what we were going to do."*

Nick Mason said about the show, *"We just took a lot of props on stage with us and improvised. Quite a bit of what we did went down quite well, but a lot of it got completely lost. We worked out a fantastic stereophonic sound system whereby the sound traveled round the hall in a sort of circle, giving the audience an eerie effect of being absolutely surrounded by this music. And, of course, we tried to help the effect by the use of our lighting. Unfortunately, it only worked for people sitting in the front of the hall. Still, this was the first time we'd tried it, and like a lot of other ideas we used for the first time at this concert, they should be improved by the time we do our next one. Also, we thought we'd be able to use the props and work our act out as we went along. But we found this to be extremely difficult. I think it's important to know what you're going to do, to a certain extent, anyway. I always like to be in control of the situation."*

Mason continued, *"Another thing we found out from giving that concert was that our ideas were far more advanced than our musical capabilities, at that time, anyway. I think we've improved a lot now. Well, we've had to, obviously. And it's much easier for us to put across what we want to say. We made a lot of mistakes at that concert, but it was the first of its kind. And we, personally, learnt a lot from it. But it makes us feel good to know that what we are doing, what we have been doing for the past three years, has now been accepted, and has had a great effect upon the sort of thing other groups are doing now. It wasn't until February of this year that everything started happening for us and made us decide to turn professional, and life has been a bit chaotic for us since then. But it was worth the wait. Three years ago, no one knew what it was all about. But now the audience accepts us. We don't feel that we should try to educate the public. We don't want to push anything onto them. But if they accept what we're offering, and they seem to be at the moment, then that's great. And we feel good because our ideas are getting across to a large number of people."*

October 28, 1967 - New Musical Express (U.K.) published an ad for the Jimi Hendrix tour with Pink Floyd. The ad included tour dates and performance times.

November 10, 1967 - Los Angeles Free Press (U.S.) reported that Pink Floyd made its only appearance in the Los Angeles area with a performance at The Cheetah Club in Santa Monica, California. The concert provided an aural/visual experience with total sensual involvement of the audience. Pink Floyd's press release read, "There are no barriers, there can be no predictions."

November 13, 1967 – The Village Voice, New York (U.S.) reported that Pink Floyd gave a one-hour performance at The Cheetah Club in New York, on November 12, 1967, before flying back to London, England, that night.

November 14, 1967 - Het Binnenhof (Netherlands) published an article titled, "Psiechedelische Wierook bij Pink Floyd." Not even Pink Floyd really knows what psychedelic music is. Bass player Roger Waters said, *"If it affects the audience, it must be good. What that name means, even we don't know. For us, it's just the use of lighting effects with music. The fact that we are now the main force of this genre is not important. We just play what we like."* Guitarist Syd Barrett talked about their latest album, saying, *"Ten great songs that we are very enthusiastic about. I think it will do pretty well."*

November 15, 1967 - Het Binnenhof (Netherlands) reported on the Hippy Happy Fair held at the Ahoy Hall in Rotterdam. The article stated that on Monday night, November 13, 1967, there was a talent contest in which Pink Floyd's manager was one of the judges. At 10:00 p.m., Pink Floyd took the stage and played for about an hour, using whirling light effects to captivate the audience. Their performance was an outstanding success even though their equipment failed at times.

November 16, 1967 – Palatinate, Durham University (U.K.) reported in Pop News on the Pink Floyd concert at the Durham University Students Center on October 28, 1967. The article said, "This controversial group did not come to Dunelm House with the intention of inspiring people to skip around the floor like gay young spring lambs, but with a show that is designed to appeal to the senses." "The lighting is used to give an added dimension to the music." "A lot of their music is electronic with often totally unconnected harmonies and constructive use of feedback, not indiscriminate wailings."

November 18, 1967 - Melody Maker (U.K.) reviewed the Pink Floyd single, 'Apples and Oranges.' It is an easier but heavily electronic song, with tinkling, whirring electricity. However, the song is pretty hard to get a hold

of. The flip side, 'Paint Box,' has a hollow 'Day in the Life' feel, but is more interesting and commercial. A good record with exciting sounds.

New Musical Express (U.K.) published a review of the Jimi Hendrix concert at the Albert Hall in London on November 14, 1967, that featured the Pink Floyd as one of the support acts. The reviewer wrote that Pink Floyd played a subdued instrumental set, with a toned-down light show, and crashing gongs, cymbals, and eastern guitar. Accompanying the article was a photo of all the musicians on the tour standing together.

Also in this issue was a quarter-page ad for the Pink Floyd single, 'Apples and Oranges.'

November 25, 1967 - The Bristol Evening Post (U.K.) reviewed the Jimi Hendrix/Pink Floyd concert at Colston Hall, Bristol on November 24, 1967. The article said that Pink Floyd played weird music, shattered eardrums, and lost themselves in a swirling cloud of colored lights.

Disc and Music Echo (U.K.) published tour dates for the Jimi Hendrix/Move/Pink Floyd/Amen Corner/Nice tour.

New Musical Express (U.K.) reviewed the Pink Floyd single, 'Apples and Oranges'/'Paint Box.' They wrote that this is Pink Floyd's most psychedelic single so far, with rising vocals, falsetto harmonies, a perpetual growling sound, and a reverberating organ. Most of the song is way—out, but it has a catchy chorus. The B-side has interesting lyrics and a hammering beat.

Top Pops and Music Now (U.K.) reported that on their nationwide tour with Jimi Hendrix, the Pink Floyd were concerned about using their light show in the big theaters. Syd Barrett explained, "*Our lighting expert usually works from a platform at the back of a hall, with a cable leading up to the stage. This is impossible on a tour, so he's working on the idea of having the lighting equipment on stage. Certainly we don't want to have to appear without lights. We've never worked without them before, and we wouldn't be happy about it.*"

Talking about their new single, 'Apples and Oranges,' Barrett said, "*It's unlike anything we've ever done before. It's a new sound. Got a lot of guitar in it. It's a happy song, and it's got a touch of Christmas. It's about a girl who I saw just walking around town, in Richmond. The apples and oranges bit*

'Er stond gewoon een podium midden in die zaal'

is the refrain in the middle."

As for their live performances, Barrett commented, *"We are going to play a lot more songs now. Our organist, Rick, is writing a lot of things, and I am still writing."*

November 28, 1967 - The Chatham Standard (U.K.) published an article titled, "Pop fever grips the towns," about the upcoming Jimi Hendrix/Move concert with Pink Floyd also on the bill. Tickets are selling

out rapidly. Reviews of the tour are wildly complimentary, although Melody Maker's Chris Welch thought the shows were too loud.

December 5, 1967 - The Chatham Standard (U.K.) reported on the Jimi Hendrix/Pink Floyd tour stop at the Central Hall, Chatham, England on December 1, 1967. The reviewer reported that Pink Floyd were a disappointment. They performed in near darkness, played unrecognizable numbers, and were overshadowed by a "man in a bear skin jacket whose task seemed to be to leap about the stage adjusting amplifiers, twisting knobs, and retrieving the odd cymbal and microphone."

December 9, 1967 - Melody Maker (U.K.) published an article titled, "Hits? The Floyd Couldn't Care Less" by Alan Walsh. Asked what they thought about their new single, 'Apples and Oranges,' not doing well, Syd Barrett replied, "*Couldn't care less. All we can do is make records which we like. If the kids don't, then they wont buy it.*"

Barrett thinks that groups should record their music, press their own records, distribute and sell them themselves, adding, "*All middle men are bad.*" As for the Beatles and the Stones, Barrett explained, "*That's why the kids dig them, because they do what they want. The kids know this.*"

The interview took place at the Central Office of Information in Lamberth where Syd Barrett, Roger Waters, Peter Jenner, and Andrew King were watching a color promo film for the song, 'Jugband Blues,' that was made for a magazine program on Britain. Peter Jenner had wanted to release this song as the single, instead of 'Apples and Oranges,' and said, "*The group has been through a very confusing stage over the past few months and I think this has been reflected in their work. You can't take four people of this mental level, they used to be architects, an artist, and even an educational cyberneticist, give them big success and not expect them to get confused. But they are coming through a sort of deconfusing period now. They are not just a record group. They really pull people in to see them and their album has been terrifically received in this country and America. I think they've got a lot of tremendous things ahead of them. They are really only just starting.*"

Asked if they are abandoning their light show as being out of style, Roger Waters replied, "*Not at all. With us, lights were not, and are not, a gimmick. We believe that a good light show enhances the music. Groups who adopted lights as a gimmick are now being forced to drop them, but there's no reason why we should. In this country, groups were forced to provide their own light shows, whereas in the States, it was the clubs who provided the*

lights." Syd Barrett continued, "*Really, we have only just started to scrape the surface of effects and ideas of lights and music combined. We think that the music and the lights are part of the same scene. One enhances and adds to the other. But we feel that in the future, groups are going to have to offer much more than just a pop show. They'll have to offer a well-presented theater show.*"

December 12, 1967 - The Chatham Standard (U.K.) published a letter from reader M. Buswell replying to the review printed on December 5, 1967. He wrote, "Your reporter seems to have gotten some of her facts wrong. Firstly she said that the Pink Floyd were a disappointment. Perhaps they were, but this was through no fault of theirs. For a start they were handicapped by having no means of erecting their cinema screen behind them, which is an essential with their light show. Secondly, she says that they played in near-darkness most of the time. Well, they had their light show with them, and I am sure she will agree that you cannot enjoy a light show, except in darkness. She also says that they played some unrecognizable numbers. I suggest that she should have listened to the Floyd's LP before she went to the show and then maybe she would have recognized them. About the "young man in a bearskin jacket." In the first place, there was no mention of the same person jumping about the stage while Jimi Hendrix was playing, retrieving a cymbal and putting up falling "hi-hats." Finally I think that it is an insult to the groups to play in the hall. What's wrong with one of the cinemas? It was good enough for the Rolling Stones and there were no complaints."

December 16, 1967 - Disc and Music Echo (U.K.) published an ad for the Christmas on Earth Continued festival, to be held at the Kensington Olympia on Friday, December 22, 1967. Among the bands performing will be the Pink Floyd. Tickets were £1 in advance, and £1.25 the day of the show.

Record Mirror (U.K.) reported that Pink Floyd have resigned with the Bryan Morrison Agency for one year, and have split with Peter Wynne-Wilson, their light man, on friendly terms. Currently the band are on Christmas

1968
A Saucerful of Secrets

holiday, and are spending time in the recording studios finishing their next album and a new single, which is due out in January. Pink Floyd will be touring Europe in March, and the U.S. in April or May.

December 30, 1967 - Melody Maker (U.K.) published letters from readers about the recent Pink Floyd tour. D.R. Lamb of Newcastle wrote that he was disgusted by the jeering at the Pink Floyd show. Jim Connor of Glasgow wrote that the audience clapped for the Amen Corner's diabolical act, and later had the gall to jeer the Pink Floyd's brilliant performance. Dave Bunday of Cornwall wrote that if any readers are intending to see the Pink Floyd, my advice is don't. They played here recently and were so unbelievably bad the supporting group had to be brought back early. It was the opinion of most of the 1,000 students at our dance that they were the worst group ever to appear in Cornwall.

Also in this issue is a letter from Peter Jenner and Andrew King that stated, *"Pop music is a rugged plant and is able to stand up well to the periodic episodes of self-torture and internecine warfare which characterize it. Now the Pink Floyd are accused of 'killing pop music.' No doubt, they are about the ninety-seventh group to be accused of this, ever since Ida Barr went electric. A lot of people, from poor old Engelbert Humperdinck to Ravi Shankar, Dave Clark, and John Lennon. If you have a sufficiently closed mind, anybody can be seen as a threat. So yes, the Pink Floyd are killing pop music because there are a large number of people whose minds are too closed to accept what the Pink Floyd do as anything other than a threat to most people's ideas as to what pop music is. To them all, boring, repetitive, false glitter, the leers, the swinging clothes and rave gear, in other words, the expensive packaging is music and is worth their hard-earned cash and worth protecting and getting excited and hysterical about. The Floyd are not packaged, they just are. Eighty percent of Pink Floyd music is improvised. Many people don't seem to realize this, and many sets include numbers never played before or since. So the Pink Floyd are largely unpredictable, both to the audience and themselves. They can be sublime. They can be awful. So can audiences and, generally, the audiences get what they deserve and what they feel. The Pink Floyd is you. If you feel they are killing something for you, then you are their accomplice."*

Record Mirror (U.K.) reported that Pink Floyd will be appearing on the BBC television show, 'Tomorrows World,' on either January 3 or 10, 1968. Mike Leonard, the originator of "Light-Sound," will also be on the program. Pink Floyd have a new light man, Terry Yetton, who replaces the departed Peter Wynne-Wilson.

January 13, 1968 - Fabulous (U.K.) published an article titled, "Born Psychedelic" by Sally Cork. Cork interviewed Syd Barrett and Nick Mason, who both have birthdays in January, in a studio not long after the Jimi Hendrix tour had finished. Mason talked about his birthdays, saying, *"When you are little, each birthday means so much more to you. Or rather, your parents and family make it a special occasion. I could have anything I wanted, even if it was roast pork and strawberry jam. Having a large family with lots of young sisters, I always came in for a number of presents on my day. And I still get a fair number."* Syd Barrett remembered his childhood birthdays, saying, *"Parties and games that you play in the dark, when someone hides and hits you with a cushion."*

January 20, 1968 - Rolling Stone Magazine (U.S.) reported that British groups such as Pink Floyd, who have gone into electronics, have "tripped up." Pink Floyd, with their electronics, are simply dull in a concert hall following Big Brother and Janis Joplin.

January 27, 1968 - Disc and Music Echo (U.K.) reported that 21-year old singer/guitarist David Gilmour has joined Pink

Floyd. Gilmour is currently recording with the band, which will begin their first European tour on February 18, 1968, including a performance at the Rome International Pop Festival.

Melody Maker (U.K.) reported that 21 year-old guitarist/singer, David Gilmour has joined the Pink Floyd line up. Gilmour is a childhood friend of Syd Barrett and Roger Waters, and has been rehearsing with the band for several weeks. He will be joining them for their first European tour, beginning on February 18, 1968.

New Musical Express (U.K.) reported that the Pink Floyd has become a five-man band "to explore new instruments and add further experimental dimensions," with the addition of twenty-one year old singer-guitarist David Gilmour. Gilmour has been rehearsing with Pink Floyd for several weeks and is presently recording with them.

Record Mirror (U.K.) reported that Pink Floyd is now a five-person group with the addition of singer/guitarist David Gilmour. His addition will allow the band to maintain their four-piece organization, while one musician will be free to explore new instruments and add new dimensions to their sound. Gilmour is a close friend of Syd Barrett and Roger Waters, and has been rehearsing with the band for several weeks. The five-piece group will begin a European tour on February 18, 1968, that will include a performance at the First European International Pop Festival in Rome, Italy.

February 10, 1968 - Record Mirror (U.K.) reported that Pink Floyd's new single, tentatively titled, 'Corporal Clegg,' is nearly finished. It was written by Roger Waters and is scheduled for release in four weeks. On February 12, 1968, the band will begin their tour of Europe, with a German television appearance on the 13th.

April 20, 1968 - New Musical Express (U.K.) reviewed the Pink Floyd single, 'It Would Be So Nice.' They explained that the version of the single that the reviewer received included a message on it indicating that it is a specially edited and shortened version for radio purposes. The song is a Kink's-like jogging good time that features a pulsating chorus, changing tempo, cymbal crashes and fuzz guitars. It has a catchy melody line, and interesting lyrics, and could be a big hit. Also in this issue is an ad for the single.

Record Mirror (U.K.) reviewed the Pink Floyd single, 'It Would Be So Nice' / 'Julia Dream.' A shortened version was released for DJs. The song is good, with a nice rolling sound, lots of surprises, and a compact production by Norman Smith. Their best yet.

April 27, 1968 - Melody Maker (U.K.) reported that Pink Floyd, who have returned from Rome, Italy, were "mystified" that there was so little advertising for the upcoming Rome Pop Festival.

May 11, 1968 - Mirabelle (U.K.), a British teen girls magazine, published a picture of the Pink Floyd and the following letter to the editor. A fan wrote, "I am livid! It isn't fair. Everybody is making a lot of fuss of big-time groups like the Herd, the Bee Gees, Monkees, and Beatles, etc. Why has nobody recognized the talent of a really fantastic group who have made some great singles and a fabulous LP? They are the Pink Floyd. They can knock spots off any of those top groups, yet why is it we never hear anything at all about them? Please try and do something about this just for the Pink Floyd fans."

May 18, 1968 - Melody Maker (U.K.) published an article titled, "Pink Floyd work on a new art form" by Tony Wilson that featured an interview with Nick Mason and Roger Waters.

Talking about singles, Nick Mason explained, "*It is possible on an LP to do exactly what we want to do. The last single, 'Apples and Oranges,' we had to hustle a bit. It was commercial, but we could only do it in two sessions. We prefer to take a longer time.*"

As for their new single, Roger Waters commented, "*Live bookings seem to depend on whether or not you have a record in the Top Ten. I don't like 'It Would Be So Nice.' I don't like the song or the way it's sung. Singles releases have something to do with our* scene, but they are not overwhelmingly essential. On LPs, we can produce our best at any given time." Mason added, "Singles are a funny scene. Some people are prepared to be persuaded into anything. I suppose it depends on if you want to be a mammoth star or not."

Mason thinks their ability and technique have "improved vastly, which makes a difference." Waters added, "A whole scene has gone. Light shows have gone well out of fashion, but if people still like them, there must be something in it." The band is concerned with their visual presentation. Waters had the idea of presenting them like a circus, using a big tent, with jugglers and escapologists. But cost considerations killed that idea.

Currently, the band has applied to the Arts Council for a £5,000 grant for a new project. Waters explained, "It would be a story, using other groups, written as a saga, like the Iliad, so that it doesn't just become a pop show with someone walking on and introducing groups. I don't want any of that scene. There would probably be a narrator, possibly John Peel, and there would be quality in the production of the material. It would be a non-profit making scene, nothing to do with selling records. I'd like Arthur Brown to play the Demon King with the Floyd providing the music. It would be telling a story, like a fairy tale. A definite scene with good and evil."

June 15, 1968 - Melody Maker (U.K.) published an ad that read "The Pink Floyd have now joined other top groups in discovering the sound of the Auto Rhythm. Hear the Pink Floyd in action with this unique instrument made by Delsonics."

June 29, 1968 - New Musical Express (U.K.) published two identical small ads that read, "July 1st – Pink Floyd – A Saucerful of Secrets." Also in this issue is an ad that features a picture of the album.

July 12, 1968 - International Times (U.K.) reviewed the Hyde Park free concert on June 29, 1968. Miles wrote that the concert "carried with it more love and more hope than I believed was possible. And what of the Floyd? During the past year or so, there have been many paths for the Pink Floyd and not all of them have been easy, and sometimes it seems

as though they have taken the wrong one. However, after Saturday, all is forgiven. I have never heard them play better, and those spoken with agree. I don't know whether the unique atmosphere or the closeness of the sky, the earth, and the water drew out their best. There was no anger or violence in what they did and the sounds fell around our bodies with the touch of velvet and the taste of honey. The last thing they did, which seemed to be 'Saucerful of Secrets,' was a form of transport in itself. It was a hymn to everything that can be if we don't give up, it filled the head and the air with music. I hope you were there."

July 1968 - Cash Box (U.S.) reported that Tower Records held a press party for Pink Floyd at Michael Mann's in New York on July 9, 1968. In attendance were all four members of Pink Floyd.

July 13, 1968 - New Musical Express (U.K.) published two ads picturing the new Pink Floyd album, 'A Saucerful of Secrets.'

July 26, 1968 - International Times (U.K.) reviewed the album, 'A Saucerful of Secrets.' Miles wrote, "The Floyd have developed a distinctive sound for themselves, the result of experiments with new 'electronic' techniques in live performance. However, the result of most of these experiments was presented particularly well on their first album. There is little new here. The electronic collage on 'Jugband Blues,' though it uses stereo well, has been done much better by The United States of America. The unimaginative use of a string arrangement spoils 'See Saw.' The use of electronic effects on 'A Saucerful of Secrets' is poorly handled and does not add up to music. It is too long, too boring, and totally uninventive, particularly when compared to a similar electronic composition such as 'Metamorphosis' by Vladmir Ussachevsky, which was done in 1957, eleven years ago. The introduction of drums doesn't help either, and just reminds me of the 12 1/2 minute backing track 'The Return of the Son of Monster Magnet,' which somehow got onto side four of The Mothers of Invention 'Freak Out' album, much to Zappa's horror, and which was left off the British version. In the same way as bad sitar playing is initially attractive, electronic

An EMI ad featuring Pink Floyd's A Saucerful Of Secrets album.

music turns people on at first. Then, as one hears more, the listener demands that something be made and done with all these 'new' sounds. Something more than 'psychedelic mood music.' 'Let There Be More Light' presents the Floyd at their best, as does most of side one. They are really good at this and outshine all the pale imitations of their style. With their 'Saucers' track, experiments

have an historical place and should be preserved, but only the results should be on record, at least until they bring out one a month and are much cheaper. A record well worth buying."

July 27, 1968 - Billboard Magazine (U.S.) reported that the Pink Floyd played to a packed house at the Scene in New York on

Monday, July 15, 1968. There was an emphasis on space and oriental sounds. The group displayed top-flight musicianship, inventiveness, and the ability to say something musically. David Gilmour showed that he knew how to use feedback, Richard Wright's performance was "masterful," Nick Mason provided strong drumming with both sticks and mallets, and Roger Waters produced vocals sounds from a whisper to a high pitched screech. During the song, 'A Saucerful of Secrets,' Waters shattered a glass by throwing it at a gong, providing a wild ending to the set.

August 1, 1968 - The Fifth Estate, Detroit (U.S.) reported in their column 'Mixed Media Ear' that Pink Floyd is a very weird group. The reviewer wrote, "I know that they were unbelievably bad at the Grande and I'm not about to try and excuse them other than to say that in every other performance in this country and in England they ably demonstrated that they are the best psychedelic group in the world. They have never claimed to be the world's best musicians, and they are really seen at their best with their own light show, so unless you have a light show of your own, just close your eyes and turn your amplifier fully on, and your parents fully off by putting 'Saucerful of Secrets' on. Although the album is by no means indicative of what the group is really. Oh well, there is absolutely no point in my saying this. Either you dig the Floyd or you don't. I do."

August 2, 1968 - Los Angeles Free Press (U.S.) reported on Pink Floyd's concert at the Shrine Hall in Los Angeles, California on Friday, July 26, 1968 with Blue Cheer and The Jeff Beck Group. James Martin, the reviewer, felt that the Jeff Beck Group was the highlight of the night's performances. The Shrine was sweltering and Pink Floyd was disappointing. Their live performance lacked the control, balance, and clarity of their studio recordings. Even the performance of 'Interstellar Overdrive' lacked spark and distinction. Richard Wright's organ saved their performance from disaster, with "hypnotic arabesques" during 'Matilda Mother,' "labyrinthian flights" during 'Set the Controls for the Heart of the Sun,' and "mystical mazes" in 'A Saucerful of Secrets.' Martin states that

while 'Set the Controls for the Heart of the Sun' is a "belladonna trip through the inner limits of the listeners body" on record, in performance the ethereality of the song is lost and the song is "almost embarrassingly inadequate."

August 8, 1968 - New Society (U.K.) reported that the EMI press release stated that Pink Floyd are not trying to create hallucinations in their audiences, and they are not anarchists, they just believe in people doing what they like, tempered by social conscience. Their new album, 'A Saucerful of Secrets,' is filled with irony. They are not brilliant musicians and when they play ordinary rock, they are quite ordinary. Their originality is "the composite noise they make and their musical ideas." Their music imitates light, "kaleidoscope music," and the noises they use are important. Their lyrics are often intelligible and sometimes just nonsense verse, but "language is to meaning as noise is to music." Enjoyment of art can be traced to a sense of the artist being in control, and on the new album the sound is a delicate balance of patterns and mess. The best song is 'See Saw,' a structured piece of pastoral pop. The song, 'A Saucerful of Secrets,' is ambitious and evocative. 'Set the Controls for the Heart of the Sun' is the most successfully original song, combining science fiction and the East. It is "about escapism, not about escape." The album is a cosmic elegy for anyone who seeks truth.

August 10, 1968 - Melody Maker (U.K.) reported that Pink Floyd will return to the United States at the end of September to tour the university circuit. The band will complete their current six-week U.S. tour on August 18, 1968.

New Musical Express (U.K.) reviewed the Pink Floyd album, 'A Saucerful of Secrets,' and gave it three stars. The reviewer felt that 'Let There Be More Light' was the best song, while the song 'A Saucerful of Secrets' is "long and boring and has little to warrant its monotonous duration."

Also in this issue was a report that Pink Floyd will be doing another U.S. tour in September, playing the college circuit with Tyrannosaurus Rex. The band will be returning to Britain from it's current American tour on August 18th, where it will play two concerts in London, plus television shows in Holland, Austria, and Sweden. They will also be doing work on their third album.

September 21, 1968 - Record Mirror (U.K.) published an article titled, "Pinkos Return from United States" that featured an interview with David Gilmour, Roger Waters and Richard Wright.

Commenting on their recently completed seven week U.S. tour, Roger Waters stated, "*We saw mainly the insides of hotels.*" David Gilmour added, "*It's quite a big country.*" Waters continued, "*We saw two different worlds. On our level, the people who came to hear us, everything was fine. But outside, the capitalist society, was, er, tatty. It works all right so long as you don't look too closely. But they are scared, really scared, of the new young Americans, and that's why they are reacting very violently. And it doesn't work. Police clubbings, and the beatings and shootings that are going on, they won't have the desired effect simply because there are so many young people. They aren't just weekend ravers. Many of them have dropped out completely.*"

As for the situation in Britain, Waters explained, "*The situation is much less immediate here because hippies are not being beaten. It's all a bit of a laugh. Something to discuss over a Scotch and dry ginger. There isn't, therefore, the same emotional involvement. I don't feel any more menaced by a British policeman than by a milkman. The police here, on the whole, are public servants trying to do a job. About the musical difference, well, Rick should answer that. He's our musician.*" Rick Wright answered, "*In America, the audience comes to listen. In England, they come to pick up scrubbers, though I should make an exception of a few places, such as Middle Earth.*" Waters added, "*We don't play any longer at places where people go to booze and pick each other up.*"

Asked about how well they are doing, Waters replied, "*We're not making our fortunes, but we're doing all right. We can survive by playing the kind of music, and recording the kind of LPs, that we like. And there are enough customers to make it*

worthwhile.*" Gilmour continued, "*We're beginning to find that we're booked on concerts, particularly on the Continent, where we get top billing over famous groups that we looked up to as the big stars when we were starting. It's not easy to adjust to this. We keep thinking there must be some embarrassing mistake.*"

Referring to performing in the States, Wright added, "*They don't go to dances to fight. You never see yobboes in a dance hall. They go to street corners.*" Waters continued, "*If our American listeners don't like our music, they go away. They don't stand around booing.*" Wright added, "*Yes, but they're prepared to listen to a whole set in case there's something they can enjoy.*" Waters added, "*They wouldn't dream of shouting at you in a million years.*"

Clarifying their comments about England, Waters explained, "*We can really only speak about England, and only the south of England at that. We don't know what goes on up North. London is our scene.*"

October 26, 1968 - Melody Maker (U.K.) published part three of a series called "Pop Today and Tomorrow" that examined musical revolutionaries. The article was titled, "Don't laugh, but the next step could be pop as a political power," and featured an interview with Roger Waters. The article stated that Pink Floyd is a band that is concerned with new ways of producing and presenting sounds. Waters explained, "*We are working on a 360 degrees stereo system. We want to throw away the old format of the pop show, standing on a square stage at one end of a rectangular room, and running through a series of numbers. Our idea is to put the sound all around the audience with ourselves in the middle. Then the performance becomes much more theatrical. And it needs special material. It can include melodrama, literary things, musical things, or lights. The basic format is laid down on four-track tape. The things we do live, songs, movement, etc., are cued by the tape, so things run for a set time. Basically, you make a four-way stereo record, and play with it.*" Talking about Pink Floyd, Waters added, "*We are probably not part of the pop scene, though we impinge on the pop market to a certain extent. We are releasing a single, for example, but we* *don't function from the usual pop stimuli. We aren't really prepared to compromise over what we are doing, but then I don't think we could, even if we wanted to."*

October 30, 1968 - News of the World (U.K.) published an article titled, "Acid Pink Star" by Mick Hamilton, that reported that Syd Barrett had turned into a "pathetic, crazed Zombie," who sets fire to his mail, shaved off his eyebrows, can no longer talk, and has been heard barking like a dog.

November 1968 - Beat Instrumental (U.K.) published an article titled, "A Saucerful of Quiet Success for the Pink Floyd." They wrote, "After the initial blaze of publicity for being "the group for the freakies" last summer, the Pink Floyd have managed to stay pretty much out of the limelight, which is surprising when you consider the amount of success they've had with records, two best selling singles ('Arnold Layne' and 'See Emily Play'), and two even bigger-selling albums ('Piper At The Gates of Dawn' and currently, 'Saucerful Of Secrets').

    The Floyd are very much musicians, as opposed to pop personalities. Even in the early days, when they gained their reputation as the hippies' musical spokesmen, the group had a role thrust upon them. Says Rick Wright, organist, *"It's hard to see why we were cast as the First British Psychedelic Group. We never saw ourselves that way. It just so happened that we started playing at UFO when it was just beginning, and people began to identify us with the club and what they thought it stood for."*

    In fact, the Floyd as a group started when Wright, Nicky Mason and Roger Waters were architecture students together. They started a band to play at local colleges, doing mostly R and B stuff. After a time, Syd Barrett, whose place in the group is now occupied by David Gilmour, joined up and gradually the blues were superseded by a new sort of music. *"We realized that we were, after all, only playing for fun,"* said Rick Wright, *"and we were tied to no particular form of music. We could do what we wanted. And so our own, more individual music started to come through, and we've developed on those lines ever since. The emphasis was, and is, firmly on*

spontaneity and improvisation."

    Perhaps one of the reasons for their being labeled 'psychedelic' is the group's use of light shows. Theirs was the first in Britain, and the hallucinatory, visionary colors of the slide projections were bound to be linked with the new craze for mind-expanding, acid, Aldous Huxley, and all stations east. The Floyd have one of the few effective light shows, another case of original being best. *"We got the idea from a lecturer at Hornsey Art School. This man had been working for some time with lights as an art form, and he wanted to do something with a group, an integrated show. As it happened, we didn't do anything with him. But the idea stuck in our heads, and later on we started our own lights."*

    Wright continued, *"It's sad to see all the mediocre light shows you get now. Even at Middle Earth, they were using techniques which they've had in America ages ago and discarded. There are too many people doing the same unremarkable things, but with a bit of imagination, you can get some amazing effects. Light shows, when they're good, are fine. But the majority aren't very good at all."*

    The Pink Floyd were the first with lights. Another new idea on which they're working is the use of all-round sound. Wright said, *"We want sound coming at the audience from behind as well as from in front. Surround*

1969
More, Ummagumma,
and Zabriskie Point

them with music. At the moment, we're trying to get the Planetarium, which would be ideal. A circular auditorium with us in the middle facing out and speakers placed around the walls. This is the sort of scene we'd like. Unfortunately, this type of show just couldn't be done at ballroom gigs, which we aren't keen on anyway. Our ideas aren't right for an audience that wants to have a rave. Ideally, the group would stick to concerts, recording, film scores and that sort of thing."

Films are figuring prominently in the band's current program. They have already done the music to one movie. Two more are in the pipeline, and Rick sees the future concentrating on this field. As far as recording is concerned, they will shortly be starting work on a follow-up album to 'Saucer.' It's intended to divide the record into four segments, one for each member of the band to do his own ideas, thus presenting four individuals, and at the same time, one group. The Pink Floyd are certainly a group with a constant flow of ideas and ambitions. It's a bit unfortunate, perhaps, that they have to be really listened to hard if you're to get the best out of them. And a bit unfortunate that they should have the millstone of one-nighters in distant ballrooms hanging around their necks. They simply aren't that sort of group. Pop nowadays covers such a wide field that we really need a new name for its' various parts. And it seems quite probable that in 10, 20, or 100 years' time, groups like the Floyd will be considered classical. Boundaries are being extended almost daily by the Floyd. Long may they progress."

November 1968 - Creem Magazine (U.S.), reported on the Black Magic Rock and Roll Festival that took place at the Olympia Stadium in Detroit, Michigan on October 31, 1968. The article, titled, "A Fiasco of the Black Arts," stated that the festival was a disaster, and many of the performers that were advertised to appear, including Pink Floyd, never showed up. The promoter, Mike Quatro, advertised

these acts even though he did not have signed contracts from them. The concert drew 14,000 people.

December 14, 1968 - New Musical Express (U.K.) reviewed the Pink Floyd single, 'Point Me at the Sky.' The article stated that, after its' ballad type opening, the song features psychedelic effects such as echo vocals, jet-stream effects, oscillations, and distortions. The effect is shattering, a wall of sounds with a commercially catchy riff. There are also breaks in the tempo where the music assumes an air of tranquility. Intriguing and absorbing, the best Pink Floyd single in a long time.

Also in this issue is an EMI ad with a picture of the album, 'A Saucerful of Secrets,' and a full back-page ad from the Bryan Morrison Agency that includes an ad for the single, 'Point Me at the Sky.'

January 18, 1969 - Melody Maker (U.K.) published an ad for a Pink Floyd concert at the Middle Earth Club on Saturday, January 18, 1969. "Turn on the Tap Zap. An Event by The Pink Floyd." Admission was 16/- for members, and 26/- for guests.

January 25, 1969 - Record Mirror (U.K.) published an article titled, "Pink Floyd Force Themselves in Doing New Things" by David Griffiths. Currently the Pink Floyd are receiving mature responses from happy college audiences. They are writing for the Ballet Rambert, and for a Dutch ballet company. They also plan to perform with a symphony orchestra.

Their next album, due in March, will feature each member on their own for a quarter of the record. David Gilmour is still at the ideas stage for his section, but Rick Wright has finished his and it includes him performing on organ, guitar, percussion, and mellotron, with a few extra percussion sounds added by Norman Smith. Wright explained, "There are no electronic sounds, no juggling with tapes.

Theoretically you could do it live, and the only reason I did virtually all of it myself is that it was quicker that way. I didn't write out scores, I drew graphs." According to Gilmour and Wright, Roger Waters is composing one or two songs about conception and birth, with a science fiction touch. The band members are all fans of the movie, '2001-A Space Odyssey.'

Talking about their new material, Gilmour explained, *"We won't let the kid fans down. Obviously, we would like to make a bit more money, draw more people, put our price up. But if we had hit singles, we might have little girls coming in and screaming while we're playing, and that would be a drag."*

As far as the band's musical morale, which is not well, Wright stated, *"We've lost things. Two years ago we were genuinely experimental. Now we go on stage knowing what is going to happen. We are getting into a live rut, relying on known factors. In the old UFO days, we had the feeling the audience was with us, helping us to experiment. We might play one number for half an hour, and 25 minutes of that would be quite boring, but during the other five, something really exciting would happen."* Gilmour continued, *"When I joined the group, nothing was arranged and I thought it would be better if things were more together, more rehearsed. They went that way, and now I'm further away from that position than I was."* Wright added, *"Yes, we're going to force ourselves to do new things."*

February 8, 1969 - Disc and Music Echo (U.K.) published a picture of Pink Floyd arriving at the London premiere of the movie, 'You Are What You Eat,' which was a comment on the hippie lifestyle in America.

February 15, 1969 - Disc and Music Echo (U.K.) published an article titled, "How the Pink Floyd defeated psychedelia," that featured an interview with Nick Mason.

Talking about the fact that the Pink Floyd have come a long way since they were a hit group with 'See Emily Play' on the charts, Mason said, *"It may sound strange, but we're now so much more secure, and we're making more bread then when we had the hit."*

The previous week the band were in a recording studio every night from midnight to 8 a.m. recording music for the soundtrack to

a French movie. Mason explained, *"We have to do it in a week, which is very cool because otherwise we'd spend three months doing it, going back and changing things all the time. Our music is quite well integrated into the film, like every time anyone switches on a radio or is in a bar with a jukebox or anything, it's the Pink Floyd which comes out."*

Commenting on their still-unfinished new album, Mason said, *"It's our usual annual album, but it is quite an elaborate affair. What we've agreed to do is take a quarter of the album each, on which we can all do the things we really want to do. It's hard to say what's going to come out of it at the moment, because everyone's being incredibly secretive about their bit till they've got it all together. I've done my quarter twice over. The difficulty is, doing something so totally egocentric as this, you keep wanting to go back and do something completely different."* Asked if it will be a double album, Mason wasn't sure if the record company would be willing to pay for it. He added, *"There's still hope that we can do one, though, which would be really great because then we could do our quarters on one album, and on the other have one side of straight songs and one side of a major work involving all of us."*

The band has been recording for three months, plus playing concerts at universities instead of ballrooms. Mason said, *"It's so nice compared with how it was when we had 'Emily,' when we were all suffering from acute paranoia, being chased round the country by angry pop lovers. At the time, everyone hated us, and we hated everyone, but now it's really nice. Like everyone says about the Pink Floyd, 'Gosh, psychedelic! That was flower power two years ago, wasn't it?' But there are people all over the country who just want to hear sounds. It's not a matter of blues fans against pop fans or anything like that. They all just want to listen to music. It's very much like it was in America last summer."*

Talking about the band's new live sound system, which they describe as "sound in the round," Mason explained, *"It's very complicated because you have to have a vast mixer onstage with tapes and so on, into which the live sound is fed. The bloke who built the original prototype has just finished a proper, giant one, which we're hoping to premiere at*

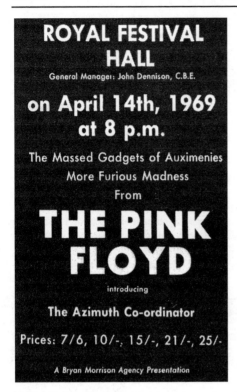

ROYAL FESTIVAL HALL

General Manager: John Dennison, C.B.E.

on April 14th, 1969 at 8 p.m.

The Massed Gadgets of Auximenies
More Furious Madness
From

THE PINK FLOYD

introducing

The Azimuth Co-ordinator

Prices: 7/6, 10/-, 15/-, 21/-, 25/-

A Bryan Morrison Agency Presentation

the Festival Hall in April."

March 29, 1969 - Melody Maker (U.K.) published an ad for a Pink Floyd concert at the Royal Festival Hall on April 14, 1969 at 8 pm. "The Massed Gadgets of Auximenies – More Furious Madness from The Pink Floyd – introducing The Azimuth Co-ordinator." Admission was 7/6, 10/-, 15/- 21/- , and 25/-. A Bryan Morrison Agency Production.

April 1969 - Beat Instrumental (U.K.) published an article titled, "Azimuth Co-ordinator – The Pink Floyd." They wrote, "If anyone still doubts the fact that the best of pop today stretches way beyond the traditional realms of pop music and the entertainment business in general, take them to the Royal Festival Hall on April 14th. Not to listen to the Pink Floyd in concert, but to listen in the middle of the Pink Floyd, for this will be no ordinary old gig. The Floyd will be all around you as this concert with the group providing the whole of the evening's music, will happen in 360-degree stereo sound, and should show once and for all who is moving music forward

these days.

Just a few short years ago it would have been inconceivable for a pop group to do a formal concert at the Festival Hall, and even if it had happened it would have been a two-hour deluge of the latest hit, the one before that, the one that got them going, and a couple of show-biz standards thrown in for good measure. It won't be like that on the 14th, for the Floyd are serious musicians as well as entertainers and probably need something with the scope and flexibility their concert will give them. I spoke to the group's drummer Nicki Mason about the concert and the new stereo system, which is said to make normal stereo seem like mono.

"*This concert will be a big, elaborate affair and I think it points the direction in which music is going to move,*" Mason said. "*The sound will be coming from all around the hall. We will be doing this by using an Azimuth Co-ordinator.*" A what, I thought? Mason explained, "*Well, it's basically a mixer unit that allows an immediate mix. We're building a giant double one that will have four channels and which will really throw the sound round the room, it really can throw the sound in all directions.*" And how does the Azimuth Co-ordinator work? "*You have two control sticks in front of you and it's all done from there,*" said Nicki. "*You can center all the speakers, change the direction of the sound, change channels, and so on. You can place a sound in any part of the room you want. For instance, you can have one thing going round and round the place, and another moving up and down, going round on a vertical plane.*"

Nicki sees this is the start of a new sound system. "*It's moving towards something that will happen in twenty years' time, probably sooner. Records will be totally obsolete and people will be buying their own four-track tapes. They'll have home sound-in-the-round, with a set of speakers at each corner of the room. A domestic set-up like that would cost little more than normal stereo, but the effect would be so different.*"

The group is working on new material for the Festival Hall, to use the new system to the full. They will be using a variety of instruments and different balancing. You might, perhaps, hear a pure piano or acoustic guitar coming from the stage, and a full-blown organ coming from the back of the hall. Who knows? *"We're still working on the system,"* said Nicki, *"so I don't really know exactly what will be happening yet. But we will be feeding in channels of taped stuff, a rhythm loop perhaps, lots of percussion. Anyway, the point is that we will be able to place sounds where we want them in the hall."*

This is not the first time that the Pink Floyd have undertaken this kind of project, nor the first appearance of an Azimuth Co-ordinator. (An azimuth, by the way, is an "arc of the heavens extending from the zenith to the horizon, which it cuts at right angles," according to my dictionary.) *"We built an Azimuth Co-ordinator once before,"* said Nicki, *"but it was stolen at the only concert we used it for, but it's no use to the bloke who's got it because ... well, I'll tell you but don't write it down because I'd hate to have him read this and be able to work it because of what I said."*

Mason continued, *"We did a concert at the Queen Elizabeth Hall, which is smaller than the Festival Hall, about eighteen months ago, but we lost money on it even though it was a sell-out because of all the equipment we had to pay for and so on. We couldn't afford to get it together properly but we can do that now. You know, we really are incredibly lucky to be in a position to do this kind of thing. Now we are past the stage of having to live in transits running up and down the country, we are getting established with proper places to work and get together. With what we are doing now, you need a base to work out ideas and to house your equipment."* Does this mean that the days of Pink Floyd gigs are over? *"We want to concentrate on concerts,"* said Nicki, *"but perhaps we'll give people a choice of concert or a normal sort of show. The atmosphere in concerts is so different, they're more formal, you have to lead the audience and let them know what's happening so that they don't get embarrassed. It's very satisfying because, with a concert, there is no suggestion of a hop. We'll be spending a long time setting the Festival Hall up with our equipment, getting everything as we want it, none of this arriving half an hour before you go on."*

Mason continued, *"The audiences enjoy what we do nowadays, they're right there with us. Back in the days of 'See Emily Play,' we were doing ballrooms and they'd dig Emily*

and dislike the rest. A good gig was one when they didn't throw bottles. They'd come to drink, dance, pull chicks, and have a couple of fights if it was a really good night. I'm doing them an injustice saying that, because most of them do go to dance and hear the group and I'm not putting down the bands that are on that sort of thing. We are all musicians and are really so close because we are all in the pop scene." Now, however, the Floyd reach a wider audience, and wider than the hippy scene they reached in the heydays of flower power.

A number of classical musicians have expressed interest in the Floyd's work and a couple of hi-fi journals have asked them about their new sound system. *"Classical composer's have been interested, too,"* Nicki told me. *"They haven't flipped and said, 'Yeah man, that is really cool,' and they haven't said we should be taken away and shot either. They have listened and expressed interest."* And that, I think, is the mark of where the Floyd are today.

At one time, their kind of experiment and exploration was the prerogative of a small group of avant-garde enthusiasts who left people outside their small sphere way behind. But now, such experimental music is no longer purely experimental, and thanks to groups such as the Floyd, it reached a wide audience who think the same way and who appreciate what is going on. This awakening and real listening to music must be largely attributed to the influence of the hippy scene, LSD, and so on. These were the people who listened to the rest of the Floyd's show once they had played Emily, and who bought their two LPs, 'Piper at the Gates of Dawn' and 'Saucerful of Secrets.' These are the people who find as much depth in the Pink Floyd's music as many classical composers' compositions, for the Floyd's music is a new phenomenon, popular, serious music.

And soon there will be another LP to listen to, quite different from anything the group has attempted before. Said Nicki, *"We've just completed the music for a film, which we did in a week, really hard at it, but we are working on an album which will be split into four quarters, each one of us doing what he wants on his piece. Mine, naturally, will be purely percussion and very much stereo orientated, using a wide range of instruments.*

If you can hit it, I might use it. I have tried to hang it together, it has movements and so forth, a construction. Few drum solos move me on record and I'm not as good as many other drummers, so it would be pointless for me to hammer away as fast as I can for ten minutes.” The rest of the group are similarly basing their pieces of the album on their instruments. Rick Wright's keyboard section is "pretty major" according to Nicki, using every track of an eight-track set-up. Roger Waters' contribution won't be all bass guitar. In fact, it is probably the nearest of the set to electronic music in that he has set himself very strict limits to work within, while David Gilmour's is in some ways the closest to Nicki's in conception, using a variety of guitars from acoustic to bowed. *"There is a problem here, though,"* said Nicki. *"'Saucerful' was more than just the sum of the four of us. It was us and what we make together, which is more. We would like the new album to be a double one, with half of it live or semi-live, us as a group. This would then show both what we can do together, and what each of us can do individually."* And I think the Floyd are one of the few groups who not only could fill a double album successfully, but actually need a double album to give them enough space to move in.

The new LP should be well worth waiting for and will, no doubt, show how far the group has moved, even since 'Saucerful.' As Nicki said, the group are in an extremely fortunate position, having established themselves, of being able to move on to new things. And movement is an essential part of the Floyd. From pioneering psychedelic music and light shows in Britain, they have now reached the point of filling the Festival Hall with their music in a way that has never been heard before. Just who can say what the members of the Pink Floyd will have produced in two, ten, or twenty years time? The mind boggles, which is, after all, part of the idea."

April 19, 1969 - Melody Maker (U.K.) reported on the Pink Floyd concert at the Festival Hall, London, on April 14, 1969. The show was described as "Artistry in pop technology." Basic instrumentation was combined with electronic effects that moved around the hall. Pink Floyd performed two pieces of music, 'The Man,' and 'The Journey.'

Bird sounds signified daybreak, followed by band members hammering and sawing amplified logs, which symbolized work. This was followed by sleep, nightmares, and daybreak once again. In the second half, a creature appeared in the audience, as they were beset by creatures of the deep. The show was "a novel concept, brilliantly executed."

April 26, 1969 - New Musical Express (U.K.) **published** an ad for Nottingham's 1969 Pop & Blues Festival to be held at the Notts. County Football ground on Saturday, May 10, 1969, from noon to 11 p.m. Pink Floyd is one of the featured acts. Tickets are 17/6.

May 3, 1969 - Melody Maker (U.K.) **published** an article titled, "Now It's Pink Floyd Plus the London Philharmonic" by Chris Welch that reviewed the Pink Floyd concert at The Royal Festival Hall in London on April 14, 1969. The concert was experimental and used various sound effects and pre-recorded tapes.

Referring to a review of the concert, Roger Waters commented, *"I thought the MM review was a bit over generous. It was a nerve-racking experience for us, and probably the audience. A friend of mine who comes to see our normal stage act was very disappointed and felt cheated. He thought it was like paying fifteen bob to see us rehearsing. He was right, in a way, because we were rehearsing. The people were watching a happening. I was unhappy with the performance. In the first half, we didn't get into anything. We just didn't have time to balance the sound. I would say twenty percent of it worked really well."*

Asked about the machine they use for the sound effects, Waters explained, *"The machine takes an electronic signal, either from a tape, guitars, or vocal mics. We've got four units, but, for example, you can put three signals into one unit, and select any one with a switch. There is a joystick on the box, and four outputs, each going to a 100-watt line-source amplifier connected to the speakers. What's inside the box is a secret. But as you push the stick around, you can fade in and out the speakers placed all around the hall. What you need to do is to take over the Festival Hall for a month, go down there every morning at 9 a.m., and set the balances. We call the machine an Azimuth Co-ordinator. We had the idea of* taking a signal and using it in a four-way stereo system. We approached a technician we knew who said he thought he could do it. And we used it for the first time at a concert at the Queen Elizabeth Hall. But the prototype was stolen about 18 months ago. Since then, we had to go through the whole thing with Syd leaving. Since Dave Gilmour joined, we have got better and better. Our show now is very together and professional."

Waters continued, "We could go on doing the same old numbers, which are very popular, and we would enjoy doing that. But that's not what the Pink Floyd is all about. It's about taking risks and pushing forward. We want to do other things. In June, we'll be doing another concert at the Albert Hall, and one at the Fairfield Hall, Croydon, on May 30th. I think people will notice the difference by then. Among the other things we want to do is use an orchestra. We've already had preliminary discussions with the Royal Philharmonic, and they are really keen. They really want to do it. Huge buzz. We're also in contact with the Boston Philharmonic. It's not that we are such an incredibly successful group. It's just that our name has got about to people who want to do strange things. It's fun. That's what it's all about. What a strange thing for a 90-piece orchestra, into Berlioz, to want to work with us. It's a gas."

Asked about their last single, 'Point Me at the Sky,' Waters replied, "That was the last of the unknown singles. I don't know why we did it. It was a constructed attempt, and it didn't happen. But we will be releasing another one. It can't do any harm."

Asked about their latest recording sessions, Waters explained, "We've finished an album on which we have done a quarter each, and a live album. We're negotiating with EMI to get them released as a double album to sell at fifty shillings. We hope to get that out as soon as possible. We also have an album of music which was the soundtrack for a film, but we'd like to play that one down. Here we go, all the excuses. Actually, I quite dig it. We did sixteen tracks in five sessions, which for us is silly, and they suffered from it."

Commenting on the state of their light show, Waters explained, "You saw our light shows back in the old days. They were probably as together as most, but it began to bore us. There are two types of light shows, one where the lights are specifically concerned with the music, as in Fantasia, and the more prevalent light show, where you set up a load of equipment and many projectors, and do things over the group, pretty patterns that don't have anything specifically to do with the lyrics. We like the first kind, and maybe we can have it together in about five years, maybe two. It's a very difficult thing to do. I lie in bed and ponder about it. I thought of using shadows and the things you could do with them. We're still trying to progress, and while the last concert upset a few people, we can't stand still. We're not an underground group. We're very much an overground group."

Also in this issue is an ad for a Pink Floyd concert at the College of Commerce, Manchester on Friday, May 2, 1969. Also on the bill were Roy Harper, and Principle Edwards Magic Theater. Admission was 15/-.

May 10, 1969 - Melody Maker (U.K.) published an ad for "Bryan Morrison Agency presents . . . The Massed Gadgets of Auximenies, Some Musical Calisthenics from The Pink Floyd featuring the Azimuth Co-ordinator." The tour begins at the Town Hall, Leeds on May 16, 1969, and ends with "The Final Lunacy" at the Royal Albert Hall in London on June 26, 1969. The concerts will be presented in 360-degree stereo.

May 17, 1969 - New Musical Express (U.K.) reported that the Tony Palmer pop documentary, 'All My Loving,' is being shown again on BBC-2 TV on Sunday the 18th. Originally broadcast on BBC-1 last November, the documentary includes footage of the Pink Floyd.

Also in this issue is an article giving Pink Floyd tour dates. The tour opens at Leeds Town Hall this Friday. On the tour, the band will be using five tons of equipment, including twenty-five speakers.

Top Pops and Music Now (U.K.) reported on the Pink Floyd performance at the Camden Arts Free Festival on May 9, 1969. The festival was organized by Blackhill Enterprises. 11,200 people attended the concert, and Pink Floyd were "just beautiful."

Bryan Morrison Agency presents . . .

The Massed Gadgets of Auximenies
Some Musical Callisthenics

from

THE
PINK
FLOYD

Featuring

The AZIMUTH CO-ORDINATOR

May 16   Town Hall, LEEDS
May 24   City Hall, SHEFFIELD
May 30   Fairfield Hall, CROYDON
June 8   Rex Cinema, CAMBRIDGE
June 10   Ulster Hall, BELFAST
June 14   Colston Hall, BRISTOL
June 15   Guildhall, PORTSMOUTH
June 16   The Dome, BRIGHTON
June 20   Town Hall, BIRMINGHAM
June 21   Royal Philharmonic, LIVERPOOL
June 22   Free Trade Hall, MANCHESTER

and

THE FINAL LUNACY
June 26, ROYAL ALBERT HALL, LONDON

(Box Office opens Monday, May 12)

(Concerts in 360° stereo)

June 14, 1969 - Melody Maker (U.K.) reported that Pink Floyd's new album, 'More,' is music they wrote for the soundtrack to the movie. It is scheduled for release by Columbia on Friday, June 13, 1969.

June 19, 1969 - The Bristol Evening Post (U.K.) reported on the Pink Floyd concert at the Colston Hall, Bristol on June 14, 1969. The article stated that the band unleashed "modern electronics, modern pop ideas, and modern violence." The show was electronically brilliant, using prerecorded tapes and four-channel stereo sound. Their ideas were exciting and followed a musical storyline. But the music was only "intermittently good," and there were silly moments, such as when a Caliban walked on stage and began a "music hall lavatory joke routine." But David Gilmour played an exciting blues solo, and there were some "weirdly viscous rock and roll climaxes." The band received a standing ovation at the end of the concert.

June 21, 1969 - New Musical Express (U.K.) reviewed the new Pink Floyd album, 'More,' writing that it features startling melodic sounds, raving blues numbers, weird out-of-the-world music, and Spanish, folk and jazz sounds, all interesting.

July 5, 1969 - Melody Maker (U.K.) reported on the Pink Floyd concert at the Royal Albert Hall on June 26, 1969. The article said that the crowd was silent and attentive as the band played brilliant and original music. They used a huge gong. Joining the band was a section from the Royal Philharmonic Orchestra and women from the Ealing Central amateur choir. It was an unforgettable musical experience.

July 19, 1969 - Melody Maker (U.K.) published an article titled, "Floyd take a shot at the moon," that reported on Pink Floyd doing music for television shows about the moon landing. The band is appearing on the BBC TV show, "What If It's Just Green Cheese?" on July 20, 1969, and they have written a piece of music for the show and the theme music. They will be playing music on a German TV Show about the moon landing on July 22, 1969, and are providing music for the

Dutch television show, "On Man On the Moon," on July 24-25, 1969.

The article also states that Pink Floyd's new double album is scheduled for release on September 1, 1969. One of the records will be live recordings from Mothers Club in Birmingham, England, and from Manchester College of Commerce.

July 1969 – Grass Eye (U.K.) reviewed the Pink Floyd album, 'More.' They wrote, "It is difficult to assess the true value of this album without first seeing the film from which it is taken. Unfortunately, this is still in the hands of the censor, apparently as it contains a drug sequence (protecting the morals of British Youth, you understand), and it is hardly likely to be put on general release, not for some considerable time at any rate. It would be unfair to the Floyd to judge this as the best of their work at the present time. Though the material, admittedly, is new, their treatment of it is radically different to their music as heard on stage. Some of the songs were used in their now-legendary concert tour. 'Green is the Colour' and 'Cymbaline' are here in foreshortened form, seeming to end abruptly just at the point when, in concert, they were beginning to take on an independent life of their own. Possibly, I am being over critical. This is an album of understatement and, therefore, unprecedented for them. Certainly there is a sensitive atmospheric arrangement in some parts, and Roger Waters is writing some beautiful songs. Summery and romantic the lovely 'Crying Song,' which he sings so that you'll never forget it, with acoustic guitars and David Gilmour's wavering harmony. Gilmour's six miles high guitar work is therefore, of course, on the more usual Floydian tracks. 'Quicksilver' is the standout, and both the dramatic and Main Film themes are also in this vein. All have the power to move your mind. The most curious cuts are the pure rock 'Nile Song,' with fuzzy growling voices, and 'More Blues,' which speaks for itself. The overall texture of the album is sensuous. Sensuality is the hallmark of the Floyd's music making. Because it's not head, heart, or stoned-sex music, it's all of these and more at the same time. Even, it would seem, when they're not at their best. Have this album, if you must, though it will, I think, sound

9TH NATIONAL
JAZZ·POP·BALLADS &
BLUES FESTIVAL
Previously at Windsor and Sunbury

An NJF/MARQUEE presentation

will NOW be held near to the SOUTH COAST at beautiful

PLUMPTON
RACE COURSE near LEWES, SUSSEX

Friday 8th August   8 - 11.30 p m   Tickets 15/-

THE PINK FLOYD
SOFT MACHINE
EAST OF EDEN · BLOSSOM TOES
Keith Tippett Jazz Group
JUNIORS EYES · THE VILLAGE

TRAVEL: By road about 45 miles from London. Take A23 or A22(A275) turning off at B2116. Special Southern Region Trains. **SPECIAL LATE SERVICE** back to Victoria and Brighton.

Saturday 9th August   ☐ 2 Sessions

☐ Afternoon
2 - 5.30 p m
Tickets 10/-

BONZO DOG BAND
Roy Harper
THE STRAWBS · BREAKTHRU'
JIGSAW · PETER HAMMILL

For Special Party or
TRAVEL RATES
and all enquiries contact the NJF
Secretary at the MARQUEE. 01-437-2375

☐ Evening   7 - 11.30 p m   Tickets £1   The Jazz Sound of

THE WHO · CHICKEN SHACK · FAT MATTRESS · JOHN SURMAN
AYNSLEY DUNBAR · YES! · The Spirit of JOHN MORGAN
KING CRIMSON · GROUNDHOGS · DRY ICE
Introducing from Belgium THE WALLACE COLLECTION

Sunday 10th August   ☐ 2 Sessions

☐ Afternoon
2 - 5.30 p m
Tickets 10/-

THE PENTANGLE
Long John Baldry
RON GEESIN · JO-ANN KELLY
MAGNA CARTA · NOEL MURPHY

For advice on
TENT HIRE
and details of camping facilities
contact NJF Camp Secretary
at 01-437 6603

☐ Evening   7 - 11.30 p m   Tickets £1   The Blues Sound of

THE NICE · THE FAMILY · London Cast of 'HAIR' · CHRIS BARBER
KEEF HARTLEY · ECLECTION · Mick Abrahams' BLODWYN PIG
CIRCUS · HARD MEAT · AFFINITY · BABYLON
Introducing from Holland CUBY'S BLUES BAND

FESTIVAL VILLAGE — — — — Open all day to Ticketholders
Including mornings and between shows — Coffee Shop — Discotheque
Book and Record Shops — Equipment — Clothes — Souvenirs — Dairy Shop for Campers

---

To **NJF BOX OFFICE, MARQUEE '90** Wardour Street, W1
Please send me the undernoted tickets for which
I enclose a cheque/postal order for............................
I also enclose a stamped addressed envelope

FRIDAY (8th) ....@ 15/- Evg

SATURDAY (9th) ....@ 10/- Aft......@ £1   Evg

SUNDAY (10th) ....@ 10/- Aft......@ £1   Evg

Name ....

Address ....
....

SPECIAL TICKETS
(IN ADVANCE ONLY)

WEEKEND
(Sat & Sun)........................@ £2

SEASON (Fri, Sat & Sun)
                                        @ £2.10.0

Office:
P

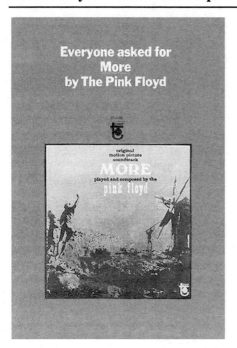

Everyone asked for
More
by The Pink Floyd

record was recorded live during concerts in Manchester and Birmingham. The second record consists of new studio recordings by each member of the band.

Pink Floyd will begin a 12-day Continental tour on September 17, 1969, with shows in France, Belgium, and Holland. On October 12, 1969, they will be performing at the Essen Festival in Germany.

September 15, 1969 - Top Pops and Music Now (U.K.) published an interview with Richard Wright. Reflecting on change, Wright stated, *"Drastic change. The sort of thing we just couldn't visualize when we started. In the early days, it always used to be a battle between us and the audience, and they normally won. They had the beer bottles you see."*

Wright continued, *"Audiences listen now, so it's a joy to play. When we started out, you had to have a hit single or nobody would listen to you. But it's different now. The non-hit groups are drawing bigger crowds. I suppose at the time of 'Emily' we had a bit of a teenybopper image. And then we did try and make a couple of singles after that, but they failed. Looking back on it, it just wasn't important. Nowadays there's just no need for us to try and have a hit single. In fact, if we had a number one record, it would be a hang-up. It would restrict us. I'm not saying that we won't ever release a single again. If we do something that would make a nice single, then we'd release it. But we'll never consciously try for a hit single. I think they're slowly becoming obsolete anyway. What can you get musically out of four minutes?"*

Wright explained, *"I'm glad of the change, obviously. In those days, music was to dance to. Now people go to see a group to listen. But it's a pity people don't dance, in a way. At the moment audiences are involved in their heads and not physically. But it's bound to change again. We noticed this at UFO. When we started there, the whole audience used to dance, and gradually they stopped dancing and started listening."*

Wright said, *"UFO played a very big part in the change, I think. It used to be held in a church hall in Powis Gardens, very much a sort of workshop atmosphere. It was all very experimental, and, at that time, we were*

infinitely better when you get it together with the film in your mind. Perhaps we could bring it to John Trevelyan's attention that our moral welfare is our own responsibility."

August 30, 1969 - Record Mirror (U.K.) reported on the Pink Floyd concert at the Plumpton Racecourse on August 8, 1969. Approximately 20-25 thousand people attended the festival over the course of three days. Pink Floyd, who were the last act on Friday, produced an atmosphere of mysticism, with droning organs and hollow guitar chords. The song 'Cymbaline,' was pretty and inviting, conjuring images of a sea shore and communication with nature before building up to new heights of electricity. However, this song was followed by improvised effects that distracted from the presentation.

Melody Maker (U.K.) reported that Pink Floyd will begin a 12-day Continental tour on September 17, 1969, performing in Holland, France, and Belgium.

Record Mirror (U.K.) reported that the new Pink Floyd album, 'Umma Gumma,' is a double album, set for release on Harvest Records at the end of September. The first working things out with music and lights. I suppose our whole life was centered around UFO then, but it was a complete way of life. It all came out in the open, and that was such a nice feeling. The whole thing was an entity in itself, you know, the Floyd were on stage, but the audience and everything else that was happening was just as important."

Wright explained, "It was an experiment in those days. Money had nothing to do with it. Now we've had to adopt a more professional attitude. We still experiment a lot, but it isn't the same. People know about us now, and they know what to expect. The audience feeling now is nice, but there's that thing behind us that we had to fight through to get established. Then, we just played basically to dig the music, and the future didn't concern us. We didn't think about it. But now we have the confidence in ourselves to know we'll be going for some time."

Asked about the future direction for Pink Floyd, Wright responded, "We're going more and more into films, doing film music. We've always wanted to get into that, and now it's beginning to happen for us. We did the music for 'More,' and that's doing well abroad. It's supposed to be the most popular film in Paris at the moment."

Wright added, "In the beginning, it was important for us to play to earn money, gigging all over the country. But now we're trying to work things out film-wise. It's a good way of working because it leaves us a lot more time than if we had to travel all over the country every night, and we can go into other things. It'll leave us more time for recording and writing. We want to release a lot more albums than we have done in the past. We'd like to do more concerts rather than straight club venues. Eventually, we'd like to make our own films."

Wright explained, "Doing the music for films is a very challenging thing. It means that we have to express facts and scenes in music. And, as I say, financially it pays off, and so it leaves us more time on our own to develop our own individual ideas. Gigs take up so much time, and they're very hard work. I'm not saying that gigs aren't satisfying. We'd never give up playing clubs. There's a good feeling when you're playing to an audience in a small environment. But personally we need time so

that we can formulate ideas on our own. For example, I would very much like to make an album, but it would take time to get together. It's good to work on your own so that you're totally responsible for whatever you create. So films seem to be the answer for us at the moment. It would be nice to do a science fiction film. Our music seems to be that way orientated. I don't know how conscious that is. I suppose a lot of it is because Roger is fairly well into science fiction. We're doing the music for a cartoon by Alan Aldridge called Rollo. It's about this little character who goes round in outer space collecting animals for his zoo."

Wright said, "I suppose much of what gives our music a space-like quality is that it's very free-form, especially on stage. We work out basic formats, but it's all improvisation on known themes. A lot of people seem to think that on stage we work with tapes, but that's just not true. We spend a lot of time looking for new sounds, especially when we're in the recording studios. A lot of it just happens. You know, spontaneous, random sounds that happen when we're on a gig, then we remember the sound and use it afterwards."

Wright said, "We start recording again in December. The idea for the album will probably come out of our next concert tour. We haven't released all that many albums, we've only done four since we started. We'd like to try and release one a year from now on, and I think we shall probably be able to. We should have a lot more free time from now on."

Wright explained, "Eventually, we'd like to build our own studio. At the moment we have to record everything in the EMI studios, and that does tend to restrict us a bit. Not that the studios aren't good, but the record company sets aside a period of time, say two weeks, in which we have to record. It can quite easily happen that we aren't feeling our best over some of that time, or we can't really work out all our ideas as we'd like to. It's impossible for us to just phone up and say we'd like to do some recording. Anyway, we're all going to build our own little studios where we can work out our ideas and record them."

Commenting on Pink Floyd's influence on music, Wright said, "I suppose we did have an influence on a lot of what's happening now. We were lucky in that working with UFO in the early days we had a freedom to do what we wanted that nobody else had. Looking back on it, we were doing some extraordinary things, the sort of things that would just be accepted now. But, at the time, we were experimenting, and we were very aware of that. But because of that, because we did that very early in our careers, it changed things so that now we have no fear whatsoever of ever having to just play pop music. Chart music. And we're confident in the fact that what was originally an experiment has now been accepted on its own level. I suppose, in some ways, because we started early on, we have influenced a lot of people and helped to change things to what they are today. But I've no doubt that a lot of people influenced us to go in the direction that we did."

September 27, 1969 - Melody Maker (U.K.) published an ad for the First German Blues Festival, The Essen Pop And Blues Festival at the Gruga Halle, Essen, West Germany on October 9-11, 1969. Pink Floyd was scheduled for Saturday, October 11th. Admission was 30/- per day, or 70/- for all three days.

October 18, 1969 - Melody Maker (U.K.) published an ad for the First Paris Music Festival organized by BYG Records and Richard Anisette. The festival was scheduled for October 24-28, 1969, and featured Pink Floyd on Saturday night, October 25, 1969. Frank Zappa and Pierre Lattes were the MCs. Admission was 60 francs.

November 1, 1969 - Melody Maker (U.K.) published an interview with Roger Waters by Richard Williams. Asked whether the live version of the song 'Set the Controls for the Heart of the Sun' on the new album 'Ummagumma' was intended to put the listener right there, at the controls of a giant spacecraft heading into the heart of the sun, Waters replied, "I don't tie it down to real images. I did when I wrote 'Set the Controls' for example, but now it's more of an abstract kind of sound picture. Most of these things are abstract. The titles are just tags which are there because that's what it meant at the time. 'Set the Controls' still has relevance to the sun as the life-giving force, but perhaps it was never a real image, more of a head image. Two or three years ago I used to read a lot of science fiction books, and that's where it must

have come from. But now I feel that we're getting closer to real experience, rather than ideas generated by reading science fiction."

Asked about the relationship between the songs 'Grantchester Meadows' and 'Cirrus Minor,' Waters explained, "They were both bits of memory, I suppose. They're about living in Cambridge. Grantchester Meadows are fields south of the town, and it just happened that I wrote two songs about the same thing, although 'Cirrus Minor' is about something else as well."

As to the reason for recording live versions of old numbers, Waters stated, "The four songs on the first album are a set of numbers that we'd been playing all round the country for a long time, and we decided to record them before we jacked them in. And they've changed a lot since we first recorded them."

Asked why a live version of 'Interstellar Overdrive' is not on the album as well, Waters said that the song "we don't dig very much." There are plans to press 2,000 acetates of the live recording of 'Interstellar Overdrive' that was left off 'Ummagumma' and give them to people who are interested in it. Waters explained, "We gave one to John Peel and he really liked it, so we may make up these acetates for people."

Since Pink Floyd is into modern electronic music, will they be responsible for the disintegration of conventional harmony in pop music? Waters answered, "I can't see us ever getting into complete disintegration. We're interested in experimenting, of course, but not in intellectual academic pursuits. If it comes out sounding academic and modern, I think it means that whichever of us has done it, has failed. I don't think it was ever our intention to go that way. To put it a better way, you may experiment with some kind of modern technique, but if you get it right, the feeling behind the music comes through, assuming that the listener has the capacity to hear it. I think we've got a very strong feeling for rhythm, and I'm not so keen on things that come out sounding clinical. We may move in different directions, and the moves you make depend, to a certain extent, on what you're asked to do. For instance, there's nothing I'd like to do more than the music for Arthur C. Clarke's next screenplay. The possibility exists

Ummagumma album cover front and back.

for science fiction films, not the cops and robbers in space type, but some of Theodore Sturgeon's stories would make incredible screenplays. That may or may not happen."

Waters continued, "We're now going to do the music for an Alan Aldridge TV cartoon series, called 'Rollo,' which will be in 25 half-hour installments. It's being put together by a private company for sale to the States, and I saw the pilot program recently. It's rather Yellow Submarine-ish, about a little boy in space. We're not going to sit down and tape 13 hours of music, of course. What we'll probably do is record a four-hour 'kit' of music, which can be fitted to the film, like there'll be so many take-offs, so many landings, so many impacts, and so forth. We'll be doing the dubbing ourselves, and that takes a hell of a long time."

The band did the soundtrack for the film, 'More,' which is doing well in France and America, but has not been released in Britain yet. Said Waters, "But it might not do so well in Britain, because the dialog in English is a bit odd. But to the French audiences, reading the subtitles, it's probably OK."

Asked about future recording and concert plans, Waters replied, "We'll be in the studios for ten days in December. I don't know exactly what we'll be doing, but it will probably be a life-cycle thing of some kind. The concerts we did with the 360-degree stereo gear earlier this year were a gas, and we're going to do some more, maybe around Easter time. We'll be improving the Co-ordinator

equipment, because we've discovered that many of the principles on which it was built were wrong. I'd like to get a bit more quality, because involving the audience depends to a large extent on it being real, and the better equipment, the more real it becomes."

Waters then explained various recording techniques, and took the reviewer to his Islington garden recording studio. Waters said, "You know, there must be thousands of people in this country who have the ability to create if they're given the chance to use tape recorders and things like that. They just don't have the facilities."

New Musical Express (U.K.) published a full-page ad for the new Pink Floyd album, 'Ummagumma.'

November 5, 1969 Record Mirror (U.K.) reviewed the Pink Floyd album, 'Ummagumma,' writing that it is a truly great progressive album. They mix psychedelic and classical patterns, and explore sounds, music, and gimmicks to their fullest extent. The recordings are beautiful. Roger Waters' song, 'Several species of small furry animals gathered together in a cave and grooving with a Pict' has to be heard to be believed.

November 14, 1969 - Melody Maker (U.K.) published an ad for the AFAN Festival of Progressive Music in South Wales on December 6, 1969. Pink Floyd will be among bands performing. Tickets are 25, 20, and 15.

November 22, 1969 - Disc and Music Echo (U.K.) published an article titled, "Are spacemen Floyd on the way back to earth?" by Roy Shipston that featured an interview with David Gilmour. Asked what the point of Pink Floyd is, Gilmour responded, "*We just want to get on and get through to people with the things we do. We want to get through to every person in the country, to every person in the world even. It's just communication, that's what it's all about.*"

Gilmour continued, "*I suppose we all want to improve the world, make it a better place to live in, like everyone else. There is a great revolution taking place at the moment, which seems to have emerged from the pop movement, the underground scene. The same thing is happening in all the Arts.*"

Gilmour continued, "*We all have very strong views, differing views, but we try, to keep it out of our music. Some of it comes through in our writing, obviously, but we are mainly concerned with just communication with people through our songs.*"

Gilmour explained, "*I don't think it's wrong if someone well-known uses his position to get over his beliefs, or influence people. Why shouldn't he? It could be wrong if it is a bad belief. We're just not very good at writing that sort of song. We never really set out specifically to protest about violence or anything. We don't want to come across with some incredible message.*"

Asked to define their music, Gilmour explained, "*There's not really much to explain. I don't know why it works out like it does. There's no special thing that we deliberately work at. We are just trying to move ahead, to get things done for enjoyment and soul. We find that people dig what we are doing, and the way we work is to do things that we like at the time, rather than things they will like us to do. It's always been that way and it seems to work. Of course you have to do some numbers that they know, but they're ones that we still enjoy doing.*"

As to why Pink Floyd's music is space oriented, Gilmour said, "*We don't deliberately try and make everything come out like that. It just works out that things happen that way. We all read science fiction and groove to '2001.' It's all very good. But some of*

our things happen completely accidentally."

As to how Pink Floyd are progressing, Gilmour explained, "*I don't know how its going to go. It's tended to get a little less spacey lately. It's just a matter of doing new things, new pieces of music, and seeing what happens. You can have an idea, then, when the whole group gets together, it will change completely. How a song is originally, and how it eventually turns out, may be two different things. The group has changed a lot since the early days, and come a long way. The worst period was after the two hit singles. We went right down then because people expected us to do them and we wouldn't. Now we are as busy as we want to be. We do two or three gigs a week and that keeps us going. But I never seem to have any cash. It's such an expensive business. We are also a bit slow, especially on recording. It takes us months to get out an LP. We get in the studio for a couple of days, then someone like the Beatles wants to record and we get shoved out. So a couple of weeks later we go back and we've forgotten the mood. It takes a lot of time getting back into the thing. What we really need is a block session to get something done in one go. We have great fun in the studios mucking about. But I don't think I could go on recording without doing appearances. It's great to do a live gig, but we can do so much more recording. I don't see why we should limit ourselves on record to what we do on stage.*"

Gilmour continued, "*There are a lot of things we haven't really touched on yet, television, for instance, which is good publicity. We have been approached about doing programs, but nothing's ever come of it. I thought we had some nice ideas for a TV show, they'd probably still be OK. But TV generally is so boring. I suppose everybody's ego would be satisfied by a lot of fame, but it seems that if you have a record in the charts, you are rejected by the so-called underground movement. Hit parades do spell death for our sort of group. But if we did a single, I'd be quite happy if it got into the charts.*"

Gilmour explained, "*Our main thing is to improve, and we are trying all the time. We are striving to improve our amplification, on stage and in the studios. We want to clean up the sound equipment. But I don't foresee any drastic changes. We've used a choir and a brass section and we tend to play any strange instruments that happen to be lying around. We don't feel limited. One of our hang-ups is that people who haven't seen us come along believing that we're going to be good before we start. And we're not always quite what they expected. Myself, I don't think we'll ever get through to the masses."*

November 29, 1969 - Melody Maker (U.K.) published an ad for "Etceteration Further Thoughts of The Pink Floyd," a concert on Sunday, November 30, 1969, at the Lyceum. Shows at 7:30 and 11:00. Admission 20/-. Also in this issue is an ad for the Arts Festival Weekend, with Pink Floyd at Brunel University on Friday, November 28, 1969. Shows at 7:30 and 12:00. Admission 10/- in advance, 15/- at the door.

Also in this issue is an ad for the AFAN Festival Progressive Music at the AFAN Lido Indoor Sports Centre, Port Talbot, South Wales on Saturday, November 6, 1969, featuring Pink Floyd. Shows at 6:30 and 12:00. Admission 25/-, 20/-, and 15/-.

December 6, 1969 - Disc and Music Echo (U.K.) reported that Pink Floyd will be doing a new British tour, beginning February 5, 1970, at the Liverpool Philharmonic Hall, followed by dates at the Manchester Free Trade Hall on the 6th, London's Royal Albert Hall on the 7th, and at the Birmingham Town Hall on the 11th.

December 13, 1969 - Melody Maker (U.K.) published an article titled, "Floyd write major film score." Pink Floyd will write the soundtrack music for 'Zabriskie Point,' a new movie by Michael Antonioni. It will be premiered in the U.S. and Britain simultaneously next February. Steve O'Rourke said, *"The sound track album may be released on MGM who are distributors of the picture. The Floyd have composed and are recording eight new numbers for the film, and the LP will be released in January. Although groups have been used for music on films, as in Easy Rider and, of course, the Beatles for their films, this is the first time a British group has done a sound track for a major production. The music is costing MGM in excess of $200,000."*

The band will also be doing music for an American cartoon series of seventeen

half-hour shows by Alan Aldridge. And negations are underway for them to do the music for a new Rita Hayworth movie currently being filmed in Paris.

New Musical Express (U.K.) reported that Pink Floyd have been commissioned to write the music for two more films and an American cartoon series. The band is currently working on the score for the Antonioni movie, 'Zabriskie Point,' tentatively scheduled to open on February 10, 1970. Carlo Ponti is the producer. Following their work on the film, Pink Floyd will stage a brief French tour with two shows in Paris on January 23, 1970, followed by a British tour in February, and a two-month U.S. tour in March.

Before leaving for the U.S. tour, Pink Floyd will begin work on the music for an American cartoon series called 'Rollo,' that will comprise 17 half-hour shows to begin airing on U.S. TV in November 1970. The series will be done by Alan Aldridge. Pink Floyd are also writing music for a French movie titled, 'The Road to Salina' starring Rita Hayworth.

Also in this issue is an article titled, "Pink Floyd Have the Last Laugh" by Nick Logan that featured an interview with Richard Wright. Recalling the early days, Wright said, *"When we started in UFO, it was a beautiful place to play. But when we went outside London, nobody wanted to know. People used to throw bottles at us. At the same time, we had a slight hit with 'See Emily Play,' and people expected us to play Top 20 stuff. Instead, we came along with this strange music they didn't understand. People just didn't believe in us. I think they regarded us as a huge joke. They saw us as a lot of freaks getting up on stage and playing freakish music. I'll never forget Pete Murray saying on Juke Box Jury that we were just a cult and would last for six months."*

Asked whether he foresaw the progressive music boom, Wright explained, *"I knew it would happen sometime, but I didn't know if it would happen quickly or slowly. I don't think we could have seen it happening to such an extent where today the underground is now the overground, and underground groups are getting better money than the teenyboppers. Yes, I would agree that it is today's pop music, and it is really nice because*

STRAND   W.C.2

Sunday, 30th November

ETCETERATION FURTHER THOUGHTS OF THE

PINK FLOYD

AUDIENCE
CUBY'S BLUES BAND

LIGHTS — ITYS

SOUNDS — ANDY DUNKLEY

Concert 7.30-11.00

Admission 20/-

Extras: Licensed Bars and Food. Enquiries: 01-734 9186

ADVANCE TICKETS AVAILABLE ONLY AT THE FOLLOWING
BRANCHES OF MUSICLAND

44 Berwick Street, W.1	734 5626
230 Portobello Road, W.11	229 3077
153 Kilburn High Road, N.W.6	624 0507
11a Church Street, Kingston, Surrey	546 7372
226 High St., Hounslow, Middx.	570 2854

1970
Laughing Madcaps
and Atomic Heart Mothers

there are so many groups playing good music and it is accepted everywhere. Well, there are still a few places where a few people will walk out. But, generally speaking, it just gets better and better. Even Glasgow, which you might expect to be an incredibly bad scene for a group like us, is a really beautiful place to play."

Asked about what caused things to change, Wright said, "It was UFO. It was groups like us, and the whole hippie philosophy that was connected with it, and because the pop thing was then so shallow and empty, and people wanted better things. Now, because of it, even straight pop is becoming better. Audiences now demand that you must be able to play your instrument. It's not just a question of having a pretty face or wearing way-out clothes. I should think it's pretty hard to establish yourself as a teenybopper group now. It's nice, too, that what has happened in the past three to four years has encouraged really good musicians to care about what is happening in pop and to form their own bands. It is very encouraging to find that what you believe in is commercial."

Although Pink Floyd has become popular through their albums, Wright was asked if they had any desire to release any more singles. Wright answered, "Well, we had that one hit, and then two after that didn't make it. Then we came to realize that it was not important to get hits and that, in fact, a Number One for us might be a bit of a drag. I find the whole business of pop, and Top of the Pops, a drag, and the singles scene is a dying market, anyway. I'm not putting it down. If we got a single that went to Number One, it might be nice. But it wouldn't be important because that's not what we are about."

As for other groups releasing singles, Wright added, "It is rubbish to say they have gone commercial. Bands like Jethro Tull and Fleetwood Mac believe in what they are playing and, in the end, it always comes down to the music. It's not a question of a sell-out. It

means, in fact, that pop is growing up. From now on, I believe pop music will be good music. There will be still more change. But the standards have been raised and I cannot see them going down again."

Speaking about doing music for films, Wright explained, "Film scores are very hard work. On the Italian film, we worked solidly day and night for two weeks to produce twenty minutes of music. But it is very satisfying work, and we'd like to do more of it."

On their future plans of working with an orchestra, Wright said, "We want to write a complete work for the orchestra and ourselves, so that the group is another part of the orchestra."

December 1969 - Rave Magazine (U.K.) published an article titled, "The Rave Pop Directory." Under "P" is an entry for Pink Floyd. "Although no longer a top pop attraction, Pink Floyd has already qualified as a life member of pop's unique anti-establishment. They ensured that the word underground was no longer a stigma, more a recommendation. Recommended LP listening: More."

January 3, 1970 - Disc and Music Echo (U.K.) reviewed the Syd Barrett album, 'The Madcap Laughs.' They wrote that the album features songs in the same vein as those Barrett wrote with Pink Floyd. The songs are mostly about love, and the cover is "terrifyingly surrealistic." An excellent album. Four stars.

New Musical Express (U.K.) published a half-page ad for the Syd Barrett album, 'The Madcap Laughs.'

Record Mirror (U.K.) published an article titled, "No more singles from Pink Floyd." The article states that the new Antonioni movie, 'Zabriskie Point,' is scheduled to be shown in Britain next month. Pink Floyd were commissioned to write the music for the film, and it is the second film score the band has written.

David Gilmour explained, *"We did the music to a film called 'More' a few months ago. It's due out here sometime. It's a big film in the States and France at the moment. It's about drugs, sex, and stuff. Since then, we've been asked to do a couple of film scores, including Antonioni's 'Zabriskie Point.' The album of the music should be out shortly. We like to do film scores because it's an overall concept, not just a string of songs. But the film I'd like to have produced the music for was '2001-A Space Odyssey.' We could have done it and done it very well. But as it was, of course, it worked out very well. We'd heard about the film before it came to London, so when it came, I knew what it would be like. The music's tremendous. But the film companies have this basic problem. Either they use an orchestra and research all the music carefully, or they commission people like us to write the music. I suppose we come quite high on people's lists for writing film music these days."*

Talking about writing singles, Gilmour continued, *"We've found it difficult to produce singles. We've needed to think that they have to be perfect. So we've decided to concentrate on LPs. In the studio, there are so many things you can do. One person in a studio can do things that would require ten people on stage to do. 'Ummagumma' was a bit difficult, though, because it was partly recorded live at a session we did in Manchester. We did two takes, and the second best of the two at the time came off better on record. The better of the two didn't come off on record."*

The band plans to tour the States in February or March.

January 10, 1970 - Melody Maker (U.K.) published Blind Date with Roger Waters, in which Waters was played a song without being told who it was, and he then commented on it.

Canned Heat - 'Let's Work Together.' Waters said, *"It's got some quite nice slide guitar on it. It reminds me a bit of Leadbelly. I know it's Canned Heat because I saw the label when we were trying to mend the record player but I admit I wouldn't have sussed it out. I quite like this. In fact, I like this sort of blues record, although I feel that most*

of it has been done better before. I mean, I don't think this says it any better than it was said 30 years ago. It has an optimistic lyric."

The Rascals - 'Hold On.' Waters said, *"Well I never! When I listen to things like that and don't know who they are, I start to wonder if they are black or white or gray. There's the old Ray Charles piano, or pianette, in there, and the drums at the front in the modern mode. I have never seen Delaney And Bonnie but I imagine this is rather how they sound. It's not really the kind of thing I'm interested in."*

Flaming Youth - 'Guide Me, Orion.' Waters said, *"Good Lord! What a laugh! I think that sums that up, without wishing to be glib. For a start I didn't like the harmonies on the vocals. It's all a bit sunshine-is-goldenish for me. I can't believe the lyrics were written seriously, there must be a bit of tongue-in-cheek going on. It's very contrived. To be fair, I suppose it was a sincere attempt to aim something at an imagined public state of mind which doesn't in fact exist. All that pastoral stuff gleaned from things that have come out over the past five years and stuck together!"*

New York Rock and Roll Ensemble - 'I'm too Busy.' Waters said, *"Is this at the right speed? Well, er, well er, well, er. They nearly got the bass line from the Righteous Brothers' 'Lovin' Feeling' right at the beginning. Then it sounded like an understudy for Jimi Hendrix coming through a Selmer Little Giant. With all that alliteration, the lyric sounds like something Pete Townshend might have written, when he was four. It's very weedy."*

The Art Movement - 'For As Long As You Need Me.' Waters said, *"I've no idea who it is, but it could be any one of five million groups. It's the old conception of taking an Artist, with a capital A, and a Song, with a capital S, written by Pop, with a capital P, Song Writers, with a capital S and W, and a Tune, with a capital T, and mix them all together. And what do you get? A load of rubbish. That is the other path of pop music. That really is the other side from all the performers who are staggering about, making sounds they think are good, making sounds for reasons. This seems to be reasonless. It's not really worth talking about."*

Kenny Clarke-Francy Boland Big Band - 'Solarisation.' Waters said, *"That second section sounded very Ellingtonish, though the rest didn't. I do like that sort of music, though I don't know what I can say about it. It's the kind of thing that, if we heard it on the way up the M1, it would get us all miming, if you know what I mean."*

Syd Barrett - 'Terrapin.' Waters said, *"This is a track I didn't produce because it didn't need anything doing to it. This song makes everything else you have played me look completely sick and silly. I think this is very beautiful. Don't take it off, I'm going to listen to it all the way through. I think that is a great song. In fact, all the songs on this album are great. No, some of them on it are GREAT, in capital letters, and all of them are good. Syd is a genius."*

Black Sabbath - 'Evil Woman.' Waters said, *"There you go! Well, well, well! I'm speechless, well, almost. It's got that kind of Dragnet, Peter Gunn, American detective series beginning. You keep thinking it's going to start. You think that for the first minute but then, if you are really perceptive, you realize it isn't going to start, and that's all there is."*

New Musical Express (U.K.) reported that two new concerts have been added to the Pink Floyd tour, at the Manchester Opera House on the 8th, and at the Liverpool Empire on the 15th.

Record Mirror (U.K.) published an article titled, "The return of Syd – a year after leaving the Floyd." Syd Barrett is back with a new single, 'Octopus,' and a new album due out this month. Syd Barrett was interviewed in an off-Oxford Street office.

Talking about leaving Pink Floyd, Barrett said, *"When we parted, I had written everything for the group. My leaving sort of evened things out within the group. Since then I have been doing lots of things, things interesting for me. I've done a lot of traipsing around. I've been back to Spain, Ibiza. I first went there with Rick three years ago. It's an interesting place to be. I've written quite a lot, too."*

Speaking about the UFO Club and what has followed, Barrett explained, *"Everything was so rosy at UFO. It was really nice to go there after slogging around the pubs and so on. Everyone had their own thing. It's*

been interesting to see things turning out the way they have. During the past six months, there have been some very good things released. The best things I've bought are the new Taj Mahal album, Captain Beefheart, and The Band. I don't think any of them have influenced my writing, though. I've been writing in all sorts of funny places."

Talking about his new album, 'The Madcap Laughs,' Barrett said, *"They're my particular idea of a record. It's very together. There's a lot of speaking on it, but there's not a very recognizable mood. It's mainly acoustic guitar and there are no instruments at all."*

As for future plans, Barrett stated, *"I'm just waiting to see how the records do, what the reactions are, before I decide on anything else."* And commenting on the Pink Floyd album, 'Ummagumma,' Barrett said, *"They've probably done very well. The singing's very good and the drumming is good as well."*

January 1970 - Beat Instrumental (U.K.) published an article titled, "Floyd still progressing, but starting at top again." They wrote, "The Pink Floyd have been playing together for five years. During all this time, there has been but one personnel change, when Syd Barrett was replaced on guitar and vocals by Dave Gilmour, and the group continually experimented, entertained, and pushed their theories into practice. Roger Waters on bass, Nick Mason on drums, Dave Gilmour on guitar, and Rick Wright on piano and organ, have achieved a lot. I recently went to Rick Wright's Bayswater flat where, for a couple of hours, we talked about the Pink Floyd, Rick Wright, the weather (it was a cold day), and what the group hope to be doing in the future.

First, the group's latest venture. *"We've just done the music for a film,"* said Rick. *"It's Antonioni's latest one, 'Zabriskie Point,' and we've done the complete score with the exception of a few bits of canned music."* Antonioni is famous for his previous film, centering on the world of the trendy, 'Blow Up,' which also featured rock music, supplied then by the Yardbirds.

How did the Floyd approach the job? Wright said, *"It's all improvised, but nonetheless it was really hard work. We had each piece of music and we did about six takes* of each, and he'd choose the best. Antonioni's not hard to work with, but he's a perfectionist. He was with us in the studios every night for two weeks, from nine in the evening until eight the next morning, every night for two weeks to get 20 minutes of music. It was hard, but it was worth it."

Do the group expect to do any more film work? Wright said, "Yes, definitely. It's one of the things we've always wanted to do. We did 'More,' which, well, we didn't really like the film. 'Zabriskie Point,' which is partly about the violence in America, seems to be an excellent film. It's hard to say what I thought of our music in 'More,' since I didn't see it with the film, but apparently, it works quite well. As an album, I don't really much like it."

A further film job for the group is that they are doing the sounds for a new cartoon series called Rollo, by Alan Aldridge, which has already, on the strength of the pilot show, been sold all over the States. "It's really incredible," said Rick. "You know what Aldridge's drawings are like. It's about a boy, Rollo, who goes around space with Professor Creator, I think that's his name, who collects galactic animals for his zoo."

The Floyd put many science fiction elements into their music, anyway. Their song titles, alone, are a giveaway, with such names as 'Interstellar Overdrive,' and 'Set the Controls for the Heart of the Sun.' And there are also elements of witchcraft and ritualism. Wright said, "It's funny you should pick on that. While we were in America, we were asked to play at a voodoo convention. Sadly, we couldn't make it because the American Musicians' Union wouldn't let us play. It would have been marvelous. All the voodoo cults from all over the world meeting up with all the science-fiction writers."

'Ummagumma' is the name of the group's latest recording. A double album, one record is live Floyd, the other being each of the four members doing their own musical section. How did Rick like the record? Wright said, "I was pleased with it. It was an experiment. I don't really know if it worked or not. But I like it." Some people were disappointed that the live section includes numbers already released on previous albums, 'Astronomy Domine,' 'Saucerful of Secrets,' and 'Heart of the Sun,' with only one new one, 'Be Careful With That

Axe Eugene.' Wright said, "We did them because so many people were asking us if we'd made any recordings of our stage act. The next one, I'm sure, will be completely new stuff."

Is 'Ummagumma,' presently high in the charts, the groups best-selling album? Wright said, "I would have thought so, though Piper and Saucer both sold a lot. It probably is the best since it's selling very well in America. It's the first time we've sold over there."

The group have twice been to America, once in 1967, "a nightmare," and once in 1968, "good." Wright said, "We should be going back in either March or April next year. It hasn't been set up yet, but a lot of people are offering us tours, and we're waiting to pick the best one."

Back to 'Ummagumma.' Wright explained, "The four pieces on the LP are very different, though there are pieces in all of them which link together. There wasn't actually any attempt to connect them all. We didn't write together, we just went into the studios on our own to record and then we got together to listen to them. We all played alone on our pieces, in fact. Again, we couldn't all agree on this. I thought it was a very valid experiment and it helped me. The result is that I want to carry on and do it again, on a solo album. But I think that maybe Roger feels that if we'd all worked together, it would have been better. That's something you just don't know, whether it would or not. I think it was a good idea."

Wright continued, "The live part of the album we had to record twice. The first time, at Mother's in Birmingham, we felt we'd played really well, but the equipment didn't work so we couldn't use nearly all of that one. The second time, at Manchester College of Commerce, was a really bad gig, but as the recording equipment was working well, we had to use it. Parts of Saucer on 'Ummagumma' came from the Birmingham gig, which we put together with the Manchester stuff. But the stuff on the album isn't half as good as we can play."

As far as studio recording is concerned, the group are tied to using EMI studios, though they did once do some stuff in Pye, as part of their contract. Wright explained, "Sessions are generally a bad scene. You have to book up ages ahead and then, whether the material is ready or not, you have to go in all the same. Also EMI's equipment hasn't been good for us. There are some really good studios where we'd like to record, but we can't. Places like Olympic and Morgan."

The group recently left the Bryan Morrison agency for NEMs, a deal with which they're well pleased. Wright said, "At last, we've got a really good agency. We're doing as much work as we want to. There's plenty of it, too much in fact. It's hard to say how much we do in one week. We may do five gigs. Another we may do one. One or two a week is really all we want."

Are they still enjoying playing live? Wright replied, "Oh yes, very much. We all dig going out live. In fact, we have very few disagreements really. But we do want to spend more time doing films. 'Zabriskie Point' should attract more offers, because working with Antonioni is starting at the top for us. He's brilliant. But generally speaking, I am happy with the way the group's going. I think a lot about what we're doing and, well, sometimes when I'm on stage I suddenly wonder, what the hell I'm doing up there. Have I got the right to have 5,000 people there in front of me? And what have I got to say? Is it important enough? I get doubts, I think everybody must, and in the middle of playing I just get a mental block. And because I'm questioning what I'm doing, I can't think of what to play."

Wright continued, "I'm very happy in what I'm doing. But I would like to try lots of other things. Sometimes I feel like leaving the business completely, doing something else, but always connected with music." Rick doesn't feel all that many connections between the Floyd and other groups. They are something of an odd-men-out in that "we started together, and we're still together. We haven't gone through the usual stages of everyone in a band having played with millions of tiny little bands, with the best of the people surviving and slowly building up into the best groups. We started off as the Floyd and that was it. We really had no experience other than the Floyd. I played trombone in a trad band years ago, but we haven't worked our way through, so we haven't had that much contact with other groups."

In their time, the Pink Floyd has come in for a lot of criticism amid the acclaim. At one time, their stage act was slated often,

though the problems here were resolved when Dave joined the group. The group is now generally reckoned to be one of the best four or five for live shows. Do they worry about criticism? Wright said, "Yes, if it's valid. If someone points out something that we haven't realized before, that's good. It makes you think about things and maybe change them. We have a lot of friends who'll come back stage and tell us what they think. This is valuable because, as a group, we never agree on how well we've played. We'll come off, and Dave will maybe say it was incredible, and Roger may think it was really bad. Occasionally, very occasionally, we'll play a gig where we all walk off feeling good. But our musical attitudes are probably fairly different, which is good."

It is also, probably, one of the reasons why the group manage to achieve so many varied moods and textures with their music, which spans an amazingly wide number of styles in one go. The Floyd play, within the overall context of "their sound," traces of rock, country, and the classics. Rick very rarely plays any rock records for his own amusement. It's all Beethoven and Berlioz at the moment. And every member of the group is giving all he's got to expand, refine and generally improve, both individually, and as part of the Floyd. The result is, after many years of trying, that the group are prospering, "Well, we're not actually losing money, which is nice," and winning the respect, both here and abroad, that they deserve."

January 14, 1970 - International Times (U.K.) reviewed the Pink Floyd album, 'Ummagumma.' Mick Farren wrote, "This double album package is above all an essential purchase for anyone who has ever got into the Floyd at any time. I must confess I came to dig The Floyd somewhat late in their career, but having made that step, I can only say that these two albums are a really magnificent package. The first disc comprises four pieces from their live repertoire, beautifully played and really well produced by Norman Smith. I think it is probably one of the best live recordings I have ever heard. The second disc consists of a section by each member of the group. The first side starts with Richard Wright's 'Sysyphus,' which begins with a slow dignified theme, goes through some rather strange progression on piano, then harpsichord, mellotron(?), and finally returns to the first organ theme. Roger Waters' section is split into two tracks, the first a song accompanied by guitar and simulated birds and bees, while the second is an amazing piece of lunacy, which can be described as a literal interpretation of the title 'Several Small Furry Animals Gathered Together In A Cave And Grooving With A Pict.' The second side opens with Dave Gilmour's track, which is much more what one would expect from The Floyd, except with a great bias towards guitar. The final piece, Nick Mason's, opens with a baroque flute theme, which is followed by a long percussion sequence with extremely effective use of stereo and a final return, in true Floyd manner, to the original theme."

January 23, 1970 - The Croydon Advertiser (U.K.) reported on the Pink Floyd concert at Fairfield Hall, Croydon on January 18, 1970. Richard Wright played organ, piano, trombone, vibraphone, and "unhurried, halcyon piano" in 'Niagara Dellof.' Other effects used by the band to change the atmosphere of the show were timpani, violent cymbals, flogging a large gong, and continuous microphone thumping by fingers. It was a three-hour concert at a frightening volume that lacked lighting effects, and was "just lacking."

January 24, 1970 - New Musical Express (U.K.) reviewed the Syd Barrett album, 'The Madcap Laughs.' They wrote that it contains a modest, meandering selection of songs. There's a good dose of Pink Floyd in the instruments and in influence. Some of the vocal effects are reminiscent of the Incredible String Band, or Donovan. It could grow on you, but it sticks too much in the same mood.

January 31, 1970 - Melody Maker (U.K.) published an article titled, "Confusion and Mr. Barrett" that featured an interview of Syd Barrett by Chris Welch. Asked how his new single, 'Octopus,' was doing, Barrett replied, "*I haven't noticed. I don't think it was necessarily a good idea to do a single, but it was done. It's a track off the album. I've spent a long time doing it since I left the group. But it was done at a reasonable pace.*"

Barrett continued, "*Yes, my time has been fairly well spent since leaving. I haven't had a particularly hard time and I was OK for money. I've heard of a few plans for me to do some appearances, but there is nothing positive enough to talk about. There are vague ideas about a group as well. I've just spent my time writing fairly regularly. I've certainly not been bored and there are still a lot of things to do.*"

Barrett continued, "*When I was with the Floyd, the form of the music played on stage was mainly governed by the records. Now I seem to have got back to my previous state of mind. With the volume used, they inclined to push me a little. Yes, there were hang-ups when I was with them, although it was not due to the traveling or anything, which you just put in the category of being a regular activity in that kind of job.*"

Asked if he likes the music industry, Barrett replied, "*It's beautiful here. I never go anywhere else. Top of the Pops is all right. You meet interesting people and there are always people around I know and are prepared to like me. That's very nice.*"

Barrett continued, "*There's no gloom or depression for me. It's been very exciting, especially when I went to America for two weeks before the split up. Then we came back and played at the Albert Hall and it was very much a crescendo and I felt very good. I miss playing to audiences, although I haven't missed it so much recently.*"

Asked if he was satisfied with his album, 'The Madcap Laughs,' Barrett answered, "*Well, no. I always find recording difficult. I can only think in terms of . . . Well I'm pleased with forty minutes of sound. But I can't in terms of the pop industry. It's only a beginning. I've written a lot more stuff.*"

Referring to the exceptional lyrics of 'Octopus,' Barrett said, "*Octopus is a particular example of recording being discussed as something exceptional because it takes an unusual metre. I don't read much, but I think I picked up Shakespeare as a book that just happened to be lying there to read. It was meant to be verse. I like to have really exciting, colorful songs. I can't really sing. But I enjoy it and I enjoy writing from experiences. Some are so powerful they are ridiculous. The straight scene is the best.*"

Barrett continued, "*What happened*

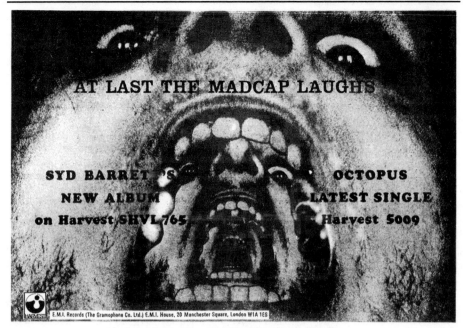

An ad for Syd Barrett's album, The Madcap Laughs.

at Tottenham Court Road when we started was a microcosm of what happened later. I think pop today is a bit difficult to take in some ways, but it's fine. I've never felt I have been left behind. I'd like to play sometime on the scene. Got to do something. It would be a splendid thing to get a band together."

February 7, 1970 - New Musical Express (U.K.) reported upcoming Pink Floyd tour dates at the Royal Albert Hall on February 7, 1970, the Manchester Opera House on the 8th, and at the Birmingham Town Hall on the 11th.

February 9, 1970 - The Times, London (U.K.) reported that Pink Floyd used the Albert Hall during their concert on February 7, 1970 as a "vast sounding chamber." Their music built slowly and gradually. The second set started with reverberated drumming, like amplified heart beats, was overlaid by hissing and growling, faded back to the sounds of a soft vibraphone, and eventually returned to a hard rock theme. This was followed by a long, soft piano interlude. Their sounds "merge and change like abstract images," similar to the colors in a light show.

February 14, 1970 - Disc and Music Echo (U.K.) published an article titled, "Pink Floyd

stay one-up" by Caroline Boucher that reviewed the Pink Floyd concert at the Albert Hall in London on Saturday, February 7, 1970. Nearly 6,000 people filled the Albert Hall to see Pink Floyd and their unique equipment set-up that sent the sound spinning around ones head. They also had an amazing array of percussion on stage, including racks of gongs, and a percussion section for Nick Mason that took up most of the stage and featured a frame hung with bells, tambourines, and dustbin lids.

Their music is beautiful and grabs at you when they play basic melodies, but this was limited primarily to the beginning of songs, including one that they have not given a name to. However, after the melodic beginnings, the songs develop into rambling un-together breaks that were too long, before concluding with a gem of an ending. Their two-and-a-half hour performance included the 'theme from More,' 'Careful With That Axe Eugene,' 'Saucerful of Secrets,' 'Set the Controls for the Heart of the Sun,' 'Embryo,' 'Sysyphus,' and music from the soundtrack to 'Zabriskie Point.'

Melody Maker (U.K.) reported on the Pink Floyd concert at the Albert Hall on February 7, 1970. Richard Williams wrote that, although Pink Floyd come close to playing the "Music

of the Spheres," they aren't perfect. They are fallible and capable of playing bad at times. During 'Sysyphus,' David Gilmour's slipshod pitching ruined the opening and closing themes, and the band were not in time with different downbeats. An untitled piece in the second half of the show used too much random noise on gongs and percussion. However, other than that, the concert was beautiful.

The show began with sirens and searchlights leading into 'The Embryo,' a song with a simple melody and interesting lyrics. Gilmour's guitar "slashed and whined," and his vocals were perfect. 'Main Theme from More' used "blipping" keyboards from Richard Wright, and 'Eugene' was a "far-out trip." 'Sysyphus' ended the first set with some excellent thundering piano by Wright. The second set consisted mainly of a long multi-sectioned piece that included a vibe solo and some blues. A slower than usual 'Set the Controls for the Heart of the Sun' ended the second set. They encored with 'A Saucerful of Secrets' that featured a heavenly organ and some chanting by David Gilmour.

Record Mirror (U.K.) published a review of the movie 'Zabriskie Point.' The article stated that the film is a love story in contemporary America set to the music of the Rolling Stones, Grateful Dead, Pink Floyd, John Fahey, Kaleidoscope and the Youngbloods. Pink Floyd wrote three original songs for the film, and an MGM soundtrack album is due out shortly. The film stars Daria Halprin, a 19-year old San Francisco student, Mark Frechette, a 20-year old Boston carpenter, and veteran actor Rod Taylor. The film opens in London on March 5, 1970.

February 21, 1970 - Disc and Music Echo (U.K.) published an article titled, "Pink Floyd – the electrical wizards who care!" by Caroline Boucher, that featured an interview with David Gilmour.

Talking about their equipment and the Azimuth Co-ordinator, Gilmour explained, "*We're all engineers by now. We weren't to begin with, but it's by necessity, really. The Azimuth Co-ordinator was a very simple idea. Once you've got the desire to make the effect, the actual making it isn't difficult. We just got an engineer to do it for us.*" Presently the Pink

Floyd are working on quadraphonic recording.

Gilmour lives in a flat in Earls Court, while the other members of the group live north of the park. Asked about replacing Syd Barrett in Pink Floyd, Gilmour explained, "*That wasn't easy. There was a bit of a Syd Barrett legend about. It wasn't easy for me or the rest of the group.*" However, they still are in contact with Barrett, who attended their concert at the Albert Hall, and who is working with Gilmour and Roger Waters on his solo album.

As far as Pink Floyd music being different, Gilmour said, "*It's different from everyone else because we work hard at it and think of the whole concept of music in a different way from other people. We try hard to do new things that are us. We don't try to be different from everyone else consciously, thinking 'Oh, god, we've got to be really way out and different.' The noise is something to do with the people in the group, the way we play as individuals. Rick plays in a very strange manner, and so on.*"

The band composes their music jointly, and songwriting gets credited to them all. Gilmour said, "*Roger is very extrovert on stage, which none of the rest of us are. He's a pushy sort of person. He does the announcing and the flamboyant extrovert stuff, but he doesn't do any more in the musical direction than the rest of us.*"

They are currently working on a third film score, following 'More,' and 'Zabriskie Point.' They were disappointed that so much of their music was not used in 'Zabriskie Point.' Gilmour stated, "*My parents live in New York, and I asked my mother to see the film twice when it opened over there to see what we sounded like and how much of us remained. I have yet to hear from her.*" Their latest film music will be for a cartoon called `Rollo' by Alan Aldridge who did the visuals for the Beatles' Yellow Submarine.

Gilmour played the interviewer some studio outtakes, including some excellent Country and Western music that the band played "just for fun." Gilmour commented, "*I don't think our sound has progressed. It changes, I suppose, but it's just another thing, a new sound, a new mood.*" Pink Floyd won't play these Country and Western songs live or

ANTONIONI's

FIRST FILM SINCE "BLOW-UP" IS A BOLD LOOK AT AMERICAN YOUTH TODAY

Metro-Goldwyn-Mayer presents A Carlo Ponti Production A Michelangelo Antonioni Film "ZABRISKIE POINT" Starring MARK FRECHETTE, DARIA HALPRIN and ROD TAYLOR Written by Michelangelo Antonioni, Fred Gardner, Sam Shepard, Tonino Guerra and Clare Peploe Executive Producer, Harrison Starr Produced by Carlo Ponti Directed by Michelangelo Antonioni Panavision & Metrocolor "X" (London)   MGM

on an album. Gilmour explained, "*We don't want to get over our own heads or anybody else's. We want to widen people's horizons, but we don't want to go beyond ourselves. A few groups have and it's easy to do. The music we play is what we are doing and we do feel it.*"

February 1970 - Beat Instrumental (U.K.) reviewed the Syd Barrett album, 'The Madcap Laughs.' They wrote, "Syd Barrett, ex-member of Pink Floyd, has produced this beautiful solo album. The sound is relaxed and quiet, and kept relatively simple, like on the first track, which comprises vocals, guitar, and washboard only, making late night music. The lyrics are not only audible, but well worth a serious listen in their own right, and the guitar is played with feeling rather than technical brilliance. The use of drums on some tracks definitely heightens the atmosphere, for, even though they're pounding out, they never get frantic. And there's also some very nice electric piano backing. Although Syd's voice is not

exceptional, it is pleasant, and he doesn't try anything out of his range."

March 14, 1970 - New Musical Express (U.K.) published an article titled, "Syd speaks out – at last!" by Richard Green, that featured an interview with Syd Barrett. Talking about what he has been up to since leaving Pink Floyd, Barrett said, "*After I left the group, I just spent a year resting and getting the album together. I didn't do much else at all, some painting and thinking about getting a band together. I've got a lot of ideas I want to explore later.*"

And speaking of his solo album, 'The Madcap Laughs,' Barrett explained, "*Making my own album was fine because, after two years away from the group, I didn't have to lead on from anything. I want to discover now if it's possible to continue some of the ideas that came from a couple of tracks on the first album.*"

March 20, 1970 - Fusion (U.K.) reported that Pink Floyd used thrilling effects and music, but a bit too much noise and running around the stage, during their sold-out concert at the Albert Hall. The stage was filled with exotic gongs and percussion equipment, and they used a 360-degree sound system. They played excerpts from 'Ummagumma,' some older songs, plus music from the soundtracks to the films 'More' and 'Zabriskie Point.' They are currently in the studio, and will be leaving on an American tour shortly.

March 21, 1970 - Disc and Music Echo (U.K.) reported that a new Syd Barrett album is being completely produced by David Gilmour, with guest musicians Rick Wright and Jerry Shirley. David Gilmour said, *"No one else can do it. It has to be someone who knows Syd, someone who can get him together."* The album should be released by the end of the summer.

Also in this issue is an article titled, "Floyd are 'dead' upset" that reported that the band was upset about the soundtrack to the film 'Zabriskie Point,' and the fact that they spent 10 days writing music for the film, only to find out that the Grateful Dead were flown to Italy to record some of the songs. Pink Floyd was proud of their version of the song, 'Love Theme,' which was not used. The soundtrack album that has been released only contains three Pink Floyd songs on it. David Gilmour commented, *"The drag is that MGM have a whole can of our music, enough to make an album of, left."* MGM have no plans to release the rest of Pink Floyd's music.

New Musical Express (U.K.) published an A-Z Guide to Sound of the 70's, which featured Pink Floyd, with group photo, under the letter P.

March 1970 - Beat Instrumental (U.K.) reported that Britain's art colleges have turned out a disproportionate number of successful musicians, John Lennon, Jimmy Page and Pete Townshend among them. It was while Syd Barrett was studying fine art at Camberwell School of Art in South London that he started playing with the Pink Floyd, the rest of whom were all, at that time, potential architects at the Regent Street Polytechnic. And the influence of the avant-garde art world was apparent in the Floyd's stage act, the first to make stroboscopes and oil-slide projections standard equipment for an evening's music.

But now Syd has his own solo best selling album, 'The Madcap Laughs,' which has provided a clear answer to that much-asked question, "Whatever happened to Syd Barrett after he left the Floyd?" At present Syd is living quietly in his sparsely-furnished London flat among his stereo equipment, piles of paintings, and a heap of battered LPs. He's taking things easily, as he has been doing for

the last two years, composing, writing, and painting as inspiration comes, and making some plans for the future. He will soon be working on another album and he also plans to get a group together, but beyond that he seems to have no particular intentions.

Syd was pleasantly surprised to find the LP had sold well, especially as there was no great hype involved. *"Yes, it's quite nice,"* Barrett said in his soft-spoken manner that sometimes becomes so soft that he's not talking to anything but his chin, *"but I'd be very surprised if it did anything if I were to drop dead. I don't think it would stand to be accepted as my last statement. I want to record my next LP before I go on to anything else and I'm writing for that at the moment."*

It was while Syd was at school in Cambridge that he started learning the guitar. He played in a number of groups in that area from the age of 16 onwards, doing Bo Diddley and Jimmy Reed numbers especially. *"Then I had to come up to London,"* Barrett said. *"I didn't mean to play for ever. It was painting that brought me here to art school. I always enjoyed that much more than school, although it had nothing to do with the music. After three years in London, I started playing with the Pink Floyd. Bo Diddley was definitely my greatest influence. Around that time, one came across so many unheard-of records that one felt one was really discovering something."*

Barrett continued, *"The Floyd's music arose out of playing together. We didn't set out to do anything new. We worked up to 'See Emily Play,' and so on, quite naturally from the Rolling Stones numbers we used to play. None of us advocated doing anything more eccentric. We waited until we had got the lights together and then went out."* The group secured a recording contract with EMI and found chart success with their first two releases 'Arnold Layne' and 'See Emily Play,' both of them written by Syd Barrett. And it was, of course, at London's first psychedelic dungeon, UFO, that the Floyd found their initial following among the early freaks, when flower power was something very real to a lot of people. However, the Floyd moved away from their starting place to tour Britain in the usual rounds of clubs and ballrooms.

After their first album, 'Piper at the Gates of Dawn,' and their third single, 'Apples

And Oranges,' had been released, the group made the now customary trek around the United States. It was on return from that great country that Syd split from the Floyd. "*I spent a year relaxing,*" Barrett said, "*and another getting the LP together. It's been very slow, like looking back over a long time and playing very little. When I went away, I felt the progress the group could have made. But it made none, none at all, except in the sense that it was continuing. To make my album was a challenge as I didn't have anything to follow.*"

Now Syd is looking to form his own band, which he hopes he will have going within a year. Barrett said, "*This is the most interesting thing to do now, to see whether it would have been possible to retain the 'Emily' sort of things that were there and on maybe two tracks of the first album. I've been writing consistently for two years now and I have lots of undeveloped things lying around. I'm still basically like I've always been, sitting round with an acoustic, getting it done. I never get worried about my writing.*" And so Syd Barrett, now back in the public eye after two years, carries on in his own way-doing what he wants as he wants to.

March 23, 1970 - Ekstra Bladet, Copenhagen (Denmark) reported on the Pink Floyd concert at the Tivoli Koncertsal in Copenhagen, Denmark on March 21, 1970. "The songs were like hymns in a fantastic cathedral." "The guitar playing got a little too savage (and too loud) and you could not give yourself away to the music."

Information, Copenhagen (Denmark) reported on the Pink Floyd concert at the Tivoli Koncertsal in Copenhagen, Denmark on March 21, 1970. "I do not think of the sound level as anti musical. The loud sound levels can add a new dimension to the music, and Pink Floyd understand the dramatic in building up a dynamic piece."

Politiken, Copenhagen (Denmark) reported on the Pink Floyd concert at the Tivoli Koncertsal in Copenhagen, Denmark on March 21, 1970. "Pink Floyd's concert last Saturday was perfect." "They belong to the few surviving beat groups, like the Rolling Stones and the Beatles."

March 28, 1970 - Melody Maker (U.K.) reported that Extravaganza 70, a large Pop and Fashion Festival, will be held at the Empire Hall, Olympia, London, England from May 29th to June 6, 1970. Syd Barrett is booked to perform at the festival with his own group.

April 11, 1970 - Melody Maker (U.K.) published an article titled, "Floyd - in the Pink!" that featured an interview with David Gilmour and Richard Wright by Chris Welch. The interview was done at Wright's Bayswater flat, just before the band was leaving for their third American tour. David Gilmour said, "*We open at the Fillmore East on Thursday. Our last tour was okay, pretty good really. This time we are taking the Azimuth Co-ordinator with us. They have never heard it before. This tour should be a lot better organized. Last time we staggered about trying to get gigs. There were so many hangups. We are renting the Fillmore ourselves, and it has sold out. Originally, Bill Graham, who runs the place, offered us a 40-minute spot with three other groups. I don't know if the tour is important to us or not. I like America, for short spells, but not too long. Last time we lost money. If you can make it through a first American tour intact, the chances are you will survive anything.*"

Wright continued, "*I'm not looking forward to it. I don't like living in hotels for weeks, and there is a lot of violence in America. And the chances are you will get involved, especially with long hair.*"

Gilmour added, "*We're not an agro. We have a lot of self-control, although Roger can get through some violence on stage. If we were a violent group, we would have had some punch-ups by now. We have been in a few bother-ups.*"

Asked about new material, Gilmour responded, "*We've got some new material. There is one new number which will last half an hour, which hasn't got a title yet.*"

Wright added, "*I feel we are getting stale. We tend to play on stage what we have been playing for years. But we don't just generate one mood in our performances. In fact, our music is a lot less on one level than in many other groups. That's something I find boring about a lot of heavy groups who are just very heavy and very loud. We had a lot of opposition to us from the business at first. The business just didn't like us at all. They thought the whole thing was a joke, and that the whole UFO thing was a joke. Our only real problem is the time factor. We just don't have enough time to do all the things we want. We are working too hard, incredibly hard since November. Our next album won't be out for some time, and in the meantime, we are working on producing Syd Barrett's next album."*

Commenting on the music they will be producing for an Alan Aldridge animated TV cartoon series called Rollo, Wright said, *"It'll be a lot of work, but we'll give them a stock of music to draw from for each episode. And after the American tour, we'll be doing six festivals in Europe. And there is some talk of a British tour. We'd like to do a theatre in London for a week, with theatrical effects and good lighting. The trouble is we are already a little too overworked in actual performances, which is slowing down our output and progress."*

As to whether Pink Floyd still has a strong musical direction, Gilmour concluded, *"I don't know. Possibly. I can't really say which way we are going. We'll just carry on and produce a new Pink Floyd classic or two."*

May 16, 1970 - Melody Maker (U.K.) reported that Pink Floyd's performance at UCLA in Los Angeles helped calm down a riot situation. Attendance was 10,000, including National Guardsmen with helmets, riot shields, and helmets.

May 25, 1970 - Great Speckled Bird, Atlanta (U.S.) reported on the Pink Floyd concert held at the Municipal Auditorium in Atlanta, Georgia on May 12, 1970. Pink Floyd used a 360-degree sound system with speakers throughout the auditorium and on the stage.

Roger Waters stated, *"We want to throw away the old format of a pop show standing on a square stage at one end of a rectangular room and running through a series of numbers. Our idea is to put the sound all around the audience with ourselves in the middle. Then the performance becomes much more theatrical."*

The reviewer, Charlie Cushing,

stated that the sound system was "beyond belief." Describing the music as "the natural merging between of electronics and psychedelics," Cushing explained that the music is produced on conventional instruments but are electronically altered, and the sounds are hard to associate with the instruments being played. In addition to the instruments, Pink Floyd also used tapes, with tape loops of rhythmic bird calls, giant stereo footsteps that walk around the hall, doors opening and closing, and a fly that gets swatted.

The four musicians include Roger Waters, the bass guitarist, who is the mastermind of the group along with Nicki Mason. Mason is the drummer, but is also involved with operating the electronic gadgets. Rick Wright, the organist, lists Stockhausen as his chief musical influence. David Gilmour plays lead guitar and vocals. The promoter, Rich Floyd, wants to bring Pink Floyd back to Atlanta for a three-hour concert in the summer. Ticket prices would be $3 and $4.

May 28, 1970 - Down Beat (U.S.) reviewed the Pink Floyd album, 'Ummagumma.' They wrote that the album "fails," but because it is striking and arresting, they declined to rate it. The songs are "more impressive for their potential that their realization."

June 27, 1970 - Melody Maker (U.K.) published an article titled, "Easy Riding with Pink Floyd," by Chris Welch. Pink Floyd just returned from a tour of the United States where they had all their equipment stolen, and later recovered by the FBI.

On seeing the Fats Domino Band in a night club, Nick Mason said, *"They had the greatest brass section in the world, until they played together."* Roger Waters added, *"And it got better to the accompaniment of clinking glasses and bottles from the crowd. The band were playing instrumentals in their tuxedos. Then Fats Domino came on, and he was great."*

About New Orleans, Waters said, *"We found that New Orleans was the worst music scene in the world. It's just full of strip joints and there was no jazz at all. Just drunks. All the jazzmen have split."* And about the rest of the U.S. tour, Waters added, *"We spent about seven weeks in the States, and it was a good trip for what it was meant to achieve in terms of promotion. We did the Fillmore in the mid-week, and, considering that, the attendance was very good. Generally, in the States, it's like it was for us here a couple of years ago. But all the audiences said that they had never seen anything like us before."* Mason added, *"We got good reviews everywhere. And we certainly didn't feel depressed. But we're glad to be back. We're a home oriented group."*

On their current plans, Mason said, *"Oh, we'll be recording, and boring things like that you wouldn't want to know about. Let's talk about football. Everybody else does."*

Continuing on about the U.S. tour, Waters stated, *"We did a concert at the University of California, just after all the campus violence. The administration had closed the school, but we did our concert, which was very nice. It was sad to note that the students had really got themselves organized in readiness for trouble. There were field dressing posts available for casualties."* Waters continued, *"Students here attempt to live out a situation that doesn't exist. I feel strongly about English students who wreck debates when they should accept it as a medium of communication."*

Asked about their equipment being stolen, Waters explained, *"That was nearly a total disaster. We sat down at our hotel thinking, 'Well, that's it. It's all over.' We were pouring out our troubles to a girl who worked at the hotel and she said her father worked for the FBI. The police hadn't helped us much, but the FBI got to work, and four hours later it was found. £15,000 worth."*

Looking ahead to their next U.S. tour, Waters said, *"Next time we go back to the States, we play at the Lincoln Center in New York, which is like moving up from UFO to the Albert Hall."*

July 4, 1970 - New Musical Express (U.K.) reported that Pink Floyd is set to appear at the Hyde Park free concert on Saturday, July 18, 1970. The concert is being organized by Blackhill Enterprises.

Also in the issue is a review of the Harvest sampler album, 'Picnic – A Breath of Fresh Air,' which includes 19 tracks, one of which is the Pink Floyd song, 'Embryo,' and another is Syd Barrett's, 'Terrapin.'

Also in this issue is a Bath Festival Special about the festival held at Shepton Mallet on the weekend of June 26, 1970. Over 150,000 people attended the festival. Pink Floyd performed excellent versions of 'A Saucerful of Secrets,' and 'Set the Controls for the Heart of the Sun.' A choir and brass section joined them in performing a new piece called 'Epic,' that sounded like the soundtrack to a movie, and reached a climax with flares exploding in the sky and colored smoke filling the stage.

July 16, 1970 - The London Times (U.K.) published an article titled, "Nuclear drive for woman's heart," that reported that a pacemaker with a nuclear battery was implanted in a woman's heart on July 15th at the National Heart Hospital in London, England. [Ed. note: This news story influenced Pink Floyd to name a song, 'Atom Heart Mother.']

July 18, 1970 - Disc and Music Echo (U.K.) reported that Pink Floyd are working on their new album. Roger Waters was quoted as saying, *"One side is a complete 25-minute piece on which we're using other musicians for the first time. We've played it on stage, but we decided it would be nice to use a choir and a brass section. None of us write music so we approached Ron Geesin, who is a friend of ours, and asked him if he'd like to be involved getting all the brass together. So we're working as a five-piece for that."*

Also reported in this issue is that an island owner in the Canaries has asked Pink Floyd to write music for a film. The band has been asked to go to the island, wander around, and write music from their impressions.

Melody Maker (U.K.) published an ad for the free concert in Hyde Park on Saturday, July 18, 1970, between 12 and 6 pm, featuring Pink Floyd, Third Ear Band, Kevin Ayers, and the Edgar Broughton Band. The Pink Floyd album, 'Ummagumma,' is pictured in the ad.

July 25, 1970 - Disc and Music Echo (U.K.) reported on Blackhill's Garden Party, a free concert in Hyde Park, London, on July 18, 1970. The festival was put on by Blackhill Enterprises, attracted 50,000 people, and featured Kevin Ayers and the Whole World, the

Edgar Broughton Band, Roy Harper, and Pink Floyd, who performed an hour of "southing and inspiring" music. Songs played included 'Green is the Colour,' 'Careful With That Axe Eugene,' 'Set the Controls for the Heart of the Sun,' and 'Atom Heart Mother,' which featured a brass section and choir.

Also in this issue is an ad for the Yorkshire Folk, Blues & Jazz Festival to be held at Krumlin, Barkisland near Halifax on August 14-16, 1970. Pink Floyd is scheduled to appear on Sunday the 16th. Tickets for all three days are £2.10 or £3 the day of the show. Tickets for Sunday only are £1.10 or £2 the day of the show.

Melody Maker (U.K.) reported on the Pink Floyd concert in Hyde Park, writing that the beauty of Pink Floyd's music was lost to the birds and trees. Their set included 'Green is the Colour' and 'Set the Controls for the Heart of the Sun,' but half the sounds just disappeared.

Also in this issue was a letter from a reader who asked about Pink Floyd's equipment. Road manager Peter Watts answered that Richard Wright uses a Hammond M102 and a Farfisa double duo, played through a Binson echorec and two 100-watt Hi Watt amplifiers. The Hammond also uses a Leslie 147 speaker cabinet run through the WEM PA system with four 4 X 12 speaker cabinets and another Binson echorec. Roger Waters uses a Fender Precision bass guitar and two 100-watt WEM amplifiers and four 12 X 15 WEM reflex bass cabinets. Nick Mason uses a Ludwig double drum kit with 22-inch and 24-inch bass drums, 12-inch and 14-inch mounted tom toms, 14-inch and 16-inch floor toms, a 14-inch snare drum, a 12-inch hi hat, and 16, 18, 20, and 22-inch Zildjian cymbals.

New Musical Express (U.K.) published photos from the Hyde Park free festival on the cover, including a picture of Pink Floyd performing on Saturday afternoon. 100,000 people attended.

August 1, 1970 - Disc and Music Echo (U.K.) reported that Pink Floyd will be playing at the Krumlin Festival in Yorkshire on August 15, 1970, instead of the Who. A clause in Pink Floyd's contract for the festival prevents them from playing at any other festivals in Britain

for the rest of the year.

Also in this issue is a letter from reader Mark Ditton-Kelly, who wrote in about Pink Floyd's 60-minute appearance on Peel's Sunday Show, saying, "I listened to the above mentioned and I can honestly say I don't think I have ever heard such a boring row. I emphasize this because from what I heard, they were supposed to be in the same class as Taste, Zeppelin, and Ten Years After. I would prefer to hear the Archies or Pickettywitch, and that's a sad thing for a progressive music lover to say."

August 6, 1970 - Rolling Stone (U.S.) reported on the Bath Festival of Blues and Progressive Music at Shepton Mallet, England. 150,000 people attended the three-day festival. Pink Floyd "destroyed," playing avant-garde music, and left to a blitz of flares and smoke bombs.

August 8, 1970 - Disc and Music Echo (U.K.) published an article titled, "Waters in the pink . . . Wild on stage, but Floyd's extrovert really loves home!" by Caroline Boucher that featured an interview with Roger Waters at his home in Islington.

Roger Waters can seem menacing, obnoxious and self-indulgent, yet at home he is a reserved, intelligent, home-loving person. Waters explained, *"This is because I'm frightened of other people. I don't think I know anybody at all who isn't frightened of other people. People know that if you lower your defenses, someone jumps on you. I find myself jumping on people all the time and regretting it afterwards, blowing your horn at other people in the car, small things like that are all part and parcel of everything getting more uptight."*

Roger talked about the early days of Pink Floyd, saying, *"I'd had a guitar in Cambridge, but I never really played it much. Nick and Rick were both there doing the same course and we had a kind of blues group when we were in our second year. Then Syd came up to London. He'd lived round the corner from me in Cambridge but I didn't really know him very well because he was a couple of years younger than me. And there was another guy from Cambridge, Bob Close, on lead guitar. We played together occasionally. We'd go out and do £10 gigs, and play at peoples parties, and* we bought some gear, and gradually got a bit more involved."

Waters continued, "We were called Pink Floyd pretty early on, and then at some point we stopped adhering rigidly to the 12-bar blues thing, and started improvising round one simple root chord. I think Bob leaving had a lot to do with us stopping playing blues. He was a man with a great wealth of blues runs in his head, and when he left we hadn't anyone who had any blues knowledge, so we had to start doing something else."

Waters continued, "Syd took over as lead guitar, and I'm sure it was the noises that Pete Townshend was making then, squeaks and feedback, that influenced Syd, so we started making strange noises instead of doing the blues. We did something at the Marquee one afternoon, and Pete Jenner and Andrew King heard us and rang us up and said we should do it professionally, but as we were all about to go on holiday we said no, ring us in the autumn, which they did, and became our managers." The year was 1966 when UFO started. Admission was 2s, and the Pink Floyd were paid £6 the first week. After playing there for four weeks, the club was packed.

In February 1967, Pink Floyd turned professional and Roger dropped out of college. He had completed five of the seven years in the architecture. After turning professional, they recorded 'Arnold Layne,' which was a hit. Roger explained, "Then we did 'See Emily Play,' and a year followed doing ballrooms and clubs. We went down terribly badly because everyone expected us to do 'Emily' and we didn't. We were doing lots of other stuff off the first album. We were incredibly bad and we knew what we wanted to do but we couldn't do it. The whole Floyd sound wasn't an intellectually contrived thing, it was just improvising the sounds, and the sounds suggested the lyrics."

Waters continued, "The idea of a light show came when we did a gig at Essex University and someone showed a film on the wall next to us while we were playing. We thought that was rather good. Then we discovered how to do it with bubbles and oils at Powis Gardens when a bloke came down with some."

Waters continued, "Everything we've done, we've done because it seemed the obvious thing to do next. There was a great glut of those sort of things shortly after that time, but they'd been doing light shows, etc., in America before us far more efficiently, and better."

After their two hit singles, Syd Barrett left. Waters recalled, "It was a very bad period. People were saying we'd had it. I don't think any of us thought so, but it was just a question of coping with the Syd situation. The original idea was that Syd should stay on and write songs, but not do live gigs, but it became obvious that that wasn't going to work at all. But with Dave joining, it became a group again, and since then it's been good all the way."

Currently, Waters lives in a nice terraced house in Islington that he bought last year for around £8,000. It has a huge studio in the garden. Waters and his wife, Judy, are fixing the house up gradually. Right now, they are living in the basement. They have divided the studio into two parts, one a soundproofed section for Roger that includes an ancient harmonium, and a larger section for Judy to work on her sculpture. She is currently teaching art and sculpture, but will stop teaching at the end of the term. Roger bought her a large kiln for her pottery work. Judy said, "I don't want him to start doing pottery himself, though, because he's so good at everything, he'd probably be better then me." Roger does want to make some sculptures of his family of Burmese cats, George, Abie, and four kittens.

Roger also owns some golf clubs, and according to Judy, he plays golf at every opportunity. Roger admits to playing "about twice a month, if that," with Ron Geesin. Roger and Judy were married a year ago, but had previously known each other for about 14 years. Roger explained, "Being married, I think, makes things much simpler. It makes it easier to cope with what's important, and what isn't. It sorts out your priorities. A family is the most important thing in life, even if only in terms of one's biological function of having kids, which is all life's really about, because I can't believe in life after death or any of that stuff. Assuming that fact, you ask yourself what else is there in the world? The answer is a lot of people and a few trees and grass and cows and things, and there's you sitting in the middle of it, alive for an unspecified period of time. And so, assuming that you haven't just accepted that life is all about getting a good job and buying Rolls-Royces, you're faced with trying to sort out what it's all about so you can then decide what to do to fill in your life. And it seems to me that what is important is to cope as best you can with the rest of the people, primarily because I think people are more important than trees and grass. So although it would be simpler to sit in a shed in a wood and wander about in the dew, I choose the alternative, and I haven't even really begun to find out how to relate myself to the rest of the world and the people, and what to do about them, so I'm nowhere, really. But I do have a kind of nagging optimism about the possibility of people coming together. It would appear that most of us can agree on some things, like saying nobody wants war. One of the exciting things about pop is that it's a new media and a vehicle for communication with a very relevant percentage of young people in the world, whereas the other media, like radio and TV, are much more involved with the system."

Waters continued, "*I think there are thousands and thousands of people in this country, let alone the rest of the world, who could and would be doing the kind of thing that I'm doing and the rest of the Floyd is doing, if it wasn't for the way the system is geared. I really believe that everybody needs a creative outlet. Obviously, quite a lot of people find it in their work. I'm not suggesting everyone should be rock-and-roll musicians, but a hell of a lot of people go to school, and the great boot comes down on top of them, and they never get out from under it again. My school was all for getting me to university, no reasons. If you asked why, they'd say it was to get a degree, and a good job. They don't tell you it's in order to be better equipped to cope with your environment. I could have been an architect, but I don't think I'd have been very happy. Nearly all modern architecture is a silly game as far as I can see. Anyway, to get on in architecture you either have to have a daddy that is in the business, say the right things at the right times, or be a whiz kid. I'm happier the way I am, and I can always build a house for myself one day if I want to. I just hated being under the boot so much, I got out. But I think a lot of people can cope with being under*

it much better than I can. Take people who decide to become accountants for example. I don't believe people sit down and say 'Wow. Wouldn't it be great to became an accountant and work out how to get money off people's taxes for the rest of my life.' I believe they go into accountancy because it's bloody well paid."

Waters continued, "*I think my music could do things for other people because I like it, and music does things for me. If Berlioz pottered through the garden gate, I'd sit back and look at him for hours, because I get a great buzz out of his and a lot of other music. I can't sit down and make a piece of music and not play it to anyone or just listen to it myself and say 'gosh, it was good.' Music is a very real way of communing with people, communicating emotions, and must be used as such, because we have such highly sophisticated defenses these days that there are not many ways of communicating left.*"

Pink Floyd, as a group, get on well together, but they don't get together socially when they are not working together. In fact, they rarely see each other. Waters commented, "*The defensive barriers that are apparent in a small group of people who work together are almost heavier than everyday contact with the general public. Like people in shops, which is a very easy situation, because they can't really hurt you or you them, but in a small group you feel more susceptible. The individual pieces we did on 'Ummagumma' weren't really very soul bearing and difficult to show to each other, because we'd agreed before we started that we'd do it like that and just come up with the finished product. 'Ummagumma' was a gamble, which I think paid off. It would have been a better album if we'd gone away, done the things, come back together, discussed them, and people could have come in and made comments. I don't think it's good to work in total isolation.*"

Pink Floyd have also been working on doing film scores. They did the music for the movie, 'More' which they did in 10 days, and for the movie 'Zabriskie Point.' They currently have another offer to do music for a film later this year in the Canary Islands. Waters explained, "*I personally like films. I think I get more out of going to the cinema than going to the theatre. But that's the other thing we want to do, something in the theatre, probably using some film and actors moving about."*

Roger also is concerned with communication. *"I wonder if there's anything to say which I'm capable of articulating. There's words, obviously, but unless you know someone very well so you're not at all frightened of them, it's very hard to communicate with words. But we don't say what we mean half the time. We say either what sounds right, or what the other person wants to hear, of any number of things."*

As for how long the Pink Floyd will stay together, Waters said that they have a very good work relationship, and doesn't see why they shouldn't get together when they're 40 if something interests them.

August 15, 1970 - Disc and Music Echo (U.K.) published four letters from readers who responded to the letter from Mark Ditton-Kelly in the August 1, 1970 issue of Disc and Music Echo.

Keith White wrote, "I was very sorry to read that Mr. Ditton-Kelly was disappointed with the Pink Floyd. After what he said about them, I suggest that he set the controls for the heart of the sun, take the Archies and Pickettywitch with him, and leave the 'boring row' for everyone else to enjoy."

Peter Rafferty wrote, "How Mark Ditton-Kelly can call himself a progressive music lover is beyond me, when it would appear that he had not heard the great Floyd previous to July 18. As for Led Zeppelin and Co., it is true that the Floyd are not in the same class, being the same distance ahead of them as a Saturn V is to a Spitfire. Their beauty, subtlety and togetherness are infinitely preferable to the fitful virtuoso performances and tired blues riffs of the others."

Tony Lamb wrote, "I was shocked to read Mark Ditton-Kelly's remarks concerning the Pink Floyd's concert on the John Peel Show. In all respects, the Floyd were tremendous listening, and were up to their usually brilliant standard. Their music is ten years ahead of anything that has ever been done. The music of the group is, to those with limited minds, obscure, but to their true fans, they stand out as the true progressive group. Thanks John Peel."

Linda Lewis wrote, "I don't really think Mark Ditton-Kelly knew what he was talking about. I, too, heard the John Peel Sunday Show, and the day before had also gone to the Hyde Park concert, where Pink Floyd topped the bill, and enjoyed every minute of both. The final work in the program called, I believe, 'Atom Heart Mother,' lasted about 30 minutes and was a sheer masterpiece. It was made so by the addition of the brass section and the male and female choir. This is an extremely unusual combination, and I think one can regard the Floyd's music as truly progressive."

September 12, 1970 - Melody Maker (U.K.) reported that Pink Floyd will be writing music for a ballet featuring Russian ballet dancer Rudolph Nureyev. Ballet producer Roland Petit will stage the ballet at the 10,000 seat Grand Palais in Paris, France, next year.

David Gilmour stated, *"It's pretty amazing. It's something we have never done before and no one from our field of music has ever done. It poses a whole lot of problems but opens up a lot of scope. We have got quite a lot of ideas, but we can't discuss them at the moment. We are still very much at the beginning of things. We have never worked with a large orchestra before, only with small ones. There will be the problem of transferring what we think onto paper and merging with what the other musicians think. There may be some scope for improvisation, but it will be limited. None of us have met Nureyev before, but we have met the producer. We will be discussing ideas with him next week."*

Manager Steve O'Rourke explained that Roland Petit was bored with the typical ballet material and was looking for something new, adding, *"He has contacted Nureyev and wants the Floyd to write the music. It will be performed over a period of ten days from June 1 to June 10, and on the last night it will be televised throughout Europe, including England. The group have a 108-piece orchestra at their disposal and Nureyev will have 60 dancers with him. It is a big step for the group to be working with musicians of this caliber and a big step for the ballet people to approach a group to write their music. We are meeting Petit next week to discuss the details. The group will actually play with the orchestra.*"

The article also reported that the new Pink Floyd album, 'Atom Heart Mother,' will be released on October 1, 1970, and will feature a side of the band playing with brass and choir from the Hyde Park free concert.

September 19, 1970 - Melody Maker (U.K.) published the 1970 Pop Poll results. In the British section, Pink Floyd were the #4 group, and had the #5 album with 'Ummagumma.' In the International section, Pink Floyd were the #8 group, Rick Wright was the #5 pianist/organist, Roger Waters was the #5 bass guitarist, and 'Ummagumma' was the #10 Album of the year.

September 26, 1970 - Melody Maker (U.K.) published an article titled, "The Floyd on rock today" by Michael Watts that featured an interview with Richard Wright. Talking about intellectual rock music, Wright stated, "*We are just four musicians playing music, using a lot of things from rock, and then bits from other media. It is just good and bad music. We do not care about being intellectual.*"

Pink Floyd have written a French ballet for producer Roland Petit, and will perform it with a 108-piece orchestra at the Grand Palais in Paris, France, from June 1-10, 1971. The score will be more melodic and rhythmic, and less improvisational, than prior works. Their new album, 'Atom Heart Mother,' will also be more melodic, as compared to 'Ummagumma.' Wright explained, "*'Ummagumma' had more emphasis on pure sound. This one is much simpler to listen to. It is more emotional, a sort of epic music in fact, because we have added brass and a choir. This will sell more than the last, I think.*"

Asked about their attempts to blend classical and rock music, Wright replied, "*The only way I believe this can work to achieve a valid partnership is for someone to write for the electric guitar, organ, bass, and drums as part of the orchestra, and not separately as a rock group playing with an orchestra. It requires someone who can understand all the instruments. At present, rock groups and orchestras are performing together, and it does not work at all, because people are trying to combine rock and classical music. The two go together like oil and water. Jon Lord has*

written for an orchestra, and this was the closest thing so far, but it still did not work. It was very clever. It was an odd mixture of music, a lot of it that was strongly romantic, but then you had the rock group come in and crash. He tried and failed. And he will always fail because he has not got the right approach."

Wright also explained that he thought the days of the light show and strobe lights as an effective visual statement were over, and that the band were interested in producing a more theatrical show. On their British tour when they performed 'The Journey' they used a man in a gorilla suit in the audience.

Wright continued, "*We also want to make our own film. We have done three or four film scores in the past. We have turned as many offers down, in fact, but there was some definite talk about us doing a film and then writing the music around it.*"

Wright also commented on their live sound, saying, "*We want to really perfect the sound live, and then release it on a four-track tape, and hopefully get EMI to sell four-track tape recorders for home use. This might not be so far in the future as you might think, because in America it is happening now. In terms of playing live on stage, all of us want to get a superb hi-fi sound, although we do not have those thousands of boxes of tricks that people fondly imagine we do. Essentially, with us, it is not a question of volume, but of the quality of the sound. Up to now, groups have just added equipment to become louder, but they have not tried to get that high quality. I don't think the Who, for instance, who get excellent volume, have ever achieved that quality of sound.*"

As for festivals, Wright said, "*We really feel happy playing at festivals, but I think concerts suit us better because you can never get a good sound at festivals, and a lot of people can often not only not hear, but cannot see. The point about festivals is that they are events. If you are a group and you go out on stage and see that number of people, it is an incredible feeling of power, in the sense that it is the audience which is giving out the power. Hyde Park, to me, when it started, was a beautiful idea. But promoters are killing off festivals, generally, because they are finding they do not always make money. We have had a* lot of trouble with festival crowds in France, where we were supposed to play at Aix-en-Provence, and the reason these riots develop is that a lot of people believe they should get in for nothing. There is nothing wrong in that, it is good, but only if they can offer a way of paying for the groups. We say, if you want to come in for nothing, you should pass around the hats, because we need the money to live. We cannot afford to play for free all the time."

September 1970 - Circus (U.S.) conducted an interview (originally published in 1971, and again in October 1980) with Pink Floyd that took place in a Howard Johnson Motor Lodge on the morning of their second appearance at the Fillmore East on September 27, 1970.

On their previous American tour, in May of 1970, the band had all of their equipment stolen in New Orleans, causing the cancellation of the end of the tour. When Nick Mason was asked about this and their return to the States, he said, "*I was afraid to step off the plane. I shudder to think what it will be like down South.*"

Asked about the violence in America, David Gilmour stated, "*When we have a punch-up in England, someone gets a bloody nose, not stabbed to death.*"

Although the band was confident playing in New York, they weren't too sure about the rest of the country. Roger Waters explained, "*I don't think many people know us in some of those places, and that can work both ways. They might hate us right off, or then again, they might just relax and really get into it.*"

Talking about their equipment, Mason said, "*It's always breaking down and there are a lot of songs we're working on now that just can't be done right until we get newer stuff. We have some friends that are working on developing customized amps and the like, using transistors to cut down on size and weight, but that whole thing gets really expensive. We'll just have to make do with what we've got.*"

At present, they don't use a light show. Rick Wright explained, "*What we need is a light show that can be projected on all of the walls and on the ceiling at the same time. Also, it should be done by someone who understands our music so that it would help us,*

not detract. We are pleased with the job that the Fillmore is doing with its regular stage lighting."

For their show at the Fillmore East, they used their own sound system because they didn't like the acoustics in the hall. Waters explained, "*When you have a hall with a high roof like that, you need baffles to absorb the sound or it just gets lost up there. One of the best places for sound is the Albert Hall in England.*"

Talking about their work on the soundtrack to the movie, 'Zabriskie Point,' and the fact that a long flowing piece of music that Rick Wright had written for use during the scenes of the Berkeley riots was not used, Wright said, "*Antonioni changed his mind during the filming. He decided he didn't want to use the piece after all. We really dug the film, but we didn't agree with the way he used the music.*"

October 3, 1970 - Melody Maker (U.K.) reported that Nick Mason produced an album by Principal Edward's Magic Theater. It will be released on John Peel's Dandelion record label.

October 8, 1970 – Sabot, Seattle (U.S.) reported on the Pink Floyd concerts that took place at the Moore Theater, Seattle, Washington on October 2-3, 1970. The article said, "They produce a sound that at once give me fantasies of outer space." "At times, the guitarist was seated with his back almost directly to the audience, doing things to his instrument in a manner reminiscent of the ape with the bone in 2001, and playing his own instrument panel on his amps."

October 10, 1970 - Disc and Music Echo (U.K.) reviewed the Pink Floyd album, 'Atom Heart Mother,' with an article titled, "Floyd, plus grunting apes." The title track consists of six movements, and features the John Aldiss Choir sounding like angels and grunting apes, a brass band gone wrong, a nice organ-cello section, war noises, a motor bike, a train, and a beautiful main theme. The other side of the album is relaxing. On 'Alan's Psychedelic Breakfast,' you can almost smell the eggs and bacon frying. They gave it four stars.

Melody Maker (U.K.) reviewed the Pink Floyd album, 'Atom Heart Mother,' with an article titled, "Floyd's best yet." The song, 'Atom Heart Mother,' is the most mature and finished song the group has ever produced. The scoring of the piece for brass, strings, and choir is superb, and it is very satisfying the way they combine with the rock instruments. The mood of the piece is superb relaxation, similar to Vaughn Williams' 'Fantasia on a Theme of Thomas Tallis.' The reviewer also compared a section of the song to Booker T., and Gilmour's guitar work to that of Steve Cropper. The other side of the album includes the pretty pastoral song, 'If.' Also in this issue is a full-page ad for the album.

New Musical Express (U.K.) reviewed the Pink Floyd album, 'Atom Heart Mother,' with an article titled, "Funky Floyd: Most grandiose work to date." The reviewer questioned whether Pink Floyd were concerning themselves with man's eternal conflict with machines. The title track takes up a whole side of the album, and is split into six movements, including 'Breast Milky' and 'Mind Your Throats Please.' Ron Geesin is a fifth composer. It is a mixture of contrasting themes, opening with a western theme that passes through electronics into a more pastoral section. The John Alldis Choir adds voices before it becomes funky soul. As a whole it is a testimony to a progressing band. Side two features songs by the band members that are gentler and pretty. It concludes with the song, 'Alan's Psychedelic Breakfast,' that features piano, acoustic guitar, and Alan talking to himself, washing, pouring coffee, and crunching his breakfast.

Sounds (U.K.) published an article titled, "Floyd, Petit, and the ballet" by Steve Peacock. The news that Pink Floyd were going to write a ballet for Roland Petit created a furor in the press. But it posed a new challenge for the band. Petit has given the band a basic theme to work from, that everything is past and the present is only fleeting. The ballet will be performed for ten days next June at Le Grande Palais in Paris, France.

Peacock spoke with Roger Waters about the ballet during rehearsals for their American tour. Waters said, "*I think the idea is to broadcast it on Eurovision one night. On that evening, there will be another ballet with music by Xenakis, who is well known as an avant-garde composer in France. We shan't be in an orchestra pit or anything. We'll be on stage somewhere, probably on a different level from the dancers. Playing live means that we've got to be note perfect each night, otherwise the dancers are going to get lost, and we won't be using a score, we'll be playing from memory. That might be a bit difficult, but it's not really that far away from what we've been doing over the past year or so, because we've tended to play more or less the same things on stage. When we get back from the States, we'll have to start working out what we want to do, and rehearse it quite a lot, then go into a studio and record it with no overdubbing, and send the tape over so that he can choreograph the ballet from our music. But we can use anything we want, really. It's almost a 'money is no object' scene. So if we wanted to use an orchestra for a bit of it, we could. It's going to be about a 40 minute piece.*"

Pink Floyd have just released their new album, 'Atom Heart Mother,' the title track recorded with brass and choir in Hyde Park this summer. Side two includes the song, 'Fat Old Sun' by David Gilmour, which was written around the same time as Waters' 'Grantchester Meadows,' and was inspired by the same Cambridge settings. Waters talked about the album, saying, "*The album is less experimental than 'Ummagumma,' much nicer to listen to. I think it's by far the best, the most human thing we've done. I wasn't fantastically amazed with the live album of 'Ummagumma,' but I think the idea for the studio side, doing one track each, was basically good. I personally think it would have been better if we'd done them individually, and then got the opinions of the others, put four heads into each piece instead of just one. I think each piece would have benefited from that, but by the time they were done, we'd used up our studio time. I was quite pleased by the way it came out, though. It sold a lot, which is something.*"

The band's rehearsals for the American tour were used to work out concert arrangements for the new songs. They will be using an American brass section and choir on the song 'Atom Heart Mother' for three shows, but the song that is the most problematic is 'Alan's Psychedelic Breakfast.' Waters explained, *"On the record, it's a carefully set up stereo picture of a kitchen with somebody coming in, opening a window, filling a kettle, and putting it on the stove. But instead of the gas lighting, there's a chord, so he strikes another match, and there's another chord, and another match, and so on, until it finally goes into a piece of music. It was the usual thing of an idea coming out of the fact that we'd almost finished an LP, but not quite, and we needed another so many minutes. We were all frantically trying to write songs, and initially I thought of just doing something on the rhythm of a dripping tap, which is something that everyone's had experience of. Then it turned into this whole kitchen thing."* The sounds for the song were recorded at Nick Mason's house, then they recorded an interview with their assistant roadie Alan, and they recorded the music in the studio, before splicing it all together. But they plan to play it live in America, with boiling kettles, popping crispies, and sizzling eggs. Waters added, *"The logistics of doing it live are quite difficult. We can't obviously take a set of a kitchen around with us and do it all, but we'll have to have some table arrangement to fry eggs on, and boil kettles, and everything. I think Nicky's going to do that."* Asked whether they could use a tape instead, Waters replied, *"Yes, but it wouldn't be as much fun. It would be much easier, in fact it would be incredibly easy to do it with a tape. But that's not really the point."*

Future projects for the band include the ballet, making a film, hiring a theater for a time, and they are making plans for their next album. But there is the time factor. Waters explained, *"When we do something we've never done before, like the last album, with all that brass and choir and things, you make a lot of mistakes and it takes a lot longer than it would if we were to do something like that again."*

Also in this issue is an article titled, "Pink Floyd's most human LP" by Steve Peacock, that reviewed the Pink Floyd album 'Atom Heart Mother.' The music is mellower than most of what they have done before. It still has a mysterious feel to it, and a rich, gentle atmosphere. The song, 'Atom Heart Mother,' with a brass and choir is an ambitious

idea that works. 'If' is a subdued song. 'Summer '68' is reflective, with memories of Sgt. Pepper and others. 'Fat Old Sun' has "a lazy, pastoral feel." 'Alan's Psychedelic Breakfast' is "a pleasant piece of music." The album has "a very subtle impact."

October 14, 1970 - The Vancouver Free Press (Canada) published an interview with Roger Waters and David Gilmour by Mike Quigley. The interview was done prior to the Pink Floyd concert at the Vancouver Gardens in Vancouver, B.C., Canada, on October 7, 1970.

Asked how long they have been performing together, Roger Waters said, *"Professionally since January 1967. We started out before that as a completely blues and Bo Diddley oriented rock and roll band from a school of architecture."*

Has anyone in the group had any classical music training? David Gilmour replied, *"Richard's had a little bit of classical training, but the rest of us haven't had any training of any sort."* Waters added, *"But we've all been through the great Music College of Life."*

When did they start playing experimental music? Waters answered, *"In June or July of 1966. By that time we'd already started to do the things that we continue to do. Even though we were still amateur, we stopped playing blues and started thrashing about making stranger noises and doing different things. Some people saw us and they said, 'We think you boys can be big,' and we said, 'Too much!' and they said, 'Let's get started' and we said, 'We're terribly sorry, but we're going off on a holiday, and we'll be back in October.' And so we did. And then we raised two hundred pounds and went into a studio and cut a record and took it to EMI and said, 'Look, we can be bigger than The Beatles.' And they said, 'Golly, gee whiz, we think you're right!' and we signed a stupid contract with them, which we're still bound by, and they released the album and it was a medium-big seller. Then we went professional."*

Did they play their album in concerts? Waters answered, *"We didn't do concerts in those days. Nobody did concerts in those days. And we hadn't done an album anyway. There weren't concerts in those days.*

There were ballrooms. If you were a working group with a hit single, you played in ballrooms. It was a hall like this, but without seats, and it was all screaming girls. . ." Gilmour continued, *"and jiving, twisting..."* Waters added, *"We cleared more ballrooms than you've had hot dinners. We didn't play the singles on stage, which was all they wanted to hear."* Gilmour explained, *"The only reason you'd get those bookings is because you had hit singles. That's how you'd get the work. And we didn't do them."* Waters added, *"We had a very rough year or so...,"* and Gilmour continued, *"apart from a few gigs in London."* Waters said, *"We had a very rough time until the second album came out, and people were coming to see us because of 'Saucerful of Secrets,' not some hit single that they'd heard."*

Asked if they played shows on the continent, Gilmour answered, *"Not for a very long time."* Waters added, *"We came to the States very early on just for a week or so."* And Gilmour added, *"We came to the States right in the middle of 1968, when the second album came out, for seven weeks. But that was pretty bad because we didn't have any of our own equipment. We hadn't got it together, either to cope with any equipment problems or things like that."* Waters said, *"But the Continent has just exploded for us now, particularly France. It's all quite new. France is maybe a year old right now, since we started getting anywhere in France. What really made it for us in France was the film 'More,' for which we did the soundtrack. It was playing in Paris at two next-door cinemas at once it was so popular."*

What about playing modern classical music? Waters replied, *"Not really. On our new album we've used some written music, some other musicians,"* and Gilmour continued, *"ten symphonic brass players and a choir of twenty."* Waters added, *"But the result is kind of a very direct attempt at hitting emotions, touching off emotional reactions with fairly ordinary sounds."*

What about playing with a symphony? Waters replied, *"Well, we've had our talks with people. But the economics of working with an orchestra are prohibitive."* Gilmour explained, *"Like this thing we've got on the next album uses thirty musicians, which isn't a lot of musicians, but it cost us five thousand dollars a night to put it on."* Waters

continued, *"We're writing a ballet for Roland Petit, which will be in Paris next June, and the sky's the limit for that. They're spending so much money on that that they'd be quite willing to pay for an orchestra. But it might take it out of our hands to a certain extent if the stuff had to all be written down, because we can't write it down ourselves. And there's always a communication gap involved between what you can sing or play on a piano, and what gets written down as music. And then you never hear it until you've got the orchestra there at the first rehearsal. And you probably only get two rehearsals anyway, so by the time you hear it, it's too late to change it. Whereas our stuff is all based on doing something and then throwing out and using something else."* Is Pink Floyd going to play with the ballet themselves? Waters replied, *"Yeah, it's going to be on for about ten days. Nureyev is dancing the male lead. On the program we're doing, we're doing one ballet and Xenakis is writing the other."*

Some people think of Pink Floyd as cosmic. Waters answered, *"Yeah, I know what you mean. That's the reaction we get from lots and lots of people, but I think the new album's going to come as something of a surprise, because it's not 'cosmic.' All they mean really are that the sounds we make evoke images of deep space."* Gilmour added, *"There are a lot of other things we do that do evoke quite strong images in the same way, but not about space."* Is this just the interpretation of the music by the audience or is it a group philosophy? Waters replied, *"Not really. There is a general feeling, I suspect, in the group that music that really works is music that touches your emotions and triggers off something unchanging, some kind of eternal response. Like, it's really difficult to describe your reactions to a piece of music that hits you, gives you a particular kind of feeling, a particular kind of feeling that transcends the normal ups and downs and ins and outs."*

Asked about their equipment and about the rumor that it is worth a hundred thousand dollars, Gilmour answered, *"That's probably a bit of an exaggeration. It's probably worth about thirty thousand dollars."* How many speaker systems do you use? Gilmour replied, *"We have a quadraphonic sound system around the hall, and there's a P.A.*

system which is quite powerful. And we all have regular amps on stage." What about the quadraphonic speakers around the hall? Gilmour answered, "Well, you can feed tape into them or you can feed the organ into them. You could feed the guitar or the vocal into them, but we don't because they're very hard to work like that." Who controls the sound effects? Gilmour replied, "Richard, the organist, has a quadraphonic sound mixer on his organ, and he can play the organ and the sound around the auditorium as he's doing it. The tape recorder's operated by Pete, our road man." Asked how they learned to use their special effects and whether someone taught them, Water replied, "No, they just happened, really. We just thought, 'You ought to be able to do this,' and then we went and saw somebody who knew something about electronics and asked, 'is it possible?' Like the quadraphonic thing, we just went to one of the maintenance engineers at Abbey Road in London where we record, and we said, 'Look, we want to do this. Can you build it?,' and he said 'Yes,' and he did."

What about EMI releasing their album on the new four-track tapes? Gilmour answered, "EMI will do it when everyone else has done it." Waters added, "They'll do it in a couple of years after everyone else. They're so technically far behind the other studios."

How many albums are they contracted with EMI for? Waters replied, "It's not a question of albums. We're under contract to them for another eighteen months." After they finish their contract with EMI, will they start an independent label? Waters answered, "We don't know. It depends. We might build our own studio."

Asked about playing festivals, Gilmour replied, "This summer, that's all we've done between our last American tour and this American tour, festivals. The Bath Festival. The Rotterdam Festival. Two in France." Waters continued, "One in Germany. Not many. About half a dozen. We haven't done any in the States. I don't like them. The sound is generally so bad, and there are too many people." Gilmour added, "The atmosphere is always very difficult for us, because we like people not to just think, 'Well, here's the next group coming on,' and then get straight into it, because it's very difficult to get straight into

our music like that. We like to set an atmosphere. We like to have a place where we're the only people performing." Waters said, "I really don't like them because I know that I would never go to one as a member of an audience, because festivals aren't really all to do with music. It's a lot to do with camping out and all that stuff, and the music is just a common factor. It's very hard for people to hear it, or for everybody to hear it. I just think they're wrong conditions for listening. Well, not wrong, but not the best conditions for listening to music."

In Europe, are there problems with people not wanting to pay to see festivals? Gilmour replied, "There's a lot in France." Waters added, "It's much the heaviest in France. It's very heavy in Germany as well. In France they've had several festivals that just didn't go on because people tore them to pieces." Gilmour said, "One we were supposed to play at, was wrecked," Waters continued, "the first day. We weren't supposed to play until the second day." Gilmour added, "They broke down the stage, threw pianos off the stage, turned recording vans over, started to set fire to them." Waters said, "They did set fire to them. It was sponsored by Radio Luxembourg, and they had two vans recording, and they burned those. The promoters had got hold of a Yamaha grand piano and they smashed that to pieces." Gilmour added, "Threw it off the edge of the stage."

As musicians, how do you feel about the idea that music should be free? Waters replied, "I think it's a bit unfortunate that these people pick on rock and roll as the start of their process to get rid of profit-oriented society, presuming that music is something they're interested in and something they enjoy. It would seem wiser if they picked on some other area where they wouldn't mind so much if the whole thing just stopped happening, because that's what they're doing, just stopping the things happening. It serves no function to come to a festival and tear it to pieces, shouting, 'Music should be free!'" Gilmour continued, "They're not going to get music for free by doing something like that because it's totally impossible." Waters added, "Well, for a start, it completely alienates those who might possibly be in a position to give it to them for free. But it can't be free. It costs fortunes to put on festivals." Gilmour said, "*It costs us, just one band, to go and do a festival in the south of France, for instance, between two and three thousand dollars just to go and do it. And they shout that they want it for free and that they should pass a hat round for money, which in fact, they tried at one festival.*" Waters said, "*Out of twenty thousand people,*" Gilmour added, "*thirty thousand people,*" Waters continued, "*they got about two hundred pounds,*" Gilmour continued, "*which is like five hundred dollars. Out of thirty thousand people.*" Waters explained, "*That's why that particular festival broke down, because the promoters hadn't got any money to pay the next group which was going on, which was The Soft Machine. And The Soft Machine just refused to go on. And then they passed the hat around and collected two hundred pounds, and The Soft Machine still refused to go on. And then they tore everything to pieces. If they want music to be free, well, it can't be free. There's no such thing as fucking 'free.' Presumably what they mean is that it should be paid for out of government funds. At least that's what I assume they want.*"

October 15, 1970 - The Berkeley Barb (U.S.) published ads for Pink Floyd concerts at Pepperland, California, on October 16 and 17, 1970, for $3.00, and at the Fillmore West on October 21, 1970.

October 16, 1970 - The University of Regina Carillon Student Newspaper (Canada) published an article titled, "The Pink Think with the Floyd," that included an interview with the band prior to their concert at the Centre of the Arts in Regina, Saskatchewan, Canada, on October 11, 1970.

Asked how long the group had been together, Steve O'Rourke replied, "*The group's been together, professionally, for three years. The first album is titled 'Piper at the Gates of Dawn,' the second album is 'Saucerful of Secrets,' the third album was 'More,' a soundtrack to the film of the same name, the fourth album was 'Ummagumma,' and the fifth album, which should be out by the end of the week, is called 'Atom Heart Mother.' The fifth one is interesting as it involves the use of a twenty-piece brass section. Three of them met at architects college, and at that time there was* a guitar player called Syd Barrett, who left after the first album, and the group was joined by the present Dave Gilmour.*"

Asked where they are from, David Gilmour replied, "*I'm from Cambridge, Roger's from Cambridge, and Nick and Rick are from London.*" And what about the group's headquarters? "*London.*"

How long has the tour lasted so far? "*A couple of weeks, two weeks, three weeks, three weeks on Tuesday.*" What cities have you been to? "*New York, Philadelphia, Seattle, Vancouver, Edmonton, Saskatoon, Regina, and from here to Winnipeg, Salt Lake, San Francisco.*"

What messages are in your music? "*Keep smiling. Peace. Get together. And what, and what, and what... I don't think we actually have specific messages, which we intend to broadcast. No, I don't think so.*"

How do you relate to the revolution and the alternative culture? "*We relate to them the same as anyone else does? You can't generalize about it.*" Asked if they sympathize with the goals of the revolution, Nick Mason replied, "*Well, some revolutionaries in this country have been kidnapping British diplomats, and your politicians on the side. And I don't understand a thing about it, at all, really. But if I was the English diplomat I'd be, well uptight, not to mention possibly dead. And, well, I know nothing about that, but my emotional reaction is that I don't go along with it.*"

Do you believe in violence as a means to cause change? "*It's an impossible question, because if you picked a specific goal. . .*" Roger Waters continued, "*Yes, it is an impossible question because somebody could postulate the hypothesis at you, that, if you had been, for instance, living in Paris during the German occupation, and some Gestapo man is about to blow your head off because you were a Jew, and you happened to have a knife in your hand, and you had the chance to stick it in him, would you?*" Richard Wright added, "*Well, the question is of survival, isn't it? A lot of Americans in Vietnam . . .*" Nick Mason continued, "*It's very hard to say, you know. We're not a committed band. We're not committed to a cause because no one has stomped on us, but . . .*" Roger Waters continued, "*they are stomping on lots of people terribly hard. And I don't feel, myself, personally, in a position, the actions that people take when they're getting stomped on, like the people, those guys in Chicago, they were getting pretty heavily stomped on, and they reacted to the whole thing pretty violently. And I was behind them one hundred percent because they'd have just sat quietly by and let the whole kind of cracked justice scene take its course. No one would have taken any notice of it at all. And, obviously, that whole kind of completely phony judicial set-up has been working in Chicago, for instance, for years and years and years. And nobody's really taken notice of it. And now, because people are reacting violently to it, it's coming out. They would say anything. They were told to 'shut up.'*

'Careful With That Axe Eugene' was used in 'Zabriskie Point,' a film about violent American society. Was that song written about the film's themes? *"We've been performing that song for years before 'Zabriskie Point' was ever made. But on the other hand, we were all quite happy to put that piece of music on that particular piece of film because we felt close, emotionally, to what the film was saying."* Were you with Antonioni when the film was made? *"Constantly. Sixteen hours a day. It was too much."* Was 'Careful With That Axe, Eugene' the only song you did for the film? *"We did the whole soundtrack. He only used three pieces. He didn't like the rest of the stuff. He was afraid of Pink Floyd becoming part of the film, rather than it staying entirely Antonioni. So we were quite upset when he used all these other things. I mean if he had used things which we found better. There were only two pieces of music in the film that we did, really, and the other piece of music we did was like any other group could have done, really, a direct imitation, really, of the Byrds, Crosby, Still and Nash, or something."*

Are you influenced by other groups? *"No, not really. No one in particular."*

How do you happen to play the kind of music you play today? *"It was all a mistake. Really, there was no plan. We just did what seemed right at the time."* When you perform, is it spontaneous or are you rehearsed? *"No, we're pretty well rehearsed."* Do you use drugs when you perform? *"Sometimes. Usually. But not much."* Did any of your songs result from

the use of drugs? Gilmour replied, *"No. There is more alcohol consumed than dope before we go on stage, you see, because, when you're high, you can sit on your own and play for hours and hours and hours, and if you put it on tape, if you come back to it when you are straight, and it's a load of shit. I think what really we do, is that we all like to get that little bit of relaxation from smoking a small amount. For myself, I like a small smoke before I play, it relaxes me."*

Do you use opening acts? *"No, we avoid back-up bands as much as we can. Unless we're absolutely forced to by circumstance, we don't, because we like to create our own atmosphere. We believe that music isn't variety, if you see what I mean."* Does this mean that you won't play at music festivals? *"We do play for festivals. And if there's some reason why a back-up band is required, like everyone needs four hours of music or something, then sure, we'd work with back-up bands. What we are saying is, if we have the choice, our ideal presentation of our music is a concert hall rather than a cattle shed, or something. Somewhere where people can listen and respond directly to the music, with no rubbish going on, sort of, no hot dog sellers, or beads, or people talking, which is one of the disadvantages of a lot of places. Just that everyone goes there to chat, and mutter, and crumple papers. And also, if we play on our own, we run much less risk of people who are there for some other reasons, other than wanting to hear us play. The only reason we're there is to play."*

Has your record company ever refused to release any of your music? *"No. People are always surprised. Compared to most people, we've got a pretty good scene with our record company because it's a very big one in England, the biggest. And people imagine that it means it's the most straight-laced, but in fact they're so confused by what we do, and so totally aghast at every move we make, that they've just given up and they just say 'well we don't know, you do it boys.' Whenever they've said this should, or shouldn't, be on, they've always been completely wrong. So they've just given up. They don't know any more about what we're about than we do."*

What is the girl screaming about on

Ummagumma? *"The chick screaming is a very beautiful chick. She's very tall and thin and dresses in black. And she sits and drinks, and smokes cigarettes. And her name is Roger Waters. 'Ummagumma' was the thing that we had the most hassle with our record company about releasing. That was the final time when we realized that they didn't know anything, because they didn't believe in 'Ummagumma.' They didn't believe it would sell at all. And it came out and sold better, far better, than anyone thought."*

What type of questions do professional interviewers normally ask you? *"We had a big press conference once, years and years ago, when we were first starting at EMI House, in London. And everybody got drunk, and I think only one piece of copy came out of it. And it had no promotional value whatsoever. It didn't mention the name of the group, or the record company."* *"The true professionals ask questions they should be able to read off our biography, if we had one."* *"Every interview I've ever seen has vanished, generally, with a very glazed expression that people get when they've smoked a lot of dope, like you people have got, and their tape recorder breaks."*

Have you ever considered writing for the Top 40? *"If we come up with something we know is going to be a top single, we'll issue it like a shot. But we're not very good at it. I mean, we've had a few attempts at it, and for the last two years they've gone off very badly."*

Did 'Ummagumma' get you off the ground? *"No. The group originally got off the ground in England with a hit single, and we had one in the States as well. But we came back down. 'Saucerful of Secrets' got us up again. Up, down, up."*

What do you think of Woodstock? *"Good question, one that all the professionals ask. It's very good for everyone except for the musicians. Great for the Hell's Angels, great for all the people that like camping out, great for anyone selling sandwiches and cigarettes. Great for people who like to get together with another 200,000 long hairs, dope freaks."*

A criticism of festivals is that ticket prices are too high due to what the groups charge to play. *"No. Most of that is put about by festival organizers who make up totally, fictional figures that they've made. They*

usually fix their prices first. They know what their gross is liable to be, how many people, etc. Then all the groups charge accordingly." *"No, that's not true. I guess most of them work out what their figures are and reckon to spend ten percent on groups. That's the sort of margin they'd like to work to. But the groups come on very strong. I mean, I need a lot of money to go through that sort of aggravation that a festival provides. It's absurd, really. It bears no relation to the performance of music. It's for people who are built like hickory-logs or whatever it is that Canadians are built of. It's for lumberjacks and grizzly bears and people with stamina, but not for people like me. It's really for creatures of the wild. Three days exposed to volumes of wind and rain. I think they should advertise and say, 'This is the greatest experience since the first world war.'"* *"You can't pretend that music has anything to do with it, because the equipment never functions after 12 hours of playing."*

What was the reaction to your performance in Saskatoon? *"They just sat there. We played some good stuff, and the acoustics were brilliant. Calgary and Vancouver were good. Edmonton was really nice."*

Concerts in Regina don't sell too well. The Vanilla Fudge only drew 800 people. *"It's too bad, really. The Vanilla Fudge, Blue Cheer, and Grand Funk are really underrated. I think they're really good."* Do you know many other groups? *"Yeah. But us, and King Crimson, and the Moody Blues all kind of work on the outside, if you know what I mean."*

Asked about the voices in the song, 'Several species of small furry animals gathered together in a cave and grooving with a Pict,' Waters replied, *"It's not actually anything. It's a bit of concrete poetry. Those were sounds that I made. The voice and the hand slapping were all human generated, no musical instruments."* So you just wanted to get into a persons head? *"And just push him about a bit. Nothing deliberate. Not a deliberate blow on the nose. Just to sort of mess him around a bit."*

October 17, 1970 - Disc and Music Echo (U.K.) published an article titled, "Electric Pink Floyd employ a conductor!" by Lisa Mehlman that reviewed the Pink Floyd concert at the Fillmore East on September 27, 1970. Mehlman wrote that the first set was "less than inspired." Richard Wright used the Azimuth Co-ordinator to send sound around the hall during the first set, which included the songs 'Saucerful of Secrets,' 'Astronomy Domine,' and 'Set the Controls for the Heart of the Sun.' For the second set, Pink Floyd were joined on stage by ten horn men, approximately twenty singers, and a conductor to perform a "rock-classical fused composition" that the reviewer did not particularly like.

Also in this issue is a full-page ad for the Pink Floyd album, 'Atom Heart Mother.'

October 23, 1970 - The Los Angeles Free Press (U.S.) published an ad for a Pink Floyd concert at the Santa Monica Civic Center in California on Friday, October 23, 1970. Tickets were $5.50.

October 30, 1970 - The Los Angeles Free Press (U.S.) reported on the Pink Floyd concert at the Santa Monica Civic Center, on October 23, 1970. Using a 360-degree sound system, and beginning with their quieter numbers, Pink Floyd managed to make the crowd of 3,700 people sit down and listen. They opened the concert with 'Astronomy Domine,' followed by 'Green is the Colour,' which segued into 'Careful With That Axe Eugene.' The next song, 'Fat Old Sun,' indicated that they have "not completely forsaken melodic structure." 'Set the Controls for the Heart of the Sun' is their showstopper. It began with a gong solo, and utilized the 360-degree sound system. 'Cymbaline' followed, which included a comic interlude of sound effects. The reviewer, Chris Van Ness, felt that the band had gone a bit too far with this. The set ended with "an exercise in structured electronic sounds," referring to 'A Saucerful of Secrets.'

The second set was 'Atom Heart Mother,' and the band added a ten-piece brass section and a twenty-voice choir. The reviewer called it a symphony, and "the most successful integration of rock and formal music I have heard." Stockhausen's influence is prevalent, although the main influence on the piece is Carl Orff, with the textures and sound balances reminiscent of some of Orff's earlier works. The new Pink Floyd album, 'Atom Heart

Mother,' includes this piece but it pales in comparison to the live performance. However, it is still an important record to own. The second side of the album contains melodic songs like 'If,' as well as electronic sound pieces, 'Alan's Psychedelic Breakfast,' but compared to 'Atom Heart Mother,' they seem like "little more than throwaways."

After the performance of 'Atom Heart Mother,' the concert was supposed to be over, but the crowd reaction forced the group to return and they performed 'Interstellar Overdrive.' An exception among rock groups, Pink Floyd don't seem to be too concerned with the monetary aspects, as the current tour has got to be an expensive one. They are paying an orchestra and choir for each performance, plus they bring all their own equipment and engineers. And their music seems to be "the sound of the future."

November 1970 - The Long Beach Free Press (U.S.) reported on the Pink Floyd concert at the Santa Monica Civic Center in California on October 23, 1970 in their column, Comments from the Mescaline Gallery. The reviewer wrote, "I had always thought that Pink Floyd was just another rock & roll band. I was certainly very shocked on the night of October 23 when I heard them at the Santa Monica Civic. They played their own highly individualized space music in between spots of dialog with the audience. "Aaaaarrggh." (from the rafters somewhere) "We haven't got to that one yet," said the groups' guitarist. The program was divided neatly into two parts. The first was a bunch of songs they had done before, interspersed with comments from the mescaline gallery, such as "Get it on!" and "Do it!" The second half began after an intermission, during which time a small orchestra was dragged onstage, followed by a chorus. Someone smashed a French horn over someone else's skull, "Far out!" came the approval of the audience. "Guerilla theater." Then we were introduced to the orchestra's conductor, who was named Peter-Something-or-other. He was about 35 and had on a bright pink shirt and bell-bottoms. He and the various musicians performed the Atom Heart Mother Suite from Pink Floyd's recent album. (They did so without much interference from the band itself.) This was followed by an encore, more space music. Then the concert was over. The orchestra staggered off into the wings, stepping over a few bruised and battered musicians and limping slightly. The chorus fell off its platform and crawled backstage. Apparently it was closing-up time. On the following Monday morning I read a review of the concert in the L.A. Times. It was by John Mendelsohn, who had apparently dropped a nasty pill. "Ultimately one can scarcely keep from wondering why the four human components of Pink Floyd bother to come out on stage at all when computers could hardly fail to make as interesting use of their arsenal of gadgets," he wrote, which probably made a lot of Pink Floyd's fans very sad. But we know your type, John, you write for Rolling Stone." "Pink Floyd was excellent."

November 7, 1970 - Music Now (U.K.) published an article titled, "The Fantastic Floyd Encore" by Pete Senoff that reviewed the Pink Floyd concert at the Santa Monica Civic Auditorium on October 23, 1970. Senoff wrote that 'Astronomy Domine' was powerful and dynamic. Roger Waters' screams during 'Careful With That Axe Eugene' were preceded by anticipatory crowd screams, but they could not compete with Waters' quadraphonic screams. 'Set the Controls for the Heart of the Sun' and 'Cymbaline' were impeccable in their use of the quadraphonic sound system. 'A Saucerful of Secrets' ended the first set and displayed dynamics and some excellent gong-work by Waters. 'Atom Heart Mother' was performed with a horn section and 20-piece choir and received a 15-minute standing ovation from the standing room only crowd of 3,000. They encored with a reworked version of 'Interstellar Overdrive.' Rick Wright played a new Moog synthesizer.

November 13, 1970 – BT, Copenhagen (Denmark) reported on the Pink Floyd concert at the Falkoner Centret, Copenhagen, Denmark on November 12, 1970. Pink Floyd impressed an audience of 3,800 with their cosmic sound. They dominated their technical equipment to a "scary degree."

Ekstra Bladet, Copenhagen (Denmark) reported on the Pink Floyd concert at the

Falkoner Centret, Copenhagen, Denmark on November 12, 1970. The reviewer wrote, "I do not think that Pink Floyd is dedicated to the trip." "I feel that they miss one dimension. The body is not involved in the trip, no spontaneity."

Politiken, Copenhagen (Denmark) reported on the Pink Floyd concert at the Falkoner Centret, Copenhagen, Denmark on November 12, 1970. The reviewer wrote, "Breathless they left us for two and a half hours, with open mouths and pressed throats."

Jyllands-Posten, Copenhagen (Denmark) reported on the Pink Floyd concert at the Falkoner Centret, Copenhagen, Denmark on November 12, 1970. The reviewer wrote, "Pink Floyd's concert is still a confrontation between planets." "Best of all is that it is a combination of modern technique and the sound of the future."

November 14, 1970 - Aarhus Stiftstidende (Denmark) reported on the Pink Floyd concert at the Veljby-Risskov in Aarhus, Denmark on November 13, 1970, calling it an "Electronic Superdance." 3,000 people attended the show.

Disc and Music Echo (U.K.) published an article titled, "A touring circus-that's what Floyd want next" by Caroline Boucher that featured an interview with Nick Mason.

Talking about the direction of the band, Mason stated, "*A lot of people are always looking for a new direction for us, and saying, 'Oh, this is your new direction, lads.' There has always been a tendency to fix labels. Our direction has always been erratic, and I think we've managed to fool most of the people most of the time. But it's odd that people want to describe our music. I wonder if it's necessary to do that at all?*"

Talking about 'Atom Heart Mother,' Mason said, "*I'm not greatly enamored of a choir and orchestra. We've used it live several times, including at Bath when someone put some beer down the tuba, which added to the chaos. It does limit you because you have to worry about them all the time. It detracts from your enjoyment. We'll probably find different ways of orchestrating so that there's more freedom. The whole thing was put together for the band with this feeling that specific parts should be orchestrated. We did it for about six or eight months, playing without any orchestration and Ron Geesin was asked to help. 'Atom Heart Mother' is just a piece of music. There really isn't a very strong theme. It's very sectionised and a mood runs through it. It's not the story of the Bible to music or anything."*

Mason is happy with the album, and the only other album he was really pleased with was 'Saucerful of Secrets.' Mason stated, *"If you put a lot of time into something it ceases to be a piece of music and becomes a sequence of memories of when you were making it."*

The band have just returned from their fourth American tour and have a busy schedule ahead of them. Mason remarked, *"We'd all rather stay at home than tour America. We're all too domesticated and much too old for all this."*

Asked about his role as a producer for Principal Edwards, Mason replied, *"I don't envisage retiring to become the Phil Spector of Camden Town."*

As for the Pink Floyd stage show, they feel that they have been playing their old songs for too long a time. Mason explained, *"We enjoy playing them, and people do like hearing things they're familiar with, but it's important to do some new things. We made 'Ummagumma' in the belief that we wouldn't have to perform those numbers any more. It's just like the Who's 'Tommy.' For our own good, as well as for everyone else's, we must start on new things."*

In the future, the band would like to stage a theatrical performance with a bigger concept that they could perform in one place for a week. For a few shows, they have already tried using a monster that crept through the audience from the back of the hall and hissed down people's necks. Mason explained, *"We've always had this bigger concert concept in mind. There have always been big plans. But it's only this year, really, that we've become financially stable so we can start organizing things to suit us rather than let it all go on around us. Playing live is good for the soul."*

Melody Maker (U.K.) published Blind Date

with David Gilmour. Gilmour was played a number of songs without being told who the bands were, and he stated his opinion of the songs.

Deep Feeling – 'Do You Wanna Dance.' Gilmour said, *"Not a clue. I don't know who that is. I liked it better when you played it at 33. It didn't appeal to me much. I like the funny instrument coming out of the speaker over there, sounded like it was a Moog. Nice steel guitar, and that's about it. It seems strange updating old songs these days."*

Tir Na Nog – 'I'm Happy to Be.' Gilmour said, *"No. Will you take it off? I will probably insult someone terribly if I say it sounded like the Settlers or the new Seekers. But I don't like it. If they're mates of mine, then I'm sorry for them, which sounds a bit coy, I suppose. Not bound for Number One, I don't think, and I don't know who it was."*

Velvet Opera – 'She Keeps Giving Me Those Feelings.' Gilmour said, *"Yeah, I like it after the chorus. I like that sort of production. I've no idea who it is. It's new to me. It's a bit repetitive, isn't it? Quite a nice voice, but when the chorus bits come in, I tend to lose interest. I like the backing and I'll give it five."*

The Voices of East Harlem – 'No. No. No.' Gilmour said, *"Play something outrageous now, something really good. I can't imagine anyone sitting down and making a record like this. It baffles me the way records do go up the charts. No, I have no idea if they will make it. I can't really relate to it myself. They sound as if they are having fun, and that's the important thing. Voices of East Harlem? Yeah, I think it's them. We played with them in Paris, and I wasn't all that impressed. I think they could be a really amazing band if they were handled right, with all those voices. But they are handled rather unimaginatively. No, take it off. They were quite good live, but nothing like they could be with the right direction."*

Sol Raye – 'Welcome Stranger.' Gilmour said, *"Take it off. No. It's horrible. That is like factory music. That's the sort of thing they churn out for the Engelberts of the world. All the little people and their ilk. It's a completely different field of pop than the one I am in. It's like asking me to give a lecture on Trad Jazz. I don't know who that was, but it's got a pretty label."*

Tim Rose – 'I've Gotta Get a Message to You.' Gilmour said, *"They all sound like they are in the same key, and all in the same rhythm. The voice is a bit like Richie Havens, but the material is very different from what he would do. Very catchy, the same as the last record. It always seems a bit more when they are sung by dark gentlemen. Lovely bass player. All stereotyped stuff, isn't it?"*

Titus Groan – 'Open the Door Homer.' Gilmour said, *"Lovely song, but what a horrible singer. God, I haven't liked one yet. I prefer it by Bob Dylan. Then you're bound to, aren't you? Yeah, I've had enough of that one. Come on, thrill me for God's sake. There has to be something better than that lot out this week."*

Smith – 'Back to Me.' Gilmour said, *"Tiny bit better. Not quite what I mean, but I do prefer this, I suppose. I suppose it might grow on me if I ever heard it again, but I don't think that's likely. It's very hard to relate to the Top Ten for a lad like me."*

Danny La Rue – 'Fanlight Fanny.' Gilmour said, *"I think this could easily be a giant hit. It's got rhymes that Radio One will like, and drive us all mad with. That's not to say that I like it, of course. Horrible. Take it off, there's a good chap."*

Harold Muir – 'The Fence.' Gilmour said, *"Sure has got rhythm. Yeah, nice, I like it. But once again I have no clue as to who it is. I ain't got a clue. Nice, though. Nice sax blowing. I could listen to this for a long time. It's nice. Can I have the record please? Yeah, that's all for that one. Come on, tell me who it is and I might buy it."*

John Renbourn – 'The Lady and the Unicorn.' Gilmour said, *"When does the singing start? Where's the hook? This isn't going to make the Top Twenty. This is too nice. Can I have this one? Yeah, I like this. I might even buy it. Can't see this as a single, really. I have no idea who it is. Not a clue. I've only got one so far. Fab. Ask me another."*

The World – 'Not the First Time.' Gilmour said, *"I think I ought to recognize this one, but I don't know who it is. Is this the last one? Oh. No, please take it off. What can you say. What can I say about a record like that except that I wouldn't like to listen to it more than once or twice. I'm sure I'll know who it is*

when you tell me."

Hannibal – '1066.' Gilmour said, *"Sounds like someone is strangling him, poor old chap. Yeah, you can take that off. I give up. I'm baffled and bored. I've got no idea who it is, like the others. It's not very inspiring, is it? My mind's a blank. God, I got some shockers. They all sounded the same."*

November 16, 1970 - Rock (U.S.) reviewed the Pink Floyd album, 'Atom Heart Mother,' calling it "a new step for Floyd," and "a fusion of rock and romanticism. . ." "They've succeeded in breaking out of the 'cosmic' mould and into a conscious earthiness."

November 21, 1970 - New Musical Express (U.K.) reported that Pink Floyd is writing a score for a Rudolph Nureyev ballet that will be performed for ten days at the Grand Palais in Paris next summer, with the final performance to be shown live on Eurovision satellite. Roland Petit, who is choreographing the ballet, asked the Pink Floyd to write the music. Pink Floyd are flying to Paris, France on December 4, 1970, to contribute to a two-hour TV special on the life of Roland Petit. Thirty minutes of the program will exclusively be Pink Floyd music. Pink Floyd are currently on tour, with concerts in Holland, Sweden, Denmark, Germany, Switzerland, and Austria, plus a performance at the Dagenham Roundhouse on December 12, 1970.

November 26, 1970 - Rolling Stone Magazine (U.S.) reported on the Pink Floyd concert at the Fillmore, San Francisco, California, on October 21, 1970. The article said that the band performed, for the first set, 'Astronomy Domine,' 'Fat Old Sun,' 'Careful With That Axe, Eugene,' 'Cymbaline,' 'Set the Controls for the Heart of the Sun,' and 'A Saucerful of Secrets.' For the second set they played 'Atom Heart Mother' with the Roger Wagner Chorale, three French horns, three trombones, three trumpets, and a tuba, all conducted by New York composer Peter Philips. It costs Pink Floyd $5,000 in musician fees to stage these concerts with chorale and brass. As an encore, the chorale performed 'Ave Maria.' Tickets cost $3.

The article also included an interview with Nick Mason, who commented on working with Antonioni on the 'Zabriskie Point' movie, saying, "*He's a fucking crazy man to work for. We ended up not doing anything in the film that much. That's why he wasn't working with experienced actors. The Zabriskie actors were ordered to do everything. They had no freedom.*"

Asked about the cows on the cover of the Atom Heart Mother album, Mason explained, "*They're just basic. Everyone's trying to put out complicated, super-hip album covers. We just wanted something plain. The title of the album came from a news headline about a pregnant woman who had been kept alive with an atomic heart. There is a connection between the cows and the title if you want to think of the earth mother, or the heart of the earth.*"

Also in this issue was a report that Pink Floyd have been working on a ballet based on Marcel Proust's 'Rememberance of Things Past,' with producer Roland Petit and dancer Rudolf Nureyev. The ballet is to be performed with Pink Floyd playing the score live for ten days in June 1971 at the Grand Palais, Paris, France, with the final show broadcast live over Eurovision to an audience of 70 million in Europe.

November 28, 1970 - Disc and Music Echo (U.K.) published an article titled, "Pink Floyd 'Atom' to Explode in Britain." The article reported that Pink Floyd will be performing 'Atom Heart Mother' with a complete brass section and the John Aldis Choir for four concerts in Britain, beginning on December 18, 1970, at the Birmingham Town Hall, followed by Bristol Colston Hall on the 20th, Manchester Free Trade Hall on the 21st, and Sheffield City Hall on the 22nd. NEM's Peter Bowyer, who is arranging the shows, stated, "*The group's management decided not to play London, as people there had already seen the work performed in Hyde Park.*"

Melody Maker (U.K.) reported that Pink Floyd will be performing 'Atom Heart Mother' with a 10-piece brass band and an 18-voice choir in four cities in Britain in December. The first of these special concerts will take place at the Birmingham Town Hall on December 18, 1970. Promoter Peter Bowyer stated, "*It is costing the group about £6,000 to put on these*

shows because of the large number of people traveling with them. It will probably be the last time 'Atom Heart Mother' is performed live in this country. The group have no more dates in the near future, and by the time they appear again, they will probably have written something new.*"

Also in this issue are ads for Pink Floyd at the Regent Theater Concert Hall, Brighton, England, on Friday December 11, 1970, admission 25/-, and at the Village, Roundhouse, Dagenham on Saturday, December 12, 1970, admission 25/.

Music Now (U.K.) published an article titled, "Outside the rock machine" that featured an interview with David Gilmour by Dai Davies.

Pink Floyd recently toured America and made a profit for the first time. David Gilmour explained, "*We had a tour of the States in 1968, but it was a bit diabolical. We used rented equipment, which didn't really work out. We had a few good gigs, but it didn't put the prices up enough to make going a really viable proposition. We didn't make a fantastic amount of money this year, but we did establish ourselves. Our reputation depends very largely on live gigs. While we were there, we performed 'Atom Heart Mother' three times, which was fantastically expensive. We wouldn't have been able to do it if we hadn't had a subsidy from our American label, Capitol. They thought it would be good P.R. to help us out. We performed the piece at the two Fillmores, and in Los Angeles. Getting the choir and musicians together for those three concerts cost an extra $15,000. The first time we played it was at Bath and that was a bit of a mess, well far from ideal, anyway. Personally, I don't like festivals, at least I don't like being a musician at festivals. I'm sure it's a lot of fun spending a weekend in the mud looning about, but for the musician there are lots of hassles. After three days at Bath, the sound equipment they were using had practically worn out, and playing out of doors to that many people really does present difficulties. There were loads of people milling about behind the stage and someone even poured a pint of beer down one of the tubas. Something on the scale of 'Atom Heart Mother' really takes a lot of getting together. The problem is that we've never done it more* than twice with the same people. The choirs are usually alright because they're used to working together. But some of the brass people have been really hopeless. In the studios, they were pretty annoying sometimes. They always used to rush off to the canteen whenever they had the chance, and split right on the dot when the session was over. Performance wise, it was a lot better in the States, but we're going to do it around a few halls in this country when we tour later this year. Towards the end of recording the album, it all seemed to get a bit warped. Some of it seems a bit messy when I listen to it now, little things jump out at me and I think, 'Shouldn't have done that.'"

The song, 'Alan's Psychedelic Breakfast,' shows a bit of Floyd humor. Gilmour said, "We do take our music seriously, but that doesn't mean it all has to be serious."

As far as album sleeves, their covers are done by two friends, Storm and Poe, who call themselves Hipgnosis. Gilmour explained, "We try and keep everything we can within the framework of our own friends. We give EMI finished tapes and artwork, and that's about all we have to do with them. We're really quite separate, or as separate as we can make it without disappearing from the whole of the rock music machine. None of us really fit into the role of rock stars. We have as little to do with the machine as possible."

Gilmour continued, "Most of our friends are people we've known from before the time when we were successful, rather than other musicians. I'd always known the Floyd, even before I joined. I went to the same college as Syd, and knew them through him. So when he split, they asked me to join rather than go through the awful auditions bit. The rock scene is very narrow-minded. Most people on the scene know and respect other people on the scene. Although, obviously, we must respect other musicians, we don't know many of them. People in groups seem socially insulated from people that aren't in the business. I think our attitude helps us see it from other angles."

Gilmour continued, "All these movements that are supposed to be all encompassing are just tripping steadily along, taking themselves far too seriously. Such a lot of bands can't see beyond themselves, even some of the bands I dig immensely. Rock musicians seem to be the victims of rules that

they have created for themselves."

Gilmour continued, "We try and get into things just outside the music. We've done a lot of film scores, but we would like to do our own films. Doing scores is fine, but you're not really your own boss, though I suppose being forced into frantic work schedules is good for you. As a band, we've done scores for 'More' and 'Zabriskie Point,' and Roger Waters worked with Ron Geesin on the score for 'The Body.' Ron asked him to help out, as Ron doesn't write songs, just themes. He helped us on 'Atom Heart Mother.' 'More' was a forced score. We wrote, recorded, and mixed it all in eight days. We hadn't seen the film as a whole when we did it. The film had rather a bad reputation, probably because of the dialog. They were saying things like 'Groovy man, let's get high.' Schroeder was a foreign director, and though he spoke English, he didn't know the subtle difference between what slang was acceptable and hip, and what wasn't."

Gilmour continued, "For 'Zabriskie Point,' we did the entire score, which, as a whole, was rejected. Antonioni is something of a megalomaniac. He used people who weren't actors so that he could get them to do whatever he told them. There was some very good music there, and although bits of it have been absorbed into the stage act, most of it we leave alone. It's essentially mood music, and if we were to put it out as a Floyd album, people would, I think, feel a little deprived. MGM hold the tapes and I don't know what they might do with it. We worked on the score in Rome, three weeks in a primitive Rome studio, working through the nights."

Gilmour continued, "We'll start work on our next album in about January, I should think. But before then, we've got the tour and we have to start thinking about the ballet that we're doing in Paris in June. Another thing which we've had in our minds for about a year, which is bound to break out soon, is a theatrical project. It's still in its vague stages, but we have enjoyed the theatrical stunts that we've used in the past to turn the audiences on. We don't like being held back by the fact that we're a rock group. We don't really have a positive direction as a group. We're not trying to peak. We've always meandered and zigzagged, so nothing we do *necessarily has to be related to anything that we've done before."*

Recently, Gilmour produced Syd Barrett's second solo album, 'Barrett.' Gilmour explained, *"Syd was the songwriter of the original Floyd for a very good reason. He is an incredible songwriter. Although the songs were his, the sound belonged to the band because they evolved it. At the moment, Syd has returned to Cambridge. He says that he wants to leave the whole rock business behind him and learn to become a doctor or something. I don't know how long that feeling will last. He is an incredibly talented songwriter. He never has to sit down and write because songs just seem to fall out of his head. It's just that he's on a different level of existence from the rest of us mere mortals. He's right up there with the McCartneys and Dylans of the world."*

Gilmour continued, *"I produced his last album, and had a hand in the first one. He's a producer's nightmare. He'll never play the same song the same twice. I've found that the only way to record him is for him to lay down the basic song with acoustic guitar and voice, and then overdub. He's only played live once since he left the band. That was at Olympia earlier in the year. Jerry, from Humble Pie, and myself got up and played with him. He seemed to go down quite well, but he was very nervous and he never has been much good at the dynamics of stage playing. The fact that he never plays the same things twice also rules out him playing live very often. He finds it very difficult, impossible in fact, to play within the discipline of a band."*

Pink Floyd hasn't played many shows in England this year. According to Gilmour, he and Nick Mason would like to play live more often. Gilmour said, *"Not every night, but about once a week."* And when they do perform, their sets usually last over two hours. Gilmour added, *"With sets of that length, a band needs a lot of material. Not all our album numbers are suitable for stage, so we tend to use old numbers like 'Careful With That Axe, Eugene,' which have been through so many changes that they're completely different to what they were when recorded. Someone will think of something one night and change it, and the change will stay. There's a place for individual improvisation in most of our stage numbers, but we've played some of them so*

often that they tend to take on a pattern and sound the same. On occasional nights, we will feel really inspired and come up with something amazing. It doesn't always coincide with important gigs, although sometimes the pressure of a big gig pushes your brain."

December 1970 - Beat Instrumental (U.K.) reviewed the Pink Floyd album, 'Atom Heart Mother.' They wrote, "With this utterly fantastic record, the Floyd have moved out into totally new ground. Basically a concept album, the A-side title track utilizes Pink Floyd, orchestral brass, and mixed choir. All blend to form a totally integrated theme, which is the great strength of this LP. Great, great, great, and I'd love to hear it in quadraphonic."

December 5, 1970 - Disc and Music Echo (U.K.) published a full-page ad announcing that "Atom Heart Mother is going on the road." The ad included upcoming tour dates with venues.

Melody Maker (U.K.) published an article titled, "Troubled Waters" by Michael Watts that featured an interview with Roger Waters at his home near Shoreditch, England. Asked about the Roland Petit ballet, Waters stated, *"We haven't started work on it yet."* Asked whether he had a basic idea for it, Waters replied, *"No, none at all. I'm madly reading all Proust, because that's the basic idea, so they tell me. That's Roland's idea, the choreographer and producer of the thing. It's based on the twenty volumes of his 'A La Recherche Du Temps.' Roland thinks there's some good gear in that, which there undoubtedly is. So very loosely, the ballet will be based on certain episodes."*

How difficult will it be for Pink Floyd, a band that improvises a lot, to do the score? Waters replied, *"You see, they don't really rely, to a large extent, on improvisation. But I know what you mean. In fact, it won't necessarily have to be note for note as long as the timing is the same every night. The melody isn't as important as the timing of the thing, because they all dance to counts, right? I can't see that it should provide any problem, really, because people who play music without reading do it constantly, all the time. All rock and roll groups do it. It's just that we tend to do*

Birmingham Town Hall
Dec 18

Bristol, Colston Hall
Dec 20

ATOM HEART MOTHER is going on the road

Manchester Free Trade Hall
Dec 21

Sheffield City Hall
Dec 22

The Pink Floyd also appearing at: Big Apple, Brighton, Dec.11 & the Roundhouse, Dagenham, Dec.12.

it less than most. And all this thing about improvisation is a bit of a joke, anyway, because people tend to have certain riffs and phrases and ideas which they use, and they string them together."

When Pink Floyd started, the music was melodic, but now it is musical streams of consciousness. Waters said, "*Originally, you see, I wasn't doing anything apart from being a student of architecture and spending money on buying bass guitars. But in terms of music,*

I wasn't doing anything at all. 'See Emily Play' and 'Arnold Layne' are Syd Barrett's songs, right? And it wouldn't matter who it was who played the bass or did this or that. It's irrelevant. They're very strong songs and you just do it. It's nothing to do with music, playing that stuff. It has to do with writing songs. And that was Syd who wrote those songs. I don't think we were doing anything then, if you see what I mean."

So, in those days, it was The Pink

Floyd, and Syd Barrett? Waters said, *"Right. But I wasn't thinking about musical policy in those days. Not that I think much about it now. Most of the stuff on the first album was Syd's. The only thing on that album that was much like what the group was going to do later was the thing that we all did together, 'Interstellar Overdrive,' which we don't like playing much now."*

Is the reason that you don't play it much anymore because you are bored with it? Waters said, *"Yeah. I'm bored with most of the stuff we've done. I'm bored with most of the stuff we play."* Does that include the new songs? Waters replied, *"Well, there isn't very much new stuff, is there, if you look at it. I'm not bored with doing 'Atom Heart Mother' when we get the brass and choir together, because it's so weird doing it. It always comes out as so odd because of the problems of rehearsing musicians. It's like everybody throwing their lump of clay at the wall and seeing what it looks like when it's happened. It depends on so many other things, as well. It depends on how it mixes, you know? And we're working with this ludicrous situation where we don't have somebody out mixing the sound in the audience, which we obviously ought to. It's ludicrous to mix the PA from the side of the stage when you are mixing brass and a choir and a group, but we do it. But it would cost a bloody fortune to get it together in another way, but I think we ought to. I'm beginning to come to a position now where I don't think we ought to play any more on a kind of Heath Robinson level, go and do it, play the numbers, do the stuff, get the money, and go home. We should not go along and play a whole load of numbers, most of them old and some of them new, with things patently wrong, like with some people balancing from the side of the stage. I think we, and a hell of a lot of other groups, are in a position now to start raising standards a bit. But we don't. Well, we haven't. But we're always intending to. The reason that they haven't is that the money's there, and people are prepared to spend it on them doing what they're doing now. So they go on schlapping around the country, doing it all, and maybe they get a new and wonderful buzz out of it, communicating with the audience every night. But I don't believe it. It's a job, a fucking well-paid job, with all the ego-boosting stuff, and* everything. And I think it becomes very mechanical. I'm going on a ten-day tour tomorrow, right? Frankfurt, Vienna, Montreux. But why am I going? To spread the gospel? To make people happy by playing them wonderful music? No, it's not true. I'm going to make bread. I'm going because I'm caught up in the whole pop machinery business, and so are the majority."*

All the members of Pink Floyd had E-type Jaguars at one time. So the band members are not just in it for the music? Waters said, *"Yes, but some of us are trying to fight it. I had mine for two months and I've just got a Mini now. But I think there's a great danger in getting into that sports car bit. It's all very, very, very tricky and hard, and we had great arguments in the band about it, because I proclaim vaguely socialist principles. And I sit there spouting a lot of crap about how having a lot of bread worries me. And we are earning a lot of bread now. I couldn't feel happy in an E-type Jaguar because it just seems all wrong, somehow. I mean, who needs four point two litres, and a big shinny bonnet, and whatever else it is. I know the answers to all the questions, like who needs hi-fi. And look at your house with all the tapestries on the wall. OK. I take that point. But I have all these feelings. I do. All about it. I don't rush around helping people desperately, and I don't give away all my bread to everybody. But the argument we are constantly coming up against is that you can't have the luxury of socialist principles and compassionate feelings about people who are less well off than you are, you can't sincerely have feelings for them, and you can't sincerely feel the system's wrong, and wish there was some kind of a socialist system here and elsewhere, and still have five grand in the bank, or whatever, which is an argument we're constantly having."*

Asked why he doesn't just give all his money away, Waters replied, *"Because I'm the same as everybody else. Everybody, except for Christ and Gandhi and one or two others, has got the acquisitive instinct to a certain extent. The tragedy of the whole thing is that it's multiplied. The interesting thing is, if we are born with it. If we're not born with it, that means that it's foisted upon us by the system, and that, by the time we grow up and start leaving home or get pocket money, we have*

```
┌─────────────────────────────────────────────────────┐
│              VILLAGE, ROUNDHOUSE                      │
│              LODGE AVENUE, DAGENHAM                    │
│              SATURDAY, DEC. 12th                       │
│                                                       │
│           PINK FLOYD                                  │
│                                                       │
│           Advance tickets 25/- ONLY                   │
│  Available from: Dagenham Roundhouse on Saturdays, or │
│  Romford King's Head on Mondays, or by post (send     │
│  s.a.e.) to: Asgard Enterprises, 645/7 High Road,     │
│  Seven Kings, Ilford, Essex. Please send P.O.s (no    │
│  cheques) crossed and made payable to ASGARD          │
│  ENTERPRISES.                                         │
└─────────────────────────────────────────────────────┘
```

developed it. *The possibility exists, even if it's only a possibility, that we're not born with it, and that, given a different environment, the kids might grow up into people who get their kicks in another way. I mean, it's impossible in our society because you're pumped full of personal acquisitions.*"

Will Pink Floyd be including more of a theatrical element in their performances? Waters said, "*This is what I was saying earlier on. I want to stop going out and playing the numbers. I personally would like to stop doing that now, today. I would like to be creating tapes, songs, material, writing, sketches of sets, whatever is necessary to put on a complete theatrical show in a theater in London sometime, and see if the people dig it. They may not. They may come on and say, well, it's all right, but it's not rock and roll, is it? They won't do that because they're all terribly well spoken students, all our fans, so they tell me. But it's quite possible that the whole thing could fail horribly. I don't think it will. I have great faith in giving the audiences more than music. There is just so much more that you can do to make it a complete experience than watching four, long-haired youths leaping up and down, beating their banjos. Not that I'm saying that's wrong. But why not try and push yourself a bit further. Why just go on doing the same thing night after night? And believe me, groups are bored with it, whether they'll admit it or not. It is boring to them. It's not quite as boring to the audience because the audience probably only see it once a year.*"

Also in this issue is a full-page ad announcing that "Atom Heart Mother is going on the road."

New Musical Express (U.K.) published a full-page ad announcing that "Atom Heart Mother is going on the road."

December 12, 1970 - Melody Maker (U.K.) published an article titled, "Ron's got it taped" that featured an interview with Ron Geesin by Roy Hollingworth. Geesin explained how he got involved in recording the soundtrack for 'The Body' movie, saying, "*Well, the film people just couldn't find the right people to do the score for a film completely about the human body. As a last resort, and I mean a last resort, the producer, Tony Gardner, phoned John Peel, who knew I had done some documentaries and a few commercials in my spare time. Well, the thing appealed to me, and I got a few ideas together. But when the film people came round, I played them all the wrong things, just the sort of thing I would do. Well, they were already puzzled out of their minds, and that threw them completely off their feet. I knew they needed songs, plus atmospheres, and multi-dimensional pieces. I saw it as the propaganda of the misuse of the lower class body, compared with the higher class body. I didn't know really what they wanted. Neither did they. I offered maybe one of ten rights. But I leapt into it, as always, with enthusiasm.*"

Geesin continued, "*I was getting on well with Roger as a human, you know, we played golf together. It's a pity more people don't play golf, you know. And, well, I asked him if he would like to join me. I dashed forth with me goods, and Roger did four songs. I actually did all the fill-in bits, funny sputtering noises, then classical, and cellos, and guitars. I worked myself to death. The strain nearly exploded my mind. Maybe it did explode my mind. But we did it."*

Geesin continued, *"After the film, Roger sort of proposed to me that I should help Floyd with their next album. He said he would like me to write the brass and choir pieces for 'Atom Heart Mother.' Well, I knew Roger, but the rest of Floyd were virtually unknown to me, and I didn't really want to tamper with the working of a fine group of collaborating musicians. But I must admit, the idea was very exciting. Floyd were off to the States then, and Roger left me with a skeleton tape of rhythm and chords. 'Atom Heart Mother' was to be a 25-minute piece, and that's a hell of a lot of work. With them in the States, I just couldn't do anything with the tape. It wouldn't have been right, and besides, I didn't really know what they wanted. But when they came back, the panic was on. You know, everyone wanted it in a couple of weeks or so, typical show biz bloody panic. Nobody knew what was wanted. They couldn't read music. Rick could a bit, but on his own admission, he's lazy. I'm lazy too, due to the working percentage of the brain. The only way we could force something to happen was to do something I didn't want to do, and that was to force myself into being in charge of that aspect of the album. It was the only way it could be done. It wasn't the big ego thing. If you want ten brass instruments playing, you can't do the bloody thing on a piano, and you can't damn well sing it. I think they got frightened."*

Geesin continued, *"Dave proposed strict ideas for melodies, and then we did the choir section together, both at keyboards, collaborating with Rick. We all had sleepless nights worrying about what was going on. What the bloody hell were Floyd doing, working with this mad Scotsman? Well, it got done. But then the thing had to be recorded with the brass band, orchestra, and choir. I could see the orchestra tuning up and the band playing in all bloody directions, playing different tunes, because I'm not a conductor, simply because I'm self taught. Conductors are*

now essential in modern music. I was incapable of telling them what to do. Things were looking terrible. Nobody knew what was going to happen. But then John Aldis, who was in charge of the best modern choir in the classical area, came to collect the choir parts, and saw our plight. I became advisor, and he the conductor-advisor-composer, something like that, and it happened. But the fright, the tension! We were all friends, Floyd and I, by then. And what I was doing for them I wanted to be good. I wanted to present them with something that would be uplifting and good for them."

After 'Atom Heart Mother,' Gessin began work on 'The Body' album. Geesin said, *"I had bad staggers of the brain by then, and took to the seaside to play with pebbles. I have a bee in my bonnet about soundtrack LPs from films. I mean, an LP is something different. You can't just lift the soundtrack and put it on record because the music for the film was mono, and the LP was to be stereo. I reconstructed the whole thing. My brain had to draw upon resources, and I nearly went too far."*

December 19, 1970 - Disc and Music Echo (U.K.) published an ad for the album, 'Music from The Body,' by Ron Geesin & Roger Waters.

Melody Maker (U.K.) reported that Pink Floyd will be performing Atom Heart Mother at the Birmingham Town Hall on Friday, December 18, 1970, complete with brass and choir. Dates are also listed for Bristol on the 20th, Manchester on the 21st, and Sheffield on the 22nd.

December 26, 1970 - Melody Maker (U.K.) reported on the Pink Floyd concert at the Birmingham Town Hall on Friday, December 18, 1970. Dennis Detheridge wrote that the concert was an unqualified success, and that Pink Floyd filled the hall with "glorious sounds." "A moving experience." Also in this issue is an EMI ad "Have a Heavy Christmas," that includes the Atom Heart Mother LP.

1971
𝔐eddle

January 2, 1971 - New Musical Express (U.K.) reported on the Pink Floyd concert at the Birmingham Town Hall, England, on December 18, 1970. A whistling kettle and the smell of bacon accompanied the "Psychedelic Breakfast" that began the first set. Other effects heard at the show included crying babies, galloping horses, gongs, crash cymbals, aircraft noises, and feedback. An audience of 2,000 were also treated to a choir and horn section during the performance of 'Atom Heart Mother' in the second set. "The use of choir and horns enhances their musical abilities."

January 23, 1971 - Sounds (U.K.) published an article titled, "Floyd's breathing space" by Steve Peacock. At the moment, Pink Floyd have no firm commitments. Nick Mason explained, "*It is completely up to us what we do next, and we are totally responsible for whatever comes out of the next few months which, I must admit, is slightly alarming even though it is what we have always said we wanted. In the past, we have always done things by a certain time, and if they haven't come out right, we could say that we had to rush or something. Hopefully, this time, we will be able to take our time and write the ballet music in advance, instead of three days before or something, and it would be nice if we could come through the next three months with an album and a new live act, no, not exactly a live act, but the ideas for a stage project of some kind.*"

Asked about a new album, Mason said, "*We've already done two blocks of sessions to rough out ideas for the album, ideas for sounds and chord sequences and things like that, and we'll be doing two more before the end of the month. I thought 'Atom Heart' was poorly executed in places. I think it was done a bit too piece-meal, but the faults are basically in details and I thought, overall, it was good. It has a very strange feel to it. Parts of it, like the ending, are real ham, which I like. I suppose you could say that it wasn't as mystical as other things we've done. I don't know what the feel of the new album is going to be, but it would be nice to go completely the other way and use the freedom of just having the four of us, lose the restrictions of the orchestra and*

choir."

In addition to working with Pink Floyd, Mason has just completed producing an album for Principal Edwards Magic Theater. He has also co-produced an album for two girls called the Chimers, which has not yet been released.

Pink Floyd are still considering a theater project that would involve a performance with music, dancers, and visual effects. Mason explained, "*The 'theater project committee' has had preliminary meetings, and we've talked very vaguely about some very vague ideas. Ideally, we'd like to spend February sorting out the ideas, and March doing the album, and April and May, if necessary. So far, we've got down about fourteen different ideas for the album, including one for a piece involving acoustic objects. Bottles, felling axes, saws, that sort of thing.*"

As for working together or working as individuals, Mason commented, "*I think 'Ummagumma' proved that group activities are much stronger than individual activities. It sold well, and to some extent continues to sell, but of them all, I think that one is the one I'd be least likely to buy. I know Dave would disagree with me though.*"

February 1971 - Beat Instrumental (U.K.) reviewed the second Syd Barrett album, `Barrett.' They wrote, "Syd Barrett is capable of much greater things than this. He sounds flat on most of his vocals and the instruments give the impression that only one track of the stereo is actually working. 'Gigolo Aunt' borders on early Floyd, but that is the best thing to be said about the entire album."

February 20, 1971 - Record Mirror (U.K.) published an article titled, "Could too much work be suicide for the Floyd?" by Lon Goddard.

Pink Floyd no longer have to play concerts every week in order to maintain their reputation. But they are not a lazy group. Nick Mason explained, "*There are some absurd scenes going on about how often a band should work. It's alright for musical suicide, but I*

An ad for the single "Point Me At The Sky" in New Music Express.

An ad for Atom Heart Mother featured in New Music Express that includes various other albums on EMI.

don't see why a group should work 30 days out of 30 on the road, unless it's to prove some point about stamina. What's the point? It isn't even worth it for the money. We do a lot of work abroad, but we're even cutting that down because we don't want to keep playing our favorite tunes from the past three years. It gets on you. When we come up with something that we can stand to do often, we'll take it on the road because Dave and I, and the others to a lesser extent, do want to play a lot. What we'd like to do is get into a position where we have complete control of what we do, based on a

different set of values. Get to the point where we don't have to make excuses and blame the record company for things that go wrong. I don't mind admitting that 'Atom Heart Mother' was very rushed. We had to go on an American tour right after that. The LP could have been technically better, but the effect is there, and that's very important. The title track was particularly rushed. Generally, we go into the studios with a plan, but with the idea of making an album. Practically the first note becomes part of the finished product. We'd like to think about it longer next time. Another LP is being made now, but we go into the studios with the idea of putting down rough ideas instead of actual tracks. We're consciously approaching this one differently."

Talking about the 'Underground,' Mason stated, "The 'Underground' became a highly commercial venture. It's changed drastically. It's much more crowded and all the TV stars have sweaty T-shirts and dirty hair. We're thinking of becoming a popular, chart-busting combo, not really. Businessmen have realized the market. A lot of these record company businessmen know nothing about music, so they always have a few long haired advisors to help. Advertising seems to be just for informing people a record is out, or in America, the space bought appears to convince people how much the management is behind the act. It was totally overdone, and 'Underground' became an overworked phrase. But it was a jumping off point for us. Technically, there was nothing to underground music, for us, anyway. It was just another way of playing rock music, and on a little higher level than 'Sugar, Sugar.' It used a lot of power and volume, and you lost melody, but melody will never really die. It seems pretty strange looking back on it, really hard to describe. Endless rock groups, that's what 'Underground' meant to the people. But that wasn't what it really was. It was a mixture of bands, poets, jugglers, and all sorts of acts. The poets and jugglers were left out because they didn't make much money for anyone. Not that there's anything wrong with making money. Gradually it was accepted, and bands made more money. People outside London used to hate us and throw bottles, and it was pretty bad. You had to have the atmosphere, or it didn't work."

March 1971 - Circus Magazine (U.S.) reported that Pink Floyd concerts are being bootlegged, and that one bootleg issued in a plain white sleeve contained an extended version of 'Atom Heart Mother.'

March 27, 1971 - Melody Maker (U.K.) published an interview with Syd Barrett by Michael Watts. This was Barrett's first press interview in about year, and it took place in the office of Barrett's music publisher.

Asked about his activities since he left the Pink Floyd, Barrett replied, "Well, I'm a painter, I was trained as a painter. I seem to have spent a little less time painting than I might've done, you know, it might have been a tremendous release getting absorbed in painting. Anyway, I've been sitting about and writing. The fine arts thing at college was always too much for me to think about. What I was more involved in was being successful at arts school. But it didn't transcend the feeling of playing at UFO and those sort of places with the lights and that, the fact that the group was getting bigger and bigger."

Barrett continued, "I've been at home in Cambridge with my mother. I've got lots of, well, children, in a sense. My uncle, I've been getting used to a family existence, generally. Pretty unexciting. I work in a cellar, down in a cellar."

Asked if he would rather be a musician or a painter, Barrett answered, "Well, I think of me being a painter, eventually."

Did you spend the last two years getting yourself together? Barrett replied, "No. Perhaps it has something to do with what I felt could be better as regards music, as far as my job goes generally, because I did find I needed a job. I wanted to do a job. I never admitted it because I'm a person who doesn't admit it."

What about the stories of you going back to college or working in a factory? Barrett replied, "Well, of course, living in Cambridge I have to find something to do. I suppose I could've done a job. I haven't been doing any work. I'm not really used to doing quick jobs and then stopping, but I'm sure it would be possible."

Asked how the Pink Floyd began, Barrett replied, "Roger Waters is older than I am. He was at the architecture school in London. I was studying at Cambridge. I think it was before I had set up at Camberwell. I was really moving backwards and forwards to London. I was living in Highgate with him. We shared a place there, and got a van and spent a lot of our grant on pubs and that sort of thing. We were playing Stones numbers. I suppose we were interested in playing guitars. I picked up playing guitar quite quickly, I didn't play much in Cambridge because I was from the art school, you know. But I was soon playing on the professional scene and began to write from there."

Asked about his song writing in the Pink Floyd, Barrett said, "*Their choice of material was always very much to do with what they were thinking as architecture students. Rather unexciting people, I would've thought, primarily. I mean, anybody walking into an art school like that would've been tricked. Maybe they were working their entry into an art school. But the choice of material was restricted, I suppose, by the fact that both Roger and I wrote different things. We wrote our own songs, played our own music. They were older, by about two years, I think. I was 18 or 19. I don't know that there was really much conflict, except that perhaps the way we started to play wasn't as impressive as it was to us, even, wasn't as full of impact as it might've been. I mean, it was done very well, rather than considerably exciting. One thinks of it all as a dream.*"

What did you think about Pink Floyd's music moving away from songs like 'See Emily Play?' Barrett replied, "*Singles are always simple. All the equipment was battered and worn. All the stuff we started out with was our own, the guitars were our own property. The electronic noises were probably necessary. They were very exciting. That's all really. The whole thing at the time was playing on stage.*"

Were you the only one in Pink Floyd who wanted to produce singles? Barrett replied, "*It was probably me alone, I think. Obviously, being a pop group one wanted to have singles. I think Emily was fourth in the hits.*"

Why did you leave Pink Floyd? Barrett replied, "*It wasn't really a war. I suppose it was really just a matter of being a little offhand about things. We didn't feel there was one thing which was gonna make the decision at the minute. I mean, we did split up, and there was a lot of trouble. I don't think The Pink Floyd had any trouble, but I had an awful scene, probably self-inflicted, having a mini and going all over England and things. Still...*"

Did the glamour go to your head? Barrett replied, "*I dunno. Perhaps you could see it as something that went to one's head, but I don't know that it was relevant.*"

What about the stories that you left Pink Floyd because you were freaked out on acid? Barrett replied, "*Well, I dunno, it don't seem to have much to do with the job. I only*

know the thing of playing, of being a musician, was very exciting. Obviously, one was better off with a silver guitar with mirrors and things all over it than people who ended up on the floor or anywhere else in London. The general concept, I didn't feel so conscious of it as perhaps I should. I mean, one's position as a member of London's young people's. I dunno what you'd call it, underground wasn't it, wasn't necessarily realized and felt, I don't think, especially from the point of view of groups."

Barrett continued, "*I remember at UFO, one week one group, then another week another group, going in and out, making that set-up, and I didn't think it was as active as it could've been. I was really surprised that UFO finished. I only read last week that it's not finished. Joe Boyd did all the work on it and I was really amazed when he left. What we were doing was a microcosm of the whole sort of philosophy and it tended to be a little bit cheap. The fact that the show had to be put together, the fact that we weren't living in luxurious places with luxurious things around us. I think I would always advocate that sort of thing, the luxurious life. It's probably because I don't do much work.*"

Were you involved in acid at the time? Barrett replied, "*No. It was all, I suppose, related to living in London. I was lucky enough, I've always thought of going back to a place where you can drink tea and sit on the carpet. I've been fortunate enough to do that. All that time, you've just reminded me of it. I thought it was good fun. I thought The Soft Machine were good fun. They were playing on 'Madcap,' except for Kevin Ayers.*"

Asked if he was trying to create a mood in his songs, rather than trying to tell a story, Barrett replied, "*Yes, very much. It would be terrific to do much more mood stuff. They're very pure, you know, the words. I feel I'm jabbering. I really think the whole thing is based on me being a guitarist and having done the last thing about two or three years ago in a group around England and Europe and the States, and then coming back and hardly having done anything, so I don't really know what to say. I feel, perhaps, I could be claimed as being redundant almost. I don't feel active, and that my public conscience is fully satisfied.*"

Do you think people still remember you? Barrett replied, *"Yes, I should think so."* Then why don't you put a band together and play some concerts? Barrett replied, *"I feel, though, the record would still be the thing to do. And touring and playing might make that impossible to do."*

Wouldn't you like to play live again? Barrett replied, *"Yes, very much."* Then what is the problem? Is it finding the right musicians to play with you? Barrett answered, *"Yeah."* As far as musicians, would it be more important to you that they were great musicians, or that they got along with you? Barrett replied, *"I'm afraid I think I'd have to get on with them. They'd have to be good musicians. I think they'd be difficult to find. They'd have to be lively."*

Were you a difficult person to get along with? Barrett replied, *"No. Probably my own impatience is the only thing, because it has to be very easy. You can play guitar in your canteen, you know, your hair might be longer, but there's a lot more to playing than traveling around universities and things."*

What about going out and playing acoustic by yourself? Barrett replied, *"Yeah, that's nice. Well, I've only got an electric. I've got a black Fender which needs replacing. I haven't got any blue jeans. I really prefer electric music."*

Asked what records he listens to, Barrett replied, *"Well, I haven't bought a lot. I've got things like Ma Rainey recently. Terrific, really fantastic."*

Will you be writing more blues then? Barrett replied, *"I suppose so. Different groups do different things. One feels that Slade would be an interesting thing to hear, you know."*

Will you be recording a third solo album? Barrett replied, *"Yeah. I've got some songs in the studio, still. And I've got a couple of tapes. It should be 12 singles, and jolly good singles. I think I shall be able to produce this one myself. I think it was always easier to do that."*

April 1971 - Beat Instrumental (U.K.) published an article about Pink Floyd. They wrote, "As a band, Pink Floyd have always proved difficult to define. One of the few surviving forces from the Flowerpower period of our youth, Floyd have always managed to remain all things to all men. They made a hit single in 1967 called 'Arnold Layne.' They had the first professional light show seen in this country. They were the creators of a UFO-preoccupied science fiction music that rapidly became the center of a growing cult.

In the less-than-balmy days since that halcyon age, Floyd have done a singular thing. They survived. More than that, they succeeded in producing, at discreet intervals, several important progressions from their original, more lighthearted, sound. The first of these was 'Saucerful Of Secrets,' which can be considered as a direct polishing of the earlier, spookier Syd Barrett sound. Barrett's influence waned, he left, and 'Saucerful' was the second-generation Floyd's first venture onto record. So successful was it, and so much did it mould their act, that up until 1970 they were still staging one of the album's strongest numbers, 'Set the Controls for the Heart of the Sun.' This piece also survived onto their consolidation album, Ummagumma. There was an older survivor on Ummagumma as well, 'Astronomy Domine' from the first Pink Floyd LP. The second side of this record, however, contained a few tentative Floyd steps in a further, as yet unseen, direction.

Enter 'Atom Heart Mother.' Floyd first produced this lengthy and much-praised piece at the Bath Festival, later taking it on tour to America and around England. 'Atom Heart Mother' is an event for four-piece psychedelic band, brass orchestra, and 40-piece mixed voice choir. When Pink Floyd took this around California, there were 40-foot billboards along Sunset Boulevard bearing the well-known cow. On stage, in addition to the above ensemble, Pink Floyd made use of their own well-tried instruments, plus the Azimuth Co-ordinator device. This, drummer Nick Mason describes as "a sort of quadraphonic pan-pot." The 'Atom Heart Mother' tour of the U.S. was in full quadraphonic sound, and American audiences were suitably fascinated by the eerie effect of sound swooping round the auditorium. Floyd lost money on that tour, as in most other on-the-road projects they have done in recent months. In, England it set them back £2,000 every time they did a show. In America, the cost must have been excruciating.

"This year we've achieved a certain financial independence," said Nick Mason.

"The band still doesn't make money, but we're not fighting to pay back debts." When was this point of financial independence reached? Mason replied, *"Some time last year, I think. I don't really know what caused us to get suddenly solvent, but for years previously we'd been paying off enormous debts. All our royalties and everything else just being used to pay off running costs. At least our royalties cover us now."*

Mason feels that the 'Atom Heart Mother' album, released to coincide with the tour, was another time job. The B-side, containing 'Alan's Psychedelic Breakfast,' was *"definitely rushed,"* and even the cover track was not what it could have been, in his opinion. He added that he doesn't think it would have made much difference to the overall effect, saying, *"I don't feel that there is a definite course of progress in our music. People see continuations and progressions, obviously, but it's not apparent to us. We get an idea for something and we try to do it."*

There has been much talk of a new, Super-Floyd extravaganza. The word downtown was that the group would shortly tackle a ballet representation of Proust's 'Remembrances Of Things Past.' As the title indicates, this monumental, 12-volume novel is a long, dreamy ramble, and very difficult indeed to reduce to concrete form. How were tile Floyd coping with this ambitious task? *"Proust,"* said Mason, and quoting bassist David Gilmour, *"has been knocked on the head. Marcel has indeed been given the ballet, and director Roland Petit has now got 'A Thousand And One Nights' as a working title, which might prove equally difficult to handle. Originally he was going to do a complete program, a piece by Zinakist, a piece by us, and a new production of Carmen. I think he has now decided to do just two pieces, Zinakist's, and ours, which has meant doubling the length of the thing we are going to do."*

It's not the first time that Pink Floyd have had a hand in somewhat esoteric production. They also did the film score for Antonioni's 'Zabriskie Point.' And now they have plans of their own for a new all Floyd idea, to be staged in theater form, locale as yet unknown. Mason said, *"Hopefully, it'll be something that settles in one place for one time, the idea being that we choose what we*

want to do, music, films, video, theatre, mime, or dance, and then do it. We've been trying to do something like this for years, but we've only just achieved the financial independence necessary."*

The germing of this particular seed has lifted Pink Floyd out of a slough of despond in which they have found themselves wallowing ever since the close of the 'Atom Heart Mother' tour, and possibly before that. Mason said, *"Until very recently we were in acute danger of dying of boredom."* Some months ago Roger Waters was interviewed by Melody Maker. They, in their wisdom, headlined the feature, 'Troubled Waters.' *"But,"* continued Mason, *"this depression has lifted a bit because we have finally got a very rough basis for this new project."*

Meanwhile, inactivity saps initiative. Mason said, *"Our thing now is to press on as fast as possible. At the moment we are doing a few odd gigs. Roger really feels that we shouldn't be working at all, but it is a great release to play the drums once in a while, all the same. What we must do is get ourselves together in every sense of the word, because we've always previously had a scene where people are telling you 'do this,' or 'do that,' or 'you ought to go out on the road and promote the album,' and all the time you're desperately trying to stop and take stock."*

The Floyd have already started a new album. At least, they have *"gone into the studio and put down some ideas, something we've never been able to do before."* They intend to record in quadraphonic, and should be one of the first bands to do so in this country, although quad records are to be with us soon. EMI are bringing in quadraphonic equipment to Abbey Road when the music is ready, and Pink Floyd are also having a special quad mixer built for their own onstage use *"in an attempt to get a better quality of sound."* They already have the Azimuth Co-ordinator, and Nick has a Putney VCS3 synthesizer in his studio-workroom. Although not integrated yet, it seems like a predictable step for them to take.

Apart from their own obscure imagery, Pink Floyd have managed to stay apolitical, using the unworldly character of their music to preserve this carefully chosen distance. No "message" lurks in the Floyd's music. Mason said, *"Messages are too* specified and they become a drag, like preaching. I think one of the worst possible beliefs is that pop stars know more about life than anyone else."

"The thing to do is to really move people," said Mason, speaking of the legendary Floyd stage-acts, "to turn them on, to subject them to a fantastic experience, to do something to stretch their imagination." But the music can, after all, do that unaided? "Yes," said Mason, "but we can back it up."

April 10, 1971 - Disc and Music Echo (U.K.) published an article titled, "Pink Floyd Do Nothing" by Caroline Boucher. The article stated that Pink Floyd are now able to do what they like, and featured an interview with David Gilmour at his house in Essex.

Gilmour explained, "Basically, we're the laziest group ever. Other groups would be quite horrified if they saw how we really waste our recording time. We did a whole lot in the studio in January. And we've got twenty-four things down in all, under the working title, 'Nothing-Parts One to Twenty-Four.' We might call the album 'Return of the Son of Nothing,' but then we never know what an album will be called or what it will sound like right up until the finish."

Gilmour continued, "'Atom Heart Mother' wasn't conceived for brass and choir. It started off as a theme for a western with the chord sequence. Nor was it called 'Atom Heart Mother' until we did it for the John Peel program and had to hurriedly think of something to call it, so we got out an evening paper and there was a story about a woman having a baby who had this thing put in her heart."

Asked about live performances of 'Atom Heart Mother,' Gilmour explained "We've performed it about thirteen times now live, and I don't think we'll be doing it much more in England. We don't want it to become a millstone round our necks. It's funny. Leonard Bernstein came to one of our American concerts and he was bored stiff by 'Atom Heart Mother,' but he liked the rest."

Gilmour then talked about performing old audience favorites, saying, "Rick practically refuses to play some things on stage. 'Astronomy Domine' I don't mind because it gets me off. It's like loud rock and

roll to me. But some numbers I hate doing. That's one thing we're trying to do with this album, do a lot of new stuff we can do on stage."

For their next album, Pink Floyd want to use household objects to make all the sounds, such as glasses, knives, and a saw, and experiments along these lines have already yielded some impressive results. Tours of the East and Australia are upcoming in July, and Nick Mason's and Rick Wright's wives are expecting babies later this month.

April 24, 1971 - Disc and Music Echo (U.K.) reported that Pink Floyd will release a compilation album at the end of the month, titled, `A Collection of Antiques and Curios.' It will cost £1.15 and will feature the unreleased song, 'Biding My Time.'

Sounds (U.K.) reported that Pink Floyd will perform at "The Garden Party at the Crystal Palace Bowl" on May 15, 1971. They will play for 45 minutes and will perform some new music. Only 15,000 tickets will be sold for the show at £1.25 each.

May 1, 1971 - Sounds (U.K.) published an interview with David Gilmour by Steve Peacock. Asked about new material for their stage show, Gilmour said, "We tend to add the new stuff on to what we already do. So all this means is that we usually play for much longer at each gig. We usually do about two and a half hours now."

Asked about performing 'Atom Heart Mother' without an orchestra, Gilmour explained, "But then, when we recorded it, we orchestrated it, and since then it has been hard to go back to doing it without the orchestra. We still do it on stage, and it sounds good because all the ideas for the orchestration came out of things we were doing anyway. But we certainly do feel the lack of the other instruments."

Gilmour continued, "The problem with the old numbers, and it has been becoming pretty difficult of late to keep on churning out the same old ones, is that each of us enjoys doing one or two of them. But they're not the same ones. So there's a good chance that in each of them, at least one of us will be bored. Actually, it doesn't happen all that much on stage. When we're playing, we all just get

working on music using only household objects, Gilmour was asked if this music would appear on the new album. Gilmour replied, "*I don't think it will be for this album now. We got a lot of stuff down, enough for a whole side I think, but had some disagreement over it and I think the general opinion seems to be that it is not quite right for this LP. We got some jolly good sounds though, and it would be fun to show people what, with a little thought, they could get out of things they've got lying around the house.*"

Asked about taking their time in the studio and refusing to be pressured to release new material, Gilmour replied, "*We don't seem to be very worried about what other people would see as wasting time in the studio. We spent about a month in the studios in January, playing around with various ideas and recording them all. Then we went away to think about them. Now we are letting things take a natural pace. We're refusing to take any pressure on the album. If people ask us about a release date, we just tell them that they can have it when it is ready.*"

Also in this issue is a report that Pink Floyd's performance at Crystal Palace on May 15, 1971, will not be limited to 45 minutes.

May 15, 1971 - Disc and Music Echo (U.K.) reported that Pink Floyd will play for two hours at the Crystal Palace concert on May 15, 1971, and will perform a new 45-minute piece. A new Pink Floyd compilation album, 'Relics,' will be released on May 14, 1971 on the Regal Starline label. It will cost £1.15.

Melody Maker (U.K.) published an article titled, "Another first for the Floyd," that reported that Pink Floyd will headline the first concert to be held at the Crystal Palace in London on May 15, 1971. The band will be performing a new piece at the show.

Richard Wright, who was interviewed in his Bayswater flat the previous week, explained, "*We have nearly finished recording it and it will take up the whole of one side of our next album. At the moment, it's called 'The Return of the Sun of Nothing,' but the title will probably be changed on the album. We went into the studio in January to put down a lot of ideas and called them all bits of nothing, which is where the title came from.*

into it and it's OK. But between gigs, we're all going around saving 'We must get some new numbers.' I'm sure the audiences don't mind hearing the old stuff because, obviously, they don't all see every gig. It's just us.*"

Asked about foregoing performing to work on new material, Gilmour stated, "*I don't think any of us could do without playing live. Roger and Rick think they could more than Nick or I, but I'm not sure that I believe them totally.*"

The band are planning on performing some new material at Crystal Palace on May 15, 1971. Asked about the new material, Gilmour responded, "*You can never hope to describe music. All you can do is make comparisons about the general sound of a group with the general sound of other groups, and the comparisons you've used in the past are still valid. It's Pink Floyd music.*" So is it like the music on previous Pink Floyd albums? Gilmour replied, "*I wouldn't make a comparison.*" What about the mood? Gilmour replied, "*It goes through a lot of moods. It changes a lot. I suppose you could say that it sounds more like the Pink Floyd in general than 'Atom Heart Mother' did.*"

Noting that Pink Floyd have been

It's twenty-two minutes long and it's a piece which we can do live without any of the problems of 'Atom Heart Mother.' We tried it out at a special gig at Norwich University, and it went down well, but that was behind closed doors. Now we will put it on in public for the first time. We are also planning a few other surprises during the act. We are getting quite a lot of money so we are spending it on some extras to add to the act. This is the first major concert we have done in London for some time, and it will probably be the last before next Christmas, at the earliest. We are doing various things abroad during the summer, and there is an American tour lined up for five weeks around the September period."

Asked about reports of Pink Floyd overcharging for concerts, Wright responded, "In the papers, there has been a lot of talk about us charging £2,000 for each concert, but we have gone out recently for as little as £400. If a university can only fit 1,000 in to the concert, then we will only charge £400. Universities have put it around that we charge £1,800, and are frightened to approach us because they think that they won't be able to afford the group. We want to keep tickets down to around the 75p mark, or £1 at the maximum."

Wright continued, "The money we live on comes from record royalties and the gig money is almost all spent on the upkeep of the band. This past twelve months we have just about broken even as far as income from gigs and expenditure on putting them on is concerned. We have a huge amount of equipment to keep up to scratch and have just bought a new mixer for £2,000."

As for playing fewer concerts recently, Wright said, "We went through a stage of depression during the last few months, a sort of stagnation which occurs to everybody. But now we are going ahead again. It's very important for the band to keep together musically and not drift apart."

Commenting on the Crystal Palace as a place to play, Wright enthused, "A venue like this is something we need in London. The Roundhouse is nice, but it's a bit small and I don't like the acoustics. Then there's the old Albert Hall, but that Frank Zappa business was really bad. The Festival Hall is all right but there's a very cold, clinical atmosphere about

it. With most places where there is room for 15,000, most people can neither see nor hear. But from what I hear about Crystal Palace, everyone will be able to see well."

Finally, Wright is asked to comment on their upcoming concert at the Montreux Classical Musical Festival where they will be performing 'Atom Heart Mother' with 40 other musicians. Wright explained, "This is just the kind of thing we like. A lot of people who normally listen to classics will be able to hear us, and a lot of young people will probably be hearing a symphony orchestra for the first time. It will be good for both."

June 1971 - Beat Instrumental (U.K.) published an interview with Syd Barrett. They wrote, "In every great revolution heroes are created who in turn are often killed by the very ideals that they fought for. The "psychedelic revolution" of 1966-67 has been no exception. Some are dead and some are living. Hendrix, Wilson, Joplin and Jones aren't living. Syd Barrett isn't dead. However Barrett isn't quite the person he was in those early days of the underground, when the Pink Floyd were the acid kings of British rock. He now has his hair cropped to 'Love Me Do' length but compromises with a purple satin jacket and stack-heeled boots.

During the interview, Barrett relights each cigarette from the remnants of the previous one and pivots his eyeballs at an incredible speed as he speaks. "I've just left a train and had to pay an awful taxi ride," Barrett said, slowly tipping his ash into an empty coffee cup. "I've come to look for a guitar. I've got a neck in the other room. Quite an exciting morning for me."

Something about him makes you think that this may well be right. His talk is slow and unrevealing. The answer given often bears no relation to the question asked. Particular areas of his life he carefully avoids mentioning. "It was only two years ago," Barrett said of his departure from the Floyd, but as to what happened immediately after, he added, "It's really difficult to relate. There's much more interesting things happening right now. There's quite a sense of freedom in doing it as well."

In these two years, he has returned to his home in Cambridge where he now lives in a cellar. His time is spent listening to records and playing his own music. "*I mainly play the guitar,*" Barrett said. "*It's very comfortable playing and it sometimes gets very interesting. I'm writing songs with it as well. You can play it all day, though, and you're not really saying much.*"

His opinions of life back at home seem to vary during the interview. "*Cambridge is very much a place to get adjusted to,*" Barrett said early on. "*I've found it difficult. It was fairly unusual to go back because it's the home place where I used to live, and it was pretty boring so I cut my hair.*" Later on his feelings change. "*It's quite fun,*" Barrett smiled. "*It's a nice place to live really, under the ground.*"

Barrett, like Stones Richard & Watts, Lennon, Ray Davies, Townshend, Clapton, Page and Beck, is an art school product. His songs, like paintings, are used essentially to convey a mood. Throughout the interview he speaks of "relating to a mood" when referring to his work. His recorded work possesses a lazy quality, an almost dreamlike state of consciousness. 'Dominoes,' on his second album, is a beautiful portrayal of meaninglessness and alienation, which is sung in a voice sounding aptly weary of life. 'You and I in place/wasting time on dominoes/a day so dark, so warm/life that comes and goes on. You and I and dominoes/time goes by.' Other tracks convey lightheartedness as on 'Effervescing Elephant,', bounce as on 'Gigolo Aunt,', chaos as on 'Rats,' last year's love as on 'Wined And Dined,' and fear as on 'Wolfpack.'

His first album, 'The Madcap Laughs,' is of a similar quality although he himself disagrees. "*They've got to reach a certain standard,*" Barrett said of the albums, "*and that's probably reached in 'Madcap' once or twice, and on the other one only a little, just an echo of that. Neither of them are much more than that.*"

Barrett was always more of a writer of songs than the electronic extravaganzas that the Floyd have become known for. Think back to 'Piper At The Gates Of Dawn' and you'll remember that Syd was in there singing about Lucifer Sam and mice called Gerald. It is possible people still expect Barrett to produce work in the Floydian mould and are slightly disturbed to hear this slightly stoned voice

singing very often with only an acoustic guitar. "*It puts people off their guard,*" Barrett said. "*I think that people miss the fact that it's obviously a gentler thing because it's clever and it's into that more than content. The message might be a bit lost because people find it hard to grasp.*"

Present plans for Syd include a new album and a new single. Also there is a possibility that he'll get a band around him and do some gigs. "*It'd be a groove wouldn't it,*" Barrett smiled as he mentioned the idea. "*I'm still in love with being a pop star really. As a job, it's very interesting but very difficult. You can be pure enough to talk about it where you can actually adapt to the grammar of the job. It's exciting. You channel everything into one thing and it becomes the art. I don't really know if pop is an art form. I should think as much as sitting down is.*"

August 14, 1971 - Sounds (U.K.) published an article that offered a comparative analysis of the Pink Floyd with Syd Barrett with the latter day Pink Floyd, concluding that they are always excellent. An equipment list was also published.

September 1971 - Phonograph Record Magazine (U.S.) reviewed the two Syd Barrett solo albums, `The Madcap Laughs' and `Barrett,' with an article titled, "Madcap Laughs" by Bobby Abrams.

`The Madcap Laughs' is "a body of love songs to make even Elizabeth Barrett Browning jealous." The song `Terrapin' leaves Abrams speechless, `No Good Trying' is "every great rock jam contained in three minutes," `Here I Go' is "so commercial Elton John could successfully record it," `Octopus' is "a Dave Mason tune left off the Mr. Fantasy album," `Feel' is the "never written Bob Dylan song," and `If It's In You' is "possibly the best cut on an album in the last year." `The Madcap Laughs' is "everything promised, everything delivered and more still."

The album `Barrett' is "so eclectic it has something for everybody and a little more too." `Baby Lemonade' recalls `I Want Candy' by the Strangeloves, `It is Obvious' is "the song Ray Davies forgot to write for Something Else," `Dominoes' is "Happy Together with an English accent," `Love Song' "could've been the theme song from Love Story," `Wined and Dined' recalls Traffic, and `Effervescing Elephant' is Abrams' favorite song on the album and is "an updated version of that childhood ditty `The Elephants on Parade.'"

October 9, 1971 - Melody Maker (U.K.) published an article titled, "Deep Waters" by Chris Welch that featured an interview with Roger Waters. Waters began, "*I work to keep my mind off a doomy situation. All over the globe, it gets crazier every day. And the craziness seems to be accelerating at a fantastic rate. But it might just be that, as you get older, your perception gets faster, until the whole thing seems unreal, as I leaf through my Guardian each morning. It's running a series at the moment on the new taboos. I read the piece on Lord Longford, which seemed quite a laugh. One gets the impression everything has got completely out of control and nobody is in control of anything. There's so much going on it's hard to evaluate anything specific. That whole festival of light business. It's hard to evaluate how important it is. From my personal standpoint, it is of very little importance. But you can't tell its effect on other people. They are trying to 'clean up the country.' But the whole thing is pathetic. So many more important things need doing. Well, it's all been said. But why get worried about the odd pubic hair on TV and the growth of dirty bookshops when they could put their energies into something that clearly needs reforming? And a job here and there would be nice. The whole tenor of their movement is repression, on the basis that people are corruptible and need protecting, which I don't believe. A lot more harm is done through repressing people's sexual attitudes than by public displays of pornography.*"

Waters continued, "*We actually went to a live show in Denmark which was extraordinary. It went on too long, and certainly long before the end we were ready for hamburgers and chips. Let's go now. It was all very schoolboyish and patently obvious it was for people who didn't have the right schooldays. The shows are just a tourist thing, anyway. I can't imagine the Danes going. It's only for old geezers of about fifty. It's all unreal.*"

Asked about what he would do for a

better world, Waters replied, "*Well, I'd like to help the revolution when it comes. It would be nice if somebody could visualize the revolution so we could have a slight idea of what to do.*"

Asked about existing revolutionary theories, Waters replied, "*The trouble is, they all smell a bit. I'd sooner live here than in Russia and I'm not really into Soviet Marxism. The double bind is that the people who tend to involve themselves in politics do it for strong personal motives. Some have a social context, but very largely it's an ego thing and the people who should be running the country are just pottering about in their gardens and reading the Guardian. Altruism and power politics just don't go together.*"

Asked what Pink Floyd have been doing lately, Waters answered, "*We've been rehearsing a John Peel show and recording. We go to America this week for our fifth tour, and we'll be gone five weeks. We'll be playing Carnegie Hall. The first time we went, in 1967, we played the Scene Club in New York. We've got three new pieces and much stuff as before. We've just started to rehearse again. I can't remember the last time we had a rehearsal. I think that often the cause of groups splitting up is when people freak and can't come up with new stuff, which has nearly happened to us. The Who flipped once and did that New Vic thing, which fell through. But no, we're very healthy now.*"

Waters continued, "*We'd like to get into a theater thing. We'll do it sometime, but I can't see it happening yet. It's really back to the old mixed media trip. The logistics of it are so complex. You have to get the quadraphonics and projectors together, and you need a clear vision, rather than a vague idea, that it would be nice to do something different. Creating something like that would be bloody hard.*"

About moving large amounts of equipment, Waters said, "*We're trying to cut it down. In January, we'll be doing a whole tour of England, about twelve days, and we may do the Festival Hall, London, again.*"

Asked about the future of Pink Floyd, Waters answered, "*I dunno, really. I have no idea what is going to happen next. We're just going to be much lighter and more efficient.*"

Sounds (U.K.) reported that Pink Floyd will

be touring Britain in the coming year, and will be performing songs from their upcoming album, 'Meddle,' to be released on November 5, 1971. The album's major piece, 'Echoes,' will be previewed on October 17, 1971 at the Roundhouse, London, in quadraphonic sound.

October 1971 - Circus (U.S.) reviewed the Pink Floyd album, 'Relics.' They called it "a greatest hits package." If you want to get into Pink Floyd for the first time, this would be a good album to get.

October 16, 1971 - Melody Maker (U.K.) reported that the Pink Floyd concert at the Birmingham Town Hall on Monday, October 11, 1971, was planned to be a warm-up for the American tour, but the new equipment they were expecting to use failed to arrive. The set started 25 minutes late, and there were long gaps between numbers. The show began with 'Careful With That Axe, Eugene,' and the rest of first set featured songs from 'Atom Heart Mother.' Quadraphonic sound was used to good effect. They previewed songs from their upcoming album, 'Meddle,' in the second set, including 'Echoes' and 'One of These Days,' which both used the same wind effects. They also performed 'Set the Controls for the Heart of the Sun' and 'Saucerful of Secrets,' before ending with an impromptu blues number.

November 5, 1971 - The Augur, Eugene, Oregon (U.S.) reported on the Pink Floyd concert at the National Guard Armory in Eugene, Oregon on October 19, 1971. Tickets were $3 at the door and the show was put on by Evergreen Productions. "Floyd was slow, cluttered, mechanical." But as the reviewer closed his eyes, the music began to open up and they "put together their collective energies to create the magic ethereal substance of music." "Floyd gave nothing but what they are . . ., thanks to Pink Floyd for sharing their beauty."

November 13, 1971 - Melody Maker (U.K.) reviewed the Pink Floyd album, 'Meddle,' with an article titled, "Pink's muddled Meddle" by Michael Watts. The Pink Floyd are so much sound and fury, signifying nothing. They have created a space rock sound, combining electronic effects with standard

musical instrumentation. The music doesn't stand up as anything more than competent rhythmic rock and the electronics are not as adventurous as they may seem on first listening. 'Meddle' shows all their faults, as well as their successful points. Side one is comprised of songs, with drippy vocals and old-hat instrumental workouts. The song, 'One of These Days,' is a throwback to the Ventures' 'Telstar.' Side two of the album is the song, 'Echoes,' which is a series of effects without any underlying depth. It is like listening to background noises in a Radio Three play.

New Musical Express (U.K.) reviewed the Pink Floyd album, 'Meddle,' with an article titled, "Pink Floyd 'meddle' to good effect." The Pink Floyd have produced another brilliant album. Side one is three themes, linked together by wind. 'Echoes' is "a zenith." "An exceptionally good album."

Also in this issue is the NME Top 30 album chart, where the Pink Floyd album, 'Meddle,' has entered the chart for the first time at #17. Also on the chart for the first time is the Family album, 'Fearless,' at #19, and the Hawkwind album, 'In Search of Space,' at #26.

Record Mirror (U.K.) reviewed the Pink Floyd album, 'Meddle.' "Marvelous." "Typically professional use of studio effects, and excellent musicianship." 'Fearless' is superb. 'Echoes' is an "expertly devised musical life cycle." "Their best album yet."

Sounds (U.K.) reviewed the Pink Floyd album, 'Meddle.' Side one is full of "surprises." Side two, the song 'Echoes,' is "one of the most complete pieces of Pink Floyd music they've done." "A very relaxed, very complete album."

December 11, 1971 - Disc and Music Echo (U.K.) reported that Pink Floyd will be going on the road again, performing their first British concerts in two and a half years. Promoter Peter Bower said, "*It'll be a remarkable tour. They have some new material ready, as well as familiar recordings. They'll have their own lighting with them, too, portable columns and pneumatic gear, operated by Arthur Max, from America's Fillmore. There'll also be quadraphonic sound.*"

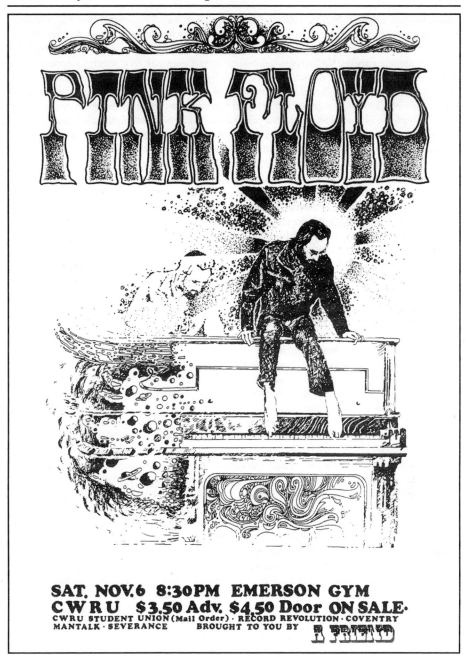

Also in this issue was a report on the Pink Floyd concert at Carnegie Hall, New York on November 15, 1971. The sold out audience of 2,900 people witnessed a show of almost three hours. Commenting about their music and the differences between concerts in the U.S. and the U.K., David Gilmour said, "*We're really making emotional music. I wouldn't say it's intellectual. In England it's different. We can do anything we like, really. We've often gone onstage and done material that we've never done before and the audiences are used to us and they love it. But in the States, it's more or less like we have to play our hits.*" At the concert, the crowd yelled for Pink Floyd to play, 'Astronomy Domine' and 'See Emily

Play,' to which Roger Waters replied, *"You must be joking!"*

New Musical Express (U.K.) reported that Pink Floyd's upcoming British tour will include 13 dates, with performances in London and other major cities. The shows will feature new material, quadraphonic sound, and lighting specialist, Arthur Max, who used to do the lights at the Fillmore East in New York.

Sounds (U.K.) reported that Pink Floyd will be doing a new concert tour of Britain that will feature "an entirely new program." The tour will begin at The Dome, Brighton on January 20, 1972. Asked if they will be performing in London, Steve O'Rourke stated, *"It's pretty sure. We are just working on a London venue now."* Their set will consist of songs from 'Meddle' plus new material, and will be the debut of the bands new PA and quadraphonic sound system in Britain.

December 20, 1971 - Rock published an interview with the members of Pink Floyd. Although all four members of the band were at the interview, the responses were listed as just from 'Pink Floyd.'

The first album had songs with mad humor and social satire, but by the time of 'Saucerful of Secrets,' a space metaphor of mystical, psychic, and spiritual themes took over. Why was there this change? Pink Floyd replied, *"Just a transfer of focus when Syd left. We never consciously set out to do that. Let's get cosmic, and all that."* But the space exploration metaphor fits your music. Pink Floyd replied, *"It's nothing intellectual, really. All it is, is a manifestation of us responding to the sounds we make, much in the same way that you would. We just set out to make a piece of music, right? 'Saucerful of Secrets' was written first, then we came up with a title. We don't plan it out."*

What about the song 'Astronomy Domine?' Pink Floyd replied, *"That's Syd's song."* But the version on 'Ummagumma' doesn't have that much to do with Syd. Pink Floyd replied, *"Well, we all were very much into science fiction. It gave us materials for songs, good subjects."*

'Ummagumma' seems to be about a different consciousness, an alien state. Pink

Floyd replied, *"We never thought of it that way. You don't have to write a song called 'kill the pigs' to have something to do with people. Of course, there are great depths of space in terms of the sound. A lot of it is more abstract, I suppose. Look, there is no fucking sound in space. It doesn't make any noise. The reason everybody has tied our sound in with space is, like, as soon as the echo chamber was thought of, and when they started making science fiction movies, the sound became associated. Actually, the sound is more like caves, large buildings."* But it has nothing to do with whether there is sound in space. Pink Floyd replied, *"What I'm trying to say is that it's because of the equipment that people pick up on those kind of connotations, and that what he said about caves and big cathedrals is much more what it's down to. How about '2001?' The music Kubrick used in that is nothing like one would imagine space music to sound like, but it worked."*

On 'Saucerful' and 'Ummagumma' there is the impression of mind-bending consciousness stretching. Is this connected to psychedelia? Pink Floyd replied, *"No. We never deliberately set out, it was never designed to reach a certain audience or affect them a certain way, just an exploration of our own. No conscious effort to make anything elevating."*

Do you relate to your audience just as entertainers? Pink Floyd replied, *"Yes."* Just as rock performers? Pink Floyd replied, *"We're musicians. We may not call it rock, but we make music just like any other musicians. We play for an audience for two hours, and they're with us for two hours."*

Rock music generally relates to its audience through the use of melodies, in particular scales, song structures, etc., but you have moved away from that. Pink Floyd replied, *"We draw on lots of other things, other kinds of music. I'm into big religious choral works, Berlioz, Te Deum, for instance."*

Is the moving away from song forms a symptom of moving away from rock music? Pink Floyd replied, *"It's a symptom of the fact that we're not good songwriters, or not that prolific. We do the other thing better."* Would you write more songs if you were better at it? Pink Floyd replied, *"If one of us were Bob Dylan, I should think we'd do a lot of Bob*

Dylan songs." But aren't you dissatisfied with the limitations of rock music? Pink Floyd replied, "*No. Not really. I wouldn't say that.*"

In some of your music there is an element of anxiety or terror. Did you do that on purpose? Pink Floyd replied, "*There's a lot of fear about. We're reflecting it.*" But your terror isn't a common variety. Pink Floyd replied, "*Whatever the terror is, it's a very good way of getting through to people.*"

In many of your songs, there is a catharsis, a journey that ends in heightened consciousness after facing perils. Pink Floyd replied, "*That's one way of looking at it.*" There is also great loneliness, and a solitary nature in your musical explorations. Pink Floyd replied, "*There's something to that.*"

What does each member of the band contribute to the quality of Pink Floyd? Or would you rather skip that question? Pink Floyd replied, "*No. No. It's a very good question. No one's ever asked us that before. I think we'd all be very hesitant about describing exactly what each of us . . .*" Well then, how do you compose a song? Pink Floyd replied, "*There are occasions when one imposes his intentions on the others, and other occasions when all work together. It could be someone arrives at the studio with a complete song, all planned out, or else it might be worked out collectively from the germ of an idea.*" How did you compose for 'Ummagumma?' Pink Floyd replied, "*That's easy. We did those in total isolation. At separate times, each of us did our own thing. We played everything ourselves, with minor exceptions. We never even heard what the other three did. But that's something unique, an idea we set ourselves to do. We didn't even consult each other. That was very much a manifestation of where our heads were at the time.*" What about composing songs on other albums? Pink Floyd replied, "*We don't usually do anything. There's no one method or formula. Once we did a thing where we took a piece of tape, and everyone had to record a track on it without hearing what the others had done. We put a count on the beginning, one, two, three, four, and then silence. We planned it as a minute of up-tempo, a minute of slow stuff, and a minute of whatever we wanted. Of course, it sounded terrible.*"

What about 'quadrasonics' and your live sound with a 360-degree sound system? Pink Floyd replied, "*Of course, we'd like to duplicate those effects on records. We've actually done a 4-track mix on 'Echoes,' but that's all up to the record company.*"

What do you think of synthesizers? Pink Floyd replied, "*We're getting into that.*"

Did you enjoy working on the soundtrack for the movie, 'More?' Pink Floyd replied, "*We liked it, although it was an incredible rush job. The guy came in and asked if we could do it right away. After viewing the footage and timing the different scenes, we went into a studio late at night, writing nearly all the material and recording it in six sessions. Just got it done in time. Later, we took some more time out in the studio to do the tracks up a bit for the album.*"

Will you be doing other films? Pink Floyd replied, "*There's a guy named Adrian Maben who's making an hour-long film, ostensibly for television. Just before we came over here, we went to Naples and recorded a whole lot of stuff at the amphitheater which was filmed, also some stuff of us walking around the city, etc. We have about 40 minutes of music, with about 20 minutes to do in December. It'll possibly be sold over here as a short or a second feature.*"

Will you be doing any other classical-oriented projects, like 'Atom Heart Mother?' Pink Floyd replied, "*We have no similar plans at this time.*"

Do you ever regret moving away from the raunchy rock and roll beat in your music? Pink Floyd replied, "*We never really had it. We were never that good at it, actually. Anyway, there are so many people doing that sort of thing.*" As a result, do you relate to your audience differently, or do you find that your audiences differ from a normal rock audience? Pink Floyd replied, "*We don't really know very much about who they are, what they're doing. The general feeling I get is that, on a good gig, they seem to be responding to it very much the same way we are.*" Does the audience's reaction affect you? Pink Floyd replied, "*Yes, the audience reaction affects us, but almost always we strike the first blow. If we are playing well and they dig it, that makes us play all the better.*"

Do you mind that people take you seriously? Pink Floyd replied, "*We don't mind*

1972
Obscured By Clouds

being taken seriously. We take our music seriously, but not sour-faced serious. One can be serious without being intellectual."

Do you read the critics reviews of your music? Pink Floyd replied, "Sometimes. Usually, you know, most of the stuff that's written is shit. There was that very nice man in Stockholm who said how beautiful our music was, when our concert had been fantastically bad. Fucking idiot."

Will you all say your name and add something for posterity? "Nick. It's very hard to think of anything. I would describe our music as sort of jazz-rock." "This is Richard. I would describe our music as cosmic Booker T." "I'm Dave, and I've heard our music described as cosmic reggae." "I'm Roger. I see our music as . . ."

December 25, 1971 - New Musical Express (U.K.) reported that Pink Floyd cancelled their show at the Plymouth ABC Cinema on February 6, 1972, because the hall lacks the necessary licensing cover.

January 1, 1972 - Sounds (U.K.) published an interview with Roger Waters by Steve Peacock. Asked about audience reactions to Pink Floyd, and whether it affects their performances, Waters answered, "Not at all. The only thing that affects the way we do things is what we think about them. It's, in fact, very depressing to do a bad gig and get a good reception, because, obviously, it takes the edge off doing a good gig and getting a good reception. But this is one of the amazing things about rock and roll at the moment, that if you've got a name, it seems that the audiences have been lulled into a frame of mind where they'll clap anything, and applause and encores and everything have become part of the décor almost. But there is a difference. One can tell the difference between an audience that have been really turned on, and one that's just clapping, because that's what you do. On our last tour, I went to the first Jeff Beck concert, and the band on before him were really so dreadful, I mean, they were really

unbearable. They were using Beck's PA and everything, and it really was fantastically loud, really unbelievably, excruciatingly loud. You couldn't hear anything at all. It was Redbone, actually. Quite a large proportion of the audience were clapping. Maybe they really did dig it, but I can't imagine that they did. You can hear things that you personally dislike quite intensely, like Des O'Connor or something, but which you can see that somebody else might enjoy if they enjoy that kind of song, and he does it quite professionally. But this was like being hit over the head with a large lump of wood, again and again and again. It was real boneshaking senselessness. That whole volume thing is just getting completely insane, and that's another thing we've done. I'm happy to say, we've got quieter."

Asked if loud volumes were painful to their ears, Waters replied, "No, not our ears. But everyone's going on about pollution and how ghastly all these industrialists are, pouring effluent into the Rhine, and then they go out on the road and play at these enormous volumes which, well, nobody knows, it's too early to say whether the people who go and sit in the front rows at rock concerts and/or rock musicians are going to be stone deaf in ten years time, or at least have dreadfully impaired hearing. Nobody knows. But lots of doctors have said it's probable, and that, apart from hurting your ears, that kind of volume is very bad for your nervous system, that the body isn't equipped to cope with it. It isn't a hearing thing at those volumes, it's a sensory thing. I was talking to Ron [Geesin] about it last night and he was saying it's like being in the feelies, some rock bands actually shake your body, the volume is so intense. So maybe it's satisfying a lack of sensual experience for people. But I'm 28 now. If by the time I'm 40 I suddenly discover that my hearing's going, or I can't hear, I'd be so sick. And so would everybody else. And they'd turn around and think, 'What was all that about,' especially when there are so many warnings going out through the media all the time. One always thinks, after the latest loud band, that it can't get any louder, but then

Roger Waters

after The Who comes Grand Funk."

Some of these bands say that they intentionally try to damage their audiences. Waters said, *"True. I've never actually seen them, but I've heard lots of reports, and that's a very neurotic situation to be in, isn't it? It's those kind of things that totally belie the idea, and there is this strange idea around that rock and roll is in some way revolutionary, and has some kind of social implications, and somehow, in some strange way, might be pointing to some kind of alternative society. I suppose, though, in terms of some of the good people's lyrics, people like Dylan occasionally have something interesting to say, that might be true."*

Don't some musicians attempt to live what they write? Waters asked, *"Well, who? I mean I can't think of any."* What about John Lennon? Waters replied, *"Yeah, well, Lennon's lifestyle isn't dominated so much by his philosophy, in my opinion, as by his income. 'New York's the only place to live.' That's great if you've got the income to support yourself in New York. But there's such fantastic contrasts. On the one hand there's all this 'Give Peace a Chance' and all his thing with Yoko, the whole peace trip. And then, on the other, he's fighting a major war in all the papers with Paul McCartney. To me, that could show that it's all so much hot air, because that is what's close to home, that's the only conflict any of us can see, that's the only fight he's got, and he's in there like a fucking terrier. And all the other stuff about Viet Nam and whatever is all third person abstractions. It's got fuck all to do with him. There are people you could point to and say they were living an alternative lifestyle, but they ain't in rock and roll. I personally think that, by the nature of rock and roll and by the very nature of getting up on stage and playing an instrument, it seems to me most unlikely that the kind of people who get involved with rock and roll groups and who are successful are likely to be the kinds of people who are selfless enough to really live out some of the things that some rock and roll people say."*

Is that due to being a star, the caste-system? Waters replied, *"It's partly that, but that's a pressure that develops once you've made it. I was really talking more about the kind of personality make-up that you need to have to make it in the first place. You have to want to do it pretty badly to be prepared to put enough energy into it to do it. There are probably lots of people who are very talented musicians or writers or whatever, who never actually become rock and roll stars because they haven't got that kind of egoey drive to get up there on a stage and do it. You've got to really want to be up there on the stage and have people looking at you, otherwise you'd never do it. There's so much stopping you, so much competition involved, you've got to be competitive, and aggressive, and egocentric, all the things that go to make a real star."*

Are the members of Pink Floyd stars to their audiences? Waters replied, *"I don't know, I really don't know. I'd like to think that it was possible to get away from the whole rock and roll adulation kind of thing, and I'd like to feel that it was really simple, straight down the line. They listen to the music, and if they dig it, they come again or buy the records, and if they don't, they don't. But I suspect that it really doesn't work quite like that. And I suspect, in fact we all know, that people are swayed by vogues and by what everyone else is thinking. If a journalist could convince enough people that we were over the top and that we were never any good anyway, and that became a vogue, then I'm sure that we'd have a much harder job showing people that what we were doing was good. It's not insurmountable. I think if you ever do anything really good, it gets through. But I think it is possible to get through with very mediocre stuff if people are digging you. There are people who buy the latest record as soon as it comes out, just because they buy rock and roll records, and they have enormous collections. I'd like to think that we could get away from that a bit. But I think, if anything, it's getting more hysterical and less close to reality."*

Is it hard to decide the next direction you are going to take? Waters replied, *"Yes, it*

is hard, but on the other hand it isn't very hard because there's so much to be done in exploring various techniques, like quadraphonics, which we've only just scratched the surface of. But I wasn't really talking so much about specific musical things, but more in terms of what seems to be happening in the minds of the group, certainly in my mind. There's this realization of the fact that one has, to a large extent, got hooked onto the successful treadmill, you reach a point where you can't bear to turn the gigs down. Maybe it's something to do with age, but I've definitely reached a point now where I'm not young anymore, my life isn't before me still. When I was at school, and all through college and everything, I always looked upon my life as something that was about to start. It would be possible, if you get hooked on the next stage, and then the next stage, to live your whole life not really living it. I'm beginning to feel more and more that it's more and more important to really evaluate, as far as one can with the information available, what's going on, and do the right things, make the right decisions. We've got to step back from that whole career/money thing and make the right decisions, and take as little notice of all those pressures as possible. And I think that would cause us to make better music."

January 1972 - Circus Magazine (U.S.) reviewed the Pink Floyd album, 'Meddle,' saying that it carries on the Floyd tradition. "This is another masterpiece by a masterful group."

January 29, 1972 - Melody Maker (U.K.) reported on the Pink Floyd concert at The Dome, Brighton, England, on January 20, 1972. Although they received a "tumultuous applause," they weren't impressive. Nick Mason's drumming was fresh, but the music lacked "framework and conception." They had problems with the speakers breaking down, and this affected the show.

Sounds (U.K.) published an article titled, "Pink Floyd have gone mental" by Steve Peacock that included two interviews with Roger Waters.

In the first interview, done in December 1971 during rehearsals, Waters was asked about the upcoming tour. Waters replied, *"The old stuff is being phased out, but there are still a couple of them that are still fun to play. The two that spring to mind are 'Set the Controls,' and 'Careful with That Axe.' But the first half, hopefully, won't be a great kind of epic. You know, 'Atom Heart Mother' and 'Echoes' are both kind of odysseys, epic sound poems. I think we're coming down to earth a bit. I hope we are getting a bit less involved with flights of fancy."* As far as the sound levels, Waters added, *"The whole thing is getting completely insane. And that's another thing we've done. I'm happy to say, we've got quieter."*

In the second interview, done after the start of the new Pink Floyd tour, Waters talked about the new show, saying, *"At the first gig, we had a terrible technical disaster during the first half of the set which is 50 minutes long and is one whole new piece, and we couldn't finish it. The tape we were using just wouldn't play on to the end. But I think that's been sorted out now."* About their new piece, Waters explained, *"It is more theatrical than anything we've ever done before, more into the whole theater/circus thing. And in concept, it's more literal, not as abstract as the things we've done before. It's more mental. We've gone mental."*

February 5, 1972 - Disc and Music Echo (U.K.) published an article titled, "Mr. Wright" by Caroline Boucher that featured an interview with Richard Wright at his house in Notting Hill Gate.

Wright said, *"Contrary to what a lot of people might think, as you get bigger, so the pressures get bigger, because the more you do, the more you have to think about what you're going to do next. If you're a band that plays basically blues, all you have to do is develop your technique and develop along known lines. Whereas, we're completely in the dark, and we're forever searching for what we're going to do."*

Talking about the new tour, Wright said, *"It has brought us down quite a lot having to play some numbers which we've done for so many years. Often you can sense it in the audience, 'Oh, we've heard these numbers too many times,' so we had to change the act for our own good. Obviously, we do some of the*

old numbers because some of them we enjoy doing, like 'Careful With That Axe, Eugene,' because it can be different each time. There's not much else I like playing, 'Saucerful of Secrets,' perhaps."*

As for inspiration, Wright explained, *"We did get into a lazy period. There was a point when we sat about not knowing what to do. That was before and during 'Atom Heart Mother.' After that, we wondered what to do. Then 'Meddle' came, and since then we've been quite excited about what we've been doing."*

The song 'Echoes' was developed out of 30 pieces of music that they either wrote or brought in to the studio. Wright stated, *"I think our best music comes from that method of working because, in a studio, everyone is throwing in ideas and rejecting ideas. Saucer was done in the same way."*

Songs like 'Careful With That Axe Eugene' show a viscous streak in the band. Wright commented, *"But there is this schizophrenic half to the group, definitely a sort of macabre relish of titles like that."*

Last autumn, the band made a film in 35mm with a director in Paris, that shows them playing live in an amphitheater in Pompeii, with additional scenes of sulfur mines, Magritte paintings, and shots of Paris, France. They have also done the soundtrack for the film, 'More.' Wright explained, *"We'd like to sit down and make a film ourselves, too, instead of someone coming to us and asking us to use our music for their film."*

They are currently working on music for a ballet again, and Wright added, *"But we're having six weeks holiday this year. We've decided that it is imperative because, as it is, one just lives and thinks Pink Floyd the whole time. It's ridiculous."*

February 12, 1972 - New Musical Express (U.K.) published an article titled, "Things just somehow happen to us – we don't plan" by Tony Stewart that featured part one of an interview with Nick Mason.

Asked about the development of Pink Floyd, Mason said, *"I don't think that there's some important pattern that relates, but obviously you can draw patterns with the music and our development. I don't think it's very important, though. The future is much* more important than getting bogged down in what's happened. In fact, there is a real danger in getting stuck in the 'Golden Oldies' routine of old numbers and old attitudes."

Asked about the bands policy when they first started, Mason replied, "We had absolutely no policy, whatsoever, and we don't really have one now, apart for the old age thing of not doing other peoples material. Obviously, our own interests us more. But in the early days we had very little idea of what we were doing, or really how to do it. The sort of lucky break, though it's not a lucky break at all, that got us off the ground was the fact that Syd Barrett wrote songs. But we could have spent years playing old Stones albums, and Bo Diddley tunes, and anything else. And we wouldn't have achieved anything. The fact that Syd was a songwriter changed the whole thing." Reminded of the fact that they had a light show, Mason added, "Yes, at a slightly later stage."

Many believed that Pink Floyd represented a new art movement in London. Mason replied, "Yes, that's true. It has a lot to do with the media. The press, at the time, had discovered the Underground, and we were the sort of house band of the Underground, because of UFO and the Gardens and so on. It was the beginning of talk about mixed media events, music and light shows, and we happened to have a light show. It just somehow happened in the same way that everything somehow happened. I mean, there was no direction, policy, planning, or anything. Things just happened. The light show was due to various influences, like someone coming over from the States, heard the band, and liked it, and had got a projector and knew how to make a water slide up, and did so. Like the gig at Essex University where someone had built a flashing light system, and controlled and showed a film at the same time. Like some work at Hornsey College of Art, where they were into a much more serious mixed media thing of light and sound workshop with special projectors and special equipment. We never really got into that in the same way that they did. They were taking it seriously, and we were far too busy being a rock and roll band who were getting some success."

Asked whether the light show was an essential part of the act, Mason said, "Well, it

became a very essential part of us. It represented Pink Floyd and an attitude in life." Did the music eventually become linked to the light show? Mason replied, "Well, not really, because at the beginning there was the music, with a few people flashing light over it. But the lights were insignificant because no one had got into powerful bulbs and so on. When the idea got taken along further, it was slightly more balanced. And then it would fluctuate wildly between a smaller place where there was a high intensity of light, and a good balance between light and sound. Otherwise it can just be sort of murky, inky, darkness."

Asked how important Syd Barrett was, Mason stated, "Very important. I mean he wrote everything. Everything except a couple of numbers."

Did you want to release 'Arnold Layne' as a single? Mason replied, "It's very hard to describe the complete open madness of us at that time. We just had no idea what was going on at all, really. We knew we wanted to be rock and roll stars. We wanted to make singles. So we thought 'Arnold Layne' was a great single. After the 'Emily' single, when Syd had left that, we hadn't a good follow up. We were being asked to produce a new single by our label, but we couldn't find anything suitable. By the time we'd done 'Saucer,' we realized that we couldn't write singles, and our interest switched much more to long tracks and more elaborate pieces." Is that why you did electronic things like 'Interstellar Overdrive' and 'Echoes?' Mason replied, "Yes, perhaps that is a part of it, part of us. But I mean, there is also the songwriting part of us. I don't know what to add to that. OK. So this is really what I mean about history. OK, you can look back and say, mmmmm, yes, there's a pattern there, long track, 'Interstellar,' a sort of number that seems a bit constructed, but 'Interstellar' is the least constructive of the pieces."

When Syd left, did it put a strain on the songwriting aspect of the band? Mason replied, "Yeah. Everyone was umm, well, we weren't really frightened because I think we'd agreed that we thought we could manage, you know, do something. But it precipitated the sort of next stage that might not have happened if Syd had stayed."

The band dropped the light show and concentrated on performing after Syd left. Was this the next stage? Mason replied, *"Yes, it was. The light show had stagnated by then. We hadn't got any new equipment. We didn't want any new equipment. It was becoming such a circus, anyway, with the amount of audio equipment. This is interesting, in terms of what we're doing now, because on the British tour, we're using lights. It won't be the same sort of light show, but we've just bought our own complete lighting set up. And it's six times as strong as our original effort."*

Although you said you originally wanted to be rock and roll stars, you began composing films soundtracks with emotion. Mason replied, *"Yes. You used the term rock and roll star a bit loosely. In the early days, that was our goal. Our goal was to be on Top of the Pops. We wanted to be stars, the whole lot, fantastic."*

In 1969 you began linking sounds with the music. How important was this? Mason replied, *"I think the most important thing was the move towards concert appearances, of taking the whole evening and creating some sort of awareness. It's much better to take a concert hall, get the audience comfortable, and, hopefully, the sound system right. And do it all properly, with nothing to break the mood, with no other bands different sort of things. I think the best nights are when there's a huge feeling of togetherness, and not one of the audience looking at the stars, although there are personalities involved. The occasion can become wonderful. And when those four wonderful lads on stage have done it, the audience become involved in helping them make it good. I felt that very strongly on a gig we did at the Albert Hall about two and a half years ago, and it all felt like a wonderful occasion."*

1970 was a stagnant year for you, when you did Atom Heart Mother. Mason said, *"Yes, well, 'Atom Heart Mother' was a specific exercise. I don't think it was a stagnant period, really. I think it was very well worth doing. It wasn't entirely successful, but I think some people were frightened we were going to stick with a choir and orchestra."* The exercise was what? Mason replied, *"Just to work with it, and try."* Was this another phase? Mason replied, *"Yes. It was just something that seemed like a good idea at the time."*

'Atom Heart Mother' was the first album with one song on a whole side. Was this a conscious effort? Mason replied, *"We didn't consciously set off to do it, but it became apparent that we'd need at least a side to get it all down. You have, to some extent, to work in album terms, which means that a piece can't be longer than forty minutes. Maximum unbroken length is about 23 minutes, or whatever."* Do you feel that it was a success? Mason replied, *"Well, we'd all like to do it again. We'd all like to re-record it. It wasn't entirely successful. But it was extremely educational."*

This interview was continued in the February 19, 1972 issue of New Musical Express.

February 19, 1972 - New Musical Express (U.K.) published an article titled, "Floyd – Simple but not Banal" by Tony Stewart that featured part two of an interview with Nick Mason. Asked how their equipment developed, Mason explained, *"The same way as with everything else, by a gradual process of acquiring an enormous quantity of gear. One is desperate to have good sounds, like most bands. In the first place, it became a matter of getting enough equipment to be able to drive everything, but not to its limit. It's almost impossible to describe how it came about, because it's a process of an increasing interest in the sound that's put out, coupled with an increasing awareness of how to achieve it. Today, there's nothing really new in the system. It's basically a mixing desk, which is taken out into the hall so that it gets a true balance. At the moment the thing is to try and make the whole system extremely compact and versatile, so that organ, guitar, vocals, or drums, or anything, can be put through the system and everything goes out via the mixing desk and can be switched through quadraphonic or stereo or double track. It's enormously expensive and time consuming to get involved in it. The Who have been heavily involved in mixing and finding methods of mixing. They started ahead of us and they're still struggling. I know they were having their deck built by the same people who did ours, but it's difficult, and they've got a much bigger problem than we have because they've got a much more powerful sound to organize. If bands of that caliber get hung up, then it's obviously quite difficult."*

While 'Atom Heart Mother' was an exercise, 'Echoes' is very similar. Mason replied, *"Yes, I think there are similarities between 'Atom Heart Mother' and 'Meddle.' I don't think we could have done 'Meddle' without doing 'Atom Heart Mother.'"* Isn't the construction of the two pieces very similar? Mason answered, *"You're obviously right about the construction. There are various things that have a Pink Floyd flavor, but are also very dangerous Pink Floyd clichés. One is the possible tendency to get stuck into a sort of slow four tempo. And the other thing is to take a melody line, or the chorus, or something, and flog it to death. Maybe we'll play it once slow and quiet, the next time a bit harder, third time really heavy, which tends to come a little bit into 'Meddle' and in 'Atom Heart Mother.' But it's slightly more forgivable with the choir and orchestra because it's nice building an orchestra and bringing in extra brass and playing more complex lines. There are various sections on 'Atom Heart Mother' that I'm very happy with. I love the choir section, both the singing and the spoken choir section. The constructing of 'Echoes' is rather similar in terms of it running through various movements. But the movements are so different that I don't feel that we've had to milk 'Atom Heart Mother' to produce 'Echoes.'"*

Asked how much they discuss during the creative process, Mason replied, *"Lots. We do more talk than anything else, really."* How did you compose 'Echoes?' Mason replied, *"Well, 'Echoes' was a specific attempt to sort of do something by a slightly different method. What we did, in fact, was book a studio for January, and throughout January we went in and played. Anytime that anyone had any sort of rough idea of something, we would put it down. At the end of January, we listened back and we'd got 36 different bits and pieces that sometimes cross related and sometimes didn't. 'Echoes' was made up from that."*

How does the band get involved if, for example, David Gilmour writes a song? Mason replied, *"Well, it depends very much. We'd have to talk about each piece specifically. Dave maybe comes in with song A, which he's recorded already at home. He's got guitar, possible drums, and vocals on it. In the case of 'San Tropez,' Roger came in and the song was* absolutely complete. There was almost no arranging to do on it. It was just a matter of learning the chords. On other songs the thing is pretty loose. We may have a bass line, and a rough idea for the chorus, and not for the middle eight."*

Asked whether the band asked David Gilmour to join for his writing ability, Mason replied, *"No. Dave Gilmour was brought in because we knew he could sing and we knew he could play the guitar, which was what we badly needed. We also thought he was someone we could get on with. It's probably more important to get people you can get on with than it is to get good musicians. That's certainly true of us. I think the reason we're still running is because, after a fashion, we can all live together."*

Asked whether the simplicity in Pink Floyd's music is a strong point, Mason answered, *"Yeah, there's nothing very elaborate there. There's no wonder whiz kid electrician on any of our equipment, no Stockhausen. There obviously is a simplicity, but it's not banal. It's very hard to try and talk about the music and say 'right, that's jolly good,' because obviously I think it's extremely good. That's what I'm doing, that's what I'm interested in. There's a lot of reasons why I think what we do is better than what other people do. I mean, otherwise, we'd probably be copying."*

Do your older songs, like 'Set the Controls' and 'Careful With That Axe, Eugene' develop as you continue performing them? Mason replied, *"Yes, but I think they're old now. They are likely to trap us in a morass of old numbers. Audiences are a bit divided between getting bored with old numbers and reliving their childhood, or reliving their 'Golden Era of Psychedelia,' or even wanting to hear what it was all about. These are OK reasons for wanting to hear something, but they ain't very valid for us."*

Are you happy with the music Pink Floyd is currently playing? Mason replied, *"Well, I'm not in a state of depression about it, which can happen. At the moment we are writing some great new stuff. Yes, I'm happy."*

Asked whether there have been any pressures on the band that may have affected the music, Mason replied, *"In terms of working too hard, yes. It's very difficult to find the right* way of working, anyway. We don't know whether to give ourselves lots and lots of free time, or to put on a lot of pressure, specifically for new material, or something like that. This seems to work and has done in the past, but it's a much less pleasant method of working."

Why hasn't the band written any songs recently with concerts in mind? Mason replied, "We've only once composed specifically for live appearances. The album is usually a sort of pressure thing, which is why things are built up in album form." Only one album has been released in a year. Mason said, "Yeah, we'd love to issue more if we could possibly write more, and record it, and do everything else. But we haven't been able to."

Why don't you do more tours of England? Mason replied, "The reason for that is a lot to do with knocking off new material, or being embarrassed of standing on a stage for the fourth year running, and playing 'Set the Controls,' 'Careful With That Axe,' 'Saucerful of Secrets,' etc., etc. I don't like it. I like it occasionally, but not enough to do a British tour with it."

Asked about the ballet they have been asked to compose, Mason explained, "We haven't started work on it yet. We've had innumerable discussions, a number of lunches, a number of dinners, very high powered meetings, and I think we've got the sort of story line for it. The idea is Roland Petit's, and I think Roland is settled on the ideas he wants to use for the thing, so I think we're going to get started. Ballet is a little like film, actually. The more information you have to start with, the easier it becomes to write. The difficulty about doing albums is that you are so totally open, it's very difficult to get started."

Has the fact that Pink Floyd can play anywhere they want in the world, except perhaps America, put too much responsibility on the band? Mason replied, "Obviously, it's a great position to be in. I don't think it puts a great responsibility on the band. There's nothing magical about the position, really. It has to be seen in terms of agencies and managers and promoters. In America, for instance, we've still got a lot of work to do. There's still very few bands who can command any price. Any other place in the world, we can ask our price, but only every so often. You have to decide how you want to use the power. You

can either use it to extract maximum cash on a sort of hit and run level, or you can use it to try and fortify your position, which is obviously the most sensible thing to do. The fact that you want to go back again is the governor on the whole thing, because it means that when you're organizing a tour, you want to get the best halls, because you want to get as many people as possible. France, for example, is a huge problem for us, because it's somewhere that we're popular and we'd like to work, but we cant get the places to work. We haven't worked in France for so long that it isn't true, because it's so difficult to find the places to work. French audiences tend to destroy the good places, so they won't have rock and roll groups there, and there's no point in us working in bad places."

February 26, 1972 - Melody Marker (U.K.) published an article titled, "Floyd's star trek" that reviewed the Pink Floyd concert at the Rainbow Theater, London, England, on February 19, 1972. A sold-out crowd witnessed a show featuring "burning flashlights, wind-blown sparkle dust, the pre-recorded voice of Malcolm Muggeridge, and a trip to the dark side of the moon." Songs included 'Careful With That Axe Eugene,' 'A Saucerful of Secrets,' 'Dark Side of the Moon,' and three encores, one of which was a blues jam.

New Musical Express (U.K.) reported on the Pink Floyd concert at the Rainbow Theater, London, England, on February 20, 1972. It was a mind and sense stunning experience. The show began with 'Dark Side of the Moon,' complete with gigantic light towers, banks of quadraphonic speakers, and recordings of Muggeridge. It ended with police sirens, revolving red lights, and a moving light tower, all leaving the audience stunned. The second set began with 'Meddle,' accompanied by wind machines as silver dust was tossed into the fans to make the air sparkle. The next song, 'Careful With That Axe, Eugene,' used magnesium flares. This was followed by the song, 'Echoes,' which began with Roger Waters at the organ. The encore was 'Saucerful of Secrets.' It was a magnificent production, and the sound quality was fantastic.

February 27, 1972 - The Sunday Times (U.K.) published a concert review by Derek Jewell of Pink Floyd's concerts at the Rainbow Theater. The music is "overlaid with a maze of extra tapes which titillate the ears from all sides with extra-terrestrial electronic sounds, whispers, cries, snatches of prayers, chugs, glugs and the surrant keening of wind and rain." Pink Floyd "have structure to their music, beauty of form . . . and an uncanny feeling for melancholy of our times." "Floyd strikingly succeed. They are dramatists supreme."

March 4, 1972 - Melody Maker (U.K.) published a review of Syd Barrett's band, Stars, debut concert at the Corn Exchange in Cambridge on February 24, 1972 by Roy Hollingworth. "Hey, Hey, Saturdays in the hay, you know you can't do these things, hey, hey," are quoted as lyrics sung by Barrett, although Hollingworth claimed he couldn't hear too well because Barrett wasn't too interested in the microphone. Barrett would stop playing, scratch his nose, and then start playing again, change time by the minute, play out of tune, and play chords that didn't make sense. The crowd didn't understand, and people left during the show. A crowd of 30 heard Stars play.

May 27, 1972 - New Musical Express (U.K.) published an article titled, "Floyd Joy for All" that reviewed the Pink Floyd album, 'Obscured by Clouds.' Syd Barrett's writing style could have been an influence on this album. There are no musical epics, just beautiful songs. The music was composed and performed for the movie, 'La Vallee' by Barbet Schroeder. Roger Waters plays some melodic bass guitar, while David Gilmour's playing is impeccable, particularly on the song 'Burning Bridges.' Richard Wright plays electronic effects, as well as piano and organ leads. 'Free Four' is happy, country rock. 'Wots . . . Uh, The Deal' has strong vocals but the lyrics are full of clichés. Although there is some poor production work, the album is satisfying.

Also in this issue is an article titled, "The Floyd Complex" by Simon Stable that featured part one of an interview with Richard Wright. Asked if he ever wished that Pink Floyd could play small clubs again, instead of to audiences of 10,000 or more, Wright replied, "*We're not into 10,000 and above, but I know what you mean. In fact, we do gigs to 2,000-3,000 in concert halls. But in answer to the question, no, that was a very special time. Those early days were purely experimental for us, and a time of learning and finding out exactly what we were trying to do. Each night was a complete buzz because we did totally new things and none of us knew how the other would react to it. It was the formation of the Pink Floyd. So if you say, do I wish we could play in that kind of atmosphere again, the answer is yes, because it was really a gas. But I'm not really interested in playing to that number of people again.*"

Does the expense of moving your equipment prevent you from playing in halls of less than 1,000? Wright replied, "*We do gigs for nothing. But generally speaking, going to play in small places to a few people is just not possible, anymore. The organization involved in getting a gig together now takes weeks of work, hours and hours of setting up, and it's just not feasible to do it in a church hall. It's one of the prices you pay for being successful, I guess.*"

Asked if their show at the Roundhouse with a choir was fun, Wright replied, "*A lot of fun and not too successful. It was OK, but we've changed quite a lot since then. All sorts of things have happened.*"

Stable told Wright that he thought the song 'Paintbox' was one of their nicest songs. Asked why they never play it live, Wright explained, "*At a concert, we're not interested in playing old material. We're desperate to play new material. It's never been performed live on stage because, I suppose myself and the rest of the band have never had that interest to play it live. It doesn't strike any of us as a good number to do live, anyway. It was a single, a three-minute piece of music. There's lots of material we've recorded that we've never played live, lots of it.*"

Asked why they perform some songs live, but not others, Wright answered, "*Because some numbers are better suited to being performed live. Things we do live tend to be longer, so we have time to develop them. As a group, we've never been interested in going on stage doing three minutes, then stopping, and then going on to do another three minutes.*"

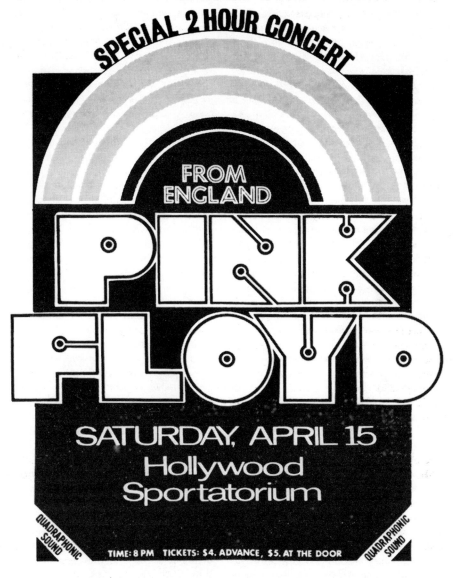

The whole tradition of the group has been to go on stage and improvise. In the old days, we used to do a hell of a lot of it. Some numbers we'd do for half-an-hour. 'Interstellar Overdrive' has a theme, but that's it, and you can go wherever you like in between."

Stable stated that he thought 'Paintbox' was a better song than the A-side of the single, 'Apples and Oranges.' Asked if the band were able to choose which song to put on the A-side, Wright said, *"Yes we did. We also had Norman Smith, who was producing us at the time, and he suggested what should be the*

A-side. But it was a group decision and we'd definitely set out 'Apples And Oranges' as a single. We all thought it was a really good song, but the recording didn't come up so well. I didn't think 'Paintbox' would make a great single, actually. I know it wouldn't, in fact. We've never been a singles band. 'Arnold Lane,' which was a great single, I thought, and 'See Emily Play,' which wasn't a great single, did very well, and those are the only two that we've ever had."

Asked how the band chooses what films to write scores for, Wright explained,

"We don't choose. What happens is that people come to us. We haven't done that many film scripts, but we're rejecting things now. We've done 'Zabriskie Point,' 'More,' 'La Vallee,', 'The Committee,' and 'In London Tonite Let's Make Love.' Up to now we've said, here's a film script, great, because we're interested in doing music for film, we'll do it."

Asked about composing songs, and whether they pick a theme and improvise on it, or whether they write it out, Wright replied, *"Yes and yes. There is no way that we write music, there are lots of ways in which we write music. For example, the extremes are, we go into the studio with absolutely nothing and we sit around saying, look we're going to write something. From then on, it's people giving ideas, people saying look I've got this thing in my head, and playing it. And from nothing you create a whole piece. 'Saucerful of Secrets' was one of those where we went in the studio saying, 'right, let's do something,' with no pre-conceived ideas. The other extreme is someone coming in with a song, which is all the chord sequences, all the words written, ideas for the arrangement, everything, in which case he says we do this, this, and this."*

How did you compose when you first started out? Wright replied, *"When we first started writing music, Syd Barrett wrote most of the music. For example the first album was all Syd except for one number by Roger, 'Doctor Doctor,' and 'Interstellar,' and we didn't do any writing, in fact, we just played and improvised. The first major piece of writing the group did was 'Saucerful of Secrets,' apart from 'Interstellar Overdrive.'"*

Do you compose pieces in a similar way that classical music and jazz music are written, by writing a theme and improvising? Wright replied, *"We used to. The improvisation started on stage and now improvisation happens in the studio and then it's written and taken on stage. We improvise on stage all the time, but we know exactly where everything is going and where it's come from. It's not improvisation, as such, where we don't know what's going to happen. We work on very strong themes now, still improvising, but on very well known patterns."*

Are your songs different in live performance than they are in the studio? Wright replied, *"No, not anymore. I mean,*

'Echoes' on the album and on stage is exactly the same. But 'Echoes' suits itself to being performed live anyway. It's an easy number to play live."

Do you get ideas from other composers? Wright replied, *"The only writers we borrow from are ourselves, and we do quite a bit of that. I can't think of anyone we've borrowed from. There's obviously lots of influences in the group. You can hear them, but it's not conscious. That's what made our music in the beginning. No one could recognize where it had come from, although we did start off like any other band on R & B, and blues, and rock and roll. The influences for me in our music are immense, but they're all subconscious right down the whole spectrum of music. But we've never based ourselves on one particular type of composing. There hasn't been any single one that we've wanted to copy."*

Are there any plans for making a movie about Pink Floyd? Wright said, *"We haven't got a clear idea of what we want to do, but we do want to make a movie. What interests us, really, is making our own movie, and writing the music for it. If we make a film, I'm pretty sure it wouldn't be anything about us, as such. It would be about something else. What, I don't know."* Would it be like the Frank Zappa movie? Wright replied, *"Zappa's film was about him, but it was about the whole scene, the whole rock and roll business of traveling around as a musician in a group. I really felt what was going on in that film. It felt very real to me. The film we make will not be about rock and roll, but we've no ideas at the moment."*

Pink Floyd are always successful even though you don't have a lot of publicity. Why is that? Wright replied, *"I don't know the answer to that question. We do get publicity, but we're not hyped. Like Grateful Dead, we've made it on word of mouth, which is a much nicer way of making it."*

What is the average age of your audience? Wright replied, *"The only people we see are the people who come back-stage, who we meet and talk to, and they tend to be around 18-22 year-old college students. But one can look in the audience and see people of 50, and very young people. That question, if I was Marc Bolan, I could answer immediately. We're in the rock and roll business, and so* basically we have the college students because it's their music."

When you perform, do you hear the music on stage the same way the fans hear it in the audience? Wright said, *"Yes, we do hear it in a different way, particularly now that we have a balance engineer working in the audience. The drummer is always going to hear it in relation to his drum kit. Not so with bass, organ, and guitar because we try to set up the amplifiers so it all balances. I have a stack on my side from Dave, and he likewise with my organ, but it's balanced to us. But we don't hear how it is out front. You could be singing into the PA, and not really hearing the vocals, but knowing that out front they are in balance. So it's learning to listen and not judging on what you hear but what you imagine out front. We tried monitoring it, and it doesn't work. We haven't tried headphones, but it wouldn't work. The whole point about rock and roll is the volume of it, and when you play loud you're not only listening to the actual note, but to the harmonics coming out of it. And if you've got earphones on, you loose all that."*

This interview is continued in the June 3, 1972 issue of New Musical Express.

May 1972 - Light Music (Japan) published an interview with the members of Pink Floyd. Asked whether their music can be called pop music, they replied, *"We dislike being called pop musicians, although, if pop music is defined as that which is popular, we are pop musicians because of our popularity."* The Japanese people feel that your music is very original. Pink Floyd replied, *"Probably because we don't write music while listening to someone else's music. We compose from the inside where we create from our experience."* Are technology or emotions more important to you? Pink Floyd replied, *"I want to say that emotions are more important. Technology is a mere tool. You can give someone a big canvas and some oil paint, but if they don't feel it in their own way, they can't create a beautiful oil painting."*

June 3, 1972 - New Musical Express (U.K.) published an article titled, "The Floyd complex, Part 2" by Simon Stable that featured part two of an interview with Richard Wright.

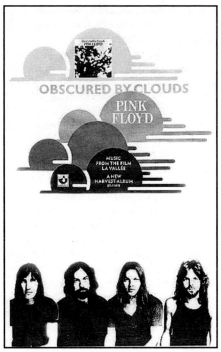

Obscured By Clouds advertisement.

Asked if the band's mixer is considered a member of the band, Wright replied, *"No. But he's an extension of the band. Maybe I've put it too strongly, because when we're playing on stage we do know what's going on out front, its not up to the mixer 100 per cent. We are giving him instructions. He's not the fifth member of the band, he's just mixing what we ask him, but we are relying on his ears to know that it's going right."*

Do you have difficulties reproducing the music from you records on stage? Wright replied, *"If any, not really any difficulties. We have had difficulties. For example 'Alan's Psychedelic Breakfast' we tried on our English tour and it didn't work at all, so we had to give it up. None of us liked doing it, anyway, and we didn't like it on the album. It's rather pretentious. It doesn't do anything. Quite honestly, it's a bad number. A similar idea, in that idiom, we did at Roundhouse another time, I thought was much better. Practically on the spot, we decided to improvise a number where we fried eggs on stage and Roger threw potatoes about, and it was spontaneous, and it was really good. 'Alan's Breakfast' was a weak number. We don't have that much problem producing things on stage. We work on our four instruments, which is all we have on stage, and adapt accordingly."*

Asked if Pink Floyd use instruments that have been specially built for them, Wright answered, *"Yeah, we don't have any specially-built instruments to produce sounds. We use normal instruments, apart from the VCS3, which anyone can buy. One of the myths about the Pink Floyd is that they have all this amazing electronic gadgetry when, in fact, we all use the same as any other group. It's our technique of using them in a different way."*

Asked what equipment the band uses, Wright explained, *"It's a Kelsey Morris PA using Phase Linear amps, and the mixer built by Alan and Heath, HiWatt amplifiers through WEM cabinets, Binson echo machines, Hammond organ, Farfisa organ, Fender electric piano, Fender guitars, Ludwig drum kit, 4-track machine, and seven quadraphonic speakers. That's what we use. We are constantly looking for new things. The whole five years has been spent in improving our equipment, not for volume, but for quality, and we've got an excellent system now, but we'll go on improving it. It's the first time we've arrived at a system that we really like, that's capable of producing a quality of sound that we really want. We've got it now, but it takes a long time."*

How much of your profits go into your equipment? Wright replied, *"In our case, a great deal. In a certain year we might earn a lot of money, but you look into the expenses of, say, the equipment and the people to look after it, and it cancels it out. There are no profits. The money we earned and the money we put in was exactly the same not so long ago. Some buy a certain amount of equipment and that's it. But we've always been concerned about the sound and trying to get it better, and we've spent a lot of bread on it."*

Have you ever had a band argument where one band member has left? Wright replied, *"We have arguments, certainly, about everything. One of the things that must keep us together is that we're successful at what we're doing. We're not successful in a huge way, we're not enormous, we sell a maximum amount of albums in Britain, but we're small in America, but it's getting bigger all the time. There is a great danger, you find something*

that's successful so you go around doing it and then people say we don't want to know anymore."

A year ago the Soft Machine played at the Promenade Concerts. Would Pink Floyd ever consider playing at a Prom concert, if you were invited? Wright replied, *"Well, we couldn't appear at a Promenade concert because they are held at the Albert Hall, and the Albert Hall have banned rock groups."*

What music do you listen to at home when you relax? Wright replied, *"Where do I start, because I listen to all sorts of things. My listening time is spent in listening to favorites that I have, listening to music that people have said is really good. Most of my time is spent in listening to stuff I've never heard before, which I may not like. A lot of it I don't like, and rarely do I have time to put on music that I do like, which is Berlioz who really lifts me up, Symphony Fantastique and Te Deum, Mahler, Bruckner, and Beethoven, Carl Orff, Steve Miller, Bernstein, Miles Davis, Messaien, Copland, and I could go on and on. The music I like, finally, is music that appeals in a very emotional way, so I guess you could say romantic."*

Did Pink Floyd ever make an appearance on 'Top of the Pops?' Wright replied, *"Yes, in 1967 with our Number 3 hit, 'See Emily Play.' We appeared on, I believe, four occasions."*

Was 'See Emily Play' on one of your albums? I know that it is on 'Relics. Wright replied, *"It appeared on the American album. You might have an import copy of the first album, in which case it's on it, because in America they put it on together with 'Arnold Layne,' I think, and took some other numbers off."* Why did they do this? Wright replied, *"Because, in America, at that time and even now, they are very concerned about the A.M. market, as opposed to the F.M. market. From every album we issue in America, a single is taken from it and played on A.M. stations in order to sell the album. None of the singles make it, of course."*

Since we don't have A.M. and F.M. stations in England, can you explain the difference? Wright explained, *"A.M. plays the Top Forty constantly, and any record they think will make the Top Forty, plus a few oldies which they play from time to time. And F.M. is any individual who happens to be on the air at that time, playing whatever he fancies playing, which isn't related to charts or anything."* Is A.M. similar to Radio One in England, and F.M. like Radio Two? Wright answered, *"No, because Radio One isn't anything like A.M. in America. Radio One isn't really a Top Forty station. They play a lot of Top Forty material, yes. But they also play a lot of other stuff, like Jimmy Young singing his little songs, etc., etc. In America, its A.M. is related solely to hit parade. Radio Two is nothing like F.M. in America. The only thing I can think of is Radio Three, which is more like F.M., although F.M. in America is a lot more radical. Radio Three is a classical station."*

If you release another single, would you appear on 'Top of the Pops?' Wright said, *"Well, first of all, I have to say that Top Of The Pops was definitely one of the worst things I did. It was horrible to be on it and it was a real drag doing it. On the other hand, if we had a single that we all liked very much, then we would go on Top Of The Pops, but only on our terms."*

This interview is continued in the June 10, 1972 issue of New Musical Express.

Sounds (U.K.) published an article titled, "Floyd: Wright on cue," in which Steve Peacock interviewed Richard Wright. Asked about the current use of machines by Pink Floyd, Wright said, *"It still could be improved a lot. Not the actual equipment, but what we put into it. There's still an awful lot we could do. At the moment, we've just been able to use tapes and effects in quad. And now I'd like to be able to have the whole band playing in quadraphonic so that the stage is no longer the center of the sound. It's just a bit worrying, sometimes. You can get very involved with sound and equipment and so on, which is a really good thing. It's really exciting to work with. But at times I miss the simplicity of just going out and playing. At times, you're so worried about everything working, about whether everything's going to come in on cue, that the actual performance can suffer. And I think it does with us sometimes. Occasionally, I feel I'd like to go back to just having a stage and us playing. I'm not trying to put down what we do, because I think it's really good that we should be trying to do it. It's just*

Obscured By Clouds album cover.

sometimes I feel it's overwhelming us. I don't know how the others feel. Maybe it inspires them to play better, and it does me when it's working well. But sometimes I look at our huge truck, and tons and tons of equipment, and think 'Christ, all I'm doing is playing an organ.'"

As far as having time to work on ideas, Wright said, *"I just feel like I've been rushing around, not knowing where I am, living in hotels, in planes, on American tours. It all got highly confusing, doesn't do your head any good. I thought I'd get away for a couple of months and not think about the Floyd at all. Well, I will, of course, but I'll have the freedom not to think under all the pressure."*

The Pink Floyd are in the process of recording a new album, called 'Eclipse.' It was to be called 'Dark Side of the Moon,' but they changed it when they discovered Machine Head already had an album by that name. Wright added, *"And also 'Eclipse' is a better title for it."*

They are also working on a ballet with Roland Petit. Wright explained, *"He's decided to use 'Eclipse' as the music for that. We've been talking with him about doing something for years and years, and he'd bring up an idea and then decide not to use it. It went on and on until we practically gave it up as a lost cause. But we sent him a tape of a live performance, and he said it was what he wanted. So we'll be doing that in Marseilles with him, and, hopefully, a French tour as well."*

Talking about future plans to incorporate films into their concerts, Wright commented, *"With 'Eclipse,' it's very important to be able to hear the words. And it works very well in England and America. But playing it abroad, they just don't understand what's happening, obviously not, because they don't understand the words. So the next thing we want to do is to use film, so that it's an international thing. It's visual, so everyone can understand it. But then, once you start getting into film, it takes a lot of time and a lot of money. I don't know how long it'll take, but I hope we'll be able to set aside enough time early next year to do it."*

June 10, 1972 - New Musical Express (U.K.) published an article titled, "The Floyd complex, concluded" by Simon Stable that featured part three of an interview with Richard Wright. Asked if Pink Floyd would consider appearing on a television show, such as The Old Grey Whistle Test, Wright replied, *"Not in its present form. What we would like to do is an hour TV show with the sound transmitted on FM Radio Three. People could watch their television and have their radio on, giving a good stereo sound with a picture. That is the only kind of broadcast I would be interested in doing. We have, by the way, made an hour-long TV film, which is still being edited. That, to me, is the answer."*

What is your opinion of Radio One? Wright replied, *"Well, there's plenty of bad pop music on it and very little progressive. There are a few shows a week as though the BBC is doing us a favor. This appears to be their attitude, and it doesn't work. There should be a radio station that is a complete alternative to BBC, but I can't see that happening for some time. It's a great shame. In America, it's a pleasure to listen to the radio and I miss this in England. Radio Three is good if I'm feeling in that mood. But if I just want to be entertained, the FM radio in America with the buzz of getting into one guy who's choosing from an enormous range of music is a gas. This doesn't happen in this country. Here, it's very formal and predictable. In America, you switch on an FM station because you want to be turned on to sounds you've never heard before, the good ones."*

When you listen to electronic music, what are you listening for? Wright replied, *"I don't know that much about electronic music, no more than anyone else, i.e., I know Stockhausen, John Cage, and Verez, and listen to them. Some of it is good and some bad. In my opinion, a lot of it's bad in terms of music, although they are interesting experiments in sound. I heard a piece recently, called 'Black Coast' by William Bolcom, which is really good, but then that isn't true electronic music because it's organ and electronic tapes. Pure electronic music I'm not really interested in."*

What is your definition of pure electronic music? Wright replied, *"I guess synthesized sounds manipulated by someone and put together. Stockhausen is good. 'Kontakte' is the first piece of electronic music I ever heard and I loved it. I still do. But since then I've listened to a lot more and I've been disappointed. Basically, it's too cold, too sparse, too technical."* Have you ever heard the Sonnee group from France that plays glass tubes? Wright replied, *"I've heard them once. It's quite nice, actually, because glass makes a beautiful sound. A lot of people would say it was electronic, but it's no more electronic than playing a violin."*

What are your plans for the future? Wright replied, *"We record our album this month and go on holiday in July and August. In September we go to the States for three weeks on the West Coast, followed by a ballet with Roland Petit using 'Dark Side of the Moon,' or 'Eclispe' as it is now called, as the music. We're rehearsing it for two days and then performing it for five in Marseilles. After that, we do a French tour and the music for a French film. We have a couple of concerts in Brighton at the end of this month, and possibility a second festival, and a couple of concerts in Europe."*

Would you be willing to perform the ballet in London if Roland Petit brought it here? Wright replied, *"The idea of doing a ballet with Roland has been going on for two years with various ideas put up and rejected. Finally, it looks like it's on, and if it's successful, we'll go anywhere in the world to do it."* Would you make a film of it? Wright replied, *"If someone came to us and could make a really good film of it, we'd do that as well. The original idea was that it would go on Eurovision, but that's not going to happen now.*

If we could do a television show, for example, which went out live throughout Europe, that would be interesting. It would last about an hour."

What are five albums that you really like? Wright said, *"'Appalachian Spring' by Copland, 'Te Deum' by Berlioz, 'Your Saving Grace' by Steve Miller, 'Surfs Up' by The Beach Boys, and Penderecki's 'St. Luke's Passion.'"*

June 17, 1972 - Disc and Music Echo (U.K.) reviewed the Pink Floyd album, 'Obscured by Clouds.' They called it "An amazing album." The title track "blasts through your head with a penetrating, burring bass background and aural sunbursts, synthesized for some dark sinister corner of the solar system." Four stars.

Melody Maker (U.K.) reviewed the Pink Floyd album, 'Obscured by Clouds.' They wrote, "It contains some of the most aggressive instrumentals the Floyd have ever recorded," as well as some dreamy, melodic songs. 'Absolutely Curtains' is unique, and builds from an instrumental to a startling climax, followed by a surreal children's sing-along.

July 8, 1972 - New Musical Express (U.K.) reported on the Pink Floyd concert at The Dome, Brighton, England in June 1972. Through the darkness came the beginning sounds of 'Dark Side of the Moon,' causing talking in the audience to stop. Dark Side, which was the entire first set, was brilliant, and ended with thunderous applause. The second set was magnificent and featured songs from the 'Meddle' album. For the encores they performed 'Set the Controls for the Heart of the Sun' and 'Saucerful of Secrets.' During 'Set the Controls' Roger Waters thrashed his gong, and at the end it was set on fire and looked like the sun.

July 1972 - ZigZag 25 (U.K.) published an article titled, "The Year of Love including the Birth of the Pink Floyd" that featured an interview with Peter Jenner. They wrote, "We've often featured articles on the San Francisco psychedelic eruption, but we get loads of letters asking us to explain how the underground movement started up in Britain, with particular emphasis to the rock aspects.

Obviously, you could fill a book, and indeed many people have, if you wanted to explore every nook and cranny, detailing how the feeling grew out of a wide variety of influences, poets, protest, folk music, the Fugs, playwrights, authors, CND, student revolution, Provos, Peace News, marijuana, Lysergic Acid, publishers, bookshops, Kesey & Leary, Kerouac & Ginsberg, Quicksilver & the Dead, and for a much more complete history, I would refer you to certain tomes on the subject. As far as rock is concerned, however, I think we can cram it into a concise 4-page nutshell, providing we don't try to dig too deeply. It'll be enough to be getting on with, anyway.

PREFACE. I lay back in the sumptuous luxury of velvet upholstery and gazed across the panoramic skyline from the penthouse suite of the Blackhill Enterprises Mayfair offices as a gorgeous nymphet poured coffee into bone china cups and offered after-eight mints. I casually mentioned the Pink Floyd, and the words seemed to cut through the vapid atmosphere like razor blades. Jenner's face, his clean cut features aglow with interest, paled as he ground his cigar butt into the big diamond studded ashtray resting on the polished mahogany desktop. *"The Pink Floyd?"* he repeated, as he casually straightened his tie and picked a stray hair off his mohair suit. That had you all going, didn't it? In actual fact, the way it happened was a little different.

I had stumbled up to Blackhill's crumbling Bayswater office to meet Peter Jenner as arranged, but had to wait on the doorstep for almost an hour before Jenner, who is half of Blackhill Enterprises, and Andrew King, who is the other half, arrived, as usual, on their tandem. As Andrew began to unload rain-sodden contracts and documents from the panniers, Peter hustled me through the chaotic mountain of strewn papers into the back room, where he invited me to make myself comfortable on one of the most austerely designed wooden chairs in the history of furniture. He disappeared, leaving me to stare out of the window at the mass of leaking drainpipes clinging to the wall of the tenement block, which backed on to the yard, and returned with a cracked Woolworths mug of tepid radiator flushings. *"Here's some coffee,"* he grunted, plonking it down on the formica kitchen table which served as his desk. He took a worn tobacco tin from his pocket, selected the half-smoked remains of a Park Drive tipped, and peered at me through his cracked national health spectacles. *"Now then,"* he wheezed with considerable hostility, *"what is it you want? Make it snappy I'm a busy man."* "It's the Pink Floyd," I stammered. "I want to know how the Underground started. I was told that no-one in England knew as much about it as you do, that you're the acknowledged authority on the subject." His chest swelled with pride below the holey vest, which hung on his bony frame, as his disposition changed to one of great charm. *"They say that, do they? Well, er, yes, of course I'd be delighted to tell you all about it, but it's a long story."* "That's ok," I replied, "just give me all the facts as well as you can remember, and I'll go back home to distort and rehash your words into a vaguely coherent article."

THE LIST OF PLAYERS. Mr. Underground - John Hopkins. An underground journalist - Miles. A shady LSE drop-out - Peter Jenner. A pirate disc jockey - John Peel. A psychedelic music ensemble - The Pink Floyd. An unemployed person - Andrew King. A finger in various pies - Joe Boyd. An East End pixie - Marc Bolan. All other parts played by Mick Farren.

THE DISCOVERY OF THE PINK FLOYD. If you can cast your mind back to the dying days of 1965, which most underground stalwarts find impossible because their drug-addled memories can't remember further back than last week, you'll recall that the chart bound sounds were 'We Can Work It Out,' 'Eve of Destruction,' 'Get Off My Cloud,' and 'Turn, Turn, Turn'. Around that time too, Smithy had just declared UDI in Rhodesia, President Johnson was showing his gall bladder operation scar to the waiting world, the Post Office tower had recently been opened, and the Government had just abolished the death penalty. Right. Now that we've established some sort of departure point we can begin our narrative.

Peter Jenner had been set for a very distinguished career in the field of education, an assistant lecturer in the Department of Social Administration at the London School of Economics, but he was bored with that. He was also a passionate avant-garde jazz freak, but he

was bored with that too. Jenner said, *"Most of it was becoming so unpleasant on the ear that I just couldn't get off on it. John Coltrane and Ornette Coleman were the last two to really interest me."* His tastes changed towards R & B, of the Bo Diddley type, where they remained for some time, approximately up until this end-of-65 period. Apart from music, his head was buzzing with ambitious notions of founding a free school and a record label on which to record his freaky-jazz musician mates whose virtuosity offended the ears of all civilized record company executives. His partner in crime in cooking up these wild schemes was a bloke called John Hopkins, later to be known as Hoppy, who he had known for years.

Now, Elektra Records had just set up an English office under the astute auspices of Joe Boyd, who Hoppy got to know, and a deal was worked out whereby Elektra would assist them in matters of finance, pressing, and distribution. Subsequently, an album by AMM was released (on the Elektra label rather than their bizarre DNA label, the logo for which, Mike Mcinnery, later a well known poster artist, had taken great pains to design) featuring Keith Rowe, Cornelius Cardew and various other musicians in the avant-garde/classical/weirdo scene, and it was a very, very good, far out record. It sold about a thousand copies, but nevertheless turned out to be the first and last album they made. However, not only did it re-open the madcap Jenner's head to electronic music, but it also set his economics-oriented mind to work on the facts, figures, and percentages of the record industry. He did his sums and came to the momentous conclusion that the only way to come out of things with a profit was to get hold of a smash hit, and even a person of his musical illiteracy, he could hardly differentiate between the Dave Clark Five and the London Symphony Orchestra, knew that freaky sax-blowing weirdies were not about to set the singles chart on fire. The problem caused a great deal of anxiety and he was on the point of consulting a psychiatrist, when it happened.

At 3 a.m. one morning, it came to him in a blinding flash. He threw the blankets from the crude framework of his camp-bed, and rushed downstairs to make a drink. He could hardly control his excitement as his trembling hands cupped the steaming Bovril "A pop group," he finally ejaculated (not a pretty sight). The fact had been staring him in the face for several months, but it was not until early 1966 that he recognized it, the ideal vehicle to strap his energies to. The previous summer, one of his closest friends had been Eric Clapton, but Jenner at that time was totally disinterested in English pop music. Compared with jazz and bona-fide American Blues, it was just a load of trite, ephemeral rubbish and, to a degree, I suppose his bigoted opinion was just about right. There was very little integrity in pop. Clapton (though this has nothing to do with our story) had suddenly decided to leave John Mayall's Bluesbreakers (in August 66, though he rejoined 3 months later) and had formed a new band which he was going to take to Europe to get it together in a Greek country cottage, man. There was Jake Milton on drums (now in Quintessence), Ben Palmer on piano (later Creams roadie), a sax player called Bernie, a bass player who subsequently became leader of the Communist party in Birmingham, and John Bailey (who was in McGuinness Flint for a while). They all went off from Jenner's flat in a big American car.

Anyway, to revert to the main body of the narrative, Jenner began to look for a tasteful pop group. No, that's a lie. He wasn't that enthusiastic. He still had his secure job at LSE and he merely decided to wait until the right group presented itself to him. His first probings were abortive, and little wonder. Hoppy had got hold of a tape of one of the Velvet Underground's first gigs in New York and it was concluded that if the Velvets played their cards right, they could enjoy the patronage of Messrs Jenner and Hopkins. Such naivety! They phoned New York and spoke to John Cale, who tactfully pointed out that a Mr. Warhol was already handling their affairs. Now, inevitably, the sequence of events is going to get a bit blurred and jumbled if we don't stick to the music, but let me just mention a few other things.

In these early months of 1966, the thoughts of various poets, painters, writers, musicians, etc., were all funneling in the same direction. The seeds of the Underground were sown and everybody was waiting for the harvest, so to speak. The Free School idea had

taken root and was being set up in Notting Hill, and the All Saints Hall was becoming the central meeting place during this fermentation period. To finance the school, which was run on donations, it was decided to put on a few concerts, and these developed into the odd gig at the Marquee in Wardour Street. Jenner said, *"It was in June, I remember, because I was in the middle of the crucifyingly boring chore of marking examination papers. I always used to leave it until the last minute so that I'd be impelled to rush through them rather than go through the laborious agonies of wondering if a paper merited an A or a B+. Anyway, I decided to pack it in for the evening and go along to this mad gig at the Marquee, which was being run by people like Steve Stollman (who's brother had started the ESP label in New York) and Hoppy. Well, I arrived around 10:30, and there on the stage was this strange band, who were playing a mixture of R & B, and electronic noises, and I was really intrigued because, in between the routine stuff like 'Louie Louie' and 'Roadrunner,' they were playing these very weird breaks, so weird that I couldn't even work out which instrument the sound was coming from. It was all very bizarre and just what I was looking for, a far out, electronic, freaky, pop group. And there, across the bass amp, was their name, `The Pink Floyd Sound.'"*

HOW TO MAKE A MOUNTAIN OUT OF A BLACKHILL. *"I didn't know anything about pop music,"* recalled Jenner. *"I just can't tell you how little I knew. I mean, I hardly knew about the Beatles even, and I didn't know anything about the Stones, and it was only at that time that I started trying to become aware of what was happening in pop music. Anyway, after thinking about it, I decided I'd like to record these Floyd geezers, and I finally tracked down Roger and Nicky who were living in an obscure flat in Highgate. It was the typical student scene. They'd bought a £20 J2 van and some gear with their grant money, but were on the point of splitting the band because 1)they weren't getting any gigs, 2)they were going off on their summer holidays, and 3)it was interfering with their studies. Roger and Nick were training to become architects, Rick was going to a music school and Syd was at art school and more interested in painting than music."* Peter merely introduced himself, said hello, and said he'd be interested in talking to them when they re-convened after their holidays, and it was only at this stage that he discovered what an amateur set-up the Pink Floyd was, no contracts, no agency or management, no gigs, and very little gear, most of which was either extremely decrepit or else encased in home made cabinets. But still, the seeds were there.

Enter Andrew King, a lifelong friend of Jenner's, who had resigned from his position as an educational cyberneticist. He, too, had become bored and found it much more gratifying to hang out on street corners. He entered into loose partnership with Jenner and jointly, as Blackhill Enterprises, they took on the management of the Floyd, which was more than they'd planned to do because the original idea was merely to find a group for their label idea. But now they determined to go the whole hog and make the Pink Floyd into a top band.

Carnival time arrived at the Free School and part of the festivities included a rock concert at the All Saints Hall, and what better choice for the group than the Pink Floyd. As well as that, some American friends of Hoppy's came along and projected colored slides on the group as they played, not moving whirlpools of color, just static slides, but it was the beginning of the "mixed media" idea, and it started Jenner thinking. Snippets of information about the San Francisco scene had been filtering over the ocean. The West Coast psychedelic scene was much more together and advanced than its Notting Hill counterpart, so why not try to find out about the sophistications such as acid, light shows, peace and love, flowers, and all the rest of the paraphernalia, and implement some of them here? The light show idea really appealed, but as no one could tell them about the refinements, they had to improvise.

Peter and Andrew, a right pair of mechanical duffers, took instruction on the way to hold a hand saw and constructed a very primitive, Heath Robinson device consisting of domestic spotlights from British Home Stores, operated by domestic light switches, shining through colored perspex pinned to this crude framework they'd nailed up out of lumps of wood. (This remarkable triumph of carpentry skill is now an exhibit in the sculpture hall of the National Museum of Early Psychedelic Art

in Chicago).

The Floyd needed help. They needed encouragement, equipment, rehearsal, roadies, work, recording contracts, direction and all the rest of it, and their new managers didn't have the first idea about the roles and attitudes of the established managers, but they waded in at the deep end. Now, there's an old adage which says, "Fools rush in, and get the best seats," and that, by a strange quirk of good fortune, is exactly what happened over the next few months. The Floyd seemed to waltz into the charts, onto the television, and into clubs and theatres without any problems at all. Here's an example of their luck. Peter was still at work, so Andrew did most of the day-to-day management and also, from the remnants of an inheritance, paid for a thousand quids worth of gear, which was promptly stolen. So they had to get another load of new gear, this time on hire purchase. By this time, things were happening fast.

In October 1966, the International Times (later abbreviated to IT) was launched and the Roundhouse was taken over for a celebration party, where 2,000 odd people (most of them were odd) were given free sugar cubes and assailed with the raw sounds of the evolving Underground's two top groups, The Pink Floyd and the Soft Machine, both of who's reputations had spread via regular gigs at the All Saints Hall. All the different factions of the Underground were represented and it was as if the net had suddenly tightened round all the loose ends, bringing them together, literally under one roof. Jenner said, *"At that time, the Roundhouse hadn't ever been used as an entertainment venue and it was just filthy. On top of that, there was virtually no electricity other than an ordinary domestic supply and wires dangled here and there so our puny light show looked magnificent in all the darkness."* Celebrities abounded. Antonioni was there, Paul McCartney was there, to name but two, and it was *"an incredibly fashionable affair, probably the most epochal party you could ever see, and the bands got noticed, particularly the Floyd, who blew up the power during their set and consequently ended the evening's entertainment. That in itself, to be cut off in the middle of 'Interstellar Overdrive' was a bummer, but at the same time it was incredibly dramatic."*

The Floyd had, by this time, dropped most of their R & B repertoire in favor of the more electronic/freaky stuff and I, in my blissful ignorance, had assumed that this was a result of acid experimentation and the like, but this was not so. It was done at Jenner's insistence. He directed them off the 'Louie Louie' trip towards the 'Saucerful of Secrets' style, and it turned out to be the perfect managerial move, although it was done largely out of ignorance. Jenner merely thought the electronic stuff sounded better than the American imitations, which he'd never really been keen on. Also, thinking that there was nothing difficult in composing new numbers, he impressed on them that they should write more original material of a "weird" nature but, at the same time, bearing the requirements of the singles market in mind. So, their style evolved to the satisfaction of their managers, who thought it was good, but had no idea how radically different it was from anything else that was happening in pop music.

IT rapidly became the official organ of the Underground (supplemented by Oz which started up a couple of months later) and then, in December 1966, Hoppy and his associates opened UFO, the first regular Underground club (and the best). Here's a brief description of what went on, borrowed from IT No. 29 and written by Miles, who's interviews and reviews had become so influential: December 23rd saw 'Night Tripper' at Tottenham Court Road, advertised by a poster and a display ad in IT No.5. There was no indication as to who would be there performing, the audience attended because they "knew" who would be there and "knew" what was happening. The name-change to UFO occurred the next week and the first UFO advertised the Pink Floyd, Fanta and Ood, the Giant Sun Trolly, and Dave Tomlin improvising to government propaganda. UFO was created by and for the original underground, posters from messrs. English & Weymouth, and an IT stall by the cloakrooms. The first UFO also had a Marilyn Monroe movie, Karate, and light-shows. It was a club in the sense that most people knew each other, met there to do their business, arrange their week's appointments, dinners and lunches, and hatch out issues of IT, plans for Arts Lab, SOMA, and various schemes for turning the

Thames yellow and removing all the fences in Notting Hill. The activity and energy was thicker than the incense.

Miles also ran Indica Bookshop in Southampton Row, a veritable goldmine of goodies, a whole new world to be discovered by emerging hippies (like me), full of books, underground papers like the San Francisco Oracle and the East Village other, magazines, posters, marvel comics. Phew! And the International Times was born out of and published from their basement, which for a while was the nerve center of the Underground. By the beginning of 1967, UFO was already bulging to the walls with freaks, and the Pink Floyd, their music becoming increasingly stranger by pop music standards, were the big musical draw. Jenner said, *"At the first two or three UFOs, the Floyd were on 60 percent of the gross to provide music and lights, and my first managerial blunder was allowing that to be altered so that we got straight bread instead of a percentage, because the place instantly became very fashionable. I've never seen anything like it, before or since. And the band had become even more fashionable, without any records or any exposure outside of a couple of places in London, we got a center page spread in Melody Maker."* If you know anything about the workings of the pop music industry, you'll know that any manager or publicist would sell his boyfriend to get a center spread in Melody Maker, but Jenner wasn't at all surprised, he assumed that this was the normal routine thing to happen to any band. But the Floyd were becoming red hot. The word was spreading like a forest fire. All the record companies were interested and suited executives were lured into the addict infested filth of UFO to see the band in action. Eventually they signed with EMI, who offered them the best deal, including an advance of £5,000, which was just unbelievably astronomical in those days, more like a telephone number than a sum of money and, surprisingly, EMI really got behind them and did an incomparable promotion job.

1967 - WHAT A YEAR! Back to the scene in general. The media was latching on to the more sensational aspects of hippieism / flowerpower / beautiful people, and what was going down in San Francisco was now on everybody's lips. There were more gatherings here too. On January 29th, IT sponsored an Uncommon Market spontaneous happening thing at the Roundhouse and a little later came the ultimate in drawing together the Underground, the 14 Hour Technicolour Dream, held at Alexandra Palace. The Uncommon Market's main attraction was a 56-gallon jelly (if you rolled around naked in jelly, you were considered very far out and groovy and gained great esteem and fame), but the Dream, which took place during the night of April 29th and was originally to be a benefit for IT which had been busted for obscenity the previous month, not only attracted 5,000 longhairs, but featured almost every underground group in England. I remember it well, the whole thing just burned into my memory for ever. It hit you as soon as you walked into the place, lights and films all over the walls and blitzing volume from two stages with bands playing simultaneously. On one stage you had the completely unknown Arthur Brown, this crazy whirling painted lunatic accompanied by a hunched up speeding organist and a thrashing drummer, and on the other you had the Soft Machine with Daevid Allen wearing a miner's helmet and staring like a weird zombie and Kevin Ayers wearing rouge on his cheeks and a black cowboy hat surmounted by giant model glider wings. I just couldn't believe it. Outside, the straights of Wood Green were watching their tellies and sipping their tea, and inside this huge time machine were 5,000 stoned, tripping, mad, friendly, festive hippies. Talk about two different worlds!

At the time, one of the things that impressed me most was the lack of any sort of physical or mental barrier between performers and audience. When a band finished its set, the members got off the stage and wandered into the crowd to sit on the floor. It was all so very unlike the usual pop gig where a group arrived on stage via a back passage, played, and went off by the same route, never mixing with the inferior rabble. What else did I see? The Purple Gang, with mandolins, washboards, and amplification troubles, bashing out their 'Granny Takes A Trip,' one of the early hippie classics. Dick Gregory and Pete Townshend and Yoko Ono were there, Savoy Brown, the Social Deviants with Mick Farren singing Chuck Berry standards against a monstrous cacophony of discordant rock, and Denny Laine was there too, but, though he had his guitar and Viv Prince with him, he didn't play (which was sad, because 1967 was his supreme year of creativity). Hoppy was there, never without a smile and Suzie Creemcheese, and they were giving out free bananas (because it was around the time of the U.S. underground great banana hoax. They conned everyone into believing that you could get high by scraping the pith from the inside skin, baking it and smoking it).

As dawn started to shine a shimmering eerie light at the windows, the Pink Floyd came on. "*It was a perfect setting,*" said Jenner. "*Everyone had been waiting for them and everybody was on acid, that event was the peak of acid use in England, everybody was on it, the bands, the organizers, the audience, and I certainly was.*" Of course, the Floyd blew everybody's mind. But this was a special occasion. The Floyd, though "the psychedelic band," were not really into psychedelics at all. They were much more booze oriented, and this was generally the case with the early underground bands. It was the pop groups of the time, the teenybop raves like The Small Faces, who were doing the drugs.

Around this time, the pirate radio stations, whose lifespan was already being limited to months by the Marine Offences Act, which was being rushed through the Commons, were at their most influential in shaping the pop charts. "We start 'em, others chart 'em." Radio London, by far and away the best, refused to play 'Arnold Layne,' the Floyd's first single, because it was about a transvestite, but Radio Caroline, once the payola had been handed over, got behind it and supplemented EMI's big promotional campaign. Before long, it had got to number 23 in the national chart, which, of course, was no surprise to Peter Jenner, who thought it was only natural for a single to go into the charts, but due possibly to the 'dirty song' ban, it never quite reached the top twenty and, thus, the essential Top of the Pops boost eluded them." Their second single, they were sure, would be even more successful, but there were doubts. Joe Boyd, who had left his Elektra job to become involved in a variety of enterprises, including record production, running UFO, and group management, had produced and made an excellent job of 'Arnold Layne,' but EMI decided to rub him out in favor of Norman "Hurricane" Smith, who had just been promoted from engineer to staff producer. It was a very unpopular move. Everybody, especially the fuming Joe Boyd, was choked off, and Norman knew it, but his experience with the Beatles, his exacting demands, his ideas and ambitions, turned up trumps and it turned out to be a very productive combination. The song they selected was 'See Emily Play,' which Syd had written (as 'Games for May') specially for a concert which our intrepid managers mounted at the Queen Elizabeth Hall. It was a staggeringly successful event, a solo performance, which was totally unheard of, because the big groups of the time would never do more than a 30-minute set, *"and we got this guy from EMI to erect speakers at the back of the hall too, which was like the predecessor of the Azimuth Co-ordinator. We had an incredible light show by then as well, and the concert, which was the first pop show ever held in the hall, was just unbelievable. At one stage, one of the roadies came on dressed in Admiral's gear and tossed armfuls of daffodils up in the air. It was just amazing, and everybody went berserk."* Everyone except the owners of the hall, who went absolutely bananas because the bubbles which had filled the place had left marks all over their posh leather chairs, and some of the flowers which had been handed out to the audience had been trodden into the carpets.

Anyway, everybody was knocked out with 'Emily,' especially Radio London, who felt that they were missing out on the flower power scene, and they went crazy. The first week out, it was number one in the Big L Top 40, a chart which bore no relation to anything other than the fevered imagination of the program director. In actual fact, far from "missing out on the hippie scene," Radio London was a distinct pioneer in that area, with John Peel's 'Perfumed Garden,' transmitted two weeks out of every three (as far as I remember) between midnight and two a.m. Prior to getting this program, Peel's "Climber of the week" was always worth hearing (among those that stick in my mind are 'Tiny Goddess' by Nirvana and 'Somebody to Love' by the Airplane), but once he got this midnight

thing going, it was compulsive listening. It was for me anyway. I used to lie there listening to the Doors, the Incredibles, Donovan, and all the others, and arrive at work the next day with great bags under my eyes. And he used to get hold of imports and play unheard of grist like Catain Beefheart & his Magic Band, and Country Joe & the Fish. It was an amazing period, one I wouldn't have missed for the world.

By the time June rolled around, the unity of the Underground was already disintegrating, with the different sections criticizing the ethics of each other, and the bread minded entrepreneurs had begun to step in and promote flower power festivals and happenings on a very obviously commercial basis. There were so many 'Underground bands' that you couldn't move for them, but the thing that caused most discomfort to the hard core of the old school was the arrest and sentencing of Hoppy for dope possession, he got nine months. Though many avant-garde musicians (not to mention people in other spheres) had been smoking marijuana for years, the public image of drugs was the wicked black man prosecuted for selling reefers to unsuspecting teenagers. But all of a sudden, all the mods were gulping down handfuls of pills, and the longhairs were either getting stoned or else trying out this incredible new acid stuff, which had newly arrived from the laboratories of America, where it was still legal until late 1966. The Sunday papers feared for the future of the nation's youth, the police got pressured into paranoia and they went berserk with their arrests. Jagger, Richard, Lennon, Georgie Fame, Joe Cocker, were all busted for possession, but the first really big purge came in the early hours of March 3, 1968, when 150 police suddenly plunged into the depths of Middle Earth, which had opened as a rival to UFO in early 1967. They took 5 hours to search 750 people and made only eleven arrests, though one heard grapevine reports of the vast tonnage of hash that was swept up from the floor afterwards.

Back to the Floyd, who were now just about world famous due to a combination of luck, talent and a miraculous series of events. Jenner said, *"If we had started out with just any old banger group, we'd have been finished within a year, because we had so little idea of what we were doing, but, fortunately, the Floyd had all this talent. Andrew and I just played everything by ear. Goodness only knows what the established record-biz people must've thought about us. I suppose that when we left their offices they just looked at each other and collapsed in disbelief at our naivety."* They cut their first album in Studio 3 at EMI whilst the Beatles were constructing 'Sgt. Pepper' next door in Studio 2, and that sold well too, so everything was going along smoothly. But at the London School of Economics, where Peter still taught, he was one of the junior staff in favor of the student revolution which was beginning to erupt and he eventually got a sharp reprimand. Either he curbed the nature of his extra-curricular activities or else he could tender his resignation. So he compromised, and took a year's leave of absence, which has so far extended itself to 5 years.

It was around this time that the pressures of the world started exerting themselves on Syd Barrett, who was really the genius of the group. He was writing, arranging, creating the sounds, singing, but he was, as everybody who ever followed the Floyd knows, cracking up a little. Peter accepts some of the responsibility for what was happening. He was always demanding greater effort, more productivity, more songs for future singles, and so forth, but the gig scene was probably more to blame. In the London long hair haunts, everything was fine, perfect vibes between audience and group. But once they got out into the world they found that their music had hardly been accepted, gigs were disastrous. Kids who turned up purely to hear a "top twenty group" could not come to terms with feedback and the like, so they booed and threw pennies. Jenner's face contorts in agony as he recalls the general miseries of touring in that summer of 1967. Finding a suitable chartbuster to follow 'Emily' proved impossible. Loads of material (much of it amazing classics like 'Scream Your Last Scream Old Woman With a Basket' and 'Vegetable Man,' which have yet to be released) was recorded, but no obvious single surfaced to keep them buoyant, and a tour interrupted the proceedings. It was an epic theatre package tour of the type we'll never see again, seven groups in one show and they did two shows a night! A roadie's nightmare! Jimi

Hendrix had 40 minutes, the Move had 30, the Floyd had 17, Amen Corner 15, The Nice 12, and so on, and it was all bound together by compere Pete Drummond, who's main success lay in alienating the fans. That tour did wonders in popularizing them, but a subsequent tour of America was decidedly very strange. They'd arrive at a gig and someone backstage would invariably induce them to sample the latest line in synthetic drugs and some extraordinary music would ensue. One of the aims of the early Floyd was to achieve the San Fran/psychedelic stance, which they thought they were doing quite well, but it transpired that their music was far removed from anything the Americans had ever seen before. With few examples of the West Coast sound to take their lead from, they had just guessed and assumed what the more progressive groups might be trying, and in doing so had evolved a style entirely their own.

THE END OF AN ERA AND THE START OF ANOTHER. Within a year of the first stirrings of love, peace, and brotherhood, the Underground had passed through its period of togetherness. UFO, under the control of Joe Boyd, had closed down, and Hoppy, just out of prison, was now much quieter and there was no one to assume his pivotal role as coordinator of underground activities. Jenner recalled, *"I think it was a tragedy for the hip community when Hoppy was put in jail and I don't think it ever recovered, because it was his energy which fired so many schemes. He held everything together and helped to maintain a unity."* Everyone withdrew into his own camp rather than think about the Underground as a whole, a very harrowing bandwagon period during which hypocrisy was around on a very big scale.

Meanwhile, the Floyd was falling apart, too. The pop press were coming out with rapturous accounts of how Syd would do a whole number strumming just one chord, but the other three weren't so much amused as troubled, and they decided to make a few changes because they could never be sure if Syd was suddenly going to change the rhythm or structure of a piece, and things stretched just a little too far. Syd stayed with Blackhill, who had plans for a solo career, and the Floyd recruited Dave Gilmour and went off to a new management in March 1968. The end of an amazing, but very weird era. Jenner said, *"We were always convinced that they were going to be as big as the Beatles, we were sure of that, but the way we ran things was so hap hazard. For instance, at one time we had the four Floyd, Andrew and me, June Child (who worked in the office and later became Mrs. Bolan), 2 roadies, and 2 lights people, they were all on salary, and we didn't keep any sort of control over expenditure. Ludicrous amounts were spent on ridiculous things, and the money scene got very unstable as a result of no hit record and no gigs, a situation which had arisen because of the reputation they'd gained for being unreliable."*

Jenner continued, *"Basically, the Floyd left us because they thought we'd have no confidence in them without Syd, which was true, even though it was a mistake for us to think like that. We just couldn't conceive how they would be able to make it without Syd, who put all the creativity into the group."* So off they went, leaving the financial position approximately as it had been 18 months earlier, everybody was broke. Jenner added, *"If I'd known then, what I know now, things would've been very different. The Floyd would have made a lot of money much sooner than they did, and I'd be a very rich man."* By this time, however, Blackhill had just taken on the management of an unrecorded duo who had no gigs and survived mainly because of John Peel's interest and help. They were called Tyrranosaurus Rex, but that's another story altogether."

September 16, 1972 - Melody Maker (U.K.) reviewed the Pink Floyd movie, 'Pink Floyd at Pompeii.' The film made its British debut at the Edinburgh Film Festival. John Gibson wrote that its technical production goes beyond perfection. The 70-minute film was made originally for television, and was filmed in a spectacular amphitheater in Pompeii. There was no audience, just the band, their technicians, and a range of lighting and sound equipment. Although the musical content is "hardly exciting," it is a visual experience using the ruins of Pompeii as a backdrop for musicians at work. The movie "jells beautifully."

September 28, 1972 - The Vancouver Free Press (Canada) reported on a Pink Floyd press conference held on the top floor of the Rembrandt Hotel. A member of the Canadian Broadcasting Company began the questions.

There seems to be a trend towards smaller concerts, like doing five small shows in one town instead of one big one. How do you feel about this? Pink Floyd replied, *"This has its advantages and disadvantages, mainly because it's hard to get the right sound in a smaller place. Anyway, we don't want to spend too much time in the states."*

How do you relate to your audiences, and how do they relate to you? Pink Floyd replied, *"Well there, we're not really stage performers. Our personalities are irrelevant, really. We're not trying to project our personalities on the audience, so it doesn't matter much whether the audience is large or small. If the band is together personally, and the sound is together, then we do a good show."*

Do you prefer live performances, or recording in a studio? Pink Floyd replied, *"We reach much higher peaks with an audience."*

You said last time you were here that you were changing your music. Have you done this? Pink Floyd replied, *"We're always changing. Anyway, come to the concert and hear for yourself."*

Would you call your music mind or body music? Pink Floyd replied, *"We don't classify music."*

Also in this issue was a review of the Pink Floyd concert at the Vancouver Gardens, Vancouver, B.C. Canada on September 30, 1972. The start of the concert was delayed a half-hour as the stage crew worked on the quadraphonic sound system. The show began with a quadraphonic "insistent throbbing beat," leading into a guitar introduction. Smoke filled the stage and reflected the various colored spotlights. David Gilmour showed his brilliance on guitar as he changed the sound electronically with a console of pedals and knobs on the floor. Rick Wright played pianos (electric and grand), organ, harpsichord, and synthesizer. Nick Mason used intricate rolls and rim shots, layers of cymbals, and a double-bass pedal organ. Later in the show, the song 'Echoes' opened with Rick Wright playing grand piano, followed by David Gilmour playing overlapping guitar leads using a steel in his right hand instead of a pick. After a duet by Roger Waters and David Gilmour, piano and guitar runs play around the hall in quadraphonic sound. This faded into strange echoing screams that "whip around the audience, passing from speaker to speaker," followed by violin-style bass chords by Waters, and finally the original theme. The encore was 'Set the Controls for the Heart of the Sun,' featuring Roger Waters on a Chinese gong. Drums and gong build up until a mighty crash on the gong, and the hoop the gong is suspended in breaks into flame. Members of the audience were reported as mumbling about celestial fires.

October 7, 1972 - New Musical Express (U.K.) reported that Pink Floyd will play a charity concert at Wembley Empire Pool on October 21, 1972. Promoter Tony Smith is organizing the show for the benefit of the Albany Trust and War on Want. Tickets are £1 and £1.50.

October 28, 1972 - Melody Maker (U.K.) reported on the Pink Floyd concert at the Empire Pool, Wembley. Calling them "the world's number one underground band," the article said that the piece 'Dark Side of the Moon' was "stunning." The band used numerous effects, including lighting towers that emitted smoke, quadraphonic sound, flash pots, and Roger Waters had a flaming gong. The concert ended with a blues jam for the second encore.

New Musical Express (U.K.) published an article titled, "Quadraphonic Smokebombs" by Ian McDonald, in which he reviewed the Pink Floyd concert at the Empire Pool, Wembley, London. The reviewer indicated that he wished he was somewhere else, and seemed to be more interested in a new Keith Jarrett record.

Sounds (U.K.) published an interview with Nick Mason by Steve Peacock. Asked whether this is the first time Pink Floyd has performed a piece before recording it, because they usually record the music in the studio first before performing it, Mason replied, *"Right, that's what we normally do. With 'Atom Heart Mother,' we had the piece a little before we recorded it and worked on it a little bit, but this was definitely a major change in terms of*

technique for us. Normally we get into the studio and stagger about for days wondering what to put down. I think this is a better way of doing it, because you spend more time making a good record. And also, usually, even if you use a late take when you're recording, the tenth take or something, by the time you've taken it out on the road for a few months you're starting to regret the way you handled it on the album."

Does this always apply to Pink Floyd? Mason replied, *"Well, it doesn't apply to everything. Some things we never perform live for a start, and some things have a different quality in the studio that gets altered. But I think 'Atom Heart Mother' is a prime example of one of the things we would have liked to have started again once we'd had it on the road for a while, because that was very much a case of learning by our mistakes. The techniques of recording it were quite extraordinary. One of the things we did on that, just as a starter, was that Roger and I put down the whole thing, just bass and drums, which was a crazy thing to do. We used parts of that, but basically it all got chopped up anyway, so it was a totally unnecessary, amazing feat of brilliance, totally useless."*

Is 'Dark Side of the Moon' more of a live concept than past works? Mason replied, *"Well, it is at the moment because it was written that way. But I think there's a lot of scope for doing other things with it. Like we keep talking about giving ourselves more time to do things like 'Dark Side of the Moon,' to get them a lot further than that was got before it was performed, though that was the furthest we've got anything, I think. That's one thing. And the other thing is that we've only recently started to get interested and find a use for synthesizers. We've had one around doing odd blips and burps for quite a time, but we've never really used it. We did a little on 'Obscured by Clouds,' and I think we'll use them more on this piece."*

What do you think about 'Obscured by Clouds?' Mason replied, *"Sensational, actually. I thought the album was an amazing improvement on the film music, and I thought the film music was really good. But then I thought the same about 'More.' It's one of the annoying things, in a way, that the difference between something we've spent a week on and* something that takes nine months isn't that great. I mean, the thing that takes nine months isn't four time nine, 36 times as good. Obviously, nine months doesn't mean nine months solid recording, but even so."

It was tighter and the playing was more intense. Mason replied, "Sure, I thought it was particularly good from that point of view. It had a good, together feel. It was a fairly relaxed album, but it was, well, tight. I like that sort of short, scheme thing. It's less disappointing in a way. Whenever we finish an album, I always think it could have been better. But with things like 'More' and 'Obscured by Clouds,' I tend to think it's really not bad for the time. Perhaps it's just there's more excuses."

Reviewing your past recordings, are there ideas that you thought were good at one time but have now been discarded? Mason replied, "Not much, actually. For instance, we haven't discarded the idea of orchestra and choir after 'Atom Heart Mother,' if that's what you mean, sort of, 'We tried it and we don't want to do that again.'"

What about your general approach? Mason replied, "There isn't much, really. We've made lots of mistakes, I know, but they've been filed under 'experience,' and there's not much that we thought of as complete disasters that we'd never go back to. I can't think of anything that really sticks out as a discard."

Is the music now less violent due to old age? Mason said, "Creeping up? Yes. I don't know. I think the thing that bothers me more than anything is that we seem to get stuck into a slow four tempo for nearly everything we do. Like the speed of 'Meddle' is the speed of nearly everything we've done for too long. That has something to do with it, that penchant for slow tempos. But again, I think, in some ways, things are becoming more aggressive. There's more aggression in the way we do 'Careful With That Axe, Eugene' on stage now than there ever was when we first recorded it. Our original recordings of that were extremely mild, jog along stuff. Even if it doesn't always come off, there's meant to be a lot of very heavy vibes coming off the stage during 'Dark Side of the Moon.' We're well into putting on a lot of effect in order to make the whole thing heavy, really, in the true sense of the word. I'm not expressing that very well, but I don't think it's getting any lighter, and I don't think the intention is to make it light, either. It's all a bit abstract, really."

How has Pink Floyd changed over the years? Mason replied, "One doesn't really feel that it has changed much because you're in it, you tend to feel you're just the same and it's everyone else that's different. I think we just take for granted all kinds of things that happen to us, things like our attitude to what the show should be like. I can't remember exactly what we were saying in 1967, but I'm sure it was something to the effect that 'there's the light show, and we're really incidental to the whole event. We should be in the background somewhere, and we don't approve of people rushing about the stage and jumping up and down.' Ostensibly, we still don't jump up and down, but the pyrotechnics and everything on stage now are arch-showmanship, really. When we were in America, we did a show at the Bowl where it was only marginal whether it was us, or a sort of Barnum and Bailey carnival night, fireworks, searchlights, the lot. I suppose the real thing is that there are so many more facilities available to us now. Five years ago we thought that you should do almost anything to increase the power of what you were doing, and it's just that now the whole thing's turned into this gigantic circus of steel machinery."

In the early days, people came to see the event, but now they come to see Pink Floyd perform. Mason replied, "Right, because there's all sorts of things to bring their attention to the stage, like the lighting towers and so on. I think that's inevitable, though, because apart from anything else, it's to do with the size of the place you're playing. At UFO, now we're really sounding like old age pensioners, but at UFO there was this kind of community feeling about it all. There were other events going on while we were playing, the light show were doing their thing as well, rather than just lighting us, and so on. But really, there's no magic in some of the horrible places we play at now, baseball stadiums and so on, so that's one reason why we center a lot more on the stage. And then, obviously, there's all sorts of other reasons as well, ego drive, and success."

The more people know you the more they may want to look at your faces, but that hasn't changed the effect you have on the audience. Mason replied, *"No, I don't think so. I think we're clearer now than we ever were about what we want to do. We used to have very vague aspirations, like when we started, all we were into was Top of the Pops and a hit single, and then we attained that. It was an amazing disappointment and very nearly exploded the band."*

At UFO, were you a part of the community, or did you play there because it was an available place to play? Mason replied, *"I think I played them because that's where we were. I didn't know what the fuck was going on. Peter and Andrew and the kind of Joe Boyd figures that were around then were probably part of it in a way that I certainly wasn't. All four of us, we were the band, that's all, rather bizarre, sometimes very inward looking people who lived in a world of our own. There was no community spirit, whatsoever. All we were interested in was our EMI contract, making a record, being a hit. At UFO, we felt like the house band. It was, by far, the nicest gig and it was what everyone asked about at interviews and so on, but I certainly wasn't into the lifestyle of the whole thing. One knew the people one came up against, of course, people like Joe Boyd and Hoppy, and once there, one ran up against people that one still sees occasionally. But I don't think I felt part of 'The New Movement' because I was too busy being part of the new rock and roll movement, which was a different thing."*

Wasn't it strange to go from the Roundhouse to Shepherd's Bush TV studios? Mason replied, *"Well, yes, obviously there was an amazing difference. But then you just took it in your stride. I think today I'd probably have a nervous breakdown because the two places are totally opposed. But then, it just all seemed part of your life."*

Is Pink Floyd's music a result of who is in the band rather than outside cultural changes? Mason replied, *"Basically, yes. But it isn't quite as simple as that. The launching of it had a lot to do with Syd. His writing and his songs were what did it, really, because as a band we probably weren't very good. In fact, I'm sure we weren't. That was part of it. And another part of it was Peter and Andrew. Like the light show was more their idea than ours, and that was an amazing leapfrog forward*

because, even if we had the worst lightshow imaginable, no one had seen anything like that before. This is psychedelia, man. I think we were all in a fairly confused state. It was only long after all that period was over that we really started to talk about what we were going to try and do. Vague attempts were made at that time, with 'Games for May,' to do a show of our own, but then we didn't manage to follow it through and do another one until two years after, and that's really a long time not to do something you were intending to do. It was just muddle and finances, and being out of control, really, just muddling along."*

Why does the band take so long to do things? Mason replied, *"Well, the trouble is that there are so many things to do and any new thing takes so much time. It's true that we do get stale if we work too much. It's very simple, really. If we work too hard then we all get very tired and we stop doing anything creative. We go into a sort of zombie, bash it out state, which is really dangerous. It's the easiest way, possibly, of blowing up a band, because the whole thing becomes pointless and you lose all interest in what you're doing. That's for us. In the words of the Scottish guru, we're all humans, and what some people get off on, others don't. There are some bands who can work 300 days out of the year doing live shows, and that's when they're happy, but it doesn't work like that for us. We try and work live as much as we can, and record, which takes so long, and so it gets very heavy to try to find really long periods of time to write new things without rushing them. Like for 'Dark Side of the Moon' we did give ourselves a reasonable amount of time, and it still wasn't long enough. We could always use more time. We don't work all that much in England, its true. It tends to be one tour a year or something. But for a long time we suffered terrible embarrassment here because we felt we were just going out all the time and doing the same things. 'Ummagumma' was supposed to be a farewell gift of all those live numbers. 'Goodbye, that's it.' We still do bits of them now, in fact, but that's because we like to do them. But for three years or something, we did them because we had nothing to replace them. I just felt embarrassed in England because people would shout out for what we were going to do next, because they knew what we were going to do next. There just wasn't anything else."*

People still request old songs, even if you have new ones. Mason replied, *"Yeah, but at least we're splitting it now. But that is one of the dangers of being an elderly band, anything over three years, and particularly the 1967 syndrome, because you're history. 'Darling, they're playing our tune. It brings back that summer in Hyde Park, doesn't it?' Really. The younger ones come along and want to know what it was all like then, because they didn't have mothers and fathers tell them about it. But they certainly had elder brothers and sisters saying, 'When we were young, there was the Pink Floyd, you know.'"*

Does it surprise you that you have stayed together so long? Mason replied, *"Yes, it does. Mainly because you always think it's your band that's got the nutters in it. You occasionally meet people from other bands and they seem very nice, and you start thinking, 'I wish I worked in a band with real people like that in it.' And then you find out that they're all much worse than the lot you're thrown in with, much worse, and they all attack each other with ice picks and so on."*

It is hard to imagine any of the members of Pink Floyd in another band. Mason replied, *"I think it could always happen. There's always various hurdles that you either get over or you don't, say the first year, or the third year, or relative to money or success or something, or people feeling that they're not getting the credit for something they've done, or they could do better by themselves. I think 'Ummagumma' was a great thing in that respect because everyone got a chance to show what they could do. There are still a lot of things, too, that we could all do together that we're all aware of, and if someone said they wanted to go off and do something on his own, then it would be cool to do that as well. There are bands where, if someone wanted to do that, everyone else would say no, but I'm sure we wouldn't now."*

Perhaps that is because you made a gradual climb upwards. Mason replied, *"True. But it's all surmise, really. I think that's one of the most interesting things about rock and roll bands, is the way they work together, the psychology of the group. It's equivalent to families and various things I've never been in*

but I'd imagine would be similar, one being a small army unit, and another a prep school. Because you can oscillate so easily between love and hate, real love and real hate. At one moment you can feel really close to them, or to one of them, or you can hate them. It's never two against two, either. It's always three against one. It really is amazing to watch sometimes. Jokes, and the way they become teasing, and bullying, that's what it gets down to. And, again, it's surmise, but I think we've been lucky in that we've used our managers when there's been a lot of aggression, instead of always ganging up on each other. Steve O'Rourke can take a lot of aggravation from us. We can be incredibly spiteful, and he can channel a lot of that from us without actually breaking, and beating us about the heads with clubs. That seems to be fantastically important."

That might be one of the manager's most important duties. You can't take it out on roadies. Mason replied, *"Right. And, anyway, that would be like going out into the audience and finding somebody very small and beating them up. It wouldn't be fair. And you couldn't pick on anyone bigger because you might lose. You need someone of equal stature. All that, of course, is particularly true when you're on the road."*

The first American tour must have been a nightmare. Mason replied, *"I'm sure that was a dream, in fact, and we all seemed to share it, which is the most alarming thing. That's it, I suppose. There's such a wealth of things that we've been through that after a certain point you feel almost obliged to stay together just so you can tell each other funny stories about, 'Do you remember when . . .?'"*

Also in this issue was a report that the Pink Floyd concert at Wembley on Saturday earned £6,000 for three charities, War on Want, Save the Children Fund, and the Albany Fund of Dulwich. For the performance, Pink Floyd used nine tons of equipment and quadraphonic sound.

November 11, 1972 - Melody Maker (U.K.) reported that Pink Floyd have just finished a new film, called 'Pink Floyd in Pompeii.' It was produced by Adrian Maben and shot on location in France, Italy, and England. The movie will be previewed at the Rainbow

1973
Dark Side of the Moon

Theater on November 25, 1972.

November 13, 1972 - Ekstra Bladet, Copenhagen (Denmark) reported on the Pink Floyd concert at the K.B. Hallen in Copenhagen, Denmark on November 11, 1972. The music was exciting but over time it became boring. Pink Floyd does not know what to do with their effects. The music often ends up in a Dooms Day roar.

December 2, 1972 - Record Mirror (U.K.) published an article titled, "Statement on Floyd fiasco." The premiere of the new Pink Floyd film, 'Pink Floyd at Pompeii,' scheduled to he held at the Rainbow Theater on Saturday, had to be cancelled. Three thousand fans showed up at the theater, and promoter Peter Boyer said, "*The notice of cancellation arrived so late that, naturally, the proper provisions for informing the public could not be arranged. I assume, therefore, that this decision by the Rank Organization resulted in many people having a fruitless and unwarranted journey on Saturday night, plus a ruined evening. It also, in my opinion, seemed to be well timed in preventing me from finding an alternative venue. I am informed that the fault lies in a clause of the lease, stating that The Rainbow must not promote any event that could be considered competitive to the Rank Organization. In this case, the Rank Organization considered that the screening of 'Pink Floyd at Pompeii,' although only a special preview, was competitive. To my knowledge, the Rank Organization never showed any interest in the film, nor did they give any minor indication that they were even aware of its existence. I, therefore, consider their microscopic examination of an infinitesimal loophole ludicrous, amounting to almost a kick in the eye for a public that, at this moment, they are trying to woo. I consider their action entirely unwarranted. I feel that people should, when assessing the severity and pettiness of their action, bear in mind that the Rank Organization are the proprietors of the circuit that is in competition with The Rainbow,*

namely The Sundowns." Edward Way, the general manager of The Rainbow, added, "*This came as a surprise to us. As late as Tuesday, Ranks' property company led us to believe that permission would be given.*"

February 10, 1973 - Sounds (U.K.) published an article about Syd Barrett titled, "Sorcerer's Apprentice" by Martin Hayman. Back in 1967, Pink Floyd's singer and guitarist, Syd Barrett, used to wear flowing capes, and waived his arms in the air to project shadows on the screen behind the band, like a sorcerer's apprentice.

Back in the very early days of Pink Floyd, the band used to play songs by Bo Diddley, and perhaps even `Louie Louie.' Manager Andrew King said, "*maybe it was just one of the number we used to sing in the car.*" King continued, "*As soon as things began to come together, they started to do more of their own numbers. It was easy to get the impression that the Floyd was Syd Barrett and anyone who happened to be playing with him. Syd started developing very rapidly as a songwriter. As soon as we got anywhere near a recording studio, songs would start popping out.*" King remembered seeing Barrett in Peter Jenner's room write two songs in half an hour. King said, "*They just came out when they were needed.*"

Talking about recording the first album, `The Piper at the Gates of Dawn,' King said, "*Everybody knew exactly how to get on with making that record. It was as easy as falling off a log.*" Barrett even contributed to the mixing and use of panning on the album. King explained, "*Syd had a unique way of mixing. He would throw the levers on the board up and down, apparently at random, making pretty patterns with his hands. He was very demanding. You see, he was a painter and wouldn't do anything unless he thought he was doing it in an artistic way. He was one hundred percent creative, and he was very hard on himself.*"

March 10, 1973 – Billboard Magazine (U.S.)

reviewed the Pink Floyd album, 'Dark Side of the Moon.' The album is "a tour de force for lyricist Roger Waters," featuring a "program of heavy, introspective statements." "This is music for intense listening."

Melody Maker (U.K.) reviewed the Pink Floyd album 'Dark Side of the Moon' with an article titled, "The Dark Side of the Floyd" by Roy Hollingworth. Hollingworth began by stating that the finest album ever made was 'Ummagumma' and to try and make it better would be like trying to re-design the sunrise. On Tuesday, he traveled to the London Planetarium to attend the world premiere of 'Dark Side of the Moon.' Life-size cardboard cut outs of the members of Pink Floyd sat behind a large desk in the reception hall. Inside the planetarium, large speakers were set up around the circular room for quadraphonic sound. 'Dark Side of the Moon' was weird. It began with blackness, and a heartbeat increased in intensity. This faded into a steam of noise that "split the room open." Starlight ended the darkness, as the music began. But ten minutes into the album, "the music became so utterly confused with itself that it was virtually impossible to follow." After 15 minutes it was "diabolically uninteresting." The end of the first side was greeted with mild applause. The second side began with the sound of coins and the music was solid and "tripped away into the night." Side two was fabulous. One song was even "Sydbarrettsian," influenced 80 percent by Barrett. It was "enormous, and massive, and overwhelmingly impressive."

The Montreal Gazette (Canada) published an article titled, "Pink Floyd's Bid for 'Top' Sound Fails" by Bill Mann. Mann wrote that Pink Floyd have never made it big, with audiences consisting only of "hard core heads." Their new album, 'Dark Side of the Moon,' is "the band's biggest disappointment artistically yet." Some songs on the album sound exactly like the Moody Blues. 'Money' is a boogie, 'Us and Them' is overproduced, and 'On the Run' is a "mediocre sound collage." At their upcoming concert at the Forum, the band employs 22 roadies, takes eleven hours to set up, uses tons of dry ice, and is rumored to hang bird cages over the stage.

Sounds (U.K.) reviewed the Pink Floyd album, 'Dark Side of the Moon.' They wrote that `Dark Side of the Moon' is the album the band has been working towards for years. It combines technical expertise with a wide range of ideas and techniques, and features Pink Floyd's best playing and composing. They have combined songs in an extended thematic piece with a rare sense of continuity. The effects add to the music without a trace of gimmickry. 'Great Gig in the Sky,' with Clare Torry on vocals, is one of the most moving pieces of music ever heard. The album is unreservedly recommended.

March 12, 1973 - The Toronto Globe and Mail (Canada) published an article titled, "Pink Floyd: space age rock 'n' roll" by Robert Martin. Martin reported on the Pink Floyd concert at Maple Leaf Gardens, Toronto, Canada, on March 11, 1973, describing it as "transplanted San Francisco acid rock complete with a middle sixties style psychedelic light show."

The Toronto Star (Canada) published an article titled, "Pink Floyd's rock has a touch of H.G. Wells" by Peter Goddard. The Pink Floyd concert at the Maple Leaf Gardens, Toronto, Canada, on March 11, 1973 was technologically advanced. An audience of 14,700 heard the show in quadraphonic, controlled by a consol in the middle of the floor that surrounded you with sound. The show was "rock based in technology," owing more to H.G. Wells than the blues, and where the visuals added extra meaning to the sound. At one point in the show, a hydraulic lift raised three banks of floodlights into the air, the stage was covered with purple smoke, strobe lights flashed from inside Nick Mason's clear drum set, and three flares were shot off behind the stage. "The machinery stole the show."

March 13, 1973 - The Montreal Gazette (Canada) published an article titled, "A sensory overload" by Bill Mann that reviewed the Pink Floyd concert at the Montreal Forum on March 12, 1973. The concert started late due to equipment problems, and Roger Waters was in the dressing room playing Official NFL Football before the show. Frisbees and beach balls were flying around inside the venue. As the lights dimmed, Richard Wright played the first note of 'Echoes,' and the crowd burst into applause. The visuals are one of the most stunning shows in entertainment, and the sound, using a $100,000 quadraphonic sound system, was breathtaking. Dry ice produced fog as a giant spinning disc reflected thousands of glints of colored lights. It started smoking during the "Dawn of Time" section. During 'Set the Controls for the Heart of the Sun,' the disc became "an angry red sun above the band." The second half of the show was 'Dark Side of the Moon,' which the audience didn't know. During 'On the Run,' four red lasers shot off the mirrored disc from behind the band like "tracer bullets," followed by four more lasers from the back of the hall, as Richard Wright made sounds like a Star Trek phaser overloading. The visuals were stunning, and the music "endlessly pleasing."

March 17, 1973 - Melody Maker (U.K.) published a letter from a fan asking about David Gilmour's equipment for the songs, 'One of These Days,' and 'Echoes.' On 'One of These Days' he used a Fender Stratocaster guitar, and a Lewis electric guitar with a plain fuzz, and on 'Echoes' he used fuzz, wah-wah, and vibrato effects.

New Musical Express (U.K.) published an article titled, "Floyd: The Great Gig in the Sky" by Tony Stewart that reviewed the album, 'Dark Side of the Moon.' Stewart wrote that `Dark Side of the Moon' has developed considerably since its first performance at The Dome, Brighton in 1972. Musically the album is similar in style to 'Atom Heart Mother' and 'Meddle,' but there has been a development in form and structure. And thematically it is stronger, with themes such as madness, death from overwork, and the separation of classes. The lyrics are enhanced by sound effects, such as hideous madman laughs. "Floyd's most successful artistic venture."

April 1973 - Great Lake, No. 2 (Toronto, Canada) published an article titled, "Pink Floyd: Mad Scientists of this age?" by Drew Metcalf. Pink Floyd's performance at Maple Leaf Gardens, Toronto, sold out 90 minutes after tickets went on sale. During 'Careful With That Axe, Eugene,' a portable

sun/moon/planet hovered above the stage, disappeared in smoke, and reappeared as a fearsome fat feline monster face. Accompanying the band during the concert were three black female backing vocalists. According to the writer, Jimi Hendrix once described Pink Floyd as "The mad scientists of our age."

Prior to the concert, Metcalf interviewed the band. Asked about the early days of Pink Floyd, Richard Wright referred to the book, 'Groupie,' saying, *"We are called Satin Odyssey in the book, and all of Syd's troubles are fully explained. Andrew King of the Blackhill agency is in there as Nigel Bishop, but the book is mainly about Family, who are called 'Relation' in the story. She's a good girl, Jenny Fabian."*

Asked about how he joined Pink Floyd, David Gilmour replied, *"I knew all the guys in the band, and they wanted to get rid of Syd. I was approached, discreetly, beforehand. It was put about in a very strange way, but what in fact did happen was that I joined the band while Syd was still in it, and for a month we were a five piece band."* *"Horrible wasn't it,"* Gilmour said to Nick Mason.

Gilmour continued, *"The whole Syd thing was a very elaborate business. In fact, they didn't exactly know what they wanted to do, except that they didn't want to have Syd performing. But they rather wanted to hang on to his talents as a songwriter. It was a drastic change when he eventually left, but I think it's probably a good thing that we didn't, in fact, carry on having anything to do with him, even if we had been able to get the thing together of having him as a part-time composer, because that would have been total . . . It's much better that we got on and did something, which, while being different, was very good."*

Asked if Barrett had left the band voluntarily, Mason said *"Yes,"* but Gilmour answered *"No."* Mason added, *"Well, I mean, it's very hard to explain."* Gilmour explained, *"In his frame of mind, you couldn't really say whether he left voluntarily or not."* Mason continued, *"I mean the whole thing was totally political. We didn't intend to get rid of him. The management we had believed that Syd was talented and he was being elbowed, so we had this sort of rough framework for staying together. But in the end he was, more or less,*

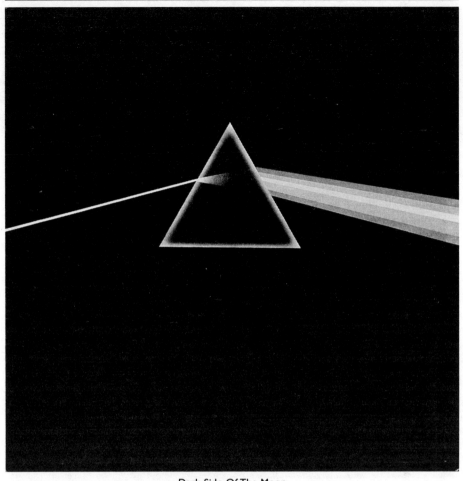

Dark Side Of The Moon

forced to leave by us. It's impossible to explain just how elaborate the whole thing was at the time because we were not like we are now in so much as we had no concept of the fact that we would have any success at all without Syd. I mean, we were terrified. We were terrified, but in one way we weren't terrified because we had been taken right to the edge by Syd. We'd really had it. We were totally screwed up. We'd all been screwed up. But then, we didn't really know what we wanted to do at all. So it was very nebulous."

Gilmour continued, *"Syd has an incredible talent for writing songs, and anybody, in getting rid of him, would definitely be losing something. And if one wasn't sure whether one was going to be able to carry on, or that people would accept that you were doing the writing, you become very*

indifferent."

Mason explained, *"The last seven or eight months with Syd had been a disaster. All the gigs had gone really badly, partly because the audiences weren't into the sort of things we were playing, and partly because the whole thing was totally, it was impossible to do it with any sort of form, gigs I mean. We just used to smash away for an hour or an hour-and-a-half. When Syd left and we started to get together, we definitely were slumping. Our price was way down."* Gilmour explained that, for the next four or five months, their price kept dropping, *"after which we did the Middle Earth gig and Hyde Park, and that really was the road back up."*

In 1968, they recorded the album, 'A Saucerful of Secrets,' that included the songs 'A Saucerful of Secrets,' and 'Set the Controls for the Heart of the Sun.' Asked if they had written those two songs for live performances, Mason answered, "*At first, it didn't occur to us really. I can remember being shocked when someone said, 'What about doing Saucer live,' you know.*" Gilmour added, "*You know, and just thinking, how on earth could we do that?*"

Lately, Pink Floyd have been releasing about one new album every year. Gilmour explained, "*The chances of us getting any faster than one album a year are negligible. We still need to spend a lot of uninterrupted time in the studio.*" Roger Waters added, "*We are getting better in terms of working together and telling one another what it's all about. 'Meddle' was the breakthrough in that respect. We haven't achieved perfection yet, but we can at least communicate with each other.*" Gilmour continued, "*With a producer, you get persuaded out of things you really wanted to do, and the sound gets transported from what you actually wanted. I can remember specific instances where I was pushed out of something I really wanted to hang on to. 'Ummagumma' was the last album on which we used a producer and he knew where his place was. We've found it works better to produce ourselves.*"

Talking about album art and its relation to the music, Gilmour said, "*The sleeve is always meant to have something. I mean, 'Saucer' is definitely related, and so is 'Ummagumma.' And there is overlap between albums. The cow on 'Atom Heart Mother' is related to 'Ummagumma.'*" Mason added, "*We were engaged in a bitter battle with Hipgnosis, and we still respect them, that is why it took so long to get 'Meddle' out.*"

Changing the subject to film scores, in 1971 Pink Floyd were approached by Stanley Kubrick for music for the movie Clockwork Orange. Waters explained, "*He wanted to use 'Atom Heart Mother,' and chop and change it about. He just phoned up and said that he wanted it, and we said, 'Well, what do you want to do?' and he didn't know. He just said he wanted to use it 'How I want, when I want,' and we said right away, 'Right, you can't use it.'*"

Talking about working with Antonioni and doing the music for 'Zabriskie Point,' Wright explained, "*Yeah, he freaked out*

when he thought our music was influencing his film, and ended up not using much of it at all.*" Gilmour continued, "*I quite enjoyed it at the time. It's quite a laugh to look back on it. We saw the unedited film before we started on it, and it was better than the final release. We all quite liked it the first time.*" Asked whether their experiences in America were reflected in the film, Waters said, "*No, not really,*" and Gilmour added, "*We only had one experience of having our gear stolen, but it was quite a small episode. It didn't last very long.*"

Mason continued, "*America is just very hard work. One tends to get into a sort of magic thing about America, you know, English bands all thinking they've got it made. We will keep on going there regularly as we have done for a while now. For us, live work slackens off in England because, at a certain point, you are doing a lot of nights on the road. Once it was, maybe, four nights a week, all over the place, but now it's, maybe, two a week, but in the same place.*"

Gilmour said, "*The increasing complexity of the gear does tend to slow you down. We could still do night-to-night work, but it would have to be close.*" Waters explained, "*You need a day, really, to get in, in the morning, and play in the evening. You need at least an hour-and-a-half sometime in between to do a sound check once all the gear is set up.*"

The Pink Floyd have always had affection for their roadies, and wrote the song 'Alan's Psychedelic Breakfast' about one of them. Mason explained, "*Alan was our road manager. He was older than us and had been in the army and was physically big, even for his job. He got to be such a star that we were afraid to ask him to do things like lifting gear. He is a real character. In the end we had to fire him. That's him on the back cover of 'Ummagumma' and in the song 'Alan's Psychedelic Breakfast' on side two of 'Atom Heart Mother.' 'Alan's Psychedelic Breakfast' was done at my place. Roger and I got it together and started it very quickly. It was a nice spontaneous thing.*"

Returning to the subject of live concerts, Mason said that the band were undecided about whether they should play more concerts in a single venue to try and get a "really nice concert atmosphere," or to continue to tour outside of England, playing to audiences of 10,000 to cover the high expenses of touring.

April 7, 1973 - Melody Maker (U.K.) reviewed the Pink Floyd album, 'Dark Side of the Moon.' They wrote that it is perhaps the best Pink Floyd album since 'Ummagumma.' "A spacey trip" that, at times, relies too much on taped sound effects. Side one lags until 'Great Gig in the Sky,' but side two is perfect.

Sounds (U.K.) published an article titled, "Floyd: At home in Radio City" by Chuck Pulin that reviewed the Pink Floyd concert at the Radio City Music Hall in New York on March 17, 1973. The concert was advertised as a midnight show, but actually began at 1:30 a.m. Elevators in the stage lifted the group into view as steam shot up through vents in the stage. There were three light towers, one with a reflecting dish, and a twenty speaker quadraphonic sound system with speakers on every level of the venue that produced "almost headphone sound." Songs included 'Careful With That Axe Eugene,' 'Obscured By Clouds,' 'Echoes,' 'Dark Side of the Moon,' and 'One of These Days.' The reviewer, Chuck Pulin, wrote that, "everything cooked, it was professional, tight, and just short of being phenomenal."

April 14, 1973 - New Musical Express (U.K.) published an article titled, "Set the controls for the heart of the Floyd" by Tony Tyler. The article compared Pink Floyd to American rock music, and concluded that there is little resemblance. Pink Floyd's appeal is enigmatic. They have a reputation of staging the most staggering stage shows, and their albums are superb. It has been suggested that there have been three different Pink Floyds, the Pink Floyd with Syd Barrett, the 'Ummagumma' Floyd, and modern day Pink Floyd.

The original Pink Floyd was entirely Syd Barrett, with whimsical lyrics and soaring guitar techniques. It's greatest triumph was their first album, 'Piper at the Gates of Dawn,' plus the first two singles, 'Arnold Layne' and 'See Emily Play.' Barrett's influence lingered through to the next album, 'A Saucerful of Secrets,' which is definitive Floyd UFOmania. It also signaled a shift musically from the Farfisa sound to the use of the Hammond organ

by keyboardist Richard Wright. David Gilmour developed his own slide and echo effects on the guitar, and Roger Waters took over writing the songs. Nick Mason redeveloped his drum patterns. The band also progressed from sonic light shows to open air spectaculars.

They entered their second period with the album, 'Ummagumma,' that represents Pink Floyd at the high water mark of psychedelia. The live side consists of UFO material plus 'Careful With That Axe Eugene,' a live visual masterpiece. The studio album part of 'Ummagumma' gave each member half a side for themselves. Waters contributed the first of his electronic jokes, which also appeared on 'Atom Heart Mother' in the song 'Alan's Psychedelic Breakfast,' with sizzling eggs, feet running across the floor, and Alan's love of Marmalade. Pink Floyd continued touring and playing majestic shows like the Bath Festival. They also wrote some film scores for the movies 'More' and 'Zabriskie Point.' 'Obscured By Clouds' in 1972, which should be considered their creative nadir, had them flirting with French avant-garde art. However, there was a certain lack of direction causing them to venture into the realms of the grandiose for the first time. They produced 'Atom Heart Mother' with a choir and brass section, which explored the earth-mother syndrome. The album was not successful, although it sold well. 'Meddle' followed, which was a return to the 'Saucerful' era for the style of composing, but it was criticized by the critics due to two previous years of unsatisfactory Floyd experimentation.

Then in 1972 they played the Rainbow Theater, which was their best ever live performance, and which was the premiere of 'Dark Side of the Moon.' This was a new direction for them, and entered them into the modern era of Pink Floyd. The album, 'Dark Side of the Moon' employed savage lyrics, with subjects like thought control, madness, and society induced brain damage. They have emerged unscathed from their psychedelic past, showing wisdom, maturity, and consistency.

April 28, 1973 - New Musical Express (U.K.) confirmed that Pink Floyd will headline a charity show at Earls Court, London on May

18, 1973.

Also in this issue, Tony Tyler examined the writing of Pink Floyd and the song, 'Us and Them.' The reviewer noted that, for the first time, the group considered their lyrics important enough to print on their record sleeve. The production of 'Us and Them' is extraordinarily clever in how the leading syllables are echoed in time with the music, adding an extra dimension to an otherwise ordinary social commentary. Some of the symbolism that Roger Waters uses has been done before, but the production makes it different. The song, which is about manipulation of the masses by a malevolent "Them," uses jingoism, media, and outright threats to convey the meaning.

May 1973 - Zig Zag Magazine 32, Vol. 3, No. 8 (U.K.) published an interview with Roger Waters and Nick Mason. They wrote, "Three years ago, when Arsenal were an interesting football team, and I had the time, I used to go to see them at Highbury. An old acquaintance from University used to meet me there and he was often accompanied by this big tall geezer who didn't say much but who looked fairly familiar. Probably someone else from University I thought. After about two years of nodding I eventually asked him what he did for a living. "*I'm a musician,*" he replied. "Oh yeah, what sort exactly," I reposted. "*I'm in a group called The Pink Floyd,*" he said, in much the same way that you might tell someone that you worked for J. Walter Thompson. It was Roger Waters. Eventually I managed to screw up sufficient effrontery to ask for a few hours of his time to answer some questions. The only problem was that he had told Michael Wale in his book, 'Voxpop,' that he couldn't stand people who asked where the group got their name from, and that seemed to me to be exactly the sort of question that I would want to ask, plus a few other not altogether trivial matters that hopefully he could clear up. We finally agreed to meet at his house, but when we arrived we were directed to a Mr. Mason's residence about 50p worth of taxi away. In conversation with Roger Waters and Nick Mason the following was gleaned. Where did you get your name from? Roger Waters and Nick Mason groaned, "*Oh no. You can make up something.*"

I) OUR HEROES RECALL THE BEGINNING. In what is quite possibly the best piece of rock music journalism that I have ever read, Pete chronicled the early days of The Pink Floyd in Zig Zag 25. The story was told from the point of view of Peter Jenner, a half of Blackhill Enterprises who discovered The Floyd and managed them for a few years. In this bit of the conversation we verify that story, and examine the parallel development of our band with those happening in America at the same time.

Was the story that we had in Zig Zag 25 about the meeting with Peter Jenner the way you saw it? Waters replied, "*Yes as far as I can remember. He must have come to a gig. Maybe it was one of those funny things at the Marquee. But he and Andrew King approached us and said, 'You lads could be bigger than the Beatles,' and we sort of looked at him and replied in a dubious tone, 'Yes, well, we'll see you when we get back from our hols,' because we were all shooting off for some sun on the continent.*"

You were all students at Regent Street Poly, right? Waters answered, "*No, just me and Nick. Rick had started at the Poly at the same year but after about a year he got a heavy elbow.*"

You had a group called the Abdabs at college during this time. Waters said, "*We had one before that called Sigma 6.*" Mason continued, "*That's right. Manager Ken Chapman. I've still got a printed card somewhere which says Sigma 6 available for clubs and parties or something.*" Waters continued, "*We used to learn this bloke Ken Chapman's songs. What did he study at the Poly? Maybe he'd left by then. Well, he knew Gerry Bron, and we used to learn his songs and then play them for Gerry Bron.*" Mason added, "*And hope to be discovered at the same time.*" Waters explained, "*They were fantastic songs. [Singing] 'Have you seen a morning rose' to the tune of a Tchaikovsky prelude or something, it was all ripped off from Tchaikovsky.*" Mason added, "*There was another one, the up-tempo one, what was that? Oh Christ, the memory has seized up. But that article you had was very good.*" Waters stated, "*We like to think that we would have made it anyway, later on maybe. We definitely don't believe in the myth of managers making* bands."

    Were you influenced by American bands, apart from the R & B stuff? For example, 'Interstellar Overdrive' seems to me to have a very Velvet Underground feel to it. Mason replied, *"We never heard much of that."* Waters added, *"That was nicked from Love wasn't it? It was a cross between Steptoe and Son, and that Love track on their first album, which I can't remember."* Mason said, *"I'd never heard any of those bands. Someone in the band had your original R & B album and that was Authentic R & B Volumes I to III, lots of Bo Diddley, but we never heard any of the other American stuff. It was a complete amazement to us when we did hear them in the States."* Waters continued, *"We heard the names, that's all."* Mason added, *"There was such a confusion. People would come over and talk about those far out West Coast bands like Jefferson Airplane and Sopwith Camel, a whole string of names, half of which were bubble gum groups."* Waters added, *"And the other half were country blues bands."* But if you were listening to Love, they were pretty unknown at that time. Mason said, *"We weren't listening to Love, Peter Jenner was. We were listening to Cream, and The Who, Hendrix, that sort of stuff. That was what turned me onto being in a band again."*

    Was it true, as Jenner was quoted as saying at the time, that he got you to drop the R & B stuff? Waters answered, *"No, that's absolute rubbish, complete crap. He had little influence over what we played at all."* Mason added, *"Nick Jones wrote that in the first review that we got in Melody Maker. It was a lie."* Waters continued, *"The idea that Peter Jenner steered us away from 'Roadrunner' into new realms of psychedelia is crap."* Mason added, *"And we've got a great battery of solicitors to prove it."*

    What did steer you away from playing R & B material? Waters said, *"I dunno. I suppose we just got bored with it."* Mason added, *"Syd wrote more songs. That was one reason."* Waters continued, *"That's true. As Syd wrote more songs, we dropped others from the repertoire. But we went on doing 'Roadrunner' and 'Gimme A Break' and all that stuff for years."* Mason added, *"But particularly when Bob Close was in the band. When he left, that was another reason to get*

rid of old material."* Waters added, *"Because we couldn't play it any longer."*

    II) THE UNDERGROUND. What was UFO like for you? Was it as magical as legend now has it? Mason said, *"It's got rosier with age, but there is a germ of truth in it, because, for a brief moment, it looked as though there might actually be some combining of activities. People would go down to this place, and a number of people would do a number of things, rather than simply one band performing. There would be some mad actors, a couple of light shows, perhaps the recitation of some poetry or verse, and a lot of wandering about and a lot of cheerful chatter going on."* Waters added, *"Mind you there were still freaks standing at the side of the stage screaming out that we'd sold out."* Mason added, *"Actually, Roger, that was usually the other band. One night we played with a band called 'The Brothers Grimm,' and that night at least, it was either the band or their lady friends. I remember that well, because it hit hard."*

    What about that other legend, The Great Technicolour Dream? Mason said, *"Oh that was a joke. That was the night we did East Deerham as well."* Waters continued, *"I'll never forget that night. We did a double header that night. First of all we played to a roomful of about 500 gypsies, hurling abuse and fighting, and then we did Ally Pally."* Mason added, *"We certainly weren't legendary there. Arthur Brown was the one. That was his great launching."* Waters continued, *"There was so much dope and acid around in those days that I don't think anyone can remember anything about anything."*

    III) THE TRIALS OF BEING A HIT PARADE GROUP. Like many bands of that era, the marketing demands that The Floyd's music made on their record company were never really appreciated. Their music was treated in the same fashion that the company had hitherto employed for everyone else, from Frank Sinatra to the Beatles. Nowhere was this fundamental ignorance of what "progressive" music required more evident than in the pressure to have successful singles, and related problems such as Juke Box Jury.

    What's the story behind 'Arnold Layne?' Waters replied, *"Both my mother and Syd's mother had students as lodgers, because* there was a girls' college up the road. So there were constantly great lines of bras and knickers on our washing lines, and Arnold, or whoever he was, had bits and pieces off our washing lines. They never caught him. He stopped doing it after a bit, when things got too hot for him. Maybe he's moved to Cherry Lynton or Newnham possibly." Mason added, "Maybe he decided to give up and get into bank raids or something."

What did you think of Pete Murray saying on Juke Box Jury that you were just a cult? Waters replied, "Now, he didn't say that. This is where the memory doesn't play tricks because it will always remain crystal clear. [Menacingly] He said we were a con. He thought it was just contrived rubbish to meet some kind of unhealthy demand." Mason added, "We thought what we think now." Which is what? Waters replied, "Well, the man's an idiot. A fifth rate idiot, and always has been." I remember David Jacobs or maybe it was Pete Murray saying about Little Stevie Wonder, that it was a disgrace the way that the record company was exploiting his blindness as a gimmick, and another time when he said in the tone of a magistrate, "I understand that there is a lot of this psychedelic stuff in America, but I very much hope that it doesn't catch on here." Mason said, "That's fantastic. That program obviously had a great impact on people. The nice thing is that we can all remember it after all these years, and see that they've all been made to look very stupid." Waters added, "But both our singles were so bloody innocuous, there was nothing difficult about either of them." Mason continued, "But people still say that. You know, 'I have to listen very carefully, and I can just about understand the music.'"

You got hassled by the BBC a couple of times didn't you? Waters replied, "We had to change all the lyrics in one song because it was about rolling joints. It was called 'Let's Roll Another One' and we had to change the title to 'Candy and a Currant Bun' and it had lines in it like..." Mason continued, "...'tastes right if you eat it right.'" Waters continued, "No, they didn't like that at all, very under the arm."

Doesn't that contradict the image of the underground a bit, that you agreed? Mason replied, "Christ no. We were a rock and roll band, and if you're a rock and roll band and

you've got a record that you want to be Number One, you get it played, and if they say take something out, or whatever, you do it. In fact what you do is exactly what was done, you make as much press out of it as possible. You ring up the Evening Standard and say, 'Did you know that the BBC won't play our record because it mentions your paper?'" Waters added, "That line was changed to Daily Standard to appease them, but nobody ever heard it because it was such a lousy record."

You used to slag off a lot of your records at the time. You once described the record, 'It Would Be So Nice,' as complete trash, and added that anyone who bought it needed their head looked at. Waters [laughing] replied, "I think that's the truth." Mason added, "It was awful, that record, wasn't it? At that period we had no direction. We were being hustled about to make hit singles. There's so many people saying it's important, you start to think it is important."

Did you get upset by the failure of your subsequent singles? Mason answered, "No. I can't understand why, actually, but we didn't." You never had a feeling that you were rubbish, that maybe they were right? Mason replied, "We may have thought that we weren't good musicians but we never thought that they were right. It's funny, but I never did feel that we'd had it when the two singles slumped horribly, that it was all over. I don't know why not, because a number of people did think it was all over." Waters added, "There was only that single, and 'Apples and Oranges.'" Mason added, "And 'Point Me At The Sky.'" Waters continued, "'Apples and Oranges' was a very good song, and so was 'Point Me at the Sky.' I listened to it about a year ago, and in spite of the mistakes and the production I don't think it was bad. 'Apples and Oranges' was destroyed by the production. It's a really good song." Mason added, "It could have done with more working out, I think."

IV) THE DAYS WITH BLACKHILL. When I was with Time Out, we ran a feature on Kevin Ayers who is still a Blackhill artist and, as is normal in such cases, we rang up to ask if there were any nice photos that we could use. Usually in such cases, the management or publicity people assure you that there are and promise instant delivery, and when you've rung off, frantically try to remember where they've put them. If they're old, they've probably hidden them under the promotional guff for whatever is about to "break." With these Blackhill cats, though, they arrived with everything we wanted and proceeded to more or less take the place apart in their efforts to ensure that the feature was good. Running up and down the stairs, making helpful suggestions. A very strange and extraordinary couple of fellows.

You applied for an Arts Council Grant in 1968. What on earth was that about? Mason explained (amid explosions of laughter), "It was another of Peter Jenner's ideas." Waters added, "It was a bloody good idea." Mason continued, "But the Arts Council just aren't into subsidizing bands."

Peter is just great for ideas, free festivals and so on. Mason said, "There's much more to it than that. Whatever we say about them now, they did discover us, and to some extent they discovered T Rex. They definitely have a talent in a way that other people don't. For example, Robert Stigwood has a talent for picking up the awards." Waters added, "Put that in. God we feel strongly about that." Mason added, "Did you know that Robert Stigwood was given an award, some golden award for putting on free concerts in Hyde Park, by some American Paper, because they thought that the Blind Faith concert was the first free concert in Hyde Park. That is the story of Blackhill in a nutshell. The whole thing had been started by Peter and Andrew."

What was the grant meant to be for, though? Mason stated, "I don't think anyone really knew, put on a film or some show, mainly just to keep the finances running, I should think. We've been heavily in debt ever since we started-up, until a few years ago, and Blackhill was at the height of our indebtedness, our debt peak." Waters continued, "At the end of the week we'd all go in to get our cheques and, week by week, people would start to go in earlier and earlier. They'd collect their cheque, dash around to their bank, and have it expressed, because there wasn't enough money to pay everybody, so whoever got their cheque first got their money. Cheques were just bouncing all the time because there wasn't enough money in the account, and if the bank manager wouldn't let the overdraft get bigger, then you didn't get paid." Mason added, "They

were usually 7 or 8, maybe 9 thousand overdrawn, but they were usually owed a fortune too."

V) ON THE ROAD: HERE AND IN AMERICA. A Floyd gig, as everyone knows, is a truly amazing experience. Majestic music impeccably presented, and shaped with their own incomparable flair for drama and excitement. Some background information.

Were the gigs in the early days really scary? Mason said, "No, not really. We got jolly annoyed but we weren't really scared. We just went on and on and on. We never said 'Damn this, let's pack it in.' We just trudged around for a daily dose of broken bottle." Waters queried, "Where was it that we actually had broken beer mugs smashing into the drum kit?" Mason replied, "East Deerham, and the California Ballroom, Dunstable." Waters remembered, "The California Ballroom, Dunstable, was the one where they were pouring pints of beer on to us from the balcony, that was most unpleasant, and very, very dangerous too." Mason added, "And things like the Top Rank suites wouldn't let us drink in the bar, which made us bloody angry. We always swore we'd never go back, but we didn't keep to it." How much were you getting for that? Mason replied, "£250, because we were a hit parade group and we could draw people." Waters added, "Went down after that though to about a ton." Mason replied, "No. It never went down that low, Rog, maybe £135 once or twice." Waters continued, "Actually, I remember the worst thing that ever happened to me was at The Feathers Club in Ealing, which was a penny, which made a bloody great cut in the middle of my forehead. I bled quite a lot. And I stood right at the front of the stage to see if I could see him throw one. I was glowering in a real rage, and I was gonna leap out into the audience and get him. Happily, there was one freak who turned up who liked us, so the audience spent the whole evening beating the shit out of him, and left us alone."

Have you ever gone in for smashing hotels and things like that? Waters answered, "No." What do you do on the road in America to combat the boredom? Waters replied, "Unlike most other bands we're not heavily into crumpet on the road. What we are heavily into is swimming pools and trips to see or do things. If we can get together any kind of *activity, we'll all be into it. We play football, go to American Football matches."* Mason added, *"Eating and talking we do a lot."* Waters continued, *"If it's in the summer, we spend all our time sitting around swimming pools reading, and playing 'get off my rope.' American swimming pools always have a rope that is slung across the pool to divide the shallow end from the deep end, which, if you stand on it, sinks down so that it's about three feet under the water. So someone gets on and the other guy climbs aboard and you can play Robin Hood and Little John all day long and the only thing that happens to you is that you get very badly bruised."* Mason added, *"And we have crazes like Monopoly and Backgammon. We also tend to work almost daily, which is important because otherwise it is so boring, but none of us are smashers."*

In the early days you must have toured with other bands? Mason said, *"We don't know any other bands really. The nearest we got to that was The Who, where we did about three gigs with them. It's a whole area of social life that we've missed out on."* Waters added, *"I think The Who are still my favorite band to meet on the road, because they're the same kind of people as we are, really. They're not all smashers. Moony's a smasher, but he's a very sophisticated smasher. He's got it down to a fine art. When he's not smashing, he's incredibly amusing."* Mason added, *"He's very good company to sit and have a drink with. A lot of people are just drunken maniacs, just lurching about, being boring."* Waters continued, *"The Who like a good chat, except for Roger Daltrey."* Mason added, *"You've never recovered from the time he thought Rick was Eric Clapton. It was in a band room somewhere."* Waters recalled, *"At the Fillmore."* Mason added, *"He came up to Rick and said 'Hullo man, good to see you.' And Rick was thinking, 'Shit, that's funny.'"* Waters continued, *"And when he realized, he slunk off and we've never seen him since."*

About 1968, Roger, you were saying that you wanted to do a rock circus. Mason said, *"The circus was quite advanced in the organization stage. We actually did have a big top, but there was some fantastic reason why the tent people pulled out."* Waters added, *"We got a bit of that feel at the Earls Court gigs last week. When we were setting up, I thought that*

it did look a bit like a circus with all these wires going into the audience. And the plane we used at Earls Court was very like those circus space rockets that people whip round and round in. It was silver and red and about six foot long, like a bloody great aluminum paper dart, flashing lights and smoke, amazing."

What is your feeling about lights now, because I remember you saying that they were OK but you'd gone off them a bit, or at least that's what you were quoted as saying. Waters answered, *"What I thought was that they were a very nice surprise device, as far as they went, but during that era, once you'd seen a good one, that was it. I went totally off the whole random thing of light shows. I felt that they should only be used to create a specific effect, and now our music is more deliberate and controlled so all our visual things now are specific and related to something in the music. When the music gets very intense we'll do some big effect, like letting off orange smoke or rockets up into the sky."*

Have you ever had problems with contracts because of the special requirements that you make on a promoter' resources? Waters replied, *"Not problems. We have to get them to provide things like 100 pounds of dry ice and so on. I haven't seen our new rider but apparently it looks like a small atlas, pages and pages. We've discovered that during our last tour of America, since our rider was like three foolscap pages, that the promoters over there don't take it seriously. And on a tour like that you desperately need things to be there when the road crew arrive, not twenty minutes later. If you stuff all that nonsense in, four locks on the dressing room door and two cases of scotch, then the bloke thinks, 'Christ I better get this together,' and then they might even get your power right and the right number of spotlights. You want the stage the right size and to be built on time."* Mason added, *"They bloody well never do it right. They always try to cut it down in size or imagine that they can get away without building the side pieces or things like that."*

Have you ever pulled out when it doesn't come up to scratch? Waters replied, *"We always mean to. When we arrive at some gig and the bastard hasn't started building the stage by noon, and we know that it's going to* take three hours to build and the gig's meant to start at seven, and the electricians haven't arrived, and we always go through a period of saying, 'If they can't be bothered then we'll go home.' But we always relent because we sit there and think that the only people who suffer are the audience." Mason added, "We've pulled out of places when it's clear, well in advance, that the bugger can't supply the power, and you can always make it clear to the promoter that you aren't going to work for or with them ever again." Do you have anyone in the road crew whose job it is to frighten promoters? Mason said, "All our people have different ways of doing things, and they have a very good reputation. The only time we jump on people is if they're stopping us from putting on the best show we can. If there's some miserable swine there who's being officious about something, then we're quite capable of getting as heavy as anybody else. All we're interested in doing is doing the show right. And if they'll let us do that, then we don't give a shit." Waters added, "Getting a bit more beer is easy, but what you can't do easily is suddenly produce two more legs of 40 amp, 110 volt, three phase, out of mid air. That's something you have to get together before you arrive. You simply can't fetch 400 feet of cable from the Chemistry block, although a lot of these people think you can. And it's all in the contract, if only they'd bloody look. And that's what makes us really angry. There are some good promoters, but most of them are just into selling the tickets and counting the money." Mason added, "A good promoter is great to work with, and he'll get a much better show. A good promoter will lay on six blokes to help with the truck, even without looking at the contract."

VI) SOME INCIDENTAL ASPECTS OF THE MUSIC. Whenever you ask a musician a penetrating question about his music, such as, 'When you used the same lyrics in two different songs, two years apart, were you consciously, with irony or humor, perhaps pointing out the metamorphosis in your work that you sensed had taken place,' you always get a reply like, 'Shit no, I only had another hour in the studio to finish it, and I didn't have the time to knock out any more words.' That is why there are no such questions here.

What do you feel is the role of sound effects? Waters answered, "Speaking for myself, I've always felt that the differentiation between a sound effect and music is all a load of shit. Whether you make a sound on a guitar or a water tap is irrelevant because it doesn't make any difference. We started on a piece a while ago which was carrying this to its logical extreme, or one of its logical extremes, where we don't use any recognizable musical instruments at all, bottles, knives, anything at all, felling axes and stuff like that, which we will complete at some juncture and it's turning out into a really nice piece."

Where do you think you most successfully used sound effects, where it was especially good. Waters replied, "Actually, I think that the simplest things are often the best. For example, just the sound of wind at the beginning of 'Cut You Into Little Pieces,' is bloody effective." Mason added, "'Alan's Psychedelic Breakfast' is quite interesting, insofar as although we've all agreed that the piece didn't work, in some ways the sound effects are the strongest part." Waters added, "We did that in a fantastic rush, didn't we?" Mason replied, "Right, but it was a fantastic idea. But because of the rush it didn't work properly." Waters added, "I'd like to think that they all worked, obviously, so I wouldn't like to try and pick out one thing." Mason continued, "'Money' I think works very well. And the interesting thing about that is that, when Roger wrote it, it more or less all came up in the first day." Waters added, "Yeah, it was just a tune around those sevenths, and I knew that there had to be a song about money in the piece, and I thought that the tune could be a song about money and, having decided that, it was extremely easy to make up a seven beat intro that went well with it. I often think that the best ideas are the most obvious ones, and that's a fantastically obvious thing to do, and that's why it sounds good."

Now what's the low down on all this science fiction stuff and space music? Waters said, "Christ I hardly ever read science fiction now. I used to read a lot, but only very occasionally now. I suppose that the reason that I liked to read science fiction novels was because they gave the writer the chance to expound and explore very obvious ideas. Sticking something in the future, or in some different time and place, allows you to examine things without thinking about all the stuff that everybody already knows about, and reacts to automatically, getting in the way. Also you get some bloody good yarns, and I like a good yarn." How does that relate to the description of your music as space music? Waters replied, "Not very much." Mason added, "That was a convenient tag." Waters continued, "Which was held over for so bloody long. People are still calling it 'space rock.' People come and listen to 'Dark Side of the Moon' and call it 'space rock,' which is crazy. Just because it's got moon in the title, they think it's science fiction, which is silly. And the other thing that they do is say that we've gone from outer space to inner space, which is daft." But it must be hard for those Fleet Street people. They have to listen to so much music that they rely on labels to tell them what they're listening to. Mason replied, "It's not hard at all. They find it very easy and just carry on." Waters added, "We haven't done many tracks that had anything to do with science fiction at all. It just depended on what you read into it. We did three songs, 'Astronomy Domine,' 'Set the Controls,' and 'Let There Be Light.'" Mason added, "'Saucerful' wasn't." Waters explained, "The title allowed you to think of anything that you wanted, and because it had echo, people went whooooo science fiction, but it could be anything."

A lot of writers have used analogies with painting to describe their feelings about your music. Do you share that at all? Waters replied, "Maybe. I think that sometimes there may be something that isn't inherently apparent in the piece because of the lyrics, so it becomes very easy to let your imagination go." Mason added, "People often listen to the music and come up with a visualization of what it is about, and when they've had it, they think they've got it, they've discovered the secret. Sometimes they even bother to write to us and say 'I've got it, I've got the answer, it's cornfields, isn't it.'" Waters continued, "And when they say it to us we tell them the truth. We just say, 'If that's what it is to you then that's what it is,' but it can be whatever you want. It doesn't matter what you visualize, it's not important." Mason added, "And they're invariably disappointed." Waters explained, "The way our music impinges on your mind

makes it very easy to conjure up some vision, very easy to imagine some scene. If you're listening to John Cage or Stockhausen it's very difficult, because the music is all squeaks and bubbles. It is more like hard edge, real abstract painting. There are definite things in it like triangles and squares. It doesn't give you an overall impression of The Battle of Waterloo or whatever, it's triangles and squares, that you respond to it in an intellectual way. Our music is non-intellectual, it is straight emotional response gear." Sensual? Waters replied, "Yeah."

What's this famous Azimuth coordinator? Waters explained, "It's just the name that we invented for the quadraphonic pan pot that we use. When we started using quadraphonic pan pots, my son, there weren't any. Nobody had made them." Where did the name come from, that science fiction geezer? Waters answered, "No, that's Isaac Asimov." Mason said, "Oh Christ, the Asimov Coordinator. Go home will you." Waters added, "Go back to the Kop will you, go back where you came from. Azimuth means direction. Where's the dictionary? 'Arc of the heavens extending from the zenith to the horizon, which it cuts at right angles.' That's it. It's vaguely relevant isn't it?"

What did Ron Geesin do on 'Atom Heart Mother?' Mason answered, "I was introduced to him through Sam James Cutler, one of the few good things Sam Cutler ever did, no that's not true. He was a Scotsman practicing in Ladbroke Grove, and then Roger met him, and you did 'The Body' with him." Waters replied, "Did I? Was that before 'Atom Heart Mother?'" Mason answered, "Yes. And then, when we started, it was agreed that it wanted orchestration, and Ron got the gig. Had we got a rough?" Waters replied, "Yes I think so. We'd got a lot of backing track, which we gave him, so he knew vaguely what we were into. Rick worked with him on the pieces for the people to sing and he wrote the introduction completely out of his Scottish head, and the other things we had vague melodies for, he worked on. That was about all. He walked out of our concert on Saturday. Did I tell you that?" Mason replied, "Yes sweetheart. Did you realize where you got that information from? From me."

VII) SYD BARRETT. Syd Barrett is

an indisputably great songwriter, and his departure from the Floyd raised doubts in many people's minds about the viability of the group as both a composing unit and a recording unit. Syd has now virtually retired to Cambridge where he works, among other things, as a gardener.

Why did Syd leave? What's the true story? Mason asked, *"What true story would you like?"* I heard that America did him in. Mason said, *"Have you heard the one about how he threatened us with a gun?"* Waters added, *"That's a good one."* Mason asked, *"Do you want the story behind the facts?"*

What were your feelings about it? Waters replied (heavily sarcastic), *"We blistered with fury."* Mason answered, *"We staggered on, thinking to ourselves that we couldn't manage without Syd, so we put up with what can only be described as an unreliable maniac. We didn't choose to use those words, but I think he was."* Waters added, *"Syd turned into a very strange person. Whether he was sick in any way or not is not for us to say in these days of dispute about the nature of madness. All I know is that he was murder to live and work with."* Mason added (sadly), *"Impossible."* Waters continued, *"We definitely reached a stage where all of us were getting very depressed just because it was a terrible mistake to go on trying to do it. He had become completely incapable of working in the group."* Mason added, *"And it seemed his whole bent was on frustrating us."* Yet you helped him on his album. Waters answered, *"That was because, and I still believe this now, he is one of the three best songwriters in the world."*

What's he doing now? Waters replied, *"I don't know. Not very much. Anyway, that's why we worked on the album. There was a great plan, and that's something that didn't come out in your Jenner article, to expand the group, get in two other geezers, some two freaks that he'd met somewhere or other. One of them played the banjo and the other played the saxophone. We weren't into that at all, and it was obvious that the crunch had finally come. One evening we went to UFO to do a gig and Syd didn't turn up so we did it on our own and it was great. We went down well, and we enjoyed playing together, it was really nice."* Mason said, *"That's fantastic, because I don't*

think that's true." Waters replied, *"Don't you? Didn't you think it was good?"* Mason replied, *"I think you're imagining a situation that never happened. Syd arrived, but his arms hung by his side, with the occasional strumming. That was the night of doing. . ."* Waters finished, *"Saturday Club."* Mason replied, *"Right, which was the breakdown, but that wasn't the end of it all. That evening was something referred to four months later."* Waters continued, *"Anyway, and Nick's almost certainly right because my memory's a bit dodgy, it was more or less that we did a gig without Syd. He may have been on the stage, but we really did it without him. He just stood there with it hanging round his neck, which was something he was prone to do, and after that we realized that we could manage."* Mason added, *"But we didn't do anything about it for some months. We had a long think at Christmas."* Waters continued, *"So it must have been over that Christmas that we got in touch with Dave and said, 'Whooaa Dave, wink wink!'"* Mason added, *"So we were teaching Dave the numbers with the idea that we were going to be a five piece. But Syd came in with some new material. The song went 'Have You Got It Yet,' and he kept changing it so that no one could learn it."* Waters said, *"It was a real act of mad genius. The interesting thing about it was that I didn't suss it out at all. I stood there for about an hour while he was singing 'Have you got it yet,' trying to explain that he was changing it all the time so I couldn't follow it. He'd sing, 'Have you got it yet,' and I'd sing 'No, no.' Terrific."*

Were you brought down by Blackhill's support of Syd? Waters answered, *"I just thought that they were wrong. We had a big and final meeting at Ladbroke Road one day, which came down to me and Syd sitting in a room talking together, and I'd worked out what I thought was the only way that we could carry on together, which was for him to be still a member of the group, still earn his fair share of the money, but Syd not come to gigs at all, become a sort of Brian Wilson figure if you like, write songs and come to recording sessions. And by the end of the afternoon I thought that I'd convinced him that it was a good idea and he'd agreed, but it didn't really mean very much because he was likely to change his mind about anything totally, in an*

hour. He then went home, and I went to see
Peter and Andrew and said that this was the
end. If this didn't work, then we were off. And
I asked them to leave it alone for a bit, for all
kinds of reasons, the main one being that they
didn't see things the same way that I saw it.
But they went round to see him and laid
various numbers on him, so that was it. We
never saw them again except at meetings to
dissolve the partnership. We had to sort out
who owned what, but that was the end, that
day. They were managing Syd for a bit, and
Peter Jenner spent about a year trying to make
an album. And they did about four tracks, all of
which were an elbow except for one. And Peter
finally gave up. And Malcolm Jones, who was
the first label manager of Harvest, said that
they weren't going to put any more money in.
And then Syd came and saw Dave and asked
him to help. And then Peter and Andrew saw
EMI and said that the boys were going to help,
give us another chance. So EMI said alright,
and gave us two days. But we had a gig on the
second day, so we had three sessions, one
afternoon and two evenings. And we went in
and recorded seven tracks in three sessions.
They were fantastic songs."

VIII) THE PITFALLS OF
SUCCESS. Whenever a band becomes
famous, literally hundreds of people approach
them with schemes to harness their music to
some other activity. Whether or not it's because
the aspirants genuinely believe that their
particular music is important or relevant, or
simply because they want to cash in on their
success, I wouldn't like to say, but maybe the
Floyd's experience will illuminate the
problem. The four episodes were 1) a ballet,
their participation in which was plastered all
over The Melody Maker, 2) a cartoon series
called 'Rollo' done by Alan Aldridge, 3)
writing the music for Zabriskie Point, which
music was chopped by the director and that of
The Grateful Dead substituted, and finally, 4)
the movie 'Pink Floyd At Pompeii', which the
Rank Organization got banned from showing
at The Rainbow last year, amid some very
suspicious and devious circumstances.

What happened to the ballet? It was
based on Proust wasn't it? Waters answered,
"It never happened. First of all it was Proust,
then it was Aladdin, then it was something else.
We had this great lunch one day, me, Nick, and

Steve. We went to have lunch with Nureyev,
Roman Polanski, Roland Petit, some film
producer or other. What a laugh. It was to talk
about the projected idea for us doing the
music, and Roland choreographing it, and
Rudy being the star, and Roman Polanski
directing the film, and making this fantastic
ballet film. It was all a complete joke because
nobody had any idea what they wanted to do."
Didn't you smell a rat? Waters replied, "I smelt
a few poofs. Nobody had any idea, it was
incredible." But you said at the time that you'd
just bought the entire works of Proust to study
them. Waters replied, "I did." Mason added,
"But nobody read anything. David did worst,
he only read the first eighteen pages." Waters
added, "I read the second volume of Swann's
Way, and when I got to the end of it I thought,
'Oh what, I'm not reading any more, I can't
handle it.' It just went too slowly for me."
Mason continued, "It just went on for two
years, this idea of doing a ballet, with no one
coming up with any ideas, us not setting aside
any time because there was nothing specific,
until in a desperate moment, Roland devised a
ballet to some existing music, which I think
was a good idea. It's looked upon a bit sourly
now."

Waters continued, "We all sat around
this table until someone thumped the table and
said, 'What's the idea then?' and everyone just
sat there drinking this wine and getting more
and more drunk, with more and more poovery
going on around the table, until somebody
suggested Frankenstein, and Nureyev started
getting a bit worried didn't he? They talked
about Frankenstein for a bit. I was just sitting
there enjoying the meat and the vibes, saying
nothing, keeping well schtuck." Mason added,
"Yes, with Roland's hand upon your knee."
Waters continued, "And when Polanski was
drunk enough, he started to suggest that we
make the blue movie to end all blue movies.
And then it all petered out into cognac and
coffee, and then we jumped into our cars and
split. God knows what happened after we left
Nick."

And Rollo? Waters answered, "They
wouldn't pay for it. We stuck some old stuff on
a pilot that they made, but when they figured
out the way that they were going to animate it
they realized that the cost would be very high.
Now, the only people with the money to back

something like that is the Americans, but the Americans can sell Johnny Wonder going at ten frames a second or something, real rubbish, and people will watch it and the sponsors will buy it. So why should they pay for Rollo, because they can sell their cornflakes with Johnny Wonder. They don't give a shit about the quality of the thing." Mason added, "*It made us aware of what crap there is, what we'll accept as cartoons now. Compared to Felix the Cat, or Mickey Mouse even, it's all such crap.*" Waters added, "*The same bit of background going by. Terrible. Alan Aldridge did most of the initial work and a team of Dutch animators did the work on the pilot, which was very beautiful.*" Mason added, "*The coloring was excellent and the animations were very complicated, with a lot of perspective in it.*"

Waters continued, "*It was a great story. The basic idea was that this boy, Rollo, is lying in bed, and he starts to dream. Or maybe it really happens? And suddenly his bed wakes up and these two eyes pop out of the bedpost and start looking around, and the legs grow and the bed bounces Rollo around, who wakes up. And then the bed leaps out of the house and goes out down the street, all in beautiful movements, and the bed leaps into the sky, and goes flying off into the sky. And when he gets up there, the moon is there and the moon is smoking a big cigar, which turns out to be an optical illusion. It's really a space ship. And then a little plane, like a bird, comes out of this space ship and scoops the bed up with its mouth. And Rollo is taken by a robot dog in the space ship to Professor Creator, who owns and runs this space ship, who turns out to be a collector of animals for an intergalactic zoo. The series was about their adventures going on these journeys to collect the rare animals. And one of the preliminary examples was about these giants who lived underground in a complex series of tunnels and corridors. One of the weird things about this planet was that gravity was different for them than it was for Professor Creator and Rollo. They got into the planet using this machine called the Mole, which bored through. And in this chase scene, where the giants are trying to get them, the giants are all running along the floor and the others are running along the wall. And things like that looked fantastic. Finally they get into* the borer and they come out to the surface of the planet, and as they come out it starts going down like a balloon. Then the ship goes into orbit around the planet, and the giants are crawling across the surface, taking great swipes at the rocket ship. It really could have been so good.*"

What about 'Zabriskie Point?' Waters answered, "*We went to Rome and stayed in this posh hotel. Every day we would get up at about 4:30 in the afternoon, we'd pop into the bar and sit there till about 7. Then we'd stagger into the restaurant, where we'd eat for about two hours, and drink. By about halfway through the two weeks, the bloke there was beginning to suss out what we wanted. We kept asking for these ridiculous wines. So by the end, he was coming up with these really insane wines. Anyway we'd finish eating, the Crepes Suzettes would finally slide down by about a quarter to nine.*" Mason added, "*The Peach Melba was good too. I used to start with Sole Bonne Femme, followed by the Roast Leg of Lamb, cooked with rosemary, and then a Peach Melba or a Crepes Suzettes, or perhaps both.*" Waters continued, "*We'd start work at about nine. The studio was a few minutes walk down the road, so we'd stagger down the road. We could have finished the whole thing in about five days because there wasn't too much to do. Antonioni was there and we did some great stuff. But he'd listen and go, and I remember he had this terrible twitch, he'd go, 'Eet's very beauteeful, but eet's too sad,' or 'Eet's too strong.' It was always wrong consistently. There was always something that stopped it being perfect. You'd change whatever was wrong and he'd still be unhappy. It was hell, sheer hell. He'd sit there and fall asleep every so often, and we'd go on working till about seven or eight in the morning, go back and have breakfast, go to bed, get up and then back into the bar.*"

And the Pompeii film? Mason answered, "*That's had a history nearly as long as the ballet. Whenever it's about to be premiered, Adrian Markham, the director, rings up and says, 'Listen, I must have just a bit more film.' We've been adding little bits to it for ages.*" Waters added, "*It's not a bad film. I saw the final version in New York.*"

What did you think of that business at the Rainbow? Waters replied, "*Rank. That is my answer. I think it's quite witty."* Mason added, *"I like Peter Bowyer's comment. He was waiting for the wounds in his back to heal before he undertook any more such assignments."*

Waters explained, *"What it is, is just us playing a load of tunes in the amphitheatre at Pompeii, interspersed with rather Top Of The Popsy shots of us walking around the top of Vesuvius and things like that. And it was a bit of an elbow. Since then he came to London and shot us in the studio for a couple of days, which has made it much more lively and it's quite an entertaining film. I think Pink Floyd freaks would enjoy it. I don't know if anyone else would. I liked it because it's just like a big home movie."*

IX) OUR HEROES TELL ROLLING STONE TO GET STUFFED, AND THEIR RECORD COMPANY. With the success of 'Dark Side Of The Moon' in America, the band were asked by Rolling Stone to do the Rolling Stone interview. On several previous occasions, when appointments had been arranged with that same paper, the interviewer had not turned up, and the band had been offered no word of apology or explanation. Naturally enough, on this occasion, Rolling Stone were told to get lost. In their next issue, they carried a vitriolic attack on the Floyd's gig in New York, full of snide remarks and cheap rhetoric. Maybe there was a connection between these two events, who knows?

What was your reaction to the put down review in Rolling Stone recently? Waters answered, *"Well you know the story. He never got into the band room. Everybody else did, but we do draw the line at people from Rolling Stone."* You think that Leon Russell, was right? Waters replied, *"Definitely. I love that song. It's hard to generalize about them all, because I don't know all of them, but from my experience of meeting people from there, they're all a bunch of power-mad maniacs. They are completely carried away with the idea that the media surrounding rock and roll, or at least their corner of it, is more important than the actual thing. Though they did print a letter in the most recent issue from someone saying, 'Dear Ed, if you didn't like it, then you were in a minority of one,' which is something the Melody Maker wouldn't do in similar*

circumstances, I can assure you."

If there is something that characterizes the career of The Pink Floyd, then maybe it's their wholesome 'no-bullshit' attitude to the tawdry world of 'da bizz,' perfectly illustrated by the story of the recent reception to launch their latest album. Why didn't you come to the press reception for 'Dark Side of the Moon' at the Planetarium? Waters answered, *"Nicky and Dave and I thought that it was so daft that we tried to get it stopped. And when they refused to stop it, we refused to go to it. I think it was pathetic."* Mason continued, *"The intention was to have the planetarium with a quadraphonic mix, which I would have been into, because I thought it was a good idea. But there wasn't a quadraphonic mix. There was only a stereo mix. And they'd got the most terrible speakers. I mean, no offence to Charlie Watkins but it was WEM, which is not what it would be about. You'd use JBLs and it would all sound pretty fantastic. I heard that it was stereo, not very well done. Cold chicken and rice on paper plates."* Waters added, *"The only point of it was to make a really first class presentation of a quadraphonic mix of the album, so that it was something special. We didn't have time to do a quadraphonic mix so we said, 'You can't do it.' But EMI wanted to do something so they went ahead. It was just stupid. The whole thing was pathetic. They spent a lot of hot air trying to get us to go to it, but we just said, 'We think it's a bad idea, we don't want to do it, we don't want to know.' Obviously we couldn't stop them doing it, but I thought it was daft."*

Final question. What would you say is the meaning of your music. No, I'm just kidding. Let's go and have a beer."

May 19, 1973 - Melody Maker (U.K.) published an article titled, "Floyd Joy" by Chris Welch that featured an interview with David Gilmour at Gilmour's house in the country. Asked what Pink Floyd had been doing recently and how long it took the to make 'The Dark Side of the Moon,' Gilmour replied, *"We did the American tour. We only ever do three-week tours now, but that one was 18 dates in 21 days, which is quite hard. We started recording the LP in May last year, and finished it around January. We didn't work at it all the time of course. We hadn't had a holiday* in three years and we were determined to take one. On the whole, the album has a good concept."

Is `Dark Side of the Moon" your best album so far? Gilmour replied, "*I guess so. A lot of the material had already been performed when we recorded it. And usually we go into the studio and write and record at the same time. We started writing the basic idea ages ago, and it changed quite a lot. It was pretty rough to begin with. The songs are about being in rock and roll, and apply to being what we are on the road. Roger wrote 'Money' from the heart."*

Are Pink Floyd cynical when it comes to money? Gilmour replied, "*Oh no, not really. I just think that money's the biggest single pressure on people. Even if you've got it, you have the pressure of not knowing whether you should have it, and you don't know the rights and wrongs of your situation. It can be a moral problem, but remember the Pink Floyd were broke for a pretty long time. We were in debt when I joined, and nine months afterwards I remember when we gave ourselves £30 a week, and for the first time we were earning more than the roadies. We hardly had any equipment of our own. We had a light*

show, but we had to scrap it for two years. We've had lights again for the last couple of years, but in the meantime we developed the basic idea of the Azimuth Co-ordinator. We did a concert at the Festival Hall with the new sound system, and none of us had any idea what we were doing. I remember sitting on the stage for two hours feeling totally embarrassed. But we developed the ideas and it was purely down to setting moods and creating an atmosphere."*

What do you think of Hawkwind? Gilmour replied, "*I don't ever listen to them. But they seem to be having jolly good fun."*

Do you like the Moody Blues? Gilmour replied, "*I'm not too keen on the Moody Blues. I don't know why. I think it's all that talking that gets my goat. It's a bit like poets' corner."*

What about milestones in Pink Floyd's development? Gilmour said, "*There haven't been any particular milestones. It's all gone rather smoothly. We've always felt like we have led some sort of a cult here, but in America it's been slow but sure. This year in the States, it's been tremendous, but I can't say why, specifically. We have been able to sell out ten to fifteen thousand seaters every night on* the tour, quite suddenly. We have always done well in Los Angeles or New York, but this was in places we had never been to before. Suddenly the LP was number one there and they have always been in the forties and fifties before."

Gilmour continued, "No, success doesn't make much difference to us. It doesn't make any difference to our output or general attitudes. There are four attitudes in the band that are quite different. But we all want to push forward and there are all sorts of things we'd like to do. For Roger Waters it is more important to do things that say something. Richard Wright is more into putting out good music. And I'm in the middle with Nick. I want to do it all, but sometimes I think Roger can feel the musical content is less important and can slide around it. Roger and Nick tend to make the tapes of effects like the heartbeat on the LP. At concerts we have quad tapes and four-track tape machines so we can mix the sound and pan it around. The heartbeat alludes to the human condition and sets the mood for the music, which describes the emotions experienced during a lifetime. Amidst the chaos, there is beauty and hope for mankind. The effects are purely to help the listener understand what the whole thing is about."

Gilmour continued, "It's amazing, at the final mixing stage we thought it was obvious what the album was about, but still, a lot of people, including the engineers and the roadies, when we asked them, didn't know what the LP was about. They just couldn't say, and I was really surprised. They didn't see it was about the pressures that can drive a young chap mad. I really don't know if our things get through. But you have to carry on hoping. Our music is about neuroses, but that doesn't mean that we are neurotic. We are able to see it, and discuss it. 'The Dark Side of the Moon' itself is an allusion to the moon and lunacy. The dark side is generally related to what goes on inside people's heads, the subconscious and the unknown."

Gilmour explained, "We changed the title. At one time, it was going to be called 'Eclipse,' because Medicine Head did an album called 'The Dark Side Of The Moon.' But it didn't sell well, so what the hell. I was against 'Eclipse' and we felt a bit annoyed

because we had already thought of the 'Dark' title before Medicine Head came out. Not annoyed at them, but because we wanted to use the title. There are a lot of songs with the same title. We did one called 'Fearless' and Family had a single called that."

Do the members of Pink Floyd argue among themselves? Gilmour replied, "A fair bit I suppose, but not too traumatic. We're bound to argue because we are all very different. I'm sure our public image is of 100 percent spaced out drug addicts, out of our minds on acid. People do get strange ideas about us. In San Francisco we had a reputation from the Gay Liberation Front, 'I hear you guys are into Gay Lib.' I don't know how they could tell."

Asked if he ever considered doing solo work, Gilmour replied, "I get all sorts of urges, but really nothing strong. Put it down to excessive laziness. No, I don't do sessions, I don't get asked. Any frustrations I might have about just banging out some rock and roll are inevitable, but are not a destructive element to our band. I have a lot of scope in Pink Floyd to let things out. There are specially designated places where I can do that."

How do you react to criticism? Gilmour replied, "React? Violently! People tend to say we play the same old stuff, that we do the same numbers for years. We don't. We are playing all new numbers now, except for 'Set the Controls for the Heart of the Sun.' The Who are still playing 'My Generation,' and nobody complains about that. We can take criticism when it's valid. But we are only human and we can only do so much. Sometimes it surprises me when we play really well, and spend some time on presenting a special show, like we did at Radio City in New York, and we get knocked. Some people dislike the basic premise of what we are all about. Then their criticism is a waste of time. For someone to criticize you who understands you, and can say where you have fallen down, that's valid. There are some people who come to our shows with no real interest in what we are doing, don't like the group, so they don't like the concert. We put all the bad reviews into a little blue book."

Gilmour continued, "I remember, after Mick Watts did his piece on us, we all gave him a complete blank in an aeroplane. It wasn't deliberate. We just didn't recognize him. But he made some snide remark in the Melody Maker, so we sent him a box with a boxing glove inside on a spring. Nick got them specially made. But it wasn't taken in good humor. Syd Barrett would never have done a thing like that. All very childish, really."

Gilmour explained, *"We don't get uptight at constructive reviews, but when somebody isn't the smallish piece interested in what you are doing, then it's no help to them or to us. We did get uptight at what Mick Watts said, it was very savage. But you can't stay angry for long. We tried to turn the feud into a kind of joke with the boxing glove. You've got to have a sense of humor. There's humor in our music, but I don't know if any of it gets through."*

Asked about the history of Pink Floyd, Gilmour replied, *"Nick Mason had got a date sheet ten yards long with all the gigs in red ink, every one since 1967. It's quite extraordinary when you look at the gigs we got through, four or five a week. We couldn't do that now, and not when you think of the equipment we carry. The roadies have to be there by eight in the morning to start setting up. It's a very complicated business. Things still go wrong, but we virtually carry a whole recording studio around with us, all the time."*

Gilmour continued, *"In 1967, no one realized that sound could get better. There was just noise, and that's how rock and roll was. As soon as you educate people to something better, then they want it better permanently. PAs were terrible in those days, but we've got an amazing one now. Before we do a gig, we have a four-page rider in our contract with a whole stack of things that have to be got together by the promoter. We have to send people around two weeks beforehand to make sure they've got it right, otherwise they don't take any notice. There have to be two power systems, for the lights and PA. Otherwise the lighting will cause a buzz through the speakers. Usually a stage has to be built, to the right size. We've got eleven tons of equipment, and on our last American tour it had to be carried in an articulated truck. Oh yes, it's the death of rock and roll. Big bands are coming back."*

Gilmour continued, *"There was a long period of time when I was not really sure what I was around to do, and played sort of,*

backup guitar. Following someone like Syd Barrett into the band was a strange experience. At first I felt I had to change a lot and it was a paranoic experience. After all, Syd was a living legend, and I had started off playing basic rock music, Beach Boys, Bo Diddley, and 'The Midnight Hour.' I wasn't in any groups worth talking about, although I had a three-piece with Ricky Wills who's now with Peter Frampton's Camel. I knew Syd from Cambridge since I was 15, and my old band supported the Floyd on gigs. I knew them all well. They asked me if I wanted to join when Syd left, and not being completely mad, I said yes, and joined in Christmas 1968."*

Gilmour continued, *"I later did the two solo albums with Syd. God, what an experience. God knows what he was doing. Various people have tried to see him and get him together, and found it beyond their capabilities."*

Gilmour recalled, *"I remember when the band was recording 'See Emily Play.' Syd rang me up and asked me along to the studio. When I got there he gave me a complete blank. He was one of the great rock and roll tragedies. He was one of the most talented people and could have given a fantastic amount. He really could write songs and if he had stayed right, could have beaten Ray Davies at his own game."*

Gilmour continued, *"It took a long time for me to feel part of the band after Syd left. It was such a strange band, and very difficult for me to know what we were dong. People were very down on us after Syd left. Everyone thought Syd was all the group had, and dismissed us. They were hard times. Even our management, Blackhill, believed in Syd more than the band. It really didn't start coming back until 'Saucerful Of Secrets' and the first Hyde Park free concert."*

Gilmour continued, *"The big kick was to play for our audiences at Middle Earth. I remember one terrible night when Syd came and stood in front of the stage. He stared at me all night long. Horrible!"*

Gilmour continued, *"The free concerts were really a gas. The first one had 5,000 people, and the second had 150,000. But the first was more fun. We tried to do two more singles around this time, but they didn't mean a thing. They're now on the 'Relics' album."*

Asked what he thinks is in the future for Pink Floyd, Gilmour replied, *"God knows. I'm not a prophet. We have lots of good ideas. It's a matter of trying to fulfill them. It's dangerous to talk about ideas, or you get it thrown at you when you don't do it. We have vague ideas for a much more theatrical thing, a very immobile thing we'd put on in one place. Also we want to buy a workshop and rehearsal place in London. We've been trying to get one for some time. No we don't want our own label, but we do have our own football team! We beat Quiver nine to one recently, and now there's talk of a music industries' cup. Oh, and we played the North London Marxists. What a violent bunch. I bit my tongue and had to have stitches."*

New Musical Express (U.K.) published an article titled, "A Walk on the Dark Side," by Tony Tyler that featured an interview with David Gilmour. The interview took place at David's home, a mock-Tudor residence in Essex with a BMW in the garage and a swimming pool in the back. Gilmour, who was wearing a T-Shirt that said "Didn't they do well" on it, was sitting in a rocking chair next to a gorgeous antique teak altar-screen. He had been to the Marquee Club the night before with Roger Waters to see Roy Buchanan perform.

Tyler congratulated Gilmour for 'The Dark Side of the Moon' having reached Number One in the States. Gilmour replied, *"Yes, it is nice, isn't it? We've never really been above fortieth position before, but, even so, we're still selling more albums there than we would in the English Charts."*

Prior to 'Dark Side of the Moon,' Pink Floyd were considered a cult band in the U.S. Gilmour said, *"I suppose we've always had this sort of underground image over there. I don't think it'll make any change. I mean, we've never had any problem selling out even the largest halls and I don't really see how that can change. We can still sell out the Santa Monica Civic two nights in succession and I'm not sure that the album will make any difference to that."*

Asked about his trip to the Marquee Club, Gilmour explained, *"In fact, I was down there that night to see Quiver."* One of the members of Quiver was in a band with David Gilmour at one time.

Asked if 'Dark Side of the Moon' is a return to a purpose, Gilmour answered, *"I suppose so. Certainly there's a sort of theme running through it, which we haven't really done for a long time. There's two opinions about this in the group. Half of us wanted to play a thematic piece, the other half wanted to play a collection of songs."* Asked which half he was in, Gilmour smiled and said, *"I didn't object, anyway. It's basically Roger's idea. We'd all written songs beforehand, and then Roger got the theme and the words together."* Tyler observed that, for the first time, the lyrics to the songs are printed on the album cover, and Gilmour explained, *"Yes, I generally don't like sleeve lyrics."* Gilmour added, *"The theme of the album is the pressure that can drive a person mad, pressures directed at people like us, like money, travel, and so on."*

The interviewer had seen Dark Side of the Moon performed at the Rainbow Theater in 1972, and since then, the piece has changed considerably. Gilmour explained that they had been performing it for six months before they went into the studio to record it, saying, *"Normally we go into the studio, often without any concrete ideas, and allow the circumstances to dictate the music."* It was suggested that this is an expensive way to record, and Gilmour replied, *"No. We don't pay. EMI do."* Tyler noted that the guitar playing on 'Money' is spectacular, and Gilmour said that he thinks his playing on 'Obscured By Clouds' is better, although he added that the song 'Money' is a guitar track. Tyler also remarked that the original taped Malcolm Muggeridge section at the end of 'Dark Side of the Moon' is not there anymore, and Gilmour replied, *"Yes. Well, you didn't really expect we'd get his permission, did you?"*

Asked about past Pink Floyd songs that he likes, Gilmour indicated that he doesn't really listen to Pink Floyd albums, but he does like the album 'Obscured By Clouds,' and some of the songs on 'Saucerful of Secrets,' specifically the title track and 'Set the Controls for the Heart of the Sun.' He also explained that 'Atom Heart Mother' was an experiment and that he would do it differently now. Gilmour explained, *"The trouble was, we recorded the group first, and put the brass and the choir on afterwards. Now, I think I'd do the whole thing in one take. I feel that some of the rhythms don't work and some of the syncopations aren't quite right."*

Asked about the ballet Pink Floyd performed, Gilmour said, *"In fact, we did that ballet for a whole week in France. Roland Petit choreographed it to some of our older material. But it's too restricting for us. I mean, I can't play and count bars at the same time. We had to have someone sitting on stage with a piece of paper telling us what bar we were playing."*

Talking about film scores, Gilmour elaborated, *"We also did the music for 'More.' We hadn't done film scores before, but they offered us lots of money. We wrote the whole thing in eight days from start to finish. We did 'Zabriske Point' for Antonioni, and, in fact, we wrote much more than he eventually used. I feel, even now, that it would have been better if he'd used most of what we'd written."* Tyler suggested that these other projects were a disappointment to some of their fans, and Gilmour angrily replied, *"That's the trouble, you can't really break out of the progression from your last LP rut. People's minds are set to expect something, and if you don't provide it, well . . ."*

Told that many fans regard the album 'Ummagumma' as their best, Gilmour stated, *"For me, it was just an experiment. I think it was badly recorded. The studio side could have been done better. We're thinking of doing it again."*

At this point, Gilmour took the interviewer into his home studio. It is described as including tape recorders, eight-track machines, a drum kit (asked if this was Nick Mason's, Gilmour replied "No, mine.") twelve guitars including a Fender Stratocaster, a 1959 Gibson Les Paul Custom, a Gibson Les Paul Junior, a Les Paul-type guitar "custom made, naturally," and a classical guitar "custom made, naturally." Also in his studio is a new EMS synthesizer that Gilmour said will never be available on the market. The synthesizer is a Synthi Hi-Fli guitar synthesizer that looks like a plastic pulpit with pedals underneath, and it includes a fader to lower a note an octave, a fuzz device, and a phase shifter. Gilmour demonstrated the device to the interviewer, who decided that Gilmour "said more about Pink Floyd in 30 seconds of

dive bombing with the Strat and the Synthi Hi-Fli than all the interviews in the world would ever do."

Also in this issue is a nationwide gig guide that featured a picture of Pink Floyd performing, plus a brief article that reported that Pink Floyd sold out their first show at Earls Court, with only a few tickets left for the second night. Members of Pink Floyd's sound crew attended the David Bowie concert at Earls Court last week in order to check out the sound. Pink Floyd will be performing 'Dark Side of the Moon' at the concerts. The gig guide also included a half-page ad for the concerts.

Also in this issue was a review of the Pink Floyd concert at Earls Court, with an article titled, "Dazzling Side of Floyd." A huge balloon was hung from the ceiling to depict the moon, with silver balls suspended on each side of it. An audience of 18,000 cheered as strange sounds began from all parts of the hall. Strobe-sparks came from the drum kit, and David Gilmour sent shivers down the spine with his guitar, as the audience sat quiet and attentive. Smoke filled the stage as the lights changed from red to yellow to orange, and Richard Wright's Hammond organ sound filled the hall. During 'Set the Controls for the Heart of the Sun,' Roger Waters played a gong, with red floodlights, and a white spotlight on Waters, forming a rainbow where they meet. The gong burst into flames as the sound traveled around the arena in quadraphonic. Waters whispered and screamed during 'Careful With That Axe Eugene' as smoke poured from above. During intermission, it was announced that unidentified flying objects were due to arrive, but they won't harm the audience.

A heartbeat began 'Dark Side of the Moon,' as the moon was illuminated, and maniac screaming was heard. The sound quality was excellent in Earls Court. During 'On the Run,' lights flashed everywhere, white searchlights scanned the audience, orange lights revolved on top of the P.A., sounds echoed around the hall, and an aircraft flew the entire length of the hall and disappeared into an orange cloud of smoke above the band. The arena was turned into a hall of clocks and watches for the song, 'Time,' and three female singers and a sax player joined the band for the song 'Great Gig in the Sky.' 'Money' followed with a raunchy sax solo, and 'Us and Them' included a sax solo and a cathedral organ. Madman screams and rockets shooting ended the piece. The encore was 'One of These Days' and ended with more fireworks. This was rock theater at it's best, music at its finest.

Sounds (U.K.) published an interview with Roger Waters by Steve Peacock. Waters began by stating, *"I certainly think it's true that a lot of bands in the past have worked themselves into the position that we're in now, seen how much money you can make, and worked themselves into the ground trying to cash in on it. They literally work themselves until there's nothing left, until they're mere shells of men, stalking the earth with staring eyes, empty heads, and full pockets."*

Asked about his current activities with Pink Floyd, Waters replied, *"I occasionally pick up a guitar and strum a few chords or jot a few words down, but when I say occasionally, I do mean occasionally. No, there aren't any concrete plans. I'm very much floating at the moment."*

Pink Floyd has done some recording work on music involving knives, forks, glasses and other objects that make nice sounds, and there has also been talk of making an album like 'Ummagumma,' where each member has a side to do what he wants. Asked if they might be working as individuals instead of as the Floyd, Waters replied, *"Not really. We're just easing back on everything. It's something we've been trying to do for a long time, but which we're now able to do."*

Asked if this was because they now have enough money to do it, Waters answered, *"I suppose that's a big part of it, if the truth be told. But also you reach various points where you want to do that because you're getting pissed off, only you don't manage to do it the first time, or the second time, perhaps. But eventually you do reach a point where nothing stops you. Someone walks in the door saying you can do a tour of so and so, and make thousands, but you've reached the point where you don't want to do it so much, that however much they offer, you say no."*

Asked about the difference between a regular gig and an inspired gig, Waters said, *"Some bands can be fantastic one night, and terrible the next, but that never happens to us.*

We never play bad gigs, and the audience response really has nothing to do with whether we play well or not. It just depends on who's there, I suppose."

Asked about the influence of technology, Waters explained, *"The more you refine it, the more difficult it becomes to do something out of the ordinary, enough to impress oneself. But even on an ordinary gig, there's a lot of energy released."*

Asked if satisfaction after a show is anything more than just a job well done, Waters answered, *"Not really. You've got to remember that we've seen every Pink Floyd gig, every one, so although there are a few surprises left, they're pretty thin on the ground. I think if it isn't a job, you'd just blow up. If it was a great emotional experience every time you played, you'd explode after about a year. I can't imagine anyone keeping it up for five years or however long it's been."*

Asked about the current slow pace of their work, Waters explained, *"The importance of this whole slowing down thing to me is to be able to do something that isn't a rush. Everything we've ever done has been a rush, and you just reach a point where you don't want to know about another deadline. The whole business is very young, it's been going a very short time, and most people really haven't found out what is actually the best way of going about writing what can be loosely defined as rock and roll. People know what they like, and they know that there have been some very good things done because they've heard and liked them. It's different for every band, I suppose, but the thing is, up to now the factor that's been foremost in everybody's minds has been that there's an enormous market and there's a lot of money to be made. Go like smoke, get the bit between your teeth and don't let go. There seem to have been only three real alternatives. Work yourselves till you're mental, which has happened to a lot of people. Work on and on until you've bored your audience away. Or wait until you've made enough money so you don't have to worry. But I suspect a lot of people who've worked their audiences into a boring grave, and have consequently faded, might not have done if they'd stopped a bit sooner and thought a bit more about what they were doing, just taken a bit more time and effort. Because until the tour happens when people stop coming to see you, you never know. And even if we can't stop that happening, at least we've tried."*

May 24, 1973 - Rolling Stone (U.S.) reviewed the Pink Floyd album, 'Dark Side of the Moon.' Loyd Grossman wrote that `Dark Side of the Moon' mainly deals with the uncommon subject matter of the "fleetingness and depravity of human life." Although it is a concept album, some songs stand on their own, like 'Time,' which is "a country-tinged rocker," and 'Money,' which is satirically played with a raunchy sax. 'On the Run' is also a standout track. The music is "lush and multi-layered while remaining clear and well structured." David Gilmour's vocals are sometimes weak and lackluster. But the album has the grandeur and flash that "comes from the excellence of a superb performance."

May 26, 1973 - Melody Maker (U.K.) published an article titled, "Floyd-a perfect moonshot" by Chris Charlesworth that reviewed the Pink Floyd concert at Earls Court, London, on May 18, 1973. Charlesworth wrote that the concert was faultless. A quadraphonic sound system allowed instruments and tapes to be heard from every corner of the hall. Roger Waters' gong burst into flames during 'Set the Controls,' and an inflatable man with green piercing eyes rose from behind Nick Mason during 'Careful With That Axe, Eugene.' During 'Echoes,' a rotating silver disc shot beams of light out into the audience. The second half of the show was 'Dark Side of the Moon,' with three girl singers, a saxophone, and numerous special effects including a large model airplane that flew over the crowd and crashed into the stage.

June 1973 - Circus Magazine (U.S.) published an article titled, "Dark Side of the Moon-Pink Floyd's Startling Leap to the Top" by Penelope Ross. Pink Floyd performed recently at Toronto's Maple Leaf Gardens. They began their set with the song 'Set the Controls for the Heart of the Sun,' and for the last half of the show played 'Dark Side of the Moon.' An audience member stated, "It was the best stage show ever in Toronto. The sound was perfect, crystal clear, and going 360 degrees around the hall." Visually, the band

used a black stage with black curtains, fog machines, red lights, dry ice, and laser-like lights. Augmenting the band were three black female background singers. The new Pink Floyd album, 'Dark Side of the Moon,' has already sold more copies than 'Ummagumma' sold in three years.

The writing sessions for 'Dark Side of the Moon,' took place in a warehouse in Bermondsey. David Gilmour said, *"When we started, we'd just discussed the barest outline of what we were going to do. Then Roger Waters came into the warehouse every day with bits and pieces of lyrics, and we all added music to them. We ended up with an album about the pressures we've been through as musicians on the road."*

For their current tour, personnel include the band, their manager, a sound man, a road manager, and two assistants. They are using eleven tons of equipment. As for touring, their manager stated, *"The U.S. is where you make it or don't. And to do well, you must do very well. Europe is made up of small countries, so it doesn't matter so much if you don't go over well in one of them. But the competition is greater here. And we want to be successful. That's why we come. American audiences are very good and the group has done some of its best shows here, in part because they get keyed up from the pressure."*

June 25, 1973 - The Detroit Free Press (U.S.) published an article titled, "Olympia's Heat Didn't Wilt the Jazzy Rock of Pink Floyd" by Christine Brown that reviewed the Pink Floyd concert at the Olympia Stadium in Detroit Michigan on June 23, 1973. Brown wrote that the crowd of 17,000 used festival seating in a hall that felt like a steam bath. Films by Peter Medak for Dark Side of the Moon could not be shown since the band's projector was ruined during a rainy outdoor concert in Milwaukee, but the music was excellent and the band did use a mirrored ball to bath the audience in a swirl of stars.

September 1973 - Circus Magazine (U.S.) reported that the Pink Floyd concert at Earls Court, London, England, was "one of the most spectacular rock performances ever conceived." The show included quadraphonic sound, a gong that burst into flames during the song 'Set the Controls for the Heart of the Sun,' an inflatable man with glowing green eyes that hovered behind Nick Mason during 'Careful With That Axe, Eugene,' and an enormous model airplane that crashed in a blazing fireball behind Rick Wright during 'Dark Side of the Moon.'

October 6, 1973 - Sounds (U.K.) published an interview with David Gilmour by Pete Erskine. Asked if he ever thought that Pink Floyd would achieve the success that it has, Gilmour replied, "*Yes. That's the short answer to that. I thought it would last a long time and I thought it would get pretty successful as well.*"

When you joined, what were the band's objectives? Gilmour replied, "*Well, it wasn't as developed then as it is now, obviously, but although we were pretty loose when we went on in those days, we had a pretty good idea of what we were trying to do.*" What were you trying to do? Gilmour replied, "*Well, even before I joined, there was an attempt to do the big production thing. There was always the idea of having a really high fidelity sound system and putting on a fully produced show, with quadraphonic sound. I mean, it was basically an audio idea then. Lighting and effects came into it, but not as much as they do now.*"

Were you aware back then how different you were from other bands? Gilmour replied, "*Oh yes, we were. We were even more different, probably, then, than now. It's always been pretty insular, I suppose.*"

How did you happen to join Pink Floyd? Gilmour replied, "*Well, I did know them before I joined, but I suppose it was through knowing Syd. I've known him since I was 14. Anyway, Cambridge is a small town.*" What was Syd Barrett doing at that time? Gilmour replied, "*Art, mostly. What he's into hasn't changed much. He has. Don't print a lot of garbage about Syd, though. We have a lot of that nowadays.*"

Was it difficult when you joined Pink Floyd? Gilmour replied, "*It was, I suppose, but I didn't really do much for a long, long time. I mean, I just sat there and played rhythm to help it all along. For a good six months, maybe more, I didn't do a single thing. I was pretty paranoid.*"

Did you know how to play lead guitar back then, or was it just that you didn't know how to make it fit in? Gilmour replied, "*I hadn't worked out how it would fit in and I wasn't at all confident of it, in any way, at all. It was mostly me, and paranoia. I don't think they, the rest of the band, had fixed ideas of what I should do, or had any fixed ideas of how I should do it. I was more conscious of knowing that I had something specific to do and thinking that I had something to follow. I guess I thought they had a more rigid idea of what they wanted me to do and be, than they, in fact, had. I was frightened to stick my neck out and change what they were doing because the way I would naturally play guitar would obviously have changed it quite a lot.*"

Are you playing your guitar naturally now? Gilmour replied, "*The way you play an instrument is down to all the influences that have affected you over the years, anyway. If I'd come through different bands up to now, I don't know whether I'd be playing the same as I do now. That's impossible to say. I think I am playing naturally. I'm free and I'm quite confident. I do play exactly how I want to play, now. The vehicles for playing over aren't always the most ideal thing for playing guitar over, necessarily. There, obviously, wouldn't be anything like that if it was for a lead guitar showcase.*"

What do you think of the early albums? Gilmour replied, "*I hardly ever listen to any of them, actually. Yeah, I like one or two bits and pieces. I like the track 'Saucerful of Secrets' on the original album. I mean, we really dug that when we were doing it, but eventually we'd been doing it so long there was nothing new ever happening. I got to the point where I was playing it completely mechanically. I just wasn't thinking about it at all. I had to really hustle for us not to play it any more. Everyone, now and then, has a real hustle trying to stop playing something. The original track for 'Set the Controls for the Heart of the Sun' is really good. They're both again on 'Ummagumma,' but I don't like them there at all.*" Why don't you like them on 'Ummagumma?' Gilmour answered, "*Well, we only recorded two live gigs and neither of them was very good. One of them was well-played but badly recorded, and the other was pretty poor playing but well recorded, but that was* done in the days of 4-track, and a 4-track recorder for a live performance, if you don't have a proper producer and really good setting up and trying out time, is completely ludicrous. We didn't try it out at all. We did about five minutes before the audience came in for mike levels and stuff, but that's all. I think they put bass and drums down together, and guitar, keyboards, and organ on another two tracks, and the vocals on one track, but we re-dubbed the vocals in the studio."

Has studio equipment gotten better since then? Gilmour replied, "A fantastic amount. The first stuff that I did with the band, the first couple of albums were done on 4-track, and trying to record a whole band with dubbing, etc., is just impossible. We were produced by Norman Smith then. It was alright, at the time, because you didn't know any better. The 8-track came along, and that was fantastically much more than 4-track, gives you a whole lot more scope. 'Atom Heart Mother' was done on 8-track, and 'Meddle' was the first on 16-track. It's developed so rapidly. Three years ago, there wasn't a studio in the country with 16-track."

What is your opinion of 'Ummagumma?' Gilmour replied, "I never thought it was that good an album. I thought it was quite a nicely balanced little thing for live and the odd little bits of, ego trips, whatever." Why do you think people find 'Ummagumma' such a landmark album? Gilmour said, "Beats me. I mean, there are some quite nice bits and pieces on it. I don't really know. I've never listened to it. I mean, I literally hardly ever heard even the other peoples' parts on it. I certainly haven't listened to my part on it, at least not since the six months directly following its release. I never really listen to any of them after they've been released because they're always completely old. By the time they get released, you know them inside, out, and backwards, and you're fed up with them."

It took you a year to make 'Dark Side of the Moon.' Did it take that long to make the rest of the albums? Gilmour replied, "No, but we never manage to put out more than one a year, though, apart from film ones which take about a week to make."

Are you planning to cut down on touring? Gilmour replied, "Yeah, we're going to cut down a bit on touring. We have done already. But we've never done that much. We've never done the heavy slogging in America that people tend to do. We've restricted it to about two three-week tours in the last three years. In fact, though, I feel in the mood for touring again. We don't want to go out and plough through all the stuff we've been doing for the past year. We still do 'Dark Side of the Moon' in one or two places, but it's really down to having something new to do."

Does the fact that your show has to be extremely organized keep you from doing it frequently? Gilmour replied, "Well, I dunno. We can do American tours for three weeks, but we do tend to start fading towards the end a little bit, but then I think most bands do."

Do you play differently on stage from show to show? Gilmour replied, "When you've lived with the material for a bit, it tends to work itself in. There's no specific part there to start with. At the beginning, when you're just starting with new material, it does vary a lot. But as you go along, you kind of cut out the rubbishy bits, and you remember the good bits, and by the time you've been playing it for a few months it's pretty much the same every night, except for a night when you really get off and start really thinking about changing it."

Are you becoming less insular from mainstream rock and roll? Gilmour replied, "I don't think it really is becoming less so. I don't know. I think maybe one or two of the people in it are maybe becoming a little less so. I think maybe I am. I'm trying to, anyway. I don't know whether that's a good thing for the band or not, though, in terms of its popularity or its appeal. I mean, I think quite a lot of its appeal is down to the fact that it's a very different band. If you get influenced by the current things, the good things that are happening, then you're tending to bring it in closer. I mean, 'Dark Side of the Moon' is closer to other people and further away from what we've done in the past in terms of the actual musical content. It's more conventional, anyway." Did that come in with 'Atom Heart Mother' and the funky segments? Gilmour said, "No, it didn't 'come in' at any time. The influence, I suppose, has come from making it largely vocal, from making the meaning about what the whole thing's about pretty clear and explicit, which it's supposed to be and doing it

David Gilmour

in a kind of vocal way. Things that sound more like us earlier on have been mainly instrumental, or they've got very spacey cosmic lyrics that don't mean anything, that are pinched out of the I-Ching and stuff."

Was 'Ummagumma' a bit tongue in cheek? Gilmour replied, "I think it's pretty serious, most of it. I can't speak for Roger, though. I don't know if he was particularly serious. The idea behind it was serious, of doing a piece completely vocally, without any instruments. Some of the pieces are meant to be open for interpretation, 'Saucerful of Secrets,' really. I mean, it kind of tells everyone a story but it could be any number of different ways it's seen in."

Have you ever thought about getting closer to what others are doing? Gilmour replied, "I think most people stick pretty closely to one thing, actually. Most of the bands who have stayed together as long as us have remained pretty constant, but you don't notice it as much because they've always stayed within a fairly narrow field, I think. Changes in fashions of playing and so on do affect us a little, but I guess we assimilate them quite well. I'm sure we do pick up on things

and use them, plagiarize them, no, sorry, forge them, into our own inimitable style."

Who decided to use the female backing vocalists on the album and in concert? Gilmour replied, "I don't know. I can't remember. It came in the making of the album. We all thought that, basically, for 'Us and Them,' we really needed girls, and once you've got them on one track, it's daft not to use them more than that, and especially when you sit and think about it you can think of all sorts of other nice things to do, and once you've done that, you might as well tour with them, mightn't you? That was a gas. It's really nice to have girls on stage. It's really added to it. It got really good, as well, in the States. We didn't have the same girls as on the album doing the solo thing on that number. That really got fantastic, some of that, and we got them doing a bit in my guitar solo in whatever it was, when it went down really quiet." Have they influenced the way you play? Gilmour said, "Not really. But it did mean that we didn't have to do the harmonies as much. On the last three sets of gigs, we've had the girls, but Dick Parry, the horn player, couldn't make the last but one American tour, but he did the last one.

If we toured again with 'Dark Side of the Moon,' we'd have them all with us."

How much longer do you want to perform 'Dark Side of the Moon?' Gilmour replied, *"We don't want to do it, really, any more. We've done it enough in the States. We could do another West Coast tour, I suppose, but I don't think we will. We've taken it to Japan, but not since the album came out, which changes it because they don't really know what we were doing then. We might go out there and do it in March, but I'm not sure. We haven't really got any gigs outstanding except for a couple in Germany this coming month, Germany and Austria. We're starting again in the studio this Monday, for two months."*

Do you have any new material? Gilmour replied, *"No, not really."* Do you always go into the studio without any material already written? Gilmour explained, *"Not always. Usually. It wasn't the way we went in and did the last album. If we go in this next week and start doing something new, it will be recorded maybe in December. It'll be like using studio time for rehearsals. There's some stuff we've done that we haven't listened to for a long time that might form the basis of what we do, but it's hard to say at this juncture what it might be like. We might change our minds, anyway."* Do you ever develop ideas at home and take them into the studio for the others approval? Gilmour replied, *"No, the stuff we tend to do, the stuff I do, tends to go into my head."*

Are there any plans for individual work? Gilmour replied, *"We did have an idea for doing another 'Ummagumma' style album, each of us taking turns doing our own stuff, like, maybe, half a side each, but I'm not sure what's happening now. I think some of us, me and Rick especially, do have vague aspirations to making solo records, but we're not very urgent. I mean, actually, there's not a lot happening now, generally. I think musicians are getting a better deal nowadays. I mean, I think something really different will come along in time. We were like the first to come along with something that was so different, and I guess we've always been able to hang on to it, although I've heard some other things sound remarkably like us then, stuff on the radio that sounds fantastically like how we used to sound, German bands. I heard one two weeks ago that*

sounded so like 'Saucerful of Secrets' I couldn't believe it. It was good, but however good it gets on that level, people will never respect it. It's always best to be original."* Didn't you copy anybody when you started? Gilmour said, *"Oh, yeah, I'm sure, Hank Marvin. As a band we never pinched anything specifically. It's just one of those strange amalgams that happened. Maybe some of it was inspired by old SF movie film scores or something, that and Bo Diddley mixed together."*

How have you been able to maintain such a high level? Gilmour replied, *"That's one of the reasons, I think, that we've managed to sustain it, because we've built gradually and fairly unobtrusively, rather than zooming up to a great peak very suddenly. We've been selling out since 1968, but it's only happened very gradually in the States. Actually, it's quite a test now for us, because we've only just gone up to a really high peak in the States, the album going to number one and having a top ten single, it'll be interesting to see what happens there, whether we can maintain it. I think, strategically, our best thing to do next would be something weird, far out, and the kind of thing that nobody could possibly understand. I think to try and follow up 'Dark Side' with similar things, it'd be placing a heavier burden on our shoulders every time. It'd just go on building up, and we do like to feel fairly free in what we like to do. It's awful to get something out, follow it with something that's the same sort of thing, and then get trapped into that. It's so easy."*

Have you covered that side of it now so that you will be going back in the other direction? Gilmour replied, *"I dunno. I don't ever think of it as a direction like that, really. I just think of them all as one-offs."* So you don't see a connecting thread in them all? Gilmour answered, *"Well, I guess there is a thread running through, though just because of the way we are and the way we've developed. There's only a very bare, thin thread, if there is one at all. I'm sure a lot of people would say otherwise, though. I suppose the closest to a connection comes between 'Atom Heart Mother' and 'Meddle,' but it didn't seem anything like that to me at the time. I heard that again, recently, 'Meddle.' 'Echoes' is quite good."*

Do you ever take time to practice the guitar? Gilmour replied, "*Not as such. I play guitar a lot, though, nothing constructive, though. I just bang around. I know musicians who practice rigidly every day, though.*" Like the guitarist in the band, Focus. Gilmour said, "*I don't doubt that. Occasionally, before a tour, I play keyboards to loosen my fingers up. I don't think my coordination is good enough to get that sort of fluidity and speed and running around the keyboard like that guy does, because I'm convinced I couldn't ever do it, and I don't like it anyway. I suppose, if I liked it, I would try and do it. Maybe if I had a gift for it, then I would learn to like it and therefore practice it and do it. As it is, those high-speed guitarists have never impressed me as much as people who hardly ever do stuff fast. Jeff Beck's one of the ones who can pull it off really well, the high-speed guitar, but he overdoes it sometimes.*"

November 3, 1973 - Melody Maker (U.K.) reported that Pink Floyd and the Soft Machine will be performing two benefit concerts together at the Rainbow Theater in London on November 4, 1973, to help Robert Wyatt who was injured earlier this year. Pink Floyd will be playing 'Dark Side of the Moon' at the two shows, which will take place at 5 p.m., and at 9 p.m.

Sean Murphy, manager of the Soft Machine, stated, "*These two bands started at the same time in the same situation at UFO and Middle Earth. They're both marked out by the public as being extra ordinary, different groups from the general theme. They have similar attitudes and are quite similar people. Robert and Nick Mason are particularly close, and the rest of them have always been friendly. The Floyd felt a great attachment to the Softs and Robert's predicament.*"

Nick Mason explained, "*The scheme is to help Robert get off the ground with another band. That's what it's all about. It's no funeral. It's a special occasion. We're not into doing half-shows like this, but there's a good reason for doing this one.*"

Mike Ratledge, the keyboard player for the Soft Machine, said, "*We and the Floyd haven't played on the same bill for years and years, so it's apt that the time we get together, it's for Robert. We're glad to be able to do*

something. *It's fantastic that it's going ahead.*"

Robert Wyatt is currently hospitalized at the Stoke Mandeville Hospital, and is paralyzed from the waist down. Wyatt said about the concert, "*Isn't it amazing? It's a dream. I still can't quite believe it. It's quite an extraordinary thing for them to do.*" Asked about his plans, Wyatt replied, "*Sometimes I get very depressed and think I can't do anything if I can't drum. Other times I get excited, because singing, playing keyboards, and making tapes, my secondary interests, have been forced to the front by circumstances. I've got lots of ideas for recording, but it costs money, it doesn't make money. I've had to think about the problems of rent, and the cost of living. But with any luck, this benefit will give me a few months breathing space. I can do recording and not have to worry about the rent or anything like that until I get out of hospital.*"

New Musical Express (U.K.) reported that Pink Floyd and the Soft Machine will play two concerts at the Rainbow Theater in London, with all proceeds donated to the Robert Wyatt Benefit Fund. Ticket prices are £5, £2.50, £2, £1.50, and £1.

November 10, 1973 - Sounds (U.K.) published an article titled, "Dark moon eclipses Rainbow" by Martin Hayman that reviewed the Robert Wyatt benefit concert at the Rainbow Theater on November 4, 1973. John Peel explained, "*Wyatt's a nice man and he's going to use the money, which will be about ten thousand pounds, to live on and make records and things. He's going to write songs and play keyboards, and he's feeling positive about the whole thing. He's not here this evening because he thought he would be a bit embarrassed about being the center of attraction.*"

The Soft Machine opened the show. Pink Floyd followed after an intermission. The hall got dark, a heartbeat began, and a demented voice muttered, "I've been mad for years." An instrumental section followed with red lights and electronics. Then searchlights scanned the audience as a silver plane dive bombed the stage and exploded. Clocks went off with sounds from the front and back, leading into 'Time.' During the second half of 'Dark Side of the Moon,' a moon rose behind

1974
Crazy Diamonds and Unicorns

the stage, smoking eerily. "And as everybody knows, there is really no dark side of the moon."

November 1973 - Hit Parader (U.S.) published an article titled, "Pink Floyd: Color Them Angry." While premature announcements of their death are printed in the newspapers at least three times a year, Pink Floyd continue to grow and change. Reports that Pink Floyd were "slowly but surely on their way out" came just as their new album, 'The Dark Side of the Moon,' hit the charts. A group member was quoted as saying, *"You know, there are some people who cannot judge a sound that isn't already established. They already know what they're supposed to think about an established sound, it's been judged for them by public reaction. But give them a new sound, and instead of judging themselves about whether it's good or not, they begin wondering what they're supposed to think as professional reviewers. Give me an audience of non-pros with honest gut reactions anytime. I'd rather be hated by them than loved by the pros."*

November 24, 1973 - Melody Maker (U.K.) published an article titled, "Pink Floyd: the true progressive band" by Michael Oldfield. Pink Floyd's first multimedia show was at Essex University in 1966 when they performed while a film of London was shown behind them. Since then, they have experimented with lights and sounds. They are a "model of what a good rock band should be, progressive, inventive and forever willing to absorb new ideas."

January 19, 1974 - Melody Maker (U.K.) reviewed the Pink Floyd album, 'A Nice Pair.' They wrote that `A Nice Pair' is a repackaging of the first two Pink Floyd albums, and is "crucial in understanding the importance of the early British underground." Syd Barrett's songs "still stand out as being devastatingly witty, incisive, and original."

February 16, 1974 - New Musical Express (U.K.) reported that Syd Barrett is alive and well, and his fan club, The Syd Barrett Appreciation Society, is in full flower. The fan club issues a newsletter called Terrapin. It was reported that Syd Barrett was seen crop-haired in Kings Road by Roger Waters recently.

February 23, 1974, New Musical Express (U.K.) published an article titled, "Bleak side of the world" by Ian McDonald. McDonald wrote that 'Dark Side of the Moon,' was voted as the number one album in Britain and the world in the New Musical Express poll. But it is too serious and hopelessly slow. So what makes it so successful? It is a record about unease and a passively compassionate view of the world. It is a "thinking fans album," and a work of art. The album "transmutes Roger Waters' unease into an artistic construct that touches on issues of social reality without becoming impersonal."

February 1974 - Circus Magazine (U.S.) published an article titled, "A Nice Pair – The Pink Floyd LPs that Failed." The article stated that the first two Pink Floyd albums are being re-released with a new cover under the express consent of Pink Floyd manager, Steve O'Rourke.

March 1974 - Circus Magazine (U.S.) reviewed the Pink Floyd album, 'A Nice Pair.' They wrote that the album 'Piper at the Gates of Dawn' was "the most innovating and the most exciting," and the album 'A Saucerful of Secrets' was "less gnome-like and more ethereal."

April 13, 1974 - New Musical Express (U.K.) published a cover story titled, "Syd – What Ever Happened to the Cosmic Dream?" by Nick Kent. Kent began the article by telling the story of how Syd Barrett, at one of the last shows he did with Pink Floyd, emptied a bottle of Mandrax on his head, mixed it with Brylcreem, and took the stage. As he played, the Mandrax-Brylcreem mixture began to melt under the heat of the stage lights, and as it melted, it ran down his face, making it look like his face was melting. This is just one of many strange stories about Barrett that may, or may not, be true.

At present, Barrett is alive and well. He sometimes makes appearances at Lupus Music, his publishing company and the place where he gets his royalties. Bryan Morrison, the manager of Lupus Music, asked Barrett to write some new songs recently. Barrett said that he didn't have any new material, but agreed to do something. On his next visit, a week ago, Barrett was asked if he had written any songs, to which he replied, "No," and disappeared. Barrett spends most of his time watching television in his two-room Chelsea apartment, or walking around London. He was spotted at a shop in Kings Road where he tried on three different sizes of the same trousers, said they all fit perfectly, but left without buying any. Although there are many such stories of Barrett's activities, the reality is that he was, at one time, a brilliant songwriter, but his genius was cut off, and he is left in a lonely limbo with stunted creativity and a helpless illogical schizophrenia.

The article then explored the beginnings of the Pink Floyd. Storm Thorgerson, of design company Hipgnosis, recalled, "It was the usual thing really. 1962, we were all into Jimmy Smith. Then 1963 brought dope and rock. Syd was one of the first to get into The Beatles and the Stones. He started playing guitar around then, used to take it to parties or play down at this club called The Mill. He and Dave went to the south of France one summer and busked around." Thorgerson said that Syd was a "bright, extrovert kid. Smoked dope, pulled chicks, the usual thing. He had no problems on the surface. He was no introvert as far as I could see then."

Before the Pink Floyd, Barrett had three main interests; music, painting, and religion. At one point, Barrett wanted to get involved in "Sant Saji," a form of Eastern mysticism, but was rejected for being "too young" at 19. This is said to have affected him deeply. Peter Barnes explained, "Syd has always had this big phobia about his age. I mean, when we would try to get him back into the studio to record, he would get very

defensive and say 'I'm only 24. I'm still young. I've got time.' That thing with religion could have been partly responsible for it."

As for his painting, both David Gilmour and Thorgerson claimed that it was exceptional. "Syd was a great artist. I loved his work, but he just stopped. First it was the religion, then the painting. He was starting to shut himself off slowly then."

The early Pink Floyd played versions of 'Louie Louie' and 'Roadrunner,' with breaks of staccato freakout. Peter Jenner talked about one of their early concerts, saying, "It was one of the first rock events I'd seen. I didn't know anything about rock, really. Actually the Floyd then were barely semi-pro standard, now that I think about it, but I was so impressed by the electric guitar sound. The band was just at the point of breaking up then, you know. It was weird. They just thought 'Oh well, might as well pack it all in.' But we came along and so they changed their minds."

First they added a light show, then they began playing all original material, and Barrett began writing songs. Jenner explained, "Syd was really amazing, though. I mean, his inventiveness was quite astounding. All those songs from that whole Pink Floyd phase were written in no more than six months. He just started and took it from there. Well, his influences were very much the Stones, the Beatles, Byrds, and Love. The Stones were the prominent ones. He wore out his copy of 'Between the Buttons' very quickly. Love's album, too. In fact, I was once trying to tell him about this Arthur Lee song I couldn't remember the title of, so I just hummed the main riff. Syd picked up his guitar and followed what I was humming chord-wise. The chord pattern he worked out he went on to use as the main riff for 'Interstellar Overdrive.'"

As for his guitar style, Jenner said, "Well, he had this technique that I found very pleasing. I mean, he was no guitar hero, never remotely in the class of Page or Clapton, say."

The first Pink Floyd single was Barrett's 'Arnold Layne.' The second single was 'See Emily Play,' and Barrett explained, "I was sleeping in the woods one night after a gig we'd played somewhere, when I saw this girl appear before me. That girl is Emily."

Their first album, 'Piper at the Gates of Dawn' was being recorded at the same time as the Beatles 'Sgt. Peppers,' but negative influences began to appear, such as ego problems and prima donna fits. Jenner recalled Pink Floyd's three appearances on Top of the Pops to promote 'See Emily Play.' Jenner explained, *"The first time Syd dressed up like a pop star. The second time he came on in his straightforward fairly scruffy clothes, looking rather unshaven. The third time he came to the studio in his pop star clothes, and then changed into complete rags for the actual TV spot."* Apparently, Barrett had been influenced by John Lennon, who had stated that he would not appear on the program, and Barrett felt that he shouldn't either. Barrett was comparing himself to Lennon, and Barnes explained, *"Syd was always complaining that John Lennon owned a house while he only had a flat."*

Also at this time, Barrett was seeing a girl named Lynsey. One day she showed up at Peter Jenner's house beaten up. Said Jenner, *"I couldn't believe it at the time. I had this firm picture of Syd as this really gentle guy, which is what he was, basically."* To make matters worse, Barrett's eyes were fixed into a terrifying stare. Barrett was coming unhinged. Some think it might have been the drugs, since Barrett was consuming vast quantities during this period. Others believe it is traceable to childhood traumas, such as the death of his father when he was twelve years old.

In an interview with Rolling Stone magazine in 1971, Barrett is quoted as saying, *"Everyone is supposed to have fun when they're young. I don't know why, but I never did."* Peter Jenner said, *"I think we tended to underrate the extent of his problem. I mean, I thought that I could act as a mediator, you know, having been a sociology teacher at the L.S.E. and all that guff. I think, though, one thing I regret now was that I made demands on Syd. He'd written 'See Emily Play' and suddenly everything had to be seen in commercial terms. I think we may have pressurized him into a state of paranoia about having to come up with another hit single. Also, we may have been the darlings of London but, out in the suburbs, it was fairly terrible. Before 'Emily,' we'd have things thrown at us on stage. After 'Emily,' it was screaming girls wanting to hear our hit song."*

An American tour showed Barrett's psyche getting worse. Dick Clark's Bandstand TV Show was a disaster because "Syd wasn't into moving his lips that day." On The Pat Boone TV Show, Barrett responded to a Pat Boone interview with a catatonic stare. Tour manager Andrew King stated, *"Eventually we cancelled out on Beach Party."*

After returning to England, the band went into De Lane Lea Studio and recorded three Barrett songs, only one of which has been released, 'Jugband Blues.' Jenner commented, *"You see, even at that point, Syd actually knew what was happening to him. I mean, 'Jugband Blues' is the ultimate self-diagnosis on a state of schizophrenia."* The other two songs they recorded were 'Scream Your Last Scream' and 'Vegetable Man,' the latter being a sing along. Jenner said, *"Syd was around at my house just before he had to go to record and, because a song was needed, he just wrote a description of what he was wearing at the time and threw in a chorus that went, 'Vegetable man, where are you?'"*

The band then embarked on a nationwide tour supporting Jimi Hendrix, and during this tour, Barrett sometimes wouldn't show up or just wouldn't play on stage. Nice guitarist, David O'List, would play with Pink Floyd when Barrett wouldn't show up. Asked if Barrett and Hendrix socialized, Jenner replied, *"Not really. Hendrix had his own limousine. Syd didn't really talk to anyone. I mean, by now he was going on stage and playing one chord throughout the set. He was into this thing of total anarchistic experiment and never really considered the other members of the band."*

At this point, David Gilmour was asked to join the Pink Floyd. Jenner recalled, *"At the time, Dave was doing very effective take-offs of Hendrix-style guitar playing. So the band said, 'Play like Syd Barrett.'"* Asked if Gilmour had his own slide-echo style, Jenner replied, *"That's Syd. On stage, Syd used to play with slide and a bunch of echo boxes."* After five shows as a five piece, Barrett was ousted from Pink Floyd. Asked how Barrett reacted, Jenner said, *"Yeah. Syd does resent the Floyd. I don't know, he may still call them 'my band' for all I know."*

After leaving Pink Floyd, Barrett stayed with Storm Thorgerson in South Kensington. Thorgerson recalled, *"Syd was well into his 'orbiting' phase by then. He was traveling very fast in his own private sphere and I thought I could be a mediator of some sort. You see, I think you're going to have to make the point that Syd's madness was not caused by any linear progression of events, but more a circular haze of situations that meshed together on top of themselves and Syd. Me, I couldn't handle those stares, though."*

Pink Floyd parted with Blackhill Enterprises, their management company, and Peter Jenner decided to go with Barrett instead of the Pink Floyd. Barrett took a year to record his first solo album, 'The Madcap Laughs.' The album is a unique work of genius. Jenner recalled, *"I think Syd was in good shape when he made 'Madcap.' He was still writing good songs, probably in the same state as he was during 'Jugband Blues.'"* Thorgerson added, *"The thing was that all those guys had to cope with Syd out of his head on Mandrax half the time. He got so 'mandied' up on those sessions, his hand would slip through the strings and he'd fall off the stool."*

His second solo album, 'Barrett,' was recorded in a much shorter time period. David Gilmour, who produced the album, recalled, *"We had basically three alternatives at that point, working with Syd. One, we could actually work with him in the studio, playing along as he put down his tracks, which was almost impossible, though we succeeded on 'Gigolo Aunt.' The second was laying down some kind of track before and then having him play over it. The third was him putting his basic ideas down with just guitar and vocals, and then we'd try and make something out of it all. It was mostly a case of me saying, 'Well, what have you got then Syd?' and he'd search around and eventually work something out."* The album feels like a one-off demo. However, songs like 'Dominoes' are exquisite and show what Pink Floyd might have sounded like with Barrett in control. 'Dominoes' ends with a typical Pink Floyd minor chord refrain. Gilmour explained, *"The song just ended after Syd had finished singing and I wanted a gradual fade, so I added that section myself. I played drums on that, by the way."* Gilmour may have been the only person able to communicate with Barrett at this time, although Gilmour said, *"Oh, I don't think anyone can communicate with Syd. I did those albums because I liked the songs, not, as I*

suppose some might think, because I felt guilty taking his place in the Floyd. I was concerned that he wouldn't fall completely apart. The final re-mix on 'Madcap' was all mine as well."

During Barrett's solo period, a number of press interviews were set for Syd. Most of the interviewers couldn't make any sense out of Barrett's ramblings, and many attributed it in their articles to Barrett's condition. Peter Barnes, who did one of the interviews, stated, *"It was fairly ludicrous on the surface. I mean, you just had to go along with it all. You know, Syd would say something completely incongruous one minute, like 'It's getting heavy, innit?' and you'd just have to say 'Yeah, Syd. It's getting heavy.' And the conversation would dwell on that for five minutes. Actually, listening to the tape afterwards, you could work out that there was some kind of logic there, except that Syd would suddenly be answering a question you'd asked him ten minutes ago while you were off on a different topic completely."*

Another thing that happened during this time was that Syd decided to shave his head. Jenner recalled, *"I can't really comment too accurately, but I'm rather tempted to view it all as a symbolic gesture. You know, goodbye to being a pop star, or something."* Barrett was living in his mother's cellar in Cambridge. In an interview with Rolling Stone Magazine around Christmas of 1971, Barrett was quoted as saying, *"I'm really totally together. I even think I should be."*

After this, Barrett tried recording again. Barnes explained, *"It was an abortion. He just kept overdubbing guitar part on guitar part until it was just a total chaotic mess. He also wouldn't show anyone his lyrics, I fear actually because he hadn't written any."* Jenner added, *"It was horribly frustrating because there were sporadic glimpses of the old Syd coming through, and then it would all get horribly distorted again. Nothing remains from the sessions."*

Barrett also formed the band Stars with Twink of the Pink Fairies. They played a gig at the Corn Exchange in Cambridge in support of the MC5, but it was an exercise in musical untogetherness that ended with Barrett unplugging his guitar and walking away. Since that time, rumors abound that Barrett may have worked in a factory for a week, worked as a gardener, attempted to enroll in architecture school, grown mushrooms, spent time busking in New York, and tried to become a Pink Floyd roadie.

All the while, Barrett is the number one mystery figure in the music business. He has a huge cult-appeal in America, and there is fanatical interest in Japan and France. There is also a Syd Barrett Appreciation Society in Britain. Barnes stated, "*I mentioned the society to Syd once. He just said it was OK, you know. He's really not interested in any of it. It's ironic, I suppose. He's much bigger now as the silent cult-figure doing nothing, than he was when he was functioning.*" Yet many people still want to get Barrett back into the studio to record, such as Jimmy Page, Eno, and Kevin Ayers. Even David Bowie is an admirer. Jenner said, "*Syd has always said that when he goes back into the studio again, he will refuse to have a producer. He still talks about making a third album. I don't know, I think Dave is the only one who could pull it off. There seems to be a relationship there.*"

David Gilmour said, "*I don't know what Syd thinks, or how he thinks. Sure, I'd be into going back into the studio with him, but I'm into projects like that anyway. Period. I last saw him around Christmas in Harrods. We just said, 'Hi,' you know. I think, actually, of all the people you've spoken to, probably only Storm and I really know the whole story and can see it all in the right focus. I mean, Syd was a strange guy, even back in Cambridge. He was a very respected figure back there in his own way. In my opinion, it's a family situation that's at the root of it all. His father's death affected him very heavily and his mother always pampered him, made him out to be a genius of sorts. I remember I really started to get worried when I went along to the session for 'See Emily Play.' He was strange, even then. That stare, you know?*"

Gilmour continued, "*Yeah, it was fairly obvious that I was brought in to take over from him, at least on stage. It was impossible to gauge his feelings about it. I don't think Syd has opinions, as such. He functions on a totally different plane of logic, and some people will claim 'Well, yeah man, he's on a higher cosmic level,' but basically there's something drastically wrong. It wasn't just the drugs, we'd both done acid before the*

whole Floyd thing, it's just a mental foible, which grew out of all proportion. I remember all sorts of strange things happening. At one point he was wearing lipstick, dressing in high heels, and believing he had homosexual tendencies. We all felt he should have gone to see a psychiatrist, though someone, in fact, played an interview he did to R.D. Laing, and Laing claimed he was incurable. What can you do, you know?"

Gilmour continued, "*We did a couple of songs for 'Ummagumma,' the live tracks, we used 'Jugband Blues' for no ulterior motive, it was just a good song. I mean, that 'Nice Pair' collection will see him doing alright for a couple of years, which postpones the day of judgment. I don't know, maybe if he was left to his own devices, he might just get it together. But it is a tragedy, a great tragedy, because the guy was an innovator, one of the three of four greats, along with Dylan. I know, though, that something is wrong, because Syd isn't happy, and that really is the criteria, isn't it? But then it's all part of being 'A legend in your own lifetime.'*"

May 18, 1974 - New Musical Express (U.K.) published an article titled, "The band who ate asteroids for breakfast" by Roy Carr and Nick Kent, that featured a consumers guide to Pink Floyd songs.

'Arnold Layne'/'Candy and A Currant Bun,' released in March 1967, merits 5 stars and is an absolute classic. 'Arnold Layne,' is a Barrett composition, and tells the story of a pervert transvestite named Arnold Layne. The lyrics were so good that The Oxford Book of Verse used them as an example of contemporary lyrics as fine art. 'Candy and a Currant Bun' is one of the best cosmic rockers from 1967.

'See Emily Play'/'Scarecrow,' released June 1967, merits 5 stars and was a successful chart single. It was produced by Norman "Hurricane" Smith and was a blast of summer psychedelia. The lyrics are similar to something Lewis Carroll would have written.

'Piper at the Gates of Dawn,' released September 1967, merits 4 stars. It has a sound that is under-eclectic, and featured songs that were archetypical heavy metal ('Astronomy Domine,' 'Interstellar Overdrive'), jazzed freak outs ('Pow R Toc

H'), but mostly Barrett's awed whimsy. It is in the spirit of 1967 cosmic adventure.

'Apples and Oranges'/'Paint Box,' released November 1967, merits 3 1/2 stars. 'Apples and Oranges' was a commercial follow-up to 'Emily,' and bombed. 'Paint Box' is an interesting song by Rick Wright. It is one of his best songs, and shows his melodic inventiveness with over-precious lyrics.

'It Would Be So Nice'/'Julia Dream,' released in April 1968, merits 4 1/2 stars and is Pink Floyd's first release after Syd Barrett left. 'It Would Be So Nice' is charming 1967 deja-vu. 'Julia Dream' is Roger Waters' fairy tale imagery and sound effects. At the end of the song someone can be heard whispering 'Ssyyyddddd.' Played at 78 rpm it sounds like the Strawberry Alarm Clock.

'A Saucerful of Secrets,' released July 1968, merits 5 stars. 'Remember a Day' and 'See Saw,' two of Rick Wright's songs, pick up Barrett's child-like whimsy. Roger Waters' 'Let There Be More Light' and 'Set the Controls for the Heart of the Sun' are doom laden 2001 songs. The title track displays Pink Floyd's change towards electronic compositions. Many fans consider it Pink Floyd's best post-Syd Barrett record.

'Point Me at the Sky'/'Careful With That Axe Eugene,' released December 1968, merits 2 1/2 stars. 'Point Me at the Sky' is a turgid metal psychedelic song that never got off the ground. 'Careful With That Axe Eugene' is a studio recording that was later re-released on 'Relics.'

'More,' released in July 1969, merits 4 stars. It is a film soundtrack album that is a mixture of music and muzak. Roger Waters' 'Crying Song,' 'Green is the Colour,' and 'Cymbaline' are impressive.

'Ummagumma,' released November 1969, merits 3 stars. The front cover is an exquisite representation of J.W. Dunne's concept of infinite regress. The live album consists of old Pink Floyd songs. The studio album is self-indulgent, pretentious, and tedious. Only 'Grantchester' is pleasing. It is "Ye olde cosmique flatulence."

'Zabriskie Point,' released March 1970, merits 2 stars. It is a movie soundtrack about teen revolt meeting avant-garde quasi-fantasy. Only three Pink Floyd songs were used in the movie, and they are uninspired.

'Crumbling Man' is third rate Grateful Dead. 'Heart Beat, Pig Meat' is sonic muzak. 'Come in Number 51, Your Time is Up' is 'Careful With That Axe Eugene' again.

'Atom Heart Mother,' released October 1970, merits 3 stars. 'Atom Heart Mother' showed that Pink Floyd were lacking as serious contemporary musicians, and contained very little substance. On the B-side, only 'Alan's Psychedelic Breakfast' was interesting. It was rumored that this song was written to allow Syd Barrett to return the to stage with Pink Floyd.

'Meddle,' released November 1971, merits 3 1/2 stars. The song, 'One of These Days' is psychedelic wind tunnel music. 'A Pillow of Winds' is ethereal, while 'Echoes' shows Gilmour is committed to his echo and slide guitar styles, and Rick Wright is competent at exploring sonic meanderings with his keyboards.

'Obscured by Clouds,' released January 1972, merits 4 stars. It is a soundtrack album for a lousy film. The title track and 'Free Four' are continued experiments with wind tunnel sounds, while 'Wots . . . Uh, the Deal' is one of Pink Floyd's best songs, sounding like classic Byrds and John Cale.

'The Dark Side of the Moon,' released March 1973, merits 4 1/2 stars. It is an important and brave departure for Pink Floyd. "A magnum opus."

'A Nice Pair,' released December 1973, merits 5 stars. A re-release of the first two Pink Floyd albums.

'Relics,' released May 1971, merits 3 stars. A cop out, as this album should have included all the songs from the first five singles.

'Scream Your Last Scream' and 'Vegetable Man' from the Syd Barrett era are unfinished and unmixed.

A song called 'Apologies' was reportedly to be the B-side for the single, 'Jugband Blues.'

There is also an alternate recording of 'Pow R Toc H' that features an organ, instead of a piano, playing the theme.

Various bootlegs are also mentioned, including 'Big Pink,' 'Omayad,' and 'With/Without.'

June 22, 1974 - Melody Maker (U.K.)

published an article titled, "Moodies, Floyd - a bore!" by Allan Jones. Jones wrote that, looking at the current album charts, all you see is redundant music. The post-Syd Barrett Pink Floyd never had much to say. They have produced beautiful music, but when they released the song, 'A Saucerful of Secrets,' they created Classical-Rock, and rock and roll was the loser.

July 27, 1974 - Melody Maker (U.K.)
published an article that explained how Pink Floyd transport their equipment during concert tours. Eleanor Angel, who worked with Steve O'Rourke to set up Pink Floyd tours, stated, *"We have worked with the big companies, like Avis, who are very good, but just recently we have worked with Edwin Shelly Trucking who take over everything for us, including loading and unloading the equipment, providing the drivers, and sorting out the paper work, like green insurance cards and ferry bookings. The Floyd have 20 tons of equipment, and nowadays they use three 48 foot articulated trucks which take everything and travel in convoys. We have instruments, lights, cases, and special effects to transport, and, including the group, we have 25 personnel on the road, each tour with 15 road managers. On long tours, it's better for the company to supply us with drivers because they have the heavy goods vehicle licenses that ordinary roadies don't always have. The road crew stops overnight in the same hotel as the group, and we make sure they get plenty of sleep."*

Angel explained some of the problems groups encounter, saying, *"You need a green insurance card for any vehicle traveling abroad, and if you're traveling in France or Italy, you need a special permit which can be obtained only from Newcastle. The licensing authority is there, and you have to get the permit from them well in advance. It's a nuisance, but if you don't have it, they can send a group back at the border if the customs are feeling finicky. As we are carrying musical equipment around, a Carnet is necessary as well, and every item of equipment has to be listed and broken down in serial numbers. It's just so that bands don't have to pay import duties, and they guarantee not to sell any of it abroad. Lately, it's been very difficult at the Carnet office, and the procedure*

can get complicated. We usually plan a tour at least two months ahead, arranging and negotiating. Lots of countries won't allow large trucks to travel the roads on Sundays, and you need another permit for that, and you have to check whether the customs posts are open on Sundays as well. There's always a last minute panic, usually when the musicians want to add another bit of equipment. But Europe is no harder to tour in than America, and when you've done it once, it's quite easy and things just follow through. To America, we ship all the equipment out by air, and it has to be cleared at Heathrow customs where they can be very fussy and want to open every box. Some bands hire their equipment in America, but the Floyd insist on using their own and having it air freighted. If it went by sea, it would take too long, and might get damaged. In America, they hire trucks, either from Avis or UHaul. Trucking is quite expensive, but the amount of equipment grows all the time, and we couldn't keep buying trucks ourselves. In the old days, the band would buy their own van, when there was only a small amount of load. But all the big bands, like The Who, E.L.P., and the Floyd, hire their trucks."*

Stuart Masterton, who was the local market manager for Hertz Europe, stated, *"The most popular truck is the three ton box, because it needs only an ordinary driving license, and is suitable for the average big group. Then there are the weekend lads who get together to form a group, and they use the 18 cwt transit. The Box takes 3.6 tons and is hired on a time-mile-age basis, at £11.55 a day and 5p per mile. The Transit is £6.95 per day including 100 free miles, and 5p per mile over that. The three tonners are often used to go to the Continent, and we help with the necessary documentation. The branch managers will help out the drivers in supplying a green insurance card, and there is an additional charge for that. We also supply documents showing the right to have the vehicle, but the driver is responsible for the Carnet de Passage, which lists the equipment. As for insurance, we can insure loads at £1 per £1,000 value, to a maximum of £10,000. We don't supply locks for shutter doors, but there are latches for locks supplied by the driver. If we supplied locks, one could well go missing."*

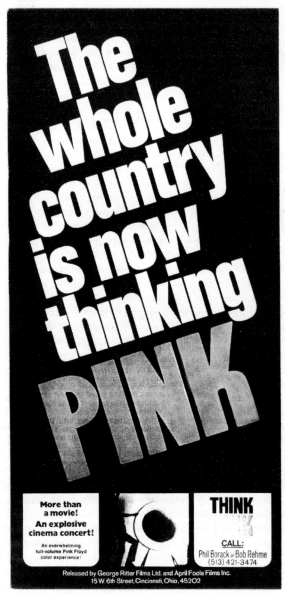

August 3, 1974 - Melody Maker (U.K.) reported that Pink Floyd are planning a British tour, likely for November. The band have been working on two new pieces of music, and are currently on holiday until the end of September.

New Musical Express (U.K.) reviewed the film, `Pink Floyd Live at Pompeii.' Charles Shaar Murray wrote that he fell asleep at the Screen On the Green cinema in Islington on Friday while watching the Pink Floyd movie. He was underwhelmed by the film. The band don't play well, and they are pictured out of context in an amphitheater. The best part is when Roger Waters smashes his gong. Rick Wright has a beard that appears and disappears throughout the movie, and David Gilmour looks like Rick Wakeman. It is an intergalactic turkey to be avoided. This issue also included a full-page ad for the Robert Wyatt album, 'Rock Bottom,' that was produced by Nick Mason.

August 10, 1974 - Melody Maker (U.K.) published an article titled, "Gilmour meets a Unicorn" by Jeff Ward. Ward wrote that David Gilmour met the band Unicorn last summer at Rick Hopper's wedding reception in Kent, where the band was playing. He was impressed enough with their music to become their producer. Gilmour explained, *"They were out of work, like so many others. But the songs were nice. They asked me if they could come and do some demos in the studio I've got at home. That's what got me interested in it, I suppose. Afterwards, we booked some sessions down at Olympic, and went from there."*

Asked what impressed him about Unicorn, Gilmour said, *"Well, I don't suppose I'd have done anything straight away. In fact, I know I would not have done anything off my own bat just from having seen them at the reception. But Rick Hopper had told me about them before and said they were good. I did listen to them and I did think they were quite good. But, largely, it's down to their songs, and songs don't usually strike you so hard the first time. We went into the studio and it was then I really began to dig it. After three days, I think it was, we'd got 20 tracks down. They worked very fast, they were very nice songs, and they played well."*

Although Gilmour produced the sessions, he doesn't see himself as a record producer, saying, *"I'm not swotting up on it for when I get pensioned off, or anything like that. It was just that I hadn't got a lot to do at the time and here was something I could do positively to help them, and they seemed like they were well worth being helped. They needed a bit of help. They were very down and out. You know how it is when you've been flogging away for years against a brick wall. I thought, well, I can't lose money on it because it's good enough for me to be able to go in and record an album, and I was sure I'd be able to get a record deal together, or Steve would, and Steve did."* Steve O'Rourke was able to get a record deal for the band with Charisma.

The new album, called 'Blue Pine Tress,' will be out this month. O'Rourke is now Unicorn's manager, and Gilmour is also assisting the band with their stage gear.

Gilmour said, *"It's the first time I've ever seen this sort of thing from the word go, gone into it, and committed myself to completing it like this. In those three days they came over to my house, each day made me more and more convinced. It was obvious that their writing was consistent. It wasn't just a couple of songs that were good. They were consistently able to put out quite a lot. I was convinced they could do it, and that there was enough good material there to be worth anyone's while to put up the money and go in and make an album. Obviously, I thought it would be better and cheaper if I was in there supervising it. That's how I come out as being producer, really. They haven't got a lot of experience of recording studios, though, anyway, I have. For me, with Unicorn, the process of getting what there was there on record didn't look difficult. It didn't look as though it would mean a lot of work, whereas Roger's thing did. He tried to get something together with some friends at Island but it didn't seem to work in the studio. They weren't really a working unit. I mean, last June was the last time the Floyd toured properly, in the States that was, and after that we were going to take some time off. But I got very bored not doing anything, and this thing came up at the right time, and took up some of my wasted leisure hours."*

Gilmour, who also plays pedal steel guitar on the album, has his name as producer in big letters on the album. Commented Gilmour, *"I told them to change the big letters to small letters because it looks a bit silly, but they haven't done it."*

As for the record selling, Gilmour added, *"I don't know much about whether things are gonna sell any records. I just know I like it. It's very hard to tell. I often sit and wonder whether it will have any success. I'm sure there won't be any disrespect for it. I'm sure most people will think it's good. Whether a lot of people will buy it is another matter. It's much more to them than their previous recordings."*

Pink Floyd's last appearance in Britain was at the Robert Wyatt benefit concert at the Rainbow Theater on November 4, 1973. Gilmour said, *"We haven't toured anywhere now for over a year, apart from in France last month. It's not that we don't see ourselves as a touring band. It's just that we don't want to* keep on. We don't need to be in the position of having to go out and keep on playing things that we don't really want to play. Up until now, if we'd gone out, we would have been forced to play all the stuff we didn't want to play. We're thinking in terms of, in the not too distant future, dropping 'Dark Side of the Moon,' let alone the other stuff."

As for the upcoming British tour, Gilmour said, "A lot of people say it's impossible to get all the gear into the little venues but, obviously, we can take a lot less gear with us, and I guess we could still play almost anything. When we did the Rainbow last year, it was the smallest gig we'd played in ages. But the plan now really is, and this is what we'd prefer to do, to select three or four places around England, quite widely spaced, and do several nights at each one."

Talking about their new songs, tentatively titled, 'Shine On' and 'Raving and Drooling,' which they debuted in France, Gilmour said, "They're tons better now than how we had them on the French tour. But it seems to have got harder. It takes a lot longer to get things done now. I suppose it's because we're trying to go one better every time. I think it's always the idea to improve on what we've done before."

As for playing live again, Gilmour said, "I'd look forward to the prospect of doing almost any tour right now, except a French one."

August 17, 1974 - Sounds (U.K.) published an article titled, "A Pre-Season Report on Pink Floyd" that featured an interview with Nick Mason. Mason began, "In the studio, we haven't really been doing anything because, there was a general feeling after 'Dark Side Of The Moon' that that was a preferable way of working, to get the pieces organized first on the road, before recording them."

Asked about the household objects project, Mason replied, "I think it will happen one day, because most of the ideas we've tried seem to work really very well so far. It's in very random form at the moment, not in pieces. There are things like 16 tracks of glasses tuned to a scale across the 16-track. It can be played across the faders. But what it really needs is each one going through a VCS3 or something, and then coming in to a keyboard. I suppose,

really, it's a very, very, very, very crude mellotron. There's a whole load of things we've done, some of them just down as sounds that work, others as bass lines, tunes."

Asked about the two new Pink Floyd pieces, one by Roger Waters, and the other a group piece, Mason replied, "We've taken them to France to road test them," and they will "almost definitely be part of whatever we do next."

What about new treatments of 'Dark Side of the Moon' for the upcoming British tour? Mason replied, "Wouldn't really like to say. I suppose they'll be roughly along the lines of what we did in France, which was use a lot of back projection films. But it's mostly ideas at the moment and I don't want to discuss them and then be very embarrassed to find that they don't exist."

How do you feel about the French tour, which covered five cities and three shows in Paris? Mason replied, "I think very well, all things considered. It was a bit thrown together at the last minute for the usual reasons, not because we didn't know about it well beforehand, but because, until it's close, it doesn't seem very real."

Pink Floyd agreed to help sell a Bitter Lemon drink in return for sponsorship of their French tour, but it didn't work out. What happened? Mason explained, "It all sounded so, sort of, once removed, that in a fit of madness we all agreed that we'd do it. We thought we'd rip them off for loads of cash, when, in fact, of course that didn't happen, and it was us who lost. It just got so confused. We'd intended them to subsidize the tour so we could make the tickets cheaper, and in the end no one could work out whether the tickets were cheaper or not. It was all such an unnecessary complication. It was quite interesting in what it brought out, though. We expected much more aggravation from people saying 'What the hell do you think you're doing?' than there in fact was, which was rather disappointing in a way, because we'd got so worked up about it by then. We ended up giving all the money away to some French charity, which made it all the more confusing."

What do you think about the new Pink Floyd movie, Pompeii, that has just been released? Mason replied, "I don't think we perhaps took quite the interest in it that we should have done, although Adrian, the guy who made it, was quite interested in having us say what we thought about it all along. It's not bad, but I'm not entirely happy about it. With the interviews particularly, I think perhaps we should have got more involved in trying to really say something about what's happening and what we do as a group, something that would be interesting and would last."

How come it took so long to be released to the theaters? Mason replied, "*God knows. I think it was because everyone thought rock and roll films were not very good news, but, in fact, it has turned out to be very good news. And then you get this ridiculous thing of everyone ringing up, saying, 'Great, fantastic, it worked, let's do another one exactly the same, immediately.' There really is this thing of when something is successful, people always want to do the same again, as near as damn it, a different song or two, but essentially the same idea, the chaps playing.*"

Pink Floyd have always wanted to be able to take their time, do things at their own speed, and get them right. Is that what you are doing now? Mason replied, "*Except that it's now too relaxed. We've found that working at our own pace gets so little done that we all get a bit frustrated. I certainly feel that as the sort of non-writer, because I can't retire to the studio and knock out a few songs. I think we all feel now that we'd liked to have done more in the last, well, we're glad we checked it out, but I think that next year we're going to do a lot more work and struggle in a sense to meet deadlines. The thing is not to swing back madly, but to try to hit a balance, and the balance does lie somewhere in between the two. You've got to find out for yourself how much you want to work, and the only way is to stop, and then see if you want to go back working, which we do.*"

Asked about the beginnings of Pink Floyd, Mason explained, "*I didn't know what the fuck was going on. Peter and Andrew, and the kind of Joe Boyd figures that were around then, were probably part of it in a way that I certainly wasn't. All four of us, we were the band that's all, rather bizarre, sometimes very inward looking people who lived in a world of our own. There was no community spirit whatsoever. All we were interested in was our EMI recording contract, making a record,*

being a hit. At UFO, we felt like the house band, and it was, by far, the nicest gig, and it was what everyone asked about in interviews, and so on. But I certainly wasn't into the lifestyle of the whole thing. I don't think I felt part of the new movement, because I was too busy being part of the new rock and roll movement, which was a different thing.*"

One day you were playing for the BBC, and the next day at the Roundhouse. Mason replied, "*Obviously, there was an amazing difference, but you just took it in your stride then. I think today I'd probably have a nervous breakdown. But then it just seemed all part of your life.*"

Talking about the early days, and when David Gilmour first joined Pink Floyd, Gilmour is quoted as saying, "*I didn't do much for a long time. I just sat there and played rhythm to help it all along. For a good six months, maybe more, I didn't do a single thing. I was pretty paranoid. I hadn't worked out how it would fit in, and I wasn't at all confident in it in any way at all. It was mostly me and paranoia. I don't think they, the rest of the band, had fixed ideas of what I should do, or any fixed ideas of how I should do it. I was more conscious of knowing I had something specific to do and thinking that I had something to follow. I guess I thought they had a more rigid idea of what they wanted me to do and be, than they in fact had. I was frightened to stick my neck out and change what they were doing, because the way I would naturally play guitar would obviously have changed it quite a lot. Even before I joined there was an attempt to do the big production thing. There was always the idea of having a really high fidelity sound and putting on a fully produced show with quadraphonic sound. I mean, it was basically an audio idea then, lighting and effects came into it, but not so much as they do now.*"

Nick Mason continued, "*It was a strange period, with Syd leaving us, and us leaving Blackhill, and then us being on what was really a bit of a downhill slope. Dave was settling in. I don't think that, musically, we were down. I think musically we started again, higher up, but there was the whole thing about our standing with Syd gone. And it all was fairly boring. Not much happened for six months. We were working quite a lot, but not really getting anywhere. But we were working on 'Saucer' and then, what was really nice was, we played the free concert in Hyde Park where we played 'Saucer,' and that was a lovely launch. It re-introduced us. It was one of our lucky breaks. Then we went to America and started on all that business, which actually was another thing Bryan Morrison did for us. Then Steve took over and we never looked back."*

How long was it before Pink Floyd started to make any money? Mason replied, *"I suppose it was about two years ago. We began to make it before then, but we also started spending. Essentially, the only way to make big money is by big hit records, so really I suppose it was 'Dark Side of the Moon' that made a real difference. The trouble is that we're now launching into yet another multi-million dollar magnificence. But there's no way we could have done a whole load of things without 'Dark Side of the Moon.' Everything else had sold OK, but it was the first big American seller. That's the real difference. There's also the extraordinary thing of 'Dark Side of the Moon' doing a million, and then the others, like 'Meddle' and 'Ummagumma,' start catching up again."*

Asked about life as part of Pink Floyd, Mason said, *"It's equivalent to families and various things I've never been in, but I'd imagine would be similar, one being a small army unit, and another a prep school. You can oscillate so easily between love and hate, real love and real hate. At one moment you can feel incredibly close to them, or to one of them, or you can hate them. It's never two against two either. It's always three against one. It really is amazing to watch sometimes, jokes, and the way they become teasing, and bullying, that's what it gets down to. I think we've been lucky in that we've used our managers when there's been a lot of aggression, instead of always ganging up on each other. Steve can take a lot from us. We can be incredibly spiteful, and he can channel a lot of that from us without actually breaking and beating us around the head with clubs. I've been really ashamed of myself, but unable to stop myself joining in. It's partly this thing of being with the band together. Yes, the gang syndrome. But it definitely makes me behave in a way that I wouldn't normally do as an individual."* Asked if he has a role, Mason replied, *"I'm an eggeronner. I sit there, encouraging Roger or Dave to get in there."* Who is likely to initiate things? Mason replied, *"It depends what it's all about. And it depends where we are. It depends what's at stake. If it's a restaurant scene, then Dave probably takes the golden biscuit for making trouble, if trouble is in the offing. But really, it comes back to this old thing about being asked the same question all the time, which tends to happen when you've been at it for a couple of years. What really builds up these terrific scenes is when you get a reporter who doesn't really know when to drop it, and thinks that perhaps if he pressures it he might get something important. So you get, 'How would you describe your music?' 'Grunt, don't want to discuss it, grumble, grumble.' 'Well, sort of folk/jazz, or psychedelic jazz, or the new classical music?' There's a whole range of questions interconnected with that, and we're off. But I think sometimes an interview can be a really good thing and it can help you to sort out things in your brain that perhaps you hadn't particularly thought about. Either that or a few good jokes."*

How do you react to criticism in the press? Mason replied, *"It depends. If I'm with the band, we all go 'urrh, remember his name, bloody check, what does he know about music.' But if I'm just reading it, I tend to think 'Oh dear, wonder if he's right.' I think I tend to worry about it more than the rest of the group. They're more hard bitten, probably. People always pay lip service to the idea that if it's good criticism, they don't mind, but it is true. I remember one occasion where everybody said they liked a show and one guy said it was pretty shabby, which was what we all felt as well. It was really nice to think that he was interested enough and knew us well enough to grade it, especially when you get to the point where people see you so rarely, particularly abroad, that as long as it more or less works, it's OK."*

Pink Floyd appears to be impervious from attacks. Mason replied, *"That might be because we had our worst attacks during out first year of existence, attacks from the audience, as well as everything else, which is the worst thing. I can't imagine how we got through that first year. I think that might have something to do with it. The other thing is that it's quite often patently obvious that these attacks are mounted by people who patently*

Nick Mason

don't know what they're talking about. They praise things that are terrible, and so on. And there's the thing of stirring up the readers' letters. Often they're based on this extraordinary thing of, there's only one right way of making music. It's either 'progressive' or it's 'pop.' You get articles opening 'In this era of pretentious music, how nice to get a fresh glitter-rock artist,' and obviously vice-versa. I remember this particularly related to my heroes of yesteryear, especially Cream. There was a thing where they were the golden group, and then, well, it does seem to move in phases really. Stevie Wonder seems constantly to be going up and down, often quite unrelated to what he's actually turning out, to my ears anyway."

It has been sixteen months since the release of 'Dark Side of the Moon.' Mason said, "It was a huge jump forward in the organization of making an album. If we made it again today, I'm sure we'd do a better job, but all the right ingredients were there, i.e., the concept is clear and the songs, the songs are all there. Probably Roger and Dave and Rick feel they could write better songs now, that's the feeling I get, but it's still a huge step

forward in construction from our previous albums. I think, also, the message got across to quite a few people, what it was about. Messages from rock and roll stars have to be, not exactly taken with a pinch of salt. But it is difficult telling people to watch out when you're sitting there making a million dollars and having a wonderful time. But it's not a hype. Roger, who did most of the writing, definitely means what he says in the words."

What are your plans for the future? Mason replied, "We haven't had a technical command meeting recently. That would suggest that the household objects album would have been the wittiest thing to do next, and it would have been if we could have knocked it out. But I think what we'll do is what we've always done in the past, which is to struggle away at whatever we've got, and see how it comes out."

Pink Floyd have their own inimitable style. Is insular the correct word? Mason replied, "Yes, I think that's quite a good word, and in fact I think it's rather a pity. We have allowed ourselves to be out on a funny limb of our own. And also not had too much contact. Dave is a bit more involved with other bands, *knows a few more people. I'd really like to do that more. Just recently I've been thinking that, but I think for me it's partly paranoia."*

What caused you to be isolated and not have contacts with other musicians? Mason replied, *"I think partly because of the kind of people we are, and also, at the time we started doing solo concerts, it was not the normal thing to do. Most of the musicians I know I got to know five years ago, when we used to share gigs with people. You'd all be on the road and you'd turn up at some university and there would be Fairport Convention. The other day this was brought home to me fantastically strongly when a friend of mine was over from America and invited us over to tea. And it developed into a kind of soiree. And Richard Thompson was there, who I hadn't seen for five years or something. It was really nice to see him again. But unless a similar thing happens, I probably won't see him for another five years. It's partly because one gets hung up for time, partly laziness I suppose, and partly all the other activities you get involved with. Also, I'm not a Speakeasy raver, which is the other place you come into contact with people."*

Recently, Mason produced Principal Edwards Magic Theater, and Robert Wyatt. Are these sessions a conscious effort to get involved with other musicians? Mason replied, *"No, not conscious. I was just delighted to have the chance, partly because you learn a lot, and partly because it's nice to work outside group decisions. If it works out, everyone gains a lot from it. It's really good because everyone learns more about the trade."*

September 14, 1974 - New Musical Express (U.K.) published a review of the Robert Wyatt concert at Drury Lane in London on September 8, 1974. The concert featured a guest appearance by Nick Mason on drums.

Also in this issue are three ads for the double album reissue of the two Syd Barrett albums.

September 28, 1974 - Melody Maker (U.K.) reported that Pink Floyd will be playing four extravaganza concerts at Wembley Empire Pool on November 14-17, 1974, as part of an upcoming British tour. The tour will begin at Edinburgh on November 3rd and 4th, followed by Newcastle, Stoke, Cardiff, Liverpool,

Birmingham, Manchester, and Bristol. Tickets will go on sale on September 30, 1974, by mail order only for one week, after which the remaining tickets will be available from the various box offices.

New Musical Express (U.K.) reported that 20 shows have been confirmed for Pink Floyd's British Winter tour in the autumn. Tickets prices for most shows are £2.20, £1.80, £1.40, and £1.

October 5, 1974 - New Musical Express (U.K.) published an article titled, "Floyd void: lunar probe lost in space" by Pete Erskine that featured an interview with David Gilmour. Asked about the follow-up to the successful Pink Floyd album, 'Dark Side of the Moon,' David Gilmour said, *"It's just been jolly hard to get together between holidays, football, and having a good time. Last June, we came back off a U.S. tour and decided to take a rest. For some reason it seemed to last a bit longer than expected, eight or nine months. We all thought that 'Dark Side of the Moon' was a good package, that it appeared at just about the right time, and for a while there didn't seem to be any point in carrying on."*

Asked if they were trying to get the most mileage out of 'Dark Side of the Moon,' Gilmour replied, *"No. Not consciously."*

Earlier this year, Pink Floyd did begin work on an album, tentatively titled, 'Household Objects,' that was to be performed entirely on items such as elastic bands, woodblocks, and coal shovels. They spent several weeks working on two songs, before abandoning them.

New material that will be performed during the upcoming British tour was first played during a French tour, and featured backing vocalists the Blackberries, and Dick Parry on saxophone. Asked about the new songs, Gilmour answered, *"I can't really describe them. I really don't know."*

Asked if they might release an album consisting of studio outtakes, Gilmour explained, *"No, we never get anything finished to that point. We don't work on anything unless it's going to be used."*

Also in this issue is a full-page ad for the upcoming Pink Floyd tour, complete with venues and tour dates.

Also in this issue, in the letters column, is a letter about the recent appearance of Robert Wyatt on Top of the Pops, with guest musicians Fred Frith, Nick Mason, Dave MacRae, Richard Sinclair, and Phil Miller.

Also in this issue, in the Teazers column, it was reported that promoter Harvey Goldsmith said that the upcoming Pink Floyd tour is a virtual sell-out by mail order only.

October 1974 - Raves (U.K.) published an article titled, "Pink Floyd's Barrett Resurfacing?" that reported that plans for a double album re-issue of Barrett's two solo albums are underway. Barrett reportedly has taken an interest in the project and wants to contribute cover art. According to the article, Barrett showed up at the Hipgnosis offices for a photo session, which did not take place.

November 9, 1974 - New Musical Express (U.K.) published a review of the Pink Floyd opening night concert at Usher Hall, Edinburgh on November 4, 1974. Pink Floyd premiered three new songs, 'Raving and Drooling,' 'Shine On You Crazy Diamond,' and 'Gotta Be Crazy,' which appeared to be "awful tedious" to the audience. The sound system didn't function properly as the sound was too loud, produced feedback, and was mixed poorly. David Gilmour's singing was sometimes dreadful on the new material. For 'Dark Side of the Moon,' the band used dry ice and films to augment the music, plus the extra vocalists, the Blackberries who are Venetta Field and Carlena Williams, and Dick Parry on sax. They had problems gelling, and didn't come together until the song 'Money,' when they started to burn. The performance of the song 'Echoes' was magical.

Sounds (U.K.) published an article titled, "The moon in . . November" by Steve Peacock that reported on a Pink Floyd rehearsal in a hangar-like building at Elstree, three days before the start of their British Winter Tour. Peacock wrote that Pink Floyd's jamming sounded like a cross between Booker T. and the MGs, and The Who. Arthur Max, the road crew chief, will be coordinating the show, which will feature three new songs in the first half, 'Shine On You Crazy Diamond,' 'Raving and Drooling,' and 'Gotta Be Crazy.'

The second half of the show will be a performance of 'Dark Side of the Moon,' with brand new films that they worked out during the summer. These will be back-projected on a large circular screen. At the start of Dark Side, when the heart-beat starts, a moon grows larger and larger until it fills the entire screen. This is followed by a sound wave pattern, similar to that on the inside of the album cover. The film for 'On the Run' begins with street lights, car lights, flashing police car lights, and aircraft lights, all in succession, followed by a cloud tunnel leading to a planet. As the surface approaches, animation begins, flying over cities and between buildings, edited together with scenes of urban destruction. A clock sequence introduces the song, 'Time,' and 'Great Gig in the Sky' uses underwater scenes from the movie, 'Crystal Voyager.' For the song 'Money,' notes and coins are shown, along with the people that use them. And for 'Brain Damage,' scenes of politicians are projected on the screen. Dark Side has been changed musically as well, with the addition of Venetta Field and Carlena Williams on backing vocals, and Dick Parry on saxophone.

A new tour folder will be available at the shows, in the shape of a comic book that includes a cartoon by Gerald Scarfe.

November 16, 1974 - Melody Maker (U.K.) published an interview with Richard Wright done at the Caledonian Hotel November 4, 1974. Asked how Pink Floyd songs are composed, Wright answered, "*We always like to write numbers, go on the road with them, and record them later. We did this with 'Dark Side of the Moon,' and we think it's easily the best way to go about it. A number changes so much when we do it live over a long period. 'Shine On' has changed a lot since we started, already. I can't think of any other bands that work this way. Usually bands record songs, and then play them. But we feel that if you do a few tours with a number, then that number improves immensely. We will probably record them after the tour. There's enough material in the three songs for an album, but I don't know yet. We may do something else as well, which we haven't actually played yet. There are things I am working on in my studio that I would like to put on the next album.*"

Asked about a new Pink Floyd

album, Wright replied, *"It'll be a two-year gap between Dark Side and the next one, and that's too long in my opinion. We have never been a prolific group in terms of records. We average about one a year over our whole career. It's not a policy to work like that, it's just the way it happens. We have a deal with the record company that makes us do about seven albums in five years, which is one album a year and maybe a couple of film scores. It's very easy to make that deal."*

What do you think about the success of Dark Side of the Moon? Wright replied, *"It's been in the English charts ever since it was released, which is quite amazing. We all felt it would do at least as well as the other albums, but not quite as well as it did. All our albums have done well in this country, but Dark Side was number one in the U.S. and we never dreamed it would do that. It was probably the easiest album to sell in that it was the easiest to listen to, but it's success has obviously put some kind of pressure on us, and that is, what to do next. We have always tried to bring out something different with our next release and it would be very easy now to carry on with the same formula as Dark Side, which a lot of people would do."*

Wright continued, *"It's changed me in many ways because it's brought in a lot of money and one feels very secure when you can sell an album for two years. But it hasn't changed my attitude to music. Even though it was so successful, it was made in the same way as all our other albums and the only criteria we have about releasing music is whether we like it or not. It was not a deliberate attempt to make a commercial album. It just happened that way. Lots of people probably thought we all sat down and discussed it like that, but it wasn't the case at all. We knew it had a lot more melody than previous Floyd albums, and there was a concept that ran all through it. The music was easier to absorb and having girls singing away added a commercial touch that none of our other records had."*

After being informed that 'Dark Side of the Moon' sold 700,000 copies in the U.K., and three times that in the U.S., Wright replied, *"I never know about things like sales. I know that it was the first gold record that we had in America. And since its release, our other albums have picked up in sales over there. We*

have made a lot of new fans as a result because it was the first time we ever had an AM airplay in America. 'Money' was played on AM radio and, for a lot of people, it was the first time they'd heard us."

Wright continued, *"I like to think this hasn't put a pressure on us in terms of what we write next, but for a whole year we never did anything. We all sat around and got heavily into our reasons for being and our group. We got into a bad period when we didn't do anything at all creatively. We all still enjoy playing Dark Side, and any time one of us didn't enjoy it, we wouldn't do it again, ever. The first time we played it at the Rainbow, it was totally different from today, but it's remained virtually the same since we recorded it. There's a solo in' Money,' which varies according to how Dave feels, and 'Any Colour You Like' is just improvisations, but various parts are very arranged, and it's almost like a score."*

Asked about the visual and audio aspects their concert, Wright answered, *"It was hard work for Roger, Nick, and Arthur Max, the sound engineer, but it's still not right. I think we are still at the experimental stage in finding out what visuals work, and which don't, even after all these years. It's so easy to have a film that is distracting and, of course, I've never any idea what the effect of the film is. I'm always on stage playing. People always expect the Floyd to come up with something different, new and better, when it comes to visuals. And it's very difficult to keep thinking of new ideas. The projector for the film was incredibly expensive, and we got a new mixing desk too, which was also expensive. Buying those will probably mean we lose money on this tour, but that doesn't matter because we'll recoup it on later tours. We can never make money in England with 25 in the crew."*

Wright continued, *"We have got a new guy mixing the sound and he is used to working in a studio. Last night was the first time he's worked with a live band and that's why the first half of the concert wasn't right. The second half was easier because he'd got to know us and the board by then."*

Wright continued, *"We spent two weeks rehearsing at Elstree before this tour, but in the end we couldn't spend one whole day playing because of problems fitting the new*

Rick Wright

system together. Also, it demanded a lot of attention getting the notes for the first half of the show, which we hadn't played much before this tour. Dave had to have the words of the songs stuck on to the top of his guitar."

The interviewer commented that he thought the new Pink Floyd songs were "harsher, heavier numbers." Wright agreed, "Yes. It's the way the numbers have been written and it's the way we played them. We always play heavier when we don't know songs so well. When we first performed Dark Side, it was heavier and harsher than it is now. As we get to know a song better, we tend to play it quieter."

Wright then brought up the subject of Syd Barrett, saying "Did you realize that 'Shine On You Crazy Diamond' is about Syd? We don't see much of him now since he left, and we're definitely a different band since his day. Thank God we're not the same. I know that it's very fashionable to like Syd these days, but I think we have improved immensely since he left, especially live. He was a brilliant songwriter, and he was fantastic on 'Piper,' but he was in the wrong state to play any music. I am all for people trying to keep his name

going, but he hasn't written anything for years. His two solo albums show the way he was going. The first album was better than the second, and since then, no one has been able to get him into a studio."

Asked why Pink Floyd no longer play live as often as they used to, Wright replied, "We all differ in opinions about how much we should play live. Dave and I would like to do more live work, but Roger and Nick are happy with the way it is. It's such a headache going on the road, and all of us, except Dave, are married with kids. I believe it's very important that I am a good father and I am around with my children. We limit ourselves to three-week tours, and this has saved us from going mad. I feel that if we worked for weeks and weeks on the road all the time, we wouldn't be producing such good music. Bands who work live all the time do it purely for the money, I think. No band can really enjoy playing one-nighters, week after week. So it must be a financial rather than a musical motive."

Wright continued, "Last year, apart from a French tour, we didn't go out on the road at all, and we had a number one album in the States. We could have gone over then and made a fortune, but we would have made ourselves mad at the same time. We will probably do two three-week tours of the U.S. next year, and take a two-month break in between. But even so, I don't think we have played enough recently. You get to the point where you don't play and then you lose the whole reason for being in a band in the first place. And that, after all, is to go out and make music for people."

Wright continued, "*I would like to reach a situation where we would devote six months in a year to the Floyd and six months to whatever we like. If, for one of us, this meant going on the road, then he could play with another band, and I think we might be reaching that stage now. There are many things I would like to do which would not involve the Floyd, and this attitude could well save the Floyd in the long run. Every one of us wants to do other things, but at the moment we don't have the time. I feel this would be a good idea. Any band is a compromise between four individuals, but a compromise for a whole year isn't a good thing. It's only time that has prevented us doing solo projects, and if I had six months away from the group, I would certainly make an album of my own. The others feel the same way. I couldn't visualize going out with my own band on the road, but I would probably do a film score or maybe produce another artist. I know I would like to try playing with other musicians for a change.*"

Asked about why Pink Floyd avoid the media so much, Wright replied, "*We are not trying to sell ourselves, just the music. Right from the start we adopted this policy. We have never had a publicity agent, and we've never found one necessary. We don't go to all the 'in' parties, and we don't go to be seen in clubs in London. People don't recognize us on the streets, and even if they did, it wouldn't be a problem. That kind of thing has changed since I moved out of London to Cambridge where people don't know anything about the Floyd. Sometimes I get people tramping through my garden and asking for an autograph because they've heard I'm in a pop group, but they don't know what the Floyd do. They probably think we're like Gary glitter. It's a very nice situation to be in. Rod Stewart has the kind of personality that encourages all the*

fan worship, but we don't. We're just not that kind of band. Incidentally, I think Rod Stewart makes great music, too. I like all sorts of music myself. I listen to my old favorites. And I listen to records that people bring to me if I respect their taste. I ignore the way pop is going. I have completely lost touch with the singles charts. I don't listen to what is being played on the radio. I don't watch Top of the Pops, and I don't watch The Old Grey Whistle Test. I don't even know how the rock business is going, except that I think the bubble will burst fairly soon. It's already burst in the States where Joe Public has decided he's not going to pay such enormous ticket prices anymore. I don't agree with these huge shows in front of tens of thousands of people. Wembley Empire Pool is the biggest place you can play before you lost the effect.*"

And finally, Wright expressed his feeling as to how long he thinks Pink Floyd will last, saying, "*It could last forever. There's no reason why it shouldn't. But then we could have a fight tomorrow and split up tomorrow. If we carry out that idea of being a group for six months and individuals for the next six months, then there's no reason why we can't carry on for a long time. As a group, we still have much to do and much to do together. We probably do things much better with each other than we ever could with anyone else. We are basically happy with the situation at this time. Roger is very keen on sports, which suits his competitive spirit. And Nick is keen on sailing. And that's another thing that helps us survive. We're not underground anymore, despite what people say. At the UFO, it was underground. But you can't be underground when you sell out every concert hall and your album goes to number one. No, the Pink Floyd can't claim to be underground anymore.*"

Also in this issue was an article that reported that David Gilmour and Richard Wright appeared with the Sutherland Brothers/Quiver at their concert at Newcastle Poly the previous weekend.

Sounds (U.K.) reported that Pink Floyd are the most popular group for background music for live sex shows in Amsterdam.

November 19, 1974 – The Daily Mail (U.K.) reported that Pink Floyd are not an average

pop group. They haven't had a Top 30 hit in a decade, the band members go unrecognized on the street, and they turn down interview requests. But Wembley was deluged with ticket requests when they announced their concerts. Their music merges different styles with extraordinary visual effects and a theatrical performance.

November 23, 1974 - New Musical Express (U.K.) published an article titled, "Floyd juggernaut . . . the road to 1984?" The article featured a review of the Pink Floyd concert at the Empire Pool, Wembley on November 14, 1974 by Nick Kent, plus an interview with David Gilmour by Pete Erskine.

Kent called the Pink Floyd concert at Wembley "hell" and stated that he was infuriated, angry, and depressed over it. He called certain lyrics from the new songs "shit" and "offensive," and wrote that the band members were limited as musicians. He said that it was "the most boring concert I've ever been forced to sit through for review purposes." He also claimed Gilmour's hair was filthy.

The interview with David Gilmour by Pete Erskine took place at David Gilmour's newly-renovated Notting Hill town house on November 15, 1974. Erskine began his interview by asking Gilmour about his low profile, laissez-faire attitude towards the fans and critics, and whether he was being cynical. Gilmour answered, "*Cynical? No. I mean, last night on stage I was just hung up, because it wasn't very good.*" What about the long spaces between songs, and Roger stalling over lighting a cigarette? "*Oh yeah. But I don't really think that's what it's down to. It's just, ah, well, I dunno. Roger likes smoking cigarettes. He can't get through a gig without a few straights.*"

Gilmour stated that Thursday's concert was "*probably the worst we've done on the whole tour. The first half, when that wasn't very good, it didn't particularly worry me because they're all new things and we're not doing them very well yet. But we have done them better than that. I thought the second half would click into place because it has done on a couple of other nights when the first half wasn't good.*"

What about the low quality of musicianship at the show? Gilmour replied, "*In the first half, the sound wasn't very good and the vocal mics were pretty terrible, which makes it that much harder to sing and that much harder to work. And also, it didn't sound as if there was any bass and drums. Unless there's a bit of that 'ooomph,' you can't really get off. It was just one of those nights where you bumble around and don't really get anything together. It sounded ragged all the way though. It doesn't worry me particularly, it just happens sometimes. Just chemistry*

really, isn't it?"

What about the audiences reaction? Gilmour replied, "*I think they enjoyed it reasonably. But I think a lot of people didn't really think it was very good. There's a difference between going home and thinking it was pretty good and going home and thinking 'wow.' And I know we do get that pretty often. More nights than not, I know that most of the people there are going to go home and say 'what a groove!' I think they probably want to convince themselves that they did have a groove, just so that they don't think they hit on a bad one, and wasted their money.*"

How did you feel about people who worship the band? Gilmour replied, "*It's a drag.*" You could release a double album of Roger tuning his bass guitar and it would sell. Gilmour said, "*I'm sure there would be people who'd react that way, but I'm sure sales figures would reflect a bad album in the end. But I don't mean that 100 per cent. I'm sure that if we put out an album of pure tripe, it would sell vastly more than lots and lots of other band's records. But in relation to our sales, a bad record would sell badly. It has done in the past.*"

Which album sold badly in the past? Gilmour replied, "*Well, 'Atom Heart Mother.' I'd say that was the worst record we've made. I didn't like it and I don't like it much now. I'm not very keen on 'Ummagumma' either.*"

What about 'Dark Side of the Moon?' Does the musical content deserve all the praise it has received or was it popular just due to the interest in the band? Gilmour replied, "*Quite possibly. You may be right. But it certainly was a very good all-around, uh, package. Everything about it was very well done. It was one continuous idea. It was recorded well, it was pretty well mixed, had a good cover and all that sort of stuff. But I've always felt, right from the word go, that the musical side of it wasn't that hot in some parts. And I still feel that. Some parts are a bit weak. We'd have a lyrical idea, but no real idea of a musical piece to put to it, so we'd just make something up and take the first thing that came, rather than being critical about the musical side as it was being done. But then some of those bits got knocked out during the months we were playing it on stage before we recorded it. The original travel section we played for months onstage and even recorded it before deciding to scrap it and start again."*

As far as blind acceptance of the band, aren't you getting to a point where you could walk on stage, throw a couple of switches, walk off, and the audience would still love it? Gilmour replied, *"Oh, I don't think so, no. I don't think that the audience have a very great participation in what we do, but I don't think that's a bad thing necessarily."*

Doesn't the fact that your audience loves everything you do promote blind acceptance? Gilmour replied, *"No. Listen, we still have to get off. I mean, you know what the difference is between a good gig and a bad gig. And it's not mechanical. We're quite capable of blowing a gig and we're also capable of doing a great gig."*

But doesn't it promote a glazed 'okay feed-it-to me' attitude? Some people fell asleep during your concert. Gilmour said, *"You think so? I think it's up to them. I think they're free to take it any way they want. A lot of people don't, though. We had someone the other night who must've known that we're football fans who was shouting 'cyyyyomon you Floyd!!!,' just like they do on the North Bank."*

The new songs sounded recycled. Are you having trouble with new ideas? Gilmour replied, *"Umm, yeah. I don't know. 'Raving And Drooling,' the middle one of the three, sounds a bit recycled to me, but they're not there yet. I'm not very keen on that one at the moment, but, I dunno, these things get worked into shape. I know that one or two of them are gonna sound great recorded. I think the last one, 'Gotta Be Crazy,' is very different to a lot of stuff we've done, but I don't think the words go right at the moment. I mean, the singing thing's been worked out a bit too quickly. Roger wrote the words to fit over a certain part and I'm not sure that we did it quite the right way."*

How can you relate to 'Gotta Be Crazy,' or 'Money,' considering the secure position you're in as a band? Gilmour replied, *"Well, 'Money' is obviously a satire on money. And it is a self-satire, obviously. It's easy to tell that because a lot of the lyrics relate specifically to things that various of us have done, but I mean, I don't think we're as capitalist as ... I think it mocks us, the song*

says that we're more than we are, in fact. It just keeps us aware of it all. 'You Gotta Be Crazy' is about business pressure really. It does relate to us, I'm sure. You'll have to ask Roger really, he wrote it. The way I understand the words is that I guess you have to harden yourself up to, uh, you know 'Make It' in this world, if that's what you call 'Making It.'"

The new songs sound safe. You haven't taken musical risks for years. Gilmour replied, *"Ah well, I think that 's all down to what you want to do. I mean, I certainly don't want to do a lot of things we did earlier on. I'm just interested in actually writing music and getting the music done that we do. You know, I think that everyone's interests have gone more towards that sort of thing rather than some of the old rubbish that we used to do, although it was good fun. But, I dunno, I don't think anyone's got any great interest in it now. You can't do that sort of thing forever. Like there are lots of things we used to do. Like we used to do an encore where we'd just go on and not decide what we were going to do until we'd started."*

How long ago did you do that? Gilmour replied, *"Oh, four years ago, at least. But I don't really want to go through that thing of doing five loads of rubbish and just once getting something that's pretty good and new. Or getting a half-hour number with about three minutes of worthwhile music in it."*

Don't you think that if you had continued improvising, you would have progressed to a personal empathy that would have eliminated the rubbish? Gilmour replied, *"I don't know. I really don't know. I've just got memories of standing onstage farting about, plonking away on stuff and feeling terribly embarrassed for long periods of time, and looking across at everyone else, realizing that they were all obviously feeling the same way. Maybe guaranteeing that what you play is something that you'll enjoy is playing safe. But I don't think we've got an intentional play-safe policy."*

Also in this issue, Teazers reported that the trucks used by Pink Floyd on their current tour are three 32-ton Mercedes tractor trucks that are rented from Avis Rental.

1975
Wish You Were Here

January 11, 1975 - New Musical Express (U.K.) published an article titled, "Dirty hair denied" by Pete Erskine. This article was a response to the New Musical Express article of November 23, 1974 that accused David Gilmour of having dirty hair. Asked if he had washed his hair, Gilmour replied *"No, and if he can find any split ends in here then ..."* Gilmour told Erskine on the telephone, *"I've just read the piece, and I'm very angry about it,"* referring to the previous article in New Musical express.

But what about the blind acceptance of the band? Gilmour replied, *"I don't think anyone on our level feels deserving of that kind of superhuman adulation number. But then a lot of them probably dig it. Sure, I'm cynical of our position. I don't think we deserve it. But I'm no more cynical of our position than I am of anyone else's on our level. I mean, to try and maintain your own perspective on what you are is totally different."*

The song 'Gotta Be Crazy,' has a great deal of cynicism in its lyrics, such as the line "Gotta keep people buying this shit." Is this a sneer at the audience? Gilmour replied, *"Mmm. Yeah, it is possibly a sneer, but not at the audience as a whole, but at the type of adulation bands like us get. I mean I think there is something wrong with that, people needing hero-figures like that, thinking that rock musicians have all the answers."*

Are bands like Pink Floyd compounding the problem by not challenging it? Gilmour replied, *"Yes. Probably. But I think we're less guilty than most. I mean we've made conscious attempts at fighting it."*

What attempts have you made? Gilmour replied, *"In things we've said in interviews and things like that. We've always said that we don't believe in that whole number, but it's very hard to get away from the image people put on you."*

The article by Nick Kent made Gilmour mad, especially the first eleven paragraphs that featured descriptions of Gilmour's personal appearance and that of a member of the audience, who was described as a typical Floyd fan who "smokes dope, prattles

on about the cosmos and gets off on the stereo production quirks inherent in all Floyd albums." Gilmour said, *"I don't see any of it being in any way relevant. So there's a guy like that in the audience, what? There were probably others like him, but you find people like that at any concert. But then Kent probably set out to find one and he did."* The interviewer claimed that there was no intention before hand to do so. Gilmour said, *"Well, I just don't believe it of Nick Kent. I really don't. He's still really involved with Syd Barrett and the whole 1967 thing. I don't even know if he ever saw the Floyd with Syd. He goes on about Syd too much and yet, as far as I can see, there's no relevance in talking about Syd in reviewing one of our concerts."*

Reminded that one of their new songs is about Syd Barrett, Gilmour replied, *"Yes, but that's all. In the beginning the songs were all his, and they were brilliant. No one disputes that. But I don't think the actual sound of the whole band stems from Syd. I think it stems just as much from Rick. I mean, Syd's thing was-short songs. The band just before Syd departed had got into a totally impossible situation. No one wanted to book them. After the success of the summer of 1967 the band sank like a stone. The gigs they were doing at the time were all empty because they were so bad. The only way out was to get rid of Syd, so they asked me to join and got rid of Syd."*

Erskine previously asserted that the band had gotten their persona from Barrett and, when he left, they held on to the momentum he provided. Gilmour replied, *"By the time Syd left the ball had definitely stopped rolling. We had to start it all over again. 'Saucerful of Secrets,' the first album without him, was the start back on the road to some kind of return. It was the album we began building from. The whole conception of 'Saucerful of Secrets' has nothing to do with what Syd believed in or liked. We continued playing some of his songs because none of us were getting good enough material fast enough to be able to do without them, which also, therefore, meant that I had to fit in with his style to an extent because his songs were so rigidly structured around it. Oh, and by the way, the band, when I joined, never ever said 'play like Syd Barrett.' That was the very last thing they wanted!"* This was a reference to a statement by Peter Jenner that the interviewer had accepted as fact.

Erskine had also stated that "The familiar slide and echo-boxes were purely of Syd's invention," which was also based on a quote by Peter Jenner. Gilmour said, *"Why didn't you ask me about things like that during the interview? The facts of the matter are that I was using an echo-box years before Syd was. I also used slide. I also taught Syd quite a lot about guitar. I mean, people saying that I pinched his style when our backgrounds are so similar, yet we spent a lot of time together as teenagers listening to the same music. Our influences are probably pretty much the same, and I was a couple of streets ahead of him at the time and was teaching him to play Stones riffs every lunchtime for a year at technical college. That kind of thing's bound to get my back up, especially if you don't check it. I don't want to go into print saying that I taught Syd Barrett everything he knows, because it's patently untrue. But there are one or two things in Syd's style that I know came from me."*

Erskine asked Gilmour if he was spreading himself too thinly as a guitarist, capable of most things, but not particularly outstanding at any one thing. Is this what he intended? Gilmour replied, *"No. But I work within my limitations. But then, whether I'm a good or bad guitarist isn't really relevant. I mean I try my damnedest to do my best, although certainly for the first half of that tour I was, well, rusty. I hadn't played for a long time and my fingers were really stiff. But also I would say that I got very good by the time we were halfway through."*

Erskine had also accused Pink Floyd of being unable to relate to the average fan due to the way the band lives. Gilmour replied, *"If you're referring to that bit which says something about our 'desperately bourgeois existences,' well, I mean, how do you or he know how we live our lives, apart from you, marginally, about me? Do you? Does Nick? He hasn't been to any of our houses. He's got absolutely no idea of how I spend my life apart from what you might have told him. And you*

don't know how the others live. Do you think my life is so desperately bourgeois? My house is not particularly grand. Have you seen Roger's house? He lives in a five-grand terraced house in Islington. So I really can't see how Kent can sit there and say things like that. He's no idea of what he's talking about."

What about the band's individual instrumental prowess? Gilmour replied, *"In terms of musical virtuosity, we're not really anywhere I think. Individual musicianship is well below par."*

Talking about the bands new material, Gilmour stated that they are not *"bereft of ideas,"* just taking their time. 'Dark Side of the Moon,' *"trapped us creatively."*

As for their lyrics, Gilmour explained, *"We tried to make them as simple and direct as possible and yet, as we were writing them, we knew they'd be misunderstood. We still get people coming up to us who think that 'Money, it's a gas' is a direct and literal statement that we like money."*

Asked about the appeal of Floyd being associated with the sophistication in stereo equipment, Gilmour replied, *"Six years ago, we still sold albums and yet hardly anyone in this country had a stereo. It was all Dansettes then."*

Does packaging take priority over contents? Gilmour replied, *"No. That's ridiculous. I suppose the same criticism would then apply to Stevie Wonder records?"*

Nick Kent, in his previous article wrote, "What the two Floyd shows amounted to in the final analysis was not merely a kind of utterly morose laziness which is ultimately even more obnoxious than callow superstar 'flash', but a pallid excuse for creative music which comes dangerously close to the Orwellian mean for a facile soulless music that would doubtless rule the airwaves and moreover be touted as fine art in the latter's vision of 1984. I mean, one can easily envisage a Floyd concert in the future consisting of the band simply wandering on stage, setting all their tapes into action, putting their instruments on remote control and then walking off behind the amps to talk football or play billiards." Gilmour responded, *"Personally, I don't believe any of that rubbish about 1984. But I mean what difference is there between our sort of music and anyone else's, apart from the fact that maybe most of the other bands just play music for the body? And they're hardly progressive at all. Not that I think we're wildly progressive either."*

How do you feel when the audience doesn't care as much about your music as a bucket of dry ice? Gilmour replied, *"Yeah. That's all part of dramatic effect, isn't it? We went through a period where we blew out our entire light show for two years and there was no real difference. I personally know for a fact that it wouldn't make any difference if we did it again. We've never been hyped. There's been no great publicity campaign. It's built up purely on the strength of gigs. I don't think we're remotely close to that thing about tapes, do you?"*

On the basis of the Wembley concert, Erskine thought that they were. He said the band looked "bored and dispirited." Gilmour replied, *"Not bored. Definitely dispirited. It gets very depressing when you're fighting against odds like dud equipment. Energy soon flags. We weren't pleased to do an encore because we didn't deserve it."*

Asked why he didn't tell the audience this, Gilmour said, *"I'm not interested in disguising my feelings on stage with showbiz devices. I've seen hundreds of bands do that. Does anybody respect them? From what he writes, Nick Kent seems to believe in it all, the old thing of The Show Must Go On, Never Let The Public See Your Feelings and things like that."*

Wouldn't doing that help your attitude? Gilmour answered, *"No. When I'm standing there I'm conscious of trying to give the most I can, and I don't need to have clean hair for that."*

February 8, 1975 - Melody Maker (U.K.) published a letter from Anthony Fletcher of London, who wrote that Pink Floyd are not over-rated. "When Syd Barrett left, they changed from light evening music to good rock music."

March 5, 1975 - Billboard Magazine (U.S.) reported on the Pink Floyd concerts at the Cow Palace in San Francisco, California on April 12, 1975. They wrote that the concerts were true multimedia experiences, and

featured a spinning mirrored wheel, a missile that flew over the crowd from the back of the hall, explosions, smoke, a large circular film screen, and quadraphonic sound. However, the music was tedious at times. The band was accompanied by a saxophone player, and two female backing vocalists.

March 8, 1975 - Melody Maker (U.K.) reported in Raver's Hot Licks that Pink Floyd have been working on their new album at Abbey Road Studios for five weeks so far.

March 22, 1975 - Melody Maker (U.K.) published a half-page ad for the movie, 'The Valley,' now showing at the ABC Bloomsbury and the ABC Fulham Road theaters. "It allows a willing audience to supplement it's own phantasies," said Time Out. "A film for sensate enjoyment. Astonishing in imagery and sound," wrote the Evening Standard.

April 9, 1975 - The Vancouver Sun (Canada) published an article titled, "Pink Floyd: like technicians for the land of gadgetry" by Don Stanley that reviewed the Pink Floyd concert in Vancouver, Canada on April 8, 1975. Stanley wrote that Pink Floyd used a 360-degree sound system, four light towers, and spotlights to transform the Coliseum into "psychedelic concrete earphones." The sound effects were heightened by keeping the music simple, and the gimmicks were impressive. A large disc revolved above the stage in a spotlight, and films were projected on a circular screen during 'Dark Side of the Moon. The films showed flying clocks, silver coins during 'Money,' and a close-up of a human eye. A silver model airplane that was suspended in one corner of the Coliseum and was supposed to fly over the crowd, never moved. "A fitfully pleasing, consistently dull show."

April 1975 - The Phonograph Record (U.S.) published an article titled, "The Pink Floyd Void – Will They Make it To 1984?" by Nick Kent in which Kent recalled the 1974 British Winter tour as uninspired. He wrote that the two shows he attended at Wembley were tedious and gave him a headache.

April 14, 1975 - The State Press of Arizona State University (U.S.) reported that the Pink

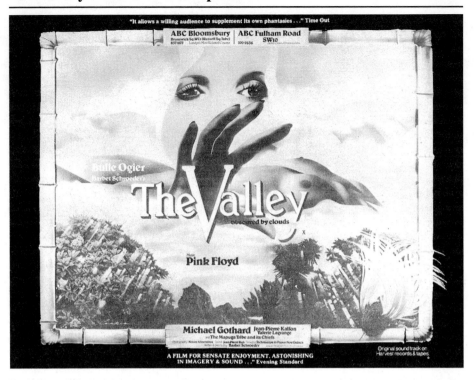

Floyd concert scheduled for April 15, 1975 at the Arizona State University Activity Center had to be rescheduled to April 20, 1975, due to the fact that the A.S.U. electrical facilities required by Pink Floyd could not be available on time. The band also claimed the stage was inadequate to hold the weight of Pink Floyd's equipment, which totaled 32 tons.

April 19, 1975 - Melody Maker (U.K.) published a letter in their mailbag reporting that 'Dark Side of the Moon' was missing from the Melody Maker's Top 30 album chart in the April 12, 1975 issue, the first time it has not appeared since its release in March 1973.

April 22, 1975 - The State Press of Arizona State University (U.S.) reported that the Pink Floyd concert at the Arizona State Activity center on April 20, 1975, was a financial success, even though 1,000 people bought counterfeit tickets. Tickets costs $7.50 and $8.50, and total attendance was 10,000.

A second article, titled, "Gimmickry detracts from excellent show," reviewed the performance. They wrote that there was a lack of enthusiasm for Pink Floyd's new songs, but the audience enjoyed the light show and special effects, including a parabolic mirror, smoke, imitation snow, a 10-foot airplane, and movies that accompanied the piece 'Dark Side of the Moon.'

A third article featured a brief interview with Roger Waters who explained why the new album, to be released in June, was two years in the making. Waters said, "*We've been doing a lot of other things.*" Asked about when the group first started using a quadraphonic sound system, he answered, "*It's too long ago to say.*" Asked for his response to someone saying that Pink Floyd were too gimmickry, Waters replied that a person "*is entitled to his opinion.*" And asked about their origins and why they quit school, Waters answered, "*Jargon, it's bullshit. They treated you like children. They were still in charge.*"

April 26, 1975 - Melody Maker (U.K.) reported that Pink Floyd will headline the Knebworth Festival on July 5, 1975. Tickets will cost £2.75.

New Musical Express (U.K.) reported that promoter Fredrick Bannister has confirmed that Pink Floyd will perform at the Knebworth Festival on July 5, 1975. Pink Floyd will be performing new material from their upcoming album at the show.

April 30, 1975 - The New Times, Arizona (U.S.) published an interview with Roger Waters and Richard Wright. The interview was done after their concert at Arizona State University on April 20, 1975.

Roger Waters commented about doing interviews, and about Rolling Stone Magazine, saying, *"We used to do interviews years and years ago, but we gave it up. We used to get asked bloody stupid questions. Unless you've got something important you want to say, it's just a hassle. Personally, I just don't prefer an interview. The Rolling Stone is just about selling records now. When we were in no position to sell their paper for them, they didn't want to know about us. I don't read the paper."*

Asked about his early days at the Regent Street Polytechnic School in England, Waters said, *"I hated it. I quit after four years. They just wouldn't talk to us. It was a joke. I mean it's just all jargon and loaded with aesthetic bullshit that has nothing to do with anything. It was just a game to them. You don't really learn in architecture school. They still treated you like fucking children. They wouldn't talk to you about anything that they thought was outside the curriculum. They were still in charge. It was still the same type of authoritative number going down. I quit when our first record, 'Arnold Layne,' came out."*

Asked about other groups owing their start to Pink Floyd, Waters said, *"Certainly. Most of the theatrical effects have been picked up very fast."*

As for madness being a theme to their music, Waters commented, *"This is true,"* and as for it being a part of life, he added, *"It's a part of life for everybody."*

Richard Wright was asked about using a VCS3 synthesizer. Wright said, *"The VCS3 is basically the same as the mini-Moog. We don't use it very much. Well, Dave uses it. It's got three oscillators. It's very hard to play. It's very versatile and you can get amazing sounds out of it. But they're not very good for live performances. One of the problems with the instrument is that it gets out of tune quite easily."*

Asked about outside musical

influences, Wright replied, *"Well, I listen to music but I've spent very little time listening to that side of it in terms of what's going on in other bands. No, I don't listen to that too much. Our influences come from things that happened a long time ago."*

Reminded of Syd Barrett, Wright said, *"He left in 1967,"* and asked whether he just split, Wright replied, *"No, we threw him out. He got totally fucked up just by the whole idea of . . . I don't know why he got fucked up, but he did get fucked up and we couldn't play with him. He couldn't play with people. In simple language, he went mad, over the edge. It's a very sad thing."*

Asked why he got out of architectural school, Wright replied, *"Why did I get out? Because I was no fucking good at it. The reason I went into it was because they said, 'Try architecture.' I didn't know what I wanted to do. I split after a year. Architecture meant nothing to me. It was just an excuse to get into college and get grants. What I really did was music, and it just so happened that we met each other."*

May 3, 1975 - Melody Maker (U.K.) published an article in their column 'Caught in the Act America' titled, "Floyd: Amazing Heroes" by Todd Tolces. The article reviewed the Pink Floyd concerts at the Cow Palace in San Francisco, California, on April 12 & 13, 1975. Tolces wrote that the audience total for both nights was 27,000, and the show was pretty amazing. The first set consisted of new songs. 'You've Got to Be Crazy' was the best of the three new songs, a beautiful song with stinging guitar work by David Gilmour, Nick Mason's cymbal tippings, and Richard Wright's spectacular keyboard bonanza in the middle. The second set was 'Dark Side of the Moon.' During 'On the Run,' a 30-foot long spaceship flew over the crowd and exploded while the band controlled the sound of the ship's thrust in quadraphonic, and the movie screen showed vast amounts of destruction in slow motion. 'Time' followed with a screenfull of endless quadraphonic alarms, and 'Money' was accompanied by visual currency. Roger Waters' bass line was timeless. The encore was 'Echoes,' during which Waters froze the crowd with a couple of 'Eugene' vocals screams.

May 8, 1975 - Rolling Stone Magazine (U.S.)

published an article titled, "Space by the Ton: Album, U.S. Tour for Pink Floyd." They reported that Pink Floyd will be touring the West Coast of North America, beginning in Vancouver, Canada on April 8, 1975. On April 23, 1975, the band will play the Los Angeles Sports Arena, where 67,000 tickets for four shows sold out in one day before a fifth show was added. For this tour, the band will be using 30 tons of equipment including rear film projection equipment, a chartered plane, and a 17-member road crew.

A spokesman for the band said that the band "*has four or five things that they're going to do differently. It will be a big, overpowering show, really massive.*" He added, "*No, they don't dress up on stage. But judging by the amount of equipment, the show will be amazing.*" Following this tour, the band will return to England in May, followed by an East Coast U.S. tour.

May 25, 1975 - Ciao 2001 No. 20 (Italy) published an article titled, "Pink Floyd: intervista a Los Angeles" that featured an interview with Nick Mason done in Los Angeles by Armando Gallo. Asked about the success of `Dark Side of the Moon' and whether the band was prepared for it, Mason replied, "*No. At the outset I didn't expect this. Looking at it now, there are two particular reasons for its success. First of all, the album was released at precisely the right moment. It has some well-written songs that fit together well as a conceptual piece. The second reason for the success of the album is that people bought it because of its success. When people buy six albums a year, 'Dark Side of the Moon' is one of them, sometimes just to test a new hi-fi.*"

Is it hard to follow up Dark Side of the Moon? Mason replied, "*No. We haven't made a new record because Dark Side is still selling a lot. So EMI isn't pressing us for a new product. We have been recording very carefully. We eliminated some pieces that we might have recorded if we were under pressure. But right now we are recording just the best material. The album will be ready in June.*"

Have you recorded the songs that are the first part of your live shows? Mason replied, "*Yes, in part. The third piece will be on the album.*"

Asked about the title of the piece about Syd Barrett, Mason replied, "*We haven't settled on the titles yet. What we have are only temporary titles at the moment.*"

How much of the song is about Syd Barrett? Mason explained, "*Roger wrote the piece so maybe he could explain it better. But he doesn't like to speak with journalists. In the beginning, it was entirely about Syd, but since then, it has changed. Now it describes, generally, what happened to Syd, and the way people reacted to his madness. Its a sad piece.*"

At one time Pink Floyd didn't want to talk about Syd Barrett, but now you are writing a song about him. Why is that? Mason replied, "*Perhaps because now we can. Syd was, without a doubt, the one who started the Pink Floyd. At the beginning he wrote almost all of the songs. He was the creative force of the group. But at that time, Pink Floyd was interstellar rock music. Now, I think that 'Dark Side of the Moon' has shown that the Floyd aren't interstellar rock music and we haven't been for years. And now that this has changed, we feel that we can do a piece dedicated to Syd Barrett without any fears of misunderstanding.*"

Some songs from 'Dark Side of the Moon' are regularly played in discothèques. This wasn't the case a while ago. Does this bother you? Mason replied, "*No. We play music for ourselves. That is why we spend such a long time recording, because it is hard to satisfy ourselves. In many countries, the song 'Money' has been issued as a 7-inch single because of its length and because it is a rock and roll number. But we didn't record it to be a single.*"

When you perform, why don't you dress for the show? Mason replied, "*Because we are convinced that dressing for a show doesn't help the music we perform. The images and the lights help you to perceive the music. The public watches the images on the screen and doesn't have time to divert their attention to our dress.*"

Who is the person who created the wonderful films for your performance? Mason answered, "*Peter Medoc, who is a cinematic producer. We are very satisfied with his work.*"

Why don't you like to talk to the press during your tour? Mason said, "*There aren't a lot of honest journalists. They often want to put down your work. I can't accept that. Our work is for the public, not for journalists."*

June 5, 1975 - Rolling Stone (U.K.) published an article titled, "Space Rock: Floydian Slip" that reviewed the Pink Floyd concert at the Los Angeles Sports Arena on April 23, 1975. They reported that Pink Floyd began the show with 'Raving and Drooling,' 'You Gotta Be Crazy,' and 'Shine On You Crazy Diamond,' which were only adequate compared to how they played them previously in Seattle. The second set was 'Dark Side of the Moon,' which suffered from poor song transitions, missed soloing opportunities, over-reactive bass playing, and uninspired drumming. The film for the song 'Money' was edited to take out the female nudity. The sound at the show was good, but the volume was too loud. For an encore, they played 'Echoes.'

Also in this issue was an article titled, "L.A. Rock Uproar . . . One Bust over the Line, Chief Davis?" The article reported that during the five Pink Floyd concerts at the Los Angeles Sports Arena, the police arrested 511 people, primarily for possession of marijuana. Los Angeles Police Chief Ed Davis is now under criticism by the mayors office, the city attorney, the city counsel, and the Los Angeles Times for the actions of the L.A.P.D. Davis, who became Chief of Police in 1969, has intensified police actions at rock concerts, causing mass arrests over the years. Managers of concert halls have accused the police of harassment and discriminatory application of the laws. Promoter Sepp Donahower stated, "The police have taken an overly aggressive law enforcement policy. It discourages concerts from coming into the city." Chief Davis, however, appears to be convinced that smoking marijuana is leading to a decline of traditional American values and could lead to us "losing the damn country."

After the Pink Floyd concerts had been organized and permits were granted by the police commission, rumors began circulating a few moths before the concerts that the police were planning to bust the event. A Shrine Hall concert attendee claimed that a police offer had told him at a prior concert, "If you think this is something, you ought to see what we are going to do at the Sports Arena."

The police commission and deputy police chief denied the rumors, and the mayor urged the police to concentrate on crimes against people and property. However, Davis said, "I'm the meanest chief of police in the history of the United States," and publicly disagreed with requests to leave victimless crimes alone. He also made headlines on the night of the first Pink Floyd concert by saying that people should buy guns to protect themselves.

The day of the show, attendees were given handbills that read, "This is not a sanctuary for pot smoking. The Los Angeles Police Department is making arrests," and sound trucks were used to broadcast this message to arriving fans outside the venue. Jim Hardy, the general manager of the Sports Arena, claimed he saw people lined up against the wall and cars being searched, and stated, "The plainclothesmen were arresting people as fast as they could." Newsmen on the scene witnessed shoving and arm twisting by the police. On the first night there were 88 arrests, the second night 134 arrests, and the third night 105 arrests. Chief Davis said on the day of the third concert, "Tonight at the Sports Arena, under three governmental agencies, they have a dope festival. It's called a rock concert or something. I think they're operating illegally. They don't have a rock permit. Don't you have to have a rock permit?" Davis then had his deputy try to stop the concerts, but the mayor, city attorney, and a councilman interceded and the final two shows went on as scheduled. 118 arrests were made on the fourth night, and 67 at the final show.

After the concerts were over, Hardy accused the police of harassment. He stated that the attendees were, "the best behaved crowd we have ever had here. By no common sense, rationale, or logic, can I understand the deployment of this massive police power for this peaceful event. It is the objective view of the general manager and all present that the effort was designed simply to put us out of the concert business."

The promoters of the Pink Floyd concerts announced that they would not be promoting any more concerts at the Sports Arena. The Los Angeles Times reported that on the same night that police arrested 134 people at the Pink Floyd concert, a boxing match at the Olympic Auditorium that yielded an unpopular decision which caused fans to light fires, damage seats, break windows, and throw objects into the streets, resulted in just three arrests. The City Attorney has since stated that the Arena's permit for the event was perfectly valid, and the mayor and others are questioning the priorities of the police.

June 7, 1975 - New Musical Express (U.K.) published an article titled, "Bootleggers Slice Floyd's Cake" by Roy Carr. The article reported that a bootleg album of 'Dark Side of the Moon' performed live has sold enough to go gold, but a new Pink Floyd bootleg, called "The Pink Floyd's British Winter Tour '74" is selling well enough to surpass the sales of any previous Floyd bootleg. The new bootleg was recoded live at Trentham Gardens, Stoke on November 19, 1974 and consists of three new Pink Floyd songs, 'Raving and Drooling,' 'Gotta Be Crazy,' and 'Shine On You Crazy Diamond.' Reliable sources estimate that 60,000 copies have already been sold in Europe, and sales could reach 100,000-150,000 by next month. The problem stems from the fact that Pink Floyd perform songs in concert before they are available on record. Harvest Records label manager, Stuart Watson commented, "*I really don't know what to say.*" Asked when the new official Pink Floyd album would be ready, he said, "*As far as I know, one side has been completed and the Floyd are in the studio at this moment mixing the remaining tracks. I don't think it will be ready for release for at least another two or three months.*" Another source stated, "I've found that well over half the people who have bought this bootleg think that it is the new Floyd album and the official follow-up to 'Dark Side of the Moon,' and I don't think that they will buy the official one when the Floyd get around to releasing it."

June 28, 1975 - Melody Maker (U.K.) published an article titled, "The Big Show will vanish" in which Allan Jones talked with Peter Jenner and Andrew King of Blackhill Enterprises, Ltd. Asked why there is a lack of new talent in the last year and a half, King replied, "*There have been a lot of strong second-raters like Cockney Rebel and Pilot. It's a matter of opinion whether or not you think they have any real talent. The really*

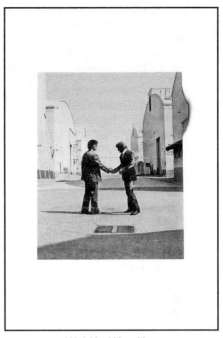

Wish You Were Here

exceptional people tend to filter through pretty slowly as a rule." Peter Jenner added, "*One of the basic problems is that there's been a continuity in musical development since the psychedelic movement, and pre that, the blues scene. Those scenes threw up a whole plethora of English musicians and bands and started a tradition, which is still continuing. Things like the Pink Floyd, which started nearly ten years ago, and Yes, who started almost as long ago as that, and the Who and the Stones who go back even further, all these bands haven't yet become obviously a Frank Sinatra scene. In this context, therefore, you've got these monster bands who've built up over the last ten years who are just sucking all the money from the market, which obviously affects the future of new bands who might turn out to be another Floyd or another Yes, or another whoever.*"

What about bands like Henry Cow, who are new and invigorating? King replied, "*But how old are Henry Cow? As a group, they've been together for something like seven years. New talent is emerging there, but aren't we looking for some new and exceptional teenage talent?*" Jenner continued, "*Or a new cycle, a new psychic thing. Because I think that the importance of what happened in 1965,*

1966, 1967 was really down to the fact that drugs came into England for the first time in considerable quantities. Marijuana and acid became very, very important to music. A lot of things which were being done in 1966, say, were weird minority tastes. Like John Mayall, oh yes, that's the blues, how quaint. Or the Floyd, oh yes, that's psychedelic, that's kaftans. It always comes down to something more than just the music. The time is always important. Basically part of the problem is that there's too much good music about, a lot of bands lingering on playing fairly well. What we need is for a lot of bands to go absolutely down the drain and be forgotten about. I think that then something much more within the nature of the times will emerge. The whole showbiz thing will alienate the kids in the end. The Big Show will vanish. I would say, as a totally random guess, that something which might well have a good chance in the future, if the economic thing continues to get ghastly, which it probably will, there'll be some revolutionary vibes which will get going, there'll be a big depression, and there'll suddenly be a wave of very Marxist, very committed, very politically-oriented groups coming on playing for workers or something like that, which is going away from the whole capitalistic big business structure. In that sense, there is a scene like the sixties. There is no way, at the moment, of doing things other than through the standard procedures of doing the pubs, leading to colleges, leading to town halls, to Odeon Cinemas, leading to American tours, leading to gold records, leading to hundreds of thousands of pounds being spent on 'A Product.' Everything is product oriented. And I think that the political thing is a possibility. As the world collapses around us, then the new music will reflect that collapse and the panic involved."

Are there any musicians already on the periphery of this change? Jenner answered, *"I suspect not. I'm thinking of someone who's like 16, say, who's going to start saying 'Look, all this stuff that all these bands do with these huge PAs and lights, that's not where it's at. It's down to the people. And I'm going to get out my acoustic guitar and I'm going to sing revolutionary songs, in pubs, or working men's clubs, or factories.' A vibe will get going sufficiently revolutionary so that people will*

catch up on it, and suddenly that kid will be the new messiah. And he'll end up playing at all the internationalist and Socialist rallies. I dread the thought of that coming. Nothing could strike me as being more horrible. But it does seem to be a plausible scenario. And if that's not going to be the scenario, I think it will be something with that kind of inter-relationship between society and the music. That was what the sixties was all about. It was about the liberation of the late teenagers, and the liberation of their purchasing powers. You could say the Wombles and the Osmonds are a reflection of the liberation of the purchasing powers of the sub-teens."

Andrew King continued, *"I think the other thing is that, when one talks about talent, one has to make a definition between acts, or bands, and songwriters. I think that, statistically, with songwriters of exceptional talent, there are bound to be ups and downs. You do get eras when vast amounts of composing genius seem to emerge. The writers all seem to have been born within a period of 50 years or something. But exceptional composing talent, on a wider basis than just writing three minute songs, comes through in an irregular and unpredictable way."*

What type of bands contact Blackhill for advice? Jenner answered, *"Basically, we spend most of our time telling people to forget it. You've got to be so absolutely sensational to make any impact. We've just had a case of someone walking in the door with some good songs, and we really believed that he was good, a very good songwriter. So we thought, 'Right, we'll sign him up.' Then we thought, 'Well, what can we do for you? We can give you a publishing contract, and then, yeah, we can do some demos. Gigs? No, that would be difficult. Records? A record deal? Ooh.' You suddenly realize that there's not much you can do for someone, even when they are very talented."*

June 30, 1975 - The Hamilton Spectator (Canada) reported on the Pink Floyd concert at the Ivor Wynne Stadium, Hamilton, Canada, on June 28, 1975. Jim Smits wrote that, from a musical standpoint, it was a great disappointment. Theatrically, it was more successful. The band used a circular projection screen, smoke bombs, dry ice, flares, various lighting devices, and an awesome sound system. "An evening of tawdry technical effects and undistinguished music." For $10 a ticket, one deserves something better than Pink Floyd.

The Toronto Globe and Mail (Canada) reported on the Pink Floyd concert at Ivor Wynne Stadium, Hamilton, Canada, on June 28, 1975. They reported that it seemed few of the people were listening to the music. It was an event, and just an excuse to get ripped. Gimmicks were necessary as the music had little to offer. A spaceship flew across the stadium, and films were projected on a circular screen. Quadraphonic sound effects were impressive. Idiots were throwing sparklers. 50,000 attended the show in a stadium that holds 36,000 for football games. "The whole thing smelled of greed."

The Toronto Star (Canada) published an article titled, "Ho hum in Hamilton at Pink Floyd show" by Bruce Kirkland. The Pink Floyd concert at Ivor Wynne Stadium, Hamilton, Canada, on June 28, 1975 was "boring and banal." They played songs from "Bad Side of the Moon," and used a ridiculous-looking rocket device that flew over the audience. The band seemed as bored as the audience was. Some fans had bleeding hands from climbing over the barbed wire barrier into the stadium. The band did receive a standing ovation, which is just the "Alice in Wonderland illogic of the rock culture."

The Toronto Sun (Canada) published an article titled, "Floyd on the bright side" by Wilder Penfield III. Penfield wrote that 55,000 attended the Pink Floyd concert at Ivor Wynne Stadium, Hamilton, Canada, on June 28, 1975. It was the first rock show held at the stadium. "The music was an excuse for a happening that didn't quite happen." This was the final concert of the tour, and at the end of the show, the roadies threw pies at the band members.

July 5, 1975 - Melody Maker (U.K.) published an article titled, "The Pink Floyd Story" by Allan Jones. On the eve of their performance at the Knebworth Festival, Jones recounted the rise of the Pink Floyd, from its beginnings in 1965 and the Syd Barrett era in 1967, to the present day Pink Floyd.

Sounds (U.K.) reported that, at the Pink Floyd concert at Roosevelt Stadium, New Jersey on June 15, 1975, the flaming airplane that sails above the audience got stuck about 50 feet from the stage and burnt out there. There were also wind difficulties that caused their pyramid-covered stage to almost blow away. An audience of 40,000 witnessed a performance that included films and quadraphonic sound.

July 12, 1975 - Melody Maker (U.K.) reported on the Knebworth Festival on July 5, 1975, with an article titled, "Plane sailing for the Floyd" by Chris Charlesworth. Approximately 100,000 attended the festival, which was well organized. Roy Harper threw a fit after he learned that his chauffer driven Rolls Royce had driven away with his stage costume in it, and he destroyed one caravan in the process. Pink Floyd provided the stage and the PA for the event. They began their performance with two WWII Spitfires flying low overhead. Their first set consisted of new material and was poor, due to tuning problems. During 'Crazy Diamond' the band was bathed in a sea of colors from their lighting columns. The second set was 'Dark Side of the Moon' and began with a model plane flying across the audience on a wire. Movies were shown on the circular screen during the set. The song 'Any Colour You Like' was a tremendous jam with David Gilmour trading licks with Roger Waters and Richard Wright, but the last two songs, 'Brain Damage' and 'Eclipse' suffered from poor vocals. They played an encore of 'Echoes,' which was superb.

Also in this issue is an article titled, "Cover Story" by Allan Jones. This article takes a look at album covers and their design. The design company, Hipgnosis, are mentioned along with the excellent covers they have designed for Pink Floyd and Syd Barrett.

New Musical Express (U.K.) reported on the Knebworth Festival on July 5, 1975. They wrote that Pink Floyd had problems tuning their Hammond organ, their PA was inadequate for Knebworth, and their playing was below normal. A couple of Spitfires flew over the crowd to begin the show, and they used quadraphonic sound, but Nick Mason' drums were inaudible. A member of the band said, "It'll be better when it gets dark." The second set, 'Dark Side of the Moon,' lacked professionalism, and the vocals were off key.

Sounds (U.K.) published an article titled, "Knebworth Report – Floyd fly high with support" by Mick Brown. Brown wrote that spitfires flew menacingly across the sky as a prelude to Pink Floyd's set, and the atmosphere became electric. They presented a spectacle that bombarded all the senses. They began by playing songs from their upcoming album, using quadraphonic sound and an elaborate light show. For the second set, they performed 'Dark Side of the Moon,' which was simply breathtaking.

Also in this issue is a review of the Pink Floyd concert at Knebworth by John Peel. He said that he liked hearing the old songs and enjoyed the special effects, but "wasn't too sure about their new stuff."

July 19, 1975 - Melody Maker (U.K.) reported in Hot Licks that Blackhill XI, with Roy Harper as captain and Chris Spedding as a member, defeated the Pink Floyd cricket team in a pre-Knebworth match. Also in this issue was a letter in Mailbag claiming that the Knebworth Festival was a rip-off. The writer claimed it was oversold, the music was poor, the PA was too loud, and Pink Floyd wasn't very good.

July 26, 1975 - Melody Maker (U.K.) reported that Syd Barrett was seen at a recent Pink Floyd recording session weighing 15 stone, and with all his body hair, including his eyebrows, shaved off.

August 9, 1975 - Melody Maker (U.K.) reported that Pink Floyd's new album, 'Wish You Were Here,' will be released on September 5, 1975.

August 23, 1975 - Disc (U.K.) published an article titled, "The Pink Floyd Story," that reviewed the history of Pink Floyd and included a discography and interviews. Asked why they changed the name of their first single from 'Let's Roll Another One' to 'Candy and a Currant Bun,' Nick Mason said, "*We were a*

rock n roll band, and if you're a rock n roll band and you've got a record that you want to be number one, you get it played, and if they say take something out, or whatever, you do it."

David Gilmour talked about replacing Syd Barrett, explaining, "*Following someone like Syd Barrett into the band was a strange experience. At first I felt I had to change a lot and it was a paranoid experience. After all, Syd was a living legend, and I had started off playing basic rock music, Beach Boys and Bo Diddley stuff. I wasn't in any groups worth talking about. I knew Syd from Cambridge since I was 15 and my old band supported Floyd on gigs so I knew them all well.*"

Talking about the first single after Syd Barrett left, 'It Would Be So Nice,' Nick Mason explained, "*That record was awful. At that period we had no direction. We were being hustled about to make hit singles. There's so many people saying it is important, you start to think it is important.*"

About 'Dark Side of the Moon,' Roger Waters stated, "*People come and listen to 'Dark Side of the Moon' and call it space rock, which is just crazy. That's just because it's got moon in the title they think it's science fiction, which is silly. And the other thing that they do is say that we've gone from outer space to inner space, which is daft.*"

On concert effects, Waters added, "*I feel that lights should only be used to create a specific effect. Now that our music is more deliberate and controlled, so all our visual things now are specific and related to something in the music. When the music gets very intense, we'll do a big effect, like letting off orange smoke or rockets up into the sky.*"

September 1975 - Circus Magazine (U.S.) published an article titled, "Pink Floyd: More Gritty, Less Giddy" by Alan Betrock that featured an interview with Pink Floyd's sound and recording engineer, Brian Humphries. Talking about the change in Pink Floyd's attitude on stage, Humphries said, "*Just watching them onstage you can see the difference. It's not as much 'cosmic sounds' as it used to be. There's a little more grittiness now. They're more of a true funk/rave-up type band today.*"

Humphries, who left Island Records

to work exclusively with Pink Floyd, explained, "*I think now that this is the trend of the future, for an engineer or producer to work exclusively with one band. I had worked on 'Ummagumma,' 'More,' and 'Zabriskie Point,' with the band, but I hadn't really seen them in the years since then. Last year I was called in to oversee the recording of some live tracks, and wound up staying at the soundboard all night. They were unhappy with their sound mixer and it just snowballed from there. They asked me to work with them permanently in November 1974, and I've been with them ever since.*"

Asked about the lack of new albums since 'Dark Side of the Moon,' Humphries said, "*For one, the record was selling and, in fact, is still selling very well, so there was no real need for a follow-up. Secondly, I think the band was a bit apprehensive about the reaction to a new album following such a worldwide smash as 'Dark Side.' So they took their time and I think the wait has really been worthwhile. You'll agree when you hear the new album.*"

Talking about recording the new album, 'Wish You Were Here,' Humphries explained, "*The album was started in January 1975, and was recorded at EMI's Abbey Road Studio. Usually EMI does not allow outside engineers to work at Abbey Road, but for the Floyd, they waived the ruling and I was allowed to work the board. The main problem was that they had just installed a new console in a new studio, and we were the very first ones to use it. It was a 24-track desk and though it's usually a fairly simple task to get accustomed to a new setup, this one was really difficult. We went through a lot of hard times there, to the extent that, in the first three weeks, we recorded 'Shine On You Crazy Diamond' three separate times. Once because the band didn't like it and thought they could play it better, and once, through somebody's fiddling, monitor echo was added on the tom-tom tracks. Consequently, the whole 'Shine On,' some twenty minutes of it, was wasted. We couldn't use a note.*"

The recording sessions for 'Wish You Were Here' took place four days a week, from January through March. In April, the band toured America. They returned to work on the album in May. Humphries explained,

"*We spent the entire month working five days a week. We finally finished the album on the fifth of June, and our Eastern American tour began the next day.*"

Asked about the tour, Humphries recalled, "*Most of the venues are 15,000 to 25,000, with some larger outdoor gigs included as well. We played a 50,000 seater in Atlanta, for example. Our entire entourage includes about forty people, and there is a lot of preparation involved in getting ready for a date. The crew usually gets there a day before a performance, where possible, and they start setting up at 8:00 in the morning to be ready for a 5 p.m. soundcheck. The outdoor gigs pose additional sound problems, like at Roosevelt Stadium, the wind was blowing a lot of the top sounds away, you couldn't hear any of them at all. We never have an opening act either, and sometimes that's a little unfortunate for the kids who come in the early afternoon, as the Floyd don't go on until 9:00 or so.*"

The tour also featured films that accompanied the music, including segments from 'Zabriskie Point' and other original films. At the conclusion of the tour, the band went to London for final mixing of the album at the beginning of July.

One upcoming project for Pink Floyd is working with director, Alexandro Jodorowsky. Humphries explained, "*It's just at the talking stages at present. Jodorowsky's next film will be 'Dune,' and he came to London to meet and hear the band in the studio. If we do it, it will mean at least a month in the Sahara with a mobile unit, because that's where Jodorowsky is shooting the film. He wants to film to the Floyd's music, so we'll be marooned for a while doing that, but it is an exciting challenge.*"

The new Pink Floyd album, 'Wish You Were Here,' opens with a piece called, 'Shine On You Crazy Diamond,' followed by a three-minute piece titled, 'Machine Song,' which consists of machine-like sounds. As to electronic gimmickry, Humphries explained, "*There are truly very few sound effects on that track. It's mostly the Floyd themselves playing, and although there are little bits like creaking doors closing and the like, it's basically the VCS 3 synthesizer which Roger plays. Some of the noises he gets out of it are really out of this world.*"

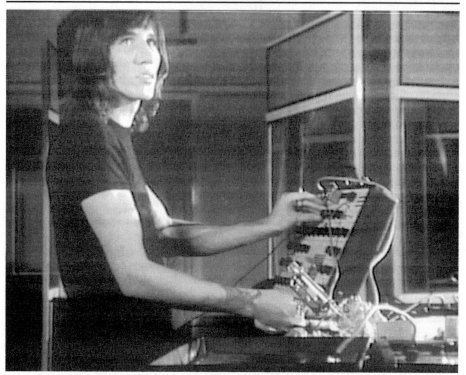

Roger Waters shown here experimenting with the VCS Synthesizer.

The first side of the album finishes with the song, 'Have a Cigar.' Side two begins with the title track, 'Wish You Were Here,' which is followed by 'Shine On You Crazy Diamond, Part II,' and an outro piece. Humphries explained, *"They had been playing the same set since last Christmas, so the songs were well worked out. Still, there were changes in the studio from the original ideas. They weren't exactly sure whether they should record the three new tracks they do live all in one album. There was some pressure because the fans had heard them all onstage and, in fact, some bootlegs were selling very, very well in Europe. But Roger got this idea about machine throbs, so only two of the new live numbers appear on this album. I don't know if the other one will ever surface, but I'm really glad to hear that Roger came up with the machine conception. In a way, the whole album is about machinery, the machinery of the music business, executives and the like, and I don't know if it's a very flattering portrait."*

In recording the album, the new 24-track board was *"utilized to the fullest. There was really so much involved in this album,* *from the basic rhythm tracks on up through the various solos, guitars, Moogs, sax, as well as the numerous vocal tracks, that if you use a track for every solo, you're gonna use up those 24 very quickly. So we had to put a few solos on one track. If we used an individual track for everything, we'd probably need at least a 40-track machine. It's a bit difficult in mixing, but we break the whole thing down into different sections and work it from there."*

Humphries also explained about Pink Floyd mixing their albums, *"On Dark Side, everybody mixed. Floyd were the first band I ever met that did their own mixing. When they explained to me that since they write and play the music, they must know how they want everything to sound all mixed, I agreed with their viewpoint. Eventually though, on Dark Side, they got so fed up with the mixing process that they finally called somebody else in. On 'Wish You Were Here,' I think it will mainly revolve around Dave, Roger, and myself. Nick's contribution is fairly minimal on this one, and Rick will be involved somewhat, I think. In the end, I leave it down to Roger. I think of Roger actually being Pink*

Floyd, as much as I regard and respect the other three. He's really in control of the studio part of the group. After all, he does write all the songs."

Asked if the band has disagreements on what to play or how their records should sound, Humphries replied, *"Well, they all listen to various kinds of music, a really wide spectrum actually. Dave is a real rock and roller at heart, and Nick is interested in producing other artists, like Robert Wyatt who he produced recently. But really, despite their varied listening tastes, there are very few musical differences within the group framework. Insofar as mixing goes, there's never any bickering or anything of that sort. They all usually agree quite easily."*

Two things that bother the band members are the idolatry of Syd Barrett and bad press commentaries. Humphries said, *"As far as Syd goes, the band really want to let the past lie. That was then and now is now. At a recent gig someone yelled out '68,' meaning that the band should do some of Syd's old songs. Well, Roger yelled back, 'this is 1975, not 1968'!"*

As to a critical British music weekly, Humphries said, *"They called us the electronic caravan. Some of it was true and needed to be said, I guess, but just the way it was said and how it was presented really upset the band, especially Roger. It seemed as if it had gotten to the point where they weren't giving a damn about anybody but themselves. It was sort of, 'Well, we're Pink Floyd and we're the greatest.' But they learned a lot from that slagging, and I think they're much more able to communicate now. They're a bit more easygoing and not quite so high and mighty. They never really were comfortable with that superstar attitude anyway. They still feel strange when getting into limos after gigs. They're a bit more normal now."*

September 20, 1975 – Billboard Magazine (U.S.) reviewed the Pink Floyd album, 'Wish You Were Here.' The album is the band's most commercial effort, featuring "typically good guitar work," "easy going synthesizer and keyboard work, and occasional hypnotic background vocals." Possibly their best album since 'Atom Heart Mother.'

Melody Maker (U.K.) reviewed the Pink Floyd album, 'Wish You Were Here' with an article titled, "Floyd in creative void" by Allan Jones. The album took six months to record, and Jones wrote that he was not enthralled. He also stated that he did not like 'Dark Side of the Moon.' `Wish You Were Here' lacks imagination and is quite predictable. The omission of two of their new songs played on the last tour, 'Raving and Drooling' and 'Gotta Be Crazy' indicates a lack of confidence in their material. The special effects on the album are artificial and contrived. There has been no development in Pink Floyd's material since 'Ummagumma.' The theme of the album is a tirade against the music business, and is merely petulant due to Waters' dubious qualities as a lyricist. The technique of using special effects throughout the album shows as much sophistication as a 1967 psychedelic band making their first concept album. The standard of musicianship on the album is extremely poor. Only the beginning of the song 'Have a Cigar' shows the band playing with any vigor. Roy Harper's guest vocals add little to a colorless song. The song 'Wish You Were Here' has inadequate acoustic guitar and Roger Waters' vocal performance is weak and forgettable. 'Shine On You Crazy Diamond' trivializes Syd Barrett's predicament with insensitive lyrics.

Also in this issue, in Mailbag, is a letter from Simon Bean stating that he is disgusted with Pink Floyd's new album, 'Wish You Were Here.' He wrote that every song is played at the same speed, and the drums and bass are unimaginative. The best thing on the album is Dick Parry's sax. Pink Floyd are stuck in a commercial rut.

Also in this issue are the 1975 Reader's Poll results. Pink Floyd is the #5 band, and the #4 live act in both the British Section, and the International Section. Richard Wright is #7 under Keyboards, Roger Waters is #7 under Bass, and Pink Floyd are #8 under Producer. In the International Section, Dark Side of the Moon is the #8 album.

New Musical Express (U.K.) reviewed the Pink Floyd album, 'Wish You Were Here' with an article titled, "How Pink Floyd learned to stop worrying and make another album" by Pete Erskine. Erskine wrote that the band must have felt extreme pressure to repeat the formula used for the successful 'Dark Side of the Moon,' leading to Roger Waters feeling cynical about the nature of their success. Having to perform 'Dark Side of the Moon' over and over for the last two years must have had a negative effect on the bands morale and musical abilities. However, despite these negative influences, 'Wish You Were Here' is concise, melodic, and very well performed.

The album cover is clean, amusing, and positive, with Magritte inspired graphics. The pictures are supposed to represent impossibles. Brian Southall of EMI explained, *"The faceless man in the desert is a record executive. The split with the sand coming out of it is supposed to represent the slipping away of the sands of time. The photograph of the guys shaking hands is supposed to represent earth, wind, and fire. The tress with the bit of red rag is to fill up white space."* The mechanical handshake logo stuck on the cover is a pair of hands shaking, one metal, the other plastic, representing the affiliation of earth with the machine.

The album's theme is represented by three thematically linked songs. 'Welcome to the Machine' is an acidic view of the record business as a mechanical conveyor belt. 'Have a Cigar,' featuring vocals by Roy Harper, has lyrics representative of record company manager rap. 'Wish You Were Here' is about tedium, routine, and hopelessness. The playing on this album is better than on any of their previous albums, although parts of the album are melancholic and depressing.

September 27, 1975 - Melody Maker (U.K.) reported that Pink Floyd's record company cannot keep up with demand for the new album, 'Wish You Were Here.' Although the pressing plants are working to capacity, record stores are only being provided with fifty percent of their orders. The album has qualified for a gold disc due to advance orders of a quarter-million in Britain. The bands previous album, 'Dark Side of the Moon,' has sold 750,000 in Britain and has earned a platinum disc.

September 1975 - Creem Magazine (U.S.) published an article titled, "Nova Express or Exploded Stars?" by Michael Bloom, that included a brief history of the band and expressed the opinion that the band has been in a "virtual slump."

October 4, 1975 - Melody Maker (U.K.) published a letter in Mailbag titled, "Floyd outstay their welcome" in which reader J. Parker wrote that Pink Floyd have outlived their creative life. He agreed with Allan Jones' criticism of 'Wish You were Here,' saying it was inevitable, and that anything following the success of 'Dark Side of the Moon' was bound to be an anti-climax. But even 'Dark Side of the Moon' wasn't so amazing in the context of the band's overall achievement. 'Ummagumma' remains a milestone. Subsequent albums demonstrated the bands' failure of nerve, not imagination. Pink Floyd and the whole progressive rock scene have reached a crisis point. The current terminal malaise of Pink Floyd is just a symptom, with the real problem being a lack of tradition to build upon. Although Pink Floyd have created a lot of worthwhile musical experiences, unless they can find a new direction, a new, radical approach to electronic music, they may as well go back to bashing out 'Dust My Broom' because that's what it's all about.

October 11, 1975 - Melody Maker (U.K.) answered a question in the 'Any Questions?' column about Nick Mason's drum kit and how he tunes his drums. Mason uses Ludwig 22 and 24 inch bass drums, 13 X 9 and 14 X 12 inch tom toms, 14 X 14 and 16 X 16 inch floor toms, Rogers pedals, a Rogers hi-hat stand, Remo roto toms sized 4, 6, 8, 10, and 12 inches, Premier cymbal stands, Paiste 16, 18, and 20 inch medium cymbals, Paiste 15 inch hi-hat cymbals, and Ginger Baker drumsticks. To get his heavy sound, he puts pillows in the bass drum, tunes deeply, and uses matt finish skins.

Sounds (U.K.) published an article about Syd Barrett titled, "Where Are They Now? – The cosmos and the caravan." The article traced Barrett's known activities since leaving the Pink Floyd, and reviewed many of the rumors that have circulated about him ever since.

November 1975 - Records and Recording reviewed the Pink Floyd album, 'Wish You

Were Here.' They wrote that 'Wish You Were Here' was Pink Floyd's best album since 'Ummagumma.' "Form outstrips content," with 'Shine On You Crazy Diamond' the kernel that would be a three-minute filler on other albums.

November 1, 1975 - Melody Maker (U.K.) published a letter in Mailbag by a fan who was shocked and disappointed by the direction Pink Floyd have recently taken. He was embarrassed after convincing friends to see the band in New York. He wrote that their sound system needs to improve if they are going to play big stadiums.

November 6, 1975 - Rolling Stone (U.S.) published an article titled, "The Trippers Trapped: Pink Floyd in a Hum Bug" by Ben Edmonds that reviewed the Pink Floyd album, 'Wish You Were Here.' Edmonds wrote that advance orders for the album topped 900,000, which was one of the biggest advance orders in the history of Columbia Records. The music on the album shows them as "just another conventional rock and roll band." David Gilmour indulges in protracted solos, thinking with his fingers instead of his head. The song, 'Wish You Were Here,' is the most successful on the record until the band comes in, and it "nosedives to ho-hum level." The effects on the album sound gimmicky, and do not compliment the music. The potential of 'Shine On You Crazy Diamond' to confront the subject of Syd Barrett goes unrealized, and "they might as well be singing about Roger Water's brother in law getting a parking ticket."

November 15, 1975 - New Musical Express (U.K.) published an article titled, "Mystery of the Floyd's Missing Tape." Three hundred people showed up at the Olympia Audio fair to hear the world premiere of a quadraphonic version of 'Wish You Were Here.' Brian Humphries, Pink Floyd's engineer, mixed this quad version, although the stereo version was mixed by the band. Humphries said, "*I could have mixed the album better than they did, but they are my bosses and they have the last say.*" Asked if what will actually be released as the quad version will be different, Humphries replied, "*Yes and no. They have their ideas. I have mine. We'll see.*"

Humphries also discussed a problem they had while recording the song 'Shine On You Crazy Diamond' in Abbey Road Studio 3. While recording the song, the monitor echo had been left on and it inadvertently was recorded onto tracks 1 and 2, which were the Tom Tom tracks. As a result, the tracks had to be completely re-recorded. Humphries explained, "*We didn't fully understand the deck.*"

Humphries also discussed what happened to the Zabriskie Point soundtrack album that Pink Floyd went off to record in the autumn of 1969. The band worked on it for two weeks before the movie's director, Antonioni, decided he didn't like the music. As a result, the songs have never been released, other than the three tracks on the movie soundtrack album.

Also in this issue is an article titled, "Is it possible, too, that Syd has risen from the grave?" by Nick Kent, in which Kent reported that Syd Barrett wandered into Abbey Road Studios during the mixing of 'Shine On You Crazy Diamond.' He recalled other times that Barrett made appearances at Pink Floyd recording sessions, such as when Barrett waited in the lobby, guitar in hand, while 'A Saucerful of Secrets' was being recorded. Peter Barnes recalled some brief 1974 studio recording sessions that Barrett did, saying, "*I think Syd didn't even bother to turn up again after the third day.*" Kent ended by reporting a Barrett sighting outside Harrods Department Store wearing a Yogi Bear bow tie.

November 22, 1975 - Melody Maker (U.K.) published a letter in Mailbag, from a reader who wrote that he understands how bands can get bored by playing an exhausting circuit, but should this give them a ticket to be complacent and sit on their behinds? Roger Waters does this and produces sardonic music like 'Welcome to the Machine.' If he is so bored with the system and "playing the same old tunes" why the hell doesn't he devote his time to writing more beneficial lyrics that can inspire instead of inducing apathy as he does? If this song is also a "profound comment" on society today, then, if the rock musician can offer no more than criticism on his own medium that he has created, one wonders why he bothers at all. Satirical comments can

1976
Productions and Flying Pigs

sometimes induce a beneficial reaction from authority, but as it is a comment on his own musical world, where is the logic?

November 29, 1975 - Melody Maker (U.K.) reported on the 1975 International Audio Festival and Fair, held at the Olympia in London. The Fair featured the world premiere of the Pink Floyd album 'Wish You Were Here' in SQ quadraphonic.

January 3, 1976 - Melody Maker (U.K.) published a letter in Mailbag from a reader who wrote that he does not accept the criticism that Pink Floyd "have been producing more or less the same kind of music" for the past nine years. 'Wish You Were Here' bears very little resemblance to 'Piper at the Gates of Dawn.' Their past two albums are similar, but by no means identical. They both stand as excellent pieces of music.

January 24, 1976 - Street Life Magazine (Canada) published an article titled, "Really Wish You Were Here – The Politics of Absence" that featured an interview with Roger Waters by Philippe Constantin. This interview was originally published in French in the French magazine, Rock and Folk.

Asked about the press, Waters said, "*I've just done an interview for French radio about a month and half ago, and it was a kind of farce. They weren't interested. There wasn't any common ground.*"

Asked how he reacts to criticism, Waters replied, "*In an emotional way. I find it frustrating that people criticize me.*"

Is recording a response to criticism? Waters replied, "*Perhaps I'll get to that stage. Still, I'd have to find a piece of criticism that really interests me, that gives me something. And I don't think it's really essential to institute a dialogue with the rock critics, there are more interesting minorities. I get a little fed up with what they tell me. It hurts me because I see it all written in black and white. I don't like the feeling of being attacked. Even if, with a handful of exceptions, they don't really get to*

the bottom of things"

Asked why he was hard on Syd Barrett in a recent French interview, Waters replied, "*Really? My violent reaction there is explained by my getting snowed under with gossip and snippets that each and everybody put out about Syd. These wouldn't even have been brought up if Syd had had some success, or if we hadn't had any ourselves.*"

Refusing interviews with the press makes you appear arrogant. Waters replied, "*I don't care about appearing arrogant in the eyes of rock critics. They are not an explanatory medium between us and the public. I don't think we appear arrogant towards the public, and that's what concerns me.*"

In public, Pink Floyd appears as a unit, but is there a leader of the group? Waters replied, "*Let's forget about that question. It's got no interest whatsoever. You know the answer. Everybody knows it. In any case we're against having leaders.*"

As for influences, did you turn your backs on mainstream rock music? Waters replied, "*We haven't ever turned our backs on anything. We've never departed from a musical tradition. Quite the reverse, perhaps we've simplified all that. It's true that several of our pieces were different, like 'Saucerful Of Secrets,' for example. Maybe we simply wanted to get away from the system of reiterating 16 or 32 beats, and to work instead on sequences. What the four of us were listening to, what we immersed ourselves in, was definitely rock, and some jazz as well. But above all Johnny Hodges, very cool you see, and Mingus. All of us were definitely listening to more or less the same kind of thing. I was simply obsessed about Berlioz at one stage, but not any more.*"

Is rock music a limited form of expression? Waters replied, "*That's a question to put to those who play it. The answer's probably no. Too limited for what anyhow? What are people really looking for in it? Who can say? If one's talking about a means of expression, then the most you can say is that it's adapted. It's of no importance whatsoever* whether it's limited or not. What I object to in rock journalism is this habit of giving things an importance that differs from the amount they really have."

Has Pink Floyd ever considered touring without visual effects? Waters replied, "Not with Pink Floyd. It wouldn't make much sense. Although it'd be true to say that a closer contact, a less sophisticated one, does interest me. David feels the same way, too. Perhaps we'll do it, but not with Pink Floyd. In the past Nick played out front with an amateur group that won the Melody Maker contest, along with Laurie Allen and others."

Do you care that your music gets used for jingles and TV movies? Waters replied, "I don't care. It doesn't thrill me. But what can I do about it?"

What do you think of German rock bands? Waters replied, "I know very little about German rock. I don't listen to it. I heard a bit of Kraftwerk on the radio the other day. It bored me. It's possible or probable that we might have been the root of all that, Tangerine Dreams, etc. If we hadn't been successful, they probably wouldn't have tried it. There wouldn't have been any action on that front."

Why did it take you longer to catch on in America? Waters replied, "Because more than anywhere else, the Americans follow the crowd."

Do you prefer playing live or in the studio? Waters replied, "The fact is that we've toured a lot in the past year. Also that I felt more at home in the studio. In addition, I haven't felt that well, inside myself, all this year, and the studio suited me better in as much as it's an enclosed space. But I won't generalize over and above that."

Pink Floyd's music depends a lot on electronics and the studio. Waters replied, "I see just where you want to go. You're going to tell me that Pink Floyd is space rock. You know perfectly well that's rubbish. There are two or three Floyd songs that have to do with science fiction. The critics have seized on this chestnut unfailingly because they can't make up their minds about our music. Sure, 'Saucerful Of Secrets' is a song that has to do with sci-fi. Also 'Astronomy Domine,' and, stretching it a bit, 'Machine.' So what? They all get classified as space rock, just like that. It obviates the need for critics to look any further, to see what's in

fact said."

'Wish You Were Here' is one of the few love songs you have written. Waters said, "Yes, that's true, it's a love song, and still one on a very general and theoretical level. If I was undergoing psychoanalysis, my analyst would tell you why I don't write love songs. In fact, I've done one or two others, but always in a very impersonal way. If I haven't really spoken about love, perhaps it's because I've never really known what love was. I'm just like someone who's had a constant love relationship since the age of 16 and who then changes all that 15 years later. What can I say about love that'd be meaningful? To write love songs, you have to be sure about your feelings. Maybe I could write about it now, but maybe just for myself, not for Pink Floyd."

Do you find the early Pink Floyd records dated? Waters answered, "Well, I don't listen to them often. I listened to the first one again the other day. Dated isn't quite the word. I just don't think much of it'll last, that's all."

Does musical technique impress you? Waters replied, "Not at all. Technique doesn't say anything in music. Nick is the most influenced by technique of all of us, without a doubt, because he's the drummer. The drums are, undoubtedly, the least liberated instrument in rock music. But that's a minor problem. I'm not in favor of all these discussions about technique. What's the point in deciding whether Alvin Lee or Eric Clapton is the fastest guitarist? Wouldn't it be more interesting to ask them what they're putting across in their music? Bruce Springsteen is a fantastic technician as far as entertainment is concerned. The start of his show is really amazing with this disheveled guy surrounded by very well-dressed musicians, with his leaps into the orchestra pit, and so on. You're stunned for the first half-hour. Then you see the system. You notice that he manufactures an authenticity for himself, and that authenticity is plastic. And then they go on to say he's the new Dylan, when in fact he's nothing but a talent maker. After two hours of it, a guy in the balcony jumped out of his seat, shouting 'Genius!' It was all too much for me to take. So, as far as technique goes, I'm mistrustful of it."

Why is 'Wish You Were Here' based on the theme of absence? Waters answered,

"We didn't start out with the idea of making a record based on the theme of absence. What happened was that we began to put the music for 'Shine On You Crazy Diamond' together, and from that we got a very strong feeling of melancholy. That's what happened first. Anyway, when I wrote the words, I don't know why, but I began to write about Syd's demise. And then a few other sections got written. I wrote one of them, 'Raving and Drooling,' and another with David called 'You Gotta Be Crazy.' Then we began to record 'Shine On.' The first six weeks in the studio were extremely difficult. I felt that, at times, the group was only there physically. Our bodies were there, but our minds and feelings somewhere else. And we were only there because this music allows us to live and live well, or because it was a habit, to be in Pink Floyd and to operate under that banner."

Don't other groups do this as well? Waters replied, *"Evidently. But that situation frustrated me. We discussed it, but I don't remember that too well because it was a long time ago. Then we discussed this particular subject, mainly David and me, what to do about it. He just wanted to record the two sections that were already written. That didn't seem a good idea to me. I wanted to force myself into what I felt at the time and to write something about it all, cutting 'Shine On' into two and projecting my feelings about what was going on inside me. Nicky and Rick thought it was a good idea, and so that's what we did, eventually."*

Why did you write 'Shine On' as a homage to Syd Barrett? Waters replied, *"Not really homage. Syd is one of the forerunners of life in the West today. Syd was close to the three of us because we were working with him, and also to Dave because he needed him when he was young in Cambridge. I really don't know why I started to write 'Shine On.'"*

Did it have do with what the critics wrote about Syd Barrett? Waters replied, *"No, nothing to do with that. I'm certain about that. I mean, I don't know, maybe. For my part I've never read an intelligent piece on Syd Barrett in any magazine. Never. No one knows what they're talking about. Only us, the people who knew him, who still know him a bit, only we know the facts, how he lived, what happened to him, why he was doing certain things. They*

make me laugh, these journalists with their rubbish. In actual fact, I wrote that song, 'Shine On' above all to see the reactions of people who reckon they know and understand Syd Barrett. I wrote and rewrote and rewrote and rewrote that lyric because I wanted it to be as close as possible to what I felt. And even then, it hasn't altogether worked out right for me. But, nonetheless, there's a truthful feeling in that piece, I don't know, that sort of indefinable, inevitable melancholy about the disappearance of Syd. Because he's left, withdrawn so far away that, as far as we're concerned, he's no longer there."

What did you want to put in the middle of 'Wish You Were Here?' Waters replied, *"The song of the Machine. It's simply a game with aural images."* Is it about being trapped without any control over things? Waters replied, *"No. Not really. It's even more simple than that. It's simply about being absorbed, breathed in by something and being carried away by it, the individual who follows what goes on about him."* Is it about being trapped in Pink Floyd? Waters replied, *"In actual fact, it's wanting to fall into a trap. It's about our society, about the motivation that makes everything work, as far as it does work. Now it's collapsing, but what made it work during the past fifty years, since the First World War maybe, those are dreams which people often aspire to. No, that's not what I wanted to say. It's that people are very vulnerable to their own blindness, their own greed, their own need to be loved and appreciated."*

What is the Machine song about? Waters replied, *"Let me think. It begins with a saxophone that fades into the distance and the appearance of a machine. It's really a song from the point of view of our hero, of an individual. And the opening of the door, if you like, symbolically you know. It's a phrase that gets used all the time in English, 'and the doors open to . . .' The symbol of doors, keys, the symbol of discovery, of advancement, of progress, of agreement. But progress towards what? Towards discovery, or something else? In this song it's in the direction of nothing at all, except the aim of becoming part of a dream that's trapped you, and to follow this road first and foremost. And the Machine is self-perpetuating, and so much so because its fuel* consists of dreams. The rock machine isn't oiled and doesn't actually run on people's appreciation of the music or on their wish to interest themselves in music and listen to it, in my opinion. At the base of it all, it runs on dreams. It's for that reason people throw themselves into it, not to make music. And that's faulty reasoning. Many people believe in it, but I don't. That's not why I got into it at all."

Why do people go into the music business? Waters replied, "*For several reasons, the most important ones being that they need to win applause and to be loved.*" Is that why you got into the business? Waters said, "*I wasn't aware of it. Yes, perhaps, because a musician's basic drive is to be successful, although you have to work very hard for that. It's true that there are people who join groups and who aren't interested in success, but who are interested in the music itself or by the process of writing songs. But these people won't be very successful. To be successful, success has to be a real need, a very strong need. And the dream is that when you are successful, when you're a star, you'll be fine, everything will go wonderfully well. That's the dream and, as everybody knows, it's an empty one.*"

Earlier in your career you used to act violent on stage, such as when you played the gong in 'Careful With That Axe Eugene.' However, after 'Ummagumma' you changed. Waters said, "*Maybe that has something to do with my age. The need to be violently aggressive gets less. It's reduced itself to virtually nothing in my case. Now I'd feel ridiculous if I broke things up onstage. Maybe it's because I'm 32. Although in the past I wanted to do things like that really badly.*" Is it because now you are a respected group? Waters answered, "*It's possible. I'm as unsure about everything as I was back then. I haven't discovered anything, anything that helps me along in my life. Every new thing I accomplish, or everything I get, doesn't satisfy me as I imagined it would do when I was young. I've realized that such ambitions are only illusions.*"

Are you progressing towards your truth? Waters replied, "*Well, yes, I hope so. Otherwise I wouldn't do anything. If I wanted to, I could let other people work for me right to the end of my life, stretch out on a beach and*

fish all day long. I don't think I could bear that because, from time to time, I feel the need to write things. But I still haven't explained the song of the Machine. It's a question of what causes a feeling of absence. 'Wish You Were Here' is a song about the sensations that accompany the state of not being there. To work and to be with people whom you know aren't there anymore. The song of the Machine is about the business situation, which I find myself in, which creates this absence. One's encouraged to be absent because one's not encouraged to pay any attention to reality, everywhere, not only in the rock machine, but in the whole mechanism of society. This mechanism encourages you to reject things. From the moment you're born, you're encouraged to reject the realities of the things that surround you and to accept the dreams and the codes of behavior. Everything is coded. You're asked to communicate through a series of codes, rather than to communicate directly. And that's called civilization, custom.*"

Why is there crowd noise at the end of the song? Is it a party? Waters replied, "*Yes, it's like a party. That was put in there because of the complete emptiness inherent in that way of behaving, celebrations, gatherings of people who talk and drink together. To me, that epitomizes the lack of contacts and of real feelings between people. It's very simple, obvious even. He gets up from where he was, ready to confront the festivities, and he's ready because that's what he was trained to do.*" These are relationships between people while the machine is nearby? Waters answered, "*Yes. He's surfacing if you like. The idea's that the Machine is underground. Some underground power and therefore evil, that leads us towards our various bitter destinies. The hero's been exposed to this power. One way or another he's gone into the machinery and he's seen it for what it is. And the Machine has admitted the fact, telling him that he's being watched because he `knows,' and informs him that all his actions are Pavlovian responses, that everything's only conditioned reflexes, and that his responses don't come at his own instigation. In fact, he doesn't exist anymore, except to the extent that he has the feeling deep down inside himself that something just isn't at all right. That's his only reality. So he goes off, leaves the machinery and enters the room. The* *doors open and he realizes it's true. The people there are all zombies. That's not very serious, you see. As for the album, critics have said it was very cynical."*

In France, the record is viewed as honest. Waters said, *"I think it was Melody Maker that said it was cynical. And the record's anything but cynical."* They may have been referring to the song, 'Have a Cigar.' Waters replied, *"I don't know. 'Have a Cigar' isn't cynicism, it's sarcasm. In fact, it's not even sarcasm, it's realism. I know a guy who works in a clinic for drug addicts, alcoholics, and child molesters. I met him in my local pub and he'd heard the song 'Time' where there's the phrase 'hanging on in quiet desperation.' That moved him a lot because it had a bearing on what he himself felt. That made me realize if I were to express my feelings, vague and disturbed as they are, as honestly as I could, then that's the most I can do. At present, I'm not very interested in art, and I only interest myself in music insofar as it helps me express my feelings."* How is that? Waters replied, *"Well, for instance, I've become accustomed to being very successful. And you cling to an established order, because one's used to success. During the start of the recording of 'Wish You Were Here,' the alternative point of departure was to try to express what I felt about that particular subject, and it worked out fifty-fifty because we were touring the States at the time and the experience drains your energies a bit. So it isn't as powerful as I'd have liked it to have been. It could have been much stronger. I'd like to have heard us argue and talk things over on this record. I'd like to have heard extracts of the conversation that took place during the recording."* That may not have been good for the music. Waters agreed, *"True. But we used bits of conversation on 'Dark Side of the Moon' in such a way that they mixed in well with the music, at least in my opinion. Maybe a transcription of those conversations could be published. It might interest people."*

David Gilmour's playing on the last record is fantastic. Waters replied, *"I agree."*

If one of the members of Pink Floyd wasn't as technically proficient as the rest of you, would he have to leave the band? Waters replied, *"No, simply because I haven't got that kind of need musically. As far as I'm*

concerned, you don't have to be technically good to express feelings."

Did you have to take some time after making 'Dark Side of the Moon' to sort out some problems? Waters replied, *"I don't think we sorted out any problems."* But on the new record you have made a statement. Waters said, *"Yes, that's true. It's hard to say, because I wrote all the words and organized all the ideas for the pieces we've done in the last few years. And it's hard to say what we'll do now. I know that Dave and Rick, for example, don't think that the subject matter or theme of the record and the ideas developed are as important as I think they are. They're more interested in music, as abstract form as much as anything else. There's something unavoidable about each of us working on his own solo project. Three of us, certainly. As for Nicky, I don't know. Personally, I've got enough material to start making a record straight away. I don't know where Dave'll find the necessaries to make a record, but I'm sure he will find them. I think he'll make a fantastic record, but nothing like we've done ourselves. We'll see."*

The myth of Pink Floyd as saints was destroyed in France by the Gini affair. Waters said, *"If Gini had succeeded, then the story wouldn't have been at all unfortunate. I wrote a song about it at the time, something that I haven't recorded. It's called 'How Do You Feel.' I was going home from Morocco by plane and I felt very bad as a result of the episode with Gini, so I wrote the first part of the lyric."*

Were you trapped in the Gini episode? Waters said, *"The song's called 'Bitter Love.' Trapped in? Certainly not. It was simply a sort of assignment for us."* Was the opportunity for money too great? Waters replied, *"No. In the beginning it was as if we were winning a prize. They wanted to give us £50,000 to take our photograph. Good God, fantastic! It was only later that I told myself, who needs that? But I'd do it if I wasn't well off, for sure. Not doing publicity is a luxury for me because I am well off. But if I was working in an architect's office for 40 quid a week and someone said to me 'Listen, we like your face a lot, we'll give you 500 quid to use it for an advert,' I'd do it."* It partially ruined your reputation in France. Waters said, *"That's fine by me, great."* But the implications against

Pink Floyd are not fair. Waters said, *"But life isn't fair, is it? If one waited for life to become fair . . . And I read the pieces they write about me."* What did they write? *"Everything. For instance, like saying I shouldn't sing."* Considering the music you wrote, that is stupid. *"Waiting until the journalists or whoever are fair, nothing in life is based on the idea of fairness."* Sometimes people base their appreciation of music on facts that have nothing to do with the music. Waters said, *"If their enjoyment of the music rests on this misleading idea that we're saints, then I'd rather they didn't like the music. It's precisely this kind of dreamery that you and me, Pathe-Marconi, EMI, etc. make fortunes from."*

Are you pleased with 'Wish You Were Here?' Waters replied, *"No. I'm not unhappy with it. It's not bad. By comparison, 'Ummagumma' is pretty awful."* What don't you like about 'Ummagumma?' Which album? Waters answered, *"Both, especially the studio one. The live recording is also very poor."*

What about 'Obscured by Clouds?' Waters replied, *"For what it was, I think it wasn't bad for all that. It was something else, we made it in a few weeks. Given what we put on it, I don't find it bad. As for the other two, I don't know. 'Atom Heart Mother' and 'Meddle' are half good. I like 'Echoes' and 'Atom Heart Mother' themselves. But we made a right mess of it on the other sides."*

What are your future plans? Waters replied, *"I'd really like to record 'You Gotta Be Crazy,' and 'Raving And Drooling,' which we played live in the States, and then some other things. Those songs are still fresh. I'm working on another piece, 'Flight From Reality,' which is very strange. But I'd like to release 'You Gotta Be Crazy' because, once again, it's a reply to the English press. Plenty of people in the press have come down really hard on us saying the lyrics are awful. Sometimes I think those people couldn't do any better themselves. They tend to forget that people who buy records and get into the music haven't all got degrees in English literature and don't read that many books either. The same goes for the people who write the music. It's quite possible that some of my lyrics are banal, because I'm just like anyone else in that respect, nothing out of the ordinary."*

May 8, 1976 - Melody Maker (U.K.) published an article about David Gilmour as a producer. The article began by reporting on a mixing session that David Gilmour was doing at the London Roadhouse studio. Gilmour stated, *"I'm just giving a hand with mixing a couple of tracks for these Hawkwinds."* Hawklord bassist Paul Rudolph watched as Gilmour adjusted the faders on the studio desk.

Pink Floyd are one of Britain's most technological bands, using £200,000 worth of equipment when they tour, and playing through a spectacular PA system in six-channel quadraphonic sound. And Gilmour has a home studio that is filled with equipment. Gilmour explained, *"Well, it's just for fun really. It's only an eight-track studio which I have in my garden, for demos and such like, nothing more."* Gilmour is an excellent guitarist and plays a Fender and a pedal steel guitar. He admits he is *"something of a collector, at least I was until someone nicked a load of stuff from my house."* On April 1, 1976, someone stole £6,500 worth of equipment, including his Telecaster, a sunburst Fender Precision bass, a Les Paul Custom 3PU, a blonde Gibson TV, a Rickenbacker 12-string, a D12/28 Martin, a Lewis guitar, plus a Hi-Fli prototype, and an EMS Synthi.

Gilmour has been involved in producing the band, Unicorn, which he met at Rick Hopper's wedding in 1973. Gilmour explained, *"They were the first band I've ever taken up and produced. I took them to my own studio and did about 20 demos. And then, eventually, I went to produce their first album, 'Blue Pine Trees,' for them."*

Talking about being a producer, Gilmour said, *"I've never had any particular ambitions to be a producer. I would never have actually set about it for the sake of it. I enjoy producing, certainly, although I do find it a little frustrating at times, and it's hard work as well. Frustrating because you're sitting on the other side of the glass watching a group of musicians having a blow and you have to sit there and not take part."*

When Unicorn takes a break, Gilmour sneaks into the studio to play himself. Gilmour said, *"They usually come back and throw me out."*

Gilmour believes that a song should create a picture in the composer's and listener's mind. Gilmour said, *"But, naturally, no pictures are the same. What Ken sees in his mind when he writes a song and what I see when I hear it are two different things. But as producer it is merely my task to get down on tape what the band are trying to say. There's rarely, if ever, complete agreement between the producer and the band. It's a matter of compromise, which satisfies both. Sometimes we do have quite solid conflicts between what we're aiming for, but it's hardly ever impossible to solve."*

Gilmour admits to having learned things by producing Unicorn, saying, *"Essentially, I've learnt a lot of technique, the actual things you have to do to transfer a sound onto tape in a large studio. Certainly, I wouldn't say I've learnt anything about production with a capital P, if you know what I mean. Besides, that's not the main thing I do or I want to do. But I do like, generally, to be able to do things. Along with a lot of other people I've been through those years of frustration in studios when I've not been able to explain exactly what I want to change. Working on the other side of the glass in the studio gives you a different point of view, a different perspective."*

May 15, 1976 - New Musical Express (U.K.) published an articled titled, "Who Flew Out of the Cuckoo's Nest? – Early Years of Pink Floyd" in which Miles recalled the early days of Pink Floyd. He remembered the London Free School, the IT launch party, benefit concerts at the Roundhouse, and the release of the first Pink Floyd single, 'Arnold Layne,' produced by Joe Boyd.

Boyd recalled, *"I was theoretically going to be their record producer and we had a deal with Polydor. Then their agents told them they would make more, they'd get a bigger advance, if they made the record first and sold the master to EMI. And ultimately, this was true. At the time, most major companies, and particularly EMI, were very leery of independent producers. What happened was that EMI said, 'We'll give you this contact and £5,000 and we want you to use our studios and our staff producers and everything.' So they immediately went in and said, 'Thanks a lot for doing 'Arnold Layne,' Joe. See you around,' and at the time I didn't really fight it. I didn't really know what to do*

about it. It was a bit galling to have Norman Smith suddenly appointed as their record producer, and I remember at the time I was very conscious of the fact that they went in and spent a great deal of EMI's money and studio time trying to get the sound I got down at Sound Techniques on 'Arnold Layne' for their follow-up, 'See Emily Play,' and ended up having to go down to Sound Techniques and get the same engineer to get the same sound."*

Miles also recalled Pink Floyd playing the Technicolour Dream concert, and the Games for May show at the Queen Elizabeth Hall. After various British tours, people began to notice a change in Syd Barrett. Joe Boyd recalled, *"The Floyd hadn't played at UFO for two months or something, and they came back for their first gig after they'd really made it. They came back to play at UFO and I remember it was very, very crowded. It was June 2, 1967, and because of the crowd and everything, there was only one way in. They had to go through the crowd to the dressing room. And they came past me, just inside the door, and it was very crushed so it was like faces two inches from your nose. So they all came by, kind of 'Hi Joe! How are you?' 'Great,' you know, and I greeted them all as they came through, and the last one was Syd. And the great thing with Syd was that he had a twinkle in his eye, I mean, he was a real eye-twinkler. He had this impish look about him, this mischievous glint. And he came by, and I said, 'Hi Syd,' and he just kind of looked at me. I looked right in his eye and there was no twinkle. No glint. It was like somebody had pulled the blinds, you know, nobody home. It was a real shock, very, very sad. Though who's to say? I don't think you can delineate and say, 'Well, one minute he was this and the next minute he was something else.' All sorts of changes like that are just the surface manifestation of something that must have been going on for a long time. People talk about acid casualties and everything, but who knows what really goes on?"*

'See Emily Play' was released on June 16, 1967, reaching Number 5 in the charts. Their first album, 'Piper at the Gates of Dawn,' was released on August 5, 1967, and reached Number 6. The rest is history.

August 28, 1976 - Melody Maker (U.K.)

reported in The Raver that seen backstage at the Knebworth Fair were Paul McCartney, Jack Nicholson, and David Gilmour.

October 2, 1976 - Sounds (U.K.) reported that Pink Floyd have completed work on their new album and are making plans for a tour next year.

October 1976 - Recording Engineer/Producer (U.S.) published an interview with Alan Parsons during which he talked about his work with Pink Floyd. Asked if he had worked with Pink Floyd before 'Dark Side of the Moon,' Parsons replied, "*I mixed the 'Atom Heart Mother' LP, of which my favorite track was Rick's 'Summer of 68,' I think. 'Atom Heart' was a hairy mix, probably the hairiest mix I had ever done up to that point. We had a lot of ADTs, a lot of echoes, a lot of tapes running, a lot of extra sound effects going on in the mix. I remember we had a problem with the drums coming through the fold-back speaker when we over-dubbed the choir, there was a bit too much leakage but we changed some things and it came out OK in the mixing stage.*"

Who supervised the mix? Parsons replied, "*It was usually the guy that had written the song.*"

Were you involved with the recording of 'More' or 'Obscured By Clouds?' Parsons replied, "*No. I think they were done at AIR London, Morgan, or in France. In comparison to 'Dark Side,' they were done fairly quickly.*"

Were Pink Floyd prepared when they went in to record 'Dark Side of the Moon?' Parsons replied, "*Well, they were prepared for what they thought they wanted to do when they first came in. Because they had been on the road performing the piece in one form, three or four months previous to the studio, we could work on the backing tracks rather quickly, but then everything would change and they'd say, 'Let's try this, let's try that.' That's when the time started piling up.*"

How was Chris Thomas involved? Parsons replied, "*Chris came in the last week as a fresh ear, because we'd all got so close to it. I didn't think it was strictly necessary to bring him in. I would have been happier doing it myself, as I had when the Floyd used to go* home early from the studio to watch the football matches. One thing that upset me was that Chris wanted to limit drums on some tracks, which I hate. It could have had a better drum sound. So I'm not saying 'Dark Side of the Moon' was bad, but it could have been better from my viewpoint.*"

How did they make the heart beat at the beginning of the record? Parsons replied, "*That was bass drum Kepexed with a lot of EQ around 100 Hz.*"

Where did the sound effects come from? Parsons answered, "*The sound effects came from the EMI library at times, and the rest were actually created in the studio by tearing up strips of paper or pouring money out of dust pans for 'Money.' The loop for that track was actually harder than we thought it was going to be because, even if the tape was off 1/4 inch, the rhythm would sound off, and we ended up cutting it by length rather than by sound. The sounds came off a 4-track tape for the quad mix. On the segues, I had to be careful of Dolby alignment. Editing from a copy back into a Dolby master, you can have all sorts of problems because the Dolby alignment can differ. For that reason, I generally don't mix Dolby. Hiss never stopped any record selling. Like when the Beatles did 'Sgt. Pepper' four-to-four, they preserved signal-to-noise by using elevated levels and one-inch tape for the 4-track.*"

Asked about the use of synthesizers, Parson explained, "*They all play synthesizers. David is pretty much the wizard at programming them. He programmed the travel section in 'On the Run.' On 'Any Colour You Like,' he was being fed a long tape loop that he was playing to, so he was playing DA DA DA, and it would come back da-da-da, da-da-da. We did it in stereo and I patched it in such a way that I used two echo-sends, the second of which is fed from the first return, and the first echo-send is fed from the second return, and you get a bouncing back and forth. Another thing you can do is to feed each echo-send to its own channel, but feed a small amount of the first channel into the second channel, and have the second channel set slightly above the first one, then, on each repeat, it will move from left to right. Another thing I've also done is when I've run out of tracks or wanted to save some tracks for something else, is just take off on to*

1/4 inch tape the track that you don't want. In that case, you would have to either mix the material at the same time or note the machine numbers so you could use the machine at a future session and hope it stays in sync with your multi-track. But after 'Dark Side,' we did some work on what could have potentially been the Floyd's greatest LP featuring non-musical instruments, things like bottles and the plucking of a rubber band into a mic for the bass."

What were the Household Objects sessions like? Parsons replied, *"I figure it was a great shame that they didn't go on with it because it had the makings of becoming a tremendous album. At the time we were doing it, four to five months after 'Dark Side,' it was literally all experimentation. While we were recording the rubber band, for example, we were encountering some problems in that, when you record it, you're dealing with a fixed-pitch. We discovered, almost by accident, the best way of getting the rubber band right was to sort of prop it up on matchsticks on a table. Then we found if you put your finger in-between, it would change pitch, of course. And then you found you got an even better sound by sticking matchsticks in the middle, which was the re-discovery of the fret. The mic was literally about 1/8 inch away from the rubber band. The rubber band was about a foot long to get a low note. Eventually, we ended up with a riff that had been played with this rubber band, made a tape-loop of that, and dubbed on a sweeping-up brush banged on a floor as a high hat. Amazing hi hat sound. Really quite authentic."*

Did you get the bristles or wood sound on the floor? Parsons replied, *"It was probably about a foot away, so it was a bit of both."* Was this on a parquet floor? Parsons answered, *"Yeah."*

For recording the rubber band, were you using an 87? Parsons replied, *"No. It was an 84. Oh, that was another thing. We decided to record the album on one mic. It would obviously be over-dubbed and over-dubbed, but I kept the mic in a place where I knew where it was, just praying that it wouldn't break down, so at the end of it we could say we used one mic."* And the mic you used was an 84 for everything? Parsons said, *"Yes, mainly because the capsule is very near the end. An*

87, the capsule is a good 1/2 inch away from the face of it, and to record the rubber band, you'd have to be absolutely on top of it because it's so quiet."

What kind of EQ did you use on the board? Parsons replied, *"A fair amount of bottom end, around the 150 sort of mark, probably +12, and probably filtering off a bit of top to get rid of the plucking sound. The snare drum was done with aerosol spray, shhh-shhh-shhh, but you couldn't get it short enough by pressing it, so I had to record a long spray and then cut it to 1/2 inch lengths of tape between white leader into a loop to get sh-sh-sh. It was a really good snare drum sound."*

Did you record all these sounds on a 1/4 inch tape? Parsons replied, *"We made the bass loop, then I dubbed on the brush, then each individual beat of the snare had to be dubbed in after that, and then another loop was made on the 24-track. So it went, click track on 24-track, then the brush, then a couple beats of the snare individually keyed-in, then a bass drum which was just footsteps on the floor using a lot of EQ."*

Was this someone walking in Plimsole shoes? Parsons replied, *"Probably was. Yes it was. Then a loop was made of the 24-track so you had a continuous thing. The whole thing took about two days."*

How much material did you end up with? Parsons replied, *"Very little. A lot of it was also compiling tapes of wine glasses vari-speeded at different pitches so you could make up different chords by combining different tracks on the 24-track."*

Was there liquid in the wine glasses? Parsons replied, *"No. It was a matter of scraping your finger on the edge and then vari-speeding it from a loop. In order to make the edit not jump in a loop, you have to make a very long cut. The splice would have to be about 2 1/2 inches."* So you would have to cut the tape at a greater diagonal than a 45-degree cut? Parsons answered, *"Right."*

What else was used? Parsons replied, *"Blowing into bottles."* What sound does blowing into bottles make? Parsons explained, *"It's sort of like an organ if you have lots of them and use VSO. We also had electric razor and egg slicer, using the wires for plucking."*

Did any of these recordings turn into

a song? Parsons replied, *"They kind of tried, but there were never any vocals to it. Oh, another thing was footsteps. We overdubbed footsteps to simulate footsteps. Rick was holding the mic by his feet while he walked around the studio. Each group member tried it, and it turned out that Rick had the most suitable shoes. But it really is a shame that album didn't surface. It could have been really something."*

How much came out of the sessions? Parsons said, *"Well, that's the thing. We ended up with virtually zero. And it's a shame because there was a lot of time spent on it, but to do that, some of it became very tedious. We probably spent in excess of a week doing it, and the majority of that was spent VSOing. Later the Floyd wanted me to set up their studio and continue to go on the road. I had done three American tours with them and it was they that brought me to America."*

Did you work with the Azimuth Co-ordinator? Parsons replied, *"The Azimuth Co-ordinator was a very early object which became superceded when people started building quad pan-pots. But it was literally the first quad pan-pot I had seen."*

When you were on tour with Pink Floyd, did you use a Teac 4-track for sound effects? Parsons replied, *"Yes, we literally just went into the studio for a day or two and put everything on the Teac we thought was necessary for the P.A. It seems odd to me that they were able to play to that at all because all the sound effects, the way the mixer was hooked up, went straight into the quad P.A. and they didn't reach the stage P.A. at all."*

Did Pink Floyd bring their own mixing board on tour with them? Parsons replied, *"Yes. It was built by Allen & Heath."* How was it configured? Parsons answered, *"I think it was 24 in, a four-way stereo out, plus the quad buss. So when you selected the quad outputs, it didn't reach the P.A. If it was in a hall with two levels, then you would have two levels of quad speakers."* That could have caused reverberation problems for the cues. Parsons said, *"Yeah. Another thing was the fact that the poor people that had to sit near the speakers had to endure that loudness."*

In their movie, they had that problem, as well as a problem with the EQ. Parsons replied, *"With the Floyd, the way the*

P.A. was set up was, we were careful to avoid that, that excessiveness in the 3 to 4k range, which is the sort of hurting range. We wanted to make sure that when we had an 'S' sound coming through the mike, that it didn't sound k-k-k, that it really did sound s-s-s. In fact, sometimes to get around that, I would often take mid frequencies out and add at top end around 8 to 10k and subtract around 3k with the equalizer on the board."*

What P.A. mics did you use? Parsons replied, *"All dynamics in P.A., mainly for their proximity effect. I think dynamics have a much better lack of distant pick-up than condensors. You have to EQ them a lot more. They don't 'pop' and they're more reliable."* What kinds of dynamic mics were they using? Parsons said, *"About 3/4 of them were Shure, and the vocal mics were Sennheisers."* How many mics were used? Parsons replied, *"There never seemed to be enough. One seemed to find that one mic a night would go out and, in the general panic of the road, it would always get put back with the ones that were working, so you would not discover which one it was until the next night when you'd find there was another one out."* Were there ever any problems with the vocal mics not working? Parsons siad, *"I was always paranoid about vocal mics not working, so I would literally check them seconds before the Floyd would come on stage, because that was the one thing you couldn't bluff."*

Did you have anything to do with the fact that the live versions of 'Dark Side of the Moon' had a different intro than the one on the album? Parsons replied, *"I'm fairly sure I didn't have anything to do with it. The only time I recorded anything on the road with them, it was only about half the concert. But touring with Pink Floyd was a grueling experience, traveling, up early every morning, staying at the same Holiday Inn in every city, and probably not getting more than four or five hours sleep. But, like I said, the show itself was the thing that made it all worthwhile. You felt the audience was applauding you as well as the group. I tried doing P.A. for Cockney Rebel after the Floyd, and it just isn't the same thing. There's no one I'd rather have done P.A. for than the Floyd because you're so much a part of the production. Afterwards there was talk of my recording a future LP, but Brian Humphries did it at Abbey Road as a free lance, which is somewhat unheard of for EMI, other than the fact that Geoff had done some work with McCartney. You must have special concessions from the top of the company."*

Did people there complain when Brian Humphries came in to Abbey road to do 'Wish You Were Here?' Parsons replied, *"Yes. I figure it was among the other engineers. The more junior engineers always thought that if the senior engineers didn't want to do it, they should have a crack at it."*

October 23, 1976 - New Musical Express (U.K.) reported that Pink Floyd were planning a spring tour. The band started a film production company to makes the films for their backdrop.

December 4, 1976 - New Musical Express (U.K.) reported that Pink Floyd confirmed that they will be playing four consecutive nights at Wembley Empire Pool on March 17-20, 1977, and four nights at Stafford Bingley Hall on March 28-31, 1977. The new Pink Floyd album, 'Animals,' is scheduled for release on January 14, 1977, and Capitol Radio in London will be broadcasting six weekly one-hour shows about the history of Pink Floyd, called 'The Pink Floyd Story,' beginning on December 10, 1976.

December 11, 1976 - Melody Maker (U.K.) reported in The Raver that Pink Floyd's new album will be called 'Animals.' Last Friday, the band sent a group of people to Battersea Power Station with a fifty-foot pink pig that they filled with helium and sent aloft. The pig's behavior became erratic, and it drifted over London in one of the busiest air traffic routes in the world. West Drayton air traffic control broadcast emergency signals to all incoming aircraft, warning pilots of a flying pig. The pig floated over Crystal Palace with a police helicopter in pursuit. When the pig reached the coast, the Civil Aviation Authority announced that it would either disintegrate or land in Germany. The Kent Constabulary lost track of the pig over Chatham. Maidstone Police Headquarters reported that the pig had crash-landed at the East Stour Farm in Chilham near Ashford. The farmer that found the pig tethered it to his barn to prevent its escape.

New Musical Express (U.K.) published an article titled, "Pig Ahoy" by Dick Tracy. The article reported that Pink Floyd were looking for a cover picture for their latest album, titled, 'Animals,' that will include three songs called 'Duck,' 'Pig,' and 'Sheep.'

On Thursday, December 2, 1976, photographers gathered at Battersea Power Station where the band were going to launch a giant inflatable pink pig made by Balloon Fabrik. Pink champagne was ready to toast the pig, and a marksman was ready with rifle to shoot it down if it went out of control. But due to a lack of helium, the pig could not be inflated and the assembled crowd went home.

On Friday, December 3, 1976, the crew returned in the morning with extra helium, and successfully inflated the pig. As it rose into the air, camera shutters clicked, but a line attached to the pig broke, and it floated up into the sky. A jet pilot who landed at Heathrow Airport reported that he had seen a large pink pig floating through the sky. A police helicopter was dispatched, and it tracked the pig to 5,000 feet before giving up the chase. The Civil Aviation Authority warned all pilots in the area to be on the lookout for a flying pink pig. The London Evening News began receiving reports from readers of UFO sightings. The CAA reported, "It was last sighted east of Detling, near Chatham in Kent at 18,000 feet going east before we lost it on our radar. It will either disappear into the upper atmosphere and dissolve, or continue across the Channel until it reaches Germany where it was made. You could call it a homing pig." The pig eventually landed in Kent.

Sounds (U.K.) published an article about Pink Floyd's new studio, that featured an interview with Nick Mason about the studio. The studio is a converted church hall in Islington, and was built for exclusive use by Pink Floyd. Nick Mason explained, *"The design criteria for the studio were related directly to our needs. For one thing, the building also contains our PA store, lighting store, group office and workshop. Secondly, the place is designed to be operated by one person, with lining up and preparation kept to a minimum. For example, we're using DBX instead of Dolby because it's easier."*

As to whether it is state of the art,

1977
Animals

Mason added, *"Well, it probably represents the state of the art in low budget studio design. I mean it hasn't got every wonderful innovation. After all it's primarily for our use so we looked for a cheap system to fulfill most of our needs."*

The equipment in the studio is from the American Company, MCI, with an MCI 32-into-24 track desk, MCI 24, 4, and 2 track tape machines, three Revoxes, and a Nakamichi cassette deck. There also are two stereo parametric equalizers, two digital delay lines, plus phasers and flangers. Mason explained, *"There is an attempt to leave the studio fully set up. It's all part of trying to make it as quick and easy as possible to get results."*

Asked why there were synthesizers in the control room, Mason said, *"We put in a lot of lines so people can do stuff in the control room. We often prefer to do things that way, and again it makes it as easy as possible for one person to do everything."*

The acoustics of the studio were designed by Ken Shearer. Lignacite brick is used on the walls along with baffles and rockwool. Mason said about the acoustics, *"I'm afraid it's not as good as we'd hoped, although the studio sounds quite quiet."*

On the possibility of running the studio as a commercial venture, Mason commented, *"We might set aside specific periods, say three weeks at a time, when it would be free for other bands. We'd probably charge about £40 an hour and get our customers by word of mouth."*

As for adding other comforts to the studio, Mason said, *"Well, we do have a kitchen. But, as yet, there's no lounge. There are some other facilities, but they'll only be for us really. The problem about your own studio is that it's a communal thing for you and you don't really want it to be like a public waiting room."*

December 18, 1976 - New Musical Express (U.K.) published a photo of a pig in the airwaves between the smokestacks of Battersea Power Station.

January 22, 1977 - Melody Maker (U.K.) reported that there have been problems with the sleeve design for the new Pink Floyd album, 'Animals.' The album, which was to have been released on January 14, 1977, has been delayed due to problems with the cover. Steve O'Rourke explained, *"There have been problems with the artwork for the sleeve. It's nothing serious, but it means that we've not been able to keep the original release date. We still haven't fixed a definite date, although we hope to decide that over the weekend. It looks as though the sleeve will be ready in time for us to release the album on January 28."*

Asked about the album, O'Rourke stated, *"The band spent the whole of last year recording the new album. It was finished and ready for release by Christmas although, of course, we were then held up by the sleeve problems."* To promote the album, the band will undertake a British tour in the spring, with four concerts at Wembley Empire Pool, and four shows at New Bingley Hall, Stafford, England.

January 29, 1977 - Melody Maker (U.K.) reported in The Raver that none of the members of Pink Floyd attended the EMI preview of the new Pink Floyd album, 'Animals,' held at Battersea Power Station last week. Richard Wright was in Switzerland, and David Gilmour had baby sitter problems. However, Steve O'Rourke flew in from America to attend. At the preview, the album was played twice, but the sound system rendered the vocals incomprehensible.

Also in this issue is a review of the Pink Floyd album, 'Animals,' by Karl Dallas. Dallas suggested that 'Animals' may be the third part of a trilogy, with 'Dark Side of the Moon' representing alienation, 'Wish You Were Here' representing loneliness, and 'Animals' a savage humanism, personified by animal caricatures. While the Bible separated humanity into sheep and goats, this album divides them into dogs, pigs, and sheep. The three animal sections of the album are placed in between the first and second verses of the

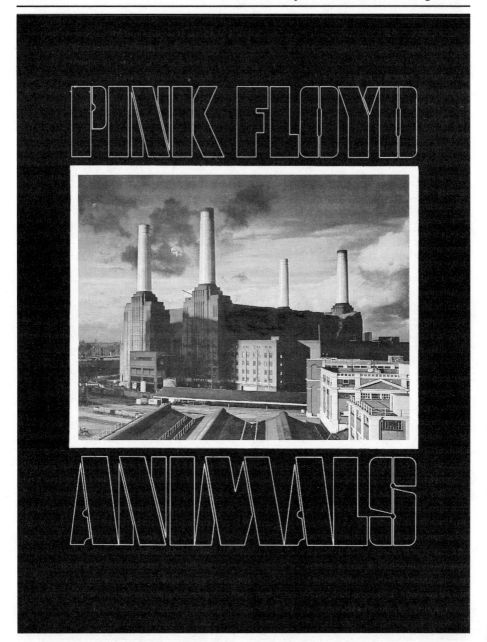

acoustic song, 'Pigs on the Wing,' that serves as a moral framework to the other songs. It is sung in a style that is so different from everything else that it serves as a splash of cold water to clear your mind for what follows. 'Dogs' depicts the modern world as "nature red in tooth and claw" where the dogs rend one another, retire, and are dragged to death by "the weight you used to need to throw around."

'Pigs (Three Different Ones)' begins the second side of the album with unflattering descriptions of public figures, including the "house-proud town mouse" Mary Whitehouse. 'Sheep' is like a mini Animal Farm, with the contented masses grazing peacefully before being sent to the slaughterhouse. During the song, a parody of the 23rd Psalm is read through a vocoder, and the sheep revolt and kill the dogs, although it is suggested that it may only be a dream or a story told by one dog to another. Perhaps the individuals that are huddling together and seeking shelter from the pigs on the wing at the end of the album are dogs. The music on the album is at times multi-layered, and at other times deceptively simple, and serves to underscore the savagery of the lyrics. Perhaps the band should rename themselves "Punk Floyd." The album will be released February 4, 1977.

National Rockstar (U.K.) reviewed the Pink Floyd album, 'Animals.' Stephen Lavers wrote that Animals is vastly superior to 'Wish You Were Here,' and shows that Pink Floyd is not done yet. The theme of the album has to do with "ravenous beasts that destroy to eat and are devoured themselves, used as images of human beings." "The next album could be their masterpiece."

New Musical Express (U.K.) reviewed the Pink Floyd album, 'Animals' with an article titled, "Floyd in Barnyard Takeover" by Miles. Last Friday, Capitol Radio ran the last part of "The Pink Floyd Story" which featured the 'Animals' album and an interview with Roger Waters talking about it. The day before, there was a press preview party for the album at the Battersea Power Station Sports and Social Club. Meanwhile, Pink Floyd will begin their European tour in Germany, with a new stage lighting system, rumored to include silver spheres with spotlights, and lighting operators on hydraulic arms above the band. A Gerald Scarfe film of a large mechanical insect will be projected behind the band.

The 'Animals' album, to be released on January 28, 1977, is simple in concept and execution, and its mood is bleak, dark, and foreboding. The first song, 'Pigs on the Wing (1)' is played on a Dylanesque acoustic guitar. 'Dogs' has angry and gutsy guitar, the drums sound like distant WWI guns, and the music swirls in abstract chords. 'Pigs (Three Different Ones)' begins with a European folk sweetness before lyrics about a "Pig Man" appear. The reviewer suggested that this is the section that EMI made the band change due to four letter words. 'Sheep' is hope after the gloom, before a warning in the lyrics. Holy prayers are electronically treated to make them

sound eerie. Terror builds upon terror. The album ends with 'Pigs on the Wing (2),' a positive message and one to think about.

'The Pink Floyd Story' on Capitol Radio traced the bands development from the beginning, in six episodes. Talking about the problems of being one of the worlds top groups after 'Dark Side of the Moon,' Nick Mason said, "There was a point after 'Dark Side' where we might easily have broken up. Well, we'd reached all the goals rock bands tend to aim for. Perhaps we were nervous about carrying on, the problems of making a follow up." Mason also added, about making the album 'Wish You Were Here,' "I really did find time in the studio extremely horrible."

Roger Waters stated that the last Pink Floyd tour was "very unpleasant, unnerving, and upsetting," and he talked about the idea of building a wall across the stage during the performance to display the true relationship between the group and the audience. He stated, "people con each other that there is no wall . . . maybe make it out of black polystyrene." As for his obsession with paranoia, Waters explained, "The quality of life is full of stress and pain in most of the people I meet, and in myself."

During the making of 'Dark Side of the Moon,' Waters had questions printed on cards, which were given to people sitting in front of a microphone. About 25 people answered questions such as "When was the last time you thumped someone?" and "What does the dark side of the moon mean to you?" One of the interviewees was roadie, Roger the Hat, who came up with the phrase "short, sharp, shock" that was used on the album. During another section of 'The Pink Floyd Story' a lighting crew tape that was recorded during the Detroit concert in June 1973 was played, on which Pink Floyd's lighting crew can be heard trying to work with the crew from the concert hall. The band can be heard performing in the background as lighting effects are cued in.

Record Mirror (U.K.) reviewed the Pink Floyd album, 'Animals' with an article titled, "Animal Yarn" by Johnny the Fox. The reviewer related the activities at the press party held by Harvest Records at the Battersea Power Station to the songs on the album. The record executives were portrayed as Dogs, while the reviewers were sheep, who were told when, and when not, to write. After the party, the reviewer was invited to a private listening of the album, noting that some sheep are more equal than others. As for the album, the lyrics are strong, bitter, and ask questions, the music is powerful at times, and the album is powerful, thought-out and may disturb you.

Sounds (U.K.) reviewed the Pink Floyd album, 'Animals' with an article titled, "Pig deal! Floyd bring home the bacon" by Hugh Fielder. Giving the album five stars which signifies a very important platter, Fielder wrote that problems with the cover art has delayed the albums release, and the writer felt that the single listening he was given at the Battersea Power Station press party was not adequate enough to give it the attention it deserved. The album has a sense of purpose and commitment that was lacking on 'Wish You Were Here.' David Gilmour's guitar has bite and aggression, and Roger Waters' lyrics have a sharp cutting edge. The album begins with the song, 'Pigs on the Wing (Part One)' that has a simple melody line. 'Dogs' occupies the rest of the first side, and features echoed vocals, slicing guitar, shifting keyboard sounds and rhythms. 'Pigs (Three Different Ones)' is musical and lyrical aggression. The third verse is about moral crusader Mary Whitehouse and echoes the writer's sentiments exactly. 'Sheep' features a classic Roger Waters bass line and some forceful lyrics. The album ends with 'Pigs on the Wing (Part Two)' that offers words of comfort.

February 5, 1977 - Melody Maker (U.K.) published an article titled, "Pigs fly over Germany" by Karl Dallas that reviewed the Pink Floyd concert at the Festhalle in Frankfurt, West Germany on January 27, 1977. Nick Mason stated, "*At the end of the last tour we felt as if we could hardly bear to see each other again. But now it feels very good.*" An audience of 12,000 packed the Frankfurt Festhalle in Germany for the second successive night to see Pink Floyd perform. Despite a generally friendly crowd, there still were some people who threw cans and bottles during the first half. At intermission, an announcer asked them to desist because delicate equipment was being damaged. In fact, Brian Humphries got

hit in the head with one, while another full can was thrown into Nick Mason's Hokasui-painted drum set and sprayed Mason in the face with foam. German police were taking pictures of the audience looking for dope smokers, while American military police combed the audience for AWOL GIs. During the song 'Pigs,' a gray inflatable pig with glowing red eyes appeared out of a cloud of smoke over the PA speakers. However, on their first three nights of the tour, the smoke machines didn't produce enough smoke so, at this show, the band decided to use a smoke bomb instead. This caused the hall to be filled with acrid, throat strangling smoke that was so thick it was difficult to see what was happening.

Technically, the sound was excellent. Roger Waters used an oscilloscope to display the waveform of his music so he could tell if his bass guitar was out of tune. He also wore headphones throughout the show to monitor the sound. Every drum in Mason's drum kit is miked through a separate noisegate, making the drums sound crisp and clean. The lighting system also was technologically advanced, with two enormous "cherry picker" gantries on each side of the stage that swooped down over band members to illuminate them in colored lights. A large mirrored glass sunburst rose from the back of the stage during the end of 'Wish You Were Here' and rotated, the center one way, the outside the other way, shooting out rays of colored light. For this tour, the band is using extra musicians, with Snowy White on second guitar, and Dick Parry on sax.

After the show, the musicians celebrated Nick Mason's 33rd birthday. Asked if he thinks their past three albums are a coherent body of work, Mason replied, "*Of course, we didn't plan it that way, but it just seemed that with 'Dark Side,' we somehow got lucky and things began to fall into place in a way that they hadn't before. This one is really my favorite. I've never been able to listen to any of our previous albums once we've finished them because we've spent so much time with them that there's no pleasure in it. But, with the possible exception of 'Saucer,' this is the only one I like playing.*" Over a dinner of frog legs, David Gilmour commented, "*Just think, someone had to kill 20 of these poor little buggers so I could eat this meal.*"

New sounds from Pink Floyd "Animals" on Harvest Records and Tapes.

February 12, 1977 - Melody Maker (U.K.) reported in The Raver that three of the songs on the new Pink Floyd album were left over from their previous album, 'Wish You Were Here.' They were, however, re-recorded. Plans for Pink Floyd to do the soundtrack for the movie 'Dune' have been scrapped. Production of the movie was cancelled when the budget exceeded 20 million dollars before any stars were even hired. Also in this issue is a two-page ad for the album, 'Animals.'

New Musical Express (U.K.) published an article titled, "Life is just a plate of meat" that reviewed Pink Floyd's new album, 'Animals.' The reviewer wrote that the album is the bands "most complete and conclusive album in years." It is "one of the most extreme, relentless, harrowing, and downright iconoclastic hunks of music to have been made available for public perusal." The lyrics, which may have been inspired by Brian Patten's poem, 'Meat,' puts humanity into three states of animality. Dogs are competitive, calculating, and aggressive, but they grow old, despair, contract cancer, and die. Pigs are 'charades,' they suppress their feelings, and are pathetic. Sheep are pushed around, misled, and abused. Waters' lyrics are honest, sympathetic,

and compassionate. Musically, 'Animals' is a revelation. The album is "great, generous, healing rock music."

February 19, 1977 - Melody Maker (U.K.) reported that Pink Floyd have rescheduled their March 20, 1977, concert at Wembley to March 16, 1977.

New Musical Express (U.K.) published an article titled, "Floyd gig switch." Wembley Empire Pool has announced that for "administrative reasons," the venue will not be available for the Pink Floyd concert on Sunday, March 20, 1977. The band were scheduled to play Wembley from March 17-20. The final night has been switched to Wednesday, March 16, 1977. A badminton tournament on the 21st may be the reason for the cancellation.

February 26, 1977 - Melody Maker (U.K.) published a letter in Mailbag titled, "Down with punk – up with Pink" that asked, what is the infatuation with morons pounding out idiot rock? We need musical literacy in the form of intellectualism, like the new Pink Floyd album, 'Animals.' This form of music makes good the potentialities inherent in musical structure and adds an extra dimension to human thought as expressed through literature. Pink Floyd uses music as a means of expressing thoughts on serious issues rather then giving lessons on how to pierce your ears with a safety pin. Also in this issue are the U.S. album charts, where the Pink Floyd album, 'Animals,' has entered the chart for the first time at #5.

March 1977 - Beat Instrumental (U.K.) published an article titled, "Pink Floyd's sound system" that explained the equipment used by Pink Floyd. They wrote, "Dave Gilmour, Roger Waters, Rick Wright, Nick Mason, individually, and collectively as the Pink Floyd, manage to remain almost totally inaccessible socially, as far as interviews, gossip columns, and general newsworthiness are concerned. Despite, but chiefly because of this, they remain amongst the largest of all "name bands" and, moreover, the name of their group has taken on near mystical proportions, and has become "a name to conjure with." This is a very wordy way of saying that the group have put themselves into a position where they live or die on the sound of their music alone, and the measure of their success is that the words, "The Floyd," have come to be synonymous with sounds that are very, very good indeed. An interesting point about the Pink Floyd is that, rather than creating their music in the studio, and then attempting to recreate an album's sound live, most of the initial musical ideas are pioneered on the road, and many pieces are first played in their entirety to live audiences. This means that the group has had to evolve a very complex, but tremendously flexible, sound system to realize their creative ideas, rather than one designed merely to reproduce them. This means that journalists have had to rationalize their developments in music by reference to the Floyd's "ability to play the mixing board like it was a fifth instrument." Whether or not anyone can actually grasp all the potential inherent in the Pink Floyd's total array of equipment, involving literally thousands of metres of wire and millions of connections, is open to question, but this article is an attempt to describe how the people that work for the group and the people who build their equipment manage to translate the Floyd's requirements for musical development into physical reality.

Mixing consoles can be played like instruments, but the fact remains that, like any other piece of electronic equipment, you only get out what you put in. In other words, for a mixing console to do a specific task, it must have been initially designed with a similar capability in mind. This article centers around the Floyd's mixer and associated electronics, as this is the nerve center of the whole sound system, and also happens to be the newest piece of equipment that the group have added to their sound system. Earlier mixers hadn't quite had the technological sophistication of construction to match their ambitious formats, which had consequently caused a certain amount of operational hassles. Say no more. The Pink Floyd had set up a company known as Britannia Row Leasing (Audio) Ltd., which hires out sections of the group's equipment when they're not using it themselves and, in early 1976, this company had ordered two monitor mixing consoles from Midas Amplification, which were subsequently used extensively with various groups, including Queen, who used the Floyd's P.A. for their Hyde Park gig. Britannia Row were well pleased with these and other Midas consoles, which include a 28 in, 8 out main desk, and a special 16 channel extension unit. Accordingly, the Pink Floyd decided to approach Midas concerning the construction of a larger mixer for their own use. Midas told me that the Floyd are now their largest, single customer, exceeding even the mighty Roy Clair, who runs the large 'Clair Brothers' American P.A. hire company.

The basis for the present Pink Floyd mixer was laid when Brian Humphries, the Floyd's engineer in the studio and live, told Robbie, who has general responsibility for the group's equipment, what facilities he wanted on the mixer. Robbie then went to see Geoff Byers, the design brains behind all the excellent Midas consoles, and together they worked out a proposed specification for the Floyd's mixer. Midas received a request for a quotation last August, and it took a month for a full specification of the console to be worked out, and for Rick Kilminster to make drawings of the intended result. The group admired the impressive half-scale drawings, admired the similarly impressive specifications, and gave the go ahead to build the desk. Before you read about what the finished item can do for Pink Floyd, try swallowing the following facts about what it actually took to make the mixer. The design of the console occupied two mechanical designers and two printed circuit board designers for a period in excess of 2,000 man-hours, considerably more time being spent on the construction of the desk. Three outside subcontractors were kept busy for two months building the basic electronic and mechanical parts of this amazing machine, and a full six weeks were spent in testing and inter-wiring the parts. Geoff kindly spent a good few minutes with his desk calculator, working out a tally of all the controls on the mixer. Hopefully this will give you some idea of why such items of equipment are so hard to construct, and why this particular one cost so much money. The electronics behind those front panels obviously contain even more components, and are even more complex to design and build.

For your amazement, the Floyd's mixer contains no less than 1,182 illuminated push switches, 447 rotary controls, 240 thumbwheel switches, 484 toggle switches, 67 rotary stud switches, 32 LED meter columns comprising 1,200 individual LED segments, 156 individual LED indicators for the separate channels, 54 mono Panny & Giles conductive plastic faders, 11 stereo Panny & Giles faders, and 5 quad Panny & Giles faders. That's a total of 70 faders in all. As a final mind boggler, the desk measures about 12 feet in length when the three separate sections are placed next to each other. Two of the console's three sections each contain 20 input channels, 4 effects groups, and four stereo sub-groups mixing into a stereo master output. The third unit contains four quadraphonic inputs, six quadraphonic sub-groups, plus quadraphonic and stereo master output groups. Robbie explained to me that the console was designed in three sections, not only for ease of transportation, but also with considerations of flexibility and future Britannia Row hiring jobs in mind. Previously, if a group wanted to hire some of the Floyd's P.A., it was often necessary to haul the complete quad board out, whether or not all its facilities were required. Now it will be possible to operate either of the 20 input consoles independently, the Quadro console being operational only when linked via the 36-way multi-core connectors to one or both of the 20 input consoles.

With the three sections all hooked up together, the following input/output facilities are provided: 40 mic/line input channels, with access to 8 effects send/return groups, which may be routed directly, or via 8 stereo sub-groups and/or 6 quadraphonic sub-groups, to either/both stereo and quadraphonic master output groups. In the numerical terminology that seems to have become standard slang in the mixing trade, that would be 40 into 8/6 into 2/4. Before I proceed any further, a word about those four outputs might not go amiss. As Mick, Robbie's partner, pointed out, "Quadraphonic is the general public's term, not ours." Although it's hard to think of another word to describe it, the Floyd's sound system does not follow the pattern that, in domestic Hi-Fi systems, is generally understood as "Quadraphonic." In Hi-Fi Quad, there are speakers positioned at left front, right front, right back, and left back, the rear loudspeakers being mirror-image in position to the pair which would normally be used for stereo reproduction. In Floydophonic sound, there are speakers at left front and right front, these being the main stereo P.A. components, and smaller loudspeaker arrays in central positions at left and right hand sides, and to the rear. To use a domestic layout for live performance in large auditoriums would involve tremendous physical problems in arranging the rear stacks of equal size and power as the front ones, and would be impossible to mix as per recorded Quad because there could be a time delay of up to half a second between front and rear. Floydophonic sound is used mainly during quiet musical passages, for prerecorded tapes, and for special effects. When a Quad joystick is in the upper and forward position, the sound is fed equally to the left and right stereo P.A. stacks. When the joystick is moved over laterally to right or left, the sound goes to right or left Quad stations. When the joystick is in the lower and rear position, the sound goes directly to the rear Quad station. Any movement between these positions will result in a movement of sound between the relevant speaker stacks, the origin of the Floyd's original, but rather confusing, term for a Quad joystick, the "Azimuth Co-ordinator."

The line drawings of the Floyd's Midas mixer are plan views. The two horizontal lines represent changes in vertical plane. The faders on the lower section are flat, and the input modules and routing modules on the two upper sections are angled in two different planes. Leaving out the upper banks of routing push-switches for the moment, concentrate on the center control sections of the input modules. There are 40 of these, and they contain all the controls for the input channels, with the exception of the faders and routing to stereo and quad sub-groups and main outputs. Starting at the top of the module, there's an input sensitivity rotary control, giving maximum gains of 80 dB for microphones or 50 dB for line inputs. Mic or Line selection is made by the left hand switch in the bank of three, situated directly below the sensitivity control. The middle of these three provides Phantom Power, a 48 volt DC supply down to the two mic cable wires to operate a condenser microphone, and the right hand switch cuts in a resistive network to reduce the gain on that channel input by 20 dB, a coarse reduction in volume to avoid overloading the channel amplifier.

The next section on the module consists of the channel equalization facilities. Treble control, offering + or - 16 dB's at frequencies of 6, 10 or 15kHz cycles per second, the frequencies being selected by a miniature toggle switch, middle control, offering a similar amount of lift or cut at frequencies of 500, 800Hz, 1.5, 2.5, 3.5, or 5kHz, selected by a rotary stud switch, and bass control similar in operation to treble, but with selectable frequencies of 40, 80, or 160Hz. Immediately to the left and below the bass control is another miniature toggle switch. This brings into operation a High-Pass filter that attenuates low frequencies, the initiation of the 16 dB per octave attenuating slope being selectable for either 60Hz, 120Hz, or not at all. These equalization controls are not as comprehensive as some currently in fashion, but considering the number of input channels, they offer ample facilities. As we shall see later, there is provision on the console to patch in more comprehensive equalizers to individual channels, to cope with really awkward sounds.

Below the tone controls on the channels there are three echo send controls, with illuminated on/off switches next to them.

Below these are three miniature toggle switches, which allow the echo send from each control to be taken pre or post the channel fader. In line underneath the three pre/post toggles are three thumbwheel 8-position switches. These allow the three-channel echo sends to be assigned to any of the effects group send/return busses, four on the LH input section, four on the RH input section.

Next on our journey down the module are three illuminated push-switches and two miniature toggles. The top push-switch is for channel mute, middle one is for channel solo (applies that channel's output to the master stereo output to the exclusion of all the others, useful whilst setting up mics). The last push-switch is marked P.F.L., which stands for Pre Fade Listen (routes the channel signal to the headphones).

The top toggle switch, next to the three push buttons, switches the equalization controls in or out of circuit for before/after comparison of their effect whilst setting up, and the one immediately below it is marked Insert/Cancel. This switch allows an effect device to be inserted into that channel exclusively, via the XLR connectors at the rear of the console. The point of insertion is after the tone controls but before the channel fader, post EQ, pre fade.

The next control down is the Left-Right pan control, perhaps the only knob that requires no explanation at all, and below this is an illuminated push switch that disables the panning function on that channel. The three round dots to the right of this control are LED indicators, which indicate peak signal levels on that channel of -15, 0, and +15 dB's (quiet sound, normal maximum level, and overload).

Next in line for consideration are the effects master modules, positioned in between the channel modules and the control module (the latter may be easily identified as there is no fader beneath it). The effects masters sum up the signals sent to them from the channel modules, and then send this combined signal out for treatment by an external device. Starting from the top of these modules, we have a send level control to set the output level from –40 dBm to +20 dBm, below this control is an insert switch operating on the send section, and below this are illuminated push-switches for solo and "check echo" (P.F.L.).

Beneath these are the bass and treble controls for the send signal, both fixed frequency controls, giving + or - 16dB's, or lift or cut at 50Hz and 15kHz respectively. Next on this module are the controls of the return from the effects device, gain, treble, middle (at 3kHz), bass, and spin. Spin returns a regulated amount of the signal, selected from either the post insert send or the pre-EQ return by a miniature toggle switch, just below the rotary control. "Spinning" the return from, say, a reverb unit, would give the effect of a soft echoing reverberation.

The four push-switches next to the spin toggle are as follows: spin mute, return mute, return solo and P.F.L. the other pan, insert, etc. Controls on this module perform the same function as those on the ordinary mic/line input channels. Both Effects master modules and Input modules have routing modules, consisting of 16 illuminated pushbuttons, above their control sections. Eight of these switches assign the output of that channel pan pot to the inputs of the 8 stereo sub-groups (four on one input console, four on the other); and another 6 push-buttons assign the post fader channel signal to any of the 6 quadro masters in the central console. These latter buttons can be preset, and then brought into operation by pressing the button marked "Q." The remaining button, marked "SM," routes the channel(s) on which it is depressed directly to the stereo master output, bypassing the sub-groups.

Each input section console contains, in addition to the 20 input channels and four effects masters, four stereo sub-groups, the stereo output, and a control module. The control module has a socket for a talkback mic, tone controls, and controls for internal and external tb levels. 6 illuminated push-buttons route the tb to either the stereo or quad master modules, or directly to any of the four individual quad stations. A similar arrangement routes the output of a six-frequency oscillator to any of the P.A. stacks (useful for lining up crossover levels). Also provided on this module are master controls for solo and headphone levels. An LED meter above this module allows any channel or effects group to be checked out merely by pressing the relevant P.F.L. button. The stereo sub-groups and master are also provided with these meters. When I saw the Floyd console at Olympia, these hadn't been installed, but when they are, these devices should be fairly unique in giving both PPM and VU indication at the same time.

The central quadro console contains, apart from the stereo and quad masters and the quad sub-groups with joysticks, four quad auxiliary input modules. These modules each comprise four discreet channels, with master fader and ganged bass, middle and treble controls. Since Rick made the drawing of this console, four individual trim pots have been added on each module, replacing the single gain control. The four auxiliary quad inputs are used up as follows. One is for a quadraphonic soundtrack in synchronization with the 35mm films that the Floyd use. Another is for pre-recorded tape tracks, the first four from the Floyd's 8-track Otari recorder, one auxiliary input is unused at the moment, and the final one is for Rick Wright's use onstage. Wright uses a rebuilt Allen and Heath mixer for his keyboards, and a "floating" quad joystick can be operated in conjunction with this to pan keyboards around the Floydophonic system, as on the Moog intro to 'Shine On.'

One of the remarkable features of the Floyd's Midas console is the amount of facilities allowing special treatment of individual channels. To give you an idea of why these are necessary, it would seem appropriate to give a run down of the Floyd's complement of "outboard" equipment. In fact, their array of what would normally be termed "accessories" is so comprehensive and sophisticated that many small studios might feel decidedly envious. They use 16 channels of DBX noise reduction - 6 on the Otari 8-track, 3 on the Master Room Reverb, 4 on the 35mm soundtrack, 1 on the Roland Space Echo "and anything else that hisses!" 2 Lexicon Digital Delay Lines - mainly used for vocals. 2 Urei Teletronix Levelling Amplifiers LA - 3A, and 2 Urei UA1176 limiters, used on sax or vocal channels via insert points. 2 DBX RM 1 60 compressors, one used on the bass guitar mic channel, the other on the bass guitar DI channel. 2 Rebis stereo parametric equalizers, used as four extra channels of EQ for problem instruments such as acoustic guitar/snare drum. 3 Gelf Electronic Auto Phasers, one for Roger Water's vocal channel, and two on the stereo master inserts - to phase the whole P.A. 1 Master Room 'B' studio spring reverberation unit, used mainly for vocals. 1 Orban Parasound 516EC Dynamic Sibilance Controller, used exclusively to tame over "ssshhy" vocals. 1 Roland Space Echo, used on instruments. 1 Allen and Heath ADT (Automatic Double Tracking) unit, used mainly on guitar. 10 Allison Research Kepex Program Expanders - very interesting - the Floyd wanted to use these on vocals but found (as the Moody Blues did before them) that they don't really work properly live. 7 Kepex are still used on the kit mics (drums provide a meaty enough signal to operate Kepex even live). 1 Otari 8-track tape recorder, 4 tracks are used for pre-recorded quad pieces, and the rest for click tracks, cues, and so on, are fed to the group onstage, via the foldback. 1 Nakamichi stereo cassette recorder for playing incidental music and recording gigs. Also in evidence were two Revox's and a TEAC 4-track, all of which seemed to be generally kicking their heels.

Typical use of the console's effects send facilities with this equipment is as follows (for a vocal channel): Channel Insert - One channel of Orban Parasound Sibilance Controller. Auxiliary Send 1 - (Via Effects Group 1) Gelf Auto Phaser. Auxiliary Send 2 - (Via Effects Group 6) Lexicon DDL. Auxiliary Send 3 - (Via Effects Group 5) Master Room Reverb. Typical of the console's live mixing facilities are the following examples. 'Wish You Were Here' - the point at which a natural sounding acoustic guitar dissolves dramatically into the same sound, but distorted as from a transistor radio. Mixing operations required: start 8-track Otari, fade out live guitar and simultaneously fade up pre-recorded "radio" tape in quad, via aux quad input on Quadro console. 'Echoes' - the point at which the dominant, repeating guitar solo suddenly goes into fuzz and increases dramatically in volume, leaping out at you from your Boots Home Lo-Fi speakers! Mixing operations required: Dave Gilmour's guitar input channel is pre-selected to one of the quad sub-groups on the Quadro console, the joystick on this sub-group is placed in a central position, and the quad fader advanced to a suitably loud position. When Dave Gilmour's foot comes down on his fuzz box, Brian Humphries' finger presses the "Q" button on the guitar channel, bringing it into the pre-selected quad position and level setting. As Robbie said, "This time the band decided to get a mixer that would do almost anything." If you want one too it'll cost you £32,000, but then you're not the Pink Floyd, are you?"

March 5, 1977 - Melody Maker (U.K.) **reported** that Pink Floyd have added a fifth show to their scheduled concerts at Wembley Empire Pool. The new date is sold-out without the box office even opening due to ticket requests already received in the mail by promoter Harvey Goldsmith. Mailbag published a letter with the title "Tickets prices: do we NEED flying pigs?" in which a reader complained about tickets prices of £3.75 and £4.25 for the upcoming Pink Floyd concerts at Wembley Empire Pool. He wrote that Wembley is not even a good concert venue. From the back, the stage looks minute, and there are also sound problems. Even if the concerts have special effects such as flying planes, thunder flashes, lasers, or even flying pigs, the ticket prices are still too high. Fans would surely prefer to see a concert without many effects if prices are reasonable.

March 12, 1977 - Melody Maker (U.K.) **reported** that Pink Floyd will perform at Wembley Empire Pool on March 15-19. All concerts, which start at 8 p.m. are sold out. The show will be a lavish production, and they will be playing material from the 'Animals' album, which has climbed to the top of the British charts and is also in the American top ten.

March 19, 1977 - Melody Maker (U.K.) **reported** that Pink Floyd are playing at Wembley Empire Pool March 16-19. All concerts, which start at 8 p.m. are sold out. The band is personally uncharismatic, and their special effects have been taken to new heights with a flying pig. But their music, which is unsurprising, is becoming just a background for their visuals.

March 20, 1977 - The Sunday Times (U.K.) **published** a concert review by Derek Jewell of Pink Floyd's concerts at the Empire Pool, Wembley, England on March 15-19, 1977. "Entertainment? Scarcely. Arguably, it's closer to somber modern conservatoire music." "Rarely, if ever, can so-called popular music have dealt so relentlessly in images of bleakest pessimism." " . . . their presentation is the ultimate in brilliantly staged theatre of despair . . ."

March 24, 1977 - Rolling Stone (U.S.) reviewed the Pink Floyd album, 'Animals' with an article titled, "Floyd's feckless fauna" by Frank Rose. Rose wrote that Pink Floyd has replaced the romance of outer space with the horror of spacing out. The songs on 'Animals' deal with subjects like loneliness, death and lies. The warm sax on 'Dark Side of the Moon' and 'Wish You Were Here' has been replaced by the poor substitute of thin and brittle David Gilmour guitar solos. The vocals are wooden, and the music is complex but lacks depth. Pink Floyd has turned bitter and morose and is being "metamorphosed into a noodle factory." Their message is "pointless and tedious."

Also in this issue, Random Notes reported that the 'Whitehouse' referred to on the Pink Floyd album, 'Animals,' is Mary Whitehouse, the British crusader against indecency who protested the playing of Chuck Berry's song 'My-Ding-a-Ling' by the BBC.

Also reported in Random Notes was the information that Pink Floyd requested that a London studio make a quadraphonic, Dolbyized, 30 ips recording of pigs grunting for their concerts. Also in this issue is a report that the price of record albums is increasing again. A year ago, prices for records increased from $5.98 to $6.98, and now they are increasing again to $7.98 for established artists. Pink Floyd's album, 'Animals,' is a $7.98 release.

March 26, 1977 - Melody Maker (U.K.) published an article titled, "Welcome to the machines" by Karl Dallas. The article was about the Pink Floyd concerts at the Empire Pool, Wembley in London, England, and began on the afternoon before the first concert when representatives from the Greater London Council (GLC) are forcing Pink Floyd to halt their light show rehearsal in order to check that the inflatable pig had been secured by a safety line as they had ordered. An annoyed Roger Waters is quoted yelling orders to the pig. "Halt pig." "Revolve pig." "Open rear vent.

Thphthphthphthphthphthphthphthphth . . . !" The GLC members ignored the final order, and Waters muttered, "Bloody wankers."

In an interview three days later, manager Steve O'Rourke explained the importance of the London concert to Pink Floyd. O'Rourke said, *"After all, other concerts are just concerts, but this is their home ground. When they play in London, it's got to be right. No half-measures are acceptable."*

Planning for these concerts began in June, when it was discovered that the preferred venues of Olympia and Earls Court would not be available. So the concerts had to be held at Wembley, a venue the band had vowed never to play at again. But with advance planning, the band hoped to make Wembley suitable for their show. By November, meetings were being held, power requirements were explained, and the GLC were consulted. A new electrical system was being installed that was hoped would handle Pink Floyd's power consumption. Their P.A. alone put out 30,000 watts.

Mick Kluczynski, Pink Floyd's production manager for the tour, explained, *"We told them we wanted 200 amps, but they didn't believe us. You'd think they would realize we know what we are talking about by now, but they always think they know better. I made a random check the other night and we were drawing over 100 amps then. When we got here, we found that instead of having a separate circuit for lights and sound, it all came in by the same cable, so we were getting the most terrible buzzes, especially when Dave Gilmour played. We brought in a 400 kVa generator so that we had separate supplies, but that didn't get rid of the noise on the first night. So that meant the power source wasn't the real explanation. After the show on Tuesday night, we went over the entire circuitry to find out what was going wrong. There are approximately 20,000 soldered joints in our entire system, so you can imagine that wasn't easy. One plug on one lamp on our projection screen can foil you if it's not wired exactly right. Do you know what we found? We had people working all night after the first show on Tuesday and eventually we discovered that, without telling us, the GLC people had gone over it on Monday night, putting these little earth wires onto everything. They said afterwards that they'd done it for safety reasons, and when we pointed out that they had ruined an entire concert, they said they couldn't care less. All they cared about was safety.*" The GLC had created a series of earth loops causing terrible humm in Pink Floyd's sound system. David Gilmour added, "*I'm the one who was most affected, because I'm the one with all the foot switches and special effects. They steam in at the last moment, when you are hoping to get the show on for 9,000 people who have paid their money, and then they do things like that without even telling you. After all the trouble and expense we go to, and then they fuck you up. In a band like this, everyone's got to be doing it, working at full efficiency on stage, technically and emotionally. I can get over things like that, but Roger can't. He gets very hung up about it.*"

O'Rourke continued, "*The position with Pink Floyd seems to be that everyone knows that we bring in a lot of equipment, so therefore they try to use us as a test case and say no to everything we want to do, in case anyone else might want to do the same. We started loading in our equipment on Friday, five days before the first concert. We'd already had long planning meetings so that they knew what we were intending to do. But because the GLC staff wouldn't work over the weekend, they refused to go through our equipment while we were setting up. Then on Monday they hit us with a list of things as long as your arm. They wouldn't allow us to use our cherry-picker lighting rigs unless they were rewired, the stage was too big, we couldn't hang the projection screen, we couldn't fly anything, they wouldn't allow fireworks.*"

Despite the complications, O'Rourke and promoter Harvey Goldsmith managed to find ways to satisfy the GLC and keep the concept of the show intact. Every lamp was secured by a safety chain, while plans to hang acoustic drapes around the hall to improve the acoustics had to be scrapped. Before the first show on Tuesday, Roger Waters supervised a lighting rehearsal. Roadies stood in place as the band while engineer Brian Humphries played a recording of the Pink Floyd concert in Dortmund from earlier on the tour. At the end of the rehearsal, Waters complained to O'Rourke, "*Is that it? Is*

that what it's going to look like tonight? Because, if it is, we're not going on." O'Rourke replied, "*They think that's what it's going to look like. We're working on it.*"

Later in the week on Thursday, O'Rourke explained, "*The last time we were here we had the whole house blacked out apart from the exit signs. Now the GLC have a new ruling which says that there's got to be a level of lighting equivalent to a bright moonlit night. That's what they told me. But apparently, the actual regulation merely says there must be a certain percentage of lighting, if possible, and providing it's not detrimental to the performance. Of course, there's got to be safety regulations, but all our stuff is designed with safety margins. Take the pig. It weighs 80 pounds, and it's carried by a three-quarter inch steel line, with a breaking strain of several tons. There is no regulation to say there's got to be a safety-line, but we had to work all night putting one on in such a way that it wouldn't foul anything as it moved over the auditorium. I asked for a copy of the regulations on Monday, and they said I'd have to write in. This sort of thing doesn't happen to us anywhere else in the world. On twenty shows in Europe, we haven't had any of these problems. Normally we set up, at a maximum, the day before, but often on the day of the show. Here we had Saturday, Sunday, and Monday before the show on Tuesday, and we still had a fucked-up show. It was really dreadful, and a large percentage of the blame is down to the GLC. Fortunately last night was close to being a very, very good show.*"

In addition to the technical problems, David Gilmour came down with the flu, pharyngitis, and tonsillitis before the shows began. But the show on Tuesday wasn't too bad, and by Thursday all the bugs had been worked out. The first set was the Animals sequence.

Robbie Williams, explained, "*Roger is the one who dreams up most of the effects.*" During the Tuesday rehearsal, Waters could be heard instructing the crew, "*I want the smoke to begin at the words 'all tight lips and cold feet' at the beginning of the second verse of Pigs. And I want as much smoke as you can give me. I don't want the audience to see the pig until the loud solo from Dave that comes after the verse.*" But the GLC stated, "*There's no way we're going to allow that much smoke in the auditorium."* O'Rourke replied, *"We'll open the doors at the back on the night and the fans will soon disperse it."*

Sound engineer Brian Humphries said, *"I prefer the pig to the aeroplane they had last time we were at Wembley. Every time it came zooming over, I used to duck. It was my first gig with the band, and it was the first time a lot of the music on this new album was played, as a matter of fact, and I was convinced it was going to crash right on to the mixer, Funnily, the GLC gave us fewer problems over that than this pig."*

Humphries runs the electronic equipment for the show from a 30-meter square section in the center of the hall. This section also houses the lighting desks, which are run by Graeme Fleming. Nigel Walker from Air Studios in London also helps control the set-up. Also in the mixing area are maintenance engineer Nigel Taylor, and Derek Unwin who records every Pink Floyd concert on a Nakamichi cassette deck. Seth Goldman mixes the monitor sound on stage and the control area. Andy Shields has a team that runs the film projector that shows Ralph Steadman cartoons. This projector is on a 17-foot tower behind the stage, and it projects onto a 32-foot back projection screen suspended above the stage. Roger Waters wears headphones during the concert that allows him to listen to the click track on the film, which keeps the band in sync with the film. During the rehearsals, an inflatable family rose from the stage. Mark Fisher said, *"This is nothing compared to what we are planning for the American tour. We'll have nine extra blow-ups. One of our ideas is a blow-up refrigerator with a door that opens and spills out sausages. Another is a VW beetle."*

New Musical Express (U.K.) published an article titled, "Eyeless in the Galaxy" by Mick Farren that reviewed the Pink Floyd concert at Wembley in London. Farren wrote that the band members were dwarfed by their hardware, such as lighting cranes, a quadraphonic sound system, and a huge circular screen. They looked more like technicians than rock stars. The visuals gave the impression of a "depressingly hopeless journey through a menacingly sterile cosmos."

On a circular screen above the band, boiling seas of blood crashed against faceless monoliths, a flower opened then closed into a steel ball, and a mechanical triceratops walked across an alien landscape. Faceless human beings tumbled through space or cowered in the corner of an energy cube. Fog slithered and billowed across the stage. When David Gilmour played his steel guitar, a lighting rig descended to a couple of feet above his head, bathing him in red light, before changing to white light and moving away. The climax of the show was a huge reflective disc that revolved in two directions, casting a web of pencil thin beams of red, blue, purple and white light into the audience. When it stopped revolving, the effect was breathtaking. Then there was darkness and the Pink Floyd were gone. The crowd roared and two small orange lights were lit on the lighting cranes on either side of the stage, which began to move towards the audience. The lights dimmed and Pink Floyd reemerged for an encore. However, despite the technical brilliance, the music was overwhelmed by the visuals. "There is too much overpowering technology and too much dull pain."

Sounds (U.K.) published a retrospective review of the Pink Floyd album, 'Meddle.' They wrote that while parts of the album are impressive, it is inconsistent. 'Echoes' had "large unwieldy portions of vague dreck," and much of it is "superfluous space muzak."

Also in this issue was a report on the Pink Floyd concert at Wembley Empire Pool, London. The concert began with quadraphonic 'baaas' to begin the song, 'Sheep.' During the song, two claw-like lighting towers came out of the darkness of the stage, trailing sparks, and shot red, blue and green lights at the audience and band, then rose to the ceiling and swooped down to head level, lighting each musician. Wind effects lead into the next song, 'Pigs on the Wing.' This was followed by the song, 'Dogs.' As David Gilmour sang the lead vocals, dry ice filled the stage with fog, and the lighting towers swooped down to illuminate him, five feet above his head. Then the lights changed to electric blue and scaned the audience. Dogs barking could be heard in quadraphonic. A hundred feet above the stage appeared an inflatable family, with white light emanating from within. They included a suited businessman, a gross wife, and a rotund evil-faced son in painted shorts. The wife and child deflated, but the businessman floated down to a few feet above head level as it deflated, and then inflated. This was followed by the song, 'Pigs on the Wing.' The next song, 'Pigs,' began as a giant inflatable pig sailed across the concert hall before disappearing into the stage. As for the music, the reviewer said that the musicians were as good as their material, but that their material was below par. At the conclusion of 'Pigs,' the band announced that they were taking a twenty minute break.

The second set opened with 'Shine On You Crazy Diamond,' and the giant projection screen behind the band came to life with images of the sea, beaches, gentle movement, and Vaseline photography. Roger Waters' vocals stumbled and ruined the song. Dick Parry's sax solo on the song was dilute and foetid. 'Welcome to the Machine' followed, with a superb film of a steel insect parading across a desert landscape. The music complimented the film. 'Have a Cigar' was the first song that was better musically than the record, with nice soloing and gritty vocals. Snowy White upstaged Gilmour with his solo. 'Wish You Were Here' was introduced with a transistor radio and more dry ice. The screen showed a film of a figure falling through blue sky, the sky cracked, the figure fell into emptiness, and into endless corridors. The set ended with the song, 'Shine On You Crazy Diamond, Part 2,' and featured a giant glass flower rising from the stage. A spotlight shone on the flower, creating a million beams of light that hypnotized, mesmerized and astonished the audience. The encore was the song 'Money,' and featured tapes, hopeless vocals, a sax solo, and a film.

April 2, 1977 - Melody Maker (U.K.) published a letter in Mailbag titled, "Pink Floyd: Them v. Us" in which a reader wrote that Pink Floyd were excellent at Knebworth in 1975, but when he saw them again on Thursday for a substantial sum of money, all he got was an inflatable pig, various animal noises, and a poor excuse for music. The sound was excellent, but the performance was clinical and uninspired. He thought he saw David Gilmour yawn at one point, and Rick Wright

seemed pedestrian. 'Taking Off' reported that Pink Floyd will be appearing at the New Bingley Hall in Stafford on March 31, 1977. The concert is sold out. The show features spectacular effects and lighting, but the music is the same as on the albums.

April 9, 1977 - Melody Maker (U.K.) published two letters from readers abut the recent Pink Floyd concerts. Teresa Wright attended the Wednesday show stating that it was a fine performance. She was disgusted by Michael Oldfield's trivial non-comments of the concert and felt that he was categorizing Pink Floyd as a rock and roll band, and was disappointed because the fans were not dancing in the aisles. The band was brilliant and obviously way above the head of reviewer Oldfield.

The second letter from Julia Stanley questioned Oldfield's comments that great performers can make their audience run riot and go berserk. Pink Floyd moves their audiences by music alone. The concert was amazing and masterful, with stirring music and a spectacular lightshow. In the future, reviewer Michael Oldfield should be sent to concerts such as Barry White or the Osmonds.

Sounds (U.K.) published a review of the Pink Floyd concert at New Bingley Hall, Stafford, England on March 31, 1977. The reviewer, Hugh Feidler, felt that the Stafford show was much better than the earlier shows at Wembley in London, because it was away from the press who generally didn't like Pink Floyd. Visually, the show featured a stunning light show, an inflatable family, a flying pig, and films. The music "built up to an almost frightening level of intensity as it swept across the hall from the front, back and sides." David Gilmour played effectively with Snowy White, the extra guitarist, who also excelled on his solo on 'Have a Cigar.'

May 5, 1977 - The Phoenix News (U.S.) published an article titled, "Pink Floyd Puts On a Circus" by Bill Boyles that reviewed the Pink Floyd concert in Phoenix, Arizona. Boyles wrote that Pink Floyd's quadraphonic sound system was operated with such precision that it sounded like a Hollywood "Sensurround" production, with pigs squealing, eerie howls, and barking dogs prowling around the arena. Giant "Fat City" balloon people with lights inside made appearances during songs from the 'Animals' album. The second half of the concert featured songs from the 'Wish You Were Here' album, and featured a giant circular movie screen playing animated films to accompany the songs. The music worked perfectly with the visuals.

May 28, 1977 - Sounds (U.K.) reported that a cloudburst nearly cancelled the Pink Floyd concert at Anaheim Stadium, California, but the rain luckily ended shortly after it began. Some fans thought the rain was part of Pink Floyd's special effects.

June 27, 1977 - The Montreal Gazette (Canada) published an article titled, "Pink Floyd just right for Olympic Stadium" by Bill Provick. Provick felt that Pink Floyd were the perfect choice to play at the Olympic Stadium in Montreal in July. The Pink Floyd sound system can make a large stadium feel intimate, and their massive visuals "compensate for the distances involved in stadium concerts." The reviewer's initial reaction to the bands last album, 'Wish You Were Here,' was disappointment because it was dull and detached, but on repeated listenings, it became hypnotic. The new album, 'Animals,' is not as distant, and the band sounds "more natural." It is an album "to be enjoyed over and over again."

The Cleveland Press (U.S.) published an article titled, "Stadium rocks, inside and out" by Bruno Bornino. Bornino wrote that Pink Floyd preformed before a world record crowd of 83,223 at Cleveland Stadium on Saturday, June 25, 1977. Jules Belkin, one of this sponsors of the event, stated, *"This is the largest crowd to ever watch a single act. We could have sold another 20,000 tickets, but it wouldn't have been fair to jam that many people into the Stadium. Pink Floyd is a band that must be seen as well as heard, so we stopped the sale so that the people with tickets could enjoy the show."* Tickets were $9.50 and $10.50.

    The show was spectacular. It started at 9 p.m. when the bands BAC-111 airplane

flew low over the crowd, shaking the stadium. Ten minutes later, the band began the first set, which consisted of songs from their new album, 'Animals.' As they performed 'Sheep,' "dozens of life-size paper sheep were parachuted on the delighted fans." Later, seven large helium balloons, one a pink pig, were floated over the heads of the audience. The second half was 'Wish You Were Here,' during which a large circular screen "showed films of beauties, beasts, bleeding buildings, UFOs, geometric figures in brilliant colors, and other symbolic pictures." For the first encore, the band played 'Money,' and followed it with a spectacular fireworks display. A second encore of 'Us and Them' followed.

The Plain Dealer (U.S.) published an article titled, "Rock: Floyd dazzles with sights and sounds" by Jane Scott that reviewed the Pink Floyd concert at Municipal Stadium, Cleveland on June 25, 1977. Scott wrote that the band arrived in eight tractor-trailers and two flatbed trucks, and had a crew of 26 people. Ten white umbrella-like trees that cost $5,000 each decorated the stage, and a 40-foot wide movie screen was erected in the back. Quadraphonic sound was used with three black speakers set up in the upper stands. A downpour delayed the start of the concert by 30 minutes. When the music began, it rained sheep, "white paper sheep with black noses and tails descended in little white parachutes." The vocals weren't as clear as the instruments, but Gilmour's guitar was clear and sweet. 83,199 fans saw a 50-foot pink pig float on wires over the heads of the audience. On the screen, movies of UFOs, beautiful women, and bleeding buildings were shown. A big metal petal with a silver center sparkled during 'Wish You Were Here.' The band returned for two encores, the second being, 'Us and Them.'

June 30, 1977 - Rolling Stone (U.S.) published an article titled, "Pink Floyd's optic nerve" by Mikal Gilmore that reviewed the Pink Floyd concert at Anaheim Stadium, California on May 6, 1977. Gilmore wrote that Pink Floyd's vision is "grandiose and lofty," and their music is "meticulous and artful." In concert they use seven helium balloons, three firework fusillades, and a giant circular projection screen, and their show is a "sensory banquet."

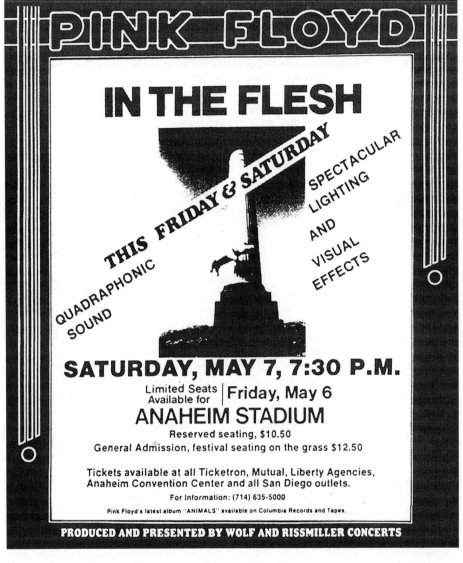

The show began with an airplane flying over the stadium with the words "Welcome, Pink Floyd" in computerized lights on the bottom. The music was full of splendor and seemed to originate from the sky. The first set was 'Animals.' David Gilmour used flangers and tape delays on his guitar, Rick Wright played synthesizer fills and textured organ, Roger Waters added repetitive bass lines, and Nick Mason played rhythmic flurries. The sound was powerful, full, and balanced. Visually, a pig was sent floating over the audience before it was sacrificed in a burst of flame. Films shown during the 'Wish You

Were Here' set included a decapitation, and a sea of blood. For an encore, they played 'Money,' complete with fireworks.

Scene Magazine (U.S.) reported on the Pink Floyd concert at Cleveland Stadium on June 25, 1977. Asked how the concert was, David Gilmour replied, *"Fine, thank you very much."* The band gave no interviews and manager Steve O'Rourke said that they hadn't given any interviews in three years. The band spent over $3,000 on fireworks for the show, and Mel Welch of Atlanta, a trained pyrotechnic, oversaw them.

July 2, 1977 - The Montreal Gazette (Canada) published an article titled, "Pink Floyd's high – on golf" by Juan Rodriguez. Next Wednesday, Pink Floyd will play the final concert of their current tour before 80,000 fans at Montreal's Olympic Stadium. They will be using approximately $2,000,000 worth of equipment, including smoke bombs, fireworks, two hydraulic cranes with attached lights, two light towers, a large movie screen, strobe lights, quadraphonic sound, plastic inflatable animals, and a huge pink pig that hovers over the audience. They employ 60 crew members, and ten trucks are needed to haul their equipment. But the band is "virtually unlistenable without the aid of mind altering condiments." With 'Dark Side of the Moon,' it was clear that "the drug taking on a mass scale was the key to Pink Floyd's success." But, according to a crew member, the band's "biggest high on the tour is playing golf on their days off."

Also in this issue is an article about Norman Perry of Montreal, who is the advance man for Pink Floyd, and the American agent for Brockum, a European pop merchandise company. He travels to cities and checks out concert venues in advance for the band. Perry said, "With a crew of 60, it's important to get everyone in and out of the hotel quickly."

July 6, 1977 - The Montreal Gazette (Canada) published an article titled, "Say, who are these guys" by Juan Rodriguez. Rodriguez wrote that the members of Pink Floyd checked into the Hotel Bonaventure yesterday afternoon, prior to their concert at Olympic Stadium. They like to remain anonymous to the public, and they generally shun the press. Their agent Allan Frey said, *"It's the total group concept that counts, not the individuals. There's nothing that they themselves can add."* A crew member added, *"They're not stuck up or snobbish. They just don't like giving interviews."* Frey also stated, *"Of course, they're looking forward to playing at the Olympic Stadium. They know how the Quebec fans feel about them and it's a special feeling for them, too."*

Spotted in a coffee shop, Nick Mason said, *"I honestly can't say that I have a different feeling playing here. During the past*

four years, the audiences have become less outstanding. You really can't tell the difference. I do know that we've always had a strong following in France. In 1967, long before we were known in America, the French supported us heavily." The Montreal concert is the last show of the tour. Asked when they might tour again, Mason said, *"Not for a long while, I hope. Physically, it's very tiring."* Roger Waters set off to play golf at a local golf course fifteen minutes after arriving at their hotel.

July 7, 1977 - The Montreal Gazette (Canada) published an article titled, "Pink Floyd: So who needs music?" by Juan Rodriguez that reviewed the Pink Floyd concert at the Olympic Stadium in Montreal on July 6, 1977. Rodriguez wrote that the Pink Floyd's spectacular light and sound effects were lost in the vast Olympic Stadium. Their lighting could not fill the stadium, but strobe lights placed in the audience helped. The stage sound was more of a rumble. The first half of the concert consisted of songs from the album 'Animals,' which used "hokey helium inflated objects" to express the mundane ideas, half-baked existentialism, and absurdity of the piece. David Gilmour's guitar solos were formless time fillers used to lead into light and sound effects. The lyrics were "weird and wandering," and difficult to comprehend. The highlight of the first half was Gilmour hassling the crowd by saying, "If you want to shout and scream, go outside. I'm just here to sing the song."

The second half of the show was livelier, with excellent quadraphonic sound. Much of their musical gadgetry sounded like gizmos from cheap science fiction films, but at times made the stadium sound like "a cathedral spaceship." During 'Shine On' they projected a film showing a human floating in the sky and turning into a leaf. During 'Machine' crawling reptiles, a beheading, and a sea of blood were shown on the screen, which seemed like a cross between Disney's Fantasia and Edgar Allan Poe. During a couple of the guitar and keyboard solos, hydraulic lighting cranes hovered over the musicians. At the end of the second set, an illuminated mirror ball reflecting blue and pink lights was "hypnotizing and spectacular." The set was followed by fireworks over the stadium. They ended with 'Money' as the first encore, and 'Echoes' as the second encore. [Ed. note - the second encore was actually 'Us & Them']

The Toronto Star (Canada) published an article titled, "Canada's largest rock audience turns out for Pink Floyd band" by Martin Melhuish. Melhuish wrote that Pink Floyd held the largest single rock concert in Canadian history at the Olympic Stadium, Montreal, on July 6, 1977. More than 85,000 fans turned out to see the band. An airplane circled the stadium with the words, "C'est fantastique." The concert grossed more than $850,000. The music was cosmic, but suffered from an inconsistent sound system. In the first half of the show they played songs from the album, 'Animals,' with giant inflatable plastic animals, cars, and human figures hovering over the stage. During the second half they played the album, 'Wish You Were Here,' and projected brilliant animated films on the circular screen. Pink Floyd is the premiere band right now.

July 23, 1977 New Musical Express (U.K.) published an article titled, "Floyd blow up cars as fans lob fireworks" by Miles that reviewed the Pink Floyd concert at Madison Square Garden on July 3, 1977. It was the eve of the Fourth of July and, even before the concert began, fireworks were being set off in the upper tiers of the Garden. Soon they were being thrown down onto the crowd below, making it very had to concentrate on the music being performed. One rolled under the reviewers seat, while another set fire to the T-shirt of a person five seats away. The tension put an edge on David Gilmour's guitar playing, but Roger Waters was not happy. The crowd roared approval when an inflatable family rose from the side of the stage, complete with a television and a car. But at that point, a firework landed on the stage near David Gilmour, causing Roger Waters to say, "*You stupid motherfucker. And anyone else in here with fireworks, just fuck off and let us get on with it.*" Then, the Garden filled with smoke, and a giant inflatable pig appeared with pencil thin beams of lights coming out of its eyes, and flew around the auditorium. This was followed by a 20-minute intermission. The second half of the show was the album, 'Wish You Were

Here,' with quadraphonic sound sweeps, movie sequences, and hydraulic lighting platforms with revolving lights. But due to the firework danger, the reviewer couldn't concentrate on the show. However, the encore, 'Money,' did come alive, with a movie of tumbling coins and scenes of gold discs.

August 1977 - Vibrations (Canada) published an article titled, "Pink Floyd – Ho hum and not much more" by Peter Overton that reviewed the Pink Floyd concert at the Olympic Stadium, Montreal on July 6, 1977. With an attendance of 80,000, it was a major happening. During the first half-hour before the sun set, Pink Floyd seemed little more than "incidental entertainment at a be-in." After darkness arrived, senses softened. Pink Floyd floated sheep down, and their inflatable pig up. But during the performance of songs from 'Animals,' the inflatable figures floated against the backdrop of the stadium instead of over the crowd, "like children's toys gone astray." And, unless you were close to the stage, the lights seemed unimportant, the smoke and fireworks were not noticeable, and the band members were invisible. The films were interesting, particularly the one shown during 'Welcome to the Machine,' but they were too small in comparison to the size of the stadium. The music itself wasn't bad, when it could be heard. The band are masters of sound textures and colors, and screaming and wooshing effects would travel around the stadium but, at times, the stadium size caused the sound system produce two beats. Furthermore, the sight lines were bad, with sound towers in the way. Even the band did not appear to care for the concert, but most of the fans seemed to enjoy the show.

September 24, 1977 - Melody Maker (U.K.) published the 1977 Readers' Poll results. In the British section, Pink Floyd was #7 under Band, and 'Animals' was #6 under Best Album. In the International section, Pink Floyd was #3 under Best Live Act, #6 under Band, and 'Animals' was #6 under Best Album.

October 1977 - Creem Magazine (U.S.) reviewed the Pink Floyd album, 'Animals' with an article titled, "Pink Floyd's Heart of Darkness: A Crash Course in Pig Latin" by Ira

1978
David Gilmour and Wet Dream

Robbins. Robbins wrote that the album is "out and out spite for the human race." It has "enough venom contained in the grooves to poison an entire sheep farm." Pink Floyd are "as miserable as any band I've ever heard."

December 10, 1977 - Melody Maker (U.K.) published a question from a German reader asking what kind of acoustic guitar, effects and amplification Roger Waters used at the Dortmund concerts for the acoustic songs from 'Animals.' Waters used an Ovation electric custom Legend through an MXR Phase 90, which was fed directly into the PA and monitor system. The sound was enhanced with an Apnex Aural Exciter.

January 7, 1978 - Sounds (U.K.) reported that Nick Mason produced the Damned's second album.

February 1978 - Trouser Press (U.S.) published an article about Syd Barrett titled, "Syd Barrett: Careening Through Life" by Kris DiLorenzo. Various acquaintances of Syd Barrett offered their insights into his career, including Glen Buxton of the Alice Cooper Band, Barrett's former flatmate Duggie Fields, Barrett's former girlfriend Lynsey Korner, Pink Floyd's former publisher Bryan Morrison, Barrett's former photographer Mick Rock, Jerry Shirley who played drums on Barrett's recording sessions, Twink who played drums with Barrett's band Stars, and David Gilmour who is Pink Floyd's current guitarist.

David Gilmour talked about Barrett's songwriting, saying, "*Syd was one of the great rock and roll tragedies. He was one of the most talented people and could have given a fantastic amount. He really could write songs and if he had stayed right, could have beaten Ray Davies at his own game.*"

Duggie Fields talked about fame, explaining that Barrett told him "*Duggie, you're 23 and you're not famous.*"

Mick Rock talked about Barrett's flat in the 1960s, saying it was "*a burnt out place, the biggest hovel, the biggest shit-heap, a total*

acid shell, the craziest flat in the world. There were so many people it was like a railway station. Two cats Syd had, one called Pink, and one called Floyd, were still lying in the flat after he left. He just left them there. Those were the cats they used to give acid to. You know what heavy dope scenes were like."

Duggie Fields talked about living above Pink Floyd, saying, "*They used to rehearse in the flat and I used to go downstairs and put on Smokey Robinson as loud as possible. I don't know where they all arrived from, but I went to architecture school and so did Rick and Roger. I don't quite remember how I met them all. I just remember suddenly being surrounded by the Pink Floyd and hundreds of groupies instantly.*"

Lynsey Korner explained the problems people have after they became stars, calling it "*chronic schizophrenia,*" and saying "*it got a bit crazed.*" Barrett began to "*act a little bonkers.*"

Duggie Fields explained, "*Oh, he went more than slightly bonkers. It must have been very difficult for him. I think the pressures on Syd before that time must have upset him very much, the kind of pressure where it takes off very fast, which Pink Floyd did, and certainly in terms of the way people behaved towards them. I used to be speechless at the number of people who would invade our flat, and how they would behave towards anyone who was in the group, especially girls. I'd never seen anything like it. Some of the girls were stunning, and they would literally throw themselves at Syd. He was the most attractive one. Syd was a very physically attractive person. I think he had problems with that. I saw it even when he was out of the group. People kept coming around and he would actually lock himself in his room. Like if he made the mistake of answering the front door before he'd locked himself in his room, he found it very difficult to say no. He'd have these girls pounding on his bedroom door all night, literally, and he'd be locked inside, trapped. He did rather encourage that behavior to a certain extent, but then he didn't know what to do with it. He would resent it."*

Glen Buxton remembered when Pink Floyd stayed with the Alice Cooper group at their house in Venice, California during the Pink Floyd's 1967 U.S. tour. Buxton said, *"Syd Barrett I remember. I don't remember him ever saying two words. It wasn't because he was a snob. He was a very strange person. He never talked, but we'd be sitting at dinner and all of a sudden I'd pick up the sugar and pass it to him, and he'd shake his head like 'Yeah, thanks.' It was like I heard him say 'Pass the sugar.' It's like telepathy, it really was. It was very weird. You would find yourself right in the middle of doing something, as you were passing the sugar or whatever, and you'd think 'Well, damn, I didn't hear anybody say anything!' That was the first time in my life I'd ever met anybody that could actually do that freely. And this guy did it all the time. The crew used to say he was impossible on the road. They'd fly a thousand miles, get to the gig, he'd get up on stage and wouldn't have a guitar. He would do things like leave all his money in his clothes in the hotel room, or on the plane. Sometimes, they'd have to fly back and pick up his guitar. I didn't pick up that he was a drug casualty, although there were lots at the time who would do those exact things because they were drugged out. But Syd was definitely from Mars or something."*

Jerry Shirley talked about Barrett's playing, saying, *"When he plays a song, it's very rare that he plays it the same way each time, any song. And some songs are more off-the-wall than others. When he was with the Floyd, towards the very end, Syd came in once and started playing this tune, and played it completely different. Every chord change just kept going somewhere else, and he'd keep yelling "Have You Got It Yet?" I guess, then, it was Roger who kind of suddenly realized, 'Oh dear!' It was getting absolutely impossible for the band. They couldn't record because he'd come in and do one of those 'Have You Got It Yet' numbers, and then on stage he would either not play, or he'd hit his guitar and turn it out of tune, or do nothing. They were pulling their hair out. They decided to bring in another guitarist to compliment, so Syd wouldn't have to play guitar and maybe he'd just do the singing. Dave came in and they were a five-piece for about four or five weeks. It got better*

because Dave was together in what he did. Then the ultimate decision came down that if they were going to survive as a band, Syd would have to go. Now I don't know whether Syd felt it and left, or whether he was asked to, but he left. Dave went through some real heavy stuff for the first few months. Syd would turn up at London gigs and stand in front of the stage looking up at Dave, 'That's my band.'"

Mick Rock remembered David Gilmour and Syd Barrett in the early days in Cambridge, saying, *"They used to play things like 'In the Midnight Hour' and Syd would go watch Dave play because I think Dave had got his chords down a bit better than Syd in the early days. Syd was always a bit weird about Dave. That was his band, the Floyd."*

Duggie Fields explained what Barrett did after he left Pink Floyd, saying, *"When he gave up the group, he took up painting again for a bit, but he never enjoyed it. He didn't really have a sense of direction. He used to lie in bed every morning and I would get this feeling like the wall between our rooms didn't quite exist, because I'd know that Syd was lying in bed thinking 'What do I do today? Shall I get out of bed? If I get out of bed, I can do this, and I can do that, or I can do that, or I could do that.' He had the world at his feet, all the possibilities, and he just couldn't choose. He had great problems committing himself to any action. As for committing himself to doing anything for any length of time, he was the kind of person who'd change in the middle. He'd set off, lose his motivation, and start questioning what he was doing, which might just be walking down the street. Sometimes he'd be completely jolly and then just snap. You could never tell what he was like. He could be fabulous. He was the sort of person who had amazing charm. If he wanted your attention, he'd get it. He was very bright. After he left the group he was very much aware of being a failure. I think that was quite difficult, coming to terms with that."*

Duggie Fields explained that visitors to Barrett's flat in the 1960s thought, *"Just give Syd mandrakes and he'll be friendly."* What eventually happened was that *"He just left them and then rang me up and said that I had to get rid of them. I said he had to get rid of them but I actually did in the end. I said 'Look, Syd wants you out. He's coming back!' They were a bit frightened of him because he did have a violent side."*

Duggie Fields speculated on whether Barrett was in control when making his solo album, saying, *"Well, yes and no. He really didn't have to have that much control before, but when you have to provide your own motivation all the time it is difficult, certainly in terms of writing a song. When it came down to recording, there were always problems. He was not at his most together recording the album. He had to be taken there sometimes, and he had to be got. It didn't seem to make any difference whether it was making him happy or unhappy. He'd been through that, the excitement of it, the first time around."*

Jerry Shirley talked about the recording session for the song, 'Dominoes,' and what happened when they played the tape of Barrett's guitar solo backwards, saying, *"It played back and the backwards guitar sounded great. The best lead he ever played. The first time out and he didn't put a note wrong."*

Shirley also talked about recording the song, 'If It's In You,' saying, *"That is a classic example of Syd in the studio. Between that and talking in very obscure abstracts. It's all going on in his head, but only little bits of it manage to get out of his mouth. And then the way he sings, he goes into that scream. Sometimes he can sing a melody absolutely fine, and the next time round he'll sing a totally different melody, or just go off key. 'Rats,' in particular, was really odd. That was just a very crazed jam, and Syd had this lyric that he just shouted over the top. It's quite nuts. But some of his songs are very beautiful. You never knew from one day to the next exactly how it would go."*

As to whether Barrett was doing some things on purpose, Shirley said, *"I honestly couldn't say. Sometimes he does it to put everybody on, sometimes he does it because he's genuinely paranoid about what's happening around him. He's like the weather. He changes. For every ten things he says that are off-the-wall and odd, he'll say one thing that's completely coherent and right on the ball. He'll seem out of touch with what's gone on just before. Then he'll suddenly turn around and say 'Jerry, remember the day we went to get a burger down at the Earl's Court Road?' complete recall of something that happened a*

long time ago. Just coming and going, all the time."

Talking about Barrett's live performance at the Olympia in London, Shirley explained, *"He was going to do it. He wasn't going to do it. It was on and off. So finally we said 'Look Syd, come on man, you can do it.' We got up. I played drums. Dave played bass and he managed to get through a few songs. It got good, and then, after about the fourth song, Syd said 'Oh great. Thanks very much,' and walked off. We tried, you know."*

Duggie Fields talked about what Barrett did after he moved back to Cambridge and tried to become a doctor, saying, *"Yes, a doctor. And he and Gayla were going to get married and live in Oxford. He had a bit of the suburban dream. That was a very bizarre sort of thing underlying him. He had lots of concepts that he found very attractive like that. He didn't really like all the one-night stands. He wanted the marriage and that bit, in the back of his head."*

Twink remembered his friendship with Barrett, explaining, *"I didn't know him closely for that long, but I was in the same space and I could understand exactly where he was at. I thought he was very together, you know. As a friend it was a very warm relationship. No bad vibes at all. We didn't have any crazy scenes."*

Twink also remembered the show Stars played at the Corn Exchange in Cambridge, saying, *"We just weren't ready for it. It was a disastrous gig. The reviews were really bad and Syd was really hung up about it, so the band folded. He came round to my house and said he didn't want to play anymore. He didn't explain. He just left. I was really amazed working with him, at his actual ability as a guitar player."*

Duggie Fields talked about seeing Barrett in London's Speakeasy Club after he quit Stars, saying, *"I wasn't sure he recognized me. I was with some people he'd known for years. We talked for about five minutes, but did he really know who we were? That was when he was starting to get heavy and he didn't look like the same kind of person at all."*

Jerry Shirley remembered seeing Barrett in EMI Studios in 1975 when Pink Floyd were recording the album Wish You

Were Here. Shirley said, *"The last time I saw him was possibly the last time the guys in the Floyd saw him, too. They were putting the finishing touches on 'Wish You Were Here.' Earlier that day, David Gilmour had gotten married and they had to work that night, so EMI had this roundtable dinner in the canteen for them. Across the table from me was this overweight Hare Krishna-looking chap. I thought maybe it was just someone who somebody knows. I looked at Dave and he smiled. Then I realized it was Syd. The guy had to weigh close to 200 pounds and had no hair on his head. It was a bit of a shock. But after a minute I plucked up enough courage to say hello. I introduced my wife and I dunno, I think he just laughed. I asked him what he was doing lately. 'Oh, you know, not much. Eating. Sleeping. I get up, eat, go for a walk, sleep.'"*

Shirley also explained what happened when Pink Floyd was listening to the playback of the song 'Shine On You Crazy Diamond,' saying, *"When the song ended, Roger Waters turned to Syd and said 'Well Syd, what do you think of that?' He said 'Sounds a bit old.' I believe Syd just got up and split not too long after that. After two years of nobody seeing him, of all the days for him to appear out of nowhere!"*

Shirley speculated on the chance of Barrett recording again, saying, *"The last person to make that sort of effort was Dave, and they barely got him to do it. It was like pulling teeth. Since then I don't think there's anybody close enough to him to get him to do it. He would have to return to the planet long enough for someone to believe that he's got it in him to actually get through the sessions. And that would just be the first step. The guys really did persevere through those sessions. God! Especially Dave. Particularly in light of the way Syd was to him before. But I don't know if anybody, if he showed that he really wanted to try for it, then maybe one of them would make the effort."*

As to whether anyone has talked to Syd about his future, Shirley said, *"Oh, yeah. No chance. You'd get some sort of sense out of him, and then he'd just laugh at you. Lots of people tried lots of different things."*

Bryan Morrison talked about how Barrett left Pink Floyd, explaining, *"He didn't leave of his own free will, really. I mean, he*

kept threatening to leave. I think in the end it was by mutual agreement, because he was having some personal problems. He wasn't able to get it together anymore and, by agreement, he left the band."*

Morrison recalled Barrett's mental state afterwards, saying, *"Have you ever met Syd? Well, one of the main things, he had psychiatric problems and was actually in a sanatorium."*

Morrison talked about what Barrett has been doing in 1978, saying, *"He doesn't have any involvement with anything or anybody. He is a recluse, with about twenty-five guitars around him. I see him very rarely. I mean, I know where he is, but he doesn't want to be bothered. He just sits there on his own, watching television all day and getting fat. That's what he does."*

March 18, 1978 - Sounds (U.K.) reported that David Gilmour is working on a solo album, to be released in the summer.

March 1978 - Circus (U.S.) published an article titled, "Pink Floyd Still Anonymous and Happy." The members of Pink Floyd like to remain anonymous, and sometimes during their tours, they put on coats and mingle with their audiences as they leave the venue.

May 6, 1978 - New Musical Express (U.K.) reported that David Gilmour's solo album, titled, 'David Gilmour,' is to be released on May 12, 1978.

June 17, 1978 - Melody Maker (U.K.) published an article titled, "Heart of the Floyd" by Karl Dallas that featured an interview with David Gilmour. The interview, to promote Gilmour's new solo album, took place on the top floor of Britannia Row Studios in London, England. Gilmour began, *"When the Pink Floyd weren't very popular, we used to do a lot of interviews because we wanted to achieve some sort of success. But when you've achieved success, the record companies can do it without you having to get involved in the slog of that kind of promotion. Our attitude, if we have a collective attitude, is that, obviously, it's nice for the music to speak for itself as much as possible. But at the same time, it is nice to promote things a little bit. But we don't*

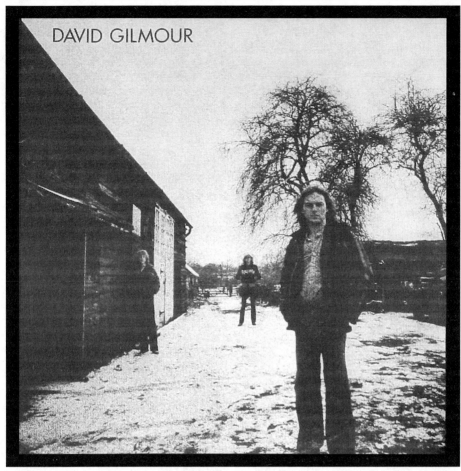

David Gilmour's first solo album.

need to do it much as the Pink Floyd. People listen, whether we promote it or not. That's what I'm promoting this new album for, so that it gets a listen. It's not so likely to get it if I don't."

How is your solo album, 'David Gilmour,' different than your work with Pink Floyd? Gilmour replied, "*I didn't try to make it the same, and I didn't try to make it different. I didn't have any intention of making a Pink Floyd sound. Some people have told me they think it sounds quite similar, and I suppose I'd have to agree that in some aspects, it does. It was less thought about than a Pink Floyd record, quicker to make, with the idea of catching a bit more immediacy, I suppose. I don't think the Floyd's music is too well conceived. I like to work that way, but if to put that amount of work and thought into it means that you lose spontaneity or immediacy, then*

that's a shame. It's not something that's deliberate, obviously. You try to keep as much of all that in as you possibly can. But at the same time, it's nice to have more than one direction to what you're doing. It's nice for me to have an alternative which is different, at least in the attitude and the way I'm going about it, even if some of it comes out sounding a little bit similar."

Have you thought about doing some solo concerts to promote the record? Gilmour replied, "*I haven't given it any great thought. I've recently done a little promo film for the album where I did some of the tracks live, and it was quite good fun, so I think I would enjoy doing that. I would hope it would be quite low key. It would be nice to have a change like that. When the Floyd is on the road, it is quite a monstrous machine, but we all do feel fairly much in control. It is fairly tenuous control at* times. There are a lot of aspects that you can't physically control all the time. The technology is all fairly well thought-out, but some of those things are very new, and it's all a bit Heath-Robinson at times. We get a few breakdowns and you start thinking you're losing control of the whole thing. The scope for musical freedom is getting less. There's always some, always bits, pieces, where you can have a blow sort of thing, but it's always the same places all the time, and consequently they start getting a bit predictable. There used to be more points where you could do that, more different points, but they are still there. I don't think it's necessarily inevitable it should be that way. I think we could change it if we wanted to. It just depends how much the emphasis of what we're trying to do is involved in trying to put over an idea, and how much of it is trying to play just music. Of course, our emphasis does change. It's different, depending upon the different people in the band. I think Roger's emphasis is more towards putting over the idea, and if bits of solo blowing get lost, then I don't think that's of any particular concern to him. My attitude is that we sometimes get a little too stuck in the presentation of the idea, and the balance is slightly tipped too far in that direction for my liking. Not much too much, but I'd prefer to see a freer area for playing."

How does the band make decisions? Gilmour replied, "*We do argue quite a lot over all sorts of things. But it's very hard to explain to an outsider how the power structure works.*"

What is the future of Pink Floyd? Gilmour replied, "*I can't see any reason why it shouldn't continue indefinitely. I don't think we've reached the full scope of what we're capable of, yet. As long as it's fun to do, and we're all enjoying it, and we think that something worthwhile comes out of it, I don't think there's any reason why we should stop or want to stop. We don't really need to. If we didn't want to, we could jack it in. I get the enjoyment of playing and making the records and doing the gigs, putting over something that's powerful and realistic to the people we play to. I get a lot out of it. Our goals were very different in the early days. We were so busy trying to be rich and successful and famous. Those were our goals, I think, mostly, as they are with most people in this business. And when you have something like 'Dark Side of* the Moon,' and all those goals suddenly disappear because you've got them, that is the point when you really have to decide what you're really in it for. That time was, really, terribly confusing for all of us, I guess. For a little while, it became difficult, because we didn't really know what we were in it for, or if we wanted to still be in it. There was definitely a danger point at that period. We could have easily packed the whole thing in after 'Dark Side of the Moon,' for a while there, and 'Wish You Were Here' was very indicative of our state of mind at the time. It was a terribly, terribly difficult record to make, simply because no one was really into it. Everyone was very confused. They weren't putting everything into the record that they could have done.*"

But `Wish You Were Here' is a powerful record. Gilmour replied, "*Yes, I think it's powerful because of that.*" Isn't the record about Syd Barrett? Gilmour explained, "*'Shine On You Crazy Diamond' was about Syd, as I understand it, but as it started growing, the rest of the album was written after that, and it grew to be a much wider thing, more about ourselves. I think 'Wish You Were Here' was more 'wish we were here,' than anything else. The 'Animals' concept didn't come up until the album was about three-quarters finished. I don't think Roger had it in his mind before, but at some point he realized how close the lyrics were on those tracks, and he changed the lyrics about a bit on 'Dogs,' which was called 'You've Got to Be Crazy' before that, and 'Sheep,' which was 'Raving and Drooling' before then. It all, obviously, fitted together in his mind, coming to mean that. It is a good thing, in the end, having to come to a collective decision, though. It knocks out some of the excesses, which might otherwise appear from us as individuals. I think I've been able to apply that lesson to my own album, though I suppose I'm naturally a fairly moderate person.*"

Only three of the songs on your solo album were written by you. Gilmour replied, "*My lyric writing being not all prolific, I sent Roy a tape of various bits and asked him if he'd fancy writing anything. This was actually after the start of the actual recording, with only like a week or two's recording time. The three that I have written started as ideas of words and music together. I can't sit down with a piece of paper in front of me and start writing words.*

I've never managed to do that. If there's a good basic idea that comes out, a feeling, then it's easier to work on from that. One song is about feeling desperate and worried and frightened about dying."

Does the fear of dying bother you? Gilmour replied, *"Yes, isn't it a thing that bugs you?"* No. Gilmour said, *"It's funny, that some people it doesn't, some people it does. It does bug me. Another one's about a particularly difficult moment in my love life, one of those things that's tricky to talk about, really, which is why they're down as songs. And another one's a slightly more positive feeling about my love life, too."*

Why doesn't the album come with a lyric sheet? Gilmour replied, *"I've never been keen on my lyric sheets because I'm not sure that my lyrics stand up."* The article also noted that Roger Waters was currently working in his home studio on a theme for the next Pink Floyd album.

New Musical Express (U.K.) reviewed David Gilmour's solo album, 'David Gilmour' with an article called "Asleep at the Wicket" by Neil Peters. Peters wrote that the songs are "alright," the rhythm section is "remarkably competent," but the album "stoops rather badly." He called it "A very Floyd-esque affair."

July 1978 - Beat Instrumental (U.K.) published an article titled, "David Gilmour – The Enigma Variations" by Tom Stock. Stock wrote that the Pink Floyd corporate reputation as an inaccessible enigma is only rivaled in rock music by that of the individual members of the band. Gilmour, Waters, Mason, and Wright embrace a policy of non-communication with the press and their public, which at times is both frustrating and self-indulgent. They require financial reward for their endeavors, yet remain unanswerable to the very people who provide that reward. They inhabit a carefully constructed cocoon which protects them from inquisitive eyes, and yet, when the time comes for the covers to be partially removed, expect the very people they've denied in the past to come running to sip the nectar for a brief moment.

What follows is a transcript of an hour-long conversation with David Gilmour in

which he explains the motives for this self-imposed exile, talks about his solo album, and touches lightly on other areas concerning the Pink Floyd. While much of the conversation involved short answers and left much unanswered by implication, it would be true to say that his body language was considerably more friendly than his oral language. He appeared, not surprisingly, to be totally out of practice communicating with a creature from the press and required prompting several times to extract anything like the information the interviewer had hoped to obtain. That said, however, once the tape recorder was switched off, he relaxed visibly, played the interviewer a couple of unheard-before demo tapes of Syd Barrett, and spent half an hour showing him around the facilities at Britannia Row Studios while playing a master tape of the solo album. This schizophrenic attitude to someone he must, by his own admission, have regarded as an invader of his privacy, seems to confirm that the self-imposed obsession with privacy has indeed become a way of life. The interviewer hoped that many readers would regret this narrow-minded view of the public, which has spent so much money placing him, and the others in the band, in this enviable position. That other major bands have managed to make their music, talk to explain their motives, and maintain healthy private lives is indisputable. If the Floyd really believe fame can be had for free they are, of course, entitled to that opinion. However, their freedom must cost their buying public some of the essential rapport that should exist between a band and its fans.

Why did you feel it necessary to make a solo album? Gilmour replied, *"It wasn't strictly necessary, it was just something to do, a bit of fun. I've always wanted to get into one, and now seemed a good time. When the Pink Floyd aren't working, it's good to have something to do."*

Is it as simple as that? Gilmour replied, *"Well, it's not quite as simple as that. There are other things, obviously, like it's nice not having to work to a compromise once in a while, which you obviously have to do in a group of any sort, unless one person is hard and fast boss. Working to a compromise is a good thing, but it's nice not to have to work within one all the time."*

So you were looking for a bit more

freedom outside the Floyd structure? Gilmour replied, "*It's not really freedom, no, it's just, no, maybe it is freedom. In a sense, it's freedom. It's not like I feel imprisoned by being within the Pink Floyd structure. I like that, and that is very rewarding and valuable. But it's nice not to be within it all the time. It's nice to have a change.*"

Did you control the album completely? Gilmour replied, "*Yes.*" From choosing the musicians to producing it yourself? Gilmour explained, "*I decided right at the beginning that I would control everything on it absolutely, just for once, from choosing the musicians, choosing the material, writing the material, the production . . .*"

Was the material pre-written, or did you write specifically for the album? Gilmour replied, "*I wrote for it. I didn't have a plan for an album right at the beginning. I jotted down a lot of short ideas, musical and lyrical, after the last Pink Floyd tour and went into our studio to rehearse and put down demos, and gradually it started taking shape. At that time, I didn't actually have any specific intention of making an album. I only decided once I had done the demos.*"

You were under no contractual obligation, so there were no legal hassles involved in making a solo album? Gilmour replied, "*Our contracts are worked so we don't have any specific time in which to produce a record.*"

Why did you choose Rick Wills and Willie Wilson to work with? Gilmour replied, "*Because they're good musicians, number one, and because they're friends of mine and we have a good empathy between us. They were very capable of doing the sort of things I wanted them to do, and also because it's partly down to them that I actually got around to doing it. They and my wife were instrumental in pushing me enough to get me started.*"

Would you take it as criticism if I said that I regard the album as being Floyd without the keyboards? Gilmour replied, "*No, I wouldn't take it as a criticism.*" Did you consciously move away from the grand keyboard structure of ... Gilmour said, "*Well, I didn't use a keyboard player, for one thing. I had to do it myself. As I said, I worked with these two guys, basically, who I know very well, and I thought working in the first place,*

at the beginning, with a keyboard player might prove restricting to some of the ideas. I did intend to get one in later on and go through all the stuff with a keyboard player, but it never worked out that I could get the right guy at the right time. So I didn't have a keyboard player. Finally, in the last count, when I was actually there recording, I didn't have a keyboard player and couldn't get one so I decided to try and do it myself. So I did it myself, and so they are very, very minimal and very basic."

The lack of keyboards does give your guitar a lot more room to work in than on the Floyd's albums, despite the superficial similarity in sound. Gilmour replied, "*This thing of it sounding a bit like the Floyd is not intentional. There was never any intention to sound like the Pink Floyd, but I do sound like me, and there's no way I can get around that. If I tried artificially to get around that, it would be pointless and it would also be pointless for me to make an album different to the Floyd unless I really wanted it. I think it is pretty different, but there are, obviously, at the same time similarities in the way I sing, in the way I play guitar. Basically I didn't try to make it the same as the Floyd, and I didn't try to make it different. I just wanted it to come out fairly natural.*"

There's also less studio trickery than on Floyd albums. Was this also intentional? Gilmour replied, "*There's quite a lot of overdubbing, but the same thing applies really. I didn't intend not to do that, or to do that. I just did each song as it felt right to me at the time, without wanting to go so deeply into it and think about it for so long that I lost the spontaneity. I did deliberately want to do it quite quickly, and do all the recording in a short space of time.*"

When I reviewed 'Animals' last year, I termed your guitar playing 'manic'. Your playing has come more to the fore on the more recent Floyd albums, and in places you've got the same demented sound on the solo album. Is this conscious? Gilmour replied, "*I haven't consciously developed it. I mean, 'Animals' was bound to sound demented because it was a demented album, right? The whole thing was, and I do try and play what I think will fit. I mean, I agree there's one song on the album where I still do a guitar passage with masses of fuzz on it, but that seemed to work at the time and appeared a reasonable thing to do."*

But 'Animals' was significant in placing your playing further out into the spotlight, so to speak. Will this be continued in the next Floyd project? Gilmour replied, *"I think there's been quite a lot of it to the fore going back. 'Wish You Were Here' had quite a lot of it to the fore. It's really a question of who's coming up with what. At the time of making 'Animals,' I was into playing a lot of guitar, and Rick was particularly into coming up with lots of ... or maybe, because of the way the songs were hard and aggressive, Rick didn't feel it suited so well. It's just a natural process, it's not anything that was preplanned."*

Can we talk about your guitars now? I take it you're still using a Fender? Gilmour replied, *"Mostly."* What kind? Gilmour answered, *"Stratocasters and Telecasters mostly."* Have they been modified in any way? Gilmour explained, *"Not really, no. Let me see. The Stratocaster that I use on stage with the Pink Floyd, which is one that I use quite a bit on the solo album, is ... the neck is from the early Sixties, the body is about 1970, and the electrics are from the same time. It's got a Di Marzio pick-up for the treble, but I don't think that makes that much difference. It's quite nice. But I also use another Strat that is perfectly standard. I always modify a Telecaster slightly because I don't like the way they're wired from the factory. Most other people seem to do the same, as it's more or less a standard modification that everyone does on the Telecaster. I also used a Gretsch, I can't remember what it's called. And I used a Gibson Les Paul as well. It's mostly between three guitars, two Stratocasters, and one variation Telecaster which is an Esquire really."*

Why do you prefer the Fender sound? Gilmour replied, *"I think whatever you start off with, you tend to stick with, and I've always stuck with it, more or less. I do like some aspects of the Gibson sound, but I find it hard to get and hard to play, hard to feel really at ease with."*

But it could be argued the Gibson produces the fatter sound, which could fit well into the Floyd's music. Gilmour replied, *"Uh-huh, it could be argued. But I think that what I do use fits O.K."*

You also have an amazing pedal-board, don't you? Gilmour replied, *"I do have a pedal-board, but it's nothing that miraculous. It's just got a whole bunch of regular effects pedals built-into it, volume controls, tone controls. It's also got send and return so that I can insert new battery things into the circuitry so it doesn't have to come out at the beginning or the end."*

The interview was interrupted when Gilmour's roadie brought in two cans of very welcome Fosters. He confirmed that the unknown Gretsch was a DuoJet, and informed Gilmour that there were a couple of Music Mans waiting for him in the studio.

What else is there on the board? Gilmour replied, *"I've got two different fuzz-boxes. One's a Big Muff and one's a Fuzz Bass, which has a tone control with it so when you switch into that circuit, you get the tone control as well. There's a flanger, a phaser, noise gate, treble, bass boost. That's basically about it. There was a Univibe, but I took it out when something else had to go in, and I use an MXR Digital Delay now instead of a Binson."*

Why did you change? Gilmour replied, *"Superior quality. I mean Binson are very good, but it's quite a job keeping them going. I used to have half a dozen, but at every gig I had to take the top off, set and adjust it all up, clean it. But with the MXR I just plug it in."*

What's your main amplification? Gilmour replied, *"I use a HiWatt generally, but I've also been using a Yamaha."*

Have you considered using a guitar synthesizer? Gilmour replied, *"I've thought about it, but I haven't got around to it yet."* Do you think that's an area you could develop into? Gilmour said, *"I've no idea until I try one out. I would like to try one out and see how well they work, and how reliable they are on stage. Most synthesizer equipment I've used has been difficult to manipulate on stage. You spend so much time trying to keep it in tune and sounding right that you haven't got time to play. But I'm not adverse to trying them."*

I've read that you're contemplating going on the road with this album. Gilmour replied, *"Contemplating it, yes. But that's as far as it goes at the moment."* Is it a serious possibility? Gilmour said, *"It is, but I've no idea when. I mean it's just entered the periphery of my brain, but that's as far as it's gone."* Do you find the prospect of touring with what would be a distinctly less complex outfit an interesting one? Gilmour answered, *"Yes, anything that's different is an interesting prospect. It would be, I would look forward to being able to, not as a permanent proposition. I don't dislike the gigs that we do in any way, I really love them. It's a terrific feeling going out in front of 50,000 people to do gigs, and be at the center of a great sound system like ours. But at the same time, it would be nice to do smaller gigs, and that would obviously be a possibility if I were to start doing stuff with a different band."*

Do you find giging with the Floyd a monstrous mechanical hassle before you can actually get out and play? Gilmour replied, *"No, not really. Sometimes it gets to feel like that. It is, but it's not a problem that I have to face. We have got lots of people to take those sort of headaches off our heads. It is a big operation in that we have to plan a tour months in advance. We can't just say 'let's pop out and do a gig,' which would be a nice thing to be able to do sometime."*

Rick is doing a solo album now, as well, isn't he? Are we going to see more of this kind of project from the members of Pink Floyd? Gilmour replied, *"I imagine you'll see one from Rick."*

Is this a sabbatical year for the Floyd? Gilmour replied, *"Well, it's something like that, yes. When you've been at it as long as we have, it's nice to be able to take short sabbaticals from time to time. Rick has done one, I think it's practically finished but I don't know when it's coming out."*

But you weren't involved in Rick's, and he not at all in yours? Gilmour replied, *"Well, there didn't seem to me to be much point in doing it if I was going to be involved with the Pink Floyd."*

There have been many instances of successful bands in which there are several writers breaking up because of the compromises that necessarily have to be made in that kind of outfit. How does the Floyd continue? Gilmour replied, *"I don't know. I guess our aims are close enough together and we're not that madly egocentric. Excuse me a mo, must go to the loo!"*

Is your own, and the Floyd's, relative inaccessibility from the public deliberate?

Gilmour replied, *"Um, let me see. It's deliberate in the sense that we want to hang on to privacy for ourselves very much. We do want to hang on to that as much as is at all possible. But when the time comes for doing interviews, and there's something to be talked about, we do do some when it's something as hard and fast as that. But a lot of the time there doesn't seem to us to be anything much to talk about that cannot be got from the music. It's different now because I'm doing these interviews to promote my album, which is a hard and fast reason for doing it. It's important to me."*

But, by the same token, if in the early stages the individual members of the band had promoted their own identities you'd probably have found there would be no reason to give interviews now. Had the band's members been better known, there would have been no need to promote the name David Gilmour. Gilmour replied, *"Yes, this is true. I want to promote the name David Gilmour a little bit so people will go and listen to the album and hear if it's worth it. But I'm glad we've done it this way around. I don't feel the loss of personal identity as such in the public eye and I don't desire it. I'm not doing this to promote my personal image as such, it's just that I want people to listen to my record, and if I don't do it, not nearly as many people would listen to it and I'd like to give it a fair crack of the whip. I wouldn't like to think in a few months' time that I could use as an excuse for its failure the fact that I hadn't done anything to help it."*

So a tour might be more on the cards than you've actually hinted? Gilmour replied, *"No, because I certainly won't be doing any touring until the success of this album is really established or lost."*

So, it really is a deliberate isolation that you and the other members of the band have placed yourselves into? Gilmour replied, *"We really don't want to become public property. There are a lot of people who have, and their lives aren't something that I envy at all. I don't want that. I don't want my life to be like that. I value being able to do anything I please, go out to concerts, to the center of the town, wander around, and do everything I want to do that I did before we were successful, without there being any great change. I hate the thought of walking around like anyone else you care to mention and having people continually staring at me and tormenting me. A lot of people are happy to trade that, to have that and lose their privacy. But I'm not, and we're not, as a group. It's not so terribly unusual these days. Lots of others are doing it. There are a lot of other bands you wouldn't recognize on the streets. The Eagles, for example. Would you recognize all the Eagles if you saw them on the street? I certainly wouldn't."* The interviewer indicated that he would. Gilmour said, *"Well, you might just about. But you're obviously a cognoscenti."*

How long do you believe the Floyd can continue producing albums of such consistently high standard? Gilmour replied, *"I can't see why the standard should drop, particularly. I mean, obviously, they'll fluctuate."*

Do you consider 'Dark Side of the Moon' to be as musically amazing as the press and public? Gilmour replied, *"No. I thought its strength lay in the idea, in the concept of the whole thing, and in it being very, very consistent. I think the musical highs were toned down a little bit and the lows were eliminated and as a record it was very, very good. But I thought at the time, and I still think, a lot of the music was, if not weak, then not as inspiring as some of the other stuff we've done. I don't think it was a perfect marriage. I think something like the quality of the music of 'Echoes' married with the quality of concept and idea of 'Dark Side of The Moon' would be better. In some ways I think the quality of the music in what's actually there in 'Wish You Were Here' is greater."*

Did `Wish You Were Here' suffer because of the overkill of `Dark Side of the Moon?' Gilmour replied, *"In a way, you could say that, but it also suffered because of us. Some of it wasn't performed as well as it could have been. Hearts weren't in all of it, all of the time."*

And yet 'Animals' is a real jump ahead, isn't it? Gilmour replied, *"Yes. 'Animals' is geared towards a smaller audience I suppose. And I never expected Animals to sell as many as 'Wish You Were Here' or 'Dark Side' because it's aimed at a narrower audience. There's not a lot of sweet, sing-along stuff on it! But I think it's just as good, the quality is just as high."*

Are you, then, that financially secure that you can deliberately aim a record at a smaller market? Gilmour replied, *"Well, we've always made records for us first, and 'Animals' was the record we wanted to make at the time. It's only looking at it afterwards, or even during the making, we knew then that it wouldn't appeal to so wide an audience."*

Did you get a vibe during the making of 'Dark Side of the Moon' that it was destined to be such an incredible success? Gilmour replied, *"We all got a vibe that it was pretty good and it would probably do better than anything we'd done before. And when we finally got the cover finished and put the whole thing together we all thought it was very, very strong. We were all fairly convinced it would do better. We thought it might do the top ten in the U.S."*

Is the Floyd's visual imagery also a cooperative effort? Gilmour replied, *"Largely, yes. We all do work on it."*

You're not really used to being interviewed, are you? Gilmour answered, *"No."*

Where do you go from the theatrics of the last tour? Gilmour replied, *"I don't know yet."* You seem to be deliberately building walls to knock down again. Gilmour said, *"Precisely."*

Have you modified your sound system since we examined it last year? Gilmour replied, *"It remains the same now, more or less. I don't know the modifications that are going on. It's always out, being rented out."*

Presumably the Floyd will be on the road again next year with the next product. Do you really feel there's an auditorium in the country that can cope with it? Gilmour replied, *"Well, there's not an auditorium in this country that compares with some of the auditoriums you get elsewhere. It's a shame that a nice sized auditorium is not of good quality because there are all sorts of auditoriums over the world where you get fifteen to twenty thousand people in a room which has good sound and none's too far away."*

Talking about sound quality, the Knebworth gig you played some years back while allowing some hundred thousand people to see the band had pretty poor sound quality. Gilmour replied, *"We had an awful lot of* problems at Knebworth, very specific problems with the generator failure, and all the keyboards going out of tune. There's nothing outside our scope at a gig like that that can't be coped with. It's just that various things went wrong at that specific time that added up to make it difficult. Also, we'd just finished an American tour and we had like a week to get all the equipment back from America, repaired, out to Knebworth, and together for a gig which involved all our guys working day and night for three days without any sleep. And also, then having to do the sound for all the other people on the gig. It was so unfortunate we were so close to the end of our American tour. We were very in practice and were playing very, very well at the time and we just got thrown. On stage we got thrown by the Hammond and all the other keyboards going out of tune because the generator wasn't keeping up 50 cycles and out front they were thrown because the equipment hadn't had time to be fixed and adjusted quite right, and lots of stuff was breaking down, and everything was against us. But there was nothing that could stop us playing, and that is a perfectly conceivable gig to do."

Is there any chance of the Floyd doing a summer festival this year? Gilmour replied, "No, there's no chance of us doing one."

The Pink Floyd, as a band, is so much on a pedestal, how much of what goes on at street level, in terms of culture and music, can actually come inside this building. Gilmour replied, "It's not the band, well, it is. But it's not how you see it, or how most people seem to see it, as four people up on a pedestal. It's the image of Pink Floyd that's up on the pedestal. But the four people in it can slip out in the shadows and leave it behind. The pedestal and the image stay there, but we're not on it all the time. We can move right out because of the way our image is, because of the facelessness of our personal publicity we can do exactly what we want to do."

What sort of music do you listen to personally? Gilmour replied, "Mostly I listen to the radio. I've had so little time to listen to records in the past two or three years. I mean literally not switching the gram on more than half a dozen times. I've got piles of new records, which record companies give me, but

I haven't listened to any of them. I sometimes get influenced by things I hear on the radio. Most of the things I hear are on the Horn, or the Peel Show when I'm driving home at night."

Later Pink Floyd albums, and your own solo album, contain less of what used to be termed the spacier passages of the early Floyd material. Is that because you've moved on, or is out of consideration for commercial realities? Gilmour replied, "It's nothing to do with it being commercial or otherwise. It's just what we want to do at the time, what it fits with, and where it feels it would be right. If it suggests itself, and we try it and it works, then we use it. If it suggests itself, and we try it and it doesn't work, or if it doesn't suggest itself at all, then we don't." I wouldn't have thought it was as easy as that.

Your more recent material is shorter, seems to have basic song structures with choruses and middle eights and all the rest of it, whereas you were into twenty minutes non-structured pieces. Gilmour replied, "Well, I mean 'Echoes' was pretty structured. 'Atom Heart Mother' was pretty structured. You're really going back to 'Saucerful of Secrets' and things around that sort of time to find that sort of thing. They were structured, but more loosely so. That is going back quite a long time, but that isn't what we want to do." But even things like 'Echoes' and 'Atom Heart Mother,' you say they're structured' but to Joe Public out there it's unstructured and something to listen to when he's out of his brain. Gilmour said, "You should be able to listen to it when you're not out of your brain. I mean, I think 'Echoes' is as structured in its way as 'Dark Side of the Moon.'"

Do you still pioneer your music on the road before you record it? Gilmour replied, "Not always. We had performed 'Dogs' and 'Sheep' under previous titles before recording 'Animals.'"

How difficult is it reproducing your studio sound out on the road? Gilmour replied, "Sometimes there are obstacles to be overcome, but we can generally think of a way of doing it."

Are you totally immune from the criticism that follows some of your gigs concerning the theatrics, the effects and the use of tapes, or does it completely wash over you because you're doing exactly what you want at the time? Gilmour replied, *"It doesn't completely wash over us, obviously. One does hear these things, but the only thing that really bugs me about it is they say we use pre-recorded back-tracks and stuff which we haven't ever used."* But the intro to 'Wish You Were Here' is on an eight-track tape. Gilmour said, *"But that's just a chord, just a basic background chord which would take up so many of Rick's fingers. I mean, we could pay half a dozen guys to stand there to play one chord, but that's pointless, isn't it? It's hardly a recorded backing track. The 'Machine' song has got a bass pulse on it, pre-recorded, but that's only to keep in time with the film because we actually synch it with the film and have to wear headphones."* Roger wears cans through the whole gig. Gilmour answered, *"Yes. That's because he likes to for his singing. He can hear his singing better, he can balance. He's got a little mixer where all the mics go through and he can balance them as in the studios."*

The Eagles last year were critically slammed for appearing as rock and roll dummies. In some respects, the same criticism could be leveled against the Floyd, that the street's idea of energy is no longer there, if it ever has been. Do you feel it necessary, or are the theatrics saying it for you, are they really relevant? Gilmour replied, *"I think they're very relevant to the music, but they're not necessary. I mean absolutely necessary. Obviously you could adapt the set if we weren't working with those things, but we could do it without them. I think there's a lot of energy and stuff going on when we play the 'Animals' stuff, particularly. It's all down to personal taste, really, isn't it? I mean, we play what we want to play. I mean, I don't know exactly what stuff you're talking about, but it's stuff that we probably wouldn't want to do, and that's our choice. It isn't anyone else's. The public's choice is to come or not come, and the critic's choice is to say it's good or not, from their personal opinion. But it's only their personal opinion."*

So what you're playing is only your personal trip? Gilmour replied, *"Yes, it is, as it is with everyone else. You can't spend your time doing things for the public. You can't eternally take into account what critics and the public want, what you think the public want, to make your music. It'd be crazy to do that. But*

I, personally, and I think we all do, but for me, I work on the philosophy that if I like it, other people will like it. One has to use one's own taste, and if it suits the public's taste, that's good. But if you start working outside your own taste, then you're completely lost, you're working in a complete No-Man's land, you'd never know where you were." I know it's miles away from the Floyd, but the Top Ten works on precisely that basis. Gilmour said, *"I know, and I've always been terribly unsuccessful at predicting what's going to be a hit single. I mean, that's not the line of work I'm in. I'm not in the line of producing top ten pap for whoever it is that buys those singles. That's not the line of work I'm in. It's as different an industry to mine as I don't know what. It's just not the industry I'm in. I'm trying to make music that I think is good music, and I have to be my own judge first, before anyone else."*

The Floyd have come an awful long way since 'Emily.' Is there a lot further to go? Gilmour replied, *"It's always a question of just something that we wanted to do and enjoy it. That's as it is now. I don't see it as linear, it's not getting from here to there, it's just carrying on. As long as we can carry on making exciting pieces up, and as long as the public will support us enough so that we can keep on doing it, we will."*

August 13, 1978 - Ciao 2001 (Italy) published an interview with David Gilmour by Aldo Bagli and Giorgio Rivieccio. Asked if the reason he recorded a solo album was because he couldn't express himself completely within the context of Pink Floyd, Gilmour replied, *"Playing with Pink Floyd has always been intense. But in addition to getting satisfaction from it, there is also a lot of responsibility. There is always the pressure that the next album has to be better than the previous one. After we recorded the album 'Animals,' we decided to take a break from Pink Floyd. Each one of us can do anything we want. I've decided that during this period, I want to work."*

Can you please explain the music on your solo album? Gilmour replied, *"There isn't a lot to explain. Creativity is something that is hard to define. When I recorded the songs for my album, it was a different time than it is today. If I recorded them today, they would be* different. It's not that I'm not satisfied with my work, but today I have more information than I had six months ago, and I've had more experiences, and so on."

What about the nature of the band? Gilmour replied, "Whoever listens to my album doesn't have to delude himself that he is listening to a Pink Floyd album. There is no sense in recreating the feelings associated with Pink Floyd."

What was it like recording by yourself? Gilmour replied, "I recorded it a lot faster. With Pink Floyd we want complete perfection. When I work alone, I prefer spontaneity. A lot of people may think that my album is superficial because I've tried to recreate the simplicity that is sometimes lost. When I am at home, I sometimes grab an acoustic guitar and begin to play, aimlessly. Well, my album was based on a desire to express myself, wanting to be as natural as possible."

Now that the album is done, what are your plans? Gilmour replied, "I'm going to follow the example of the others. I want to rest and devote my time to my private life. But in 1979, Pink Floyd will return to the recording studio." Why are you waiting so long before recording again? Gilmour said, "We aren't machines. We have our limits." What about a tour? Gilmour answered, "I can't answer that. So no comment." Why not? Gilmour said, "Because every time we comment about it, people interpret it wrong. So we prefer not to disclose ourselves."

Why doesn't Pink Floyd give any interviews after releasing their albums? Gilmour replied, "When we weren't famous, we bombarded the musical press with our interviews. However, now there is no need to. The records speak for themselves."

Do you feel happy about where Pink Floyd is today? Gilmour replied, "Sometimes I think that the band follows themes that are too exploited. I would like to explore new horizons. But it isn't easy when there are four people involved. However I'm convinced that Pink Floyd can go on a bit longer."

Do you still like the album 'Wish You Were Here?' Gilmour replied, "I can't yet give a final judgment about that album. It was a very hard album to compose. The success of 'Dark Side of the Moon' changed us in an

exasperating way."

Is 'Wish You Were Here' about Syd Barrett? Gilmour answered, "Yes. Especially the piece called 'Shine On You Crazy Diamond.' It is the nucleus of the record."

When you wrote 'Animals,' did you have a central theme in mind? Gilmour replied, "No. Up until the end we didn't know what we were going to do. The idea about animals came while we were recording the last things. Roger thought of it while noticing that the lyrics of the songs were similar. So he changed 'You've Got To Be Crazy' to 'Dogs,' as that was once called, and 'Raving and Drooling' to 'Sheep.'"

Is Roger Waters the brains of the band? Gilmour replied, "Well, I think so. I have never been successful in writing good lyrics."

What did you do for the lyrics on your solo album? Gilmour replied, "I managed three pieces on my own. For the others I had the help of outside musicians. One song was composed by Ken Baker, and another one by Roy Harper. It's incredible, but during 33 years I never wrote proper lyrics. For my album I had to choose the subjects. One piece is about death, and another is about sentimental disappointment. Maybe it's banal, but that's the way it is."

Overall, are you satisfied with your solo album? Gilmour replied, "Yeah, above all because the album has allowed me to get away from the Floyd's music. Pink Floyd, particularly in concert, is like a monstrous machine. In fact, sometimes the technology eclipses the feelings. And sometimes we seem to loose control. If you only rely on the technique alone, there isn't any real purpose to the music. At times, we may have gone a bit too far."

September 30, 1978 - Sounds (U.K.) reported that Pink Floyd have booked their studio in Islington for five months.

November 4, 1978 - Sounds (U.K.) reviewed the Richard Wright album, 'Wet Dream.' They called the album an unqualified success. The instrumentals have an edge over the songs, as the lyrics are mostly superfluous, but when the instrumentation takes shape it is worth the wait. The song, 'Waves,' is "a glorious five-minute instrumental."

1979
The Wall

November 11, 1978 - New Musical Express (U.K.) reported that the title of the new Pink Floyd album will be "Walls" and performances of the piece will include building a wall between the stage and the audience, with the band spending part of the show as part of the audience. Pink Floyd's record company, Harvest Records, confirmed that the title of the new album would be "Walls," while Pink Floyd's office denied this.

November 18, 1978 - New Musical Express (U.K.) reported that Pink Floyd have plans to take a traveling concert hall on tour with them at the end of 1979. Manager Steve O'Rourke stated, "*The halls in Britain just cannot take the band's 45 tons of equipment and 45,000 Watt P.A. system. The only way we can play to audiences in Glasgow, for example, is by taking our own hall on the road.*" The concert hall is an inflatable canvas tent that will hold 5,000 fans and a stage. O'Rourke added, "*It will take about a day to set up the tent in each city, but it should be worth it.*" Pink Floyd will soon begin recording a new album, tentatively called "The Wall," which is scheduled for June release, and will be followed by a film called "The Wall," featuring the band performing live.

February 11, 1979 - New Musical Express (U.K.) reported that, at a recent Los Angeles concert by another band, the audience was asked to stamp and cheer so that they could be recorded for use on the upcoming Pink Floyd album, 'The Wall.' However, the crowd instead responded by booing and yelling.

February 1979 - Relix Magazine (U.S.) published an article titled, "Floyd's Guitar Man Goes Solo" by Michael Branton and Greg Stone that featured an interview with David Gilmour, done around July 1978.

David Gilmour was asked how long he had wanted to do a solo album. Gilmour replied, "*It's been on my mind for a while. Quite a few years, but I never got around to it before. It took ten years, while I thought of other things to do instead, whenever we had free moments of time. But I knew I would do it eventually.*"

How long did it take to write and record? Gilmour replied, "*Well, there was a lot of time spent just going into the studio, working things out, and rewriting material and playing around. That took me from November to January, just a day or two here and there, and not all the time. The actual physical recording of the album took a month to do, during last February. It sounds like I'm underplaying it. I actually spent quite a lot of time putting it all together and writing it.*"

Had you played with the musicians you used on the album before you became a member of Pink Floyd? Gilmour replied, "*Yes, we had a band together for a while when we were teenagers. We had been in France for a year or so, and we'd had about enough of that particular band, and decided to call it a day. So I went on to London and they wanted to go back to Cambridge where we came from. Two or three months after that, I joined Pink Floyd.*"

How is your solo album different from a Pink Floyd album? Gilmour replied, "*There's really no intention for this album to be different from Pink Floyd albums, particularly, but I had no intention to make it the same, either. I just went into the studio and did it without thinking about it very deeply, just however it came out, rather than trying to make it sound like anything else.*"

Is your solo album more personal, as opposed to technical, like Pink Floyd? Gilmour replied, "*Yes, that's true, lyrically, especially. It's more personal than a lot of Pink Floyd stuff has been, because the songs are more personal for me. And I hope I captured a kind of spontaneous feeling to the whole thing. We did record all the tracks fairly spontaneously. We would rehearse them not quite a lot one day, then leave them for the night, and then go into the studio and try to bang it down first thing in the morning, without playing it through and getting stale in it. So I hope we captured an enthusiastic feeling to it. But I would also hope that you're not right if you say that Pink Floyd's stuff is technical. My playing comes from the emotions anyway, generally speaking, either in Pink Floyd or in the solo things that I do."*

Did you achieve one of your goals in making this solo album? Gilmour replied, *"Well, I don't really see that making this is achieving lots of goals and ambitions. I just wanted to do something without compromising myself in any way. And to really take the whole thing on my own shoulders and see if I could do it alone."*

Do you have plans for other solo albums? Gilmour replied, *"I will make another one. I had a lot of fun making this one and, because of that, I would like to try another one. Also, I would like to go out and play it live at some point. But before I have time to fix that all up and do it, I think we'll be working together again as Pink Floyd on our next album. But there's plenty of time."*

How would a solo tour be different from a Pink Floyd tour? Gilmour replied, *"It would give me an opportunity to do it much simpler and, of course, I would have to do it in much smaller places. It would be a pretty simple show, with just playing music, I guess. I certainly wouldn't want to go into a mammoth production like the Pink Floyd production, because it would be a wonderful opportunity not to do that for a change. But that's not meant to denote any dissatisfaction with the way we do it as Pink Floyd."*

Asked about producing Syd Barrett's solo albums, Gilmour answered, *"Syd was a friend of mine long before I joined Pink Floyd. And before he entered into groups, we learned to play guitar together in some ways. We were together in a college in Cambridge for a while, and we used to spend our lunchtimes playing and practicing. He was a close friend of mine for quite a long time. Then, in Pink Floyd, he got pretty messed up and had to get out of the whole situation. And when he wanted to do that solo stuff, there was no one else to help put it together. So he came to Roger Waters and myself and asked for help. It just seemed like a good idea to help him out."*

When you joined Pink Floyd, they were recording the album, 'A Saucerful of Secrets.' Gilmour said, *"They had a couple of tracks left over from previous recording sessions, one or two of which went on that*

album. But I joined more or less at the beginning of making that album, apart from a couple of tracks that Syd had been working on a couple of months before. Generally speaking, I played most of the guitar on that album. But, obviously, Syd is playing guitar on his stuff, and he also sort of played a slide guitar on one of the tracks."

Had you seen Pink Floyd live before you became a member? Gilmour replied, *"I'd seen them twice before I joined, I guess. That's all. I had been out of the country, mostly, before then. I didn't know what was going to happen, though I knew Syd wasn't going to stay with them very much longer. It was pretty dreadful the times I saw them because Syd was already on the down path and it wasn't very much fun. It was a different band then, you see. Syd was leading it and writing all the stuff, so its aims and directions were totally different from what they became after that. Syd was a good writer for short, snappy pop songs, a wonderful and original type, but the rest of us weren't. We wanted to put our direction toward something different than that."*

What are your favorite Pink Floyd songs? Gilmour replied, *"Lots, over the years. On most of the first few albums we did, I have one or two distinct tracks that I like, and the rest don't do much for me, like 'Saucerful of Secrets' and 'Set the Controls' on that album. But I don't think about that too much because it seems like a different era to me. More recently, I like stuff like 'Echoes' and 'One of These Days' on 'Meddle,' and all the stuff after that."*

Pink Floyd has changed over the years. Was there a change after 'Meddle' came out? Gilmour replied, *"Yes, just after Meddle, there was a turning point. There was a specific direction change when we made 'Dark Side of the Moon,' and that was one of bringing lyrical and idea content up to being on an even footing with the musical content. The ideas had always been subservient to the music. A lot of the lyrics before that time were just being treated rather like instruments, and quite pretty at times, but not of any great significance. But from 'Dark Side of the Moon' onwards, they received a different importance, and we worked to make the whole idea much stronger."*

What kind of electronics do you use? Gilmour replied, *"All the stuff that I use is fairly ordinary stuff that you can find down in your local music store. You just have to experiment with all that stuff to come up with something that sounds interesting. Whenever a new effects pedal came out, I'd try it out and see if I could fit it into the sort of things I did. And if I couldn't, I'd send it right back to the store. Onstage, I'd stick them all on the ground in front of me, joined by wires, and they'd always break down. So eventually I had them all built into a main-powered pedal board. But it's still all the original units, just stuck inside a board with bypass switching and main electricity for better quality. There is nothing particularly unusual about it."*

What do you think of Alan Parsons and other musicians who copy what Pink Floyd does? Gilmour said, *"Well, whatever they want to do, I usually take it as a compliment. Alan learned a lot from us, of course, and now he's using it to his advantage. That's all in the game, isn't it? I think he's one of the most blatant rip-offs of the sort of thing we do, in the whole concept of what he does, and the sort of material he covers and everything. We showed him how to do it, and now he's doing it for himself. I don't worry about it, though."*

Why does Pink Floyd take so long to record an album? Gilmour replied, *"Well, they don't just come out sounding the way they do by accident. An album takes a long time to make. Then you spend a long time touring. Then you maybe take a bit of time off. And then you maybe start to make another album. And it often takes at least six months or more to write and rehearse and record an album and get the sleeve done, and then get the whole thing released. So we really have to work flat out all year around to get an album out once a year. And at our age, we don't want to work that hard all the time at being Pink Floyd."*

When will Pink Floyd release another album? Gilmour explained, *"We've taken a year off from the end of our last tour. So that's already 18 months after the release of the last album. And another album might take another year from now. So I guess that would be over a two-year gap from 'Animals' to the next one. That's not a long time to us, because it may look like we're taking two years off and having a holiday, but that just isn't the way it works."*

Have you ever thought about releasing a live album? Gilmour replied, *"Well, on tour we generally play the whole side of an album. Like on the last tour, we did 'Wish You Were Here' the first set, and 'Animals' the second set. And, I mean, to do a live album, it would mean that we were just taking that whole thing and putting it back on an album again when everyone's already gotten that album in the first place. That doesn't seem to have a point to it, to me. People will just have to stick with the bootlegs. There are quite a few of those, you know. It's flattering that people want to buy them, and the only ones who aren't too pleased is CBS."*

What do you think of the latest music coming out of England today? Gilmour replied, *"Hmmmm, I'll have to polish up my crystal ball. I don't think too much about it, you know. I just go where I get taken, and whatever else is happening around doesn't really affect me too much. I haven't seen very much that's new and interesting coming out. I like Elvis Costello, and Tom Robinson, and a few other things that are going around. And some of the much older things suddenly seem to be getting a little revitalized at the moment. Like, the Stones' 'Some Girls' album I like quite a lot. And Bob Dylan's newest album."*

And finally, why do the members of Pink Floyd avoid the public spotlight? Gilmour replied, *"The media spotlight we've kept away from, yes, not the public spotlight. It's never been a considered and deliberate thing. It's not a group decision. We just don't need to do interviews as much as we used to. Unless there's something specific and interesting that we want to talk about, then we don't see the need for it. Also, we've found you've got to separate the people who are interesting to talk to from those who aren't really worth it. And, obviously, it hasn't been as necessary for Pink Floyd to promote their stuff as it is for me personally, when I'm not working under the Pink Floyd name."*

March 31, 1979 - Melody Maker (U.K.) reported that Pink Floyd will return with a new album and concerts in September. The band is currently recording tracks written by Roger Waters last year. It is believed that they have enough material for a double album. Their record company, Harvest Records, stated, *"We are expecting an album from them in late autumn, when they will also play some concerts. We haven't heard any of their work yet, but they have been re-recording some stuff that was done last year."* The band is spending most of the year abroad for tax purposes, and they will finish recording at a studio in France. This week, David Gilmour is in a studio in London producing an album with Phil May, formerly of the Pretty Things.

May 19, 1979 - Melody Maker (U.K.) reported that Pink Floyd is recording their new album in Nice, France. The album is called "Bricks," and is being produced by Bob Ezrin. The stage show will consist of a brick wall across the front of the stage, through which the audience will only be able to see the hands and instruments of the musicians performing. At the end of the third song, the wall will explode and shower the audience with bricks.

May 26, 1979 - Sounds (U.K.) reported that Bob Ezrin may be producing the new Pink Floyd album.

June 16, 1979 - New Musical Express (U.K.) reported that Pink Floyd are planning to return to the concert stage with shows at either Wembley or Earls Court in early autumn, with shows at provincial venues to follow. Their new album is finished, and is expected to be released in a month as a double or triple set.

October 13, 1979 - Sounds (U.K.) reported that the Pink Floyd is expected to release a new double album, called 'The Wall,' before Christmas. A world tour is planned for next year with possible shows in Britain in the summer.

November 17, 1979 - Sounds (U.K.) reported that the new Pink Floyd album, 'The Wall,' will be released on November 30, 1979. A single from the album, 'Another Brick in the Wall, Part II,' is to be released on November 16, 1979. A world tour is being planned for next year.

November 24, 1979 - Melody Maker (U.K.) reviewed the Pink Floyd single, 'Another Brick in the Wall (Part 2).' They called it "A

great modern single" and "An anti-education rant."

December 1, 1979 - Melody Maker (U.K.) reviewed the Pink Floyd album, 'The Wall,' with an article titled, "Floyd: the new realism" by Chris Brazier. It is "an extraordinary record." "I'm not sure whether it's brilliant or terrible, but I find it utterly compelling."

New Musical Express (U.K.) reviewed the Pink Floyd album, 'The Wall,' with an article titled, "Pink Floyd: A Band with Walls!" by Ian Penman. The album is a "seamlessly fatalistic piece of work," "a monument of self centered pessimism," and ". . . hopelessly clichéd."

Sounds (U.K.) reviewed the Pink Floyd album, 'The Wall' with an article titled, "Up against the wall" by Dave McCullough. "This is Pink Floyd's worst album ever." It is "full of tired music," features feelings of "lethargy and datedness," the solos sound senile and antiquated, and the themes are tedious. "Gordon Lightfoot meets Pete Townshend on a very bad trip."

December 8, 1979 - New Musical Express (U.K.) reviewed the Pink Floyd single, 'Another Brick in the Wall (Part 2),' saying it was "cunningly conceived, complete with easily-memorable moron-choir parts."

December 29, 1979 - Melody Maker (U.K.) published a letter from Sylvia and Tony Cooper criticizing Pink Floyd's single, 'Another Brick in the Wall (Part 2)' as being superficial for putting the blame on teachers for society's problems with adolescents. Teachers are doing their best to make school endurable for kids. Pink Floyd blame the teachers, when it is really our capitalistic society that is to blame.

1980
The Wall live

January 10, 1980 - The Daily Mail (U.K.) published an article titled, "Scandal of the Pink Floyd pupils" by Howard Foster. Foster reported that the 23 school children who sang on the Pink Floyd single, 'Another Brick in the Wall (Part 2),' are banned from having their pictures in newspapers or from appearing on television to support the record, and newspapers have received letters complaining that the lyrics of the song encourage kids to disrespect their teachers. A member of the Inner London Education Authority, Mrs. Patricia Kirwan, has condemned the decision to let the children sing on the record, stating, "It seems very ironical that these words should be sung by children from a school with such a bad academic record. It is scandalous that it should be allowed to happen in school time, and it can only lead other children who hear the record to emulate the attitudes expressed in it. The grammar is appalling, too." The children attend Islington Green comprehensive, a progressive school that has been criticized for its bad exam results. Headmistress Margaret Maden imposed the ban on television and newspaper appearances by the children, and claimed that she was unaware that the school children were being used for the recording. The song is being promoted with a video that features different children. Teacher Alan Redshaw allowed the children to sing "to get experience of a recording studio." Maden said, "He wasn't clear about the lyrics, and as soon as the children had done it, he came and told me what they were. We said, 'Oh, dear,' but decided it wasn't as bad as all that. If I had known about the recording in advance, I would not have allowed the children to do it in school time." As for linking the lyrics to the schools poor exam results, Maden said, "It is unfair to criticize those results because the children involved were of low ability. Up until five years ago, the school was very unpopular. But since then, everyone has worked extremely hard, and now we are oversubscribed with children of above average ability."

January 12, 1980 - New Musical Express (U.K.) reported that Pink Floyd are planning a world tour in February, consisting of five nights in Los Angeles and five nights in New York, during which they plan to build a wall between themselves and the audience.

January 24, 1980 - Rolling Stone (U.S.) reported that Pink Floyd is planning a two-city tour to support their latest album, 'The Wall,' partly due to the fact that they have to satisfy a contractual provision with CBS Records that requires them to tour after an album's release. The shows will take place at the Los Angeles Sports Arena and the Nassau Coliseum in New York, both of which will offer seating of 11,000 to 12,000 for the concerts.

February 23, 1980 - Sounds (U.K.) published an article titled, "All in all there are exactly . . . 420 bricks in the Wall" by Sylvie Simmons that reviewed the Pink Floyd concert at the Los Angeles Sports Arena on February 7, 1980. Simmons wrote that the show was "bloody spectacular," with 30-foot inflatable dolls, a white brick wall, a flying pig, and quadraphonic sound. It was opening night of seven sold-out nights, and some of the fireworks caught a curtain on fire, but the show was "a musical and visual sledgehammer." The show began with a partly built wall across the stage and a little pink doll leaning up against it. During the first half of the show, strobes flashed behind the drums, a plane flew over the audience, a large inflatable teacher puppet made an appearance, slides were shown on a screen, an inflatable mother with spotlight eyes appeared stage left, animations of flowers eating each other were shown, a long green inflatable monster with tongue hanging out appeared, and the wall was built. In the second half, a living room appeared in a hole in the wall, incredible films were projected on the wall, and David Gilmour sang 'Comfortably Numb' from astride the wall. As a finale, the wall came crashing down in a huge sensurround rumble, and the band played acoustic instruments in the ruins of the wall.

February 24, 1980 – The New York Daily

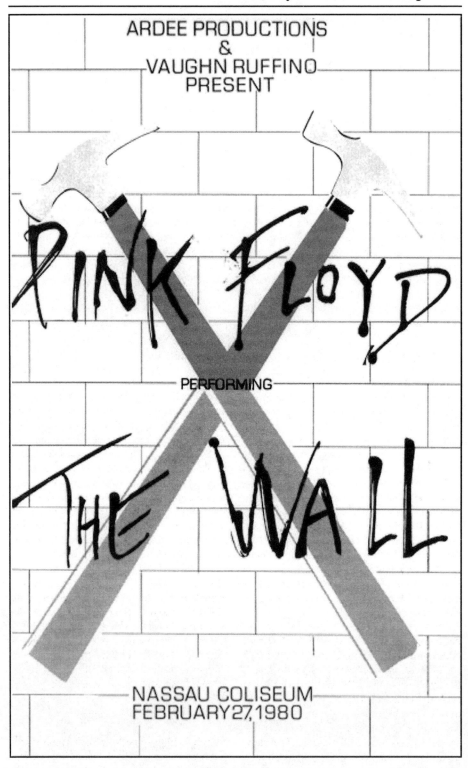

News (U.S.) published an article titled, "The Wall in New York" by Martha Hume. Hume wrote that tonight is the first of four Pink Floyd concerts in New York. All shows are sold out and people are paying any price for tickets. The reviewer "cannot figure out just what people see in a menopausal British rock band that seems to be contemplating the Guyana solution as the nearest exit from life." They are more notable for their technological excellence than for their lyrics or melodies. 'The Wall' is "an album for chumps," offering little more than the 'I am a famous rock star with lots of money so why am I not happy?' lament. The members of the band are exceptionally talented musicians, but with pedestrian imaginations.

Also in this issue was an article titled, "Pink Floyd has scalpers in the pink, uh, green," by Clint Roswell. Roswell reported that scalpers were selling tickets for the five Pink Floyd shows at the Nassau Coliseum for as high as $100 each for orchestra seats. One fan reportedly paid $60 for a $12 third-promenade seat.

February 25, 1980 - Time Magazine (U.S.) reviewed the Pink Floyd album, 'The Wall,' with an article titled, "Pinkies on the wing" by Jay Cocks. Cocks wrote that the album is spacey and seductive, full of high-tech sound stunts. Roger Waters' lyrics are a kind of libretto for Me-decade narcissism, with every avenue of Waters' psyche ending up against a wall. The album may succeed more on the sonic sauna of its melodies than the depth of its lyrics. Talking about the stage show, sax musician Dick Parry who has performed with the band, said, *"They've got everything down exactly. On stage with the Floyd, there's no spontaneity at all. They've got little pieces of tape everywhere, and if you stand in the wrong place, they go crazy."*

February 26, 1980 - The New York Times (U.S.) published an article titled, "Pink Floyd stages lavish show on wall" by John Rockwell. Rockwell wrote that 'The Wall' concert at the Nassau Coliseum on Sunday night was "the most lavish stage show in the history of rock-and-roll." One estimate of the cost for the special effects was $1.8 million. The show used visual references to the past, such as a model airplane that flew over the crowd, and an inflatable pig. The sound was spectacular and the concert "went off without a hitch."

The Toronto Globe and Mail (Canada) published an article titled, "Pink Floyd uses everything but kitchen sink and music" by Paul McGrath that reviewed 'The Wall' concert at the Nassau Coliseum in New York on Sunday, February 24, 1980. Scalpers had been asking $150 a ticket to see the large-scale fantasy. The concert began differently and ended with spectacular fake destruction, but the music was lost. Two minutes into the show a large airplane flew over the audience and crashed into the wall. Later two huge inflatable puppets, one a British schoolmaster similar to Chalkie and the other a caricature of Margaret Thatcher, danced in front of the wall. By the end of the first half, the wall was complete and the band had disappeared behind it. The star of the second half was Gerald Scarfe, whose breathtaking drawings were projected onto The Wall. Crossed hammers were the most striking. As a giant 20 X 30 foot inflatable pig moved over the crowd, the reviewer wished it would move away from him, not because the pig didn't look friendly, but because the audience was throwing garbage and bottles at it. There was little clarity in the spectacle and the reviewer was left with no clear impressions of what was meant. The finale was nevertheless magnificent, with The Wall being destroyed, and the musicians appearing in minstrel costumes with acoustic instruments. However, apart from the spectacle, the musicians were "relentlessly tedious," and the songs were slow and sludgy. But the visual carnival kept your attention.

March 1, 1980 - Melody Maker (U.K.) reported that Andy Warhol attended Pink Floyd's exclusive New York party at the Privates Club in Upper Manhattan that followed their concerts at the Nassau Coliseum. Asked whether he liked the concert, Warhol replied, "I always felt that the Velvet Underground was a good psychedelic group." Other celebrities who attended the party were Carly Simon and Mark Knopfler.

March 2, 1980 - The New York Times (U.S.) published an article titled, "Pink Floyd's Great Wall" by John Rockwell. Rockwell wrote that

`The Wall' concerts were "a serious attempt at a mass theatrical spectacle by Roger Waters." It will remain "a milestone in rock history," and is the "touchstone against which all future rock spectacles must be measured."

March 1980 - Circus Magazine (U.S.) published an article titled, "Up against the wall of secrecy with Pink Floyd" by Richard Hogan that featured interviews with Steve O'Rourke, Michael Kamen, and Bruce Johnston of the Beach Boys. Manager Steve O'Rourke is quoted as saying that the band were able to *"spend a lot of years not letting people know who they are."*

Asked about the creation of `The Wall,' arranger Michael Kamen explained, *"In the summer of 1978, Bob Ezrin went to Europe and ran into Roger. Pink Floyd was already in the middle of the project. They'd worked on it for a year and Roger wanted help. Bob buried himself in the studios for a solid year and helped Roger realize his ideas."* Kamen added that `The Wall' *"seems to have the whole aura of Pink Floyd about it."*

Kamen wasn't allowed to meet the band until after he had completed work on the arrangements for the 55-piece orchestra. Kamen stated, *"They're a brilliant bunch of guys. I'd wondered how they functioned. Were they a band, a fucking board-meeting scene, or*

what? I was out on the West Coast when they were mixing, so I got to hang out with them. They're friends, they get along, but they play together rarely, only in the studio or when they're on the road. Otherwise, they move in their separate ways, which is a nice way to collaborate."

During the recording of the album, Roger Waters cancelled a recording date with the Beach Boys who were supposed to record vocals for the album in Dallas. Bruce Johnston explained, *"Mike Love and I went over to Roger Waters' house. He and David Gilmour were there. They said, 'We started singing high parts, trying to sound like the Beach Boys, and then we decided, 'Why don't we ask them?' They made cassettes of the songs we'd be working on. But we couldn't get together on dates with the Pink Floyd. We finally set up studio time in Dallas for Bob Ezrin to fly down with Roger and bring the tapes. They cancelled the day of the session. It was just a shame to me, because it would have had a lovely impact had it been the Bach Boys singing."* Instead Johnston and Toni Tennille recorded backing vocals for the songs, 'The Show Must Go On,' and 'Waiting for the Worms.' Johnston said, *"Musically, I've gotta represent a vast amount of saccharine. Toni's gotta represent a lot of fluff. There we are, singing songs about worms on this album that certainly has to be 180 degrees from what the Beach Boys do. I had an image of Pink Floyd that was funky, like their music. It was like their whole image turned demonic as soon as they went out the door. So I went over to Roger's house and I see he's got a staff that works for him, and beautiful furniture, and a nice wife and a couple little babies, and his mother-in-law is flying in. It was really MOR. I thought, 'God! Pink Floyd! They're ultra-civilized people making this bizarre album, sitting around their million dollar house in Beverly Hills.' Roger and I talked about getting together and playing tennis. I even tried to get Waters down to the beach, but it didn't work out. I laughed a lot about that."* As for the recording sessions, Johnston revealed, *"The sessions were actually civilized. You go behind the screen, and you find out that the Wizard of Oz is about 5'4", might have two cavities, and is losing a little hair. Pink Floyd is normal."*

March 8, 1980 - New Musical Express (U.K.) reported that concert attendees for the Pink Floyd concerts at the Los Angeles Sports Arena paid $12.50 and $15 for tickets to get strafed, and see a giant plane fly across the arena, a giant pig, a 35-foot high wall, and gallons of smoke. The concerts will come to Wembley in May.

March 10, 1980 - Newsweek Magazine (U.S.) published an article titled, "Up Against the Wall" that featured an interview with Roger Waters in Los Angeles. Asked about the Montreal 1977 Pink Floyd concert that inspired 'The Wall,' Waters stated, *"It was hell. I found myself spitting on a guy who wouldn't stop yelling. It was a real war."*

Asked about the lack of audience participation at the Wall concerts, Waters said, *"I hate audience participation. It makes my flesh creep. Yelling and screaming and singing is great in church, but not at our shows, thank you."*

Asked about the current status of Pink Floyd, Waters added, *"We have been pretending that we are jolly good chaps together, but that hasn't been true in seven years. I make the decisions. We pretended it was a democracy for a long time, but this album was the big own-up."*

Pink Floyd spent $800,000 putting

on The Wall concerts, and they hope to turn it into a motion picture.

March 1980 - Guitar Player (U.S.) reviewed the Pink Floyd album, 'The Wall.' They wrote that the album begins with the menacing distortion-laden Strat guitar of David Gilmour, and features heavyweight guitar solos on 'Another Brick in the Wall, Part 2,' and 'One of My Turns.' The album has a "continuous metamorphosis of moods," and a cohesive "all-pervasive plot." Some nice acoustic guitar ditties are also included.

March 29, 1980 - Melody Maker (U.K.) reported that Pink Floyd have changed venues for their upcoming British concerts from Wembley to Earls Court. They are also considering an open-air show. Shows are planned for about three nights at Earls Court in June, plus an outdoor show near Milton Keynes. It is believed that the band thought that Wembley would be too small for their stage presentation, where nine nights had been tentatively booked in June. Additional concerts in Britain are being considered, as well as shows in Germany. Meanwhile, Nick Mason and manager Steve O'Rourke will be racing in the Silverstone Six Hour Race in May, and at the Le Mans Classic Race the second week of June.

April 3, 1980 - Rolling Stone Magazine (U.S.) published an article titled, "Pink Floyd: Up against the Wall" by Steve Pond, that reviewed the Pink Floyd concert at the Los Angeles Sports Arena on February 7, 1980. Pond wrote that the star of the show was The Wall, not the album or the concept, but the actual wall, "probably the most spectacular prop ever used by a rock band." The concert was startling, overpowering, and numbing. The wall was built by roadies as the band performed, and by the end of the first set the group was walled in. The second set was ingenious, with a living room folding out of The Wall for one song, and David Gilmour soloing from atop The Wall for another. Animation was also projected on The Wall. At the end of the show, The Wall collapsed onto the stage and the band came out playing the song 'Outside the Wall' on acoustic instruments. It was "an enormously impressive testament to a band that doesn't mind playing second fiddle to a lot of white bricks."

April 1980 - The Rag (U.S.) published an article titled, "Pink Floyd: Building Blocks for the Wall" by Cal Rudd, in which he reviewed a live performance of The Wall at the Nassau Coliseum in New York. Rudd wrote that the protagonist, "Sunshine," is swallowed up by the forces he encounters throughout the play. The music was "stylistically bleak and sparse" and fit the production. The reviewer's initial reaction was ho-hum, but he learned something from thinking about it and reading the lyrics.

April 5, 1980 - Sounds (U.K.) reported that Pink Floyd are planning a major concert at the Milton Keynes Bowl in the summer. It is uncertain if this will be instead of, or in addition to, the concerts proposed for Wembley. The new album, 'The Wall,' is the longest running Number One album since Grease two years ago. The album, 'Dark Side of the Moon,' has just eclipsed Carole Kings' 'Tapestry' as the longest running album in the U.S. Top 200 Charts.

April 1980 - Circus Magazine (U.S.) reported on the Pink Floyd concerts at the Nassau Coliseum in New York, and included interviews with Bob Ezrin and Michael Kamen. Bob Ezrin stated, "*The Wall couldn't have been done live. The live show grew from the record, but it's a copy of the record. They just don't play together anymore.*" Ezrin explained that David Gilmour had to "*bust Rogers arm*" in order to write for the project and, according to Ezrin, Roger Waters told Ezrin "*You can write anything you want, just don't expect any credit or money for it.*"

Asked about Roger Waters, Ezrin explained, "*I keep hitting these turkeys who can't put four words together in a nice sentence. To run into Roger Waters was an absolute joy. He's the finest lyricist in rock.*"

Michael Kamen said about Ezrin, "*Bobby has a gift for taking someone's concept and organizing it almost before the artist has thought of it.*"

Talking about 'The Wall' album, Ezrin explained, "*In an all-night session, I rewrote the record. I used all of Roger's elements, but I rearranged their order and put*

them in a different form. I wrote 'The Wall' out in 40 pages, like a book, telling how the songs segued. From that, the stage show grew. It wasn't so much rewriting as redirecting. I acted as Roger's editor, and believe me, his lyrics are so good they didn't need much." For example, Waters' original lyrics for the song 'Another Brick in the Wall' were, "I don't need your drugs to bring me down, down, down." Waters then wrote a series of lines that substituted other specific substances for drugs. At Ezrin's insistence, Waters made the lyrics more general for part three of the song, in order to convey Pink's alienation with more power. "I don't need no arms around me. I don't need no drugs to calm me. Don't think I need anything at all."

Ezrin explained, "*The record used to be Roger's life story, and there were dates in the lyrics that put him at 36 years old. Kids don't want to know about old rock stars. I insisted we make the record more accessible, more universal. It was kept universalized, with some very important fine-tuning by Roger. But the credits would've read like the Bible if we'd broken everybody's contribution down.*"

Asked about whether Pink Floyd and Roger Waters could be looking towards more legitimate theatrical work, Ezrin said, "*One thing we went for with the Pink Floyd vocals was an acting quality. For example, Gilmour, who's very sober by nature, sang screaming on 'Young Lust' in a way he hadn't sung in years. And all the characters and accents in 'The Trial' are Roger. When we were through, I said to him, 'We've really got to do Broadway.' He and I are seriously discussing something like that.*"

April 26, 1980 - New Musical Express (U.K.) reported that the Pink Floyd album, 'Dark Side of the Moon,' has just become the longest charting rock album in Billboard's history, at 303 weeks. And 'The Wall' album has been at Number One in the American charts for 14 consecutive weeks. Recently a New York radio station sponsored a 'Pink Floyd Night' at the Central Park Ice Rink, where some of the skaters spun, it's said, on acid.

May 1, 1977 - Rolling Stone (U.S.) published an article titled, "Pink Floyd break pop chart record" that reported that the Pink Floyd album, 'Dark Side of the Moon,' is the longest charting pop album in the history of the Billboard charts. As of March, it has been on the Billboard chart for 303 weeks.

May 1980 - Trouser Press published an article titled, "Floydian Analysis – Tripping Through the Years With the Pink Popsters" by Jim Green that reviewed of the history of the band.

Also in this issue was a small article on 'The Wall' concerts in Los Angeles and New York. Tour coordinator Nicky Hepworth stated that the band had to "cover it out of their pockets," and added that the shows "haven't made money."

June 1980 - Creem Magazine (U.S.) published an article titled, "Pink Floyd's Wall: Live and All Pink On the Inside" by Dave DiMartino. DiMartino wrote, "The Wall's brutal critical reception was as unjustified as it was inevitable, the snide work of people who didn't like it before they even heard it." Although DiMartino found the albums 'Wish You Were Here' and 'Animals' lame, he wrote that 'The Wall' was their first serious effort since 'Dark Side for the Moon' changed their career.

July 19, 1980 - New Musical Express (U.K.) reported that the Pink Floyd concerts at Earls Court will go on as planned, despite rumors that they lost almost all their equipment in a fire that happened at the Alexandra Palace. Capitol Radio had borrowed some of Pink Floyd's equipment for a jazz festival at the Alexandra Palace, but "it was only one of six or seven rigs owned by Floyd."

August 2, 1980 - Melody Maker (U.K.) published an article titled, "Up Against the Wall," by Michael Watts that featured an interview with Bob Ezrin. The article reviewed the events of 'The Wall' concerts held at the Nassau Coliseum in February 1980, the story of how 'The Wall' concept developed, and the different phases of 'The Wall.'

Explaining about how 'The Wall' began, producer Bob Ezrin said, "*I went to Hamilton in the car, Roger and Caroline, my friend and myself, in fact. Roger had a slight accident and had to go the Hamilton General*

Hospital. Luckily the friend I brought was a doctor. But on the way home, while my doctor friend and Caroline went to sleep in the back seat, Roger and I began to discuss this crazy idea he had about putting up a wall between him and the audience, because he felt this sense of separation. That was the first mention of it. It was just a very casual conversation. We were talking even about Broadway and things like that, then. And then we spoke about it at his house in London a year and a half later."

Ezrin continued, "*Having written the first draft, he realized the extent of it all. He decided it was too much work to do it all by himself, and he didn't want to go back to the old lifestyle of living in the studio for eight months. He had little kids and he wanted to be able to get home in the evening. So he decided on a collaborator. I believe he'd made a list of people and my name was first on the list because we'd actually met and spoken a few times about this. We weren't really friends, but we were acquaintances.*"

Ezrin continued, "*Roger really began the whole thing by himself at his little studio in the country. And he wrote an entire record called 'The Wall,' which was almost one song. It was a demo for the purpose of seeing if it would play, and for the purpose of sending it around to all the other members of the group to see if they'd be interested. But there was never any distinction between the actual three elements: the album, the stage show, and the film. They were all devised at the same time.*"

Ezrin explained, "*On an average day, we'd roll up to Gerry Scarfe's house at nine in the morning to look at rough animation done around a song that we hadn't even finished recording yet. After checking that out, we'd go in the studio, and at one o'clock in the afternoon, we'd have a meeting with the director of the film. It was crazy, but a very good way to do it.*"

As for being a co-producer and working with Pink Floyd for the first time, Ezrin stated, "*I was slightly fearful of finding myself in an unbearable situation.*" And about the difference in lifestyles, Ezrin explained, "*They live their own very peculiar life. I've never met a group of people that lives the way this group does. Never. They're very, very British. Their lifestyle is interchangeable with the president of just about any bank in*

England. It's anything but rock and roll madness. If you bumped into Roger on a Sunday afternoon with the kids in the park, Roger and Caroline on 'the nanny's day off' as they call it, you wouldn't know that this guy wasn't a wonderfully successful young executive marching his family into the park. Very reserved. In fact, there's such a lack of rock and roll energy throughout that getting to Los Angeles was a good idea. It's very hard to inject that sort of consciousness at ten o'clock every morning, and you're working regularly from ten till six."

As for his contributions to 'The Wall' album, Ezrin explained, *"Musically, Roger really doesn't have the vocabulary, or the facility, if you will, to zero in on the problem with the construction of a song. He needed someone who could do that for him. Usually, it has been really trial and error."*

Ezrin was responsible for reordering the songs on the album, and also suggested that they release a single from it. Ezrin said, *"In the past, I don't think it was because they had any phobia about being typed as a commercial group. They simply didn't know how singles worked. And they didn't really give a shit. They didn't really have to, did they? They were amazingly successful for guys who didn't concentrate on radio. It may seem like it, but there was no war going on amongst Pink Floyd members against radio. They just weren't really conscious of radio programming needs and formulas. So they did what they do best. And it put them in a very special class of their own. But in things like what a good tempo would be for a single, and how to get an intro and an outro, I know all those things, and they were quite open to trying them."*

Talking about Roger Waters, Ezrin said, *"He's the finest wordsmith in music right now. There's no one to touch him. Absolutely brilliant. You may not like the subject matter that he finally decides to go with, but I've seen other things he's written and he does have a capacity to write anything, right down to simple rock and roll. He has a facility with language like no one else."*

Asked about Pink Floyd's future, Ezrin said, *"They can't get any more spectacular. There's so much distance that has yet to be put between them and this project. But I don't know that it's the death of Floyd, the*

last rattle before they lie down and die. I don't think so."

The article also reported that photographer Jill Furmanovsky had her film confiscated at The Wall concert by manager Steve O'Rourke, that requests for information about the animation were denied by Waters, that Nick Mason loves to dance, that Chris Thomas was flown in from England to advise on the sound at Nassau, and that Bob Ezrin had a run in with Waters and was heading back to Toronto. Ezrin explained, *"Roger went off in a complete huff and hasn't spoken to me since. Honest to God, he's that sensitive. And we had a very good relationship, too, after working cheek to cheek like that for a year. To have something small like that throw him off . . ."*

August 9, 1980 - Melody Maker (U.K.) reported that ten original Gerald Scarfe paintings that were on display in glass frames at Earls Court during the Pink Floyd concerts there, had been stolen. They were part of an exhibition that ran during the concerts, and included the original artwork for the cover of 'The Wall' album.

August 16, 1980 - New Musical Express (U.K.) published an article titled, "And Pigs Will Fly" by Nick Kent that reviewed the Pink Floyd concert at Earls Court, London, on August 6, 1980. Kent recalled his last review of a Pink Floyd concert at Wembley six years ago, which he said was a wretchedly lackadaisical performance. Since then the group has lacked inspiration and has become non-democratic with Roger Waters as the self-appointed leader. The Wall concert makes Waters stature clear, and the concert program, which sells for £1.50, indicates that 'The Wall' was "written and directed" by Waters. He also plays the principal role of the story in concert, which is a "grave error" because he has no stage presence, he doesn't project, and his vocals are too limited. The Wall was the true star of the show. Each band member had a double, making it impossible to tell who was playing what, and Nick Mason and Richard Wright were mostly anonymous in the performance. Prerecorded tapes were used throughout the performance, and the reviewer wondered if they played during the whole concert. The show was a bloated extravaganza, and the effects, such as an airplane crashing onto the wall, a flying pig, fireworks, quadraphonic sound, and dry ice, were "stock nonsense" that won audience approval. Gerald Scarfe's cartoons were thought provoking, but they were too much for the audience's "bread and circus" mentality. The reviewer felt that 'The Wall' failed as both a record and a stage show due to a lack of direct confrontation. Waters is obsessed, and his contempt for the audience is pure smugness. Waters should deflate the farce, debunk all myths, strip the Floyd of their pathetic theatrical devices, inform the audience that the game is over, and offer them refunds for their tickets.

Also in this issue, T-zers reported that during 'The Wall' concerts at Earl's Court, thieves broke in and stole some Gerald Scarfe paintings that were on display in the foyer. The paintings are valued at £30,000, and Scotland Yard is posting a hefty reward for their return.

Record Mirror (U.K.) reported on the Pink Floyd concert at Earls Court, London, saying it was "a triumph of spectacle over substance." Possibly the most spectacular rock show ever performed in London, but the concept is "as hollow as the bricks used in the construction," and as "exciting as beating somebody around the head with a sugar glass bottle." Tickets were £9.50

Sounds (U.K.) reported on the Pink Floyd show at Earls Court with an article titled, "The grandiose dream of a paranoid millionaire" by Hugh Fielder. Fielder wrote that no other band could have conceived or executed the extravaganza that was held at Earls Court last week. The largest indoor rock venue was dwarfed by a "dazzling array of effects and a 360 degree sound system." Even expectations didn't prepare you for the huge scale of The Wall.

The beginning of the show was unexpected and deliberately confusing, with an announcer building up the audience before the band came on amid thunder flashes, and a spitfire flew the length of the hall and crashed into The Wall. But the band wasn't Pink Floyd. It was four clones performing like an Americanized version of the band. After a couple of minutes, the real Pink Floyd emerged. This had a disquieting effect on the audience. During the performance, The Wall was built on the stage, and Waters' bleak tale of indoctrination and alienation was helped by grotesque figures of schoolteachers, judicial mothers, and cartoons by Gerald Scarfe. Symbolism varied between the subtle, and a sledgehammer. At the end of the first half, Waters made one final attempt at communication through a hole in the wall, before the final brick was put into place. This was followed by a 20-minute intermission.

The second half was performed mostly from behind The Wall, but Roger Waters appeared in a living room that came out of The Wall, and David Gilmour appeared on top of The Wall to sing 'Comfortably Numb.' The MC reappeared to give his introduction in a slowed down mechanical manner while the roadies set up a back line in front of the wall and a new lighting rig was lowered from the ceiling. The real Pink Floyd then performed in front of The Wall as a giant inflatable pig glided over the audience. The Wall finally crumbled and the musicians marched across the debris in a Pied Piper style. It was "the most ambitious spectacle so far attempted under the auspices of rock and roll."

August 21, 1980 - New Scientist (U.K.) reported on the technology used for the sound at The Wall concerts at Earls Court, London. Twenty engineers operated the sound equipment, with twenty banks of speakers above the stage powered by a 20 kW amplification system. The musicians used cordless radio microphones. Films projected on the Wall were 70 meters wide and played on three 35mm projectors that were synchronized by pulses recorded on an eight-track tape recorder that also played pre-recorded music, sound effects, and a countdown/click track that was sent to the musicians through wireless headphones. Quadraphonic sound used three speaker banks above and behind the audience, with each bank using 10 kW of amplification. Hidden bass speakers were used for low frequency rumble. The mixing desk was 4 meters long, and graphic equalizers were employed for each part of the sound system to balance the sound and eliminate echo. A pre-concert test was done using white noise that was electronically analyzed.

1981
Fictitious Sports &
The Wall Rebuilt

January 1981 - Music Express (U.S.) published an article titled, "Audience Apathy Creates the Wall" that featured an interview with Roger Waters about 'The Wall' album. The interview was done by Tommy Vance in 1979.

Where did you get the idea for 'The Wall?' Waters replied, "*Well, the idea for 'The Wall' came from ten years of touring with rock shows, I think, particularly the last few years when, in 1975 and 1977, we were playing to very large audiences, some of whom were our old audience who'd come to hear us play, but most of whom were only there for the beer. All this was in big stadiums and, consequently, it became a rather alienating experience doing the shows. I became very conscious of a wall between us and the audience, and so this record stemmed from shows being horrible.*"

Did you really not want to be there? Waters replied, "*Yeah. It's all because the people who you are most aware of at a rock show are the front twenty or thirty rows of bodies. In large situations, where you use what is commonly known as festival seating, they tend to be packed together, swaying madly. It's very difficult to perform in a situation where people are whistling and shouting, screaming and throwing things, and hitting each other and crashing about, and letting off fireworks. I mean, they're having a wonderful time, but it's a drag to try and play when all that is going on. But I felt at the same time that it was a situation that we'd created ourselves through our own greed. The only reason for playing very large venues is to make money.*"

But it would not be economically feasible for Pink Floyd to play a small venue. Waters replied, "*Well, it's not going to be when we do this show because this show is gonna lose money. But on those tours that I'm talking about, the 1975 and 1977 tour of Europe and England and America, we were making money.*"

How would you like the audience to react to your music? Waters said, "*I'm actually happy that they do whatever they feel is*

necessary because they're only expressing their response to what it's like. In a way, I'm saying that they're right, you know, that those shows are bad news. There is an idea, or there has been an idea for many years abroad, that it's a very uplifting and wonderful experience, that there is a great contact between the audience and the performers on the stage. I don't think that is true. I think that, in very many cases, it's actually a rather alienating experience for everybody.*"

I've seen you in concert and it is a very uplifting experience. Waters replied, "*Well, that's good and maybe I'm just paranoid or maybe I pick on the darkest side of things to think about or to write about. What I hope is that, when people listen to this thing, there are feelings inside them so that they can understand what I'm talking about and would be able to respond to it and say, 'Yeah, I feel like that sometimes, too.' This show that I've been working on in parallel to working on this album is not going to be like that at all. I mean, it will be like that. I think a lot of people in the audience may get very uncomfortable during it because most of them won't be able to see most of the time. It will be just like it normally is for a lot of people who are packed behind PA systems. You know, like every seat in the house is sold. So there are always thousands of people at the sides who can't see anything, and very often in rock shows the sound is dreadful because it costs too much to make it really good in those kinds of halls. The sound will be very good, mind you, at these shows, but the impediment to seeing and hearing what is going on will be symbolic rather than real, except for The Wall, which will stop people from seeing what's going on.*"

Will The Wall remain there? Waters said, "*No, not forever.*" Who will knock down The Wall? Waters replied, "*Well, I think we should wait and see about that for the live show. I think it will be silly, really, for me to explain to you everything that is going to happen in the live show that we put on. Mind you, anybody with any sense listening to the album will be able to spot where about in the show it is that it comes down."* You are talking about the physical wall. What about the psychological wall? Waters replied, *"Ah, well, that's another matter. Whether we make any inroads into that or not is anybody's guess. I hope so."*

The first song on the album is 'In the Flesh?' Does this song set up what the Pink character has become at the end? Waters replied, *"That's right. I couldn't have put it better myself. It's a reference back to our 1977 tour, which was called 'Pink Floyd In The Flesh.' That was the logo we used for the tour. That is supposed to set the whole thing up. On the album, I can't imagine anyone would actually get that because when we do the show, at this point we should be recognizable."*

The next song on the album is called 'The Thin Ice.' Is this the very beginning of Pink's life? Waters replied, *"Absolutely. In fact, at the end of 'In the Flesh,' you hear somebody shouting 'roll the sound effects,' and you hear the sound of bombers. And so it gives you some indication of what's happening. So it's a flashback and we start telling the story about it, which, in terms of this, it's about my generation."* You mean the war? Waters said, *"Yeah, war babies. But it can be about anybody who gets left by anybody."* Is this related to a personal experience? Waters replied, *"Yeah, my father was killed in the war."* That must have obviously affected you. Waters answered, *"Obviously."*

In the album lyrics, the father has flown across the ocean. Has he gone away to somewhere else? Waters replied, *"Well, yeah, it could be. You see, although it works on certain levels, it doesn't have to be about the war. I think it should work for any generation, really. The father is also ... I'm the father as well. People who leave their families to go and work, not that I leave my family to go and work, but a lot of people do and have done, particularly in rock and roll. It happens in all kinds of businesses, really. So it's not meant to be just a simple story about somebody getting killed in the war, and growing up and going to school, but about being left, more generally."*

The next song, 'The Happiest Days of Our Lives,' condemns school life. Waters replied, *"Well, my school life was very much*

like that. It was awful. It was really terrible. When I hear people whining on now about bringing back grammar schools, it really makes me quite ill to listen. I went to a boys grammar school. I want to make it plain that some of the men who taught there were very nice guys. It's not meant to be a hard condemnation of all teachers everywhere, because I admire a great many teachers. But the bad ones can really do people in for a long time, and there were some at my school who were just incredibly bad and treated the children so badly. They wanted to systemize them and crush them into the right shape so that they can go to university and do well. I'm sure that still happens and there is a resurgence of it right now in England. You know, terrible panic, because the little dears can't read and write, and the resurgence of 'right, we've got to regiment them,' and this nonsense about interesting them in things and treating them as individuals. There is a resurgence of the idea that that's all rubbish, and that all you've got to do is sit them down and keep them quiet and teach them things, which is what I object to. You know, my son was three the other day and my daughter is one and a half." So they have not encountered this yet? Waters answered, *"Yes they have."* How are you going to prevent them from becoming part of the system? Waters replied, *"I'm in the privileged position of being able to pick and choose how my kids are educated. But most people aren't. Most people are stuck with a system of state education. But my feeling is that our system of state education is improving."*

You are in an elite position, but you say that you are not an elitist. Waters replied, *"Yes, there are a lot of paradoxes in all of this. But, you know, maybe we shouldn't be really talking about my political beliefs. Maybe we should. I don't mind. I've nothing to hide, really."* It's not just political. It is also sociological. Waters said, *"But for me they are the same thing, really."*

In the song, 'Mother,' what sort of mother is this? Waters replied, *"She's over-protective, basically. That's what she is. All enveloping and over-protective, which most mothers are. If you can level one accusation at mothers, it is that they tend to protect their children too much, in my opinion, and for too much and for too long. That's all. A woman that I know phoned me up the other day saying that, on hearing the album and the track 'Mother,' she liked it and that it made her feel very guilty. Now, she's got three kids. I was interested and glad that it had got through to her. If it means that much to people, then it's good."*

Does the fact that a mother is over-protective make it difficult for the child? Waters replied, *"Well, it makes it difficult, and more difficult for you as you grow up and in your later life, to respond to people as an individual in your own right, rather than being an extension of your mother. In the same way that over-bearing school teachers will crush you down. Mind you, that's completely different because I feel very antagonistic towards the teachers at my school who tried to put me down when I was a kid. I never felt like that towards my mother, although I recognize certain things that she did may have made it harder for me to be myself as I grew up."*

What is happening in Pink's life at the time of the next song, 'Goodbye Blue Sky?' Waters replied, *"Since we compiled the album, I haven't clearly tried to think my way through it, but I know this is very confusing. I think the best way to describe this is as a recap, if you like, of side one. It's like setting off from childhood at this stage."*

Is 'What Shall We Do Now' about the young adult setting off on his own? Waters replied, *"That is the track that is not on the album. It was quite nice and, although it is not on the album, we do it in the show. It's quite long, and this side was too long. It's basically the same tune as 'Empty Spaces.' And although 'Empty Spaces' is quite nice to listen to within its context, it isn't particularly strong. We've put 'Empty Spaces' where 'What Shall We Do Now?' is. The lyrics to that one are, sort of, very crude."*

Pink then jumps from the recap of side one into 'Young Lust.' Waters replied, *"No, he doesn't. He goes into 'Empty Spaces,' and the lyrics there are very similar to the first four lines of 'What Shall We Do Now?,' except here it's personalized. As you can see, 'Empty Spaces' works better there, instead of that track. What is really different between those two tracks is that list where it says, 'shall we buy a new guitar, drive a more powerful car,'*

etc. That is about the ways one protects oneself from one's isolation by becoming obsessed with other people's ideas. The idea is whether it is good to have a powerful car, or whether you are obsessed with the idea of being a vegetarian, or going to be analyzed. Whatever it might be, you are adopting somebody else's criteria for yourself without considering them."

Was there ever a 'Young Lust' period in your life? Waters replied, *"Yes, but not at that stage, funnily enough. When I wrote this song, it was actually quite different, lyric-wise. Originally, it was about leaving school and wandering around town and hanging around outside porno movies and dirty bookshops and things like that, and being very interested in sex but never being actually able to get involved because of being too frightened. That song exists somewhere on a demo, but now it's completely different on the album. That was a function of us all working together on the record, particularly with Dave Gilmour and Bob Ezrin, who co-produced the album with me. Dave didn't like the chord structure of the song that I had originally written, so we changed it and then it never seemed it could quite fit in anywhere."*

The song, 'One of My Turns,' sounds like a viscous acid song. Waters replied, *"Well, yes, it actually happened to me years ago, maybe six or seven years ago. That was a bit like me but I would have never said it, to actually come out with anything like that, because I was much too frightened of everything, really. I think a lot of people in rock and roll are, sort of, very frightened of most things."* I don't get that impression. Waters said, *"No, of course you don't get that impression. But it's one of the very safest places in the world, standing on the stage with a few thousand watts of amplification behind you. It's like driving a very powerful car. Anything with a lot of power makes you feel safer, temporarily. I referred to all that in 'Young Lust.' On 'One of My Turns,' it's all terribly confusing. At the end of 'Young Lust,' there is that telephone call. There is an enormous leap, conceptually, from 'Young Lust' to somebody calling home from an American tour. And although nothing is said, it implies a sort of 'Dear John' phone call. I have experienced that sort of thing, not that* particular phone call, because that is just a theatrical device. I love that operator. I think she's wonderful. She didn't know what was happening at all. I mean, it's been edited a bit, but the way she picks up all that stuff about 'Is there supposed to be anybody else there besides your wife?' I think she's amazing. She really clicked into it straight away. The idea is that we've leapt, somehow, into the rock and roll show. It's a lot of years from 'Goodbye Blue Sky.' So we've leapt to somewhere on into our hero's career. Then 'One of My Turns' is supposed to be his response to a lot of aggravation in his life and not really having got anything together with a woman, although he's been married. He's just splitting up with his wife and, in response, he takes another girl back into his hotel room. He's had it now. And on this song, he can't relate to this girl either. That's why he just turns on the TV and sits there and won't talk to her." He realizes the state he is in.

Waters continued, "A lot of men and women do get involved with each other for lots of wrong reasons, and they do get very aggressive towards each other and do each other a lot of damage. If you skip back from there, my theory is that they do that because they've never really been able to become themselves and there is a lot of pressure on people to get married, at least when they're in their late twenties, not earlier. I think that a lot of people shouldn't really get married until they are strong enough in themselves to be themselves. It's very easy to attempt to be things that you are not. I, of course, as far as I can remember, have never struck a woman, and I hope I never do. But a lot of people have. A lot of women have struck men as well, and there is a lot of violence in relationships that very often aren't working. This is an extremely cynical song. I don't feel like that about marriage now."

In the song, 'Another Brick in the Wall, Part 3,' he seems to get his confidence back, as the line 'I don't need no arms around me' refers to. Waters replied, "Yes." This is followed by the song, 'Goodbye Cruel World.' Waters explained, "Well, what is happening is, from the beginning of 'One of My Turns,' from where the door opens through to the end of side three, the scenario is an American hotel room. So when the groupie leaves at the end of 'One

of My Turns,' he sings to anybody. It's directed at women, in a way. It's a kind of guilty song as well. At the end of that, he is there in his room with his TV, and there is that kind of symbolic TV smashing, and then he resurges a bit out of that kind of violence, and says, 'Fuck it. I don't need any of you.' And he sings, 'All in all, you are just bricks in the wall.' So he convinces himself that his isolation is a desirable thing. I've seen that happen to people, and 'Goodbye Cruel World' is that sort of feeling."

What state is he in when he sings, 'Goodbye Cruel World?' Waters replied, "He is catatonic, if you like. That's the final thing and he's going back and he's not going to move. That's it. He's had enough. That's the end. So at the end of side two, he's finished. The Wall is finished. It's complete now. It's been built, in my case, since the Second World War, but in anybody else's case whenever they care to think of it. If they feel isolated or alienated from other people at all, then it's from whenever you want."

Side three of the album begins with a different song than is listed on the record jacket. Waters explained, "When we put side three together, we realized that . . . In fact, I wasn't there when side three was finally put together, and Bob Ezrin called me up and said, 'I've just listened to side three and it doesn't work,' and when I asked him what was wrong with it he said there were too many sound effects. I think I had been uncomfortable about it anyway. I thought about it for a bit and I thought that the thing that was wrong with it was that there was a long scene with somebody in a hotel room with a broken window and a TV, and he sings his thoughts and feelings while he is sitting there on his own. What we are talking about now is nothing, really, conceptually to do with the album. It had just to do with how the side of the album balanced and how to program the thing. I thought about it, and a couple of minutes later I realized that 'Hey You,' conceptually, could go anywhere, and that it would make a much better side if 'Hey You' is at the front of the side, and sandwiched the little theatrical scene of the hotel room between an attempt to re-establish contact with the outside world, which is what 'Hey You' is, and the end of the side three, which we will come to later on. So that's why those lyrics are printed in the wrong place, *because that decision was made afterwards. I should explain, at this point, the reason why all these decisions were made too late was because we'd promised lots of people a long time ago that we would finish this record by the beginning of November, and we wanted to keep that promise. In this instance, I am sorry they are out of place."*

Pink is now behind The Wall. Waters replied, *"He is behind The Wall symbolically, and he is locked in a hotel room with a broken window that looks out onto the freeway."* What are his plans at this point in the story? Waters explained, *"Within his mind, 'Hey You' is a cry of help to the rest of the world. Dave sings the first two verses of 'Hey You.' Then there is a fantasy piece which I sing, which is a narration of 'The wall was too high, as you can see. No matter how he tried, he could not break free. And the worms ate into his brain.' That is the first reference to worms. The worms have a lot less to do with the piece than they did a year ago. A year ago they were very much a part of it. They were my symbolic representation of decay. Because the basic idea behind the whole thing is that if you isolate yourself, you decay. So that is why there is this reference to worms there. And then I sing the last verse of the song. So, if you like, it's like going back to 'Goodbye Cruel World.' At the end of 'Hey You,' he makes this cry for help, but it's too late."*

Is it too late because he is now behind The Wall? Waters answered, *"Yeah. Anyway he is only singing it to himself. It's no good crying for help if you are sitting in the room all on your own, and saying it to yourself. All of us, I'm sure, from time to time, have formed sentences in our minds that we would like to say to somebody else, but we don't say it. Well, that's no use. That doesn't help anybody. That's just a game you play with yourself. It's useful to me, personally, because that's what writing is."* That is mentioned in the first line of the song, 'Nobody Home.' Waters said, *"Precisely. After 'Is There Anybody Out There,' which is really just a mood piece, he comes out to ask if there is anybody out there."* He realizes he needs help but doesn't know how to get it. Waters said, *"Well, he doesn't really want it. Part of him does, but part of him that makes his lips move doesn't."*

In the song, 'Nobody Home,' the

lyrics describe the various things he has, like a Hendrix perm. At the end it says, 'I've got fading roots.' What does that mean? Waters replied, *"He is getting ready to re-establish his contact from where he's started, and to start making some sense of what it was all about. He is getting ready here to start getting back to side one."* He does this on the next song, 'Vera.' Waters explained, *"On the surface of this, 'Nobody Home' is like having had the song about the non-telephone conversation. This is a re-expression of that. He is not just watching television. Sometimes he is trying to get up and trying to call her. So this is about his wife going off with somebody else. And then this is supposed to be brought on by the fact that a war movie comes on the TV, which you can actually hear. That snaps him back to then. The stuff about Vera Lynn is a stream of unconsciousness, and it precedes what, for me, is the most important track on the album, 'Bring the Boys Back Home.' The central song on the whole album is, 'Bring the Boys Back Home.'"*

Why is `Bring the Boys Back Home' the most important song on the album? Waters replied, *"It's because it's about, because it has the most to do with me, because it's partly about not letting people go off and be killed in wars. But it is also partly about not allowing rock and roll, or making cars, or selling soap, or anything become such an important and jolly boy's game that it becomes more important than friends, wives, children, and other people. That's a very, very little vague song, and that's why I like it. In a way, it's a shame for anybody who might read this, that they hear how I feel about it, because, in a way, it would be nicer if it's just vague."* So you want people to draw their own conclusions? Waters said, *"Yeah. And I hope there are lots of other conclusions that can be drawn from all of that. I'm doing this interview because I think the thing is very complicated and not very well done. But having said that, in a way, it's a shame because I don't want people to get stuck with how I feel about it. I'm sure people have their own feelings about it. I hope they will."*

Waters continued, *"After 'Bring the Boys Back Home,' there is a short piece where there are tape loops used. The teacher's voice is heard again, and you can hear the groupie saying things, and the operator again. But* there is a new voice introduced at that point. There is somebody knocking at the door, saying, 'Come on, it's time to go.' So the idea, which obviously isn't expressed clearly enough, is that they are coming to take him to the show, because he has got to go and perform. And when they come to the room, they realize that something is wrong, and so they actually, physically, bring the doctor in, and 'Comfortably Numb' is about his confrontation with the doctor." The doctor puts him in a condition that allows him to perform. Waters explained, "He gives him an injection so as to cool him out, and he can actually function, because they are not interested in any of his problems. All they are interested in is the fact that there are thousands of people, and tickets have all been sold, and the show must go on at any cost to anybody. I mean, I personally have done gigs when I've been very depressed, and I've also done gigs when I've been extremely ill, where you wouldn't do any ordinary kind of work." You did those shows because you were committed? Waters said, "It's nothing to do with being personally committed to do it. It's to do with how much money is at stake." That is what I meant. Waters continued, "Oh, yes, because the money is there in the briefcase. That's all it's about. Generally speaking, people in rock and roll don't really cancel concerts at such short notice because it costs a lot of money. To cancel a show at such short notice is very expensive. And that is worth more than that. Some of the lines on 'Comfortably Numb' and 'Nobody Home' hark back to the halcyon days of Syd Barrett. It's partly about all kinds of people that I've met. All this is about all sorts of people that I've met. But Syd was the only person I ever knew who used elastic bands to keep his boots together, which is where that line 'I got elastic bands keeping my shoes on' comes from. In fact, obviously, the 'obligatory Hendrix perm' you have to go back ten years to understand what all that was about. I never had a Hendrix perm, thank God, but they were obligatory for a while. It was unbelievable. Everybody, from Eric Clapton to I don't know who."

So the doctor gives Pink some drugs and he goes back on the stage? Waters replied, "Yes." How much of himself does he see on the stage? Waters explained, "Well, at this point, none. He is completely gone, really, except at

the beginning of 'In the Flesh' he kind of harks back. In answer to you question, nothing really. You will find that, in 'The Show Must Go On,' there are some extra lyrics because we had to edit the side an awful lot. So we just took those lyrics from the album, but left them on the sleeve. For people out there who read the lyrics, I'd tell them not to worry about it."

Pink is now on stage and is very vicious. Waters replied, "Yes. The basic idea behind it all is this story. Montreal 1977 at the Olympic Stadium in front of 80,000 people, the last gig of our 1977 tour, I personally became so upset during the show that I spat at some guy in the front row who was only doing what he wanted to do, but what he wanted to do was not what I wanted to happen. He was shouting and screaming and having a wonderful time, and pushing into the barrier. What he wanted was a good riot. And what I wanted was to do a rock and roll show. I got so upset that I finally spat on him, which is a very nasty thing to do to anybody. I got him as well, it hit him right in the middle of his face. Anyway, the idea is that these fascist feelings develop from isolation. So the symbols of decay develop from isolation. So what happens to you is that, if people who are older and wiser than you don't set you straight in the world, it's very easy to become isolated. And if you become isolated, you decay. The end result of that kind of decay is any kind of fascism that you care to think of, and any kind of totalitarianism or violence." Pink shows this from the stage. Waters replied, "Yeah, this is really him having a go at the audience or the minorities of the audience. I've picked on queers and Jews and blacks simply because they're the most easily identifiable minorities where I come from, which is England. In fact, they are the most easily identifiable minorities in America, as well. Outside the English-speaking world, I don't know, because language has a great deal to do with what you understand and what you don't understand, and I wouldn't care to comment about France or Germany or anywhere else. So this track is like the obnoxiousness of 'In the Flesh.'"

What is Pink telling the audience in the song, 'Run Like Hell?' Waters replied, "This is meant to be . . . I don't whether you have noticed, but this is disco. So it says something about disco, and it says something *about 'there is a great deal of rock and roll that is kind of unthinkingly paranoid and unthinkingly warning people about all this isolation,' and that's what 'Run Like Hell' is. Originally, when we started making the album, I wanted there to be announcements and all kinds of stuff to make this sound live, but when you try to put it on record, you realize that it would be alright if you'd listen to it once only. For instance, when 'In the Flesh' finishes, if you put in an announcement like 'Thank you very much,' and then you say 'Here is a tune for all the paranoids in the audience,' it will only last for one or two listenings because a joke wears out quickly. So it's best just to leave them out. 'Run like Hell' is meant to be him just doing another tune in a show. So that is just part of the performance, but still in his drug-crazed state."*

In between some of the songs, you can hear things going on, such as before and after 'Run Like Hell.' Waters said, *"If I don't explain this, nobody will understand it. After 'In the Flesh,' you can hear an audience shouting 'Pink Floyd.' After 'Run Like Hell' you can hear an audience shouting "Pink Floyd' on the left-hand side of your stereo, and on the right-hand side or in the middle you can hear voices going 'Hammer, hammer, hammer.' This is the Pink Floyd audience turning into a rally, a kind of fascist rally."*

The next song is 'Waiting for the Worms' which is about decay. Does Pink know he is decaying? Waters replied, *"Yes. 'Waiting for the Worms,' in theatrical terms, is an expression of what happens in the show when the drugs start wearing off and his real feelings of what he's got left start taking over again. Because he's been dragged out of the hotel room and put in that position, he is forced by the situation he finds himself in to confront his real feelings. That's the idea. In the show, we've used the hammer as a symbol of the forces of oppression, and the worms are the thinking part of the forces of oppression."*

Who puts Pink on trial? Waters replied, *"He does. He puts himself on trial. It is interesting to point out that, in 'Waiting for the Worms,' you can hear a voice being spoken through a loud hailer. That wasn't done with a loud hailer. I did it with my hands over my nose. None of that stuff was written and I did it all in one take, all through the song. It starts off*

with 'We will convene at one o'clock outside Brixton Town Hall.' It is actually describing the route of the march from Brixton Town Hall down Southwark Lane and then Lambeth Road and over Vauxhall Bridge. It's meant to be describing a route to Hyde Park Corner to have a rally by the National Front. I did that because I feel that there are enough people in the world who are isolated and alienated that they find it necessary to join those kinds of organizations, and to attempt to damage other people as much as they really would like to if they were ever to come to power. I thought twice about whether to write all that stuff down on the inner bags of the album and, in the end, I decided not to. But since then, I've realized that people who listen to it can't hear any of it, which, in a way, is a shame. But, hopefully, anybody who listens to it and wonders what it is, this interview will be able to tell them what it's all about. That is a description of a National Front march from Brixton to Hyde Park. An then, at the end of it, there is somebody who is raving, and raving about what should be done." The person raving is a fanatic. Waters said, *"Yeah, a right-wing fanatic. Although this isn't really meant to be a very political album, I suppose it is a political album in a way, and it does seem to me that right-wing politics always seem to lean more towards alienation between different groups of people, which is what, it seems to me, fucks people up. If you like, on the broadest level, side four is particularly a left-wing statement. Not in any economic terms, but in terms of ideology."*

So Pink puts himself on trial? Waters explained, *"The idea is that the drugs wear off, and in 'Waiting for the Worms,' there are bits which Dave sings, 'sitting in the bunker, here behind my wall, waiting for the worms to come.' He keeps flipping backwards and forwards from his original persona, which is a reasonable kind of humane person into this 'waiting for the worms' kind of persona, and he is ready to crush anybody or anything that gets in the way, which is a response to having been badly treated, and feeling very isolated. But at the end of 'Waiting for the Worms,' it gets too much for him, and he says, 'Stop, I wanna go home.' So he takes off his uniform and leaves the show. But he says, 'I'm waiting in this prison cell because I have to know if I've been* guilty all the time,' and then he tries himself, if you like. The judge is part of him, just as much as all the other characters and things that he remembers. They're all memories in his mind." None of his memories have any sympathy for him. Waters said, "Well, the Mother does a bit. She wants to protect him, that's all. She is only being over-protective. She's not attacking him in the way that the teacher and his wife do. There is also the prosecuting counsel. He, in fact, is meant to be the person who is on the record label on side four. He is that rather pompous lawyer figure. The idea is that he is somebody who always follows all the rules and that he ended up in the legal profession because he likes laws and that it has nothing to do with real feelings. It's always amazed me, the idea of barristers who can look at both sides of the case and be able to present either side. There is never anything impartial about it. If you're a good barrister, you've got to be able to present both sides partially. That I find very strange. I find that kind of discipline in law very strange. I think that's probably why the trial crept into this piece. Anyway, so there is this trial going on in his head, and it's really just his imagination. He's creating a courtroom for himself. At the end of it all, when he judges himself, he feels extremely guilty and bad about everything that he's been and done. And in the end, the judgment on himself is to de-isolate himself, which, in fact, is a very good thing. The wall is then torn down."

'The Wall' album is phase one, the concerts are phase two, and a film will be phase three? Waters answered, "Yes. You're right." The live performance of The Wall is an enormous project in itself. Waters replied, "It's a very enormous thing, and not easy to move from country to country. So it's a rather slow project in many ways, and can't be done very frequently because it's very complex and difficult to do." Where will you film it? Waters said, "I don't know. But I think I'd like to do it in the open air because I have some ideas for the film that would only really work in the open air. The place certainly needs to be somewhere with a kind of tutonic architecture. Any big stadium would do, really, but it would be nice if it had that kind of German/Roman feel to it because of the culture that we've grown up in. Those will become symbolic of the kind of totalitarianism that part of the record is about."

When you perform The Wall live, why don't you do an encore? Waters replied, "I've always been very against it, but everybody else says that we should. It's the writer in me that says, 'That last line is so nice that you should just leave it at that.' We definitely don't want to play any old material as an encore, first of all because it wouldn't fit in with The Wall concept, and secondly because we've played that old material so often in the past." But that's what the audience wants to hear. Waters said, "We never, over the last few years, have done old material as encores. I mean, the 1977 tour consisted of 'Wish You Were Here' and 'Animals,' and then I think we played one track of 'Dark Side of the Moon' as an encore."

What Pink Floyd song that you have written still excites you? Waters replied, "Funnily enough, I listened to the last three records all the way through when I finished mixing 'The Wall,' just because I thought it would be a useful exercise to listen to it before completing 'The Wall.' You get so immersed in a thing like a double album or a project like this that, sometimes, it's hard to see it clearly. I didn't listen to anything pre-Dark Side of the Moon, though. I know I still like 'Echoes,' as a piece, but from 'Dark Side of the Moon' till now, I liked it all. I was amazed. I expected to be annoyed or at least embarrassed by it, but I wasn't. I thought it was all pretty good, particularly 'Animals.' I was not amazed, but I was surprised that it is as good as it is because, when we did it, it was all done very quickly. It's not a masterpiece, but it's a bloody good album, and I think 'Wish You Were Here' was too."

Can you summarize 'The Wall?' Waters replied, "I wouldn't care to, really. I think we've been over everything that's relevant." Would that defeat the whole purpose of 'The Wall?' Waters answered, "Yeah. It's not all that simple."

January 31, 1981 - Sounds (U.K.) reported that Pink Floyd will be performing The Wall again for six nights in Dortmund, Germany, in February. The concerts are already sold out.

March 1, 1981 - The Observer (U.K.) published an article titled, "Pink Floyd firm is in the red" by Richard Milner. Eleven days ago, investment firm Norton Warburg announced that they are going into liquidation. Among their large clients are the Pink Floyd. An associated company, Cossack Securities, which is a venture capital organization organized by Warburg for Pink Floyd and owned by the four members of the band, is being closed.

March 7, 1981 - Sounds (U.K.) published an article titled, "Floyd's financial empire suffers £1 million blow," which reported that Pink Floyd have lost over £1 million due to the collapse of the Norton Warburg investment company. The company handled Pink Floyd's income and investments from 1972 to 1979, and has gone into liquidation.

April 10, 1981 - Now! (U.K.) published an article titled, "Lost Fortune of the Rock Superstars" by Stella Shamoon. The article reported that Pink Floyd had lost about 3 million pounds through bad investments by the financial advice organization, Norton Warburg Group, which is now being sued for one million pounds by the band, claiming fraud and negligence.

April 18, 1981 - Melody Maker (U.K.) reported that promoter Harvey Goldsmith could have rented Earls Court for the upcoming Pink Floyd shows in June for less than the £170,000 he paid, due to a cancellation by a Midlands exhibition organizer who was willing to unload it for less than a tenth of that.

June 13, 1981 - Sounds (U.K.) reviewed the new Nick Mason album, 'Fictitious Sports.' They wrote that Nick Mason has used his influence to produce a Carla Bley album, and bring business to Bley's Grog Kill Studios in New York. As for the music, the song, 'Hot River,' could pass for 'Great Gig' from 'Dark Side of the Moon.' 'Can't Get My Motor to Start' sounds like bad Captain Beefheart. 'Wervin' is a psychotic avant-garde treatment of Ornette Coleman. 'I'm a Mineralist' could have come off of Pink Floyd's 'Ummagumma.' This album "tarnishes the memory of Bley's earlier works."

June 20, 1981 - Melody Maker (U.K.) published an article titled, "Cracks in the Wall" by Karl Dallas. There were backstage problems at the first two Pink Floyd performances of The Wall at Earls Court. The second drummer, Willie Wilson got sick on the eve of the first show and had to be replaced by Clive, a Pink Floyd roadie who was a drummer. Wilson was seen feeling better backstage on the second night, and appeared ready to play again. And on the second night, two of the hydraulic lifts that raise the band and their equipment up to the stage in front of The Wall caused a large chasm between the band and some of their equipment. Although this did not interfere with Roger Waters, who is cordless, it caused David Gilmour not to be able to reach his pedal-board and vocal mike at the same time, and caused him not to be able to hear what he was playing. Roger Waters commented after the show, "*I quite like it when things go wrong. It makes it less boring, puts more of an edge on things.*"

New Musical Express (U.K.) published an article titled, "Another Pinkie Hogs the Limelight" by Chris Bohn that reported on 'The Wall' concert at Earls Court, London. Bohn wrote that Pink Floyd were back to "re-enact this cosmic farce for the sake of a movie camera." Although it is difficult not to be impressed by the spectacle, it leaves a bitter aftertaste. The music is "portentous and pedestrian," and Gerald Scarfe's animations and puppets are "as contemptuously vile as Waters' characterizations." Roger Waters, "get well soon."

June 21, 1981 - The Sunday Times (U.K.) reported on the Pink Floyd concert at Earls Court. Derek Jewell wrote that the concert was "the ultimate in expensive, grandiose, and depressive rock spectacle." The music is long on ornateness, but short on invention and originality. The "engulfing overkill" is self-defeating. Although the band try to astound the audience, they only succeed in making them numb and fail to move them.

June 23, 1981 - The Daily Mirror (U.K.) reported that Pink Floyd lost £2 1/2 million to a bad investment group. Nick Mason stated "*It's always a drag losing money, but you can't* spend your whole life worrying about it. We've tried to shrug it off." On the Pink Floyd concerts in London, Mason added, "The shows have always been more about spectacle than personalities. It makes life more pleasant and avoids all the hassles."

July 1981 - International Musician and Recording World (U.K.) published an article titled, "Nick Mason – Inside the Floyd" that featured an interview with Nick Mason. Talking about his newly released album, 'Fictitious Sports,' Nick Mason was asked why there was a delay of eighteen months between its recording and its release? Mason replied, "Because of record company problems in America. It shouldn't have taken so long at all. It just got stuck, and got really boring. I mean, it's pretty boring to live with something that you've finished. And just to have it lying around for a year, and every time you hear it, you're thinking 'I wish we could change that,' or 'I wish we'd done it in a different order.' That's the usual thing. You immediately want to change the order around as soon as the cover's been printed."

Carla Bley wrote the material on the album. Is it a burden not to write songs with Pink Floyd? Mason replied, "Not really. The others all write. And it's a fact of life really. I'm interested in writing. I'd like to be a writer but I don't feel that I've got a lot of stuff burning inside me that I've got to get out. So, in a way, it's not a burden because it means at least I'm not a frustrated Floyd composer, so to speak. The thing with this record is just that I still like making records and I wanted to make a record of stuff that I like, by musicians that I like, in which I played a hand in putting together."

Since 'Fictitious Sports' is completely different from Pink Floyd material, does this mean you are frustrated with Pink Floyd? Mason replied, "I think one doesn't do other things through frustration, but rather because you like to do them. I don't feel that I'd like Pink Floyd to suddenly adopt a rather jazzy style. It's just something I'd like to investigate in another way with some other musicians. In a way, one of the good things about the Floyd is that there is actually enough freedom to do other things outside. There isn't a feeling that commitment to the band has to be

twenty four hours a day."

Why is this the first solo album you've done? Mason replied, "Yes, well, it's partly time, and partly opportunities and ideas. I've done other bits of production for people, and, in a way, this is just a development of that. Solo album is an incorrect title for it, really. But it's part of the way that it worked. It was possible for me to finance making the album, and make it as my project, although, in lots of ways, I'd be just as happy for it to be seen as a Robert Wyatt record, which I'm sure a lot of people will see it as, or as a Carla Bley record. I don't care, really, how it's seen, as long as it was made in a satisfactory way."

Asked about his drum kit, Mason explained, "I use a fairly standard Ludwig kit. I usually use three or maybe four tom toms, and a single bass drum now, although I used to use two. The toms are 12 X 8, 13 X 9, 14 X 14, and 16 X 16, and I don't know what size the bass drum is now. I use a Ludwig black beauty snare, Paiste cymbals, Japanese stool, and AKG microphones. I don't collect drums in a big way. I've got a small Gretsch kit, which I use for some recordings, and I bought some Sonor school drums some time ago, which are terrific, because you can tune them with one handle. I've tried out various snare drums. I've got some Ludwig, Slingerland, and Gretsch snares. I'm not a drum expert but I'm beginning to feel more and more that it's down to the way they're tuned rather than the manufacturer, and that there does seem to be a strange thing with a well looked after old kit sounding better than a new. It does seem that a lot of the problems of tuning drums and getting them to sound right without rattles is something to do with how they're looked after. If the shells or hoops are, in any way, distorted, that's when the problems seem to start. I've had quite a few problems with snare drums."

Do you just play the drums, or are you involved in setting them up? Mason replied, "Well, no drum roadie in the world can ever set up a kit exactly right. I tend to fiddle around more with cymbals than drums, in terms of getting them in the right place, and trying different things. Paiste have always been very good in terms of sending me different things to try. In a way, cymbal fashions change much faster than drum fashions, sizzles and Chinese types, bigger and smaller splashes, and so on. I think it's slightly unnerving just how much I learned from James Guthrie, who was the engineer on 'The Wall.' He spent a lot of time working on the drum sound with me. And he would work at it for much longer than I've ever worked with it before, and got much better results. I was very impressed with the amount of time he did spend, and the different ways he tried to get particular sounds. He got a clean, elegant sound. Hi-fi."

What kind of drum heads do you use? Mason replied, "Remo Ambassadors, usually. I've tried those oil-filled skins and so on, but I feel if the drums are tuned nicely, and give a decent tone without rattling, so much else can be done by using the right microphones. If it's not C451s, then it's Neumanns, or something like that. Just very careful placing of the microphones to get really good separation is very important. There's always a problem with damping and resonances and so on, and quite often we stuck little bits and pieces over them. But once you've got it right, it seems to get better and better all the time, and you can just keep tweaking it. It's a very curious thing, really, because they are the last acoustic instrument of rock and roll. But they're ten times more difficult to sort out to give a satisfactory tone."

In large Pink Floyd concerts, the drums are hardly acoustic. Mason said, "Yes. But I was thinking more of the recording studio situation. But there is a difference between amplifying an acoustic instrument than amplifying direct."

Do you feel detached from your sound in large concert situations? Mason replied, "I try and work almost without monitors, if I can, and try and rely on the good placement of the rest of the band to get a decent feel of what's going on. If you're confident in the engineer, I don't particularly want to hear what I'm playing. I obviously want to hear enough to know that I'm actually playing and hitting the drums correctly. But I'm not too bothered what it sounds like to me as the sound has been set up correctly out front. I'd rather just make sure that I'm hearing the rest of the music, and get on with working with that."

Asked about Roger Waters' use of headphones in concerts, Mason replied, "Roger wears cans because it helps him to

pitch his voice. I only wear cans on the few bits and pieces where we're working with click tracks, particularly when film is involved. We did a certain amount of recording, making a click track first, and then playing on top of that, which I'd never done before and always found very difficult. But, in fact, it was a real breakthrough. I was very impressed with the opportunities you can get by working with pre-recorded stuff. You can really work out very quickly an awful lot of information by having a click track, and, perhaps, scoring the thing as well. From both, you can work some very complicated parts very quickly."

Have you ever had any drum lessons? Mason replied, "I've never had any tutoring at all. I'm entirely self-taught. And it's a real drag. I mean, it's not to be recommended. I think that if you can get the right balance of training and self-help, you can get much better results a lot faster. I think, with most instruments, there is a problem with too much classical training, which can be stultifying. Certainly it can kill off the possibilities of improvisation, which it has done for a lot of people. A good, basic technique is a much better basis from which to work on an instrument, than self-taught messing about. If I wasn't lazy, which is what it really is, as opposed to busy, which is what I say it is, I think I'd take lessons now and learn how to do it properly. But there's that horror of making a fool of myself, and having to start again. That contributes to me not doing it."

In working in Pink Floyd, how are you involved in the process? Mason replied, "Well, it's varied a lot over the years. 'The Wall' was the ultimate that we've reached in that Roger did present a virtually finished idea. I think, however, that once you start recording, inevitably, it changes, however complete it is. But that's the great opportunity, really. Once you start getting the sound down, new things develop. But it was very complete. But I feel about 'The Wall,' although I contributed far less than other albums in terms of having a say in production, how it should go, that it benefited my drumming and the drum sound enormously. I think the playing on the record is far tighter and better, and sounds better, than anything before. I'm actually quite pleased with the way the drumming sounds."

Asked why he was more pleased

with the drum sound on 'The Wall,' Mason replied, "*It's partly engineering, and partly working with click tracks, getting things right, getting the tempo steadier, and getting the actual parts played tighter and better. Being able to really score it at times. I actually got around to learning to read drum parts, which I'd never done before. It's not that Roger presents it in that amount of detail, but rather that once we've decided how it will be, we could sit down and score it. I'm not saying that it was actually scored correctly. But then it's always interesting to see how it should be done. But you might want to break it up in many different ways. But what I'm saying about scoring it is that you can actually play something which is really good, and go back, and instead of having to learn it by heart, you can just hear it once, and score it, so you can always recreate it, especially if you have an elaborate thing, like in an eight bar section where each bar has got a fill in it. And you want to try and remember that and get each one right. It's so nice being able to score sections like that.*"

Asked if he worked out his own scoring technique, Mason replied, "*No. Bob Ezrin really started it. He showed me what it should look like and taught me the basics. He then helped me to devise schemes where, if there was a tricky part, he'd re-write it in a different way.*"

After 'The Wall' album had been completed, a couple of Los Angeles arrangers were asked to score the whole piece properly, including the drum parts. Mason said, "*I didn't want to learn music in the same way that I'd taught myself drums.*"

Mason explained why Pink Floyd were repeating 'The Wall' shows again, saying, "*Because we want to film it.*" As to why it wasn't filmed before, Mason replied, "*Because we're silly billies. No, really, because we'd anticipated using the shows as rehearsals for the film, which would have been shot in a studio situation because we wanted extra light and a different sort of feel. In fact, having played the shows, and re-considered the situation, it became plain that we wanted a live atmosphere, which we simply couldn't get on the set. So, in view of that, it's really a matter of going back and doing them again in order to shoot them. In fact, things we thought would be* the case, like insufficient lighting, turned out to be wrong, as there are films which can accept lighting levels as they are at the concerts.*"

Will this postpone Pink Floyd writing new material? Mason replied, "*We were going to film in the studio even if we weren't going to film in Earls Court, so it's the same schedule, more or less.*" The concerts will keep the band in the public eye, even without new material. Mason said, "*Ah. I see what you mean. I think there'll be some more music written for 'The Wall,' for the film score. There isn't any more material yet, anyway. OK. One can say, yes, it's taking perhaps longer to, not exhaust 'The Wall,' because it's not quite the same as previous things when we've toured it, recorded it, toured it again, and finally got sick of it. I think we still feel there's more development within 'The Wall.' It was designed, originally, to be more than a record and more than a show, really. We still haven't expressed it properly, and there are all sorts of things that filming can do to help, to tell the story properly.*"

Mason denied being bored with the music, and added, "*I think the only frustration would be that we don't play enough, and that's why I'd maybe rather do some more things outside the band. Like I'd love to do some live concerts of my album, or something like that. That would be fairly feasible, I think, if there's enough interest in it, as Carla comes over fairly frequently.*"

Are Pink Floyd going to split up? Mason replied, "*Well, they are more than substantial rumors, really, as I've heard that these concerts are already being billed as 'Farewell gigs.' It's a bit like reading ones own premature obituary. I think you know a band's on the way out when they start announcing 'World Tours' with, in brackets, 'Clean-up tour.' I just don't think we've reached that point yet. You know, we are a dinosaur of rock and roll, in common with, maybe, one or two others. But we are not yet extinct.*" As to the rumors being false, Mason added, "*There's nothing like a denial from the horses mouth.*"

What are Pink Floyd's future plans? Mason said, "*What? You mean after the split? I think that Roger has got some post Wall plans, but, quite honestly, I don't know what they are. I think Dave and Rick will do solo albums. And I know Roger's got some solo* material. But I don't know what he'll do with it. I don't think it will be anything on a scale grander than 'The Wall.' We'd have to do a chariot race set to music, like in Ben Hur."

What is it like being Pink Floyd's drummer? Mason replied, "Well, it feels very nice because I think the show works. So the spirit of the musicians playing it is good. I think a band's spirit falls apart when you know you're kicking a dead horse, when you're working a set that you've played a million times before, and you're just not finding anything new in it. We used to have horrible scenes about encores because when we'd finished a couple of hours playing, we'd exhausted every number we have the least interest in playing. You know, 'Oh God it drives me crazy to think about it.' But there's none of that now. It's a pleasure to play. And there's still a lot of interest in playing it correctly. Even if there isn't the greatest scope for improvisation, it's great to just try and do the show properly. We think it works, not just as a piece of mad spectacle with a thousand different things happening, but that it all hangs together after a fashion and makes some sort of sense, although it's far less free than other things that we've done. That's why it's still a good thing to do."

Asked if the members of Pink Floyd are superfluous to what is happening, Mason replied, "Yes. But that's part of what 'The Wall' is about, the fact that you can be substituted. I think that's one of the fascinations of it. I'm sure someone will do it, even if we don't, that is, to design a show like a play in which you can use different actors to perform a 'thing.' I don't see anything wrong in that, but we haven't yet managed to make that jump."

What are Pink Floyd's motivations? Mason replied, "I think our motivation is still satisfaction with what we're doing. The thing that stops a band is when nothing new turns up and boredom sets in. I think it's more or less as simple as that." Why do you continue to play? Mason said, "Well, of course, we don't play very much. In the past year we've probably done twenty-five shows, which is not a great deal. So it's a novelty! We've invented the three-day year! All I can say, really, is because it's still fun. That's what makes you want to go out. I mean, if you're successful and think, 'God, how boring,' it doesn't take long to think

of really good reasons to retire immediately. The fact that we decided to do the extra shows in Germany indicates this. We all felt that we wanted to play."

Since Roger Waters is the primary song writer in the band, does anyone else in the band have any input in the writing process? Is there room to tell Roger it stinks? Mason replied, "Oh, yes. To a large extent I think we do have a sort of feeling for how things should go. Roger's very good about criticism. I mean, he hardly ever kills anyone! Quite often, people are let off with just a broken leg! Dave contributes quite a lot to the arrangement of things once Roger has done the basics. Quite honestly, I think one gets into dangerous ground here because there's nothing like saying who does what to make everyone feel extremely upset. I mean people do get really involved in whose idea a thing originally was. But Dave does contribute a lot to altering things. Roger also decides changes for himself. But obviously things do get modified. The stage show changed dramatically. If you've got something as elaborate as that, ideas contained within it keep showing up, which you haven't actually envisaged at the start. For instance, it was clear that the wall was going to be erected in a particular way. But until you actually see it going up, you can't be certain. I think Roger's got a very good theatrical sense. We obviously use fairly experienced lighting designers and technicians who also have a good creative sense for sorting out a lot of the effects."

When does the financial aspect of a Pink Floyd concert become too much? Mason replied, "Last year it all went completely out of control. We're extremely evasive about what it really cost, partly because I don't think we really know. All we know is that it cost us a lot more to put on than we made back on it. In theory, the film will recoup some of that, hopefully, and will make me rich as well." Aren't you already rich? Mason said, "I seem to be single handedly paying for the National Health at the moment. The thing is that, once you've committed yourself to something like that, you can't back out. You can't say, 'Let's go and do 'Dark Side of the Moon' instead,' and leave sixteen tons of equipment here. One's too cowardly to make those sensible decisions. So you crash on regardless, and hopefully it all comes out right in the end."

1982
The Wall Movie

What about touring 'The Wall?' Mason replied, "*It's not a touring show. The cost of putting it on makes it prohibitive. I mean, you can do it, and once you've paid off the capital equipment, you'd eventually make money on it. But it's such a hard way of doing it. And it has to be done properly to make it worthwhile. That means three days of set-up instead of twenty-four hours, and lots of rehearsals. It's a very impractical show, and not something I'd like to repeat in a hurry.*"

What about future Pink Floyd concerts? Mason replied, "*I think there may always be a difference of opinion between us about how much live work each of us want to do. I think especially Dave and myself like playing enough to want to go out and do something.*"

August 1981 - Hi-Fi News and Record Review (U.K.) reviewed the Nick Mason album, 'Fictitious Sports.' They wrote that the songs, all written by keyboard player, Carla Bley, are angular and a bit melody shy, but with Robert Wyatt singing, it doesn't matter. He is able to give the songs a wonderful feeling of melancholy, such as on the song 'Do Ya?' The musicians play enterprisingly and sometimes brilliantly, always maintaining interest.

October 1, 1981 - Rolling Stone (U.S.) reported that 'The Wall' album will be made into a movie, to be directed by Alan Parker. The movie will include live and animated segments. Roger Waters wrote the screenplay, and will write additional music for the film. Animation for the film will be created by Gerald Scarfe. Spokesman Allen Burry stated that the movie "is not a rock opera, it's not a rock & roll movie, and it's not a film of a concert. In fact, we're trying to figure out exactly what it is." He also added that none of the band members will appear in the film.

March 27, 1982 - Melody Maker (U.K.) reported that 'The Wall' movie will premiere in London, England on July 15, 1982. Bob Geldof compared his acting in the movie to midway between Al Pacino and Marlon Brando.

May 13, 1982 - Rolling Stone (U.S.) reported that shooting of 'The Wall' movie by Alan Parker has been completed and the movie should be ready by July. Gerald Scarfe is currently working on additional visuals, and Roger Waters is writing 25 minutes of additional music for the film at his home studio. The new music will include a new song, 'When the Tigers Broke Free,' and features a 100-voice male choir recorded in Wales.

June 27, 1982 - Sunday Magazine (U.K.) published an article titled, "Climbing the Wall" by Ray Connolly that featured interviews with Roger Waters, Alan Parker, and Gerald Scarfe. Connolly wrote that 'The Wall' movie was premiered at Cannes last month and debuts in London on July 14, 1982.

Roger Waters talked about not being recognizable, saying, "*By not having a face which is known to the public, I am able to have the best of both worlds. I get all the acclaim and rewards for the work I do without having to be aggravated by people bothering me. It's a very nice state of affairs.*"

Waters explained how 'The Wall' came about, saying, "*I was on stage in Montreal in 1977 on the final night of a tour, and there was one guy in the front row who was shouting and screaming all the way through everything. In the end, I called him over and, when he got close enough, I spat in his face. I shocked myself with that incident, enough to think, 'Hold on a minute. This is all wrong. I'm hating all this.' Then I began to think what it was all about.*"

Recalling his childhood, Waters, who was brought up in Cambridge, said, "*My parents were schoolteachers and devout Christians and pacifists at the beginning of the war. My father was a conscientious objector at first, and did his part for the war effort by driving an ambulance. But then he and my mother became converted to Communism and, after joining the Party, he thought it was right to fight. So he joined the Royal Fusiliers. He*

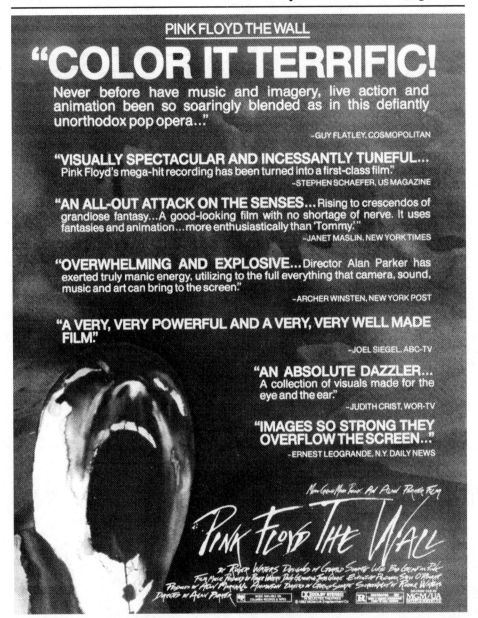

was killed at Anzio. My mother stayed with the Party and all through my childhood she would take me to things like 'Friends of China' meetings. So I had an extreme left-wing indoctrination from a very early age. In the end, of course, you find your own way."

Talking about recording 'The Wall' album, Waters explained, "We recorded the album abroad because we panicked about income tax, we had to get out of the country quickly. We didn't have £2 million to lose and

we were terrified that they'd come after us. In those days, when tax was 83 percent, it went against the grain to pay so much. I suppose it's just ones personal greed, but it led to everyone in the business joining some scheme to pay less. We were taken in by the pin-stripe suits and the smart ties. If 'Dark Side of the Moon' had been the only work I'd had in me, I'd have been finished. Luckily, I had 'The Wall' as well."

Gerald Scarfe, who collaborated on 'The Wall,' explained, *"Roger saw right at the beginning that 'The Wall' could be an album, a show, and a film. My first work on animation was to draw the hammers, a symbol of oppression, which were used in the concerts the group did when the album was first released. As soon as we had done the shows, we discussed the film."*

Director Alan Parker, who had heard 'The Wall' album, sent a letter to EMI films suggesting that it would make a good movie. Parker said, *"We're still waiting for their letter to say they don't want to do it."* MGM, however, did want to do it.

Gerald Scarfe drew a storyboard for the movie, and filming began last September. For the animation, 50 artists were used. Scarfe explained, *"You can do anything with animation. You can turn a telephone box into the Empire State Building if you want to. In live action, that sort of thing isn't possible. At the same time, I had to change my style from The Sunday Times scratchy-pen approach to cartoons, to something that could be copied by other artists. The reason that Disney drew the way he did was because everyone could draw like Disney, at least everyone who could draw. So to do this, I had to explore other areas of my work, which was very exciting. Altogether, we did about 14,000 separate drawings for the animation section."*

Personal tension existed between the collaborators on the film. Parker explained, *"There has been a clash of three egos. If you put three megalomaniacs in a room together, there are bound to be sparks."* Scarfe added, *"You could say that the collaborative process has been filled with angst. But, possibly, out of that will come something rather special. After all, we're only an artist, a musician, and a filmmaker. I wonder if Picasso and Stravinsky would ever have had these problems."*

Now that the film is done, Roger Waters plays golf and is working on a piece for theater that will be performed by musicians other than Pink Floyd. Waters explained, *"The trouble with rock and roll is that you only stay a few nights in one place and by the time you've just about got the sound right, you have to move on to the next gig and begin all over again. I'd like to do something in theatre so that it would stay for a long time in the same*

place and we could get it absolutely perfect. I'd also like to work in film again, but on a much smaller scale. I've been used to controlling what I do for so long that it's difficult to work with someone else."

July 10, 1982 - New Musical Express (U.K.) reviewed the Pink Floyd movie, 'The Wall' with an article titled, "A Wall Over Troubled Waters" by Richard Cook. Cook wrote that, as a rock movie, 'The Wall' stands high, but as a real movie it is grainy and stolid. Images are cross-referenced exhaustively. Technically it is impeccable, and Gerald Scarfe's animations have demonic energy. But the movie tells us nothing new of 1970s excesses. The reviewer can't see it as a personal odyssey.

July 1982 - Music Week (U.S.) reviewed the Pink Floyd movie, 'The Wall' with an article about the premiere of 'The Wall' movie. They wrote, "It is an escapist movie." "Everyone seemed shell-shocked." "The Wall has set the standard by which all future music-inspired films will be judged."

July 15, 1982 - The Daily Mail (U.K.) published an article titled, "The boy in 5,000 who won role with a rock star" by Mike Richardson. 14-year old Kevin McKeon won the role of Young Pink in the Alan Parker movie, 'The Wall,' even though he did not really audition for the part. McKeon said, *"I remember it was a Sunday and my friend Paul came around and said there was an audition at the church hall. We didn't know what that was. He had read it in the paper and he asked me to go with him. When we got there, I sort of joined in. They filmed me and showed my face on a video screen and said they might call me up. I didn't really take any notice, but they did call me up the next day and offered me a part."* McKeon enjoyed making the film, but said, *"There was one scene when I got right embarrassed. It was in a railway station and lots of people had to sing at me. That was bad enough, but there were lots of kids in the distance laughing at us. I blushed quite a few times."*

The Guardian (U.K.) reviewed the Pink Floyd movie, 'The Wall.' Derek Malcolm called it an extraordinary film, something no

American director could have done. A considerable achievement.

July 18, 1982 - Sunday Magazine (U.K.) reported on 'The Wall' movie with an interview with Bob Geldof who played the character Pink in the movie. Geldof said, *"I was terrified to see the film. It was only when it was shown in Cannes that I had the courage to creep into the screening. I told the director not to be offended if I walked out the first time I saw it."*

Geldof continued, *"The movie charts Pink through three stages, from a young child to a boy, and then man. I end up as this mad rock singer, who has come to represent society falling apart. When I first read the storyline I felt it was almost what I'd call naive. The point it's making isn't original, but that doesn't mean it hasn't got something new to say. I have to admit that when I first met Parker and he asked me if I'd seen 'The Wall,' I replied. 'Sure, I see it at the bottom of my garden everyday.' That was the extent of my knowledge of the music."*

Geldof explained, *"It had an amazing impact on me. I'm rarely shocked into silence. Frankly I look horrible as Pink, especially the skeleton scene with flesh falling off my bones. Sure it's disgusting, but it comes over as a strong representation of society falling apart. I start off looking reasonably OK. But like Dorian Gray, who sold his soul to the devil, I gradually get worse."*

July 19, 1982 - Record Business reviewed the Pink Floyd movie, 'The Wall' with an article titled, "Waters' view – just too black to be credible" by Brian Mulligan. Mulligan wrote that `The Wall' is a truly nasty film, and that Waters' view of mankind is totally and morbidly hopeless. It is confusing, overlong, disturbing, and offers no hope for the future. But, occasionally, the music and visuals have a stunning impact on the senses.

July 24, 1982 - New Musical Express (U.K.) reported that Pink Floyd's new single, 'When the Tigers Broke Free,' backed by 'Bring the Boys Back Home' will be released the following week. Early pressings will have a triple gatefold sleeve with scenes from the movie, 'The Wall.' 'The Wall' movie is due to go on general release in August, and includes music from 'The Wall' album, plus some new Roger Waters compositions that are to be released on August 31, 1982, as a new Pink Floyd album called 'The Final Cut.' Avon Books have just published the book, 'Pink Floyd - The Wall' that features lyrics and color stills from the movie.

August 6, 1982 - The New York Post (U.S.) reviewed the Pink Floyd movie, 'The Wall' with an article titled, "Explosive Pink Floyd flick is off its rocker" by Archer Winsten. Winsten wrote that, "as a one shot entertainment, it is overwhelming." The film is an "emotional explosion that happens in another place, a different time."

The Record (U.S.) reviewed the Pink Floyd movie, 'The Wall' with an article titled, "Pink Floyd/The Wall combines music, art to stunning effect" by Jim Wright. Wright wrote that the films' message may be cliché-riddled, but it is presented in "a most effective mix of rock and rolling cameras." It employs a "jarring narrative form," and is the latest in a long line of British movies about alienated youth. While the ideas in the movie are not particularly original, they are portrayed in "high style." Scenes of bloody violence, open wounds, and bizarre sexual imagery may be too much for some people, and "if you're not a Pink Floyd fan, the movie may leave you uncomfortably numb."

August 7, 1982 - Melody Maker (U.K.) published an article titled, "Floyd's Soundtrack Becomes New Album" by Karl Dallas. Roger Waters, who flew to the States for the premiere of 'The Wall' movie, is half-finished with a new Pink Floyd album. Waters explained, *"We were contracted to make a soundtrack album, but there really wasn't enough new material in the movie to make a record that I thought was interesting. The project then became called 'Spare Bricks,' and was meant to include some of the film music, like 'When the Tigers Broke Free,' and the much less ironic version of 'Outside the Wall' which finishes the movie, the sequence with the kids playing with the milk bottles, plus some music written for the movie but left on the cutting-room floor. I decided not to include the* new version of 'Mother' from the movie because it really is film music and it doesn't stand up. It's a very long song, and besides, I'm bored with all that now. I've become more interested in the remembrance and requiem aspects of the thing, if that doesn't sound too pretentious. Anyway, it all seemed a bit bitty when I came up with a new title for the album, 'The Final Cut.'"

Asked if this would be Pink Floyd's final album, Waters replied, "*I would doubt that very much.*"

Waters continued, "*From that title, the whole thing started developing a different flavor, and I finally wrote the requiem that I've been trying to write for so long, 'Requiem for the Post-War Dream,' which became the subtitle of the album.*"

The song, 'The Fletcher Memorial Home' from the album appears to change the subject from the personal hang-ups of a rock star to the more political issues of the movie. Waters explained, "*It's become obvious that we were attempting the impossible in trying to finish the album before I go to the States, so we have got to the stage of a rough throw-together of all the work we've done so far. After about a week's work on the American launch, I'm going to take a holiday, and when we get back in September, we'll finish the album.*"

The Toronto Star (Canada) published three articles about 'The Wall' movie.

The first article, titled, "Pink Floyd's The Wall is not just another brick" by Sid Adilman, praised 'The Wall' movie, and featured interviews with Alan Parker and Gerald Scarfe. Director Alan Parker stated, "*In fact, when we were trying to raise the financing, to try to explain what we were going to do was difficult. They had trouble visualizing it.*" Pink Floyd "*could have done a concert film and got it out quickly. But Pink Floyd has always tried to do something new.*"

In selling the movie to the British film industry, Parker recalled saying, "*Look at 'The Wall,' a number one album in goodness knows how many countries, an obvious narrative line, where is the film? Didn't anyone in the record division play the tapes to anyone in the film division?*" Parker was then put in touch with Roger Waters. Parker explained, "*At the time, I only intended to tell him who to avoid in the film industry. I said he*

didn't need another writer. He was THE writer. I had been involved with other rock n' roll film projects before, and had seen the original intention of the creators lost by the process. The most notable being the film 'Sergeant Pepper.' My advice was not to write a conventional screenplay but to follow the albums narrative links.*"

After Pink Floyd put up the first $5 million, Alan Parker agreed to do the film and United Artists backed it. Parker said, "*There are 99 minutes of screen time. A lot of images to tell a story just with music is quite complex. I shot dialog every day, but no more than five percent of it has dialog. But it's there at the back of the music. This film belongs to three people: me, Roger Waters, and Gerald Scarfe. 'Pink Floyd - The Wall' is a very painful expression. It's Roger's, but I put some of my anger into it.*"

Illustrator and writer Gerald Scarfe explained, "*This movie has got a long history. Roger wrote it three years ago, and he and I worked on the screenplay for a long time, and we realized we needed a filmmaker. It was always meant to be a complex picture. We decided not to pull our punches. When you're working on something, it's hard to know how violent the images really are. But it will be difficult to make a show bigger than The Wall.*" Parker "*likened it to Livingston going up the Zambezi. Now that it was finished, in retrospect, it felt more like going over Victoria Falls in a barrel.*"

The second article in this issue was a review of 'The Wall' movie titled, "Top-heavy with symbols, Wall collapses" by Ron Base. Base refered to the movie as bleak, a "zombie-like, punk rock" movie, and "desensitized pretentiousness."

The third article in this issue was titled, "Other projects delayed movie" by Peter Goddard, and featured a phone interview done with David Gilmour from Los Angeles. Gilmour explained, "*We had a director picked out years ago, and various other people hired, including a screen-writer, but we were trying to do too much. As it turned out, the album, the live concert, and the movie are three different projects. Each needed a lot of time to be complete. So we decided to drop the movie to get on with the making of the album. Not that the original album was intended to be a* soundtrack. It was intended to stand up fully and completely as an album. But we will likely be releasing, this fall, some music which was to be included in the movie, but had to be cut."

Gilmour continued, "The album, the concerts, and the movie all tell basically the same story, and they use the same music, but the imagery is much more specific in the movie. It's also more autobiographical. It's more about Roger, who wrote the story."

Asked about the specific references in the movie, Gilmour said, "It was Roger's and Al Parker's intention of making the story more specific, harder, and stronger. Because the album is lyrics, singing, and sound effects, it's not as specific as the movie. On the record, for instance, there's the reference 'Daddy's flown across the ocean,' rather than 'Daddy got killed' as it appears in the movie. That is the truth of the matter, though. Roger's father actually got killed at Anzio during the war, before he even knew him. Roger, Alan Parker, all of us, in fact, who worked on it, are of that generation who were born at or just after the end of the war. What Roger and Parker were trying to do with it was to be specific to that particular age group. We're not apologizing for being this specific. You can't make things for the largest possible audience, pandering to their taste. You have to do what you want to do."

August 15, 1982 - The Toronto Sun (Canada) reviewed the Pink Floyd movie, 'The Wall' with an article titled, "The Wall – Building a story brick by brick" by Bruce Kirkland. Kirkland wrote that seeing 'The Wall' movie at a theater is voluntary suicide, yet the movie is "a beautiful, brilliant film." It "overloads your capacity for negative images and feelings," and is "one of the few must-see movies of the year."

August 21, 1982 - Melody Maker (U.K.) published a letter from Sharon Taylor of Clewer Crescent, Harrow Weald, Middlesex, England, in which she described 'The Wall' movie as simply amazing. "Definitely the film of the year."

August 23, 1982 - The New York Post (U.S.) published an article titled, "Who Needs Words?" by Diana Maychick that featured an interview with Gerald Scarfe. Maychick wrote that `The Wall' movie has been breaking records at the Ziegfield Theater, where it took in $123,673 in its first week.

Artist Gerald Scarfe, who designed and did animations for the film, talked about the film, saying, "There is no gratuitous blood. The horrors depicted are necessary for a true depiction of increasing psychosis."

When he was young, Scarfe had a severe case of asthma. He explained, "All I could do is dream, and read, and draw ships sinking, volcanoes erupting, airplanes crashing. Once I got down on paper all the things I feared, somehow I tamed the fear. It's the same in the movie. I think Alan felt the same way."

Talking about the lack of dialog in the movie, Scarfe said, "Words are not necessary to impart strong images. Look at Walt Disney."

Talking about how he got involved with the movie, Scarfe explained, "One day Roger Waters called. 'I have this idea,' he said. 'It's gonna be an album, a stage show, then a movie.' Roger and I have been friends for years, but I thought to myself this is a mighty ambitious project. I just hoped we could pull it off."

The movie features both live action and animation. Scarfe talked about the animation process, explaining, "In animation, you watch 12 drawings pass by every second. Each one is slightly different. It's a painstakingly difficult process. Like in the scene where the flowers make love. Within seconds, they're fighting, and then, imperceptibly, one destroys the other. But it took months to make that melting process, one picture dripping into another, look seamless."

Ten thousand drawings were used for the 15 minutes of animation in the film. Scarfe explained, "I passed each drawing on to my animators who added the connective tissue to make them evolve. It took some time for me to get used to the idea that my art no longer came straight from my head, went down through my arm, then out of my pen. With animation, there's a whole group of intermediaries."

September 16, 1982 - The New York Daily News (U.S.) published an article titled, "What

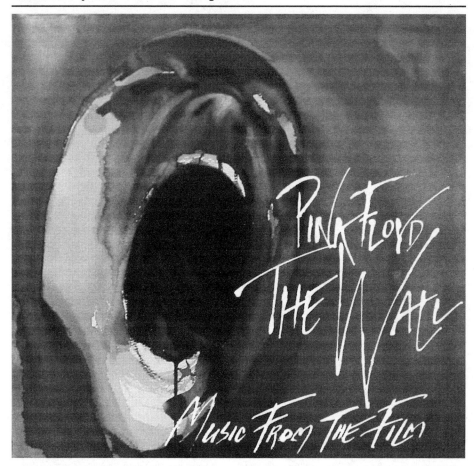

gives Pink Floyd staying power?" by Lynn Van Matre. Pink Floyd have endured, and 'Dark Side of the Moon,' which has sold 17 million copies worldwide, is their finest album and a rock classic.

David Gilmour talked about the development of their music, saying, *"We always wanted to be better in the area of lyrics, but none of us, frankly, was very good at it. So we relied on what we did best until Roger started feeling more confident and could start writing stuff, and we began attempting something with real meaning. It was around 1972 or so, I think, that he started feeling that he could say something meaningful, and that was a good thing all around for us."*

Talking about the music now being Waters' outlook on life and society, Gilmour said, *"A lot of the stuff that we have done in the past is Roger's view of life. I do write lyrics myself, but Pink Floyd albums tend to be about*

a certain subject or a certain concept, and I find it very hard to write songs that fit in with somebody else's concept. We don't all always agree with Roger's ideas, but we do recognize that most of the things he talks about, or aspects of them, do have their place."

Rolling Stone (U.S.) published an article titled, "Behind Pink Floyd's Wall" by Mick Brown and Kurt Loder. The article featured interviews with Roger Waters at his home in London in November 1981, Alan Parker at Pinewood Studios in April 1982, David Gilmour in a hotel suite on Fifth Avenue, New York in August 1982, and Bob Geldof at Pinewood Studios in November 1981.

The Wall album was inspired by Roger Waters' spitting incident at a concert in 1977, and Waters said that it was *"a very fascistic thing to do. It frightened me. But I'd known for a while during that tour, which I hated, that there was something very wrong. I didn't feel in contact with the audience. They were no longer people. They had become it, a beast. I felt this enormous barrier between them and what I was trying to do. And it had become almost impossible to clamber over it."*

Talking about 'The Wall' concerts, Waters said, *"To actually wall yourself off from people is a very belligerent, aggressive idea. But I liked doing 'The Wall' live. I felt I was making more contact because I was expressing all these ideas about what I feel about it."*

Talking about the state of Pink Floyd, Waters explained, *"We no longer pretend to one another. Back in the early Seventies, we used to pretend that we were a group. We used to pretend that we all do this and we all do that, which of course wasn't true. And at one point I started to get very resentful, because I was doing a lot more and yet we were all pretending that we were doing it. Well, we don't pretend anymore. I could work with another drummer and keyboard player very easily, and it's likely that at some point I will."*

Asked about the future of Pink Floyd, Water replied, *"Depends very much on me."*

Asked about 'The Wall' movie, Alan Parker recalled, *"Roger went on holiday for six weeks. In that period I was allowed to develop my vision, and I really made the film with a completely free hand. I had to have that. I couldn't be second-guessed by Roger, and he appreciated that. The difficulty came when I'd finished. I'd been shooting for sixty days, fourteen hours a day. That film had become mine. And then Roger came back to it, and I had to go through the very difficult reality of having it put over to me that it actually was a collaborative effort."*

Waters said that filming the movie had been *"the most unnerving, neurotic period of my life, with the possible exception of my divorce in 1975. Parker is used to sitting at the top of his pyramid, and I'm used to sitting at the top of mine. We're both pretty much used to getting our own way. If I'd have directed it, which I'd never have done, it would have been much quieter than it is. But that's one of the reasons I liked the idea of Parker doing it. He paints in fairly bold strokes. He is very worried about boring his audience. It suits us very well because we did want a lot of this to be a punch*

in the face. I wanted to make comparisons between rock and roll concerts and war. People at those big things seem to like being treated very badly, to have it so loud and distorted that it really hurts. But there is very little of that left in the film. For a long time, the script had this image of a rock & roll audience being blown up, bombed, and, as they were being blown to pieces, applauding, loving every minute. As an idea, it is quite pleasing, but it would look silly to actually do it on film. It would be hard for it not to be comic."

Referring to the demolished hotel room scene in the film, Waters observed, *"No, no, no. This isn't my room at all. Dave Gilmour, perhaps, but not me. I'm much tidier."*

Bob Geldof commented on the Pink character in the movie, saying, *"A lot of what happens to Pink is his own fault. I think he brings it upon himself. People who try to achieve something, and then, once they've achieved it, can't handle it, are essentially weak people. You shouldn't strive for something if you don't know what you want it for."*

Asked about the history of Pink Floyd, David Gilmour talked about Syd Barrett's departure, saying, *"I wouldn't put it down to drugs or LSD, necessarily. I suspect that it would have happened anyway, and maybe that stuff acted as a catalyst. He certainly couldn't handle success and all the things that go with it, as in 'The Wall' story, really. And he started going mad after the first hints of success. Toward the end of 1967, he was in a condition where he wouldn't play with the band at all. He would just stand onstage with his amp and guitar turned full up, his left arm hanging down by his side and just sort of smashing the guitar with his right hand, making a fearful racket all night long. No one would book the band back for return dates. Their career was diving downhill as fast as it could go."*

At the time, it was suggested that Barrett remain a non-performing member of Pink Floyd, but Gilmour thinks that *"was just a political way of dealing with the situation. There was, at one point, an intention for Syd to stay home and write wonderful songs, become the mystery Brian Wilson figure behind the group. But there was no point in him coming with us."*

As for Barrett's solo career after leaving Pink Floyd, Gilmour said, "*I've got a few other songs at home on cassette. But Syd was . . . The long and the short of it was that he was quite severely mentally ill. Every psychiatrist who's seen him says he's incurable, and he's still the same. He can't look after himself now. His mother has to look after him, and I expect at some point that he'll have to be institutionalized. I don't know whether he writes anything at all these days, but his romantic madcap image is entirely false. There's nothing romantic about it. He's not a happy person. He's just on a completely other level.*"

Asked about Rick Wright's departure from Pink Floyd, Gilmour explained, "*Well, you know, none of us has ever been the best of friends. I have never been a close personal friend of anyone else in the band, and neither was Rick, really. Roger and Nick have at times been fairly close. We don't not get along, but we're working partners.*"

As for his present situation, Roger Waters explained, "*I spent an awful lot of my life, until I was about twenty-eight, waiting for my life to start. I thought that at some point I would turn from a chrysalis into a butterfly, that my real life would begin. So if I had that bit of my life to live again, I would rather live the years between eighteen and twenty-eight knowing that that was it, that nothing was suddenly going to happen, that it was happening all the time. Time passes, and you are what you are, you do what you do.*"

Asked what his impression of 'The Wall' movie was, Waters replied, "*It does say quite loudly that it is bad for us when we're isolated from one another and frightened of one another. And the film gets criticized for that, either by people who say it's not true, or by people who think it's self-evident and therefore not worth saying. I believe that it is true and it is worth saying.*"

Asked about outside influences, Waters said, "*You make your own decisions, your own life. What 'they' do clearly impinges on your life, but in the end, the responsibility for what you do and how you feel about yourself is yours. You are an individual. You're alone, but that's all right.*"

September 18, 1982 - The London Free Press (U.K.) reviewed the Pink Floyd movie, 'The Wall' with an article titled, "The Wall weird, fascinating" by Noel Gallagher. Gallagher wrote that 'The Wall' is "an energy-charged hard rock opera." Its offbeat approach and in-tune soundtrack makes it "a film experience well worth suffering through its rough spots."

September 30, 1982 - Rolling Stone (U.S.) reviewed the Pink Floyd movie, 'The Wall.' They wrote that the film "celebrates the suicidal self-pity of a burned out British rock star."

October 2, 1982 - New Musical Express (U.K.) published an article titled, "Syd Get's His Trousers Back." They reported that an article in the French magazine, Actuel, by writers Michka Assayas and Thomas Johnson, reveled that the journalists had tracked Barrett to his home in Cambridge, and spoke to him briefly at his doorstep.

The interview began when the writers brought Barrett some clothes he had left in Chelsea, and Barrett replied, "*Thanks very much. Do you want some money? Did they pay you?*"

Asked what he is doing these days, and whether he paints, Barrett answered, "*No. I've just had an operation, but nothing too serious. I'm trying to go back down there, but I've got to wait. There's a train strike at the moment.*" Told that the strike has been over for several weeks, Barrett said, "*Oh, good. Thanks very much.*"

Asked if he played guitar in his apartment in London, Barrett replied, "*No. No. I watch TV. That's all.*" Asked if he wants to play again, he answered, "*No, not really. I don't have time to do very much. I must find myself a flat in London. But it's difficult. I'll have to wait.*"

Referring to his clothes, Barrett said, "*I didn't think I'd get these things back. And I knew I couldn't write. I couldn't have made my mind up to go and get them, to get the train and all that. But then, I didn't even write to them. Mum said she'd get in touch with the office. Thanks, anyway.*"

Asked if he remembers Duggie Fields, Barrett replied, "*Uh, yes. I never saw him again. I'm not going to see anyone in*

London." Told that his friends say 'hello,' he said, *"Ah, thanks. That's nice."*

Asked if they could take a photo, Barrett agreed, *"Yes. sure,"* and afterwards, *"Good. That's enough now. It's painful for me. Thank you."*

The interviewer commented that a tree in front of the house looked nice, and Barrett replied, *"Yes, but not anymore. They cut it, not long ago. Before that, I liked it a lot."*

Barrett's mother called from the house, "Roger, come and have a cup of tea, and say hello to my friends." Barrett, told the reporters, *"Good. There you are. Maybe we'll see each other again in London. Bye."*

October 3, 1982 - The Wilmington Star (U.S.) reviewed the Pink Floyd movie, 'The Wall' with an article titled, "Pink Floyd promises more than it delivers" by Ben Steelman. Steelman wrote that 'The Wall' movie has been bombed by critics, but it will be remembered as the groundbreaking movie of 1982, "the one that contained the most innovations in the way films are made." It is the first commercial movie release to combine videotape production with music. Although the film never adds up to the sum of its parts, "five minutes of it can stun you with its brilliance, 95 minutes leaves you uncomfortably numb." "The Wall suggests what the technology can do in better hands."

October 1982 – American Cinematographer (U.S.) published three articles about the making of 'The Wall' movie.

The first article was titled, "Notes on Pink Floyd The Wall" by Richard Patterson and David W. Samuelson. The movie, which reportedly cost $10 million to make, does not have a conventional plot or dialog, but it does have a logical structure. Scenes in the movie depict the life of rock star Pink, and explores his consciousness with both live action and animation. The art for the animation had to be adapted to the anamorphic format and a special camera had to be used.

Kent Houston and Chris King of the Peerless Camera Company filmed the animation using a Panatar lens that could focus on a 6 1/2 inch wide area. They also created a motorized focus control that allowed them to follow focus on computerized moves. To

overcome a certain amount of distortion appearing in the field, field charts were sent to the animation artists that allowed them to draw within the allowable frame width. King explained, *"It was never an effective problem in terms of what people were going to see on the screen, but I think because there isn't really a Panavision lens designed to shoot animation, there are probably one or two things that could be improved in the system to give us a much more even field of focus from edge to edge. But, by and large, the results were very satisfactory."*

King continued, *"There was one sequence, in the 'Goodbye Blue Skies' sequence with the warlord, where the dove was metamorphosed into a bird which becomes a bomber and flies through the sky over London. Eventually, it turns into a warlord and bombers fly out of its belly. There are various explosions and effects in that, setup over the top of London. We had a lot of mixes from one scene to another and they become very drawn out where we were doing shadow effects and then a lot of small neon effects for explosions and for glowing eyes. Each one of these effects was a separate run. We had the complication of having to use very large artwork with field sizes up to 29 to 30 inches across, and there were multiple movements of the camera, the table top, and peg bars at the same time with dissolves. I think, as far as my experience of animation shooting goes, it was the most difficult shoot I've done in all my life."*

For shooting the live action sequences, Gerald Scarfe's designs were used by production designer Brian Morris and director of photography Peter Biziou to create surrealistic scenes that blended well with the animated sequences. Biziou explained, *"I was going to go for very strong contrast. I would be using, for instance, arcs with clear glass for hard shadows, this kind of thing. I decided to let myself be affected by the mood and words of the Floyd's music and apply as much dramatic effect as possible to Brian's set designs and Alan's ideas. Technically, this involved using super speed lenses and keeping the negative as clean as possible because the 35mm squeezed negative was going to 70mm and through opticals. The Samcine Inclining Prism was also invaluable."*

Low angles were used to create a

surreal effect. Biziou explained, *"The camera pulls back from a medium close up of Pink in his armchair to a very wide angle, and we discover either the room is very large or he's very small. Then the shadow of his wife appears on the wall. She is walking towards him and growing in size, and very smoothly her form becomes Gerald Scarfe's animation, which continues growing into a gross figure that is persecuting Pink. Brian Morris had to build a very large room and cheat the perspective. We kept Pink and all the furniture the same normal size so that, as the camera pulls back, you are given the impression that he's totally alienated in this very, very large room."*

The second article in this issue was titled, "The Making of the Film, Brick by Brick, From My View" by Alan Parker. Director Alan Parker discussed how he got involved in making 'The Wall' film. Parker first talked with Roger Waters in his home studio about 'The Wall.' Parker told Waters that a conventional screenplay wasn't necessary, and that the music could be the narrative. The following day, Parker met with Waters and Gerald Scarfe, who showed him a storyboard for the film. Although Parker did not want to direct the movie, he returned every day for the next two weeks to go over the script. Later, while Parker was working on the movie 'Shoot the Moon,' Waters called and suggested that he and Parker should produce the film, while Michael Seresin and Gerald Scarfe would direct it. This was agreeable to Parker.

In January 1981, Parker's associate producer Garth Thomas and production designer Brian Morris began production preparation for The Wall. In February 1981, Parker and Seresin flew to Germany to witness Pink Floyd performing 'The Wall' live at the Westfallenhalle in Dortmund. It was "rock theater on the grandest scale." When he got back to the States, Parker was visited by Pink Floyd's manager, Steve O'Rourke, who was going to be the executive producer for 'The Wall' movie, as well as the go between for Waters and Parker.

After Parker finished editing his current movie, 'Shoot the Moon,' he returned to London to work with Waters and Scarfe on the script for 'The Wall.' They created a giant storyboard across the walls of Waters studio.

One of the ideas they had was to use scenes of Pink Floyd in places as narrators, so five additional Pink Floyd concerts were scheduled in London for the purpose of filming them. Also at this time, Parker and O'Rourke returned to Los Angeles to try and sell the movie to a Hollywood Studio. Despite numerous rejections, eventually MGM agreed to take a chance on it.

In June 1981, the Pink Floyd concerts took place in London, and three camera crews filmed the shows. But the filming was a disaster. The film crews didn't know what they were supposed to be doing, and the low light Panavision lenses had no resolution. A Louma crane that was used during 'Hey You' to climb up and over the wall and show the audience, never got the correct shot, despite five different takes. Parker realized at this point that, in order to make the film, he would have to direct it. Parker and Waters agreed to this on the conditions that Parker would have more control over the film, and that Alan Marshall would take over as producer. Parker began working on the 39-page script, while Scarfe developed his animations for the film.

The Pink Floyd concerts had convinced Parker that a narrator wasn't necessary, and that the use of live concert footage would defeat their efforts not to make it a concert movie. Bob Geldof was cast as Pink after a screen test reading the courtroom scene from the movie, 'Midnight Express.' Little Pink and young Pink were found after an open call was broadcast on radio stations in London, Manchester, Leeds, and Glasgow. Keven McKeon was picked after he turned up in Leeds with a neighbor's child who was auditioning.

Filming began on September 7, 1981 at a retired admiral's house in East Molesey that became young Pink's residence for the movie. The sequence of the teacher with his wife was also shot here. Outside the house, a second unit used six cats and three crates of doves to get a shot of a dove flying into the air. A playground in Bermondsey was used for the scenes of pink in the playground. The rugby field scene was filmed at Epsom Downs, while the outside of the Los Angeles Sports Arena was shot at Wembley Stadium using kids from the local American school. The Anzio sequences were filmed at Burnham Beaches at Barnstaple, with 200 soldiers from the local labor exchange. The first scene with Bob Geldof was shot with him sitting in a chair in an alien landscape.

A laboratory in Oxford was used for the close-ups of skin and drops of blood. The interiors of Pink's hotel room were shot on the 'D' stage at Pinewood Studios with a Los Angeles backdrop. The giant wall was also built at Pinewood with granite-like blocks and a false perspective to give the impression that the wall went on forever. A sequence had been planned for the wall to open up, as it did in the concerts, but this was discarded. An enormous air cannon borrowed from a James Bond movie blew up the wall.

For the concert scene for 'In the Flesh,' the Horticultural Hall was used with a specially built stage, and was shot on October 28, 1981, the 38th day of filming, with 380 skinheads, 24 choir members, a 21-piece brass band, six mothers with babies, 30 guards, and three guard dogs. For 'Run Like Hell,' choreographer Gillian Gregory devised a Nazi-esque disco dance.

On the 41st day of shooting, scenes of football crowd violence were filmed at Watford Football Ground, but only bits of these scenes appeared in the final film during the song, 'Waiting for the Worms.' The street violence during this song was filmed in Muswell Hill behind the remains of the Alexandra Palace.

A deserted cake factory in Hammersmith was converted into a surreal lunatic asylum, where Pink was wheeled into a room of rows of neatly made beds, but only a bit of this made it into the film during the song, 'Hey You.' The asylum scene was inspired by Roger Waters, who had originally written about a bald headed Pink eating sweets in a padded cell.

The train scene with young Pink was filmed using the Keighley and Worth Valley Railroad near Bradford. Originally, the teacher puppet was to be dangled from a crane in the tunnel in this scene, but this did not work in the context of the movie. 'Bring the Boys Back Home' was filmed at Keighley Station using local people as extras.

The school maze for 'Another Brick in the Wall, Part 2' was built at Pinewood Studios by Brian Morris, and the destructive sequence was begun here and finished at the Becton Gas Works. The riot scene at the Becton Gas Works was shot on the 57th day of filming, and used 150 rioters and police, two police vans, police cars, smoke, and tear gas guns. For 'Run Like Hell,' a Brixton Café was built in back of Kings Cross Railway Station, where it was destroyed by the 'Hammer Guard' that consisted of members of the 'Tilbury Skins.' The rape scene was unpleasant and was cut down for the final cut.

For sixteen weeks, Parker had supervised 61 consecutive 14 hour work days that included 977 shots, 4,885 takes, and used 350,000 feet of film. During post-production, James Guthrie mixed the music in the Pinewood 2 Dubbing Theater. Waters recorded the new song 'When the Tigers Broke Free' with assistance from Michael Kamen. A new version of 'Mother' was also recorded, and the songs, 'In the Flesh,' 'Outside the Wall' and 'Bring the Boys Back Home' were redone. A prelude was also recorded, but not used. An additional 7 1/2 minutes of new animation was created for the movie, making the total animation in the film 15 minutes long. Over 60 hours of film produced the 99 minute movie. A still-wet 70mm copy of the film was flown directly from the MGM laboratory to the Cannes Film Festival for the debut screening of the film.

The third article in this issue was titled, "High Speed Blood and Worms – Oxford Scientific Films Meets Pink Floyd" by Peter D. Parks. Oxford Scientific Films, Ltd. were contacted after Alan Parker saw an old promotional tape by the company. The special effects company had previously done work on the movies, 'Altered States,' 'Superman I,' 'Flash Gordon,' and 'Land Between Two Rivers.' They also specialized in wildlife photography, using high speed and time lapse photography. Alan Parker had seen a film of milk dripping into milk at 3000 fps, and he asked Oxford Scientific if they could do this with blood dripping onto a hotel carpet. They said that they could, but not at 3000 fps in anamorphic format on 35 mm film. To do it, they had to shoot it at 2000 fps to speed up the action.

Another scene that Parker wanted was a shot of Pink's head being devoured by maggots. A head was made of minced pork and was sculpted by Paul England, fly maggots were put on the head, and it was filmed at 2000 and 1000 fps. This sequence was cut into the rough edit of the film in the beginning.

Another sequence was a shot of a close up of Geldof's Mickey Mouse watch, arm, cigarette, and eye. This was accomplished using a Cosmoglide suspension system with a Galactoscope camera head. Takes 10, 11, and 12 were used in the final cut. Other sequences that were considered were tracking shots through and over Pink's personal items, a dead soldier on a battlefield covered with flies, and some dream sequences of endless hotel corridors and empty rooms.

Circus Magazine (U.S.) published an article titled, "Pink Floyd drops Rick Wright," that announced that Richard Wright was no longer a member of Pink Floyd. David Gilmour is quoted as saying, "He just gradually lost interest. But, Rick can take care of himself."

Oui Magazine (U.S.) published an article titled, "Floyd's Filmic Fantasmagoria" about the Pink Floyd movie, 'The Wall,' that featured an interview with Alan Parker from June 1982 at Pinewood Studios. Parker said, "*Certainly there will be comparisons to 'Tommy'. Ken Russell's film was brilliant, and quite influential in the creation of our picture. But it's still very traditional in style and structure when matched up against the nonlinear nature of 'The Wall.'*"

Is 'The Wall' too political for commercial cinema? Parker replied, "*I realize there's a risk here, but I felt it was important to try and examine the issues which have upset me, and 'The Wall' offered the potential for a truly original way of doing it. Pink Floyd's album of 'The Wall' was released in 1979, and it examined the barriers people put up that make it difficult for them to communicate. It was about alienation, separation, and the fears one has about breaking away from society. I thought that by using the power of rock and roll, interwoven with screen images, I could explore the fears I had about oppression, totalitarianism, and the sort of mindless activity which is very relevant to life in England today. And since England seems to represent, in microcosm, the problems that are* affecting the world, I think the picture says something about the general attitude we're taking towards right-wind extremism.*"

Parker continued, "*My generation was peddled the promise of the consumer society during the 1960s. But when the British economy proved incapable of providing all those things, the generation after mine was angered by the failure of something they had grown up to expect. So while my working-class background made me lean to the left, with a distinct Socialist bent, the younger generation revolted against the Socialist dream. And what better way to rebel than to turn to the Right? 'The Wall' expresses my fears about where this will go, because these kids seem to find their answer in destruction.*"

Parker explained, "*I read a phrase which stuck in my mind about the way the punks seem to regard themselves. A boy said, 'I want my head to look like a clenched fist.' That's scary. What kind of society has bred that mentality? I tried to show a bit of the sickness that has overtaken the working-class punks and skinheads who actually appear in 'The Wall', but as we were shooting the film, I realized that even the most horrifying, outrageous images I shot could actually look seductive to a certain part of the population, and that's scarier still.*"

Is The Wall too complicated a movie? Parker replied, "*I do ask a lot of the audience. The mind will constantly work to keep up with the eye. It's difficult to juggle all the languages of film which we use in 'The Wall,' and still hold an audience. And in a year's time we can say that we were either very brave or very reckless to try. But in my gut, I think the audience will react well to the film.*"

Parker continued, "*Music is the most important single thing in most young people's lives, much more important than literature or films or television. That's why I felt compelled to use it as a narrative form, to try and reach them. I don't think you should ever talk down to an audience, but it's important to find a common language in which to communicate your ideas. In any case, it's the job of the filmmaker to push into different areas. We tend to get very comfortable, because the language of film has been established for generations. The audience will have to struggle through a new dialect in 'The Wall', but there's no forward movement unless you gamble a bit.*"

Asked about skinheads being used in the movie, Parker said, "*At one time we had over 600 skinheads on the set for a gigantic Nuremburgesque meeting. There was one gang who had been working with us for several weeks by this time, and they were the toughest of the various groups we knew. So we assigned them the task of maintaining order. They acted as a kind of police force while we shot the scene, though we didn't use the word 'police' in dealing with them, because that would have enraged them. These are incredibly raw, working-class London kids with very extreme political points of view. They're incredibly naive, too, as proven by the time we shot a scene between a group of them and 20 stunt men we'd dressed up as police. Even though the skinheads had been informed that these weren't real policemen, just actors dressed up to 'look' like police, they either couldn't or wouldn't understand the difference. The fact that these men had policemen's uniforms on meant that they were cops, and therefore, they were to be whacked across the head with lumps of wood.*"

Parker continued, "*Even though we were appalled by their extremism, at the same time, we were amused by their natural cockney wit, and this despite the fact that, the night before, they had thrown a Pakistani off a speeding train. After a while, we started feeling responsible for them, but in the back of our minds, there was always the knowledge that this is what it must have been like to make a film with the Nazis.*"

Parker continued, "*These kids looked at the film totally superficially and got a great kick out of throwing tables through windows and getting paid for it. They got fun out of running down alleyways or smashing up a house, because, unfortunately, they weren't invested with an incredible amount of intelligence. And if they did have a question, now and again, they might pause after an evening of total destruction and ask us, "Ere, are you taking the piss out of us?' We'd say, 'No!' I kept thinking they'd catch on to what we were really trying to say, but they didn't.*"

December 1982 - Musician Magazine (U.S.) published an interview with David Gilmour about 'The Wall.' The interview was conducted

by David Fricke in a New York hotel in August 1982 after the premiere of 'The Wall' movie in New York.

Asked about the Pink Floyd concert in Montreal, Canada in 1977 that traumatized Roger Waters to write 'The Wall,' Gilmour explained, "*None of us, were aware of it at the time. I just thought it was a great shame to end up a six-month tour with a rotten show. In fact, I remember going offstage for the encore and going back to the sound mixing board in the middle of the audience to watch the encore while Snowy, the guitar player who was with us at the time, played guitar on the encore.*"

Unlike previous Pink Floyd albums, 'The Wall' features simple songs and arrangements. Gilmour explained, "*The idea of 'The Wall' was so big and there was such a lot of stuff that Roger wanted to get across lyrically that there was no other way to do it, really. As it was, we had to struggle to get it on a double album. And also, none of the stuff had ever been out on the road before. 'The Dark Side Of The Moon' was toured before the album was made. That determined things. They worked onstage before they ever got to record, and I suppose that's the big difference on this thing. It was purely made in the studio.*"

How did The Wall develop? Gilmour explained, "*Roger had done a demo, at home, of the entire piece and then we got it into the studio with Bob Ezrin and the rest of us. We went through it and started with the tracks we liked best, discussed a lot of what was not so good, and kicked out a lot of stuff. Roger and Bob spent a lot of time trying to get the story line straighter, more linear conceptually. Ezrin is the sort of guy who's thinking about all the angles all the time, about how to make a shorter story line that's told properly, constantly worried about moving rhythms up and down, all that stuff which we've never really thought about.*"

Asked about the song arrangements, Gilmour replied, "*Some of the arrangements are very close to how Roger originally had them. Most of them are just changed, perhaps, a bit. That's just the normal process we use. Bash things on and try them, move things around if you don't like it.*"

Did you telescope your musical ideas for this album? Gilmour said, "*I don't think it was a matter of telescoping. It was a* matter of being economical and making things say what they're trying to say, quite snappily, and not waste the time. That was the mood we were in and certainly Bob Ezrin helped. Very snappy and to the point."

The song 'Another Brick in the Wall (Part 2)' is simple, and it became a Top 40 single. Gilmour explained, "It was originally a very short song. There was going to be a quick guitar solo and that was it. There was only one verse ever recorded and we put the solo stuff on the end. Roger and myself sang the verse and then we thought we'd try getting some kids to sing on it. I made up a backing track with a sync pulse up on it so we could later sneak it back in with the original track. We were in L.A. at the time, so I sent the tape to England and got an engineer to summon some kids. I gave him a whole set of instructions, ten-to-fifteen-year-olds from North London, mostly boys, and I said 'get them to sing this song in as many ways as you like,' and he filled up all the tracks on a 24-track machine with stereo pairs of all the different combinations and ways of singing with all these kids. We got the tape back to L.A., played it, and it was terrific. Originally, we were going to put them in the background, behind Roger and me singing on the same verse, but it was so good we decided to do them on their own. But we didn't want to lose our vocal. So we wound up copying the tape and mixing it twice, one with me and Roger singing, and one with the kids. The backing is the same. And we edited them together."

The song, 'The Trial,' is the other extreme, with violins and orchestra. Gilmour said, "That's largely Roger and Bob Ezrin collaborating. I think it was written by Bob with the immediate intention to do that with an orchestra, although we did demos of it with synthesizers and stuff."

Pink Floyd has been known as a space band that uses special effects in the music, but your music also includes excellent sound processing techniques. Gilmour stated, "I like our music to feel three-dimensional. It's about trying to invoke emotions in people, I suppose. You feel larger than life in some sort of way. Let's face it, none of us in Pink Floyd are technically brilliant musicians with great chops, who can change rhythms, fifteen or sixteen bars here, there, and everywhere. And we're not terribly good at complicated chord

structures. A lot of it is just very simple stuff dressed up. We stopped trying to make overtly 'spacey' music and trip people out in that way in the 1960s. But that image hangs on and we can't seem to get short of it."

Asked about Syd Barrett, Gilmour said, "He was a truly magnetic personality. When he was very young, he was a figure in his hometown. People would look at him in the street and say, 'There's Syd Barrett,' and he would be only fourteen years old."

Asked if Barrett's breakdown was due to the psychedelic experience, Gilmour answered, "In my opinion, it would have happened anyway. It was a deep-rooted thing. But I'll say the psychedelic experience might well have acted as a catalyst. Still, I just don't think he could deal with the vision of success and all the things that went with it. And there were other problems he had. I think the whole swimming pool thing in 'The Wall' movie comes from one of Syd's episodes."

How were you able to deal with Syd Barrett when you produced his first solo album, 'The Madcap Laughs?' Gilmour replied, "With extreme difficulty. EMI understood Syd's potential at the time. They knew he was very talented and they wanted him to carry on. So they got an EMI producer who started recording this album and he spent ages on it. I think it was over six months. Eventually, EMI thought that too much money had been spent and nothing had been achieved. So Syd came and asked if we could help him. We went to EMI and said, 'Let us have a crack at finishing it up.' And they gave us two days to do it, and one of those days we had a Pink Floyd gig, so we had to leave the studio at four in the afternoon to get on a train and go to the show. But basically, Roger and I sat down with him after listening to all his songs at home, and said, 'Syd, play this one. Syd, play that one.' We sat him on a chair with a couple of mikes in front of him and got him to sing the song. On some of them, we just put a little bit of effect on the track with echo and double-tracking. On one or two others, we dubbed a bit of drums and a little bass and organ. But it was like one side of the album was six month's work, and we did the other tracks in two and a half days. And the potential of some of those songs, they could have really been fantastic."

There was more instrumentation on

the second Syd Barrett solo album, Barrett. Gilmour explained, "*We had more time to do that. But trying to find a technique of working with Syd was so difficult. You had to pre-record tracks without him, working from one version of the song he had done, and then sit Syd down afterwards and try to get him to play and sing along, with a lot of dropping in. Or you could do it the other way around, where you'd get him to do a performance of it on his own and then try to dub everything else on top of it. The concept of him performing with another bunch of musicians was clearly impossible because he'd change the song every time. He'd never do a song the same twice. I think quite deliberately.*"

Did Barrett show up during the Pink Floyd mixing session for the song, 'Shine On You Crazy Diamond?' Gilmour said, "*He did show up, yeah. He showed up at the studio. He was very fat and he had a shaved head and shaved eyebrows and no one recognized him at all, first off. There was just this strange person walking around the studio, sitting in the control room with us for hours. If anyone else told me this story, I'd find it hard to believe, that you could sit there with someone in a small room for hours, with a close friend of yours for years and years, and not recognize him. And I guarantee, no one in the band recognized him. Eventually, I had guessed it. And even knowing, you couldn't recognize him. He came two or three days, and then he didn't come anymore.*"

What do you think about all the attention given to Syd Barrett by fan clubs? Gilmour replied, "*It's sad that these people think he's such a wonderful subject, that he's a living legend when, in fact, there is this poor sad man who can't deal with life or himself. He's got uncontrollable things in him that he can't deal with and people think it's a marvelous, wonderful, romantic thing. It's just a sad, sad thing, a very nice and talented person who's just disintegrated.*"

The Pink Floyd song, 'Shine On You Crazy Diamond,' which is about Syd Barrett, is very sad. Gilmour agreed, "*It is sad. Syd's story is a sad story romanticized by people who don't know anything about it. They've made it fashionable but it's just not that way.*"

Asked why he joined Pink Floyd, Gilmour replied, "*I joined the Pink Floyd for*

the stardom and the girls."

Asked about the song, 'A Saucerful of Secrets,' Gilmour explained, "*I had just joined when we started doing that track. Basically it was the architecture students in the band. They'd sit down with a piece of paper and they'd start it like this, 'It's gotta go right here, and then it's gotta go right up there,' and they were drawing these peaks and troughs and things on a chart, working out where the piece was going to go. The whole first part of it was kind of like a war, I think. I didn't fully understand it myself at the time. But it seemed to me like a war. The first part is tension, a buildup, a fear, and the middle with all the clashing and banging, that's the war going on. The aftermath is a sort of requiem. The start of it was done with the edge tones of cymbals. We'd get some cymbals and put a nice microphone right on the edge of it, then beat the cymbal very gently with soft mallets. That actually produces a tone not a bit like a cymbal. The whole first section is basically that, a series of those tones, with lots of stuff tacked on top. For the next section, Nick played a drum pattern, snipped and spliced it together into a loop, and we ran it on a tape recorder for hours and hours. Then there's me playing the guitar, turned up real loud and using the leg of a microphone stand like a steel bar, running it up and down the guitar fingerboard.*" Although structured, it sounds free form. Gilmour said, "*I remember, sitting there, thinking, 'My God, this isn't what music's all about.' I had just come straight out of a band that spent most of it's time rehashing early Jimi Hendrix songs to crowds of strange French people. Going straight into this was culture shock.*"

After that, you released the album, 'Ummagumma,' with live songs plus songs from each member. Gilmour said, "*We just didn't know what else to do at the time. We were a bit short on material. Also, what we were very good at, at that time, was live performance. We were going out around England and Europe and selling out anything we wanted to. We were one of the top drawing bands, apart from Hendrix and Fleetwood Mac, in their earlier incarnation.*"

At that time, how much of your live show was improvised? Gilmour replied, "*A lot of it. There was a whole passage of time when* we would have nothing planned. We'd just say 'We're gonna do this,' and waffle away for a little while, go 'Ready for the next one?' and nod each other into it. I mean, we were doing stuff like 'Careful With That Axe Eugene,' which is basically one chord. We were just creating textures and moods over the top of it, taking it up and down, not very subtle stuff. There was a sort of rulebook of our own that we were trying to play to. And it was largely about dynamics."

Next came the album 'Meddle,' with the song 'Echoes.' How did this develop? Gilmour explained, *"A lot of the stuff we did in those days was just sitting around in the rehearsal room plunking around for ideas, searching for ideas, desperately trying to come out with little things and work on those."* Referring to 'Echoes,' Gilmour added, *"It's quite a few ideas developed together. It's quite complicated. It was the first time we'd used 16-track. Take the choir at the end, the everlasting backwards choir. Have you ever heard that musical thing where they get a tone that seems to go on, you know, like those Escher paintings where the staircases go up and up and up and never getting anywhere? Well, there's a tone and it keeps going ding, ding, ding, ding, and up and up, and the same time they are surreptitiously taking out high frequencies so that it never gets anywhere. That's what the choir at the end does, right on the very end of 'Echoes.' The whole beginning of 'Echoes' was a complete accident. There was a piano at Abbey Road and they had it miked. We'd put the microphone out through a Leslie in the studio at the same time as Rick was playing it. He was just sitting there, plunking away. Every once in a while he'd come up with this note and it had a strange resonance to it. It was kind of a feedback thing, so it would resonate in the studio 'Bing!' a complete accident. We said 'that's great' and we used it as the start of the piece. At a certain point later on where we had to go move on musically, we tried to recreate the sound and edit it together. But we couldn't get that note to resonate again in the same way."*

After 'Meddle' your songs changed. Gilmour explained, *"The big difference after 'Echoes' is, Roger started to write lyrics with a meaning. The lyrics for 'Echoes' were just an excuse to hang the music on. I think that started Roger suddenly realizing what he can do lyrically on 'Obscured By Clouds.'"*

Next came 'Dark Side of the Moon.' You recorded the sounds for 'Money' on a loop of tape. Gilmour explained, *"You're trying to get the impact from the cash register, the 'snap, crack, crssh.' You'd mark that one and then measure how long you wanted that beat to go and that's the piece you'd use. And you'd chop it together. It was trial and error. You just chop the tapes together, and if it sounds good, you use it. If it doesn't, you take one section out and put a different one in. Sometimes we'd put one in and it'd be backwards, because the diagonal cut on the tape, if you turn it around, is exactly the same. We'd stick that in and instead it would go 'chung, dum, whoosh.' And it would still sound great. So we'd use that."*

You began recording 'Dark Side of the Moon' in June 1972 and finished the following January. Did it take you nine months to record it? Gilmour said, *"It was very, very split up. The actual recording time was probably two or three months. There was touring in the middle. In fact, we did five nights at the Rainbow Theater in London. There are bootlegs of us doing 'The Dark Side of the Moon' a long time before we ever started recording it, and the differences are unbelievable. The whole 'On the Run' section with the synthesizer was completely different. 'Time' was, like, half the speed. I think the 'Time' vocal was me and Rick singing in harmony very low. It sounded terrible."*

How did you do the guitar solo for the song 'Time?' Gilmour explained, *"It's a Strat worked through a fuzz box and a DDL for the echo effect. If you just have a fuzz directly through an amplifier, for me, it's usually too fuzzy. But if you put a bit of DDL on it, it smoothes it out a bit and makes it sound more natural."*

On the song, 'Any Colour You Like,' the guitar sounds like it was put through a Leslie speaker. Gilmour said, *"I think that's through a Univibe. In those days, there were Univibes."*

Equipment back in those days was quite different than it is now. Gilmour explained, *"I think the people out there who are looking back think that the synthesizers and all that stuff came out a long time before it did. In studios, up until really the middle*

1970s, there weren't any effects units. They didn't exist. The choices you had were to get the tape players to run tapes against each other. You could take a track on a multi-track machine and play it off the sync head, through another tape recorder, and play with the speed of it with a vari-speed. Now to vari-speed a tape machine in those days, EMI had to wheel in an enormous box with oscillators and output bars and God knows what, with great big knobs on it, and you spent three hours plugging it into a tape machine and playing with the knob and the tape machine."

With 'Dark Side of the Moon,' did you intentionally try and make a state of the art sounding record? Gilmour answered, *"We always were. But that was the first time we actually got someone else in to give us an extra opinion on the mixing of it, Chris Thomas."*

Overall, what did you think of the music on 'The Dark Side of the Moon?' Gilmour replied, *"I thought 'The Dark Side of the Moon,' at the time, was a little weak musically. Some of the songs I didn't think were that good as chord structures. My argument after 'The Dark Side of the Moon,' when we went to do 'Wish You Were Here,' was to try and get some of the feeling and musical power of 'Echoes,' with the lyrical power of 'Dark Side of the Moon.'"*

What did you think about the way 'Dark Side of the Moon' sold so well commercially? Gilmour said, *"The thing I remember most about the period after that was the incredible annoyance at these gigs. We were doing these places where all the young kids would be shouting 'Money' all the through the show. We'd been used to all these reverent fans who would come and you could hear a pin drop. We'd try to get really quiet, especially at the beginning of 'Echoes' or something that has tinkling notes, trying to create a beautiful atmosphere, and these kids would be there shouting 'Money!'"*

The pressure of following up the hugely successful 'Dark Side of the Moon' must have been enormous. Gilmour explained, *"The pressure was entirely our own, of knowing that we had to follow up that album. It was very difficult getting back in and working."*

What do you think about punk rock and, the Johnny Rotten 'I hate Pink Floyd' T-shirt? Gilmour replied, *"It frightened a lot of people, but it didn't frighten me. I like a good kick in the pants. It does you good."*

Listening to the lyrics on the next albums, 'Wish You Were Here,' and 'Animals,' is Roger Waters bitter about Pink Floyd and the record industry? Gilmour answered, *"You'd have to ask him really. He certainly holds a resentment of those figures and the 'attempted' control, what they tried to take over. I mean, we met some people in the record industry, we couldn't believe how they could possibly have jobs in the industry. And we still do."*

Do Roger Waters' lyrics speak for the views of the rest of the band members? Gilmour answered, *"Well, that's the world's assumption, and that's what we have to put up with, I suppose. It's entirely possible that I might write a song that would get onto a Pink Floyd album, but it's also entirely possible that it wouldn't fit in with whatever overall idea we were working with. It's 'he who comes up with the goods.'"*

What did the rest of the band think of 'The Wall' concept? Gilmour said, *"We all thought it was a very strong concept. I think there's a lot of it that's irrelevant to me. I don't feel the pressure of a wall between me and my audience. I don't ever think there's something that doesn't get through to them. I don't feel a lot of the things that happened to me in my earlier years, some of which weren't so wonderful, adversely affect my life to the extent Roger feels some of those things affected his life. Roger, for example, never knew his father. But that's his viewpoint and he's perfectly entitled to it. But I don't subscribe to it. A lot of the other stuff, 'The Dark Side of the Moon,' and 'Wish You Were Here,' I am fairly in sympathy with. 'Animals' I could see the truth of, though I don't paint people as black as that."*

The members of Pink Floyd have become recluses. Is this what you prefer? Gilmour replied, *"It's not a Pink Floyd thing. That is a case of any one individual at any one time doing whatever he wants to. That's exactly what we do and we've always done. There's never been a band policy where we do not do interviews. We have had difficult times with the press and we proved to ourselves that we didn't need them. They were constantly trying to prove to us that the measure of our*

1983
The Final Cut and Back

success was done through the publicity we were given by them. But we absolutely proved that wasn't so."

Are you afraid that Pink Floyd will become nothing more than a product? Gilmour replied, *"We still make records and tours, but none of that is controlled by anyone else other than us. No one says we have to make a record. No one says we have to deliver a record by such and such a date. We have never accepted any of those restrictions. Well, once we did, but no more than we had to. When 'The Wall' was running long overdue, the record company offered us a larger percentage and a larger advance if we would deliver it by a certain date. Apart from that, we don't have restrictions. We give the record company records, and they go and sell them to the best of their ability. The question of whether we are irrelevant or not is down to the public to decide. When and if they decide we are irrelevant, we won't be able to carry on with it."*

March 17, 1983 - The Guardian (U.K.) reviewed the Pink Floyd album, 'The Final Cut.' Reviewer Robin Denselow wrote that the album is a mini epic written by Roger Waters that includes a viscous attack on Margaret Thatcher. The record is "messy, overblown, and awkward," but it includes startling lyrics, a few good songs, and brilliant recording work. Well-worn Roger Waters' themes include World War II, the death of his father, war heroes becoming teachers, and personal madness. It also features references to the Falklands conflict and attacks on Thatcher, such as the song 'The Fetcher Memorial Home,' which puts her in a "home for incurable tyrants and kings." The album ends with a nuclear holocaust.

March 19, 1983 - Melody Maker (U.K.) reviewed the Pink Floyd album, 'The Final Cut.' Reviewer Lynden Barber wrote that Roger Waters has refused to grow old with good grace and is propping up his "personal

sense of pride with ill-conceived and myopic acts of vanity." The album is a feeble attempt to come to grips with the state of the world without the aid of "anything remotely resembling an analytical, poetic, or probing imagination." Its failure is stupefying and its self-satisfaction nauseating. Waters does not possess the political literacy or artistic sensibility needed to address issues such as the decline of Britain, and he sings about it with a colorless voice. "Truly, a milestone in the history of awfulness."

New Musical Express (U.K.) reviewed the Pink Floyd album, 'The Final Cut' with an article titled, "Over the wall and into the dumper" by Richard Cook. Cook wrote that the album, which is entirely Roger Waters' statement, juggles the identical themes of 'The Wall' with no fresh momentum. Waters' songs are flabby, inconsolable rhetoric. It is the expression of a man who loathes the demands of rock and roll, yet is unable to move beyond them.

Sounds (U.K.) published an interview with Roger Waters by Karl Dallas. Asked about how 'The Wall' concerts ended, Waters replied, *"That final song is saying 'Right. Well, that was it. You've seen it now. That's the best we can do.' That was us performing a piece of theater about alienation. This is us making a little bit of human contact at the end of the show."*

Asked about the different ending to 'The Wall' movie, Waters added, *"That final image, if it's saying anything at all, is suggesting that when we're born, we don't like Molotov cocktails. And that we learn to like them as we grow older. We learn to want to burn stuff and break things. You know, children don't like the smell of petrol and they don't like the taste of whiskey. These are tastes that one acquires. Actually, children do like Molotov cocktails. Of course, they do. I don't know why I said that. It's clearly nonsense. They like guns, and fireworks, and bangs. But they don't like killing. Certainly my children don't. They don't even like it in nature. They don't like it when Jon-Jon, our cat, kills a bird, because they identify with the bird. Killing is very worrying to children. It's something that we get hardened to as we grow older. Some of us get more hardened to it than others."*

Waters was asked about the mother figure in 'The Wall' movie, and he replied that it is *"not very well drawn. My relationship with my mother wasn't like that. In fact, my mother is one of the bad areas of characterization in the film, I think. She's full of contradictions, that character, really. I think that may have something to do with the fact that I didn't draw her directly from my own experience. I mean, I did find a dying rat on the Rugby field and take it home and try to look after it. And my own mother did make me put it in the garage. But not like that. She wasn't a crazy, overweight, hysterical woman. I think that's a very crude portrayal. It's a cliché."*

The Pink Floyd's new album, 'The Final Cut,' is dedicated to Waters' father, Eric Fletcher Waters, but Roger Waters has *"a sense that I might have betrayed him, because we haven't managed to improve things very much."*

Asked about the songs on the album and the voicing of his opinions on political issues in the lyrics, Waters replied, *"Clearly I'll get a lot of stick for this. I mean, 'Who the hell does he think he is, criticizing?' Well, thank God the one thing we have in this country is that we all have the right to say what we like about anybody, you know. Just because something's going to be a lyric in a song that lots of people may listen to doesn't mean that one should temper one's personal feelings any more than one would talking to somebody in a pub. And I do think it was wrong to not stop the Task Force in those last couple of days before the Vulcan attack on Port Stanley and before the sinking of the Belgrano. Not that I'm saying it was right for them to invade the Falklands. It wasn't. And clearly they're bastards, the Galtieris of this world. But through the offices of the United Nations, our opposing positions had drawn closer together until they were pretty close. And I don't think that the difference between the British position and the Argentinean position then, at the end, or the beginning of the war as it became,*

justified those lives. A thousand lives, or something, 800 or whatever it was Argentinean lives and a couple of hundred British lives. I suspect that there may well be a quite considerable swell of similar feelings among people who were actually there. It so often happens that the ones who come back a bit shell-shocked, for the first time in their lives having been involved in a conflict like that, suddenly think, 'Well, hang on a minute. What was that all about?' Don't get me wrong. I'm not a pacifist. I think there are wars that have to be fought, unfortunately. I just don't happen to think that was one of them. We've now got an island that's so bloody full of booby traps and landmines that you can hardly even go for a walk."

Referring back to the Pink Floyd album, 'Wish You Were Here,' Waters was asked about its reference to Syd Barrett, and he replied, *"Well, it's about him, and it's about us all, really. It could equally have been called, 'Wish We Were Here' because in the band we were going through one of our communication troughs at that point, a divergence of opinion about what we were doing, what records should be about."*

Asked about communication between the members of Pink Floyd, Waters replied, *"Not too good at the moment. With this album, 'The Final Cut,' none of us have got a very clear idea of what it is, really. I sit here, hoping that what it is will suddenly hit me in a blinding flash. I'll suddenly scribble out two or three pages of feelings, which will suddenly tie it all together, and make it all a more coherent work than it is at the moment. But that hasn't happened yet."*

Asked about the song 'Not Now John' from The Final Cut album, and whether it is a statement about the previous songs on the album, Waters said, *"Yeah, yes it is. It's a strange song, that. It's a very schizophrenic song, because there's this one character singing all the verses, who's got irritated by all this whining and moaning about how desperate things are, the Falklands and so on, and doesn't want to hear any of it any more. And there's part of me in that. Then there's this other voice which comes in and keeps harping back to earlier songs, saying 'make them laugh, make them cry, make them dance in the aisles,' which is from 'Teach.' So it's a strange*

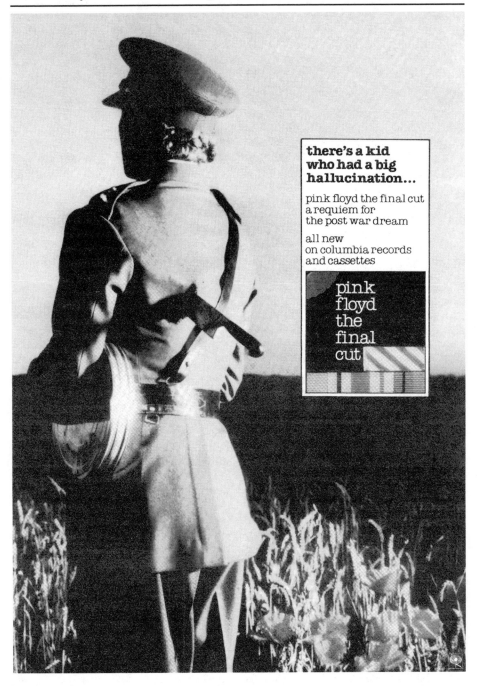

song. But what the first voice is saying is very straight forward. 'Fuck all that, we've got to get on with these.' There's no time to think about any of that. We've got to learn how to make these things quicker than the Japanese can, which is ludicrous, of course. There's no way we can compete with the Japanese. They've got thousands of years of obeying their mums and dads behind them. The Japanese people, in their religion and in all their social mores and conditioning for thousands of years, are absolutely purpose-made as workers in factories. And we're not, thank God. Now, that's something about us that I think we should be proud of, the fact that we can't become part of the machine, successfully. I think that's a natural characteristic of the British people that we should be very glad about. It makes life a bit uncomfortable if we're living a life where the ethic is to compete with everybody else and sell more goods to the Third World, or each other, or whoever it might be, you know, to win that particular race. So it makes it difficult. But it's something. It's a difficulty I'd rather be coping with than living in Japan. Mind you, this is easy for me to say. I'm not on the dole."

Asked about the effect of world politics on the children of the world, Waters replied, "The things that are done to the children in the film, well, to the main character, is that his father is killed and that clearly is being done to a hell of a lot of children all over the world, apparently more and more. I mean the pace at which carnage in the world is apparently growing, since there was a little bit of a lull after the Vietnam conflagration, seems to be increasing now. I don't know, maybe I'm becoming more sensitive to it, maybe it's not, maybe it's something that goes along on a level, but it seems to be so, clearly there are a lot of war orphans being created now, a feeling that never leaves me, really. It's always there somewhere in the back of my mind, or in my chest somewhere. I think it must have to do with something that happened in my childhood that I maybe can't quite put my finger on, is the feeling of helplessness. I can imagine in the breasts of the victims of an errant power, whether it's the people who whisk you off the streets in Buenos Aires and you're never seen again, or the Christian Phalangists in Lebanon who put you up against the wall and shoot you and kill your children, or whether it's the Nazis in the last war, or the Russians in Afghanistan. That moment when they're there and you're there, and they're saying, 'Bye, bye. I've got the gun and this is it.' And you have no recourse to anything, let alone law. It happens here a bit, but thank God and touch wood, it's still reasonably rare in this country. Generally speaking, we're lucky enough in England to have recourse to a system of law. And we are protected by it, largely, in the extremes, and I identify pretty much with people who aren't."

Explaining the song, 'Two Suns in the Sunset,' from 'The Final Cut' album, Waters said, "That was a thought I had, driving home one night, thinking 'We all sit around and talk about the possibility of accidents or, as I put it in the song, people just getting so bloody angry that finally somebody pushes a button. Well, the song's all about that moment when suddenly it happens, you know it's happened and you know it's the end, you're all dead, and it's the end of the world, and that you'll never see your kids again or your wife or anybody that you love and it's all over. And, in a way, it's the same feeling for me, which is why I mention the words 'recourse to the law,' as the idea of somebody kicking in the door and they are the law, and you know what they're doing is wrong. If you're in Argentina and suddenly one of the squad comes round and whips you off and takes you into a cell and kicks you to death, or in Northern Ireland, or wherever it might be, you know it's wrong, but there's nothing you can do about it. So, in a way, my dream is, or his dream, the gunner's dream is of that not happening, whether it's nuclear war or somebody kicking your door in. It's the same feeling of helplessness and hopelessness. It's very easy to go 'Oh yes, well, there may be an accident and the holocaust may happen,' without having the feeling of what it might be like. And that's why it says in the song 'and as the windscreen melts, my tears evaporate, leaving only charcoal to defend, finally I understand the feelings of The Few,' which is supposed to be a reference to the bomber and the gunner and all those people, my dad, and all the other war casualties. Fortunately, the people who are directly affected by war are a small minority. And I have a feeling that if they weren't, and all the people who were directly affected by war could somehow be a majority, there wouldn't be any more. It's very easy, we become inured to it, and we see it on the TV all the time, and it's very easy to harden oneself to the feelings that must be involved, easy to forget, now, all those people in Sir Tristan, and Sir Galahad, all those people. That song, I suppose, in a way is going back to the second song on the album when there's a line 'a warning to anyone still in command of their possible futures. Take care.'"

The article stated that Roger Waters

is currently at work on a solo album, with recording scheduled to begin on the day 'The Final Cut' is released.

In reply to printed rumors that Pink Floyd might break up, Waters said, "*All I said was there wasn't any reason why, at some point in the future, I shouldn't work with another drummer or another guitarist, or anybody. Of course, there isn't. Dave and Nick have both made solo albums, and they've worked with other drummers or other bass players or other writers, but they make it sound as if I'm saying that's the end of the band, which is nonsense.*"

Asked about Rick Wright, who is no longer a member of Pink Floyd, Waters stated, "*Our paths were not parallel enough.*"

As far as Pink Floyd guitarist David Gilmour is concerned, Waters added, "*If you look at the work we've done together, a lot of it's very good. 'The Wall' is very good. It's a very, very good record. I think Dave's contribution is very important. Not just his guitar playing, but a couple of really good tunes that he wrote for 'The Wall.' I'm not belittling his guitar playing. His guitar playing is fantastic. He's a very underrated guitar player, in my opinion. It's a very strange thing. People in bands always have differences and things often go in cycles. You have productive periods when you work well together, and periods when you don't work well together. It would be ludicrous to expect, in a career spanning fifteen or sixteen years, that you always agreed about everything that happened, and that it was an expression of some kind of gestalt feeling. It's never like that. No band is like that. If you want to know whose feelings they are, you look at the songs, you look and see who's written the songs. Because that's what it's about.*"

Asked whether there will be any more Pink Floyd concerts after 'The Final Cut' is released, Waters answered, "*Don't know. Definitely not 'The Wall' again. I can't imagine that, the aggravation of getting it together. You never know. We won't be certain about that for another few years when one will know that everything has rotted and all the machinery is rusty. If you haven't seen it again in the next five years, then you'll know that you're not going to, because everything will have been stolen or rusted away, the cardboard will all be* soggy. It's not something that I'd care to do again, but it's something that I'm glad to have been part of.*"

March 25, 1983 - New York Daily News (U.S.) reviewed the Pink Floyd album, 'The Final Cut.' They wrote that the album uses the Holophonic Sound technique that produces a fascinating three-dimensional ambience for the special effects. The music has a "superb sense of melodic and harmonic invention," and the use of the National Philharmonic Orchestra of England enhances the music. The songs are deeply profound and deal with world politics and the futility of war. The songs are well written and feature solid vocals, intriguing effects, and dynamic musical instrumentation. 'The Gunners Dream' is enchanting. The album is "a rock 'n' roll masterpiece."

April 14, 1983 - Rolling Stone (U.S.) reviewed the Pink Floyd album, 'The Final Cut.' Kurt Loder called it essentially a Roger Waters solo album. He gave the album five stars and said that it might be "art rock's crowning masterpiece."

May 1983 - Sounds (U.K.) published an interview with David Gilmour about 'The Final Cut' album. Gilmour was asked why he wasn't involved in the production of the album, and he replied, "*It's very, very much Roger's baby, more than any one has been before and I didn't... it's not the way I'd have produced it and we did have an argument about the production on this record, several arguments, and I came off the production credits because my ideas of production weren't the way that Roger saw it being. Obviously the way it is, is the way Roger wanted it to be.*"

Asked if he was happy with it, Gilmour replied, "*It's very, very good, but it's not personally how I would see a Pink Floyd record going. The sound quality is very good, it's very, very well recorded, and the string arrangements and orchestral stuff are very well done. But it's not me. Consequently, I was arguing about how to make the record at the beginning, and it was being counterproductive.*"

Asked why Rick Wright left the band, Gilmour answered, "*Um... What's the best cliché I can think of...?*" Gilmour was reminded that Roger Waters explained Wright's leaving by saying *"Our paths were not parallel enough,"* to which Gilmour added, *"That's good enough. You'd have to ask him really. Ask Rick one day."*

Is your path still parallel with Waters? Gilmour replied, *"Well, no they're not, really. We diverge quite a lot. But we do still just about manage to work together. And we still have got things that we can contribute to each other. I think the thing with Rick was that he didn't have anything that any of us felt was contributing to what Pink Floyd do."* Compositionally? Gilmour answered, *"In any way."*

July 1983 - Creem Magazine (U.S.) reviewed the Pink Floyd album, 'The Final Cut' with an article titled, "Waters On the Brain" by Jim Farber. Farber wrote that Roger Waters uses vinyl "as his psychiatrist's couch." According to the Columbia Records press release, the album is about "the disillusionment of a generation that saw the hopes and dreams coming out of the Second World War go unfulfilled, the frustration and anger brought to mind by all conditions of economic upheaval, impending war, poverty, or another holocaust." Waters makes these universal issues sound like individual hang-ups, and paranoid delusions. It is an artistic failure. The music is dull, and Waters' vocals often sound like the mutterings of a street lunatic. The album makes Roger Waters seem "as think as a brick in the wall."

September 1983 - Guitar World (U.S.) reviewed the Pink Floyd album, 'The Final Cut.' They wrote that this is Roger Water's latest "doomsday ballad." The album is without the adventure of Richard Wright's "psychotronic escapism," leaving just David Gilmour's "nihilistic ax implosives." This is the death knell for Pink Floyd.

September 1983 - Hit Parader (U.S.) published an article titled, "Pink Floyd – Off the Wall." The article reported on the release of the new Pink Floyd album, 'The Final Cut,' with a bit of background on the Falkland Islands conflict, and some information about 'The Wall' album and film. David Gilmour explained why Roger Waters didn't play the part of Pink in 'The Wall' movie, saying,

"When he was going to play the part, he wouldn't write scenes that were difficult to act because he knew he couldn't handle them." As to why Bob Geldof was selected even though he was not a Pink Floyd fan, Gilmour explained, *"If we had to find someone who was suitable for the part and liked our music as well, we might still be looking."* Geldof explained that he enjoyed the part even if he didn't agree with Waters' pessimism, saying, *"It's Roger's point of view and I'm allowed to disagree with it. We would talk and play snooker and have lots of arguments."*

Epilogue

Although this book ends with the year 1983, the members of Pink Floyd have continued producing extraordinary music to this day. In 1984, both David Gilmour and Roger Waters released solo albums and toured to support them. Richard Wright released a collaboration album in 1984, and Nick Mason released one in 1985. Roger Waters toured again in 1985, before announcing that he was no longer a member of Pink Floyd. In 1987, Pink Floyd returned with both an album and a tour, as did Roger Waters. In 1990, Roger Waters staged a live performance of The Wall in Berlin, Germany. 1992 brought a new solo album from Roger Waters, and in 1994 Pink Floyd released a new album and toured. In 1996, Richard Wright released a solo album, and Roger Waters performed live once again with tours in 1999 and 2000. And the story continues.

About The Author

Author Vernon Fitch is a music historian who has studied the history of Pink Floyd for over 30 years. He currently runs The Pink Floyd Archives, a vast private collection of Pink Floyd memorabilia for the purpose of documenting the history of the band. He has written numerous articles and reference works about Pink Floyd, including The Pink Floyd Encyclopedia.

For additional Pink Floyd resources, see The Pink Floyd Archives home page on the Internet at:

http:\\ourworld.compuserve.com\homepages\PFArchives

Pink Floyd shown on this Record Mirror issue, 1967.

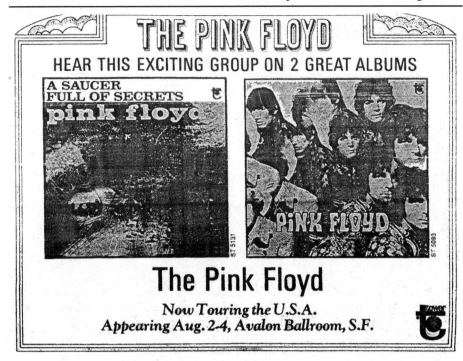

A rare Tower Records ad that mentions the first U.S. tour, 1968.

An EMI advertisement featuring Syd Barrett's first album, 1970.